A
QUICK AND DIRTY
GUIDE TO
WAR

THIRD EDITION

A
QUICK AND DIRTY
GUIDE TO
WAR

THIRD EDITION

BRIEFINGS ON PRESENT
AND POTENTIAL WARS

James F. Dunnigan
and Austin Bay

WILLIAM MORROW AND COMPANY, INC.
New York

Library of Congress Cataloging-in-Publication Data

Dunnigan, James F.
    A quick and dirty guide to war : briefings on present and
potential wars / James F. Dunnigan and Austin Bay.—3rd ed.
        p.   cm.
    Includes bibliographical references and index.
    ISBN 0-688-14152-8
    1. War. 2. World politics—1989–   I. Bay, Austin. II. Title.
U21.2.D83   1996
355'.033'0048—dc20   95–51146
                                                                    CIP

Printed in the United States of America

First Edition

1 2 3 4 5 6 7 8 9 10

BOOK DESIGN BY PAUL CHEVANNES

PREFACE TO THE THIRD EDITION

The analyses we produced for the original 1985 edition of *A Quick and Dirty Guide to War* were formulated in 1984, a year before its publication. Long lead time is unavoidable in the book business, which makes writing about ongoing conflicts and "could-be wars" a dicey proposition. Yet the analyses supporting those chapters had "legs"— over time they proved to be sensible, sound, and surprisingly resilient to the daily friction of history and events. The 1991 edition, which we referred to as the post–cold war edition, also withstood the attack of time. Such success does not "scientifically verify" the book's methodology, but it does give the book a remarkable track record. Five years later it's time to risk it—and risk-assess—once again.

The journalistic explanation and historical sections provided readers with a colorful and fast summary of many complicated and complex political situations. There was little debate on that score; even a few nit-picking types admitted the book's broad scope and thrust packed a lot of accurate and useful information into a small and available package.

But critics unfamiliar with analysis or simulations methodology have had trouble with "all the numbers" and the "Potential Outcome" projections of the various conflicts. One reviewer of the 1985 edition dismissed *A Quick and Dirty Guide* as the work of "fantasists." She was particularly amused that we mentioned "Indian" and Native American conflicts as major sources of war in the Western Hemisphere. Another reviewer was amused that we considered violence by animal rights activists as ideologically driven terrorism. In 1990 the Canadian Army battled Mohawk "warriors" in a dispute in Quebec. The nominal subject was a golf course and a bridge; the real subject was Native American rights. Since 1985, violence by animal rights activists has, in a macabre fashion, emulated that of a number of European guerrilla groups. The animal rights nuts, at least in their propaganda, speak of being at war with "science." Fantasy becomes reality, which most historians will admit is all too common. Since the 1991 edition, the reality of Indian wars has become accepted fact. The Zapatista (i.e., Maya) attacks on January 1, 1994, woke up the world.

Okay, Native Americans have real gripes and the animal rights bunch are fruitcakes and decidedly fringe, but we were looking at the seeds of conflict, the seeds that grow into greater tragedies. Our analyses challenged a few critics' points of view too profoundly. Actually, the 1985 edition received far less of that light-caliber flak than anticipated. We admitted at the outset that we were experimenting and that what we were doing was risky.

In statistical terms, what was the "success" record of the original edition over a six-year period? Remember Twain's admonition about lies, damned lies, and statistics. But using a "power-weighted" basis for analyzing the "Potential Outcomes" accuracy, where the "most likely" outcome received "x" points for occurrence, other "mentioned outcomes" received points on a sliding scale if they occurred within the time frame projected, and a penalty was incurred if "what happened in reality" was not mentioned (or modeled) at all, the first edition scored a notch above 80 percent. Not a bad hit rate. Better than anything else around, except perhaps for the major national intelligence agencies. But then you can't pick up a copy of their forecasts in your local bookstore.

The 1991 edition, over four years since its publication, ended up with a rating of 78 percent. We'll accept the slip. The end of the cold war has meant a lot more chaos. The 1991 edition scored 220 out of a possible 280 on "complete projections," i.e., those addressing likelihoods. Incomplete projections, for which we took a "far-out" possibility such as a new Iran-Iraq War (which we said had only an 8 percent chance of occurring between 1990 and 1996), and which were used as a basis for analysis of an unlikelihood, were left to the readers to ponder (which was our intent).

Here's one of our closer hits, from the chapter on South Africa (now reduced to a Quick Look for this edition). This was the first outcome in the Potential Outcomes section.

"1. 45 percent chance through 1996: South Africa establishes a new government (that works) with all citizens obtaining the vote (in one form or another). It's wide open as to just what form this would take. Some Boers push for ethnic areas for all groups, but this would not work completely—it never does. Even multiethnic democracies like Switzerland and Belgium end up with a lot of intermingling. Because the better-educated and wealthier whites tend to be where the jobs are, there would be a constant influx of blacks looking for work (and finding it). Many blacks push for "one person one vote," allowing things to be sorted out after elections. What is needed is a form of government where consensus rules. The whites will continue to control the wealth for some time, and if they feel oppressed enough, they will leave and take most of the jobs their wealth and talents currently provide. This was the lesson learned, and acted upon, in Zimbabwe. The Zimbabwe example is everyone's foundation for the new South African constitution. Still, look for the political parties to retain tribal bases."

Here's another, even more complicated projection from the 1991 edition, the "first outcome" (most likely) in the chapter on Russia. Remember the gaming behind this projection was done in 1990, a full year before publication.

"1. 35 percent chance through 1996: The USSR divides into five 'groups': the Baltic republics, a Russia-Byelorussian-Ukraine and Kazakh federation, 'Southeastern Muslim,' 'South Muslim,' and 'Christian' fragments (Georgia, Armenia)."

Did it happen? Is this a hit or a miss? As for the "big bull's-eye," the USSR fell apart in the fall of 1991, right after the 1991 edition hit the stands. The Baltics went their separate ways. The "Christian" fragments became independent, though Azerbaijan became a totally separate state rather than a "South Muslim" confederation. Tajikistan, Kyrgyzstan, and Uzbekistan became separate nations but each one suffering from the same sorts of "Southeastern Muslim" troubles.

We saw the Soviet Union falling apart but the core of the superpower maintaining some kind of federation. Russia did attempt to impose the Commonwealth of Independent States (CIS) but that became moribund. The Ukraine and Russia have argued violently over the Black Sea Fleet and the status of the Crimean Peninsula.

But the seeds for rebuilding the "core of the USSR" are now beginning to sprout. Despite Ukrainian-Russian acrimony, cooperation is returning. Russia still has a large presence in Kazakhstan. Belarus (former Byelorussia) wonders publicly why it's independent of Russia.

Even Ukrainian ultranationalists have begun to realize that Ukraine needs Russia as much as Russia needs Ukraine's immense agricultural productivity. Here's the 1995 projection.

"1. 45 percent chance through 2001: Russia stabilizes its economy; democracy survives. Minimal number of military operations in the Near Abroad (peacekeeping missions really are sent to keep the peace, not intervene on behalf of Moscow). If that occurs, there is an 85 percent chance that a de facto Russia-Belarus-Ukraine-Kazakh federation develops, based on mutual-defense treaties. That federation functions as an economic trading zone, with Russia supplying natural resources, heavy industry, and defense, Ukraine food and industry, Kazakhstan oil, and Belarus wondering why it ever left Russia to begin with.

Maybe these projections wouldn't play in the State Department, but as some smart alecks might say, close enough for *non*government work—and certainly close enough to cue readers on what to look for on the historical horizon. Most of the games for this edition were conducted within seven- (through 2001) or ten-year (through 2004) time frames.

When the hardcover edition was published in 1985, one interviewer asked coauthor Austin Bay if all of *A Quick and Dirty Guide*'s numbers and quantitative analyses indicated that political science had become a "true science." Though Aristotle used the term (and used it wisely), in this century "political science" has become an unfortunate term. The answer is no, *A Quick and Dirty Guide* isn't the harbinger of any such baloney. Politics is an art. Human beings don't reduce to mathematical thingamajigs; free will remains a hellacious statistical variable. Quantitative analyses are tools, like an understanding of a nation's language, culture, art, literature, ethnic groups, geography, and history. We'd like to propose a better moniker for studies like this one: Applied Humanities—bringing together good research, common sense, and an open, inquisitive mind.

ACKNOWLEDGMENTS

The authors would like to thank Jim Bloom, Albert A. Nofi, Connie Wooldridge, Willard Preussel, Trent J. Telenko, Tom Trinko, Kathleen Bay, Frank Bay, Larry Graham, Ben FitzGerald, Sterlin Holmesly, Phil True, and Fred Chase.

CONTENTS

PART 3: AFRICA

PART 4: ASIA

PART 5: THE AMERICAS

PART 6: DATABANKS ON WARS AND ARMIES, PRESENT AND POTENTIAL

INTRODUCTION

Wars don't just happen. Organized violence, like the weather, is never a complete surprise. There are signs and long-term trends. You cannot predict the exact outcome of a war or battle any more than you can predict exactly what the weather will be at noon tomorrow. You can, however, analyze past and ongoing conflicts and use the results to project the major trends shaping similar current and future events.

No one can predict an outbreak of war by psychic magic or mathematical hocus-pocus. Intelligence analysts, however, can estimate the likelihood of war or armed conflict in the same way meteorologists "predict" a hurricane's path. Weather forecasts collect current weather data, compare the most reliable information with evidence gained from past experience, add a large dose of intuition and probability, then stick their necks out and put a storm track on the weather map. That track is not as much a prediction as it is a projection of what could occur; still, this projection may have extraordinary utility, and is useful for activating flood control procedures, warning local populations, formulating plans of evacuation, and analyzing the vulnerability of coastal lowlands.

The daily press tends to play down the predictability of wars. This is understandable as sameness does not sell newspapers or induce one to view TV news. Wars are easier to sort out than the news suggests. This does not imply that all journalists indulge in sensationalism; that is simply not the case, though TV reporting has yet to resolve successfully the conflict between the camera's need for drama and the journalist's commitment to accurate reporting. Actually, the problem with the daily press is often that it does its job too well in recording and reporting the events of the last twenty-four hours. Such reports tend to be nearsighted. A sound historical and contextual focus is lost in the magnifications of immediate headlines.

While newspapers come to conclusions too quickly, the prediction professionals in think tanks have the opposite problem: They seem never to come to a conclusion. That puts military leaders and citizens in a predicament. The press screams out often sensational predictions and conclusions while government officials are served by think tank advisers who essentially say that definitive conclusions are impossible to reach.

It's very true that no one can predict the future with any precision. At the same time, government leaders, and the citizens who elect them, must plan for and make decisions about the probable future. Military and diplomatic analyses must be made, Defense and State department budgets must be planned. Careful projections of possible future events, linked to sound analysis of available data, have utility only if good decisions are made. Even deciding to do nothing is a decision, and often the least favorable one. How, then, do decisions usually get made?

The two primary sources of decision-influencing information, the press and the experts, are used quite differently. The free press, while often suspect because of the political leanings of reporters and editors, is highly regarded for its immediacy and the range of conclusions it provides. Moreover, press conclusions are in the open and subject to useful criticism and debate. At least this gives the government decision maker and the citizen a variety of analyses from which to choose and adapt.

Then we have the experts. There exists within the U.S. government a multibillion-dollar-a-year intelligence and analysis community. These are the experts who, with a worldwide network of agents, analysts, and electronic wizardry, are charged with creating an official analysis of events and future prospects. This group is responsible only to the decision makers they support, and this creates a curious relationship. These experts, given their enormous resources and professional pride, strive for an academic perfectionism. This often leads to an extensive, expensive, and complex analysis of every topic under study, whether the subject is Russian wheat production, bee excrement, or toenail growth rates of nineteen-year-old corporals testing a new jungle boot. The employers of the experts usually have neither the time nor the experience to grasp all the data they are given. The usual result is unfortunate. The decision makers reach their conclusions based on press information, gossip, and very brief summaries of the massive research done for them: 2,532 pages of analysis and research shrink to a single three- by five-inch briefing card. Expert information often becomes an after-the-act justification for conclusions the decision makers have already reached. Thus the tail (decision makers' conclusions) wags the dog (research done by the appointed experts).

This absurd situation is caused in part by the security requirements under which the experts operate. One must have a security clearance to work on or review all of the research. Much of this work thus is subject to very little criticism and informed debate. In addition, massive amounts of raw information often tend to blur the situation rather than illuminate it. Common sense gets lost in the metric shuffle of increasingly arcane forms of analysis.

Bureaucratic analyses also suffer from the committee problem. As in any large organization, there are more chiefs than Indians in the intelligence community. All these chiefs must justify their existence and often do so during uninformed debates on the validity of the research done and preliminary conclusions reached.

The research gatherers and analysts (the Indians) are often quite competent and dedicated. So are their superiors (the chiefs). But many potential futures are created with no easy way of choosing the "official" one. Sharp analysis dulls; clarity becomes bureaucratic murkiness.

Remember that we are attempting to project the outcome of wars that have not yet been fought (and may never, one hopes, be fought) or, if the conflicts are in progress, have not concluded. The potential outcomes have varying implications for the size and compositions of defense budgets and armed forces. The size of these budgets also has serious effects on the economies that produce the funds through taxation. Thus the decision makers' most immediate problem is not how correct their experts are, but how well any decisions can be "sold" to other interest groups within the government and nation. Accurate analysis and projection become secondary to the more immediate problem of getting enough people to agree on a course of action and move forward to a conclusion. The defense intelligence and analysis community fails so often not because of a lack of skill or resources, but because there are so few people with the ability, power, or sheer nerve to choose from the often unpleasant conclusions presented. Ugly realities are often swept aside in favor of more palatable political pictures. The officials' version is generally the more expedient, not the most accurate, product of billions of dollars of research and analysis.

Our approach in presenting a lot of data is to be open, straightforward, even simple. We try to explain, but we leave a lot of interpretation to you. Most of you are citizens, taxpayers (probably), and voters (we hope). What you have here in this book is often no more than many military and political decision makers have available when crucial decisions must be made. As several readers of the manuscript pointed out, we have given a complex body of knowledge manageable form. This is one reason we prefer to talk about "projections" rather than predictions. We give you a way of looking at current events in context. Observe and reach your own conclusions.

This book covers several current major wars and violent political conflicts, ongoing and potential. It explores the geographical factors and historical trends affecting these conflicts, takes a look at the human beings involved, then focuses on the present and possible future conflicts.

The key to understanding current wars, and their likely development, is knowledge of the fundamentals. We look at the political, ethnic, and economic makeups of the participating societies, the local geography, the societies' essential history, and the capabilities of their armed forces. This is the foundation for a conflict assessment.

If you can "predict" the past with such tools (and historians have been "predicting" the past and present for centuries), you can expect to have a better understanding of the present and future.

While this book is nonfiction, it makes many potentially, and one hopes ultimately, fictitious projections. Portraying the future is a popular spectator sport, but the spectators' wrath will fall on those who fail too often to divine events that have not yet happened.

Our primary technique in projecting the future is first to predict the past, with the idea that the future is an extension of the past. Details may differ, but patterns remain remarkably consistent. Human nature hasn't changed; time is doing its thing; some groups are winning, some losing; most people continue to suffer and reproduce.

World Wars I and II could be seen incubating in the Balkans, central Europe, and north China. Today the Middle East is a primary source of potential world conflict (though Asia is getting hotter). How do we know this? We compile data, turn the data into lists employing commonly used geopolitical factors like population and gross domestic product (GDP, or the total value of domestic goods and services produced yearly by a country), sort through the lists, then take a qualitative and quantitative look at the new arrangements of information. In some cases we applied simple statistical mathematical analyses to the information to create the conflict models that lie behind this book. Other analyses relied more heavily on geographical, historical, or political "war-gaming" to produce potential outcomes.

There is nothing mysterious or particularly difficult about this technique. Common sense, intuition, and recent headlines might tell you that the Middle East is the world's most dangerous trouble spot. However, when all the trends are laid out in a comparative manner, you begin to get a better picture of why this is true, where trouble comes from, and where the trouble might lead.

Data about armed conflict are relatively easy to find. Enterprising journalists and opposition politicians spend a great deal of energy collecting and reporting this information. An armed confrontation's causes, however, are often more obscure. History and geography give the best clues. Geopolitical interests rarely change, though sometimes the actors do. People have to eat and find shelter. Nations have to feed their people and maintain some degree of order. Our analysis of the available evidence relies on such primary human concerns. When one gets fancy and tries to guess the specific reasons for specific actions or policies, one generally walks where the ground is not. Experience teaches the analyst to guess where the ground might be.

There may be a large number of tactical options, but there are relatively few strategies. Strategy usually takes place on such a grand scale that one can guess with reasonable accuracy what strategic path a group has chosen to take. We assume that survival is the basic human strategy. A group of people can become a community of farmers; that's one strategic option for survival. Another group can become a gang of thieves. Although a couple of bad crops may turn the farmers into thieves, trends begin to emerge. The thieves, if they are to survive as thieves, must sharpen their wilier skills. Farmers forced to become thieves have to learn the trade from point zero, or hire some thieves to do their dirty work—yet another strategy. Farmers harassed by thieves can buy them off, which may work if the thieves are just hungry, or they can fight the crooks. Or perhaps the farmers can hire a few samurai to protect them from theft. The movie *The Seven Samurai* is a detailed look at this strategy. One can substitute oil for crops, nations for farmers and thieves, fighter-bombers for samurai.

This book focuses on basic strategies. Just as opposing armies keep track of each other by building up data over time, we kept track of a number of conflicts. Patterns begin to emerge. An analyst would call it a picture of the situation. A few good guesses about "state secrets" enhance the picture. Governments attempt to keep military secrets, but over time most details leak out. People can't keep their mouths shut, reporters have to write stories.

As we mentioned earlier, weather forecasting is a good analogy for this method of analysis. A computer powerful enough to model all the essential elements of a weather system has not yet been developed, and given the chaos of reality, trying to define with certainty what those essential elements are might be a fruitless pursuit. However, people can and do generate useful weather forecasts. Most of them rely on analyses of past weather events. Farming has long been dependent on such crude but useful predictions. It would be helpful, but is not essential, for a farmer to know exactly how much rain there was going to be in a given growing season. Knowledge of when the first and last frosts will occur would also be useful but isn't absolutely necessary. Farmers get by with a weather almanac of past events and an ability to judge the present situation.

Judging contemporary warfare and the potential for future wars is somewhat more complex than judging weather patterns. Herein we provide you with an almanac of past and current events. Add your judgment and you have as good a means as any for analyzing the course of present and future armed conflicts.

You can reach the authors via the Internet at JFDUNNIGAN @AOL.COM and AUSTIN.BAY@GENIE.COM.

HOW TO USE THIS BOOK

Each intelligence briefing or chapter consists of ten or eleven complementary sections, plus appropriate appendices. The authors designed the book so that the reader, usually a taxpayer putting up the bucks for the Departments of State and Defense, has a chance to play the role of highfalutin politico or military officer. In a very real sense the book is an adult role-playing game, with the reader as decision maker and the authors as briefers.

These briefings are not designed to be exhaustive. A briefing without some brevity isn't very functional. The challenge to both authors and reader is to do justice to the complexities of the issues—which entails including a certain amount of detail—while making the information readily available to someone who has to be at work on time. Most people don't have the time to become "experts." This book takes that into account. You will also find some repetition from section to section (or chapter to chapter). Rather than refer you to another page for an item, we duplicate it where needed. In most cases this repetition is a phrase or sentence. We found that readers appreciated this, so don't let it bother you (if you tend to dislike such things). Most people use this book as a reference, not something to be read straight through.

Reading each chapter from start to finish will provide a more thorough description of each conflict. We know, however, that many of you will require only certain kinds of information, such as who are the regional powers interested in a specific situation. If that's what you want to know, then go straight to the Regional Powers and Power Interest Indicator Chart(s) in the chapter. If you understand the organization of each chapter and its sections, you can then locate the information you want.

Introduction

Gives a summary of what is covered in the chapter. The section also includes a brief description of who is fighting over what.

Source of Conflict

Contains a description (often brief, sometimes more detailed) of how the situation became a conflict. Often outlines the major causes of the conflict and provides preparatory information that will be expanded upon in the Geography and History sections.

Who's Involved

Describes the important players in the conflict.

Geography

Analyzes the fundamental geographic considerations involved. Geographic considerations are of vital importance and, in geographically ignorant nations such as the United States (at least according to recent academic surveys), will, one hopes, open a few minds.

History

Describes some of the more important historical events still affecting the region and attempts to take the situation up to late 1995. In some chapters in which there is a lot of history, this portion will be more expansive.

LOCAL POLITICS

This section gives an in-depth look at some of the area's more peculiar political participants. Often this section deals with personalities and the organizations they inspire. In certain large nations like China, organizations totally predominate. In smaller nations organizations dominate but personalities get more ink. Americans in general lose sight of just how divided a population can be politically. This section demonstrates how fractured many nations are.

POLITICAL TREND CHARTS

These short charts provide a quick and quantitative look at a particular nation's (or in some cases a nonexistent but theoretically possible nation's) type of government, the stability of that government, and that government's effectiveness. The political cohesion of the nation, the comparative level of "repression" (a rough index of personal and political freedom), and the comparative education level, including educational resources (schools, universities, the cultural emphasis on learning) as of early 1995, are also rated. In most cases, figures are given for 1995 and are projected into the year 2001. These short charts have already stirred debate. That is good. Readers and critics are encouraged to construct their own.

REGIONAL POWERS AND POWER INTEREST INDICATOR CHARTS

Attempts to provide a "comparative quantitative rating" of the major national (and sometimes subnational) players' economic, historical, political, and military interests in various aspects of the conflict under discussion. Also provides an analysis of the participants "comparative Force Generation Potential" (FGP). The authors use these as a basis for conducting military/political war games of the conflict under analysis. Important note: The FGP shown on the chart is relative to the specific conflict only. A rating of "9+" means a particular player can bring overwhelming power to bear in that conflict. (There are no 9+ ratings in this book.) A "0−" would indicate that the player can't even mount a decent street demonstration.

The United States appears in many of these charts. U.S. FGP ratings are usually based on a five- to sixty-day reaction time (often that is specified in the chart). The U.S. FGPs assume (in almost every case) that the United States is involved militarily in this conflict only (i.e., the United States isn't already waging a war in another part of the world). This is an important assumption to understand, for U.S. power, like everyone else's, is limited.

Each player's ability to intervene diplomatically and politically is also rated. In several instances a nation's ability to contribute to regional economic development is rated as well. In the chapter on Mexico the reader will also find a basic power-rating chart comparing political, economic, and combat power of current and potential factions inside Mexico (as of early 1995).

Participant Strategies and Goals

This section takes a practical view of the political-military strategies and options of the players. Draws on information in the entire chapter to synthesize a view of participant aims.

This section attempts to dispense with volumes of superfluous detail that usually surround a current conflict. While not slighting the numerous undertones of a situation, a clear description of who wants what from whom goes a long way toward putting each conflict into better perspective.

Potential Outcomes

Gives the reader a look at possible futures, depending on certain events. Consider this to be the authors' betting line, and the most controversial aspect of the book. These are based on "game projections" by the authors.

KIND AND COST OF WAR

This section varies from chapter to chapter. The section underlines or encapsulates important information about the kind (or kinds) of past or potential conflicts. In some chapters it provides estimates of the fiscal and human cost of the conflict. The cost is expressed in two currencies: lives and material wealth. Wealthy nations generally fight a war of matériel. Life is precious, so they can afford to throw wealth into the battle instead of lives. Poor nations have nothing to commit but lives. Wars between nations with material resources are more likely to escalate. Warfare between less wealthy nations tends to be bloodier, assuming that the combatants can afford sufficient weapons to fight more than one or two battles.

APPENDICES

For the reader who is interested in more specific information and the sidelights involved in each conflict, "special appendices" are attached to most chapters. The "information packages" in the appendices usually provide more background information or additional analyses. In some cases, exotic items are tossed in so that the reader can spice up a dragging cocktail party conversation. In one case we tack on a newspaper essay written at the time a crucial opportunity for international action was muffed. It's there as something to think about. Most of these are tagged as Quick (and Extended) Looks. These are short (and not so short) descriptions either of interesting local situations that we felt should be especially highlighted or of conflicts that are analogs of wars more exhaustively discussed in other chapters. Several of the Quick Looks focus on nations the authors have determined are critical strategic actors in their particular region (e.g., Indonesia, Brazil, South Africa).

At the end of the book we present a chart showing the particulars of the armed forces of all the nations of the world (except the tiny ones) and give a brief description of each nation's military situation and whatever wars are going on within its borders.

A
QUICK AND DIRTY
GUIDE TO
WAR

THIRD EDITION

Part 1
THE MIDDLE EAST

For thousands of years, the Middle East, the area encompassed by Egypt, Syria, and the Persian Gulf, has been the focus of dramatic and momentous events. Epic grudges and grievances spanning centuries keep tensions high. Nothing has changed.

Chapter 1

IRAN: THE MULLAHS' MANY WARS

INTRODUCTION

During the golden age of the Achaemenians (559–330 B.C.), Persia was the center of the universe, politically and metaphysically. The Arabs knew their subordinate place. If the mountain tribes to the east and north failed to pay tribute, Persian shock troops were dispatched. If the Greeks and other Europeans couldn't be bought off, the emperor of Persia would deal with them militarily. As for the people on the vast steppes of central Asia, fortress cities and alliances thwarted the northern barbarians.

Medean and Zoroastrian religious knowledge and philosophical speculation assured Persia of its moral centrality. The rise of Christianity nineteen hundred years ago, the specter of Christian Constantinople seventeen hundred years ago, and then the stunning military and religious success of Arabian Islam twelve hundred years ago challenged that centrality. After the Arabs came Seljuk Turks, Mongols, and, only six hundred years ago, Tamerlane the Destroyer. Then in the sixteenth century, Persia's rulers rallied to the cause of Shiite Islam. The religious hubs of Qum, Meshed, Karbala, and Najaf gave Shiites a theological voice.

But centuries of conflict, oppression, and despair stalled Persia's return to glory. The nineteenth and twentieth centuries produced further humiliations, with domination by British commercial interests, occupation of northern Persia by the Soviet Russians, and a series of "westernizing and secularizing" shahs in the "Pahlavi dynasty." The reliance of the sycophant Shah Mohammed Reza Pahlavi on that most secular of nations, the United States, was a crowning insult.

Enter the Ayatollah Ruhollah Khomeini, the brains and soul of Iran's Islamic Revolution. Checkmate: removal of the shah in 1979. New game: the takeover of the U.S. embassy, with hostages held for 444 days; the subsequent failure at Desert One of the U.S. rescue mission; and the sponsorship of the Iranian brand of revolution around the globe, but particularly among nonfundamentalist Arabs. Khomeini's activist followers suggested a new era had begun: The Great Satan of the United States would fade, the lesser Satans of Russia and France would wither, and the Zionist entity of Israel would be destroyed. Once again Iran would return to the center of world history, first morally, then politically.

The new game, however, hasn't brought quick glory. The old archenemy, Iraq, attacked, sparking the terrible Iran-Iraq War (1980–88). Then economic problems became endemic. Ethnic antagonisms re-emerged. The mullahs overseeing Iran's revolution now find themselves at the epicenter of nearly two dozen armed conflicts around the globe.

SOURCE OF CONFLICT

Iran, though no global power in the traditional sense of economic, political, or military might, is globe girdling in terms of involvement in controversy, revolution, and armed conflict. While Iran generally takes advantage of preexisting frictions or indigenous problems, the list of conflicts in which Iran is involved is as interesting as it is intimidating:

1. Iraq—The possibility of renewed war with Baghdad is very real; Iran also has common political and theological cause with Arab Shiites in southern Iraq. Iraq supports armed Iranian rebels. Arab Shiites receive covert aid from Iran.

2. Strait of Hormuz—An armed chess match with Oman, the United Arab Emirates, and the industrialized world competing for control of the entrance to the Persian Gulf and oil tanker routes going through it.

3. Persian Gulf states—The entire spectrum of competition exists here among Arab gulf states, from economic, cultural, and political to armed revolution and outright war. Iran disputes ownership of Persian Gulf islands with the Persian Gulf states.

4. Turkey—Struggles with Iran for dominance in the region and in emerging Muslim nations of the former Soviet Union. Iran sponsors radical religious and political factions in Turkey.

5. Azeris and Armenians—Azeris, a Turkic people, comprise 23 percent of Iran's population. Iran has supported Azerbaijan in its war with Armenia, but Persians are concerned about Iranian Azeris' loyalty.

6. Russia—Though Russia is an old enemy, Iran is buying Russian arms and technology, including nuclear reactors. The Azeri-Armenian war could bring Russia and Iran into direct confrontation. Iran has supported Chechen rebels and Islamic radicals throughout the former USSR, particularly in Tajikistan and Kyrgyzstan.

7. Afghanistan—Iran supplies various factions in Afghanistan's continuing civil war.

8. Indonesia and Malaysia—Iran supports Islamist political groups throughout Southeast Asia. Teheran may provide political aid to the PAS Islamic party in the Malay state of Kelantan and the Filipino Moros.

9. Bosnia—Iran has provided guns, money, and political support for Bosnia's Muslims, in a major way.

10. Lebanon—Hezbollah ("the Party of God") works for Teheran and is active in Lebanon's Shiite districts. Iran has tried to extend influence throughout Africa via Arab (primarily Lebanese) communities in Africa.

11. Israel—The "Zionist entity" is an enemy for many convenient reasons. Fighting Israel gives Iran credibility with Arab radicals. Israel also traded with the shah. Iran's "anti-Zionist activity" allegedly includes support for terror strikes in South America. Iran fears Israeli preemptive attacks against nuclear weapons facilities.
12. Egypt—Iran provides support for Islamic radicals against Egypt's moderates.
13. Sudan and the Horn of Africa—Sudan's Islamic north is conducting a holy war against the Christian and animist south. Teheran supports Sudanese radicals as well as Islamic radicals in Somalia and Ethiopia.
14. Algeria—Iran provides money, guns, and training for Algeria's radical Islamists. Rebels in Tunisia and Libya also rate Teheran's support.
15. France and Germany—Muslim immigrants in France provide tinder for Teheran's cause. Iran proselytizes Turks living in Germany.
16. United States—Iran may support several religious and radical political groups in the United States. Iran sees the United States as an active foe, propping up "decadent" Arab gulf states and supporting Israel.
17. Iranian civil strife—The complex political trouble in Iran includes conflict with:

   Kurds—Iranian forces battle Kurdish nationalists in Iran and Iraq.
   Baluchis—A renewed bid for an independent Baluchistan is possible. Baluchis live in both Iran and Pakistan. That could lead to trouble between Iran and Pakistan.
   Monarchist, Communist, and democratic forces—Internal and external opponents of the mullahs' Islamic Revolution.
   Internal religious war—The mullahs' persecution of the Baha'is, evangelical Christians, and other sects continues.
   Various Islamic apostates—A conflict without geographic boundaries. Salman Rushdie is the most famous of apostate enemies of the Iranian Islamic revolution. Fatwas, propaganda,

censorship of foreign TV videos, and terror are the weapons in this war.

WHO'S INVOLVED

Iran—Perceived as "the loser" in the Iran-Iraq War, Iran sat quietly on the sidelines during the Persian Gulf War, waiting. The revolutionary appeal of Iran's brand of radical Islam gives it global leverage.

Iraq—Saddam Hussein's regime invaded Kuwait, igniting the Persian Gulf War. That war substantially damaged Iraq's military but did not destroy it. Iraq ranks in the world's top five nations in proven oil reserves.

Russia—Moscow's military power remains immense. The Russians watch the Iranian border, abutting troubled Azerbaijan. A "traditional" supplier of Iraq during the cold war, Russian arms show up in both Iran and Iraq. Russia fears nuclear weapons in the hands of Islamic radicals but sells nuclear technology for cash.

United States—The U.S. Central Command (CENTCOM) controls U.S. forces in the region. The new U.S. Fifth Fleet is CENTCOM's navy. Diego Garcia, the U.S. Indian Ocean base, stockpiles equipment for a Marine brigade and an Army armored brigade. U.S. heavy equipment is being stockpiled in Kuwait and Qatar, and possibly the UAE.

Saudi Arabia and the Persian Gulf states—The Gulf Arabs fear Persian (Iranian) domination. The UAE and Oman confront Iran across the Strait of Hormuz.

Islamic revolutionary radicals—The "Islamists" are now quite an international group. Many revolutionary religious groups are not directly controlled by Iran, for these people see themselves on a mission from God and thus free of any earthly constraints, including Iran's.

Armenia and Azerbaijan—These former Soviet SSRs are now weak nation-states locked in a bitter war on Iran's northwestern border.

The Kurds—This ethnic group (over fifty different clans and tribes) has been waging a war against Persians, Turks, and Baghdadi Arabs for over two thousand years. Saddam Hussein's Iraqi regime has fought a brutal war against the Kurds and killed thousands of them with chemical weapons.

Wild Cards

Iranian dissidents—Ideological, religious and secular groups oppose the Iranian Shiite clergy's Islamic revolution (see Local Politics).

Turkey—Friction over the Kurds remains. The Iranian radicals think Turkey's secular (and Sunni) state is heretical. Turks don't particularly care for the Arabs or Iranians. The feeling is mutual. Iran sees Turkish anti-Kurd attacks into Iraq as a sign of Ankara's wider regional ambitions.

Israel—In 1981 the Israelis attacked the Iraqi nuclear reactor at Osirak. If Iran obtains nuclear weapons, Israel would attempt to destroy them. Even the mullahs respect Mossad, the Israeli intelligence agency.

Baluchis—Aryan tribe. Like the Kurds, this ancient ethnic group never managed to achieve modern nationhood. The border-straddling Baluchis threaten the stability of Pakistan, Iran, and Afghanistan.

"Afghanis"—Islamic militants who learned to fight during the 1979–89 struggle against the Soviets. Once controlled by Pakistani secret police, they are increasingly a power unto themselves, controlled by no one. A few "Afghanis" have ended up in Bosnia.

Afghanistan—Iran at one time supported eight different Afghan mujahedeen (freedom fighter) factions. Now some of the factions fight among themselves. Teheran fears that Afghan fighting could spill over into Iran via Afghan refugee camps, and possibly stir up the Baluchis.

Syria—Iran's Syrian alliance frayed after the Persian Gulf War. The Middle East peace process has led to new tensions. Yet the Syrian Alawite regime regards Iraq as its enemy. The divisions between the Syrian and Iraqi branches of the Baath party run deep. Iran offers Syria "a second front" against Iraq.

GEOGRAPHY

Iran has an area of almost 1.65 million square kilometers (a little bigger than Alaska) and a population of some 68 million. Ninety-five percent of the people are Shiite Muslims. Iran is, however, an ethnic hodgepodge, which is one reason the "unifying" Shia faith is so important politically. Fifty-one percent of the people are Persians, 23 percent Azeris, and 7 percent Kurds. Eastern Iran's 1.5 million Baluchis make up a large and potentially anti-Teheran minority. Sixty percent of the people speak Persian or Persian dialects (Farsi and Dari, mostly); around 25 percent speak Turkic dialects (like Azeri). Prior to the revolution, the capital city of Teheran had a population of about 4 million; the current figure is 12 million. Two million Arabs live in the province of Arabistan (also called Kuzistan). The Iran-Iraq War battle sites of Abadan and Khorramshahr are in Kuzistan, near the Shatt-al-Arab.

Iran borders Turkey, Armenia (only thirty-five kilometers in length), Azerbaijan, Turkmenistan, Afghanistan, Pakistan, and the Persian Gulf. Rugged mountains cover half of the nation. The Zagros range runs from the Turkish and Azeri border region south and east. The city of Teheran sits on a high plateau. While open to ground attack from the north, as the Iran-Iraq War illustrated, Teheran is relatively immune from attack by Iraqi land forces. Teheran is well within range of Iraqi SCUD missile and air attacks. Iraq remains Iran's most likely foe.

The Shatt-al-Arab (the confluence of the Tigris and Euphrates rivers) and its delta separates southern Iraq and Iran's Kuzistan Province. Control of the Shatt-al-Arab has been a major source of Arab-Persian conflict. The Shatt-al-Arab controls access to Iraq's chief port, Basra. Terrain around the Basra-Abadan-Khorramshahr area consists of mud flats, marsh, salt flats, and salt marsh.

Seventy-five percent of Iraq's population of 15–16 million inhabits the alluvial plain running north from Basra to Baghdad. Breaking through to these population centers was an Iranian objective during the Iran-Iraq War.

Upriver, the Iran-Iraq border area turns rugged and dry. The northern region is raked with tough mountains and hills. The "Kurdistan" areas feature this rugged terrain. The mountains continue into Turkey and Iran.

At the far end of the Persian Gulf lies the Strait of Hormuz. Thirty-five to 45 percent of the world's daily oil supply moves through the strait. Islands in the bottleneck, such as Sirri, are critical military geography. Small boats, artillery, and antiship missiles can be based on those islands.

To the north Iran borders Azerbaijan, the Caspian Sea, and Turkmenistan. The Caspian Sea and its littoral are the main routes for a ground assault toward Teheran. East of Iran lie Pakistan and Afghanistan. The terrain is rugged, with open, rocky deserts rising into mountains. The Baluchi tribe inhabits eastern Iran and western Pakistan.

HISTORY

Background to Iran-Iraq War (1980–88)

The peoples east of the Shatt-al-Arab have been raiding (or invading) west of that waterway for millennia. Alexander the Great fought in the area, as did the Romans and the Byzantines. Persia (officially renamed Iran in the 1930s, though the locals called themselves Iranians for centuries, "Persia" being a Western appellation based on the name of an ancient Iranian province) has occupied Iraq three times since 1500: from 1508 to 1514, 1529 to 1543, and 1623 to 1638. Boundary disputes, specifically over the Shatt-al-Arab, and old enmities led to war. In 1639, Arabs and Persians signed the Treaty of Peace and Frontiers, a peace ensured by tribute money paid by Baghdad to the Persian shah.

In 1818 war broke out, again over the Shatt-al-Arab. The first Treaty of Erzerum (1823) failed to solve the dispute. In 1847, Britain and Russia tried to stop an impending Persian-Ottoman war over the river and imposed the second Treaty of Erzerum. Abadan, Khorramshahr, and the east bank of the Shatt became Persian; Ottoman Turkey received Zuhab Province, an area the Persians had occupied for two centuries.

The failure of the 1911 Teheran Protocols, the Ottoman collapse after World War I, conditional Iraqi independence, and Persian refusal to acknowledge the new Arab state produced a chaotic boundary situation. The Kurds exacerbated things by conducting "bandit actions" against both Arabs and Persians. In 1936 the Iraqis made several concessions and set the boundary in mid-channel on the Thalweg Line. The Iranians guaranteed that the Shatt would be open to Iraqi shipping. This pact held until Iraqi nationalists came to power in 1958. They regarded the agreement, with some justification, as a sellout. When the radical Baath party took control in 1968, its nationalist program included demands for the "return to Iraq" of the Arab-populated areas in Kuzistan. The Baathists called for Arab resistance to Iranian authority in Kuzistan.

The Iranians in turn sponsored Kurdish anti-Iraqi activity. By 1976 a full-scale Kurdish rebellion against Baghdad was under way. The Kurds received U.S. backing. Iraq also harbored a fugitive the shah of Iran didn't like: the Ayatollah Ruhollah Khomeini. The Iraqis wanted the Iranian border closed to Kurdish rebels, and the shah wanted the Ayatollah out of the region—to keep him from stirring up Shiite activists. A deal was cut; Khomeini, however, proved to be quite politically adept.

The regime of Saddam Hussein in Baghdad saw the chaos following the fall of the shah and the establishment of the extremist Islamic revolution as an opportunity to settle the border problem in Iraq's favor. Flexing of Iraqi military would also forestall any attempts by the Iranians to promote Islamic revolution among Iraq's Shiite community.

The Iran-Iraq War began in August 1980, with an Iraqi tank and motorized infantry assault into Kuzistan. While the Iraqis made initial progress, their logistical (supply) deficiencies and a rigid command structure stopped them from taking advantage of initial Iranian weakness. No "Arab rebellion," however, occurred. The Iraqis halted their invasion and called for negotiations. The Ayatollah Khomeini's regime in Teheran refused and counterattacked. The campaign became a full-scale conventional war, with the two nations locked in attrition combat within a sector basically thirty kilometers on either side of the Tigris River branch of the Shatt-al-Arab. Iran conducted lurching foot-infantry offensives, with human-wave attacks led by zealot Revolutionary Guard regiments. Iraq, realizing it was outmanned, got smart and responded with layers of trenches, fortifications, and carefully prepared traps. Iranians would break through a trench line and find themselves in a "fire pocket," enfiladed by dug-in artillery, tanks, and infantry on their flanks. The Iraqis violated international law and used chemical weapons against Iranian infantry. In general, both sides used air and armor forces piecemeal; as a result, tank and fighter-bomber forces were very ineffective.

In February 1986 the Iranians attacked and took the Fao (or Faw) Peninsula. That put "Persian" troops next to Kuwait. Iraq counter-attacked in April 1988 and retook the Fao area. In July 1988, Iran bitterly accepted UN Security Council Resolution 598 (passed in July 1987) that called for a cease-fire. In effect, both sides lost the war (as many of their neighbors had hoped). Iraq's invasion of Iran in 1980 failed miserably, and Iran's subsequent invasion of Iraq from 1982 to 1988 failed even more tragically. Iraq lost fewer troops but spent more (largely borrowed) money. Iran saw its revolution weakened by a failed jihad against Iraq, but did recover some inconsequential lost territories when Iraq sued for a final peace in the wake of the Persian Gulf War.

The "sideshows" to the Iran-Iraq War were also serious: the Tanker War, which brought the United States into the fray, the War of the Cities (also called the Missile War), and the interminable war against the Kurds. The Tanker War consisted of Iraq shooting at Iranian oil tankers, an attempt to curtail Iranian oil shipments, and the Iranians attacking the tankers of nations Iran believed allied with Iraq. Iraq began the Tanker War in 1982 when Syria closed down the Iraqi Mediterranean oil pipeline that crosses Syrian territory; the Iraqis saw this, correctly, as an attempt to strangle Iraq economically. The United States "reflagged" several Kuwaiti tankers and conducted naval escort missions in the Persian Gulf. Iran used naval mines for most of its antitanker attacks, with occasional surface attacks launched by Rev-olutionary Guards in Swedish Boghammer speedboats. The Iranians also acquired Chinese-built Silkworm antiship missiles. The most no-table Silkworm strike was launched against a stationary target: a Ku-waiti offshore oil port. U.S. and Iranian forces fought on a number of occasions. In April 1987, U.S. forces sank an Iranian frigate. The most serious attack against U.S. forces, however, was launched by Iraq in May 1987. An Iraqi fighter-bomber fired (accidentally?) two missiles at a "naval target," the U.S. Navy frigate *Stark*. Thirty-seven U.S. sailors died. One of the largest losses of life occurred in July 1988 when the U.S. Aegis guided missile cruiser *Vincennes* accidentally downed an Iranian passenger plane (Iran Air Flight 655) flying from Bandar 'Abbas across the Strait of Hormuz. Two hundred ninety civilians died. The *Vincennes* weapons officers mistook the Iranian Airbus for an Iranian F-14 Tomcat fighter.

The War of the Cities consisted of Iraqi bombardments of Teheran and other Iranian cities with Soviet-supplied, Iraqi-modified SCUD ballistic missiles. The Iranians replied in kind. At least one Iranian missile hit Kuwait. The Iraqis maintain the "cities war" was begun with Iranian fighter-bomber attacks on civilian areas in Baghdad. Several thousand civilians were killed and injured in attacks on cities. The War of the Cities foreshadowed Iraqi SCUD attacks in the Persian Gulf War.

The war against the Kurds continues to grind on. In the north the Kurds became active against the Iraqis, with support from Iran and bases inside Iran. After the 1988 cease-fire the Iraqis struck back. Iraqi troops burned and gassed several Kurdish villages using nerve agent GA (tabun) and a mustard gas. The Kurds continue to raid Turkey from Iraqi territory and attack targets in Iran. (See the chapter on Turkey.)

Iran lay low during the Persian Gulf War. Iranians smuggled goods to Iraq (despite the UN economic boycott), but when Allied air attacks began in January 1991, the Iranians made it clear they were neutral. One of the Persian Gulf War's more bizarre episodes occurred when the Iraqi Air Force began to fly en masse to Iran. Iran incorporated the best Iraqi planes (French Mirages and advanced MiGs) into its air force.

Since the mid-1980s, Iran has attempted to export its brand of revolution throughout the world. Islamic groups from Malaysia to Bosnia to the United States have received political and economic aid. Groups in Lebanon, Egypt, Iraq, and Algeria and radical Islamic factions in Afghanistan have been the primary beneficiaries. The government of the Sudan is a staunch ally of Iran and may be as close to a "puppet" ally as Teheran possesses.

The Iranian Gambols: The Mullahs' Many Wars

See the Source of Conflict section above for a list of the covert wars in which Iran is involved.

The Next Iran-Iraq War

The Iran-Iraq War (1980–88) was simply the latest iteration of an old conflict over control of the Shatt-al-Arab. This fight has raged, lapsed, then continued since at least 500 B.C.

In the Iran-Iraq War, supersonic aircraft, antiship missiles, and modern tanks mixed with human-wave infantry attacks. These high- and low-tech forces, tied to inadequate logistics systems incapable of supporting sustained offensives, produced high-casualty attrition combat along a static front. Call it World War I in the salt marshes and mountains.

The Kurds could ignite a new conflict. Iranian bombers frequently fly into northern Iraq's UN-imposed no-fly zone to strike bases of the Democratic Party of Iranian Kurdistan, an Iranian Kurd rebel group. Teheran has raided Iranian National Army bases close to Baghdad.

The possibility of another war is real. The next round of major fighting between or among Iraq, Iran, Syria, nations on the Arabian Peninsula, Israel, and others in the region, however, may not be like World War I; with the addition of chemical and nuclear warheads, and ballistic missiles (and precision-guided conventional weapons), the next round of combat might be more like World War III: nuclear warheads blistering desolate battlefields laced with nerve agent and other chemical weapons.

Regional and Global Reach: Iranian Islamic Revolution

The revolutionary appeal of Islam exacerbated the Iran-Iraq War. Iraq's secular leadership is predominantly Sunni Muslim; its overall population is, by a narrow majority, Shiite. Iran has tried to co-opt the Iraqi Shiite community; it continues to mine Shiite discontent in southern Iraq.

The Iranians send religious shock waves throughout the region. Increasingly volatile (and Shiite) Bahrain has attracted Iranian zealots. Oman and the United Arab Emirates (UAE) confront Iran across the vital Strait of Hormuz, where much of the industrialized world's oil passes every day inside the tanker hulls of very large crude carriers (VLCCs). Religious discontent isn't strictly a Shiite phenomenon. Poor Sunnis are angry with "the wealthy sheiks." In twenty years, Teheran hopes, Sunni purists could stage their own uprising—in Saudi Arabia.

Teheran sponsors Islamic revolutionaries around the Persian Gulf and the Middle East, providing radical movements in Oman, the UAE, Qatar, Bahrain, Saudi Arabia, and even Kuwait with arms and political support.

The Iranian Islamic revolution has global tentacles. The Shiite revival has given the Iranians a global ideology, an alternative to Western democracy and capitalism.

Lebanon is a stronghold of Hezbollah, the Shiite "Party of God." Through Hezbollah, Iran wages a proxy war with Israel. Hezbollah regularly battles Israeli forces in the South Lebanon buffer zone and sends guerrillas into Israel. The Israelis in return bomb Hezbollah sites.

Economic Woes: Source of Civil Instability

Iran, though a major regional power, is a troubled nation. Economic woes are real. Iran has experimented with multiple exchange rates in an attempt to control foreign currency reserve fluctuations. Subsidies and state intervention exacerbate deficits. Inflation, which hit astronomical levels during the Iran-Iraq War, remains a devastating problem.

A basic dilemma: The Shiite clerics running the Iranian government don't want to lose control over the economy; loss of economic levers, they believe, is the first step in losing political power. The properties belonging to the late shah and some belonging to wealthy Iranians who fled the revolution were confiscated by "religious foundations" run by prominent clerics. Billions of dollars in assets instantly became the personal fiefdoms of the clergy who control them. Wealth is power and even among the devout it becomes a corrupting influence. The clerics are not businessmen, but they know how to use their religious and political power to protect financial assets. Attempts by more pragmatic Iranians to run the economy on a more rational, productive basis are opposed by the now rich clerics. The population suffers, and gradually becomes aware that the clerics are the chief obstacle to a more efficient economy.

Will Iran's religious revolution be brought down by an Iranian rebellion against clerical control of the economy? Riots over increases in utility, fuel, and water bills broke out in early 1995, with reports of over one hundred demonstrators killed. Helicopter gunships from the Iranian Army reportedly fired on the crowds. Building active, effective opposition to Iran's clever religious leaders, however, takes time and money.

Nuclear Warfare, Iranian Style

Despite economic woes, Iran is rapidly acquiring an arsenal of advanced weapons, including ballistic missiles, chemical weapons, and, soon, nuclear warheads. Russia and North Korea have been prime sources for Iranian weapons.

In the early 1980s, Iran tried to buy centrifuges, heavy water, and other nuclear bomb components from Argentina. Iranian agents, seeking nuclear technology, now ply Russia, China, Western and Eastern Europe, and the states of the former Soviet Union.

The game of nuclear hide-and-seek puts Teheran on a collision course with Israel and the United States. Teheran fears an Israeli preemptive strike on nuclear facilities similar to the Israeli strike on Iraq's Osirak reactor in 1981. U.S. cruise missiles are also a threat.

Actually obtaining a nuclear weapon would drastically increase Iran's tensions with Turkey and Russia. But cash-starved Russia has contracted with Iran to build up to four nuclear reactors near Büshehr. Russia also sells weapons to Iran. Sources estimate the Russians are selling the Iranians $1 billion worth of used military equipment a year.

The United States, which constantly complains about violations of the Nuclear Non-Proliferation Treaty, is a source. In 1993, U.S. corporations sold Iran turbojet engines, gas liquefaction and separation equipment, lab furnaces, and centrifuges. The turbojets could be used on cruise missiles. When business and foreign policy collide, the smart bettor bets on business.

War in Central Asia: Return to the Great Game

With the failure of communism, the former Soviet "Islamic SSRs," such as Tajikistan and Kyrgyzstan, are fertile ground for Iranian influence peddling. Iran has sought to extend religious, cultural, political, and occasional military influence into central Asia. And from the mullahs' perspective, why not? At one time central Asia was a vast Persian satrapy.

Iran has joined what the British once called the great game—the struggle for central Asia. In the nineteenth century the players were Great Britain and Russia, the proxies various Indian, Afghan, and Himalayan tribes. Now the players are Russia, Turkey, Iran, the United States, and in the deep background Europe and China.

Teheran supports Islamic radicals with cash, training, and weapons. But the pitch to central Asia is also economic and geographic real politik. In 1994, Tehran tried to play regional peacemaker among Russian and Tajik Muslim and nationalist adversaries in Tajikistan. The economic and transportation card is on the table: In 1995, Iran completed several links of a railroad through Iran from central Asia to the Persian Gulf. Iran wants the central Asian republics to use its railways in preference to Russian transport nets.

Iran and Azerbaijan participate in a consortium to develop the multibillion barrel Caspian Sea oil reserves. Several U.S. firms participate in the consortium. The Azeris have sought and gained Teheran's financial aid for funding energy projects in Azerbaijan's autonomous enclave of Nahcivan.

Turkmenistan is particularly interested in an Iranian oil pipeline project designed to export central Asian oil and gas through Iran and

Turkey. Iran and Georgia discussed Teheran supplying natural gas to Tbilisi. Iran offers Georgia an alternative to Russian supplies.

Teheran has tried to influence the continuing civil war in Afghanistan by supplying arms to several radical Islamic guerrilla organizations. All is not simpatico, however, between Teheran and Afghanistan. In 1993, Iran began forcibly returning some two million Afghans from refugee camps inside Iran. Migrants are a volatile issue in central Asia.

Chechnya, Azerbaijan, and Armenia: The Potential for Another Russo-Persian War?

In March 1994, Iran offered to mediate in the war between Russian and Muslim secessionists in Chechnya. Russia reacted with disdain, claiming that Iran had provided the Chechen rebels with weapons.

The Chechen conflict isn't likely to bring Russia into a war with Iran. However, the bitter struggle between Armenia and Azerbaijan could, most likely by an "accident" where events in the smaller conflict escalate and suddenly Russia and Iran collide on the battlefield.

Here is an example of such a central Asian collision: At least 23 percent of Iran's population is Azeri (left inside Iran by a border drawn in 1828). The Turkic Azeris are a tricky ethnic question for Teheran. The Azeris tend to identify with fellow Turks; antipathy between Turkey and Iran is real. Iranian Azeris may come to believe they have more in common with independent Azerbaijan than with Iran, though ethnic Azeris have been successful inside Iran. Still, over one hundred thousand refugees from the Armenian-Azeri war are in Iran. Many Azeris think Teheran has been pursuing a policy of supporting Azerbaijan rhetorically but keeping it weak so that Azerbaijan does not become a beacon for Iranian Azeri nationalism. Such a policy might backfire. Trouble could occur in the Azeri refugee camps. Internal Iranian strife could ignite an Azeri-Persian conflict, which would draw Russia in on Azerbaijan's side or bring in Russian troops as "peacekeepers." Russia and Iran would then confront one another directly. Another scenario brings Russia in on the side of Armenia while Iran actively supports Azerbaijan. An even more dangerous alternative: Iran and Turkey support Azerbaijan against Russia. The veneer of Muslim versus Christian, already active in Christian Armenia's fight with Muslim Azerbaijan, could lead to a bigger war.

Russia and Iran are deeply involved in Armenia and Azerbaijan. In spring 1995, Russia signed a treaty with Armenia that allows Moscow to operate military bases in Armenia for twenty-five years. The agreement permits Russia to position forces in the northern Armenian town of Gyumri and in the capital of Yerevan. Several observers pointed out the treaty merely legalized the presence of Russian troops already in Armenia.

Iran would support Azerbaijan out of religious solidarity, because of pressure from Iranian Azeris, or, more cynically, because of a decision to absorb Azerbaijan and keep its own Azeri minority in line (a risky gambit but not farfetched by central Asian standards).

There have been battlefield incidents. Armenia's Yerevan Radio reported in February 1994 that an aircraft entered Armenia from Iranian air space and bombed targets in the Kapan and Megrin districts. Iran may have supported Azerbaijani forces in spring 1994 in combat near the Omar Pass and Goradiz. Armenian propaganda? Possibly. Incidents like these, however, seed broader conflicts.

The Terror War

The Iranian government continually denies involvement in international terrorist activities. The truth is, terror attacks are a means of "long-range strategic strike" for many nations, Iran among them. The Iranians believe terror attacks give them the ability to threaten the United States, Israel, and other enemies; terror operations become a low-tech counter to the long-range strategic weapons of more militarily sophisticated nations.

The secular Arab governments of Egypt and Algeria are terror targets of Islamic revolutionaries supported and trained by Iran. Little secret is made of Iran's support for Hezbollah's terror attacks on Israel. Iranian terror targets also include Iranian political opposition figures, many Muslim intellectuals, and Islamic "apostates" such as author Salman Rushdie, who went into hiding in 1989 after the Ayatollah Khomeini found his book, *The Satanic Verses,* to be blasphemy. Iran's ruling mullahs view terrorism as a legitimate political and military instrument. The U.S. State Department maintains that "acts of terrorism are approved at the highest levels of government in Iran."

Allegedly, the University of Dawat and Jihad (University of the Community of the Holy War) in Peshawar, Pakistan, has received significant Iranian support. Dawat is the top training facility for terrorists operating worldwide and may have been key to the training of the team that attacked the World Trade Center in New York City in 1993. The "Afghanis"—anti-Soviet Islamic fighters (not all of them Afghan) trained in Pakistan by the U.S. CIA, Pakistan intelligence, and, in some cases, Iran—provide Islamic revolutionaries with a core of experienced guerrillas and potential terrorists. In the early 1990s, training for terrorists supporting the Iranian revolution seems to have moved to the Sudan.

War in the Strait of Hormuz

From 35 to 45 percent of the world's daily oil supply moves by tanker from the Persian Gulf through the Strait of Hormuz. For the world's industrial economies, the Strait of Hormuz is a geographic choke point.

Iran has often played hard games with its neighbors across the strait. In the 1970s the shah of Iran helped Oman fight an earnest, dirty desert war with then Marxist Southern Yemen (Aden). The shah, trying to play regional warlord, promised to defend the UAE. The Persian Gulf Arabs were suspicious, for many reasons. It is one thing to have the distant Americans playing protector; it is another to have the local big guy, Iran, as protector. Then came Khomeini's revolution. Many in the UAE read "Islamic revolution" as another cover for Persian control.

The Strait of Hormuz has always been a key objective for the U.S. CENTCOM. CENTCOM regularly holds war-game operations in the strait, including a mock attack on the chief Iranian port in the area, Bandar 'Abbas.

The Iranians are very aware of CENTCOM's attention. They have improved their naval facilities in the Persian Gulf (at Kharg Island and Büshehr); strengthened defenses around their port in the Strait of Hormuz, Bandar 'Abbas; and improved air and naval facilities at Chāh Bahār on the Gulf of Oman. In early 1995, Iran moved U.S.-made Hawk surface-to-air missiles (SAMs) and heavy artillery onto Abu Musa, in the Persian Gulf near the UAE. It also deployed various SAMs (including SA-6s) and Silkworm antiship missiles on the islands of Qeshm and Sirri. Iran's loyal Revolutionary Guard Corps units man the island fortifications. Fishermen from the UAE also live on Abu Musa. The Iranians have beefed up forces on the strait islands due north of Abu Musa, Greater Tunb and Lesser Tunb. The UAE claims these islands but does not have the military power to enforce its rights.

The Iranian deployments mean that Teheran now has missiles on both sides of a deep-water channel that loaded tankers are obliged to use when passing through the Strait of Hormuz.

There are several scenarios that could lead to anything from a war of nerves to a very high intensity conflict. Iranian attempts to destabilize the UAE or Oman via surprise attack or terror and proxy political forces, attempts to hinder tanker traffic, actually firing on tankers, mining the strait or threatening to mine the strait (and sending shipping insurance costs through the roof), could trigger a U.S.-led coalition response.

If the Israelis (or anyone else for that matter) attack nuclear weapons facilities or targets in Iran, the Iranians might attempt to close the Strait of Hormuz as a form of political blackmail.

The strait is troubled water. Iranian naval forces regularly stop vessels in order to check for contraband, often using UN Security Council Resolution 661 (economic embargo against Iraq) as legal cover for the inspection. There are, however, many "freelancers" who engage in a form of piracy. The Iranians stop freighters and demand either a bribe or part of the goods in order to obtain release. Allegedly, some of the freelancers operate under direct orders from Teheran. The Persian Gulf has a long tradition of local piracy—committed by both Persians and Arabs.

LOCAL POLITICS

Islamic Republican party—Political front constructed by the now-deceased Ayatollah Khomeini; completely dominated by the mullahs and the vast wealth of the late shah (and his followers) that they now "manage." Three "subparties" are key: the Teheran Militant Clergy Association, the Militant Clerics Association, and the Fedaiyin Islam Organization. Organizations supporting the radicals include the Muslim Students Following the Line of the Imam and the Hojjatiyeh Society.

Ayatollah Ruhollah Khomeini—The Imam. Died in 1989 but still the spiritual leader of Iranian radicals.

Revolutionary Guards (also called the Pasadaran)—Iranian youths forming the Islamic revolutionary army; were used to purge the old imperial army, now operate as political and military shock troops. As of mid-1995, they were organized into eleven regional commands with a total of four motorized divisions and twenty-four infantry divisions. Many of the "divisions" have only 6,000–8,000 lightly armed soldiers and a handful of artillery pieces.

Iranian Army—Reorganized after the Iran-Iraq War. It consists of three army headquarters and ten divisions: three armored, two mechanized-infantry, and five infantry divisions. (The Iranian Army divisions are full-sized, with 15,000–16,000 soldiers and tanks, artillery, and antiaircraft artillery and missiles.) The army deploys two airborne infantry brigades, four special forces brigades, and an SSM (surface-to-surface missile) brigade armed with SCUD and advanced SCUD SSMs.

Komiteh—Islamic revolutionary secret police. The term also refers to semiofficial "squads" that patrol streets enforcing proper Islamic behavior.

Bassij—Government-backed Islamic popular militia. The Bassij counterbalance the regular army. The army has refused to fire on mobs of angry citizens; the Bassij are more willing to "keep order."

Majlis, or "Islamic Consultative Assembly"—Iranian parliament. It is divided into "moderates," who want to get the economy back in order, and religious zealots, who are more interested in revolution and maintaining power.

Bazaaris—Iranian merchant class. They are perhaps the most dangerous enemy of the Iranian clerics, for the bazaaris have money, brains, and, with their followers and employees, numbers. The bazaaris and clerics have traditionally found themselves on opposite political sides.

Organization for Human Rights and Fundamental Freedoms in Iran—One of several European-based Iranian opposition groups.

National Front—Anti-Islamic-republic group composed of a few remaining shah supporters and some liberals who supported the interim Baktiar regime after the shah's fall. It operates out of France.

National Council of Resistance—Anti-Islamic-republic group composed of liberals and leftists, a large number of whom once supported Khomeini. Former President Bani-Sadr, the only man in the entire thirty-five-hundred-year history of Persia who was ever democratically elected to any national office, was involved with the National Council of Resistance. In 1993 the National Council of Resistance elected Mujahedeen member Maryam Rajavi Iran's "president in exile." The Mujahedeen have changed from an "Islamic Marxist" organization to a Muslim nationalist movement. Many women participate in the revived National Council of Resistance.

National Liberation Army (NLA)—Anti-Khomeini Iranian group. It has fifteen thousand troops under arms, is supported by Iraq, and is associated with the People's Mujahedeen, an Iraq-based Iranian opposition group.

Al Dawa—Iraqi Shiite opposition group loyal to Iranian revolutionary regime. Its full name is Al Dawa Al Islamiyah—Islamic Call—and it is allegedly involved in numerous terrorist incidents in the Persian Gulf area and in Lebanon.

Democratic Party of Iranian Kurdistan (KDP)—An Iranian Kurd rebel group that operates from bases in Iraq.

Tudeh party—Iranian Communist party. Most members have been killed or have fled to Turkmenistan or elsewhere in the ex-USSR.

Great Satan—The United States. Lesser Satans have included France, Iraq's Saddam Hussein, Israel, etc.

Hezbollah (Hizbollah)—The "Party of God" works for Teheran

and is active throughout Shiite communities in Lebanon. It was formed in 1983.

Bishop Haik Hovsepian Mehr—Former chairman of the Council of the Assemblies of God Church. He was murdered in Iran in January 1995. Islamic extremists loyal to the Teheran government are suspected of the crime. According to Western press sources, Mehr embarrassed the Teheran regime by championing the plight of a sixty-year-old convert from Islam to Christianity, Mehdi Dibaj. According to Iran's radical leaders, converting from Islam to Christianity is apostasy punishable by death. Dibaj was held in prison for a decade until Mehr secured his release by appealing to the Vatican and the international community. Dibaj was later found murdered.

Savak—The shah's old secret police force and intelligence service. Some surviving Savak agents are now allegedly involved in the Middle Eastern drug and weapons trade.

Kuzistan—Iranian province, also called Arabistan, with a significant Arab minority (30-plus percent). It has large producing oil fields.

"Marsh Arabs"—Shiite Arabs living in Shatt-al-Arab marshes. Their area, especially around Majnoon Island (secret or "hidden" island), was the scene of some of the Iran-Iraq War's most bitter fighting.

Satellite TV—In 1994 the mullahs attempted to outlaw ownership of "dish TV" antennae, the type that pluck racy Western TV shows off geosynchronous satellites. Western TV undermines the mullahs' vision the social order: too much sex, violence, and rock and roll.

Hijab—Modest Islamic dress. In Islam, a hijab gives a woman dignity, respect, and authority. A chador is a head-to-toe cloak. Many women, especially urbanites with education, having tasted freedom under the shah, resent the religious restrictions the clerics have reimposed.

Fatwa—Religious proclamation, effective in proportion to the stature of the issuing cleric. In the West it has come to mean a death warrant.

The Iranian economy—Money woes put a crimp in even a zealot's plans. In May 1993, Iranian President Ali Akbar Rafsanjani won re-election by advocating trade liberalization and economic privatization. His reforms failed; the mullahs couldn't make the austerity measures stick. The Iranian economy is in serious trouble, notably with hard currency because oil export income is decreasing. Iran has well recovered from the earlier Gulf wars and is now the world's second largest petroleum exporter, behind Saudi Arabia. Iran's earnings are estimated at between $17 and $20 billion in 1993, while its foreign debt increased from $9 billion in the late 1980s to $30 billion. The leading cause: foreign arms purchases.

U.S. economic boycott—A selective boycott. U.S. exports to Iran climbed from $60 million in 1989 to nearly $800 million in 1992. Items sold include consumer goods (like TV videos) and oil equipment. The big question: If the U.S. embargo were to tighten, would it have any effect on Iran's ability to build nuclear weapons and advanced weaponry? The answer is yes, if the embargo included the EEC, Japan, China, and Russia. The embargo does exact a political price from Iran and makes technology acquisition somewhat harder and more expensive.

Refahs—A thousand-shop chain of discount stores that sell goods at prices guaranteed by the Iranian government (a payoff by the mullahs to buy domestic tranquillity). Plunging oil revenues have made even these shops less attractive because of shortages. This encourages unrest, as the people get a taste of what they might have more of if the nation's oil wealth were not devoted to buying weapons.

World Bank—Despite U.S. boycotts and UN denunciations of Iranian troublemaking, the World Bank remains active in Iran. It is particularly successful in financing irrigation projects, which have increased Iranian agricultural production. Iran sells produce to central Asia.

Political Trend Chart

Iran

Gv95	Gv20	PC95	PC20	R95	R20	Ec95	Ec20	EdS95	EdS20
TD5,4	CD5,5	5	5	7	7	4–	4	4	3

Gv = Government Type
TD = Theological Dictatorship (actually a coalition of religious radicals)
    (effectiveness, 0–9, stability 0–9)
CD = Coalition Dictatorship (incorporating religious and secular wings)
PC = Political Cohesiveness (0 = chaos, 9 = maximum)
R = Repression Index (9 maximum)
Ec = Comparative Economic Status (0–9)
EdS = Relative Education Status (0–9); in this case, urban population only

Regional Powers and Power Interest Indicator Charts

Iran and Iraq War II (1980–88)

	Economic Interests	Historical Interests	Political Interest	Military Interest	Force Generation Potential	Ability to Intervene Politically
Iran	8	9	9	9	5	9
Iraq	9	9	9	9	4+	9
Syria	7	8	8	8	3+	5+
Russia	5	7	7	7	5	6
Turkey	6	8	8	8	5	3
United States	7	4	7	6	3	3
Jordan	6	8	8	7	2	4
Egypt	3	7	7	5	2	4
Pakistan	2	4	6	6	2	4
Israel	2	7	7	8	3	1
Saudi Arabia	8	8	9	8	2	5
Kuwait	9	9	9	9	1–	2

Note: 0 = minimum; 9 = maximum

STRAIT OF HORMUZ

The Strait of Hormuz is a specific geographic area, rather than a nation, but one that is strategically vital. This chart focuses primarily on military capabilities. Remember, force generation potential (FGP) reflects comparative capabilities in the specific region or country.

Power Interest Indicator D+ 5*

	Economic Interests	Historical Interests	Political Interest	Military Interest	Force Generation Potential	Ability to Intervene Politically
Iran	8	9	9	9	6†	9
United States	7	5	8	6	6‡	6
Japan	8	4	7	6	1	7
Britain	7	6	6	7	2	4
Saudi Arabia	8	8	9	7	1+	8
Russia	2§	5	4	5	2−	4
Oman	9	9	8	9	2	7
Iraq	2	5	7	4	0	3
UAE	9	9	9	9	1+	8
Turkey	2	5	6	3	1	4
Israel	2	2	7‖	6	2−	0

*FGP for D-Day plus 5, i.e., five days from the commencement of hostilities. If Iranians conduct planned closure of the strait, Iran's FGP on D-Day is 5.

†An FGP of 6 is applicable for defense on the Iranian side of the strait; give "revolutionary Iran" an FGP of 5 for operations on islands in strait, FGP of 2 for operations against the UAE or Oman on mainland. The shah's forces would have had a 4+. Oman's FGP of 2 is applicable to defense in Oman. Oman has a FGP 1− for operations against Iranian islands. The UAE's 1+ is applicable in the UAE and on UAE islands. Until the arrival of new frigates, the UAE has no ability to operate offensively against Iran.

‡U.S. D-Day plus 15 strength is 8.

§Russia's economic interests could increase if Moscow needs new oil sources.

‖There has been a large rise in the past five years in Israeli political interest in this particular conflict.

IRAN VERSUS TURKEY

	Economic Interests	Historical Interests	Political Interest	Military Interest	Force Generation Potential	Ability to Intervene Politically
Iran	7	9	9	9	5+	8
Turkey	6	8	8	9	7	7
Russia	5	7	8	8	7+	6
United States	4	6	7	7	7	5
Azerbaijan	8	9	9	9	2	3
NATO*	4	5	6	7	4	6
Greece	1	5	8	8	1	3
Bulgaria	1	4	7	5	1−	1
Iraq	7	9	9	9	3	4
Syria	6	8	8	7	2	4
Kurds	7	9	8	8	1	6

*NATO other than United States, Greece, and Turkey.

IRAN VERSUS RUSSIA

	Economic Interests	Historical Interests	Political Interest	Military Interest	Force Generation Potential	Ability to Intervene Politically
Iran	9	9	9	9	6	8
Russia	8	9	8	9	8	8
Turkey	6	9	8	9	5	6
United States	6	6	8	7	5+	5
Azerbaijan	9	9	9	9	1	5
Armenia	9	9	9	9	1+	1
NATO*	7	7	8	8	3	7

*NATO other than United States and Turkey (primarily Germany).

PARTICIPANT STRATEGIES AND GOALS

Iran—Radicalizing Shiites in Iraq and in the Arabian Peninsula countries will further weaken Iraqi and Arab power. Revolutionary Iran's goal is to spread the gospel of Islamic "Koranic" government, or at least their xenophobic version of the Koran, and drive Western influences out of the Islamic world. Iran wants to be the dominant power in the Persian Gulf and in the Islamic world. Iran also has another motive: The war is a populist diversion from the revolutionary excesses by the Islamic republican revolutionaries and the resulting failing economy. The Iranian mullahs see the creation of an "Islamic republic" in Iran as move number one in the establishment of a pan-Islamic federation. Iran is still outraged by the Iran-Iraq War. Fomenting trouble between Iraq and Syria, or even Iraq and Israel, gives Teheran a chance to get even.

Iran in Lebanon and Sudan—Between the overthrow of the shah in 1979 and the Israeli invasion of Lebanon in 1982, Lebanon became the first foreign "branch office" of the Shiite Islamic revolution. Lebanon marked the westernmost reach of Shiite believers. Syria was a major power in Lebanon, thus making it easy for Iranian "holy warriors" to enter Lebanon and recruit. The resulting terrorist organization has been a constant problem for Israel and a forward base for support to Iranian-supported terrorists farther west. In the early 1990s the Sudan replaced Lebanon as the chief base for Iranian revolution. Egypt and Algeria became major targets.

Iraq—The Persian Gulf War left Iraq weak and on the edge of fragmentation. If the economic embargo ends, Iraq could produce up to 6.5 million barrels of oil a day (2.4 billion a year). The money would finance a new army. Iraq's indigenous arms industry, though affected by the embargo, is still in place. New Chinese arms are once again showing up in Iraqi army units. Iraq (with or without Saddam) is the Arab bulwark against the Persians.

Saudi Arabia—Continues to rely on U.S. and Egyptian support as a counterweight to Iraqi and Iranian power. The Gulf Cooperation Council's "Six Plus Two" (the Arab Gulf states plus Egypt and Syria) is another way to militarily counterbalance both Iran and Iraq. The invasion and pillaging of Kuwait by Iraqi troops will not be forgotten or forgiven. The big Saudi problem is internal stability.

Russia—Despite its economic and political problems, Russia maintains considerable influence in Iran, and has influence in Iraq. The Russians also have a supply "tether" on the Syrians—most Syrian equipment is of Soviet manufacture and without a steady supply of spare parts would soon become useless. The Russians' biggest objective is to try to put a damper on the turmoil in the former "Islamic SSRs." Russia wants to keep Teheran from exporting Islamic revolution to Russia. Long-range Russian strategy in the Mesopotamian and Gulf region is to guarantee Russian access to oil supplies if their own fields peter out. The Russians also fear proliferation of chemical and nuclear weapons. As for tactical ballistics missiles, they have only themselves to blame. They initially supplied both the Iranians and Iraqis with the weapons. Now they may become a target.

United States—Wants to maintain some third-party contacts within Iran and hopes that if moderates come to power they will be pragmatic enough to see that at some point even Teheran must deal with the world's superpower. Ultimately, the United States is the only certain counterbalance to Russian influence, though the mullahs may think China could replace America as a counterweight to Russia. The United States wants to ensure stable Gulf governments so that the oil flow isn't interrupted. The United States has demonstrated that it is willing to make a military commitment to the region. Operation Desert Storm showed how U.S. military might can stop a threat to the Arabian oil fields. The United States still wants to curb Iranian military power. Washington is particularly concerned about chemical and nuclear weapons and the potential for renewed troublemaking.

Other Regional Participants

Turkey—Still seeking a solution to its own Kurdish insurgency. The Turks want regional peace so they can concentrate on internal development and the potential development of "Turkic nations" in the former USSR's new Islamic nations. Turkey sees a future market in the old Soviet south. The Persian Gulf War gave Turkey a chance to be the "European army" in the field. All of Turkey is a potential target for Iranian (or Iraqi) missiles. "Secular" Turks want to minimize "Islamist" influence, regionally and within Turkey.

Pakistan—A rival to Iran for leadership of the Muslim world, Pakistan has the advantage of being mainline Sunni and thus on good terms with Saudi Arabia. Pakistan has nearly twice the population of Iran, but little in the way of natural resources like oil. There is also India, Pakistan's sworn enemy, to put a damper on any overt foreign adventures. Pakistan has serious internal political and economic problems, but in the international forum still provides a counterbalance for Iranian-sponsored terrorism and destabilization.

Afghanistan—Since the Russians retreated in 1989, the Afghans have, as is their tradition, continued the strife by fighting each other. About 15 percent of the population is Shiite; Afghan Shiites are concentrated near the border with Iran. But this area is quite poor in resources. However, about half the population speaks Dari, closely related to Persian. In the long term, Iran could have a significant influence on politics inside Afghanistan. Relations between the two nations can be expected to remain tense, but Afghan religious radicals give Iran another source for "Islamic internationalists."

Azerbaijan—The Azeris have plenty of trouble internally and with their warlike neighbors, the Armenians. The Azeris are Turks, and feel more comfortable establishing relationships with Turkey and, for economic convenience, the Russians. There is also the ancient desire to be united with the sixteen million Azeris (twice the population of Azerbaijan) in Iran, a matter the Iranians take a dim view of. Rarely independent during their long history, the Azeris now have a chance of uniting all the Azeri people, and they and Iranians both know this can only be done at Iranian expense.

Other International Participants

France—Despite French military opposition to the invasion of Kuwait, Iraq remains a major French market. The French are also active in Qatar and the UAE, both militarily and economically. French interest in Algeria is enormous.

Algeria—The Islamic fundamentalist movement is shaping up to be the next success in Iran's export-the-Islamic-renewal efforts. If the fundamentalists take power in Algeria, they can be expected to cooperate with their like-minded fellows in Iran to stir up revolution in other Muslim nations. Algeria becomes a base for waging "revolutionary war" with Europe.

Israel—As one of the principal targets of Iran's lethal foreign policy, Israel can be expected to do whatever it can to limit the impact and extent of Iran's aggressive moves. Israel is particularly concerned with Iranian moves to upset the peacemaking currently under way among Israel, the new PLO-Palestinian authority, Jordan, and Syria. Iran has everything to gain and much to lose by ensuring that peace does not break out between Israel and its Arab neighbors.

POTENTIAL OUTCOMES

Iran-Iraq War II: Iran Versus Iraq, or the "Stab in the Back": Iran and Syria Versus Iraq

There's an overall 10 percent chance (rather high, actually) through 2001 that this major conflict will reoccur. If this war erupts and Syria does not join the battle, look for the same result as in the last war, though the conflict would be of a much shorter duration. What would set it off? Another toppling of the Iraqi Baath dictatorship could lead to a power vacuum in Baghdad—and an opportunity for Iranian revenge. A fresh outbreak of the Islamic revolution might also anger the Baathist Iraqis and provoke a border war. If this war starts, there's a 40 percent chance of the "stab in the back"—Iran and Iraq square off and this time Syria decides to take Iraq down several pegs by annexing western Iraq. This could involve Saudi encouragement as well as old scores between the Baathist divisions.

1. 55 percent through 2001: An attrition stalemate results between Iran and Iraq along their border, just like in the Iran-Iraq War of the 1980s. The Syrian offensive in the west is blunted. War stops due to mutual exhaustion; then convenient diplomatic cover that allows all sides to look like victors unfolds.
2. 25 percent chance: Iranian or Syro-Iranian victory. The remnant of the Iraqi Baathist party is toppled from power. The Shiite region of Iraq falls under Iranian control. Gulf Arabs prepare for war with Iran.
3. 20 percent chance: Iraqi "victory." The Syrian offensive bogs down in the desert and the Iraqis toss them back. Gulf Arabs rally to Iraq's cause. Part of this outcome could be a big Syrian political victory where Iraq submits to Syrian demands in exchange for "peace" on the Syrian front. Iraq then turns on Iran. War sputters and turns into a new attrition conflict.

The War of Hormuz

1. 50 percent chance before 2001: Iran probes U.S. political and military readiness by increasing military forces in the Strait of Hormuz, occasionally stopping sea traffic, and conducting submarine operations. Iran continues to attempt to destabilize the UAE, Oman, and other Gulf states. Teheran sees little downside in this venture: They can always goose the price of oil if they can throw a scare into the Persian Gulf nations and the oil companies.
2. 30 percent chance: Iranian military operations prompt a series of counterstrikes by the United States and allied coalition. Iranian naval forces in the strait region are sunk and airfields destroyed. Attacks may include air strikes on Iranian nuclear facilities. The Iranian government is outraged but can do little other than promise terror attacks in retaliation.
3. 10 percent chance: A harsher version of Outcome 2. Iranian game playing in the strait gets out of hand. The U.S.-led coalition has broad support in the UN. CENTCOM forces land in Bander 'Abbas. Deep air strikes take out Iran's power grid and damage

industrial sites. An economic embargo is placed on Iran. Russia and the United States provide large-scale covert support for Iranian dissident groups. If this occurs, there is a 95 percent chance that an Iranian civil war erupts.

4. 10 percent chance: Iranian victory. Iran strikes quickly. The UAE government quickly falls and the peninsular region of Oman is secured before U.S. forces can be brought to bear. This rises to 40 percent if the United States is engaged in a war in Asia, such as a conflict with North Korea. Oil prices skyrocket.

Turko-Iranian War

This is not likely. Only severe Iranian meddling in Turkey's internal politics or overt Iranian support for anti-Turk Kurds might set it off. But if it occurs:

1. 85 percent chance: Mountain war confined to northwestern Iran. The Turkish Air Force smashes northeastern Iranian air bases. The Turkish Army makes a fifty-kilometer advance into Iran. Negotiations end the war. The Turks withdraw as big political and military winners.
2. 9 percent chance: Azerbaijan joins Turkey in war and they wrest control of northwestern Iranian Azeri territory from Iran.
3. 5 percent chance: Iranian forces stop a Turkish attack. A stalemate results. Possible Iranian missile attacks on Turkish cities; Turkish air attacks on Iranian cities. Turkish internal political troubles increase.
4. 1 percent chance: Iran announces it has a nuclear weapon and if the Turkish Army doesn't withdraw Iran will nuke Istanbul or Ankara. (Get ready for a NATO-Iranian war.)

Russo-Iranian Conflict

This theoretical conflict would be extremely dangerous. It could take several forms—of an "accidental war" where Russian and Iranian proxies bring the nations into combat, or of Russia acting as a protector for Armenia or Azerbaijan or another former SSR in central Asia. If it occurs:

1. 65 percent chance: Russian limited victory. Russians attack Iranian transportation and supply centers. Russian ground forces mass on Iranian border, perhaps launch short ground attacks into Iran. Negotiations pry adversaries apart and lead to Russian withdrawal in return for relaxation of Iranian troublemaking. Teheran government loses face at home and in central Asia.
2. 34 percent chance: Iran sucks Russia into a "big Chechnya" operation. The Russian Army meets widespread resistance in the former SSRs. Iran protects its limited air and missile assets and succeeds in creating an effective antiaircraft defense around its own strategic centers. Russia can never effectively bring its power to bear to beat an Iranian field force. Despite successful air raids on Teheran, Iran refuses to capitulate. Russian forces ultimately withdraw. Iranian political victory.
3. 1 percent chance: Iran tries nuclear blackmail on Russia. The result, however, is different than when attempting to blackmail the Turks (see Outcome 3 in Turko-Iranian War). Moscow responds with nuclear reality. The whole world comes to a stop as a brief nuclear war erupts. No one wins exactly. But Russia remains and the mullahs' Iranian government does not.

COST OF WAR

The Iran-Iraq War of 1980–88 killed over half a million people and injured several times that number (one source suggests a total of 1.8 million Iranians and Iraqis were wounded). This war cost over $250 billion in military expenses and economic damages. The 1990–91 Persian Gulf War killed far fewer people, less than 50,000 from all causes, and its cost, to all involved, was about half that of the earlier war. The 1990–91 war was cheaper mainly because it was shorter. Iran has been rearming in the 1990s to an extent never before seen in the region. Should Iran attack anyone that Western powers will defend (i.e., just about everyone except Iraq, and even that's not a sure thing), the war could be long, as well as very violent. The next Persian Gulf war could cost half a trillion dollars or more. If nuclear weapons are used, losses in lives and treasure will be even higher.

APPENDICES

Sunnis and Shiites

Arab versus Persian, Arab versus Arab. Iraqi and Iranian enmity can be traced back thousands of years to local Arab-Persian ethnic confrontations as well as political conflicts over control of river valleys (the Tigris and Euphrates, for example) and trade routes. Iranian militants also resent Arabs because historically Arab elites have exercised an often very arbitrary political and economic hegemony in Persia. As the Persians saw it, the liberality of Islam—equality before God—didn't translate into political equality in the Arab empire. This is an old anger. Other angers also affected the Iran-Iraq War, such as disputes between Sunni and Shiite Muslims and the lingering Persian, Arab, and Ottoman disputes over the Shatt-al-Arab.

A quick history of the Sunni-Shiite schism provides some background. After Muhammad's death, his earthly successors had difficulty consolidating the new Islamic political empire. Abu-Bakr, the first caliph, died after only two years in office. A period of confrontation followed between the new Arab political and military elite and the tribes of their empire. Taxes imposed by the government in Medina were one issue, but the fundamental problem was political and judicial inequality. Abu-Bakr's replacement, Umar, was killed by an angry Persian slave. The Islamic movement plunged into a political contest between Muhammad's followers, Ali and Uthman. Uthman was the choice of the Meccan power elite. Ali ibn Abi Talib, Muhammad's son-in-law, was the favorite of the Arab tribes. Uthman was murdered. Another power struggle between Mu'awiya and Ali's followers erupted into an intra-Islamic war. Ali became caliph, was murdered, and Mu'awiya took control of the movement. Mu'awiya's followers centered Islam about a Meccan elite. The Shiites, "the followers of Ali" (*shia* means "partisans") rejected this as secular. They also objected to the "citification" desired by Meccan merchants. The Shia saw in Hussein, Ali's son, killed by yet another rival for the caliphate, a heroic martyr who sacrificed his life for true Islam. Hussein, in fact, was assassinated near the present-day Iraqi city of Karbala, hence the frequent use of Karbala as a code name for Iranian offensives during the Iran-Iraq War. The name was a direct appeal to martyrdom.

Generalizing about Sunni and Shia differences is an invitation to trouble. It is accurate to say, however, that among Arabs, Shiism still retains an antiestablishment appeal, both politically and religiously. It's different with the Iranians. In the sixteenth century the Safavid rulers of Persia adopted Shiism as one more way to distinguish their empire from that of the Sunni Ottomans and the Turks' Arab fiefs. An early Persian literary movement known as Shuubiya is regarded by some as a Persian reaction to Arab dominance. Iranian Shiism blends Shiism's resentment of the Meccan secularists with the old Persian monarchical tradition. Iranian Shiism became in part a way of drawing ethnic and cultural distinctions. It also made the Persian Shiites a bit more attractive to Arab Shiites, who often chafed under the rule of Arab Sunnis. During the Iran-Iraq War, Iran's Islamic revolutionaries hoped to use this appeal to topple the governments in Bahrain and Iraq. The Shiite Arab minorities, however, seemed to prefer Sunni Arab leaders to a leadership controlled by Persians, though in early 1995 Shiite agitation in Bahrain increased dramatically as unemployed Shiite youths rioted in Bahraini villages.

Many Shiites, in Iran and elsewhere, believe in a line of twelve descendants of Muhammad, through Ali; these are the twelve Imams, or spiritual guides. The twelfth Imam, it is said, never died, but became "hidden" in the world. Until the twelfth Imam returns, Shiite clerics are directed to lead the Shiite faithful and make decisions "according to Allah's will." This belief in the hidden Imam and the clerics' specified role as interpreters and guides in the Imam's absence often puts Shiite clerics in direct conflict with temporal and secular (non-Shiite) authorities. The Shia clergy's logic is clear: God's will overrides human laws.

Shiite priests tend to have more direct political and social sway with their flocks than their Sunni counterparts. Several Middle Eastern scholars have suggested that this accounts for the often surprising strength and depth of Iran's Islamic revolution. The argument is simple: Shiite priests already enjoyed a great deal of "structured political power" among the people prior to the revolution. The rebellion against the shah merely removed the competition. The late shah's father understood this power and let the mullahs know they opposed him at their own great personal risk. Less concern for clerical authority among the Sunnis may also explain why Iranian Shiite radicals have a hard time attracting significant support in predominantly Sunni lands.

But there are even more personal and fundamental divisions. Shiism, according to some Sunnis (from *Sunna,* the "path or code," of proper or customary Islam), is also highly tainted with elements of animist religions, Manichaeism, and Persian astrological notions. In other words, in the eyes of Sunni critics, modern Shiism is a heresy, a mixed-bag "people's religion." The Shiites, in turn, deeply resent this Sunni snobbery.

The Iranian Arms Race

In 1989, Iran began to rearm. North Korea has been a key source of Iranian weapons, but various South American, European, Arab, Asian, and even African nations have all sold weapons to Teheran. Spare parts and other supplies for U.S.-made weapons have also been sold to Iran by North American companies. Various estimates, including one by the CIA, put Iranian expenditures for imported weaponry from 1990 to 1994 at $10 billion.

Since 1990, Iran has either acquired or ordered:

155 to 235 combat aircraft, including
    72 F-7 Chinese fighters
    68 MiG-29s
    25 Su-24s
    24 Su-27s (possibly not, details are murky)

24 MiG-27s

24 MiG-31s

12 Tu-22M Backfire bombers

2 Il-76 Mainstays, AWACS-type aircraft (one of these was an Iraqi aircraft that flew to Iran during the Persian Gulf War)

400–500 T-72 tanks

320 surface-to-surface missiles (170 SCUD B and C types and 150 No-Dongs from North Korea)

2,000 surface-to-air (SAM) launchers of various types including SA-7, -14, -16 (handheld), SA-5 Gammon missiles, SA-11 Gadfly missiles, SA-13 Gopher missiles

Fall 1994 saw the delivery of five Hudong missile boats from China and three Kilo-class diesel attack subs from Russia, and Iran wants more. The Ukraine also offered to sell Iran a Kilo-class sub (see below).

Iran is also expanding its internal weapons manufacturing capability. In 1991 there were 240 state-owned munitions plants, and 12,000 privately owned workshops employing 45,000 workers. This number is expected to rise to 60,000 by the end of the 1990s. Iran has armed its aging U.S.-made F-14 jet fighters with U.S. Hawk ground-to-air missiles, which may be of internal manufacture, or at least a clever improvisation from foreign-made weapons.

Iran is also starting to export weapons. In January 1992 at the Dubai international arms exhibition, Iran offered several simple weapons systems and services for sale, including contracts for maintenance of older-model U.S. jet fighter aircraft (though like Iraq, Iran is still very weak when it comes to maintaining high-tech equipment).

Possession of these modern weapons does not automatically translate into combat power. Without trained operators to use them, experienced technicians to maintain them, and ample funds to pay for training and support, all the money spent on hardware is nothing but a bigger hole in the national budget. Without basic maintenance and training, the spiffy new hardware gives a nation a false sense of combat power.

Iran's plan to expand its fleet of Russian-built Kilo-class submarines by acquiring another twenty to thirty subs is a classic example of this notion. Given the difficulty of training the crews (submariners are the most highly trained and carefully selected sailors) and maintaining the boats (subs being the most complex of all warships), it is unlikely that Iran will have a credible submarine force anytime soon. They would not be able to maintain the subs or crew the vessels—unless they hired mercenary sailors.

The Kilos' Russian-made "wake homing" torpedoes are particularly lethal, since they do not have to be aimed with any degree of accuracy to be effective. Wake homers detect the wake of moving ships and follow the wake until they hit the ship creating it. As yet there are no good countermeasures for wake-homing torpedoes—and oil tankers are the easiest of prey.

The Iranians are also acquiring the Chinese-made C-803 antiship missile. The C-803 has performance characteristics similar to the French-made Exocet.

The Silkworm and the No-Dong

Silkworm missiles are a key weapon in the Iranian arsenal. The Hai Ying HY-2 is manufactured by China Precision Machinery Import and Export Corporation and is an improved copy of the Russian-made CSS-N-2. The Silkworm can hit targets out to ninety-five kilometers. The basic Silkworm uses active homing radar, which makes it much easier to jam than Western antiship missiles like the Exocet or Harpoon, but still effective against commercial tankers. Improved Silkworms incorporate passive infrared homing capabilities. The "Seersucker" version of the Silkworm is a more reliable version. During the Iran-Iraq War, Iran deployed Silkworms in Bandar 'Abbas and Kuhestak. The deployment of additional Silkworms to Qeshm, Sirri, and other islands creates a dangerous gantlet for commercial shipping.

The No-Dong and the No-Dong II are improved Soviet SCUD-type missiles (of Persian Gulf War fame) manufactured by North Korea. The No-Dong may have a range of 1,000–1,200 kilometers. This places many Middle Eastern urban areas within range of Iranian missile fire. The No-Dong carries either a conventional high-explosive warhead or a chemical warhead. Ultimately, an Iranian No-Dong warhead may include a nuclear weapon.

The Suitcase from Allah: Nuclear Kamikazes

The Western world has been shocked by Arab and Iranian terrorists who willingly blow themselves to paradise, while taking a few enemies in the same dreadful blast. The 1983 truck bomb attack on the U.S. Marine compound in Beirut may be the most famous suicide terrorist assault; it is by no means unique. There exists a tradition, especially among Shiite Muslims, of such suicidal action. They identify with Hussein, although in the twentieth century, TNT has replaced daggers. A high-explosive blast, however, is an inconsequential firecracker when compared to "the suitcase from Allah"—a terrorist-borne nuclear weapon.

U.S. security analysts pale when confronted with the thought of terrorists acquiring a nuclear weapon either by theft or underground purchase. A nuke acquired by theft, from a poorly protected Russian nuclear weapons storage site, for example, is actually the least worrisome prospect. While the terrorists could grab a small tactical nuclear warhead, they would be hard-pressed to detonate the device unless they also stole the weapon's activation codes. Those codes, which activate and control supersecret PALs (permissive action links) on the weapon, are held in higher command channels. While U.S. codes may be safe, there are scenarios that suggest Russian and Ukrainian nuclear weapons officers might be persuaded to sell the codes—for a price.

In the case of theft of a U.S. weapon, unless the terrorist can simultaneously break into a half-dozen U.S. headquarters and then know which of several million potential codes go with the precise warhead they've stolen, the nuclear weapon is just a hunk of uranium and high explosive. But it's a hunk that's good for lots of headlines.

A weapon acquired by a terrorist group through purchase or code-velopment, with the Pakistanis, Iraqis, or Iranians, for example, presents another kind of problem. It is indeed possible to make a crude atomic weapon and carry it around in a steamer trunk. Even if it failed to make "the big bang," the target area could still be contaminated with lethal radiation.

Where would "Islamist" terrorists employ such a weapon? Getting one to the United States (to drop out of the Goodyear blimp, like one movie suggested) would be quite a feat, but it's not impossible. Mossad could slip up and nuclear terrorists could slip into Israel. Another variation is the "nuclear Cessna," where a small nuke (like the 100–200-pound variety used for artillery shells) is carried in a single-engine aircraft piloted by a suicide pilot (in the spirit of the Japanese kamikazes of 1944–45).

A major candidate for a terrorist-delivered nuke is Russia. The Russians are well aware of this. During the cold war the terrorists' scenario went something like this: (1) The terror team detonates a nuclear weapon inside a Soviet city or near a Soviet military installation; (2) the Russians think the United States did the dirty deed; (3) the two military superpowers eradicate themselves with a strategic nuclear exchange and Islamic radicals pick up the pieces. This "maximum result" was never all that probable and is less likely now; the United States and Russia would most likely contain any further escalation. But the damage done and chaos spread by such a terror strike would be immense. The terrorists' "point," however, would have been more than made.

Given Russia's political troubles, all kinds of other political improbabilities could occur in the wake of such a strike. Conceivably, hard-line military forces could assume control of one of the new (and frightened) nations of the ex-USSR or "rim" nations as the populace screams for protection. In fact, it wouldn't be beneath the ability (or philosophical inclination) of neo-Stalinists to help Islamic terrorists stage such a strike.

In terms of creating chaos and striking fear, the "spiking" of a conventional high-explosive bomb with nuclear material (or chemical or biological agents) is a frightening possibility. Radioactive material would be spread throughout the target area. In a major urban area the explosive damage would be small but the economic damage could be quite large; areas of the city would have to be sealed off for nuclear decontamination and cleanup. The terrorists could rely on the news media to call it an atomic bomb.

There has been no shortage of volunteers for past suicide missions, and there won't be a shortage of volunteers for the job of nuclear triggerman. As one Shiite Hezbollah leader told *The Washington Post* (February 3, 1984): "In one week I can assemble 500 loyalists ready to throw themselves into suicide operations. No border can stop me. We are coming to the end of the world. Presidents and ministers are eating each other up. Military men are traitors. Society is corrupt. The privileged, the notables are not worried about the poor. Only Islam can give us hope." Such millenarian thinking justifies the use of any kind of weapon—and any degree of destruction.

Poison Gas, the Evil Genie in the Bottle

World War I's trench systems and attrition battles forced tacticians to look for ways to break the deadlock. In April 1915 at Ypres, Belgium, the Germans experimented with a new mass-casualty weapon: chlorine gas. A special German engineer regiment dispersed along the front trenches. When the wind began to blow toward the British and French forces, the engineers opened the chlorine cylinders. The resulting greenish-yellow chlorine cloud opened a two-division-wide hole in the Allied lines. The Germans were as little prepared for their success as the Allies were to defend themselves against gas. After-action reports speculated that if the Germans had followed up the gas attack with a prepared infantry assault, they could have broken through to the English Channel.

Poison gas offers the would-be user a cheap mass-casualty weapon. Chemical agents like liquid mustard are relatively easy to make. A talented chemist, if provided with a college-grade lab, can synthesize even more exotic weapons, including nerve agents like sarin (code name GB). Almost every third world country can produce potential chemical agents and use them, either in aerial sprays (like crop dusting from aircraft), mines or fire pots on the ground, bombs, or artillery shells. Several regional powers in the Middle East—Iraq, Iran, Syria, and Israel are noted examples—can top off a medium-range ballistic missile with a chemical-agent-filled warhead. The likely targets are population centers or air bases. The warhead would detonate in an "airburst" over the target and the chemical agent would fall as a deadly drizzle on troops and equipment. The technical challenge to producing such missiles is not making the nerve agent, but building the complex warhead that will disperse the gas effectively.

Chemical weapons may be of dubious value, however, when used on well-trained and -equipped soldiers, like NATO troops or front-line Russian forces. NATO estimates that trained soldiers, with equipment available, would have fewer than 5 percent casualties even from a surprise attack by nerve gas. The Israelis put a great deal of emphasis on troop chemical defense training. Their units can be ready for a gas attack in seconds. But third world forces, like Afghan guerrillas or Iranian Revolutionary Guards or Kurdish insurgents, have no protection. They don't even carry gas masks.

Mustard gas (H, HD, or HN in chemical agent symbols) isn't a gas but a liquid. It is a delayed-action and persistent chemical agent. Mustard produces large and painful blisters eight to twelve hours after contact. Apparently, the Iraqis sprayed Iranian lines with mustard agent while the Iranian infantry was massing for human-wave attacks, causing death and horrible wounds (pictures of which were released to the public). Iraq may have also used tabun (GA), another nerve agent. Iraq has used a nerve agent on Kurdish insurgents and Kurdish villages and may have used liquid mustard as an "area denial agent" in Kurdish territory. Iraq's threats against Saudi and allied forces in the Persian Gulf War are well documented.

GB (sarin), a nonpersistent nerve agent developed by the Germans just prior to World War II, and GD (soman), a semipersistent nerve agent pioneered by the Germans but developed by the Russians, may also be available in the Middle East. Iraq had GB stocks. Syria may have stocks of GD.

Chemical weapons, however, are dangerous to the user as well. During the Iran-Iraq War, Iraqi troops were little better prepared to face Iranian chemical attacks. And no nation's civilians (including Israel's) are prepared for a surprise nerve gas attack, delivered either by missile or by terrorist.

And poison gas not only kills, it terrifies. This last effect is the major reason why armies have avoided using this terror weapon since 1918. When you use chemical weapons, everyone's troops tend to get demoralized.

The macabre nerve gas terror attack in the Tokyo subway system on March 20, 1995, illustrates what damage nerve agent can wreak. Though only a dozen people were killed in the attack, nearly five thousand passengers suffered from nerve agent poisoning. Hundreds required a week or more of hospital care and many of them will suffer permanent nerve damage. The death of seven people in Matsumoto, Japan, in June 1994 may have been a grotesque trial run of the Tokyo attack.

Nerve agents are chemical cousins of conventional organophosphate pesticides, such as parathion, an agricultural insecticide. A nerve agent like GB interferes with "neurotransmitter" chemicals and enzymes that relay electrical nerve impulses in the human body. The result: Muscles twitch and convulse; then flaccid paralysis occurs. When the lung muscles are paralyzed, the victim gasps for breath and dies from asphyxiation.

Atropine is the chemical antidote for nerve agent poisoning. Soldiers usually carry two or more atropine injectors inside their gas mask carriers. A soldier exposed to a nerve agent is trained to take an injector and slam it against his thigh. A spring drives the injector's needle into the thigh and the atropine counteracts the nerve agent. (Subway riders, however, rarely carry gas masks and atropine injectors.)

GB is sometimes described as a yellowish or straw-colored liquid. It can be absorbed through the skin. As a chemical weapon it is usually delivered as a vapor, from tiny bomblets in a missile or artillery shell. GB is considered a nonpersistent agent, since it will degrade quickly.

Persistent chemical agents, like liquid mustard, remain on the battlefield. Farmers in France, over seventy years after World War I, still occasionally develop mustard blisters after plowing old battlefields. Civilians continue to suffer after the shooting, and spraying, stop.

Chapter 2

IRAQ, SAUDI ARABIA, KUWAIT, AND THE ARABIAN PENINSULA: RING OF FIRE AROUND ARABIA

INTRODUCTION

The Iran-Iraq War of 1980–88 threatened everyone on the Arabian Peninsula. Even though Iraq started that particular round of warfare, the Arab states in the Persian Gulf backed Arab Iraq against Persian Iran.

Arab Iraq, however, proved to be as large a menace to the fragile Gulf states as Iran. Coveting Kuwait's oil, and with eyes on controlling global oil prices, in August 1990 Iraq invaded Kuwait, igniting the Persian Gulf War. A military and political coalition, cobbled together by the United States, smashed Iraq's army and drove it out of Kuwait.

A ring of political and military fire flashes around the Arabian Peninsula. Iran attempts to spread its explosive variety of Islamic revolution in this politically frail region. North and South Yemen, after reunification, fight a bitter war on the southwestern fringe. Iraq rearms. The political order inside the Big Prize, Saudi Arabia, becomes increasingly brittle.

SOURCE OF CONFLICT

The conflicts in and around the Arabian Peninsula are many and they are complex.

The Persian Gulf War and Iran-Iraq War are but two of several recent or simmering wars around the Arabian Peninsula and Persian Gulf. Energy and geography make political conflict and subterfuge among these countries acts of worldwide concern. The tiny nation of

Oman sits at Saudi Arabia's back door. It also covers the south side of the Strait of Hormuz, that delicate neck of the Persian Gulf.

West of Oman lies Yemen, or at least the part of Yemen that used to be the People's Republic of South Yemen. Oman and South Yemen waged a quiet little "camel war" for almost ten years, with South Yemen receiving boatloads of Russian equipment and a large number of Eastern European combat advisers. The Omani Army got a better deal—they obtained a brigade of the late shah of Iran's imperial army and a small but very effective group of British Army instructors.

The nation of Yemen is an iffy proposition. Twice within the last twenty-five years South Yemen invaded what was the royalist northern Republic of Yemen. During the 1960s, the Egyptian Army, at Egyptian President Nasser's direction, waged a bitter war in northern Yemen. Egyptian aircraft dropped Russian chemical bombs on Yemeni royalist tribesmen and inflicted huge casualties. The guerrilla resistance, under the spiritual leadership of their imam, forced an Egyptian withdrawal.

The cold war lapsed and Russian support disappeared. The year 1990 saw South Yemen and the Republic of Yemen forge a tentative "reunification." But their antagonisms went beyond the ideological divide of communism and monarchism. In 1994 war erupted, one that featured SCUD attacks and armored columns punching through the desert. Saudi Arabia and Yemen continue to squabble over migrants and a poorly defined border.

The troubles of monarchism, geostrategic change, the shape of an Islamic society in the modern world, and the impact of wealth brought by oil plague Saudi Arabia, the United Arab Emirates (UAE), Bahrain and Qatar, and a Saudi offspring named ARAMCO. They brought tragedy to Kuwait, in the shape of the Persian Gulf War.

Theology was kind to Saudi Arabia, for it was the original home of Allah's Prophet Muhammad. Geology was also kind to Saudi Arabia, leaving it with some 150-plus billion barrels of crude oil. Saudi Arabia is also the temporary home of nearly 600,000 Yemenis who are treated as very second-class citizens (some 400,000 were expelled in the wake of the Persian Gulf War). That leaves the Yemenis, along with a restive Shiite minority in Saudi Arabia and Bahrain, receptive to the Islamic revolutionary gospel being spread by Iran.

Iraq remains isolated, enigmatic, and threatening, but with its oil, population, and location it cannot be ignored. The twentieth century has put the heartland of ancient Mesopotamia back on the map.

The Fertile Crescent of ancient Mesopotamia, that extended sweep of land between the Tigris and Euphrates rivers, has played a critical role in human history: as incubator of some of the world's earliest urban centers, as nexus of religious, trade, and agricultural development. Babylon and Nineveh, Assyrians and Hittites all spread their power from this central region. In subsequent centuries the nearby state of Persia (modern Iran), or the city of Baghdad (Iraq), or the city of Damascus (Syria) was the focal point of Eurasian trade and political affairs.

In the large lens of history, the economic and social development of Western European civilization, the advent of long-distance merchant shipping (sea routes around Africa), and to some extent, the intricacies and depredations of Ottoman Turkish rule in the region after the collapse of the Omayyad (Damascus) and Abbasid (Baghdad) caliphates removed the Mesopotamian states from the center stage of trade and influence; the long caravans from the east slowly became superfluous. The region turned into a colonial eddy.

In the twentieth century, the destruction of the Ottoman Empire, Arab tribalism evolving into a kind of nationalism, the discovery of the world's largest oil fields, the intrigues of the cold war, and the creation of the state of Israel have led to intense international concern in the area—and introduced new strategic instabilities. "Mesopotamia" and the Arabian Peninsula have once more become centers of globally significant conflict.

Ancient hatreds, modern intrigue, petroleum, and advanced weapons systems in the hands of unstable regimes make the regional situation extraordinarily precarious. When the United Nations showed up for Operations Desert Shield and Desert Storm, the assault on Iraq proved to be more than just another Arabian border war.

WHO'S INVOLVED

Saudi Arabia—The Big Prize, with the world's largest proven oil reserves. The Saud dynasty faces distrust at home and border threats.

Kuwait, Bahrain, United Arab Emirates, Qatar, Oman ("the Gulf states")—Oil, sand, and religious radicalism are a volatile mix.

Yemen—Civil war erupted in 1994. Relations with Saudi Arabia are increasingly strained. Yemen sees itself as the major power in the Arabian Peninsula, but oil wealth has eclipsed Yemen's ancient population and rainfall advantage.

Iraq—Saddam Hussein remained in power after the Persian Gulf War, in part as a bulwark against Iranian expansion. No matter who is in power in Baghdad, Iraq will remain unstable.

Iran—If an Iranian regime, revolutionary or otherwise, wants to control the Strait of Hormuz, they must either politically co-opt or militarily control Oman and the UAE. Teheran has large ambitions, including domination of world oil prices.

United States—The world's only superpower still depends on fossil fuels. ARAMCO stands for Arabian-American Oil Company.

Islamic revolutionary groups—Many are sponsored by Iran but several Sunni groups in the Persian Gulf states reportedly shun Iranian Shiite support.

Wild Cards

United Nations—UN-legitimated military action demonstrates just how dependent the world's industrial economies are upon Middle Eastern oil.

Jordan—Jordan is focused on its new relationship with Israel and emerging Palestine. Geographically pincered between Iraq and Israel, Jordan was Iraq's most reliable ally during the Persian Gulf War. Jordan's ruling Hashemites (direct descendants of the Prophet Muhammad) once were the traditional overseers of the Hejaz and Mecca, until the Sauds threw them out.

Egypt—The largest Arab nation has a real interest in Saudi stability, as well as remittances from Egyptian workers in the Persian Gulf. But Egypt suffers from its own troubles with Islamic radicals. Nevertheless, Egypt would act militarily should Saudi Arabia be threatened.

Turkey—Trouble with Kurds isn't Turkey's only concern. Curtailing Iranian influence and thwarting Iraqi power grabs are vital Turkish goals.

Israel—Israel casts wary eyes at Iraqi rearmament and Iranian nuclear weapon development. In 1981 the Israelis attacked the Iraqi nuclear reactor at Osirak. Rapprochement between Israel and Saudi Arabia made the Palestinian peace process possible. If the Sauds fall from power, what happens to Palestine?

Russia—Would Russia sit on the sidelines in another war pitting Iraq against Saudi Arabia? Russia still sells arms to Iran. Yemen, absorbing South Yemen's Soviet weapons stocks, is a new Russian customer. Iraq could be another customer for cash-desperate Russia.

Pakistan—a large number of Pakistani technicians serve throughout the Arabian Peninsula. Pakistan also lies on the other side of Iran.

Exiled and underground remnants of former South Yemen Marxist government—The "socialists" have not disappeared.

GEOGRAPHY

Let's start below the ground with a little oil geography. On the Arabian Peninsula, big structural traps of Mesozoic Age carbonates (like limestone) hold the world's biggest deposits of oil. Saudi Arabia's Khawahr field holds some 80 billion barrels. That compares to the less than 10 billion barrels that were in Alaska's Prudhoe Bay. The Oman fields are in the comparatively puny 1.5 billion range, huge by any other standard.

In Iraq, Iran, and Kuwait, the subsurface is a little different—Kuwait's oil is held in sandstone deposits—but in an era of fossil-fuel-powered economies, the presence of lots of oil increases the strategic significance of the sand and mountains aboveground.

The Strait of Hormuz, between the tip of Oman and Iran, is the Persian Gulf's exit. The deepest channel lies on the Omani side, the route for outgoing oil tankers. The strait narrows to fifty kilometers in width (less if Iranian and Omani islands are taken into account). Antiship missiles on these islands can easily close the Gulf.

At the northwestern end of the Persian Gulf, near the Shatt-al-Arab, lies the emirate of Kuwait. Kuwait is 18,000 square kilometers of oil-soaked desert wedged between Iraq and Saudi Arabia. Iraq and Kuwait signed a border agreement in 1932, but in 1961 Iraq reneged and claimed Kuwait as Iraqi real estate, asserting that Kuwait had once been part of the Ottoman Empire and under Iraqi control. This spurious claim was one pretext for the Iraqi invasion of 1990. Ironically, post–Persian Gulf War international surveys have moved the border in Kuwait's favor and have given part of the Iraqi port of Um Qasr to Kuwait.

On a per capita basis, prior to the war, Kuwait was one of the wealthiest nations in the world. Of the two million or so people living in Kuwait, only 700,000 were Kuwaitis. (Among native Kuwaitis, 70 percent are Sunni Muslim and 30 percent are Shiite Muslim.) The other "expatriates" either worked in the oil industry or "served" the Kuwaitis. As of mid-1995, Kuwait has substantially recovered from the Persian Gulf War. Estimates of war economic loss and damage in Kuwait run from $60 to $100 billion.

Bahrain Island, the largest of the six islands that make up the tiny nation of Bahrain (620 square kilometers) lies near Saudi Arabia midway between the Strait of Hormuz and the Shatt-al-Arab. Almost 600,000 people live in Bahrain (around 400,000 of them native Bahrainis). Seventy percent of Bahrainis are Shiite Muslim, the other 30 percent Sunni. For many Sunni regimes in the Gulf, the high percentage of Shiites in Bahrain is a source of worry. Any government in Bahrain unfriendly to the Saudi monarchy would seriously threaten Saudi Arabia and the UAE. Bahrain, however, is a very socially relaxed place compared with the rest of the Gulf. Bahrain essentially serves as a "pleasure island" for the region. Still, there are a significant number of religious militants among the Shiite population. Unemployment and the increasing wealth of the ruling Khalifa family have fueled riots and resentment among the populace. The local police, even with the assistance of British antiterrorism experts, have a hard time keeping the lid on.

Qatar (11,000 square kilometers) consists of flat, barren desert with no arable land. Slightly less than 50 percent of the 500,000 people living in Qatar are Arab; 20 percent are Pakistani, 20 percent Indian, and some 10 percent Iranian. Qatar is dependent on desalinization facilities for water.

The United Arab Emirates (the UAE, formerly called the Trucial Sheikdoms or the Trucial Coast) are a federation of seven Arab states: Abu Dhabi, Dubai, Sharjah, Ajman, Umm al-Qaiwain, Ras al-Khaimah, and Fujairah. At 75,500 square kilometers, the UAE is about the size of Maine. Ninety-eight percent of the land is desert. Less than 20 percent of the 2.8 million people living in the UAE are UAE citizens ("Emirians"). Nearly 50 percent of the people are Indian or South Asian. There is a large east Asian and European expatriate community. Ninety-six percent of the people are Muslims (16 percent of those Shiites). The southern boundary of the UAE runs into the Rub al-Khali (Empty Quarter) of Saudi Arabia. The Omani border is undefined. In fact, most of the borders on the southern end of the Arabian Peninsula are undefined. Attempts to define these borders often led to confrontation.

The Rub al-Khali borders of Oman and Yemen were supposedly settled by a boundary agreement ratified in December 1992. Until the ratification Oman and Yemen were separated by an "administrative line."

Oman, the "elbow" of the Arabian Peninsula, is approximately 300,000 square kilometers in size—but everything is approximate since no one is sure of the borders. Part of Oman is separated from the rest of the country by the UAE. This is the Musandam Peninsula, which juts into the Strait of Hormuz. A long coastal plain stretches northwest of Muscat. Mountains lie to the interior. Foothills and dry desert extend to the south and west. Oman, bordering the Arabian Sea, benefits from the summer monsoons. Of the 1.7 million people living in Oman, almost 75 percent are of the Ibadhi Muslim sect (*ibadhi* means "community of the just"), a Shiite offshoot; the rest of the people are either Sunnis or Shiites. Sizable East Indian and Baluchi Pakistani communities live in Muscat and Matrah.

"United" Yemen has a population of nearly eleven million people and an area of over 520,000 square kilometers. Sanaa, the capital of the former (northern) Republic of Yemen, is united as Yemen's capital. At least 85 percent of the people are Muslim, but a substantial minority of the people living around the city of Aden are Hindu and Christian.

Approximately three million people live in what was South Yemen.

The terrain in southern Yemen consists of a flat and sandy coastal zone with a mountainous interior. The border region between Yemen and Oman moves from the low coastal zone through rocky, dry terrain, into the mountains and desert. Aden is the major city in the region and is united as Yemen's economic and commercial capital. Aden is unusual when compared with the rest of the Arabian Peninsula. It has a large non-Arab population, composed of people of African (Somali) and Indian descent. This reflects the more international character of the Aden area. A strong labor union movement exists in Aden. Ideology aside, the ethnic mix and more international orientation of Aden has been one of the causes of trouble with the tribes of Yemen's north.

A quarter of the eight million people living in Yemen's northern area work outside of the country as emigrant labor. Most of Yemen's north is very mountainous. There is a 64-kilometer-wide coastal strip along the Red Sea. The mountainous interior is well watered and supports intensive agriculture. "The rain in Arabia falls mainly on the Yemen" is true, but not a hit song. The mountains are over 3,600 meters in height (12,000 feet). Yemen was once part of the ancient kingdom of Sheba, and always contained the bulk of Arabia's population. Recent oil discoveries suggest modest reserves of two to four billion barrels throughout Yemen. These fields are beginning to produce and are injecting much needed hard currency into the country. Still, Yemen has resented the Saudi and Kuwaiti oil wealth. Yemen and Saudi Arabia also have some minor border disputes. That explains, to some degree, a Yemeni "tilt" toward Iraq immediately following Iraq's invasion of Kuwait.

The island of Socotra in the Gulf of Aden belongs to Yemen. Yemen controls the Bab al-Mandab, the strait between the Indian Ocean and the Red Sea. A large section of the Saudi-Yemeni border is undefined.

Saudi Arabia is approximately one quarter the size of the continental United States (2 million square kilometers). Exact population figures are hard to find, but approximately eighteen million people live in the country. Some twelve million of them are Saudis. Over 90 percent of the Saudi nationals are Sunni Muslims (the Shias with Saudi citizenship are in the Eastern Province along the Gulf). The remaining residents are almost all expatriate workers. Riyadh, with a population of over two million, is the capital. Desert of some type—sand, plain, rocky waste—covers over 65 percent of the land, and most of the rest is dry meadow and pasture. The country has no permanent rivers. There are five principal regions: the northern region near Jordan, which is desert populated by Bedouin nomads; the al-Hasa (Eastern Province), which borders the Persian Gulf; the Najd (or Nejd) region where Riyadh is situated; the Asir, a mountainous area on the southern Red Sea coastline; and the Hejaz region, which borders the Red Sea. Mecca, Islam's most holy city, is located in the Hejaz. The government is a monarchy with some three hundred princes acting as representatives and counselors of the king. Basically, a tribal extended ruling family runs the kingdom and that means running the oil business.

Iraq has an area of 438,000 square kilometers and a population of eighteen million. More than 60 percent of the people are Shiite Muslims; 75 percent of the people are Arabs, with Kurds making up nearly 20 percent of the total population. Most of the Kurds live in the north, in the region running from Kirkuk to Erbil. Iraqi Arab Christians are 4 percent of the population.

Iraq is, geostrategically, a nation surrounded. The attack on Kuwait, to seize the oil fields and obtain the best deep-water port in the Gulf, left it even more isolated. Iraq found itself boxed in from four sides, trapped within an "Iron Quadrangle" of its own making: Iran to the east, Turkey to the north, Saudi Arabia to the south, Syria and Jordan to the west.

The region west of Baghdad toward the Syrian border and on into Syria turns increasingly dry and harsh—a desert wasteland. If a war broke out between Iraq and Syria, the highway linking the Syrian town of Dayr-az-Zawr and Iraq's Al Qa'im would be a major battleground. Both cities are on the Euphrates River. A major Syrian target would be the Iraqi-Turkish oil pipeline, which crosses from Iraq into Turkey west of the northern Iraqi town of Zakhu.

The key terrain at the northern end of the Persian Gulf region includes the Shatt-al-Arab.

Upriver, the Iran-Iraq border area turns increasingly rugged and dry. The northern border region is mountainous. The Kurdistan area features this kind of rugged terrain. The mountains continue into Turkey and Iran. With the advent of the UN no-fly zone in post–Persian

Gulf War Iraq, the Kurdish region began to function as something of a separate nation.

Though Kuwait had been ruled for over 250 years by the al-Sabah family, under Turkish administration part of Kuwait had been assigned to the "millet of Basra." It was under this pretext that Iraq invaded Kuwait. Iraq also claimed Kuwait was taking more than its allotment of oil out of the shared Rumalia oil field; Iraq also wanted to control the Khawr Abd-Allah, a brine channel situated between the Iraqi coast and Kuwait's Būbiyān Island. The Khawr Abd-Allah circumvents the Shatt-al-Arab and allows access to the Iraqi port of Um Qasr. Ironically, a UN commission has ceded parts of Um Qasr to Kuwait after a postwar survey found the border between Kuwait and Iraq to be incorrect.

The Baghdad government has had a series of major projects intended to drain the Tigris and Euphrates marshes. Many Shiite dissidents live in these southern marshes between Baghdad and Basra.

HISTORY

Because of the abundant oil deposits, the historical, intertribal, and ethnic squabbles of the Persian Gulf area take on global significance.

The south Arabian states have a history of conflict between the more worldly coastal dwellers and the nomads in the hinterland. During World War I, T. E. Lawrence ("Lawrence of Arabia") made shrewd use of this fact when orchestrating an Arab "tribal rebellion" against the Ottoman Turks. Prior to Lawrence, religion was often the nominal reason for these city-dweller-versus-nomad squabbles (or "sand versus sown" in the local parlance). These bandit-level affairs tended to flare suddenly and then die a negotiated death after a half-dozen or so principals were beheaded. Negotiated settlements usually involved promises of obeisance to the sultan and some yearly tribute. "Sides" didn't really exist with any more definition than borders drawn in blowing sand. The situation has changed but the sand hasn't. South Arabia possesses a decidedly strategic position, with easy air and sea access to East Africa, the Indian Ocean, the Red Sea, and the Persian Gulf.

World War I, the collapse of the Ottoman Empire, and British-French colonial intrigues in the Middle East introduced "nationalism" as another religious cause for combat. Pan-Arabist nationalists and "tribal nationalists" (tribes with flags, as some commentators refer to the Middle East) entered the potent brew. Politics remained personal, fragile, and feudal; compromise on the complex and heterogeneous issues that plague the modern world was often impossible as eleventh-century methods met the twentieth century. Colonialism made things worse.

The southern half of Yemen, or Aden as it was known under British hegemony, is not the typical case, but it is a case in point. Fighting among leftist groups (1965–68) left the British protectorate of Aden in chaos as Great Britain withdrew from the colony. The National Liberation Front, a coalition of socialists and Communists, succeeded in winning the street battles and established a new government in November 1967. In June 1969 the radical Communist wing of the NLF took control. With certain internationalist additions, such as South Yemeni support for the Palestinian attack on an Israeli tanker in the nearby Mandeb Strait in 1971, but beneath this veneer of ideology, the old coastal-versus-nomad antagonisms continued—though in this day and age many of the nomads had traded camels for Mercedes-Benzes. The southerners have fought pitched battles with Saudi forces inside Saudi Arabia (1969 and 1973). (In the early 1970s there were a number of Palestinian guerrilla and terrorist training camps in South Yemen, supported by the Soviet intelligence service, the KGB.)

By far the longest sustained combat was with Oman. Beginning with political sponsorship of dissident residents of Dhofar, the South Yemenis began to supply arms and troops to the "Dhofar Rebellion" along with East German and Cuban military advice. They also set up an Omani "government-in-exile," indicating a bigger goal than Dhofar. The Dhofar war began in the early 1970s, with full-scale guerrilla battles in 1972 and 1973.

In 1973 the shah of Iran offered his paratroops to the sultan of Oman. In September 1973 nearly 1,000 of the 3,000 active Dhofari rebels defected to the Oman government, just as the Iranian-led offensive began to hit back. Offensive operations in December 1973 and early 1974 by the shah's paratroopers laid the groundwork for the rebels' defeat, though the fighting dragged on into 1975. Omani units in Dhofar also operated with British advisers. Jordan also sent military support units. Some Iranian Army advisers remained in Oman until the fall of the shah.

In 1979, South Yemen signed a "treaty of friendship" with Russia. Oman accused Russia of providing renewed support to the would-be rebels. In 1979 there were reported to be some 800 to 1,000 East bloc military advisers in South Yemen.

Sporadic fighting erupted in Dhofar in 1979 and 1980. In late 1980 and early 1981, South Yemeni troops made several raids across the administrative line.

South Yemen also conducted an on-again, off-again border war with the Republic of Yemen to the north. In February 1979, South Yemeni mechanized forces, accompanied by East German and Cuban advisers, attacked Yemen and took the villages of Qatabah and Harib. Fighting took place as deep as sixty kilometers inside Yemen. The United States responded by sending aid and equipment to the Yemeni government in Sanaa. Fighting renewed in October and December 1980. Occasional combat occurred throughout the 1980s.

In the fall of 1990 the Republic of Yemen and South Yemen agreed to reunify. The north was troubled by growing Islamic fundamentalism among the northern tribes; the south, having lost the support of the floundering Soviet Union, was increasingly impoverished. The process was completed in 1991 and in 1993 national multiparty elections were held. However, certain essential political problems were not dealt with, such as if the new Yemen would be a central state controlled from Sanaa or a more loosely defined federation with Aden having a great deal of local autonomy. Interestingly, the Yemeni Army was never integrated. Forces loyal to the south simply camped beside northern forces. Electoral power went with demography: The more populous northern political coalition, led by Ali Abdullah Saleh, out-polling the Socialist party (the south's party) and taking control of the parliament. The north, effectively, dominated the south. The "deputy president," southerner Ali Salem al-Baidh, resisted. In August 1993 he left Sanaa for Aden. Since 1990, significant oil reserves have been discovered in what was South Yemen (in the eastern province of Hadhramaut). Sanaa was not about to let South Yemen slip away. Several press sources suggest that Iranian intervention, in the form of cash support, on behalf of the northern-based Islamic radical Islaah party upset the balance between northern and southern leaders.

1994: Civil War in Yemen

In spring 1994 the southern Yemenis began to purchase arms, roughly two divisions' worth of tanks and artillery. In April 1994, Yemeni military forces loyal to the north surrounded southern loyalist forces around Sanaa. In May 1994 the north's forces marched south, intending to link up with a northern loyalist garrison in the town of Zinjibar, east of Aden. Southern forces stopped the initial northern attack in the Amman Mountains near the old border. The south fired SCUD missiles at Sanaa.

The north's manpower advantage made the difference, as northern forces slowly fought their way out of the mountains and down to the coast. Within two months Aden fell. Many of the southern "rebels" moved out into the provinces and Oman to form a guerrilla resistance front. Possibly, Oman and Saudi Arabia will provide some support.

Some reports suggest that the southern Yemenis concluded an agreement during the civil war to buy two MiG 29s, sixteen MiG-21s, and twelve Su-22s from Russia while the war was going on. Most of the planes did not arrive before the war concluded. One MiG-29 was captured at Aden's Al-Rayan airport. These sources suggest the Saudis financed the purchase and paid the pilots who flew the MiGs.

Iraqi Historical Background

When the nation of Iraq was established in 1931, it consisted of the three ancient (and dissimilar) provinces of Baghdad (ancient Mesopotamia), Mosul (long a Kurdish stronghold), and Basra (Bedouins and "marsh Arabs"). There was some dispute with the new Turkish Republic, as the Mosul province (and the Kirkuk oil fields) were more Turk than Arab (and more Kurd than anything else). The British gave the northern area to Iraq, partially to reward their Arab allies for

World War I services and partially to ensure that the Turkish republic did not have future oil wealth with which to entertain ideas of reestablishing another Turkish empire. In hindsight, this proved a big mistake, as the forward-looking Turks turned westward in their thinking and have been a staunch ally of the Western democracies ever since.

Great Britain imported a prince to rule Iraq from the ruling (then and now) Hashemite family in Jordan. The Hashemites were another of Britain's local allies during World War I. The British kept a finger in Iraqi politics and actually took over Iraq again during World War II when a large number of Iraqi Army officers sought an alliance with the Nazi Germans. Iraqi and Nazi officers apparently had a lot in common, at least in terms of politics and attitudes toward Jews. After World War II, the British left once more, leaving Iraq's Hashemite royalty to their fate.

Baghdad's imported aristocrats were lined up against a wall and shot when the Iraqi Army took over in 1958. With the Hashemite royal family dead and the army in control, a civil war of sorts began. While the army was a potent political power, it was overshadowed by the Arab nationalist Baath (Renaissance) party. The Iraqi branch of the Baath was founded in 1949, partially as a reaction to the creation of Israel. Initially, Baath wanted to overthrow the monarchies and unite all Arabs from Iraq to Morocco into one powerful state. This lofty ideal soon fell apart under nationalist pressures, inside both Iraq and Syria.

Iraq initially sought a Baath-controlled unification with largely Sunni Arab Syria as a way to solve their minorities problem. There was one catch: The Baghdad Arabs of Iraq would then be an even smaller minority in the united nation and the more numerous (and nearly as bloody-minded) Syrian Sunni Arabs would run the whole show. Syrian Sunnis also had a minorities problem, but not as severe as Iraq's. The Syrian Baath party members were not gentle people and dealt harshly with real or imagined opposition. Thus began the ongoing blood feud between Baath factions in Iraq and Syria over, essentially, which wing of Baath would control the other.

Saddam Hussein, author of Iraq's ill-fated invasions of Iran and Kuwait, first appeared on the Iraqi political scene in 1958 when, after the fall of the monarchy, he tried to assassinate the (non-Baath) general ruling Iraq. Saddam failed and was wounded in the incident. He found refuge in Syria. He returned to Iraq and joined in the eventual Baath takeover. Saddam was one of many from the "Tikrit clan" to rise in Iraqi politics. Tikrit is a region of a few hundred thousand people a hundred miles north of Baghdad. While Baghdad contains several warring "clans," the Tikrit group has remained fairly united, in no small part due to the skill and ruthlessness of Saddam.

In 1968 the non-Baath Iraqi Army officers were purged and Baath acquired sole control of the army, and Iraq. At the time, the second-in-command of the Iraqi Baath party, and the real power in the country, was thirty-one-year-old Saddam Hussein. Saddam waited in the shadows until he could take complete control of the country. He soon did this. Saddam's attention was diverted by problems with Iraqi Kurds and a war with Iran from 1980 to 1988. But by 1990, his attention shifted south.

1990–91: The Persian Gulf War

With a long-standing tradition of local rule under the Al-Sabah dynasty and ongoing good relations with the British, in the 1930s Great Britain guaranteed Kuwait's independence. Though many Baghdad Arabs protested that Kuwait should be part of Iraq, it was not considered worth the trouble to press the issue with the British. The new nation of Iraq had enough problems with other Iraqi minorities without taking in some traditionally hostile Bedouins. And no one yet knew just how much oil wealth there was in Kuwait.

They learned, and Kuwait became a key Iraqi objective. With the end of the cold war, Saddam saw an opportunity to take Kuwait, incorporate it into Iraq, and also gain the ability to dominate the world's oil business. Saddam gambled that the Saudis and the rest of the world would tremble, then ignore Kuwait just as the world essentially ignored Mussolini's invasion of Ethiopia in the 1930s.

Unfortunately, Saddam missed a critical bit of information: Ethiopia wasn't in the oil business. Saddam raised a dagger—an economic, political, and military dagger—to the world's petroleum artery.

The world did not ignore Saddam's attack. The Iraqi invasion in

August 1990 capped a string of strategic political miscalculations. In the historical sense Saddam's greatest misstep will prove to be his serious underestimation of Saudi political abilities. The Saudis proved to be fast, astute, and decisive in the face of Iraqi armed might. Saddam also sorely misjudged U.S. willingness to act and U.S. military capabilities.

U.S. and allied forces began building up in Saudi Arabia in August 1990. Several UN Security Council resolutions sanctioned Iraq and called for Iraqi withdrawal from Kuwait. Saddam sat tight. On January 17, 1991, massive allied air raids struck Baghdad. The air war destroyed Iraqi communication and command facilities and isolated the Iraqi Army in Kuwait. The Iraqis managed one large attack into Saudi Arabia, at the Saudi city of Khafji on January 29. Within two days parts of three attacking Iraqi divisions were destroyed by allied air and ground forces. Iraq also fired SCUD theater ballistic missiles at Saudi Arabian and Israeli cities.

U.S. and allied ground units began probing Iraqi positions in Kuwait in early February. A wide and deep left flank attack kicked off on February 23. Two allied corps swung into the desert west of Kuwait and within four days had surrounded or destroyed all Iraqi units remaining in Kuwait. Other allied units attacked directly into Kuwait City. The allies captured nearly sixty thousand Iraqi prisoners.

Saddam Hussein and his regime survived the defeat of his army, the postwar Kurdish rebellion in northern Iraq, and the Shiite rebellion in southern Iraq. United Nation inspection teams ferreted out most of Iraq's nuclear and chemical weapons programs.

In order to protect the Kurds, the northern third of Iraq became a no-fly zone for the Iraqi Air Force. A southern no-fly zone was later established. Occasionally, the Iraqis tested UN will. In December 1992 and January 1993, Iraqi fighter aircraft were downed by allied aircraft patrolling the no-fly zones. Allied aircraft have also attacked Iraqi radar and antiaircraft sites.

1994: Saddam Threatens Kuwait

In September and October 1994, Saddam Hussein rattled his cage. Approximately two armored divisions were sent to the Kuwaiti border. The United States responded by sending thirty-six thousand troops to Kuwait in a three-week period. Equipment for a U.S. armored brigade is stockpiled in Kuwait. The United States beefed up the force to division strength. Iraq retreated.

In August 1995 two high-ranking Iraqi officers (sons-in-law of Saddam and Tikritis) defected to Jordan. Saddam's son, Uday, an increasingly powerful figure in Iraqi politics, had sought to purge them from power. The defectors maintained that Saddam's regime was increasingly unstable. As 1995 ends, the northern and southern thirds of Iraq are still patrolled by U.S. and coalition aircraft based in Turkey and the Gulf states.

LOCAL POLITICS

The Arabian States

Saudi Arabia

Wahhabi sect of Sunni Islam—The puritanical Saudi and Gulf-state sect of Islam. Wahhabi law and conduct are modeled on those of the first Islamic communities in Medina and Mecca. The sect is named for the eighteenth-century Islamic religious scholar Abdel Wahhab. Wahhab became a political ally of the Saud tribe during the Saudi struggle for control of Arabia.

House of Saud—Royal family of Saudi Arabia, from the tribe of Saud. Saudi Arabia is run by the royal family in conjunction with several other aristocratic families and tribal sheiks (*ulama* and *umara*). The House of Saud follows the Golden Rule of Consultation (*shura*) and Consensus (*ijma'*). The king, princes, and aristocrats always try to hammer out a common position that will not alienate the sheiks or tribes. The regime's legitimacy relies on careful personal alliances. The House of Saud directly controls the Saudi Arabia National Guard (SANG). SANG troops come from tribes loyal to the Sauds.

Abd al-Aziz ibn Saud (also called Ibn Saud)—Founder of Saudi Arabia. He was an ally of the British in World War I. Born in 1881, died in 1953. He fathered enough sons to provide a supply of successors through the 1990s.

Saudi Interior Ministry—Responsible for internal security; it functions as an internal intelligence and police service.

Committee for the Defense of Legitimate Rights (CDLR)—This Saudi dissident group is based in London. Originally founded in 1993 inside Saudi Arabia, it moved to London as the Saudis cracked down on members. Its chief spokesman is physics professor Mohammed al-Massariold.

The Bridge over the Strait of Tiran—Saudi Arabia and Egypt are discussing building a fifteen-mile-long system of bridges and causeways that will connect the tip of the Sinai Peninsula to Saudi Arabia. This will be a land route that bypasses Israel and Jordan. Ostensibly, it's to be for tourists and to help "pilgrims on their way to Mecca." Actually, the bridge is a wedge against Iraq and Iran—a way of quickly moving Egyptian troops into Saudi Arabia. The bridge, however, faces international environmentalist opposition; it must cross some of the planet's most beautiful reefs.

Kuwait

Kuwait is an emirate, ruled by the al-Sabah family. Actually, the al-Sabahs are but one of the many clans that "rule" Kuwait; they had long simply been in charge of dealing with foreigners but had the good sense to get control of the country's checkbook once oil was discovered. Kuwait had a parliament until 1986, a noisy and freewheeling forum that was dissolved by royal decree. The parliament had fifty elected members and twenty-five government appointees. In 1989 and 1990, agitation began among Kuwait's many well-educated, well-heeled, and bucks-up citizens. The Iraqi invasion and liberation led by the United States increased the push for more democracy. The al-Sabahs, however, have been reluctant. Some members of Kuwait's new parliamentary council favor an Islamic state.

Kuwait—In Arabic, "small fort."

Diwaniya—The tradition of "open discussion" begun by Kuwaiti sailors and merchants who, in the preoil "Ali Baba" days of Gulf life, gathered to share information ranging from the price of fish and marine rope to the quality of pearls being found offshore. Kuwait is the only Gulf state with anything resembling a democratic tradition, and *diwaniya* is the basis of that tradition. Also, *diwaniya* can refer to a special room separated from the house where these discussions take place. Kuwaiti nationalists exiled by the Iraqi invasion strongly favor a democratic government in "restored Kuwait."

120 to 200 billion—Add a dollar sign ($) and get an estimate of the amount of cash and value of Kuwaiti investments outside of Kuwait prior to the Persian Gulf War. A lot of it was spent to repair the damage of the war, and much was found to have been stolen outright or through fraud. This put more strain on the al-Sabahs.

Bahrain

Officially the government of tiny Bahrain is a "constitutional emirate." The National Assembly, however, was dissolved by the emir in 1975. The ruling clan is the Khalifa family. In the face of agitation for democracy, the Khalifas appointed an "advisory council." In Bahrain the wealthy families tend to be Sunni; the poor majority are Shiite.

OBUs—Offshore banking units; the Bahraini banks do not handle local deposits, but do handle deposits for the region's troubled nations.

Royal Air Force and U.S. Navy—Both have facilities in Bahrain.

Precautionary law—Law that permits detention of political prisoners for up to three years without trial. It is backed up by thousands of mercenary (non-Bahraini) troops.

Sheik's Beach—A private pleasure preserve for friends of the emir. It is a source of social and ethnic antagonism in Bahrain. Patrolled by Pakistani guards, it is limited to "whites and Japanese only."

UAE

The United Arab Emirates is a federation of seven minikingdoms, each run by a prince ("emir") and a cohort of sheiks. All were British protectorates until 1971. Rivalry between emirs is rampant. Because of their size, Abu Dhabi (which constitutes 85 percent of the UAE's area), and Dubai, with its harbor, dominate.

Trucial Coast—Former name of UAE-area, derived from the 1853 "Perpetual Maritime Truce" between the British and tribal leaders. The "truce" was designed to curb local pirates preying on British shipping between England and India.

Qatar

Qatar is a traditional emirate. Wahhabi Islam shapes policy. The ruling clan is the Al T'hani family. Family power is somewhat curbed by the Consultative Council, whose elected members advise the ruling sheik and his Council of Ministers.

Oman

Oman is an absolute monarchy run by the Al Bu Said dynasty; no political parties, the current ruler a benevolent autocrat, Sultan Qaboos. Qaboos was educated at the British military academy, Sandhurst. The preceding ruler, Sultan Said ibn Taimur, Quaboos's father, was a medieval, and murderous, autocrat. Qaboos deposed his father by coup in 1970.

Dhofar Province—Site of the low-grade war between Oman and South Yemen; sometime home of PFLOAG—Popular Front for the Liberation of Oman and the Arabian Gulf—which later became PFLO—Popular Front for the Liberation of Oman. PFLO was a Marxist group supported by South Yemen. This organization no longer exists.

Omani Army—Strength of 25,000, with several hundred British officers and NCOs. Dhofar Province has a 3,500-troop home guard, now composed of many of the former "rebels" sponsored by South Yemen.

Kanjar—The traditional Omani curved dagger.

Yemen

The Republic of Yemen has an elected "general assembly" with 301 seats. In the north the politics outside of Sanaa are essentially tribal and the government "rules" by granting fiefs to local tribal rulers.

General People's Congress (GPC)—Controlled by Ali Abdullah Saleh, it is the northern party and largest single party.

Islaah—Yemeni Grouping for Reform, a northern-based Islamic fundamentalist party.

Yemeni Socialist party—The former Communist party, it now acts as the "party of the south." Was controlled by Ali Salem al-Baidh.

Qat—Narcotic leaf chewed in Yemen; men hang out in *qat* dens.

Jambiyas—Traditional, ornamented Yemeni daggers. The most precious have handles of rhino horn. This makes Yemeni daggers an ecological no-no, and Sanaa a market for East African poachers.

General

Emir—Title indicating a patriarchal ruler in Arabian Peninsular nations. (Also, archaic term for a military leader or provincial governor.)

Gulf Cooperation Council (GCC)—Originally organized in 1981 as a fledgling defense group for the UAE, Saudi Arabia, Qatar, Kuwait, and Oman, it is now a sort of regional political sounding board.

Mecca—Islam's most holy city, regarded as protectorate of Saudi monarchy. True Muslims must make at least one pilgrimage to the House of God in Mecca during their lifetime. Hezbollah, the Iranian-backed Shiite Muslim terrorist sect operating out of Lebanon, has called for the removal of the Saudi royal family as the guardian of Islam's holiest shrines, located in Mecca and Medina.

The Mahdi—Literally, "the Expected One," the restored leader of Islam who will lead Muslims to final worldly victory; there have been several dozen "false" Mahdis in the last century.

Caliph—The *khalifa*—the agent or successor acting on Muhammad's behalf.

Sunna—Derived from the root of the Arabic word for "custom," suggesting the customary or "the beaten path"; Islamic code of correct faith and conduct.

Sunnis and Shiites (or Shia Muslims)—Two main sects of Islam.

The Koran—Book of Muhammad's revelations through the Angel Gabriel; the holy writ of Islam. The Koran is augmented by accepted "sayings" (*hadith*) attributed to the Prophet. The Koran is the revealed word for "Islam" ("submission"), submission to the will of God.

OPEC—Organization of Petroleum Exporting Countries, headquartered in Vienna. Established in 1960 to coordinate member oil production policies, it is modeled after the Texas Railroad Commission.

Iraq

Arab Baath party—Iraqi element of same Arab Resurrection party found in Syria; bitterly at odds with Syrian Baathists.

Republican Guard Forces Corps—Corps of politically reliable troops within the Iraqi Army. They are recruited, especially the officers, from Saddam Hussein's native Tikrit region north of Baghdad.

Iraqi Special Forces—"Secret police" organized into army-type units tasked with monitoring the Iraqi Army and Republican Guard.

Kurds—Major organization is KDP, Kurdish Democratic party.

Al Dawa—Iraqi Shiite opposition group, loyal to Iranian revolutionary regime; full name is Al Dawa Al Islamiyah—Islamic Call.

The National Progressive and Democratic Front in Iraq—Coalition group of almost every flavor of anti-Iraqi Baathist opposition; includes Nasserites, Shiite Socialist party, Communists, etc.; based in Damascus.

Tikrit—Iraqi town; hometown of many of the current Baathist regime's highest-ranking members (the "Tikritis"). Now a province, it provides a larger base of loyal (and favored) supporters for Saddam.

"Marsh Arabs"—Arabs living in Shatt-al-Arab marshlands.

"Big gun"—A 131-foot-long, 39-inch-bore "supergun" designed by rogue ballistics genius Gerald Bull (assassinated in Brussels in March 1990—the killer used a silenced 7.65-mm automatic pistol). Italy, Turkey, and Great Britain intercepted parts of the huge weapon. Some sources estimate the gun would have had a potential range of six hundred kilometers and could fire chemical, nuclear, or conventional "booster-assisted" shells, or place a small satellite into orbit. Mr. Bull had designed the long-range G5 155-mm howitzers for South Africa's Armscor Company (exported to Iraq and anyone else willing to buy). Iraq's "big gun" project was destroyed in the aftermath of the 1991 war, but other nations are exploring the project.

POLITICAL TREND CHARTS

SAUDI ARABIA

Gv95	Gv20	PC95	PC20	R95	R20	Ec95	Ec20	EdS95	EdS20
AM6,5	AM4,4	6−	5−	5	5	7	6+	6−	6

Gv = Government Type

AM = Absolute Monarchy (effectiveness, 0–9, stability 0–9)

PC = Political Cohesiveness (0 = chaos, 9 = maximum)

R = Repression Index (9 maximum)

Ec = Comparative Economic Status (0–9)

EdS = Relative Education Status (0–9); in this case, urban population only

ER = Education Resources

IP = Investment Potential

NOTE: All figures apply to Saudi Arabians, not guest workers; the trend indicates a weakening political control by the House of Saud as the economy slowly declines.

KUWAIT

Gv95	Gv20	PC95	PC20	R95	R20	Ec95	Ec20	EdS95	EdS20
PM5,4	CM3,2	7	5	3	3	7	7+	7	7

PM = Parliamentary Monarchy (well, a constitutional sheikdom of sorts)

CM = Constitutional Monarchy (a democracy, after a fashion)

OMAN

Gv95	Gv20	PC95	PC20	R95	R20	Ec95	Ec20	EdS95	EdS20
AM6,4	M4,3	6	6	7	6	3	4	3	3+*

AM = Absolute Monarchy
*Oman's drive to improve education standards has not succeeded as planned.

UAE

Gv95	Gv20	PC95	PC20	R95	R20	Ec95	Ec20	EdS95	EdS20
M7,4	M6,4	5	5	6	7	7	6	4	6

M = Monarchy

QATAR

Gv95	Gv20	PC95	PC20	R95	R20	Ec95	Ec20	EdS95	EdS20
M7,5	M7,5	6−	6	5	4	6+	6	3+	4+

M = Monarchy
NOTE: New leaders may broaden political base.

YEMEN

Gv95	Gv20	PC95	PC20	R95	R20	Ec95	Ec20	EdS95	EdS20
A06,5	AD6,5	6	6	4	4	2+	4−	2	2

AO = Authoritarian Oligarchy with some democratic trappings; tribally based
AD = a very Authoritarian Democracy (rather more authoritarian than less, but some
    change from 1995)
NOTE: Look Back: The 1991 edition (most of it written in 1990) projected this line
for a theoretical united Yemen in 1996. Would local autonomy in Aden have prevented
a civil war? Who knows, but "united" Yemen opted for centralization, which meant
political control by the more populous north.

"UNITED YEMEN"

Gv96	PC96	R96	Ec96	EdS96	ER96
AC3,5	3	5	3	3	2

AC = Authoritarian Coalition of some type, probably an authoritarian oligarchy with democratic trappings and "autonomy" for locals in Aden

IRAQ

Gv95	Gv20	PC95	PC20	R95	R20	Ec95	Ec20	EdS95	EdS20
1MD6,3	1MD5,3	3	4	8	7	2+	3+	3	3

1MD = One-Party Military Dictatorship
NOTE: Iraqi economy could improve to 5 if embargo ends by 1996.

PARTICIPANT GOALS AND STRATEGIES

Arabian Peninsula

Saudi Arabia—Relies on the United States as guarantor of existence, though Saudi Arabs dislike "the West" and the presence of non-Islamic foreigners in their nation. Because of its economic clout, Saudi Arabia is wooed by the world and by other Arabs. As a comparatively defenseless nation, however, the Saudis know they are subject to intimidation by Iraq and Iran. Theirs is a balancing game. The ruling Saudi aristocracy also knows that this means, like it or not, a relationship with the world's superpower, the United States. Internal militants, such as those who bombed the Saudi Arabian National Guard headquarters in Riyadh in November 1995, must be co-opted or stopped.

Oman—Continues to improve its armed forces and buy more modern weapons. Oman is receiving new U.S. and French equipment, along with U.S. and European training groups. The British have been by far the most effective trainers. Oman relies on "back door" U.S. support to counteract Iranian intrigue. To openly embrace the United States would open Oman to Islamic reaction that could easily spread into Islamic revolution.

Regional Powers and Power Interest Indicator Charts

Saudi Arabia and Arabian Peninsula Power Interest Indicator D + 5 *

	Economic Interests	Historical Interests	Political Interest	Military Interest	Force Generation Potential	Ability to Intervene Politically
United States	8	5	7	7	4	5
United Kingdom	6	7	5	5+	1	4
France	6	6	5	5	1	4
Russia	3	4	4	4	2	3
Iraq	8	9	8	8	3†	3‡
Iran	7	8	8	7	1§	7
Jordan	8	9	8	8	2	4
Israel	1	7	8	8	4	1+
Egypt	7	8	8	7	2	7
Saudi	9	9	9	9	2+	8

Note: 0 = minimum; 9 = maximum

*FGPs as of D-Day plus 5. Excepting local armies and militias (e.g., Saudi Arabia itself), virtually all military forces require "lift" or "march time" to bring significant forces into target areas of the peninsula. U.S. FGP at D+45 is 8.

†Pre-Desert Storm D+5 FGP was 7.

‡As Iraq rebuilds from its defeat in Operation Desert Storm, it will increasingly use political sway and military might to influence regional politics (i.e., oil production, oil prices, and Iranian influence).

§If the Iranian Air Force and Army are rebuilt into a pre-1979 "shah-sized" force, give Iran an FGP of 3− for Saudi Arabia and Persian Gulf coastal area, excepting the Strait of Hormuz. (For that area, see below.)

Force generation potentials inside their own borders: Oman, 2; Kuwait, 1+; UAE, 1−; Qatar, 1−; Yemen, 2+; Bahrain, 0.

IRAQ VERSUS SAUDI ARABIA AND ALLIES (ANOTHER PERSIAN GULF WAR)

	Economic Interests	Historical Interests	Political Interest	Military Interest	Force Generation Potential	Ability to Intervene Politically
Syria	4	8	8	8	4+	6
Russia	4	7	7	7	6−	4
Turkey	6	7	8	8	6	3
United States	7	4	7	6	8	6
Jordan	9	8	8	7	2	4
Egypt	6	7	8	5	4	7
Pakistan	4	4	6	6	2	1
Israel	2	7	7	8	2	1

Kuwait—Kuwait has chosen to become a protectorate of the United States and the UN.

Qatar, UAE, Bahrain—These emirates have tied themselves to Saudi Arabia. As the Saudis' internal situation becomes more precarious, they may look for other protectors. Qatar is expanding global contacts.

Yemen—There is no basic local strategy other than repression and domination by the north. Despite the newly discovered oil deposits, Yemen's political disorder makes its economic prospects even dimmer. There is the real prospect of a guerrilla war waged by the south against northern domination. The best strategy would be for the north to re-create a United Yemen as a loose federation. Cultural and political differences between north and south argue against that kind of wisdom.

Iraq—Until they lost the Persian Gulf War and were evicted from Kuwait by the allied coalition, the Iraqis were the military leaders of the Arab Middle East. The desire for political leadership and economic leadership (dictating oil pricing in OPEC) and taking "the nineteenth province" (Kuwait) was too much of a temptation. Defeat by the UN coalition weakened Iraq. The old troubles with its Kurds, with Iran and Syria—and potentially with Turkey—have not gone away. Iraq's leaders want to rebuild the army and escape from the UN embargo.

Saddam Hussein—Iraq will have its strategic interests no matter who is in power. Without Saddam a less militant Iraq could emerge, but that is not a certainty. What are Saddam's strategic goals? Saddam is trying to stay alive and remain in power in Baghdad. He may dream of forging some type of pan-Arab coalition for another fight with the United States, but under his leadership such dreams are madness. He finally seems aware that crossing certain political boundaries and boundaries of behavior invites calamity.

Is Saddam a madman? Saddam did burn Kuwait's oil wells and massively pollute the northern Persian Gulf by pumping crude oil from Kuwaiti wells and refineries. It is possible that Iraq has managed to conceal a nuclear device or biological and chemical weapons. Iraq could obtain a nuke. Would Saddam use these weapons on Kuwait or Saudi Arabia? Don't bet against it.

Iran—Though the desire to spread Islamic revolution throughout the region has waned, especially in light of the Kuwait crisis, Iran benefits by keeping other regimes as unstable as Teheran. This unstable condition lessens the threat to the Iran "Revolution" and also gives Iran a card to trade. Hezbollah's call for stripping the Saudi royal clan of its role as guardian of Islamic shrines is an example of this strategy at work. Concerning Islamic revolution in Kuwait, Bahrain, and the UAE: Ayatollah-inspired assassinations and bombings have severely disrupted these rich Arab states. Propaganda directed at Gulf state Shiites has so far failed to ignite a revolution. Probably because the Shiite Arabs don't care too much for the Persians and the chaos in Teheran isn't as appealing as domestic peace.

United States—Washington wants to ensure stable Gulf governments so that the oil flows. CENTCOM stocks tanks and heavy equipment around the region; Kuwait has a "garrison" of sorts. The United States and the Saudi monarchy are in this together; the Saudis want to stay rich, which means sell their oil, and the United States, for the sake of its own economy as well as its allies, must blunt Islamic revolutionary destabilizations. This takes long-range planning, careful politics, and domestic political will. The Persian Gulf War and the

September–October 1994 "reinforcement" of Kuwait proved CENT-COM can do the job if U.S. troops can arrive in time.

Russia—The Russians are very sensitive about the Iranian-Azerbaijan border. The USSR was a traditional supplier of Iraq during the cold war. Russian arms show up in both Iran and Iraq, and Moscow likes the fact that Iraq pays cash. Russia also fears nuclear weapons in the hands of Islamic radicals. Despite its problems, Russia is still a military superpower. If ideology no longer runs Moscow, know that self-interest, in the advent of a nuclear war in "Mesopotamia," would.

POTENTIAL OUTCOMES

Events on the Arabian Peninsula and in Iraq will be greatly affected by those in Iran and events affecting the Israeli-Palestinian question. Still, the following events, because of the geostrategic interest in the oil-rich region, will make headlines if and when they occur.

1. Revolution in Saudi Arabia: The big If for the big prize. It seems that internally many Saudis would love an option to the Saud dynasty, but no one can produce an alternative. The Sauds aren't interested in experimenting with democracy. Chances for overthrow of the Sauds before 2001 are slim: 2 percent.
2. "Successful" Islamic revolution sponsored by Iran: 15 percent chance through 2001 in Bahrain; elsewhere in region (Oman, UAE, Saudi Arabia, Kuwait), 3 percent; possibility of Iranian-sponsored violence and terror in the region (to include more trouble in Mecca and Medina), 99 percent. Possibility of internal, non-Iranian revolt against the Khalifa regime in Bahrain: 20 percent.

Iraq Versus Arabian Peninsula

Iraq's Kuwait debacle focused the world's attention on the weakness of Saudi Arabia and the Gulf states. Only massive Western (i.e., U.S.)

intervention, and remarkable politics by the Saudis and Egyptians, thwarted Iraq's aggression. Iraq suffers from severe internal problems. That's the local political key to a 15 percent chance of a major war erupting before 2001. If a major war occurs, there's a 98 percent chance of a repeat of the allied and "United Nations" return to the Persian Gulf region (a repeat of August, September, and October 1990, but with less concern for political delicacies). As for another "bluff" Iraqi invasion of Kuwait—25 percent chance through 2001 (a repeat of fall 1994 as Iraq tests international political will). With the above as starting points, these are the projections for "the next Persian Gulf war."

1. 85 percent chance: Allied "victory" over Iraq (though oil production in the region is disrupted for a year).
2. 13 percent chance: a renewed military stalemate, but with Iraqi forces inside their pre–August 2, 1990, borders. Iraqi regime solidifies domestic political control by standing up to "the Saudis and the West." Jumps to 33 percent if United States gets involved in a war in north Asia (Korea).
3. 2 Percent chance: Iraqi military success. Iraq retains Kuwait and forces a change in the Saudi government.

Renewed Yemeni Civil War

There is a 30 percent chance through 2001 that Aden will once again attempt to separate itself from Sanaa's control. Probability of a northern victory is 80 percent. As for the odds on a guerrilla and terror conflict erupting: a 99 percent sure thing.

COST OF WAR

A recent Arab study suggested that the 1990–91 Persian Gulf War cost the Arab nations in the Persian Gulf region and those who sent major contingents to the battlefield (i.e., Egypt and Syria) a grand total of $700 billion (yes, 700 *billion* dollars). This figure includes the cost of warfare, damage, and lost oil revenues. It does not include the costs borne by other nations (though it does include payments made by Saudi Arabia to compensate for the costs borne by its allies). The war may have been short but the costs were astronomical. A big war in this region is a trillion-dollar affair in terms of global economic costs.

QUICK LOOK: Soldiers of the Queen: "Mercenary" Officers and NCOs

Most nations are understandably nervous about trusting foreigners to run their armed forces. Yet mercenary troops have long been a logical way for rulers to control their subjects while avoiding revolution spawned in the local military barracks. The only trick is to obtain reliable mercenaries. The ruler has to make sure he is buying troops who will stay bought once they sign their contracts.

The British are familiar and at ease with mercenary arrangements. The Gurkhas from northern India and Nepal still serve in the British and Indian armies. Increasingly, Gurkhas show up in other parts of the world also. In the "merc world," the British participate by supplying officers and NCOs to many nations. In the 1970s and 1980s, this old tradition was very much alive in the Persian Gulf, particularly in Oman. In the 1990s, the "soldiers of the queen," though less overtly active, continue to press on.

The rulers of the Persian Gulf states are generally local strongmen whose power the population prefers to recognize rather than resist with arms. So, raising troops from among the locals is not a good way to sustain the strongman's power. An obvious solution is to use mercenaries. Troops are easy to obtain; many groups in the area have traditionally served as mercenaries for whoever could afford them. Individual Baluchi tribesmen of Iran, Afghanistan, and Pakistan soldier for the highest bidder. Baluchis tend to be outstanding soldiers—which is one reason why they can become an internal problem for both Iran and Pakistan.

Other forces from the region, particularly Pakistan, are available (officially or otherwise) to serve appropriate foreign rulers ("appropriate" means non-Israeli). The Pakistani government has made several defense arrangements with Persian Gulf potentates, "lending" brigades and fighter-bomber squadrons for local defense. The deal is that the lendee pays for maintenance, training, and other expenses, and Pakistan gets their trained troops and well-maintained equipment when it needs them (for example, prior to a war with India).

One problem with using local, homegrown armed forces is the danger of their being lured into local political intrigues. Of course, mercenary leaders can also become involved. In December 1989, Colonel Robert Denard, a French mercenary commanding the five-hundred-man Comorro Islands' presidential guard, organized the assassination of the Comorro Island President Ahmed Abdallah. Denard, while allegedly connected to French intelligence services, was something of a classic mercenary lone wolf. In 1995, Denard tried it again, but this time the French promptly sent in troops and arrested him and his men.

The British Army, however, retains direct links to its officers and NCOs "seconded" to foreign service; the Brits remain "soldiers of the queen." For this reason, Gulf rulers have always looked favorably on obtaining British officers and NCOs to lead mercenary troops or even the local armed forces. British officers and NCOs serving in foreign armies often "resign" from the home forces for the duration of their foreign service. They just as often rejoin the British Army afterward—with their "foreign" service time conveniently counting toward retirement. What is more striking about this foreign service is that the British mercenaries actually command foreign troops in the service of a non-British ruler. This arrangement serves all concerned and demonstrates why some mercenary forces survive and will most likely continue to do so. The British arrangements are unique for mercenary service. In almost all other cases, the nation the mercenaries come from has little or no interest in regulating the activities of their freelance warriors.

As with any army, the officers and senior NCOs are the keys to effectiveness and reliability. The British Army has had several hundred years' experience in leading mercenary forces, and has acquitted itself well in this capacity. While the British government has not been averse to interfering in the affairs of the Gulf states, it has generally done so with diplomacy and tact. The United States, Russia, China, and Iran rarely display such tact. The British (most recently in the Persian Gulf War) once again showed themselves to be militarily reliable as well as discreet.

With the breakup of the Soviet Union, thousands of experienced soldiers from the former Red Army have gone abroad looking for work. Many have found it. Russian mercenaries have shown up in Bosnia, the Persian Gulf (Yemen, Iraq, Iran), Africa, Asia, and South America. The most sought after former Red Army troops are those who served with Spetznaz (commando) and airborne units. Pilots are also in demand, and are often rented when high-performance Russian combat aircraft are sold abroad. These troops are tough, well trained and, relatively speaking, cheap. Just as there were plenty of German and Japanese mercenaries available immediately after World War II, there will be plenty of Russian (and other Soviet-nationality) mercs on the market throughout the 1990s.

Former members of South Africa's antiterror forces are also showing up on the payrolls of troubled African governments. A South African firm called Executive Options went to work for the beleaguered governments of Angola and Sierra Leone in 1995. Another British-based outfit, offering Gurkha mercenaries, has also found work in Africa.

Not to be left out, a number of recently retired, but very senior, American officers formed an organization called Military Professional Resources, Inc. It is based in Alexandria, Virginia, right down the road from the Pentagon and MPRI employees include former Army Chief of Staff Carl Vuono and former Defense Intelligence Agency chief Harry Soyster. MPRI had a multiyear contract with Croatia and has been officially sanctioned by the U.S. State Department. MPRI insists that their work is strictly in the classroom. Instruction is given in the established Croat military schools, and does not cover purely military matters, but rather issues of logistics and organization. This is threading a fine line, but it is something America did before World War II in China, where several groups of "official" mercenaries aided the Chinese against the Japanese.

QUICK LOOK: Inside the Post–Persian Gulf War Iraqi Armed Forces

The Persian Gulf War was a military disaster for the Iraqi Army. The Iraqi Army remains demoralized and in disarray.

In 1994 open sources estimated total Iraqi military strength at 380,000 troops organized into six corps. Twenty-nine divisions (twelve of these are called Republican Guard divisions) and around ten Special Forces brigades man these corps. I, II, and V corps are in the north combating, or simply watching, the Kurds. III and IV corps fight Shiite insurgents in the south. From three to five Republican Guard divisions remain in the Baghdad area. These units do not begin to approach their prewar combat strength. Iraq lost most of its modern army equipment in the Persian Gulf War.

The post–Persian Gulf War Republican Guard Forces Corps still consists of politically approved troops. The Hammurabi and Medina Republican Guard divisions have been apparently reconstituted as full-strength units. Whether they are truly armored divisions is a real question. At one time the Iraqi Army could motorize up to twenty divisions. As of mid-1995 the Iraqis had the ability to motorize (effectively turn infantry divisions into quasi-mechanized divisions) for short periods of time (and short distances) approximately three Republican Guard divisions. Two of these formations were sent to the Kuwaiti border in the fall of 1994.

Four new Republican Guard divisions have been raised since the Kuwait debacle but they are apparently of brigade size (four thousand or so troops). These are named Al-Abed Division, Al-Mustafa Division, Al-Nida Division, and Al-Quds Division. They serve as internal security units.

The Special Forces (SF) brigades are assigned to watch the regular Iraqi Army and civilian population areas. Critical facilities, including dams, oil fields, pumping stations, and power generation sites, are watched by the local police, secret police, and elements of the Special Forces.

The SF brigades have been organized into large divisions for "special assignments" such as combating the Kurds and attacking Arab Shiites in the marshes. Iraqi SF units are not special operations forces like U.S. Special Forces or the British SAS; the Iraqi SF are political police units capable of conducting extended military missions.

The Iraqi Baath regime maintains itself by constant surveillance. This is reflected in the "multiple structure" of the Iraqi military. There are several intelligence and security agencies in Iraq. As of mid-1995, all of the security agencies were led by Saddam Hussein's personal allies and all had Saddam as their titular leader.

Saddam maintains absolute secrecy about his whereabouts and movements. He travels with a large personal security force, most of its troops from Saddam's hometown of Tikrit. This personal control and secrecy did not stop three reported coup attempts against Saddam in 1993, two major reported coup attempts in 1994, and at least one in 1995. The personal control did, perhaps, keep the attempts from being successful. The key unit in fending off coups appears to be the Presidential Special Guard Force (the Al Haras al-Khass, around ten thousand troops)—a tough and politically reliable formation based in Baghdad.

Saddam has purged many military commanders since the retreat from Kuwait. Eighteen generals were reportedly shot in June 1991 for attempting to overthrow Saddam's regime. Military commanders in the Iraqi Army are transferred at the least hint of disloyalty. A long-standing Russian practice, hundreds of thousands of paid and unpaid informers, is widely used and provides an up-to-date picture of who is for, or against, Saddam and to what degree. Saddam trusts no one.

Iraq's air defense system was damaged in 1991 but not destroyed. Radars have been rebuilt. Iraq could put together an integrated air defense system. However, it would rely on out-of-date surface-to-air missile systems and antiaircraft artillery (AAA). Iraq does have some five thousand AAA pieces.

The Iraqi Air Force is a shell of its prewar self. Iraq managed to keep a dozen or so MiG 29s and about 30 Mirage F1s. According to open press sources, Iraq has around 150 modern combat aircraft, but the embargo means the aircraft lack spare parts, thus limiting their ability to fly much, if at all. Iraq's Chinese-made J6 and J7 aircraft are thought to be virtually unflyable. The Iraqi Air Force has lost its access to Eastern European maintenance facilities and maintenance personnel. In mid-1993 the Iraqi Air Force was managing to fly around one hundred sorties a month. That is not enough to keep up pilot proficiency.

QUICK LOOK: What Is Saudi Arabia?

The very name of the country denotes the nation's historical origins: Saudi Arabia was initially organized as the personal fiefdom of the Saud family, one of the many Bedouin clans that have long wandered across Arabia trading and warring with each other. In the last two hundred years, three clans have dominated the Arabian Peninsula: the Sauds, the Rashids, and the Hashemites. There were also the Ottoman Turks and various European nations, but until oil was discovered in the area, these external powers did not evince great interest in the affairs of the desert tribes. Before oil became a factor, the only areas of any interest were along the Persian Gulf coast (for fishing, trading, and commerce) and in the relatively densely populated Yemen area to the south, where there was more rain and thus more intensive grazing and agriculture.

In the eighteenth century the Saud clan supported a religious revival among local Muslims (Wahhabism, still a factor in puritanical Saudi Arabia) and gained control of most of the Arabian Peninsula. But not of the Muslim holy cities of Mecca and Medina—the Hejaz area. Control of the Hejaz brought with it economic benefits, as Muslim pilgrims had money to spend. The dozens of tribes that made up the Saudi coalition were difficult to control, and the Saudis lost much of their power to intercine tribal fighting in the nineteenth century. But by exploiting the religious fervor of the tribal warriors, the Saudis regained control of central Arabia, and then parts of western Arabia (controlled by the Rashid clan) in the two decades before World War I. Taking support from the British from 1915 on, the Saudis eliminated the Rashids as a major power by the early 1920s (with a few side efforts to assist Lawrence of Arabia's "Arab uprising" against the Ottoman Turks). But Lawrence's main Arab ally was the Hashemite Arabs (of Jordan and, until 1925, the Hejaz). In 1925 the Saudis gained control of the holy cities of Mecca and Medina and the Red Sea coast. To keep the peace, the British guaranteed the Hashemite kingdom of Jordan and installed a Hashemite prince as the king of the new nation of Iraq in 1931. The Saudis renamed their larger territory Saudi Arabia in 1932 (the only nation in the world named after its ruling family).

British diplomats had not spent all their time with the Saudi clan. Treaties were also made with the ancient, and numerous, Arab emirates on the Persian Gulf coast as well as in Yemen, which was largely hostile to any Bedouin unity. Through the 1920s and 1930s the Saudis had their hands full reining in the Bedouin warriors, who had gotten into the habit of raiding into neighboring Syria, Jordan, Yemen, the Gulf emirates, and Iraq. That was their traditional sport and it took a Saudi king to bring these nasty habits under control with causing a civil war.

While the Saudi princes struggled hard to tame the tribal warriors, they were also dependent on these same men of the desert for support. What changed this ancient relationship were the first oil wells that began operating in the 1930s. The trickle of oil income began to rise sharply after World War II and became a flood when the oil cartel was formed and prices sharply increased in the early 1970s.

After World War II, Saudi rulers realized that they needed a modern army and air force. But that required educated men to fill the ranks of officers and technicians. The most likely candidates were available from the townspeople, particularly from the Hejaz (Mecca and Medina) region. The Hejaz was conquered by the Saudi-led Bedouin tribes of central and eastern Arabia. The House of Saud did not feel quite safe with so much of the military being run by Hejaz officers. That problem was solved by recruiting the Hejaz population for the army and air force and setting up a separate army (the National Guard) staffed entirely by Hejaz tribesmen traditionally loyal to the Saudi clan. Thus the Saudi Arabian Army watches foreign enemies and the National Guard watches the army. In wartime, of course, both forces would be equally fervent in defending their holy (and oil-soaked) homeland. What the Saudi princes worried most about was a military coup in peacetime. The Saudi crown prince usually commands the National Guard.

The Bedouin House of Saud and their personal fiefdom (Saudi Arabia) are unique in other ways. The Saudis are the guardians of the holiest shrines in all of Islam. Every Muslim is obliged to attempt at least one pilgrimage to Mecca, and with increasing wealth and cheaper air travel, many more do so. It is a great honor for the Saudis to guard and maintain the holy places, but they do so largely through enforcing a very orthodox (and puritanical) form of Islam in their nation. The House of Saud came to rule the holy places partially because they were more devout than their rivals, and largely because they were more astute militarily and politically. For example, they became allied with the United States because, as they put it, "America is far away and has no designs on Saudi Arabia." That may be less true as the United States becomes ever more dependent on Persian Gulf oil. But the move toward a U.S. alliance is another example of Saudi pragmatism. The Saudis manage to be one of the loudest opponents of Israel (largely because of the Muslim holy places in Jerusalem) while remaining close to Israel's most powerful ally.

The Saudis (and more worldly Kuwaitis) have managed to live well with their "gift of oil." Although Saudi Arabia is a monarchy, the standard of living of all Saudis has made spectacular gains in the last two generations. Each year, thousands of Saudis pour forth from universities around the world. Few university graduates are taught that monarchy is the best form of government. Yet the Saudi monarchy is also based on ancient tribal practices. The monarchs lead only if the people follow. Three generations ago, a bad king would have had to face the rifles of unhappy subjects. Today, unhappy subjects can still shoot a king they are dissatisfied with (as happened in 1975, while the king was giving one of his regular audiences where any subject could petition him), but they can also clamor for democracy or any other new idea that catches their imagination. The House of Saud has so far made a successful effort to merge ancient tradition with twentieth-century wealth and aspirations.

Two other aspects of Saudi wealth catch wide attention. The Saudis maintain the traditional Bedouin (and Islamic) precepts of charity and hospitality. Hundreds of thousands of Palestinians (and other Muslims in need) are direct recipients of Saudi aid. Within Saudi Arabia, no one is allowed to want for anything. Although millions of foreign workers live in the country, they are well paid and send billions of dollars home each year. But Saudi Arabia is a very puritanical nation (at least by Western standards). Alcohol and public socializing with women is forbidden (and diligently enforced). Lawbreakers are whipped, mutilated, or publicly beheaded or stoned to death. The practice of any religion but Islam is not allowed, nor are Jews allowed in the country. The Saudis, however, are also human and many of the (largely male) aristocrats (up to 10 percent of the population) spend a lot of time outside the country sinning in the Western fashion. But then, Saudi princes were always prone to living it up. Now they can afford to do it away from the scrutiny of the religious authorities and that helps keep the peace at home. However, it does not keep the peace in other Arab nations.

For thousands of years the Bedouin Arab nomads in the area were considered, well, less civilized than the better-educated Arabs living in the urban areas in other parts of the Arab world. The enormous wealth that has fallen upon these "camel herders" seems somewhat unfair to many less fortunate Arabs. There is a lot of resentment, and perhaps even more envy, in the rest of the Arab world. It was for this reason that Iraq had some popular support for its takeover of Kuwait. But the Saudis have had to live with the envy and resentment for a long time. They have made their alliances carefully and, being what they are, put their trust in God and keep their weapons and allies handy.

Chapter 3

ISRAEL AND THE MIDDLE EAST: BABIES, SHEKELS, BALLOTS, AND BULLETS

INTRODUCTION

From 1948 to 1982, Israel's wars with its Arab neighbors failed to create a stable peace. Still, the first years of the 1990s saw the Camp David "peace process" (and later the "Madrid formula") provide an alternative to relentless Arab-Israeli warfare.

Jordan has followed Egypt in recognizing Israel's status as a legitimate sovereign nation. The Israelis and Palestinians now argue over what the new Palestinian state will look like and how it will function, not whether or not a new Palestine will ever exist. Progress toward stable peace, however, is erratic. The next Arab terrorist bombing, the next murder by right-wing Israeli anti-Arab radicals, the next round of strike and reprisal in southern Lebanon, brings the process to a halt.

Everyone in the Middle East always gets more than they bargain for, and so much less. The Arab and Israeli military situation remains distinctly unsettled; the armed conflict ranges from the stones thrown by eleven-year-old Palestinians at both PLO policemen and Israeli Army troops to large-scale conventional combat in Lebanon. Armed conflict with Syria, or even Iraq and Iran, remain real possibilities.

The irony in the peace process is this: As Israel secures a measure of peace and security on its own immediate borders, with the acquisition of ballistic missiles and long-ranging strike aircraft by Iran, the possibility of a militarily resurgent Iraq, and the potential scattering of radical, Islamic fundamentalist (and anti-Israel) regimes from Sudan to Algeria, the Israelis must look to defend themselves at ever longer ranges. The potential exists for a regional nuclear war with Israeli involvement. Any full-scale war involving Israel remains the most dangerous in the Middle East.

In 1948, Israel fought Saudis, Jordanians, Egyptians, Syrians, Palestinians, and a few Iraqis. In 1956, Israel once again fought the Egyptians, who deployed Palestinian units in their army. In 1967, Israel fought Egypt, Jordan, Syria, and a host of Arab combat contingents supplied by Iraq, Libya, and Algeria. In 1973, the Israelis took on the Egyptians and the Syrians, both once again supported by a smattering of Arab contingents.

In the 1982 Lebanon War, Israel tangled with the Palestinians, the Syrians, and practically every armed faction in the entire Middle East. In late 1987, simmering Arab discontent on the occupied West Bank boiled over and the *intifada* began—the Palestinian uprising against the Israeli occupation of and Israeli settlement in the West Bank. In some ways the intifada became the cruelest and most internally politically divisive of Israel's wars.

Iraq's Saddam Hussein attempted to use the Israeli-Palestinian issue as diplomatic cover for his naked aggression in the Persian Gulf War. Because of the depth of Arab bitterness over Israel, he did have some limited success on the propaganda front.

But Saddam trumped himself when he attacked both Israel and Saudi Arabia with SCUD missiles. The Israelis took the Iraqi SCUD missile attacks and did not respond on the battlefield. Via live feeds from CNN, Israelis and Arabs could watch one another be attacked by the same brutal, common enemy. The Persian Gulf War changed the dynamics of the Arab and Israeli conflict. Rapprochement between Israel and Saudi Arabia became real and peace became a possibility.

Still, the Israelis continue to fight a terror war involving "rejection-ist" Palestinian factions, "rejectionist" Israeli extremist factions, vari-ous Iranian-sponsored organizations, and a few leftover guerrilla and terrorist contingents looking for a post–cold war raison d'être.

True, Israel stands out as the Middle East's regional military giant. Since 1991, Israel has begun to draw a better balance between eco-nomic and military demands.

But what new Palestine will be remains unanswered. The Arab pop-ulation of Israel-Palestine grows faster than the Jewish, though the arrival of settlers from Eastern Europe and Russia complicates ethnic arithmetic. Old differences between various Jewish ethnic and religious groups causes more political divisions within Israel.

Hezbollah, Iran's proxies in Lebanon, continue to make war on Israel. Syria makes moves toward negotiated peace but as always hedges its position by maintaining covert support for several anti-Israeli organizations. The issue of water rights in the region—an old source of war—is begged. Growing Islamic radicalism threatens Arab moderates in Egypt and Jordan and even Saudi Arabia. The spread of weapons of mass destruction, to Iran, to Algeria, or to other nations, increases Israeli distress.

SOURCE OF CONFLICT

The fundamental conflict is notorious: The very existence of the State of Israel and the lives of Israelis are intractably bound to the dispersal and deprivation of the region's Palestinian inhabitants.

The Middle East is a land of long memories and tenaciously held grudges. Three major, and several minor, wars have occurred over this issue since 1945. Israel has been militarily victorious in each war. Yet the basic antagonisms remain, and get worse as new hatreds arise.

Any Middle Eastern war involving the State of Israel has the poten-tial of escalating into a conflict igniting a vast swath of the world from India to Morocco. With the introduction of theater (medium-range) ballistic missiles into Iran's arsenal (and potentially, a radicalized Algeria), Russia and the whole of southern Europe could become involved in the terrible spillover of another Arab-Israeli or radical-Muslim–Israeli war.

U.S. commitment to Israel's survival is another reason any local war could expand into a larger confrontation. It is not inconceivable that a Syrian-Israeli confrontation would become a confrontation between the United States and Iran in the Persian Gulf.

So far Israel has more than held its own in the political arena and mastered its opponents on the battlefield. But there are subtler kinds of combat, the demographic and economic wars that Israel and dozens of other countries have yet to master. Ultimately, motherhood is mightier than either the pen or the sword. Demographic combat, the battle of human population statistics, begets several problems. Here are a few examples. A population boom brings more mouths to feed, as in India. There can be more workers or more dissidents. If one is building a nation out of a struggle, population growth can bring either more soldiers or more guerrillas. Zimbabwe faces this prospect with the minority Matabele tribe. A slowdown in population growth can mean there aren't enough soldiers. West Germany, prior to the events of November 1989, feared this would happen in the 1990s. The *Kinderlos* society was not producing enough *Kinder* to fill the Bundeswehr's *Garten*. The absorption of East Germany and the relaxation of tensions in central Europe mitigates the problem.

The welcome relaxation of tensions in Eastern Europe has opened up a new source of people (or, cynics might say, cannon fodder) for Israel—Russian Jews bailing out from the chaos of the former USSR. Arabs perceive this influx as a demographic attack.

In democracies a population increase can mean there are more voters to appease—and these new potential voters may be culturally and/or ethnically different from those groups currently in power. The problem isn't unique to democracies. Totalitarian societies fear rapid increases in nondominant ethnic groups. One of the causes for turmoil in the old USSR was the struggle between Russia and its emerging majority of non-Russian ethnic groups. Either traditions change or revolutions erupt.

Israel, with a Jewish population of 4.2 million, faces two kinds of potential population problems. Most obvious is Arab population increase. Arabs number 17 percent (approximately 650,000) of the population in the State of Israel proper. Some of these Arabs are Druze Arabs, who in the past have displayed pro-Israeli inclinations.

In the occupied West Bank, however, the equation changes: There, as of mid-1995, 115,000 Israeli settlers mix with at least 1.15 million Arabs. Some 15,000 Israelis live in the occupied Golan Heights and 140,000 in East Jerusalem. As of mid-1995 the number of Israelis still living in the Gaza Strip had shrunk to around 2,000.

Despite the peace process and the tentative creation of a Palestinian state, extreme Zionists talk of annexing the West Bank, calling it biblical Samaria and Judea. To annex the West Bank into Israel proper would create a huge demographic shift in the nation of Israel, unless the Israelis completely displace the Palestinians, which some right-wing radicals openly advocate. Palestinians average 5 children per family. The Israeli average is 2.7, though this may be trending upward.

Some Israelis dispute the notion of the demographic time bomb, especially since the arrival of Jews from the former Soviet Union. Approximately 500,000 Russian Jews and Jews living in the ex-USSR arrived in Israel between 1989 and May 1994.

In 1995, as the unemployment rate in Israel declined, the number of immigrants from Eastern Europe appeared to be going up again (an estimated additional 125,000 immigrants from the ex-USSR arrived from mid-1994 to the end of 1995). Many of the immigrants from Russia are described as "paper Jews"—those who buy fake Jewish identity papers in order to leave Russia's chaos. Perhaps 25 to 35 percent of the émigrés have no connection to Judaism. With the exception of a few religious zealots, Israelis don't seem to mind; the new immigrants (especially their children) will assimilate quickly.

These new arrivals now make up over 10 percent of Israel's population. This appears to be the kind of people boom that leads to economic boom: 57,000 of the new immigrants are engineers; 12,000 identified themselves as doctors and dentists; 12,000 as nurses and medical technicians; 12,000 as artists, composers, and writers. Approximately 200,000 of the new immigrants reported they had completed at least thirteen years of education.

Where do the new arrivals go? Israeli government studies show that the Israeli economy cannot absorb all of the professionals and educated. Some do move on to the United States. Others take labor jobs, displacing many Arab workers in the process. Since the establishment of the State of Israel, around 400,000 Jews have left Israel for other nations.

The other political population problem Israel faces is even more subtle. The Ashkenazim Jews of Europe, those currently in political and cultural power, are slowly being outnumbered by the Asiatic and African Sephardic Jews. The addition of Ashkenazim Russian Jews only ameliorates this a little—they do not come from a land familiar with democratic solutions to problems. Election laws, which allow for representation of even the most extreme splinter groups, exacerbate the political effects of this Israeli fractiousness.

Israel has checked the horrendous inflation rate of the late 1980s and early 1990s, but the difficult job of raising regional economic standards—stabilizing peace through prosperity—has yet to begin. The Jordanians say that if the peace process is to continue, Arab moderates must make economic gains, or Islamic radicals will take power. The economic war, which Israel began to win in the early 1990s, has changed. Israel cannot merely concern itself with its own economic success. Jordan and Egypt, and perhaps even Syria and Lebanon, must ultimately get a piece of the pie.

Peace has benefited Israel economically, which is one important reason the Israelis continue to proceed despite terror attacks. Still, overwhelming military superiority vis-à-vis one's neighbors, such as that enjoyed by Israel, can be an expensive kind of "staying ahead of the Joneses." Tanks and fighter-bombers not only exact a huge initial capital cost but also generate high fuel and maintenance bills. Do you buy tanks, build roads, buy butter, or support a government bureaucracy? War costs money. You can continue to print shekels but unless the amount of "work and value" in the country reflects the number of shekels circulating, inflation results. Losing an economic war may be slower and less dramatic than losing a shooting war, but the effect can be almost as devastating.

Thus peace for everyone in the region can mean a double win—no war and more money. The economies of Egypt and Jordan, however, continue to falter. Here is the looming crisis: The collapse of Israeli will to pursue peace and the collapse of moderate, peacemaking Arab regimes in favor of radical "anti-Zionist" organizations like Hamas.

For Egypt, now with a population nearing sixty million, the early 1990s have been a period of economic gloom. Official figures place economic growth (GDP) from 1991 through 1993 at less than 2 percent. There are good reasons to doubt official figures, but even if accurate the surge in Egyptian population and the transformation of Cairo into a nearly ungovernable "mega-city" means that low economic growth translates into no growth for the impoverished.

Ruled for more than fifty years by the same party of political and military elites (latest name: National Democratic party), Egypt is now paying a stiff political and social price for years of corruption, nepotism, and "socialist" bureaucratic bloat. The government and military sector takes up between 35 percent and 40 percent of the economy. Increased inflation is inevitable. The end of the cold war has a curious role in Egypt's economic plight. Until 1990, Egypt traded its often inferior industrial goods with Communist Europe for petroleum, other natural resources, and other products.

Egypt's social, political, and economic troubles are fertile fields for the growth of Islamic radicalism. Since the late 1980s the Egyptian government has waged an increasingly brutal internal war against the Muslim Brotherhood. The crackdowns and gun battles have moved Egypt ever closer to military dictatorship, and the Muslim Brotherhood continues to grow. The Islamist militants criticize the "peace with Israel."

Even if Egypt and Jordan fend off the challenge of Islamic radicalism, conventional and even nuclear war involving Israel remain very much in the picture. At present Israel has an overwhelming military advantage. Credible estimates give the Israelis around two hundred nuclear weapons. Analysts believe that most of the Israeli nuclear stockpile consists of bombs designed for delivery by aircraft, but no doubt the Israelis have a nuclear weapon, which can be delivered by a theater ballistic missile.

New and more sophisticated weapons are coming into the hands of Israel's potential and real adversaries. Examples are long-range SA-5 surface-to-air missiles and SS-21 ballistic missiles in Syria, and the procurement of chemical weapons, ballistic missiles, long-range strike aircraft (Tu-22Ms and SU-24 Fencers), and nuclear technology by Iran.

What does this mean and where does it lead?

Let's look at the "biblical trend": Josiah, king of Judah, fought the forces of Necho, king of Egypt, in the plain of Megiddo. Josiah took a couple of arrows and died. This is covered in the Old Testament (2 Chronicles). Megiddo is better known by its New Testament name—Armageddon. The Battle of Armageddon, according to some interpretations of the prophecy, will lead to the destruction of the earth.

Various "plains of the Megiddo" have been identified in the confining nexus of Israel, Lebanon, and Syria. Identification of the specific piece of land really doesn't matter; what does matter is that this is one of those "regional conflicts" that could lead to nuclear war and devastation. Whether you buy the Bible version or not, it doesn't take a revelation to realize how dangerous that is.

WHO'S INVOLVED

Israel—Is Israel a democracy under siege or a European colony of Jewish Crusaders? Inroads are made by "militant settlers" and fringe Jewish religious radicals as extreme in their own agendas as any radical Islamic group.

Egypt—Cairo signed a peace treaty with Jerusalem, then the peace went "cold." The intifada put the moderate Egyptian government in a political vise. Islamic radicalism, a virulent brand that is anti-Western, anti-Zionist, and anti-Arab moderate, threatens Egypt. Egypt is a country on the edge of crisis.

Jordan—King Hussein has made peace with Israel. Airline flights to Amman now routinely fly through Israeli airspace. But Hussein and Jordan's economically progressive business class are plagued by "rejectionist" radicals.

Syria—Visions of Greater Syria, a threatened dictatorship, and militant pan-Arabism lead Syria into constant struggle with Israel. Yet the Golan border remains quiet.

United States—The U.S. moral commitment to Israel remains strong. The United States wants to have Israel and it wants to have peace. The United States wants to buy Arab oil. The United States wants Arab allies. The United States wants a lot.

Iran—The successful spread of Islamic revolution could topple moderate regimes.

Palestinians—In two camps, those supporting the Palestine National Authority (PNA) and those supporting the "rejectionists," led by the Hamas group.

Wild Cards

Iraq—Saddam Hussein threatened to "burn half of Israel."

Russia—Moscow supported the creation of Israel, but Arab disenchantment gave Russia the opportunity to win friends by supplying arms. With the end of the cold war, Arabs—and now the Iranians—must pay for the arms with cash.

Saudi Arabia—Money can't buy happiness, or peace, but it can act as a prod. The Saudis have been paying everybody off because they're scared of everybody.

GEOGRAPHY

Israel is surrounded. That's the Israeli point of view.
Israel is (choose any or all):

1. a Zionist dagger in the side of Arab political unity
2. a European-Zionist-Crusader dagger in the side of Arab unity
3. an American-Zionist dagger in the side of Arab unity
4. a necessary enemy, otherwise Arabs would only be fighting one another
5. a disheartening reality that could be ignored except for those obnoxious Palestinians
6. a tough Zionist bunch that, like it or not, must be lived with, and just might help resolve the Palestinian issue

7. a potential regional economic powerhouse that could help make everyone's wallet a little fatter
8. all of the above (the Arab point of view)

The map on page 97 shows that Israel, minus the West Bank, is shaped something like a dagger, 20,000 square kilometers' worth: the Red Sea port of Elath at the point and the Negev Desert as a double-edged wasteland, Jordan to the east, and the Sinai to the west.

Up north it begins to get complicated. The Jordan Rift Valley, with the Dead Sea to the south, the Jordan River, and Lake Tiberias (the Sea of Galilee) to the north, not only separates the West Bank from Jordan but provides a militarily significant division. Operations in the valley are hindered by terribly broken terrain. It's the badlands. The Dead Sea, at a negative 396 meters below sea level, is the lowest point on the planet (see the Bible, Sodom and Gomorrah).

The central hills of Israel and the West Bank are also broken and rugged. Agriculture is an iffy proposition given the scarcity of water and the area's rockiness. In the coastal plain region, north to south on the Mediterranean coast, are the major transportation arteries and the Tel Aviv metropolitan area. The occupied Gaza Strip is also on the coastal plain. The coastal plain, like the Negev, is agriculturally productive if sufficient water is available for irrigation.

Jordan, on the other side of the river, lies on the Arabian Plateau. Most of its present territory, 91,000 square kilometers, not including the West Bank, is open desert. In fact, 88 percent of the country is desert waste. Bedouin nomads inhabit the desert. Amman, however, is a large, modern, urban area. The western area of Jordan has a large number of Palestinians and a substantial Arab Christian community. Over 90 percent of Jordan's four million are Sunni Muslim.

Jordan has few natural resources. Several oil companies have explored the eastern provinces, but, unlike Iraq to the east and Saudi Arabia to the south, Jordan has yet to show significant petroleum reserves.

The Golan Heights border region is characterized by difficult, buckling mountains, which rise from Israel onto the Damascus plain. Syrian guns on the Golan Heights shelled Israeli farms for twenty years. The 130-mm guns sited in the hills can almost reach the sea coast. That is

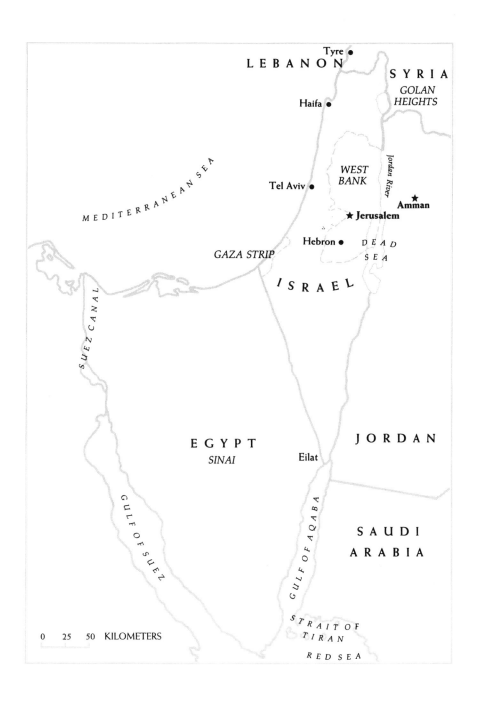

Tyre ●

L E B A N O N

S Y R I A

GOLAN
HEIGHTS

Haifa ●

MEDITERRANEAN SEA

WEST
BANK

Jordan River

Tel Aviv ●

★ Amman

★ Jerusalem

Hebron ●

D E A D
S E A

GAZA STRIP

I S R A E L

SUEZ CANAL

E G Y P T

SINAI

Eilat

J O R D A N

G U L F O F S U E Z

G U L F O F A Q A B A

S A U D I
A R A B I A

S T R A I T O F
T I R A N

R E D S E A

0   25   50   KILOMETERS

why the Israelis are very reluctant to withdraw from Golan, though Israel and Syria both talk as if the Golan were on the table.

The Israeli-Egyptian border (Negev to Sinai) is characterized by large sand plains and broken rocky terrain. The Sinai interior is broken by mountains and a number of rocky, desert mesas. The southern tip of the Sinai juts into the Red Sea. The Strait of Tiran, between Sinai and Saudi Arabia, controls sea traffic into the Gulf of Aqaba. Egyptian threats to close the strait to Israeli shipping or the actual closing of the strait, as in 1967, have figured in all three major wars.

Egypt is the land of the Nile. Over 90 percent of Egypt's population live in the Nile Valley region. With a total land area of right at 1 million square kilometers, Egypt is three times the size of the state of New Mexico. Three percent of the land is arable; 95 percent is desert wasteland. Between 1979 and 1994, the United States put $33 billion into Egypt, only slightly less than the $42 billion the United States gave Israel. In 1993, Egypt spent an estimated $3.5 billion on defense, or slightly over 10 percent of GDP.

HISTORY

Contemporary Zionism, the political movement dedicated to the creation of a Jewish state in the old biblical homelands, was given its framework in the nineteenth century by Theodore Herzl. Jews settled the Ottoman-controlled Palestinian region, always with the ultimate intention of establishing their own state. The Palestinians didn't like the Ottomans either, but they wanted a Palestinian state, as well as a Bedouin state (somewhere across Jordan and then south into the peninsula) free of Turkish control. World War I, the British and French defeat of the Turks, Lawrence of Arabia, and the conquering of Syria by Arab tribes allied to the West all created a political situation characterized by several mutually exclusive goals (just like the current situation in Israel). Britain's 1917 Balfour Declaration promised the Jews a "Jewish home." But the Brits had also promised the Arabs their own states (perfidious Albion). The way Britain's League of Nations mandate was drawn created further problems. Under the Turks, the East and West banks had been the same administrative district. Under the mandate, the west zone came under a British administrator while the east became the semiautonomous state of Transjordan, an emirate that included large portions of present-day Syria.

Essentially, the defeat of the Ottoman Turks left the Arabian Peninsula and the Holy Land vulnerable to any politician with an itch to draw new maps. Significant numbers of Palestinians ended up in four distinct political entities. Several riots and armed exchanges between Jews and Arabs occurred during the 1920s. Jewish leaders demanded that the Balfour Declaration be carried through, asserting that the emirate of Transjordan was effectively an Arab state, so where was the land for the Jews? The British and French put that demand off until Hitler's Holocaust made any Western opposition to a Zionist state impossible. Jewish rebel activities, like Irgun terrorism, also had an effect. But the Arab League didn't agree. Palestine had been Arab since the Prophet's imperialist forces overran the Jordan Valley, with the exception of Latin Crusader states that hung around for a couple of centuries. Israel looked like the work of Jewish Crusaders, backed by the West.

With postwar Great Britain and France retreating from colonies, "backed by the West" came to mean "backed by the USA." America gave Israel weapons, money, and strong moral support. Arabs needed weapons and Russia was ready. Russian willingness to send weapons has proved to be the basis of a working relationship, though almost all Arab countries had no love, and less trust, for Moscow.

The 1982 Israeli invasion of Lebanon left everybody in disarray, including Israel. The PLO was already divided into several factions, but the invasion of Lebanon left the strong anti-Arafat rebel sects in Lebanon effectively under the control of Syria. Until the intifada erupted, Arafat became the "Wandering Jew" of Middle Eastern diplomacy, but a waif with an international reputation and strong influence among Palestinians.

The peace process has transformed Arafat's wing of the PLO from active revolutionary organization to protogovernment, but it is a difficult transformation. The PLO still isn't a sovereign government in a true sense of the term. The West Bank and Gaza, the constituent elements of "New Palestine," are under nominal PLO control. Without the intervention of the Israeli Army the Palestinian national police (a paramilitary force that does contain many former PLO guerrillas) would be hard-pressed to deal with rejectionist Arab organizations like Hamas and the Muslim Brotherhood (Palestinian faction). The Cairo Agreement on the Gaza Strip and the Jericho Area (DOP) calls for a transition from the Palestinian Authority (which immediately became the Palestinian National Authority) to an elected Palestinian National Council as part of Palestine's self-governing process.

During the intifada, Jordan's large Palestinian population created a dangerous situation. Moderate factions pressed the Jordanian government for help in setting up the West Bank as an autonomous region, but radicals could turn any agreement King Hussein made into a call for his assassination and a civil war in Jordan.

The creation of a new Palestinian state has given the Jordanians an opportunity to make public peace with Israel and seek new forms of economic cooperation. Still, domestic pressures in Jordan, both from the radical Muslim Brotherhood and from Arab democrats desiring more self-government make Jordan anything but stable. The death of King Hussein could lead to civil war. The economic situation remains tenuous. Assistance from oil-rich Arab states (Saudi Arabia and UAE) has largely ceased. The Persian Gulf War demonstrated how financially dependent Jordan is on the "Iraqi trade." The highway linking Jordan's port of Aqaba to Baghdad is a modern-day caravan route, except Mercedeses and Mack trucks hump the load instead of camels. From 40 to 50 percent of the Jordanian economy was linked to trade with Iraq. Jordan's economy began to rebound in 1992. In 1993, however, Jordan still had an estimated unemployment rate of 20 percent.

During the Iran-Iraq War, Jordan was a solid Iraqi ally, supplying Iraq through its port at Aqaba (when Iraq's Persian Gulf ports were closed) and allowing Iraqi warplanes to use Jordanian air bases. Jordan also "lent" Iraq an armored brigade as a signal of its political support. As a thank-you, Iraq gave Jordan over 120 British-made Chieftain tanks captured from the Iranians and at least 30 American-made M60A1 tanks. Jordan also initially supported Iraq during the Persian Gulf War, and paid a stiff diplomatic and economic price for doing so.

Syria and Israel are at loggerheads in Lebanon and the Golani border. Syria continues to modernize its military and to occupy Lebanon's Bekáa Valley.

Egyptian criticism of the Israeli invasion of Lebanon finally provided a diplomatic opening for Cairo to the Islamic Conference, but Egyptian readmission was inevitable. Egypt's size, power, and prestige could not be ignored. And Egypt did not deny the Camp David Accords that established its peace with Israel. Camp David did a lot for Egypt; the nation regained the Sinai. The squabble with Israel over the Taba beach resort (near the Israeli port of Eilat) was resolved in Cairo's favor, a political plus. It also illustrated, once again, the Egyptian government's contention that the best way to deal with Israel is by negotiation.

By mid-1995 the Palestinian National Authority was taking control of several cities in the West Bank—and waging an internal war against the Hamas-led Palestinian rejectionists. The November 1995 assassination of Israeli Premier Yitzhak Rabin by an Israeli settler extremist did not stop the slow and bloody drive to a New Israeli-Palestinian relationship. Terror, counterterror, and assassinations, carried on by both sides, continue.

Significant Dates

May 14, 1948—Israel declares its independence; the simmering conflict between Israel and its neighbors breaks into total war, the Palestine War. Four armistice agreements are reached between and among Israel and Egypt, Jordan, Lebanon, and Syria. But no general peace agreement, or recognition of the Jewish state, is made. Trouble remains in place.

October 1956—Provoked by a huge Egyptian arms buildup and Nasserite threats, Israel invades the Sinai and occupies the Gaza Strip as Great Britain and France invade the Suez region after Egyptian President Gamel Abdel Nasser "nationalizes" the Suez Canal. The 1956 Sinai War ensues. The Israelis withdraw, and get ready for the next war.

June 1967—President Nasser sends nearly one hundred thousand troops and over two hundred tanks toward the Israeli border in the Sinai; he asks the UN to withdraw its UNEF peacekeepers and they depart. The Strait of Tiran is closed to Israeli shipping. Israel launches an "anticipatory counteroffensive" against Egypt and its war-ready allies Jordan and Syria. Israel takes Sinai, the Golan Heights, and the West Bank in the Six Day War. Israel fortifies its new possessions and prepares for the next war.

October 1973—Egypt and Syria attack Israel during Yom Kippur holiday. Egyptians cross the Suez Canal and inflict a surprise defeat on Israeli counterattackers. Light Israeli forces on the Golan are almost overrun by Syrian armor. Israelis counterattack and cross the canal into Africa. Israeli counterattacks punish Syrian forces. The October War ends with the Egyptian Army in Sinai surrounded. The Soviet Union threatens to intervene and the United States responds with a worldwide general alert, including nuclear retaliatory forces. Israelis, shaken by the lower performance compared with 1967 (a tough act to follow in any event), redouble their efforts to prepare for the next war.

November 1977—Egyptian President Anwar el-Sadat visits Jerusalem. The Camp David Agreement, brokered by U.S. President Jimmy Carter, ends the state of war between Egypt and Israel. Israel ultimately withdraws from the Sinai Peninsula.

May–June 1982—Israel launches Operation Peace in Galilee into Lebanon: at first a small series of moves on the northern border designed to destroy PLO base camps and training facilities. Many commentators believe the feints were a cover, and that from the beginning Israeli General Ariel Sharon intended to strike at Beirut and destroy the PLO in Lebanon. The attack eventually breaks out into a full-scale two-day war between Israel and Syria; Israelis shoot down eighty-five–plus Syrian aircraft with the loss of one Israeli plane. Israel eventually withdraws from the hornet's nest of the Lebanese Civil War but establishes a buffer zone in south Lebanon.

December 1987—The Palestinian uprising—the intifada—erupts on the West Bank. By late 1990, nearly a thousand Palestinians are killed in an endless series of demonstrations and civil resistance to Israeli occupation of the West Bank. (Sources conflict but the total number of Palestinians killed in the intifada from 1987 to 1994 is around twenty-five hundred.)

July 1988—Jordan's King Hussein renounces his kingdom's historic claim to the West Bank. According to the king, from now on Jordan will support the West Bank Palestinians' desire to "secede" and set up their own nation. Note: Before the 1967 Six Day War, Jordan derived nearly 40 percent of its gross national product (GNP) from the West Bank area.

December 14, 1988—The United States and Palestinian Liberation Organization agree to open direct talks as the PLO "officially" rejects terror. Hope for a negotiated and "moderate" settlement rises. Talks suspended in June 1990 after PLO refuses to rebuke and disassociate itself from an attempted sea-launched Palestinian Liberation Front (PLF, directed by Abu Abbas) terrorist attack on Israeli beaches. Israel had stopped the May 1990 attack.

August 2, 1990—Iraq invades Kuwait. Iraq announces that they invaded Kuwait to support the Palestinian cause against Israel. Most Arab states unite against Iraq, ignoring Israel for the moment.

October 8, 1990—Twenty-one Palestinians are killed near Muslim holy places in Jerusalem. Arabs turn attention to Israel once more.

September 13, 1993—Israeli Prime Minister Yitzhak Rabin and PLO Chairman Yasir Arafat agree to Declaration of Principles (DOP) in Washington.

February 25, 1994—Attack by radical Jewish settler Baruch Goldstein (originally a doctor from Brooklyn) on Muslim mosque in Hebron (the Cave of the Patriarchs), massacring three dozen Palestinians. Between September 1993 and the Hebron massacres, Palestinian terrorists kill thirty-three Israelis. The Cave of the Patriarchs is the site of the 1929 Arab massacre of Jews.

May 4, 1994—Cairo Agreement on the Gaza Strip and the Jericho Area, completing negotiations on the first phase of the DOP. The agreement says that Israel will retain responsibility for external security and internal security and public order for new Palestinian area. Within five years direct negotiations will determine the final state of New Palestine.

October 1994—Israel and Jordan sign peace pact.

Fall 1995—Israel continues to pass control of West Bank towns to the Palestinian National Authority. Yitzhak Rabin murdered by right-wing Israeli. Syria indicates it could agree to peace terms. Despite terror attacks, the peace process continues.

General Assemblages

UN Security Council Resolution 242—Calls for end of warfare by all states in region, territorial integrity, and political independence; sets guidelines for Israeli withdrawal from areas seized in 1967 war (dates from November 22, 1967).

UN Resolution 338—Calls for a lasting peace based on negotiations; followed October War (1973).

LOCAL POLITICS

Israel

Likud party (also called Likud bloc)—The right-wing Israeli party; composed of Liberal, Herut, and La'am factions. It never held power until 1977 when Likud's Menachem Begin became prime minister. Militant policies have a broad appeal among Sephardic Jews who have been oppressed under Arab or pro-Arab regimes. Emphasis on Jewish identity and power may appeal to Russian Jews who have experienced anti-Semitism in Russia. Right-wing elements demand that Jerusalem be made the capital of Israel.

"The constraint ministers"—Most hard-line members of the Likud party. In 1990 these included General Ariel Sharon, Yitzhak Modai, and David Levy.

Labor party (also called Labor Alignment)—Left-of-center party, containing Labor and Mapam factions, regarded by many in the West as the Israeli party most likely to achieve a settlement based on granting a Palestinian homeland; primarily Ashkenazim. Major leader is Shimon Peres. The Meretz party is a Labor coalition member.

Religious splinter parties—Extreme Orthodox parties that in coalition governments almost always support the Likud bloc.

Other splinter parties—These include the Communist party and socialist factions.

Ashkenazim—Jews of European origin, who compose most of the upper and middle classes.

Sephardim—Jews of Asian and African origin, less educated and wealthy than the Ashkenazim.

Histadrut—General Federation of Labor, Israel's all-encompassing labor, economic, and industrial organization. Over 65 percent of Israel's workers belong to Histadrut, making it a potent political force.

Mossad—Israel's intelligence service. The Mossad is the top intelligence operation in the Middle East; perhaps the best in the world.

Shin Bet—Domestic intelligence and security agency.

Aman—Israeli military intelligence service.

The Irgun—Underground Jewish resistance and terrorist group; it fought against the British and Arabs from 1945 to 1948.

The Stern Gang—Formally called Lohamei Herut Israel (Fighters for the Freedom of Israel); the most radical of Israeli underground organizations in the late 1940s. In September 1948, in Jerusalem, the Stern Gang assassinated UN envoy Count Folke Bernadotte, a Swedish diplomat sent by the Security Council in May 1948 to attempt to establish a cease-fire between the Israeli and Arab armies. The Stern Gang was a splinter group of the Irgun and was named for its first leader, Avram Stern. At one time Likud leader Yitzhak Shamir was a member of the Stern Gang. Arab terrorists justify their attack on moderates and those "interested in truces" by pointing to the action of early Israeli terrorist groups such as the Stern Gang.

The IDF—Israel Defense Force (the army). Only Jews and Druze Arabs are subject to the Israeli draft—the Druze decided to willingly submit to conscription.

Kahane Chai—Kahane Lives. Followers of murdered (in 1990, by Islamic fanatics) radical Rabbi Meir Kahane, another American-born Israeli rejectionist. Kahane Chai operated a paramilitary training center in the Catskill Mountains in New York State. Meir Kahane founded the militant Jewish Defense League (JDL) in the United States in the 1960s. He moved to Israel in 1971 and founded the Kach party. Kfar Tapuah is a Kahane Chai–run settlement in the West Bank. Kahane Chai has been linked to a series of pipe bomb attacks (1992) in New York City aimed at UN and Arab organizations. Associated with the Kach party.

Israeli Arabs—Officially 600,000 strong, perhaps as many as 800,000; they have Israeli passports but Palestinian origins. Generally put at 17 percent of Israeli population, Israeli Arabs only account for 5 percent of the university students. Of the 650,000 Israelis classified as living below the poverty level, half are Arabs. Seven Arab deputies sit in the 120-member Israeli parliament. They have recently formed several splinter groups, including the left-wing Sons of the Village. The Muslim Brotherhood is also increasing in influence.

Sabra—A native Israeli Jew, born in Israel. They are an increasingly decisive force in Israeli politics, which was originally overwhelmingly controlled by immigrants.

Aliya—"Ascendancy"; the movement of Jews from Diaspora to Israel. The latest aliya is that of Russian Jews.

Kibbutzim—Voluntary socialist "organizations"; many began as farms but are now involved in various industrial enterprises.

Judea and Samaria—Likud code words for the West Bank; used as a pretext for asserting historical Israeli control over the West Bank. Judea and Samaria are part of what Likud leader Yitzhak Shamir once referred to as a "big Israel" where Russian Jews might settle, part of the traditional "Eretz Yisrael," the Land of Israel.

The Israeli political system—The Israeli parliamentary system is built upon a system of representation where parties representing bare fractions of electoral opinion can win seats. Seats in the Knesset (the parliament) are divided according to the proportion of votes the party receives. Voters vote for parties, not individual candidates. That makes individual politicians directly accountable only to other party members. This system is blamed for immobilizing coalition governments. Look for electoral reform to be a major issue in Israel.

Military Order No. 158, Order Amending the Water Supervision Law of 1 October 1967—The occupied West Bank is "governed" by Israeli military authorities. This order states: "It shall not be permissible for any person to set up or to assemble or to possess or to operate a water installation unless he has obtained a license from the Area Commander." Carried to an extreme, the order effectively gave control to the Israeli Army of local agriculture by controlling irrigation development. Water is life in the Middle East, and Israel controls the water for all the Palestinians in Israel.

Gush Emunim—Bloc of the Faithful. This idealistic group of Israeli settlers believes the 1967 Arab-Israeli war was a "messianic event" and that settling the West Bank fulfills a divine purpose.

Council of Judea, Samaria, and Gaza—Radical settler group.

Syria

Arab Baath party (Socialist Resurrection party)—Dominant Syrian party, upper echelons controlled by Alawites (a minority in Syria, sort of like the Druze).

Other parties—Syrian Arab Socialist party, Arab Socialist Union, Unionist Socialist party, Communist party.

Jordan

Arab National Union—Once the only party allowed by the Jordanian monarchy; in 1992 political agitation liberalized the system.

Islamic Action Front (IAF)—Umbrella group of Islamic political parties. Israelis maintain that the IAF has close ties with Hamas. In Jordan, the Islamic fundamentalists are not as extreme as those in the West Bank and Gaza. As of early 1995 the IAF coalition (including the Muslim Brotherhood) controlled approximately 20 percent of the seats in Jordan's lower house of parliament.

The Arab Legion—Jordanian Army, man for man the best army in the Arab world, largely Bedouin, personally loyal to Jordan's king.

September 1970—Black September, when Palestinian radicals tried to take over Jordan. A Syrian unit participated, disguised as a Palestinian force; the Jordanians defeated the Palestinians and later expelled all PLO fedayeen guerrillas. Both the PLO and the Jordanians remember this date.

Egypt

National Democratic party—Official government party. Significant members include President Hosni Mubarak and Amr Mousa.

Major legal opposition parties—New Wafd party, Socialist Labor party, National Progressive Unionist party.

Muslim Brotherhood—An armed Sunni fundamentalist movement that is dangerous and devout. Its members were encouraged by the success of religious fundamentalists in Arab elections in Tunisia in 1990. It actually operates as a suppressed opposition party.

Coptic Christians—Officially 6 percent of the population, possibly as high as 12 percent. A convenient target for the Muslim Brotherhood. The Coptic Church is the largest Egyptian institution outside of government and runs many schools and hospitals.

Imbaba—Slum district in Cairo, controlled for long periods by Islamic militants. It was raided in 1992 by forty thousand Egyptian paramilitary police.

Al Ahram Foundation—Government think tank.

Factory 200—Factory that assembles U.S. M1A1 tanks; located in the desert north of Cairo.

New Palestine/Palestinian Organizations

Palestinian National Authority (PNA; also referred to as the Palestinian Authority)—Name of evolving Palestinian government in West Bank and Gaza.

Palestinian National Police—As of early 1995, the PNA had armed around seventeen thousand Palestinian policemen. Includes cadre of Palestinian Security Service.

PLO (Palestine Liberation Organization)—The most visible of Palestinian political organizations. Yasir Arafat is head of the main faction, Al Fatah, which has become the core of the new Palestinian government.

Palestinian National Council (also called the Palestine National Council)—Was the PLO's Government of Palestine in Exile. Members of this "parliament" are scattered throughout the world. Now the core of a new Palestinian parliament.

Non-PLO activists—Certain West Bank mayors have tried to carve out a separate, non-PLO international position; several of them have been accused by other Palestinians of being collaborators with Israel.

Islamic Jihad—Radical Palestinian-dominated terrorist sect (also active in Lebanon and Egypt). It has issued communiqués threatening Russian Jews arriving in Israel. Has claimed "credit" for attacks on Israelis visiting Egypt. Subunits include the Al-Suri Martyr and the Martyrdom Lovers' Battalion.

Hamas—Radical Islamic movement; possibly the most powerful of "rejectionist" factions that accept no peace or any compromise with Israel.

Izzedine al-Qassam Brigade—Hamas's military wing.

Fatah Revolutionary Council (FRC)—Terrorist band headed by Abu Nidal (literally, Soldier of Nothing; his real name is Sabry al-Banna). Now fractured.

The Palestine National Army—Formed by Arafat in mid-1989. Once called the Palestinian Army of South Lebanon, it was originally a thirty-five-hundred-man force that the PLO hoped would be the building block of a future Palestinian regular army. Some of the troops and officers were used to form the Palestinian national police force.

Fellahin—The Arab peasant farmers.

Fedayeen—PLO guerrilla fighters.

Islamic University of Gaza—Center of Palestinian political radicalism.

POLITICAL TREND CHARTS

ISRAEL

Gv95	Gv20	PC95	PC20	R95	R20	Ec95	Ec20	EdS95	EdS20
RD7,8	RD7,8	7	8	5	4	6	7*	8	8

RD = Representative Democracy
*Agriculture and comparatively educated population in cities improve investment potential, despite the lack of stability.

NEW PALESTINE

Gv95	Gv20	PC95	PC20	R95	R20	Ec95	Ec20	EdS95	EdS20
ALD	LRD	1	4	8	7	3	4	5−	5

ALD = Authoritarian Limited Self-Government (Israel dominates Palestinian decision making)
LRD = Limited Representative Democracy (limited by Israeli military veto of Arab political and Islamic radicals)

Look Back: For purposes of comparison, the 1991 edition of *A Quick and Dirty Guide to War* saw Israel 1996 (with separate Palestinian state achieved by "peaceable" means) as looking like this:

Gv96	PC96	R96	Ec96	EdS96
RD8,8	8+*	3	6	8

*The demographic time bomb is defused—and this indicates a negotiated solution is in the interests of Israelis interested in maintaining both a democracy and a "Jewish homeland." In this Israel, Jews make up over 85 percent of the population—possibly 90 percent. For this particular series of projections we "averaged" several sources and decided to use the following figures for breaking down the 1990 4.4 million Israeli population (a figure excluding the West Bank and Gaza Strip).

"NEW STATE OF FREE PALESTINE"—1996

Gv96	PC96	R96	Ec96	EdS96
AD5,4	7	8*	3	5

AD = Authoritarian Democracy
*High repression index due to repression of radicals.

Evaluation:

Israel 1996: The population time bomb has not been totally defused but the influx of Eastern Europeans has mitigated the effects of the Arab baby boom.

Free Palestine 1996: Not a good investment bet in 1995 but perhaps an improving economic prospect; our projected repression index of a high "8," as of 1995, was on the mark as the new Palestinian government battled Hamas and the Muslim Brotherhood.

JORDAN

Gv95	Gv20	PC95	PC20	R95	R20	Ec95	Ec20	EdS95	EdS20
ACM5,5	ACM6,5	5	5	4	4	3	4	5	5

ACM = Authoritarian Constitutional Monarchy

EGYPT

Gv95	Gv20	PC95	PC20	R95	R20	Ec95	Ec20	EdS95	EdS20
AD3,3	MD4,5	4	4	8	8	3	4	3	3

AD = Authoritarian Democracy
MD = Military Dictatorship

REGIONAL POWERS AND POWER INTEREST INDICATOR CHARTS

ISRAEL

	Economic Interests	Historical Interests	Political Interest	Military Interest	Force Generation Potential*	Ability to Intervene Politically	Interest/ Ability to Promote Economic Development
Palestine	9	9	9	9	1	7	6
Pal.-Rej.†	1	9	9	9	0§	8§	0
United States	5	8	8	7	5	6	7
Jordan	8	9	9	9	4	5	4
Syria	3	8	9	9	6‡	4	5‡
Egypt	6	7	9	7	6‡	6	5
Iraq	1	6	7	5	0§	1	0
Iran	3	5	7	6	2§	2	1

NOTE: 0 = minimum; 9 = maximum

*Israeli force generation potential up to 100 kilometers from its borders is a 9.

†Palestinian rejectionist organizations such as Hamas. They exist as a force of political intervention.

‡Given time for mobilization; Syria needs three weeks, Egypt ten weeks; note, both Egyptian and Syrian military force generation potential have dropped in past five years. Note Syria's rise in interest in Israeli economic development.

§A plus for Palestinian rejectionists, Iraq, and Iran due to terror. Hezbollah forces and growing Iranian arsenal of theater-range weapons account for Iranian FGP.

NEW PALESTINE/WEST BANK

	Economic Interests	Historical Interests	Political Interest	Military Interest	Force Generation Potential	Ability to Intervene Politically	Interest/ Ability to Promote Economic Development
Israel	8	9	9	9	9	7	9
Jordan	7	8	9	8	4	6	8
Syria	3	4	7	7	5	4	2

NOTE: An economically viable Palestinian state will be key to future Israeli and Jordanian economic health.

JORDAN

	Economic Interests	Historical Interests	Political Interest	Military Interest	Force Generation Potential	Ability to Intervene Politically	Interest/ Ability to Promote Economic Development
Israel	5	8	8	8	8+	5	7
Syria	3	7	7	7	8	6	5
Iraq	5	7	7	7	2	3+	4
Saudi Arabia	5	9	8	8	1	7	8
United States	4	7	8	7	4	5	7
Palestine	8	8	8	8	1	6	5
Iran	1	2	5	6	1−	1	2
Britain	4	7	5	3	1	2	3

Egypt

	Economic Interests	Historical Interests	Political Interest	Military Interest	Force Generation Potential	Ability to Intervene Politically	Interest/ Ability to Promote Economic Development
United States	5	7	8	8	4	4	6
Israel	6	8	9	9	6+	3	5
Libya	3	7	8	9	2	2	2
Russia	1	5	6	6	1	2	1
IslamRads	2	9	9	8	4	8	1
"EEC"	6	6	7	6	2	3	7

NOTE: Islamic radical (IslamRads) political intervention capability has risen 5 points since 1990.

PARTICIPANT STRATEGIES AND GOALS

Israel—There are the things Israel is good at and will continue to do: hang tough against Arab terrorist groups by continuing reprisal tactics; seek to extend political ties to Jordan (including increasing trade and technical assistance for agriculture and industry); punish Lebanese Hezbollah guerrillas and Syria when the warfare gets too hot in Lebanon.

The Israelis have begun to address the immigration challenge, but jobs remain an issue. The potential influx of 650,000 Jews from the ex-USSR in the late 1990s, while bringing more soldiers, also tests the economy. The economy may crack, making Israel vulnerable to radical politicians at home. The Israeli economy, in fact, the State of Israel itself, with a Jewish population of 4.2 million and an area of 20,000 square kilometers (80 percent of which is desert) has been sorely pressed to create new jobs for the immigrants.

Israel must continue to seek accommodations with the Palestinians of the West Bank and Gaza. Either the process of creating an autonomous, stable, and peaceful Palestine state continues or the radicals on both sides win. Israeli radicals call for "transference" (euphemism for the removal of Arabs from the West Bank); the Islamic radicals call for the removal of Jews.

Other long-term goals include the old basics: Arab recognition of Israel's right to exist as a state and the destruction of radical terrorist factions who launch attacks upon Israelis.

The Israeli strategy of counting on the United States has frayed, and it will shatter if the Israelis pursue a strategy of "transference." The United States may be less willing to provide Israel with all-out support in a regional conflict if such support might harm its rapprochement with Russia. From the Israeli perspective, part of the Israelis' strategy of helping China develop new weapons may be to hedge their bets with the United States.

Egypt—Egypt's government has to pursue a very basic yet most difficult strategy of self-cleansing and self-renewal. Egypt must control Islamic fundamentalist strength inside Egypt and continue to privatize its economy without massive unemployment—a very tough trick to accomplish (ask Russia). Corruption has driven many people to Islamic political radicalism. Egypt must also answer the question, where does its four-hundred-thousand-man army land politically when the economic perks disappear? Ethnic and religious tensions are also high. Egypt could become "another Lebanon" with Muslims and Coptic Christian factions squaring off.

Egypt must also keep a wary eye on its Western Desert frontier with Libya and an eye on events in the Sudan. Events in "Upper Egypt" (of which part of the Sudan may be considered) have always affected dwellers in the Nile Valley.

Because of Egypt's size and power it was never truly "isolated" from the other Arab nations just because it supported the Camp David Accords.

Should Egypt's "moderate" government turn to military dictatorship (as we think it could), watch Egypt slip from its role as the dominant Arab nation. An economy strangled by a corrupt bureaucracy provides little hope for the Egyptian leadership.

Palestine National Authority (PNA) and Palestinian moderates—Palestinian moderates seek a Palestinian state independent of Israel. Economic success is key to their political success. There are also important political goals. The PNA needs to get the Israeli Army out of West Bank towns. In order to do that the peace process needs to stay on track, which means the PNA has to perform. The peace process depends on improving conditions on the West Bank and in Gaza and eliminating terrorist violence against Israelis. The PNA suffers from factionalism and disorder, as well as inexperience with governance. In early 1995 the U.S. State Department criticized the PLO/PNA for failing to create "a credible system" to make certain the billions in promised aid is spent to improve the quality of life for Palestinians. The State Department feared corruption might siphon off the money. The PNA also has to prove itself to other aid donors. As of mid-1995 only a dribble or two of the aid promised to support Palestinian self-rule has shown up.

Palestinian radicals—Seek a Palestinian state and the destruction of Israel—and nothing less. The radicals will continue terror war.

Jordan—Continues to pursue a moderate line that fends off attacks by Arab radicals. Jordan must also control and suppress Islamic fundamentalist groups within Jordan. Jordan also needs to find a new economic and political benefactor in the region. Jordan is still shunned by Gulf Arabs for its role in the 1990–91 Persian Gulf War (King Hussein made the mistake of politically supporting Saddam). Will the United States be that benefactor? Jordan also must navigate its own "Palestinian" internal political problem. Jordanian Palestinians want equal rights with the Jordanian Bedouins. The Bedouins, including the king's clan, migrated to Jordan after being ejected from the Hejaz in Arabia after World War I. Jordanian Bedouins from the East Bank dominate the government and the military and control the intelligence services. Many Palestinians from the West Bank are now quite economically successful and control large chunks of the private sector economy. If cooperation breaks down, this could be a recipe for a civil war.

United States—American strategy and goals revolve around efforts to guarantee Israel's existence and resolve the question of a Palestinian state. The United States wants to see stable (and moderate) Arab regimes in power throughout the area. The relative end of the cold war leaves the United States as the only superpower, which to some degree increases U.S. leverage. The United States already has peacekeepers in the Sinai. (The unit is a battalion-sized force that operates on a rotational basis. It now includes some volunteer U.S. Army Reserve and National Guard soldiers.) The United States is also a possible source of troops for other peacekeeping assignments, including on the Golan Heights. However, stationing troops in the Golan (near Lebanon and Syria) is more of a security risk than placing them in the Sinai Desert.

Syria—Syria's Alawite regime wants to protect its ethnic base and remain in power. That means balancing internal Syrian politics with regional relationships. Syria's leadership wants the best deal possible for Israeli peace, one that is politically popular in Syria. Syria is also in the process of "digesting" parts of Lebanon. The Bekáa Valley may become a permanent Syrian fiefdom. Reclaiming at least part of the Golan Heights from Israel is an important goal.

POTENTIAL OUTCOMES

Future watchers, we offer these possibilities. However, the Middle East is a terrible place for probability equations and projections. A radical with a weapon and the will to use it is an ultimate political variable. In "gaming the situation," we've cracked up these projections:

1. 50 percent chance through 2001: What might be called "the status quo but better." The Israeli economy continues to improve. The nascent PLO-led Palestinian state gets better control over radicals in Gaza and West Bank. Israel retains "defensive settlements" in the West Bank area. The terror war continues but at a much reduced level. The PNA helps combat the terrorists.
2. 20 percent chance through 2001: Continuing terror war in New Palestine and Israel brings right-wing hard-line government into power in Israel. Radical Israeli "settlers" gain new voice. Peace process halts. Hamas and other Arab rejectionist organizations gain

in power. Israel launches new arms buildup and economy sputters. The intifada renews. Repression of Arabs in Israel increases. This might be called "the Middle Easternization of Israel." Israel would be behaving like every other country in the Middle East, i.e., favoring a particular ethnic group, waging war on its neighbors, casting off ethnic groups it didn't want.

3. 20 percent chance: Want a complicated and contingent scenario? This is it, but it may be a peek at future history. The various Islamic radical and Arab rejectionist organizations assassinate the PLO moderates and foment an armed Palestinian revolt on the West Bank.* If this occurs, 80 percent chance of a Palestinian bloodbath at the hands of the Israeli Army, 19 percent chance of "minor" massacres and a return to low-grade intifada, less than 1 percent chance of the Palestinians pulling it off.† If there is a bloodbath, there is a 75 percent chance of mass Palestinian expulsions in the aftermath (forced into Syria or Jordan). Twenty-five percent chance of an "internal" settlement between Palestinians and Israelis giving moderate Palestinians autonomy with security guarantees to Israel.

4. 6 percent chance through 2001: PLO moderate factions and Israeli intelligence organizations defeat Islamic radicals via assassination, expulsion, and improving economic and political conditions. Labor government receives overwhelming electoral victory in Israeli elections. Israel grants New Palestine total internal autonomy. You could call it peace.

5. 4 percent chance through 2001: And you could call this disaster. Egypt and Syria both come under the control of Islamic radical regimes. The 1973 war begins anew, this time with ballistic missiles.

---

*This is an outcome that extreme right-wingers in Israel would like to see happen, since the odds are 3 to 1 (75 percent to 25 percent) in favor of expulsions ("transference") of West Bank Palestinians. This gives extremists in Israel a "reason" to provoke Palestinians to even more extreme action.

†A surprise variable that could kick off this chain of events is the mounting competition for water resources, on the West Bank between Israelis and Palestinians, and between Israel and Jordan (see Local Politics, Israel, Military Order 158). Israeli settlers have dug deep wells that the West Bank Arabs claim sap their shallower wells. Depletion of water resources and the prospect of starvation could be the final push to total armed rebellion.

The Mushroom Beyond the 100th Percentile

We're not into predicting Armageddon (that's for theologians, prophets, and religious salesmen); however, there are two not-so-distinct possibilities. Case One is an Arab versus Israel nuclear war. The initial warhead could fly from either direction, though a "Baath bomb" from either Syria or Iraq is more likely. These would be small-yield, aircraft-delivered A-bombs or small warheads on SCUD-type battlefield missiles. This rates a 3 percent chance if a major war occurs. If the Arab-Israeli war stays conventional, there's less than a 1 percent chance of U.S. or out-of-region-power military involvement. If the Arab-Israeli war goes nuclear, the chance of American participation jumps to 85 percent.

Case Two: There is also a chance of the terrorist-delivered nuke. This would be the suitcase from Allah; see the appendix by that title in the Persian Gulf–Arabian Peninsula chapter. We offer no percentage on this event. Suffice to say that there are many people in the Middle East who would use a nuclear weapon if they could get one. If these people got hold of one, it's a sure thing they would try to use it. Mossad, the CIA, et al., are on the watch for this event.

KIND AND COST OF WAR

The human toll of over 120,000 dead and injured in the Arab-Israeli wars to date is dreadful. The economic toll could be considered equally grim. Most nations can get away with spending only 5 percent or less of their GNPs on defense. Israel, and its fractious neighbors, spend twice to three times that rate. Since the 1948 creation of Israel, there has been over $200 billion in war-related defense expenditures. The losses to crippled economies have undoubtedly been even higher. We estimate that the total economic cost of the Arab-Israeli conflicts have been over half a trillion dollars.

This is one of the few areas in the world where every type of conventional warfare is possible, and has actually occurred on more than one occasion. The intifada was a very low-level guerrilla war, often waged by teenagers throwing rocks. It was once waged by Palestinians against Israelis. It is now waged by Arab rejectionists against Israelis and the slowly developing Palestinian self-government. Combat in the area moves up the scale to terrorist actions by individuals and small groups and ultimately to massed tank armies slugging it out with the assistance of artillery and airpower. For the latter type of war, military analysts from all over the world keep a close eye on Israel in order to divine what might happen if other nations had to fight a major battle with modern weapons. Out of all this has emerged the Israel Defense Force, which no longer has as many combat veterans as it once had (1973, and even 1982, are many years past), but is still one of the best-trained forces in the world. They have every incentive to train and prepare effectively as, almost alone among the world's armies, they know that they are quite likely to have to fight again.

QUICK LOOK: Third World Ballistic Missiles

So-called third world ICBMs pose a serious threat to the entire globe. Though at present few of the missiles in the hands of third world nations possess truly intercontinental range, and are more correctly classified as medium-range "theater" weapons, their ability to carry high-explosive, poison gas, or—yes—nuclear warheads throws a new and extremely dangerous twist into world politics.

The terrorist potential of ICBMs is obvious. These missiles could give a religious or ultranationalist radical an opportunity to push a button and send a nuclear warhead toward Moscow or Washington. The Russians don't think this is a Hollywood fiction. Kremlin military planners are painfully aware that southern Russia and neighboring Ukraine are already threatened, given the ranges of missiles already available to Iran and Iraq.

Israel is another target. During the Persian Gulf War, Iraq fired more SCUDs at Saudi Arabia and Israel. While the Iraqis' SCUDs were militarily ineffective, as terror weapons they might have succeeded but for the presence of the U.S.-made Patriot surface-to-air missile. On live international television it sure looked like the Patriot intercepted SCUDs.

Post–Persian Gulf War analysis of the Patriot's performance showed that the missile had not been as successful in engaging incoming SCUDs as initially thought. The figures are inconclusive. Perhaps as few as three of the approximately eighty SCUDs launched were actually destroyed by Patriots. Other sources suggest that between forty and fifty SCUDs were successfully engaged so that the SCUD, had it been carrying a chemical or nuclear warhead, would not have been able to deliver and detonate the warhead. (New Patriot models fielded in the mid-1990s are more effective against SCUDs.)

In the Persian Gulf War the Patriot did work as an effective political counter to the SCUD. Next time, the Israelis argue, we will need more than political cover.

Iran has obtained advanced North Korean SCUD-type missiles, which can reach Israel; Iran is also actively seeking nuclear weapons and nuclear weapon technology. Syria also possesses several medium-range missiles. The Israelis are also wary of friendly Arab regimes. What if the governments do not remain friendly, or if they fall to anti-Israeli Arab groups? Saudi Arabia has purchased the Chinese-made CSS-2 missile. With a range of sixteen hundred miles, the CSS-2 can easily reach Israel.

Little wonder that Israel is looking for Patriot antitactical ballistic missile (ATBM) upgrades and is pressing development of its Arrow antitactical missile system as a means of countering this threat. The Arrow, a high-speed antimissile missile, is in fact a "mini-SDI" weapons system. Israel is also developing the Jericho IIb, a ballistic missile (almost certainly nuclear-capable) that has a range of over nine hundred miles. The Jericho IIb puts the cities of Sevastopol (Russian) and Odessa (Ukrainian) within Israeli missile range.

There are other dangers beyond the "terror" missile. Ballistic missiles are a means of quickly and radically expanding a border squabble into a much hotter regional or international conflict. Take this example: During the Iran-Iraq War, Jordan let Iraq park combat aircraft on Jordanian air bases beyond the range of Iranian bombers. Iran didn't have a weapon that could reach Jordan, so Jordan and Iran remained, nominally, at peace. But a "neutral" air base filled with enemy aircraft is a tempting target for an ayatollah with a long-range missile. Fire it and you've got a bigger international mess.

Easily manufactured chemical weapons give these ballistic missiles "cheap" warheads capable of mass destruction. Point One: During the Iran-Iraq War, Iran and Iraq bombarded one another's civilian neighborhoods with upgraded SCUD missiles. Point Two: The Iraqis used chemical weapons on Iranian infantry. Point Three: It's a frighteningly narrow step, in the mind of a dictatorial clique, to put a nerve gas warhead on a missile and fire on civilian targets. The warheads could burst over the targets, showering a city with a deadly rain. Casualties from one missile could reach the tens of thousands, making the Bhopal chemical plant disaster in India look like a minor problem. The terror attack on Tokyo's subways in 1995, which made use of a weakened nerve gas, may have killed only a dozen but it injured over five thousand people. The only positive spin on this is that it is difficult to manufacture high-potency nerve gas, and very difficult to manufacture the mechanism that will efficiently disperse the chemicals from a high-speed warhead.

Weapons of mass destruction won't be wished away. It's very unrealistic and naive to expect international negotiations and agreements to control their availability. There are just too many foreign exchange hungry and unaligned missile makers willing to supply a demanding market. Brazil has three missiles under development. India's Space Launch Vehicle 3 has a range of up to fifteen hundred miles and could be topped with a warhead.

Obviously, the United States is also a potential target—which leads to an ongoing debate over "thin-shield" strategic defense systems. Even a relatively simple ABM interceptor system would help stop the "terrorist" missile as well as provide a means of intercepting an accidental ICBM launch from one of those nations that have them (China and Russia). If the thin-shield system were properly sited and intelligence was timely. These are rather large ifs.

The debate over scaled-down ballistic missile defense (BMD) systems will continue. Full-scale "Astrodome" SDI systems are expensive, most likely ineffective, and with the end of the cold war probably obsolete. Many sound analysts differ on the "probably," however. Still, the threat presented by proliferating third world ballistic missiles may make a thin-shield BMD relying on advanced Patriot-type missiles or aircraft-launched "boost-phase" intercept ATBMs a bipartisan U.S. defense program.

But then we might simply see more "gunboat diplomacy," with U.S. and allied aircraft blasting third world missiles before they can be used in any long-range adventures. We can also expect to see more scientists and technology exported (legally or otherwise) to nations determined to have the best long-range missiles in the region.

Part 2
EUROPE

In this century, Europe has been the scene of the most violent wars in history. But from 1945 to 1991, there was an uncharacteristic peace. Now the peace is broken, even as the cold war has ended and many of the cold warriors have been demobilized. The many antagonisms kept in check by the superpowers are now boiling over again.

Chapter 4

BALKANS

Back to the Balkans: An Introduction

The Balkan Peninsula remains a smoldering powder house of crude nationalism, ethnic bitterness, and religious animosity—a geographically critical microcosm of the world's afflictions—and the powder house's ignition could make the twenty-first century as bloody a mess as the twentieth.

Since 1991 the multiethnic state of the "South Slavs" (Yugoslavs) has shredded into ethnic remnants. The worst of the former Yugoslavia's armed strife has been the war that began in Bosnia in March 1992. The Bosnian war has ranged from snipers to full-scale conventional combat with tanks, artillery, and jet aircraft. Europe has once again witnessed atrocity and genocide ("ethnic cleansing" in Balkan parlance). United Nations peacekeepers have proved unable—or unwilling—to stop the "creeping war of aggression" waged this time by Bosnian Serbs aided by the Serb government in Belgrade. In Balkan tit for tat, Bosnian Muslims and Croats, in an uneasy cohabitation, strike back at ethnic Serbs. NATO peacekeepers enter; the tension remains.

Is the Bosnian war (1) a civil war, (2) a war fought by Serbian ultranationalists and nationalist Communists for "Greater Serbia," or (3) one of several Yugoslav wars of devolution that may be precursors to a much larger Balkan war that could spread throughout Eastern Europe?

The answer: Bosnia is all of the above.

Bosnia is only one of several Balkan conflicts, all linked to one another in an explosive mosaic. Armed conflict among other ethnic and nationalist groups in what was Yugoslavia, old troubles renewed between Albania and its neighbors Greece and Serbia, continuing trouble over what is or isn't Macedonia, squabbling between Hungary and Romania over the sad (and strange) case of Transylvania, and the Balkan region's traditional crisis of relentless irredentism all could once again lead to a European bloodbath.

With the end of the cold war, Balkan history has begun again—with a vengeance. The Balkans (the name is derived from a Turkish word for mountain) have had a lot of "history"—if one simply totals cruel and bloody political events. To the *ghazis* of Turkey, the Balkans were the door into "the realm of war," the land of the infidel. But the inhabitants of the Balkans were at it—and each other—long before the arrival of the Turks.

The Yugoslav-Albania chapter in the first (1985) edition of *A Quick and Dirty Guide to War*—written not long after the 1984 Winter Olympics at Sarajevo (Bosnia), didn't go over well with some readers. One critic argued that projecting a Yugoslav breakup over the Kosovo issue was farfetched, given the superpower bloc division of Europe; the legacy of Tito and East-West "pressure" would keep the state together. Within the context of the cold war, the Yugoslav trouble (Serbian, actually) with Albanian natives in Kosovo Province would be resolved as an "internal" matter. Yugoslavia was modernizing, heading for a "Swedish model" socioparadise.

The Swedish socialist model didn't serve Sweden so well, and since 1991 Yugoslavia has slowly become four of the six (or is it eight?) countries it always was—a mad basket of ethnic anger.

Romania is also "back in the Balkans." Perhaps the most devilish and clever of the East bloc dictators (see Ion Pacepa's *Red Dawn* for an outline of Ceauşescu's propaganda operations in the West), Romania's Nicolae Ceauşescu took Albania's evil Enver Hoxha one step worse—and in so doing beggared a productive nation.

The Communists haven't disappeared in Romania; given the peculiar conditions in that nation, it's safe to say that, like Transylvania's most famous resident, Count Dracula, old members of Ceauşescu's Securitate secret police will be rising from the totalitarian tomb for the next three or four decades. Following the December 1989 Romanian revolt, rumors spread immediately that the rebellion was planned by dissident Securitate elements and the events in Timişoara merely kicked off the Communist versus Communist coup a little early. Witness Elena Ceauşescu's pleas (on videotape) scolding her "children" for their revolt, just before she and Nicolae are killed.

No matter what flavor of government finally roots in Romania, the new regime will face the "old histories" of the Balkans, in the case of Romania, a looming scrap with Russia over Moldova (formerly Moldavia SSR), a tug with Serbia over border regions, tiffs with the Bulgars over other border adjustments, and then, worse yet, a war with Hungary over Transylvania.

Balkan politics demand attention. World War I began in the Balkans, and throughout history the region has sparked many other wars. Over a dozen major ethnic groups live in the Balkans. Each group suffers from internal political and social divisions. In Serbia and Bosnia these factions large and small are torn between the possible advantages of unity and the desire for ethnic independence. On the rest of the peninsula the ghosts of geographic irredentism and lost populations lurk behind fragile borders.

GEOGRAPHIC ASPECTS OF BALKAN CONFLICT

Three significant geographic features characterize the Balkan Peninsula and directly affect the region's political history.

1. Most Balkan rivers follow erratic, rocky courses and are not navigable.

2. Rugged mountains are the dominant terrain.
3. There is a dramatic absence of "geographical centers" (one or two central areas with good surface routes to the rest of the country) around which a national state can coalesce.

These three geographic ingredients are a recipe for strategic isolation. Even in the latter days of the twentieth century, the absence of a significant, navigable river system makes large-scale trade expensive; prior to railroads and highway systems, the lack of navigable streams cut off the more easily developed coastline from the backcountry. The presence of mountains exacerbates the situation. Without one or two geographic centers, which even in mountain countries can exist in the form of fertile transverse valleys, every valley or hill mass becomes its own ethnic, cultural, and, usually, political center. The Turks took advantage of the geography and played divide and keep-conquered with the various Balkan regions they occupied.

Grating against central Europe, extending into the eastern Mediterranean, and in too-close proximity to the Middle East, the Balkans occupy a strategic and sensitive position. Any potential conflict in the peninsula dramatically affects the European power balance. Before the Warsaw Pact–NATO division, there existed Axis versus Allies, Grand Alliance versus Triple Entente, Ottoman Turkey versus everyone; everyone worried about the Balkans.

Geopolitical hegemony, however, is only one aspect of the problem. The threat of all-out thermonuclear war has diminished with the end of the cold war. Now the small, ugly, historically driven conflicts so typical of the Balkans resume. Local ethnic groups, some quite small, violently object to the cartographer's status quo. They see themselves as belonging to a nation-state other than the lousy one the last war stuck them in. Agitation and instability begin at the local level.

In the second decade of the twentieth century, when Turkey, "the Sick Man of Europe," finally lost control of its European provinces, a power vacuum appeared. Eighty years later, at the end of the cold war, the power vacuum left by Russia's retreat allows the old Balkan hates to surface.

The Great Yugoslav War of Devolution: The Bosnian War, the Serbo-Croat War, the Serb-Serb War, and Other Variants

SOURCE OF CONFLICT

With the Bosnian war the Yugoslav powder keg has already blown apart. Is the fuse lit to also blow apart all of the contemporary Balkans?

Bosnia has been characterized as a "pizza pie" of ethnic settlement, with "Bosnian" Serb, "Bosnian" Croat, and "Bosnian" Muslim living side by side or, in many cases, living together.

One ethnic rule of thumb says that a "South Slav" is a Croat if he's Catholic and uses the Latin alphabet, a Serb if he's Orthodox and writes in Cyrillic, and a Bosnian if he's Muslim.

There is some truth to this, as there is some truth to the notion that Yugoslavia was once functioning as a multiethnic state. Josip Broz (Tito) was the man and myth who held post–World War II Yugoslavia together. When Tito died in 1980, the one true Yugoslav passed away. The end of the cold war, and the elimination of the threat of Soviet invasion, removed another *raison d'être* for "Tito's Yugoslavia." (Henceforth in this chapter the former nation of Yugoslavia as it existed under Tito is referred to as Ex-Yugoslavia. We refer to the rump state of Yugoslavia comprising Montenegro and Serbia, as well as Kosovo and Vojvodina, as New Yugoslavia. As of 1995 the official U.S. view was that Yugoslavia had dissolved.)

There were opportunities for political change, "peaceful devolution," and the possible creation of an economic "confederacy" among Croatia, Serbia-Montenegro (New Yugoslavia), Slovenia, Bosnia, and Macedonia. But a new ration of Serb ultranationalism, of old historical hatred by Serbs and Croats for Slavs who became Muslims, and the failure of the United Nations and European nations to stop the internecine warfare produced, once again, a Balkan agony and bloodbath.

WHO'S INVOLVED

Major ethnic groups of Ex-Yugoslavia—Between 24 million and 25 million people live in the new nations formed from Ex-Yugoslavia. They are still scattered throughout the region. Of course, as this edition of *A Quick and Dirty Guide* goes to press, new borders are being drawn as the result of warfare. Ethnic demographics are changing due to genocide and exile.

The current mix includes:

Serbs—New Yugoslavia (Serbia and Montenegro) has a population of 10.9 million, 6.9 million of whom are Serbs. Total Serb population in Ex-Yugoslavia is around 8.5 million. Kosovo has around 1.7 million people (90 percent are Albanian). Serbs claim that Tito (a Croat) and Edvard Kardelj (a Slovene) engineered the 1974 Yugoslav constitution so that Serbia was "divided" (i.e., Vojvodina and Kosovo made autonomous provinces, bypassing Serb authority, and in effect making them minirepublics). New Yugoslavia is a Serb state with none of those old Yugoslav restrictions.

Montenegrin Slavs—670,000 Montenegrins live in all parts of Ex-Yugoslavia; 620,000 live in the Montenegro area of New Yugoslavia. Montenegrins divide into the *Zelenasi* (Greens), who favor Montenegrin separatism; and the *Bjelasi* (Whites), who favor union with Serbia. Montenegrins are Serbs who never succumbed to Turkish rule.

Slovenes—There are 1.9 million Slovenes scattered about Ex-Yugoslavia. Total Republic of Slovenia population is near 2 million, 1.8 million of whom are Slovenes. Located adjacent to Austria and Italy, Slovenia is the most economically and socially progressive of the new nations emerging from Ex-Yugoslavia. Slovenia's per capita personal income is nearly two and a half times higher than Macedonia's. People are predominantly Roman Catholic; a strong nationalist party is active.

Macedonians—There are 1.5 million Macedonians in Ex-Yugoslavia, almost all of them in the Republic of Macedonia. Total republic population is right now at 2.3 million, 23 percent of which is Albanian. The other ethnic fragments in Macedonia are: Macedonians 65 percent, Serbs 2 percent, Turks 4 percent, Gypsies 3 percent. The Macedonians have been caught between Bulgarian and Serbian domination, but right now they fear the emergence of a Greater Albania that will incorporate part of western Macedonia.

Croats—Some 4.5 million Croats are scattered about Ex-Yugoslavia. The population of the Republic of Croatia is around 4.7 million (78 percent of Croatia is Croat). Serbs living in Croatia demand "association" with a separate Serbia. About 600,000 Serbs live in Croatia (12 to 15 percent of the population, depending on who is counting). Many Croats are Catholics. Croats argue that historically Bosnia is closely linked to Croatia, and that Bosnia's Muslim Slavs are ethnically Croats. Croatia has a long history of political association with Hungary.

Bosnians and Bosnian Muslims ("Bosniaks")—There are 2 million Bosnian Muslims. They compose close to 45 percent of the population of the Republic of Bosnia and Herzegovina. (They made up 9 percent of Ex-Yugoslavia's population.) The Republic of Bosnia as it existed in March 1992 had a population of 4.6 million. Bosnia has been tugged back and forth by Serbia and Croatia for centuries. Most Bosnian Muslims favor a multiethnic state with multiparty democracy. There is a small but powerful group of Bosnian Muslims who favor an Islamic state. Substantial arms and cash shipments flown in from Iran make this faction stronger.

Hungarian minority in New Yugoslavia—About 550,000 Hungarian (Magyar) ethnics reside in the Vojvodina autonomous province of Serbia, or 25 percent of the Vojvodina's population of 2 million. (One million Serbs live in Vojvodina.)

Albanians in New Yugoslavia—Kosovo Province has around 1.7 million people, of whom 90 percent are Albanian.

The Contact Group—United States, Great Britain, France, Russia, and Germany: would-be problem solvers in the Balkans.

Wild Cards—see page 136.

Prelude to the Third Balkan War: Albania, Macedonia, Bulgaria, and Serbia Continue the Balkan Tradition

SOURCE OF CONFLICT

The current problem of ethnic Albanians in the rump New Yugoslavia of Serbia and Montenegro is a prime example of several dozen such conflicts that always simmer in the Balkans. Albanian unrest in Serbia has the potential of bringing war to the entire Balkans.

Yugoslavia was a fragile ethnic composite. While the New Yugoslavia of Serbia and Montenegro is in fact a Serb state, it still remains multiethnic. With the exception of a significant Greek community in its south, Albania is largely Albanian. The Albanians maintain that Yugoslavia's Kosovo Province with its 1.6 million Albanians belongs to "Greater Albania"; they feel that the Serb variety of Slavic imperialism keeps Kosovo separated from its legitimate rulers in Tiranë.

The Serbs, however, have had their quest for Greater Serbia whetted by success in Bosnia. Kosovo is also a cultural center of Serbia. It was at Priština that the Turks defeated the Serbs and subjugated them to the sultan.

The other source of Albanian-Serbian conflict is Macedonia. Macedonia is also a fracture point for Bulgaria and Greece. The Greeks, "fearing" for their own Macedonian region around Salonika, refer to the Republic of Macedonia as "the former Yugoslav Republic of Macedonia." Bulgarians insist that a Macedon is another kind of Bulgar. The Serbs have always viewed Macedonia as a Serbian satrapy. Nearly a quarter of Macedonia's population is ethnic Albanian.

If Albanians in Kosovo were the only issue, the problem wouldn't be insurmountable. But Macedonians, Serbs, Croats, Montenegrins, Slovenes, Bosnians (Bosniaks), Greek minorities, Turk minorities, Bulgars, Magyars, and even a few displaced Austro-Germans (all with strong ethnic aspirations) are part of the Yugoslav powder keg.

The collapse of communism in Eastern Europe freed Ex-Yugoslavian nations and Albania to continue the Balkan tradition of ethnic struggles, boundary disputes, and political rivalry. Throughout Eastern Europe people have replaced the lost faith of communism with ethnic and historical identifications. In the Balkans, ethnic and historical identification doesn't mean eating Italian food on Columbus Day or drinking green beer on St. Patrick's Day. In the Balkans, ethnic and historical identification means fighting with thy tribe's neighbor.

WHO'S INVOLVED

Albania—3.4 million people live in Albania (95 percent of them ethnic Albanian). The xenophobic regime of deceased Albanian maverick Communist leader Enver Hoxha (pronounced Hod-yah) kept a heavy lid on Albania.

Albanian minority in Kosovo Province of Serbia—Over 1.5 million Albanians (90 percent of the provincial population) live in Kosovo Province. Kosovo is the poorest region in New Yugoslavia.

Albanian minority in Macedonia—23 percent of Macedonian population is Albanian.

Greek minorities in Albania—With 280,000 to 300,000 Greeks in

Albania, an Albanian grab for Kosovo might shake the Greeks into reaching for northern Epirus, which is what Athens calls southern Albania; Albania officially claims there are only 58,682 Greeks in Albania.

Serbia—Has long viewed the "Macedonian region" as Serb territory.

Greece—The border claims against Albania remain unresolved. The big concern: Macedonia will claim "Greek Macedonia" and the port of Salonika.

Bulgaria—Has long held historical claims on Macedonia.

Wild Cards (for all Balkan conflicts)

Hungary—Magyars (Hungarians) live in Serbia's Vojvodina autonomous province, and, after all, the Balkans are old Austro-Hungarian (Hapsburg) stomping grounds.

United Nations peacekeepers—Peacekeeping? Don't bet on it.

Italy—Italy is increasingly willing to involve itself financially, politically, and militarily in foreign disputes, especially in those areas across the Adriatic (such as parts of Croatia and Albania) that were, for centuries, under Italian control.

Austria—Perhaps Ljubljana should still be named Laibach. These are old Hapsburg stomping grounds, but for an insight into the Austrian "attitude," recall Prince Metternich's line: "Asia begins with the Landstrasse." The Landstrasse (Provincial Road) leaves Vienna and heads toward Hungary and the Balkans.

Turkey—Geographic proximity in eastern Thrace, bitter historical memories of Ottoman action in the Balkans, and current antagonisms with Greece and Bulgaria put Turkey close to the trouble if Yugoslavia and Albania go to war or Yugoslavia disintegrates in civil conflict.

Russia—Pan-Slavism was an old Russian trick prior to the Comintern. Imperial communism is over, but imperialism isn't.

Romania—Lingering internal troubles, ethnic problems, irredentism, and proximity put Romania close to the fuse.

Wild Wild Cards for All Balkan Conflicts

Iran, Libya, and other radical Middle Eastern states—In the early 1980s, Libya was reportedly bankrolling an "Islamic" education for young Muslims from Albania and Yugoslavia. Iran has become involved in Albania and has shipped arms to Bosnia's Muslim government.

GEOGRAPHY

The Socialist Federal Republic of Yugoslavia (Ex-Yugoslavia) consisted of six republics: Croatia (capital in Zagreb), Slovenia (Ljubljana), Montenegro (Titograd), Bosnia and Herzegovina (Sarajevo), Macedonia (Skopje), and Serbia (Belgrade). Belgrade served as the federal capital. The former state of Yugoslavia occupied 250,000 square kilometers, an area about two thirds the size of California, and had a population of around 25 million (California's is 30 million).

The rump New Yugoslavia of Serbia and Montenegro (Federal Republic of Yugoslavia) has about 100,000 square kilometers, about the size of Maine and Connecticut combined. Belgrade remains the capital. Vojvodina, in northern Serbia near Hungary, remains a province of Serbia. It contains parts of the old kingdom of Hungary county (*megye*) of Bachka and half of the Banat region (the other slice of the Banat is in Romania). Kosovo, in Serbia's south abutting the Albanian border, remains a Serb province. Kosovo Province has some of those rough and rugged mountains; tough country capable of protecting insurgent guerrilla groups. The Donau (Danube) River, central and southeastern Europe's most important waterway, flows through northeastern Serbia and past Belgrade. Montenegro (Crna Gora) has several small ports on the Adriatic Sea.

Bosnia has slightly over 51,000 square kilometers, and is about the size of Tennessee. Bosnia is mountainous and crisscrossed with valleys. Bosnia has one harbor on the Adriatic, the town of Neum.

Croatia, with 56,000 square kilometers, is the size of West Virginia. Croatia is more geographically diverse. The Adriatic coast of Ex-Yugoslavia is now dominated by Croatia, including most of the multiethnic Istrian Peninsula (see Local Politics). The coastal area has a Mediterranean climate and is rocky but has good harbors. Inland terrain runs from flat plains along the Hungarian border to the typical Balkan mountains. The Dinaric Alps parallel the Adriatic (Dalmatian) coastline.

Slovenia at 20,000 square kilometers is the size of New Jersey. Alpine mountains follow the border with Italy. Slovenia possesses a small strip of land along the Adriatic coast. Slovenia and neighboring Austria have become important trading partners.

Landlocked Macedonia has 25,000 square kilometers and is the size of Vermont. Macedonia is mountainous. Key terrain features include Lake Ohrid and Lake Prespa in the southwest corner of the nation. Macedonia borders on Albania, Greece, Bulgaria, and Serbia. The Greek port of Salonika has been Macedonia's chief outlet for trade. Macedonia possesses enough indigenous agricultural and energy resources (coal) to meet its own basic, subsistence needs.

Albania has approximately 30,000 square kilometers—about the size of Maryland. Tiranë (Tirana), the capital, is the only city of any consequence. About 180,000 people live in Tiranë. Durrës (the ancient Illryian city of Epidamnus and the Roman Dyrrachium) is the only significant port, though Vlorë can handle shipping. For the most part, Albania is rural and undeveloped, despite Hoxha's insistent propaganda to the contrary. The Gheg Albanians live to the north of the Shkumbi River; the Tosk variety live to the south. (The Albanians are thought to be the last of the original Balkan peoples, the same "Balkanites" the ancient Greeks and Romans fought.)

Mountains, many with conifer forests, dominate Albania. The northern mountains are an extension of the Montenegrin Dinaric Alps. The 20 percent or so of the country that is coastal plain is infertile and often swampy; malaria once scourged visitors and, for all the World Health Organization knows, it may still.

Armies have always been able to move through Albania; the great Roman road that crossed ancient Illyria, the Via Egnatia, attests to that. The difficulty lies in controlling the mountainous backcountry and digging out the armed clans that inhabit it. Falling back into the mountains and cutting themselves off from the invader or landlord is the classic Albanian foil. The Montenegrins escaped Turkish domination using this same strategy.

HISTORY

To many minds, Yugoslavia was always a phony political entity. Yugoslavia attempted to bring together as one nation six republics and two "autonomous regions" with a population of 25 million people drawn from five major ethnic groups using two alphabets, practicing three major religions and speaking four different languages.

Yugoslavia came into existence at the end of World War I with the defeat and dissolution of the Austro-Hungarian Empire. The Great Powers wanted to solve the perennial Balkans problem of what to do with the small, fragile, yet strategic southern Slavic states, so they established a kingdom of the Serbs, Croats, and Slovenes with Serbian King Peter I as ruler. Yugoslavia combined the former Austro-Hungarian provinces of Croatia, Slovenia, Bosnia, and Herzegovina with the previously independent states of Montenegro and Serbia. Macedonia, the other present-day Yugoslav republic, was included as part of Serbia. Bulgars claim that Macedonians are Bulgars and Serbs claim that Macedonians are Serbs.

To attempt to do justice to the rich, violent, and intriguing histories of the southern Slav nations prior to World War I is impossible within the constraints of this book. But let's be pithy—the history is one of short periods of stability punctuating long sentences of petty internecine conflict over land claims and ethnic rights, and paragraph-length episodes of outside imperial powers dividing the squabbling Balkan countries. One has to recognize the date of June 28, 1389, however, when Serbia's Prince Lazar was defeated by the Turks in the Battle of Kosovo and the long period of Turkish domination began. In the main, among Yugoslavs, Serbia got the best of the others, but the Croats, Slovenes, and Macedonians have all had their turns in the driver's seat. The Montenegrins have for the most part held out in their mountainous niche against the influx of Turks, "other" Serbs, and Germans.

The Montenegrins pride themselves on being the only "Balkan Christians" who never succumbed to Muslim Turkish rule.

From an ethnic standpoint, Serbs regard Montenegrins as fellow Serbs; many Montenegrins concur that, yes, they are of Serbian stock, with the caveat that as Montenegrins they are a bit more independent, wilier, tougher, braver, etc. They are all that is left of Yugoslavia, now a Serbian state.

Between the world wars, Yugoslavia tried to create a common political ground. Still, there was much infighting. Yugoslavia frequently accused Hungary of intending to pry back its lost Banat and Bachka regions. Old League of Nations documents are filled with Yugoslav and Hungarian charges and countercharges. In 1934 the Yugoslavian government accused Hungary of covertly supporting the radical Croat Ustase terrorist organization.

In April 1941, Nazi Germany invaded Yugoslavia as part of Hitler's plan to shore up his Italian allies. Mussolini's army based in occupied Albania was bogged down in its war with Greece. In fact, the Greek forces had launched several successful attacks against the Fascists. Yugoslavia's ruler, King Peter II, established a London-based government-in-exile. Within Yugoslavia two rival partisan armies emerged: the Communist National Liberation Army under Marshal Tito, a multiethnic group; and the Yugoslav Army of the Fatherland, or "Chetniks," of Draja Mihajlovic, also multiethnic but with strong Serbian support. The Chetniks fought the Germans and the Communists, and made the mistake of noticeably cutting deals with the Nazis. Tito waged a consistently anti-Nazi, nationalist campaign, no mean feat considering that there was no such thing as a Yugoslavian national. This is the key to Tito—his communism was very secondary to his nationalist mission. During World War II, over two million Yugoslavs lost their lives, over half slain by fellow Yugoslavs. With the defeat of both the Germans and his Chetnik adversaries, Tito became premier in 1945. He severed his close relationship with Moscow in 1948 and closed the Macedonian border to Russian-backed Greek Communists who sought to topple the Athens government. As Tito saw it, the most imminent imperial threat came from the east. Western governments, the United States in particular, were slow to recognize the truly nationalist aims of Tito.

During World War II, the Nazis actively recruited Balkan Muslim populations. Two SS divisions were predominantly Muslim: SS Division Skanderbeg (named for Albania's Prince Alexander, see below) and SS Division Handschar. SS Handschar consisted of from 6,000 to 8,000 Muslims (Albanian and Bosnian), who were used to destroy Serbian partisan villages. The Germans would surround a village, then send in the Balkan SS troops for "ethnic cleansing." These memories are still very much alive in Serbia and are used to justify current Serbian policy.

Here is another World War II fact with current resonance: Tito formed the Republic of Macedonia from southern Serbia in 1944. Allegedly, Tito had in mind the creation of a larger Macedon state, one that would include parts of Bulgaria and northern Greece. (The preamble of the new Macedon constitution refers to a nineteenth-century concept of "unifying" Macedonia's three regions, i.e., central Macedonia, and Greek and Bulgarian "Macedonian" lands.)

Albania is similar in many respects to the other petty Balkan states (neighboring Montenegro in particular), with a long history of clans being able to retreat into the wilderness and maintain some degree of self-determination and a definite identity. Albania claims to be the descendant of the ancient kingdom of Illyria, a contemporary of the early Greek city-states. It is a reasonably valid claim; certainly it is an important element of Albanian national myth and Albanian pride. Albania is one of history's greatest losers. With the brief exception of 1443 to 1478, when Albania's national hero Skanderbeg (Prince Alexander, sometimes written as Skanderberg) drove Turkish forces from the country. From Roman times to 1912, Albania was occupied by some foreign power. An independent state of sorts did exist in the interior as Roman power waned, but the Byzantines soon appeared, then Venetians, Turks, and more Turks.

The Ottoman policy of passing out fiefs to soldiers and civil servants gave many countries under their reign a legacy of rapacious feudalism. There was little interest in long-term development of a country since, in all but a few rare cases, the fief could not be passed on to an heir. Albania was no exception. Already poor and backward, Albania was further impoverished by Turkish rule.

During the Balkan Wars (1912–13) and World War I, Albania was a battleground for Greek, Bulgarian, Serb, Austrian, Italian, and other forces. After World War I, a civil war among various mountain clans sputtered. When a battle stopped, the mountain clans' vendetta tradition kicked off a new round of fighting. In 1925 Ahmed Zogu declared Albania to be an independent republic. By 1928, Zogu had made himself king. Renewed Italian intrigue, sparked by Mussolini's quest for a New Rome as well as Albania's oil deposits, culminated in an invasion in 1939. Albania was the springboard for Italy's bungled attack on Greece. Germany's attack on Yugoslavia was precipitated by Italy's impending loss in the Balkans.

By 1944, Enver Hoxha's Albanian resistance group had driven out the Axis armies. The Albanians won without the benefit of an invading Russian or Allied army. In 1946, Albania declared itself to be a Communist republic with Hoxha as premier. A strict Stalinist, Hoxha broke with Yugoslavia when Tito broke with Russia. When Stalin died, Hoxha became an even more virulent Stalinist. Khrushchev and his revisionist gang had destroyed the old wartime Communist camaraderie, or so it appeared to Hoxha. In 1961, Albania withdrew from the Warsaw Pact and became Communist China's European ally. Hoxha admired Mao's revolutionary fervor and extremism. When Mao died, the Chinese relationship soured.

Enver Hoxha died in 1985. The anti-Communist revolutions of 1989 finally began to put some pressure on Ramiz Alia, the Hoxha lieutenant who took over. Alia's regime fell in 1991. Albania now has an authoritarian democracy. Massive starvation threatened Albania in 1991. The collapse of the Communist regime revealed the utter weakness of Albania's economy. Industrial output fell 60 percent in 1991–92. In 1994 the Albanian Democratic party was in turmoil. Foreign aid donors were few and the homegrown development policies that attempted to bridge fifty years of Communist misrule and overcome five hundred years of economic backwardness were failing.

Kosovo Province is particularly dear to the Serbs, though they comprise only 10 percent of the population. (As noted, in 1389, Prince Lazar's Serb Army was defeated by the legions of Turkish Sultan Murad I in the Battle of Kosovo. You begin to comprehend the Balkans when you accept the fact that these nations venerate defeats.) Serbs regard Kosovo as the cradle of Serbian civilization. Kosovo was the core of Serbia's medieval empire.

The ethnic Albanians, however, who make up the vast majority of Kosovo's population, demand to be "liberated from the tutelage of Serbia," despite large Yugoslavian (Serb) investments in the province made in the early 1980s.

The Kosovian Albanians are very wealthy compared with the Albanians in Albania, but the demands of ethnic identification don't seem to be mitigated by economic development. Belgrade thinks there must be outside agitation from Albania, with possible aid from Bulgaria, but discontent has been a long-term phenomenon. There were student disturbances in 1968, demonstrations in the provincial capital of Priština in 1976, and a number of riots, some of the worst occurring in 1981. In the last decade an estimated one hundred thousand or more Serbians have left Kosovo because of "harassment by Albanians." The Albanians claim they cannot get jobs. The "Albanikos," at first an ill-defined resistance group in Kosovo that began a series of public demonstrations in 1984, have evolved into several aboveground "resistance" groups. Belgrade fears they are the vanguard of a revolution. In 1990, Yugoslav President Slobodan Milosevic revoked Kosovo's status as an autonomous province and said it should be forcibly reintegrated into Serbia.

Finally, there is the Greek view. The Greeks refer to southern Albania as "northern Epirus." Up to 300,000 people of Greek descent live in Albania. In 1981 a number of Greek groups estimated that Hoxha held nearly 20,000 Greeks in Albanian jails or labor camps. Albania denied the accusation. Greece has never formally relinquished its claim to northern Epirus, though they seem to want to leave well enough alone. It is no secret that the Greeks fear that trouble in Kosovo could turn the Balkans into a madhouse. As communism wanes, the split between Greek Orthodox Christians and "revivalist" Islam among formerly "atheist" Albanians could lead to further trouble.

Though the Bosnian war officially began in March 1992, war came to Ex-Yugoslavia in 1991. Croatia declared independence from Yugoslavia in June 1991. In the fall of 1991, Serbian forces shelled the Croat port of Dubrovnik. The Yugoslav Army, totally dominated by Serbia and Montenegro, also launched an ill-fated invasion of Slovenia in 1991. The army withdrew. Fighting broke out across Bosnia in 1991, with small bands of partisans—Croat, Serb, and Bosnian Muslim—engaging one another, primarily in regions near the Serbian border.

But there was method behind the first signs of ethnic conflict in Bosnia. In the late 1980s several political analysts concluded that Serbian leader Slobodan Milosevic's Belgrade clique of Serb ultranationalists was a political group with a mission: to keep faltering Yugoslavia together under their brand of Serbian domination or, if that stratagem failed, to create a "Greater Serbia" out of Bosnia, Montenegro, Macedonia, and parts of Croatia.

At one time a large percentage of Serbian Serbs thought the war required to fashion Greater Serbia was not worth the questionable prize. But the dream of Greater Serbia proved to be too potent a nativist myth and too powerful a political tool in the hands of a clever politician like Milosevic.

On April 6, 1992, the EEC recognized Bosnia and Herzegovina as an independent nation. From March 1992 to early 1994, Bosnian Serbs and Croatian Serb "militias," organized and supported by the Serbian national government in Belgrade, drove Croats and Bosnians out of numerous towns and villages. Slobodan Milosevic, the Serbian ultranationalist leader, proved to be an able strategist and skillful demagogue. The Serb "militias," many of the units trained by the CRDB (see Local Politics) and supplied by the Yugoslav (Serbian) National Army, fought a "creeping" war of aggression, taking a snip of Croatia here, a niche of Bosnia there, then halting and lying low until the diplomatic outrage subsided. Many of the Bosnian militia leaders acted as local warlords. They were in fact on Belgrade's payroll.

The Serb offensives featured calculated terror and genocide, the well-documented instances of "ethnic cleansing" where Muslims in particular were executed by rampaging Serb irregular forces. There were instances of Croat and Bosnian Muslim terror and murder, but this time the preponderance of the war crimes and outright criminal acts were perpetrated by Serbs. There are many Croats who have encouraged the Serbs because they wish to divide Bosnia between Serbia and Croatia. The UN and Western response to ethnic cleansing was angry rhetoric and the insertion of ineffective peacekeeping forces.

By mid-1994 the Bosnian Serbs occupied nearly 70 percent of Bosnia. By 1995, Western press sources reported that over 750,000 Muslims had been evicted from Serbian-controlled Bosnia. A Croat offensive in August 1995 (Operation Storm, the largest military operation in Europe since World War II) forced most of the Serbs living in the Krajina region to flee to Serb-controlled territory in Bosnia or into Serbia itself. (Some of these Croatian Serbs may be resettled in Kosovo, adding more fuel to that ethnic fire.) A shaky Bosnian, Bosnian-Croat, and Croatian government alliance formed. Their combined forces pushed most Serbs out of western Bosnia and reconnected the Muslim-dominated Bihac area of Bosnia with other Muslim areas. By late fall the Bosnian and Croat alliance held around 50 percent of Bosnia's original territory; Bosnian Serbs controlled the other half. Fitful negotiations began, based on Serbian recognition of an independent Bosnian state and the Muslim-led Bosnian government's recognition of an autonomous but "federal" Bosnian Serb microstate within Serbia. The "51-49" formula (which would give 51 percent of Bosnia to the Muslims and Croats, 49 percent to the Bosnian Serbs) was once again under negotiation.

The Bosnians also have their extremists, and political Islamic radicals have increasing influence. (Iran has supplied Bosnia with arms and ammunition.) Independent Bosnia was supposed to have a collective, rotating presidency. In late 1992, however, President Alija Izetbegovic (a Muslim) refused to step down, saying he would stay until the war ended. The five major Bosnian opposition parties fear the increasing influence of "Bosnian ultranationalists," and political Islamists will mean "a weakening of Bosnian multiculturalism" (code phrase meaning increasing Muslim control).

The process of Yugoslavia's disintegration into warring tribal states served as a political laboratory for the United Nations, Europe and the United States, each bloody day asking the question, How do we deal with the historical and national fragmentation resulting from the end of the cold war?

The answer was, Not well at all. Resolutions to enforce a twenty-kilometer artillery-free zone around the besieged Bosnian capital of Sarajevo were tested by the Serbs. UNPROFOR (UN Protection Force) tried to create "safe havens" for refugees (the Muslims in particular) but these proved to be little more than surrounded islands of hostages. Despite occasional bombs dropped by NATO warplanes, the Serbs kept the pressure on the Muslims. The would-be peacekeepers and peacemakers gambled that airpower alone represents credible commitment. With the low cloud ceilings of Balkan winters, narrow valleys, mobile artillery for targets, and shoulder-fired antiaircraft missiles in their possession, the Bosnian Serbs showed it was not.

Other political options were tried. An arms embargo, dating from September 1991, originally applied to all of Yugoslavia. The Serbs did not suffer from it, since they seized most of the old Yugoslav Army's tanks and artillery. The Bosnians did, though weapons supplies began to accelerate in 1994. Running guns through the blockade was not all that difficult; estimates suggest that only 20 percent of these "illegal weapons" did not get through.

The Bosnian war generated an interesting "first." On February 28, 1994, American jet fighters shot down four Serb fighter-bombers. This was NATO's first combat action as NATO. It was also the first time the U.S. AMRAAM air-to-air missile, in development for over ten years, actually shot down a hostile aircraft.

As of early 1996, Croatia's province of Eastern Slavonia remains under rebel Croat control. The Yugoslav (Serb) Army keeps substantial forces on the Serb border across from Eastern Slavonia. Serbia and Croatia could go to war over control of the region. Eastern Slavonia is not part of the NATO peacekeeping mandate but is under UN supervision. Croatia's control of the Prevlaka Peninsula (near Dubrovnik), which restricts rump Yugoslavia's access to the Adriatic Sea (via Montenegro), is also a volatile issue.

The NATO peacekeepers divide Bosnia into three major zones. Northern Division consists of the U.S. 1st Armored Division (headquarters in Tuzla) reinforced by the Nordic Brigade, the Russian Brigade, and Balt, Polish, Turkish, and Romanian units. Western Division is policed by a British division reinforced by Dutch and Canadian troops. Malaysia and Pakistan also provide contingents. Southern Division is run by a French division reinforced by an Italian brigade.

Spain, Portugal, Egypt, Pakistan, Indonesia, and Ukraine also provide units. (The peace force is now IFOR, implementation force.)

Key areas of potential conflict remain the Sarajevo area, the Posavina Corridor (through Bosnian Serb territory, connecting Sarajevo to Bosnian government outposts near Serbia), and the Brčko Corridor north of Tuzla (which connects Serbian and Bosnian Serb territory to Serb-controlled territory in western Bosnia).

Peacekeepers who come for short periods will not create long-term stability. The world hopes for the best, but Bosnia may well be one of the twenty-first century's first battlegrounds.

LOCAL POLITICS

Serbia and Montenegro (New Yugoslavia)

Slobodan Milosevic—President of the Serbian Republic; Serbian ultranationalist leader; head of Serbian Socialist Party (SPS), the former Communist party.

Serbian Orthodox Church—A religious institution that is also central to Serbian "cultural identity."

CRDB—Acronym for Centar Resora Drzave Bezbednosti, or Center of the Department of State Security, the Serbian Interior Ministry's secret police. "Sector V" of the CRDB handles intelligence and counterintelligence. In Ex-Yugoslavia the secret police were called the SDB (Sluzba Drzave Bezbednosti). Many Serbs and Montenegrins still use the old name.

Revived pre-1941 Serbian parties—Radical party (ultranationalist), Democratic party.

Serbian Nationalist Revival (Srpska Narodna Obnova)—Ultranationalist Serbian group; advocates establishment of a Greater Serbia, which includes Macedonia, Montenegro, Bosnia, and large parts of Croatia.

Vreme—Liberal Belgrade weekly publication that opposes the Serbs' war in Bosnia.

Arkan—Nom de guerre of Zeljko Raznatovic, leader of the Bosnian Serb "Tiger" militia. Now a member of legislature in Belgrade representing Serbs in Kosovo. Western press sources report the Tiger militia has been accused of committing numerous war crimes in Bosnia.

Captain Dragan—Dragan Vasiljkovic, leader of Serb Kninjas militia.

Kosovo Province of Serbia

Albanikos—Albanian ethnic "irredentists" (in Yugoslavian political jargon roughly meaning "people we don't like") living in Kosovo Province in Yugoslavia.

League of Democrats of Kosovo (also translated as Albanian Democratic Alliance of Kosovo or Democratic League of Kosovo)—Albanian ethnic party in Kosovo.

"Republic of Kosovo"—Self-declared Albanian nation in Kosovo.

Independent Citizens party—New Serb ultranationalist party in Kosovo; Arkan is a member.

Patriarch Arsenije III Carnojevic—Serbian Orthodox patriarch who led thirty-six thousand Serb families from Kosovo to Vojvodina in 1690, after revolt against Turks failed.

Hajduk—Serbian archetypal folk hero, bearded mountain brigand with fur hat, cape, and guns. Symbol of resistance to Turks.

Cathedral of St. Sava—New Orthodox cathedral being built in Belgrade; the dome is supposed to be bigger than St. Sophia's in Istanbul.

Croatia

Croatian Democratic Union (HDZ)—Coalition of Croatian nationalist parties. Franjo Tudjman, Croatia's president, heads the party.

Social Liberals—Coalition of liberal parties.

Coalition of National Understanding—Croatian centrist party.

Social Democratic party—"Reformed" Communist party.

Independent Serb Republic of Krajina (also Republic of Serbian Krajina)—Self-declared Croat Serb separatist state that was effectively destroyed by the Croat Army in August 1995. The Krajina ("military frontier") is that part of Croatia where Austrians resettled Serbs in the sixteenth century as a barrier to the Turks.

Croatian Peasant party—Revived pre-1941 Croat party.

The Ustase—Ultranationalist Croatian movement; formed as a political party by Hitler and Mussolini. The core of the movement were members of the Ustase radical group active in Croatia after World War I; they participated in several terrorist incidents. They ruled the puppet state of "Greater Croatia" during World War II and are responsible for atrocities committed against Jews, Serbs, and Gypsies.

1526—The year of the Battle of Mohács. The Turkish victory led to the division of Croatia between Turkey and Hapsburg Austria. Strategically, the Turk victory over the Hungarian and Balkan forces assured the Ottomans long-term control of the Balkans.

"Greater Croatia"—Croat ultranationalists' dream. Would incorporate all of western Herzegovina into a larger Croat state.

Brac Island—U.S. intelligence-gathering site in Croatia; possible staging point for international peacekeeping forces' withdrawal or further NATO operations.

Istria—Major tourist region of Croatia along Adriatic. The Istrian Peninsula is multiethnic with its northern end in Slovenia. Istria is adjacent to the Italian city of Trieste (which has historically been a part of Istria). Many Istrians demand "regional autonomy" from Croatia. In 1994 the autonomists held a convention in the port city of Pula. The convention was denounced by Croatian authorities in Zagreb. Istria is Croatia's most economically advanced region. Members of the Istrian Democratic Assembly (IDS) say they want to remain within Croatia, but they demand the power to decide on issues of local development and retain their tax revenues.

HV—Symbol for Croatian government forces; HVO indicates Bosnian Croat troops.

"The map"—A map scribbled in 1995 on a piece of paper by Franjo Tudjman, which shows Bosnia being divided between Croatia and Serbia "within ten years."

Bosnia

Party of Democratic Action (SDA)—Major Bosnian Muslim nationalist party; in 1995 led by President Alija Izetbegovic, a Muslim who once called for the creation of an Islamic state.

Serbian Democratic Party of Bosnia and Herzegovina—Led by Radovan Karadzic; Bosnian Serb political party. "Typhoon" is the code name for the party's secret police. Karadzic has been indicted for war crimes.

MUP—Bosnian Interior Ministry Police.

Bogomils—Adherents of a twelfth-century Manichaean heresy, which continued to find followers in Bosnia. Believers in Bosnia and Herzegovina were numerous. Some historians believe this heritage of Bosnian religious schism paved the way for Islam's ready acceptance in Bosnia. Persecution of Bogomils by Catholics made Islam look good.

Independent Serb Republic of Bosnia and Herzegovina—Self-declared Serb state inside Bosnia. As of late 1995, could become the Bosnian Serb "Republika" but remain "federated" with Bosnian government. (According to the Dayton Agreement.)

Croatian Community of Herceg-Bosna—Self-declared Croat state inside Bosnia. As of late 1995 once more part of Bosnian-Croat confederation.

Bihac—The Bosnian "elbow" into Croatia; home of Muslim group opposed to Bosnian Muslim government. As of late 1995 part of Bosnian-Croat Confederation.

7th Muslim Brigade of the Bosnian Army—An all-Muslim unit and regarded as a potential "Bosnian nationalist extremist" organization.

October 7, 1908—The day of infamy. Austria annexes Bosnia and Herzegovina.

Sarajevo—Site of the 1984 Winter Olympics, now a remnant shell of that Olympiad city. Sarajevo experienced artillery bombardment from 1991 to 1995. It is also the site of the first shot of World War I: Gavril Princip (a Serb) assassinated Austrian Archduke Ferdinand on June 28, 1914. Mount Igman, outside of Sarajevo, commands almost all of the routes into central Bosnia. It has been the site of frequent combat.

"Afghanis"—These Islamist fighters were supposed to leave in January 1996. Approximately two thousand in Bosnia as 1995 ends.

Macedonia

Social Democratic Party of Macedonia—Former Macedonian Communist party, still major nationalist force in Macedonia.

IMRO (or VMRO)—Revived Internal Macedonian Revolutionary Organization, now an ultranationalist political party (also called Democratic Party for Macedonian National Unity).

Other parties—Democratic Party of Turks (Turk party); Party for Democratic Action (Slavic Muslim party); Alliance of Reform Forces of Macedonia/Liberal party; National Democratic party.

Tetovo University—Ethnic Albanian university set up in December 1994 in defiance of a government ban.

Democratic Prosperity party (PDP)—Albanian nationalist party.

Autocephalous Macedonian Orthodox Church—Splinter sect of Serbian Orthodox Church; not recognized by Serbian Church.

Slovenia

Major Slovene political parties—Liberal Democratic Party of Slovenia (LDS); Christian Democrats (SKD); United List (new name of old Communists of Slovenia and allies); Slovene National party.

Windisch—Slovenes favoring "Germanization"; many found in Carinthia region.

Catholic Church—96 percent of Slovenia's population is Roman Catholic.

Ex-Yugoslavia (leftovers with continuing political relevance)

Federal Executive Council—The old committee with the "rotating premier." It was essentially a nine-member collective presidency.

1974 Yugoslavian Constitution—Said that the federal state is composed of "voluntarily united nations" and implied that these nations have the right to pull out of the federation; autonomous regions, such as Kosovo, do not have such a right.

Tito—Josip Broz (1892–1980), the godfather of all Yugoslavs, even after his death. The anti-Nazi resistance hero who led the partisan movement from 1941 to 1945, Tito stressed that the only Balkan Slav state that could survive was a federation. He believed that infighting would bring in strong outsiders (i.e., Russia) to divide and conquer the Balkan Peninsula.

The Yugoslav Army—Was primarily officered by Serbs and Montenegrins.

The Blue Train—Tito's private luxury train.

Brotherhood and Unity Motorway—Main highway between Belgrade, Serbia, and Zagreb, Croatia.

Goli Otok and Sveti Grgur—Islands holding torture prisons for men and women, respectively. The prisons were run by Tito's secret police.

Illyrism—Nineteenth-century literary, linguistic, cultural, and philosophical movement that evolved into the concept of "Yugo-Slavism." Sought to bridge "South Slav" divisions and set the stage for the formation of a united "Yugoslav" state. Major figures included the Serb, Vuk Karadzic, and the Slovene poet, Jernei Kopitar.

Albania

Political parties—Democratic party; Democratic Alliance party (formerly aligned with the Democratic party); Social Democratic party; Albanian Republican party; Albanian Socialist party (formerly Albanian Workers party, i.e., Communist party).

Omnia—Greek minority party.

Ghegs—Northern group of Albanians; speak the Gheg dialect of Albanian. Gheg is the official Albanian dialect.

Tosks—Dominant southern group of Albanians; speak the Tosk dialect.

Northern Epirus Liberation Front—Right-wing Greek terrorist group active in Albania in 1994 and 1995.

Greater Albania—Many Albanians still object to the 1913 treaty that left so many Albanians outside of Albania. Greater Albania includes Kosovo, parts of Montenegro, and most of Macedonia.

Enver Hoxha—deceased Albanian Communist leader. He survived all of Khrushchev's and Tito's alleged attempts to remove him. Of Albanian Muslim background, he was violently anticlerical and opposed to all religions. He was the alleged "founder of the world's first atheist state" and fancied himself to be a philosopher.

Mehmet Shehu—Was supposed to be Hoxha's ordained replacement, but he died in 1981 from "mysterious causes," purportedly associated with a coup attempt.

Sigurimi—Old Albanian Communist secret police. Now disbanded.

Decree No. 4337 of the Presidium of the People's Assembly—Entitled "On the Abrogation of Certain Decrees," it was passed on November 22, 1967. This was Hoxha's death knell for religion in Albania; the decree finalized the creation of "the first atheist state in the world." In 1967 the Albanian government closed nearly twenty-two hundred churches, mosques, and shrines; the country was supposedly 70 percent Muslim, 20 percent Orthodox, and 10 percent Catholic. In 1990, Albania once more began allowing private religious practice.

"Law of Blood Vengeance"—A holdover feature of Albania's mountain clan past, but a feature that has survived Christianity, Islam, and communism. Serbian sources estimate that "blood revenge" accounts for the deaths of one hundred Albanian men a year in Kosovo Province. There are no current figures for Albania, other than admission from refugees that the ancient ritual continues. The "law" requires the family of a victim of a slaying (or fatal accident) to either kill an adult male from the family of the person who caused the death, or make the offender's family pay handsomely for the loss. Some Montenegrin hill clans allegedly carry on this practice.

Arnauts—Albanian Muslim troops serving with the old Ottoman Turkish Army. They often did the Sublime Porte's dirty work in the Balkan fiefs. This fact is remembered by Albania's neighbors.

Shqipri—Albanian name for Albania. Translates as the Land of Eagles. Hence, Albanians are Shqiptars, or "eagle men."

POLITICAL TREND CHARTS

ALBANIA

Gv95	Gv20	PC95	PC20	R95	R20	Ec95	Ec20	EdS95	EdS20
AD3,2	AD4,5	4	5	6	5	1	1+	1+	1+

Gv = Government Type
AD = Authoritarian Democracy (effectiveness, 0–9, stability 0–9)
PC = Political Cohesiveness (0 = chaos, 9 = maximum)
R = Repression Index (9 = maximum)
Ec = Comparative Economic Status (0–9)
EdS = Relative Education Status (0–9); in this case, urban population only

NEW YUGOSLAVIA

Gv95	Gv20	PC95	PC20	R95	R20	Ec95	Ec20	EdS95	EdS20
SA6,5	AD3,4	6	5	7	5	2+	5	5	5

SA = Socialist Authoritarian (albeit a peculiar one)

CROATIA

Gv95	Gv20	PC95	PC20	R95	R20	Ec95	Ec20	EdS95	EdS20
RD5,5	RD6,5	5	6	6	5	4	5	4	5

RD = Representative Democracy

SLOVENIA

Gv95	Gv20	PC95	PC20	R95	R20	Ec95	Ec20	EdS95	EdS20
RD6,6	RD6,7	7	7	3	3	5	5+	5	5

Look Back: The 1991 edition's "fantasy state" of Independent Slovenia looked like this:

Gv96	PC96	R96	Ec96	EdS96
RD6,7	7	2	7	6

BOSNIA

Gv95	Gv20	PC95	PC20	R95	R20	Ec95	Ec20	EdS95	EdS20
AD1,2	AD4,3	1−	4	5	4	2	5	4	5

MACEDONIA

Gv95	Gv20	PC95	PC20	R95	R20	Ec95	Ec20	EdS95	EdS20
RD4,4	RD4,5	3	5	3	3	2	3	3	3+

THEORETICAL "GREATER SERBIA" STATE
(Fantasy state includes Montenegro, Serbia, Vojvodina, Kosovo, 70 percent of Bosnia, Serb areas in Croatia, northern Macedonia)

Gv20	PC20	R20	Ec20	EdS20
SA5,4	4	8	3+	4

THEORETICAL "GREATER ALBANIA"
(ALBANIA PLUS KOSOVO)

Gv20	PC20	R20	Ec20	EdS20
MA3,3	4	7	2*	1+

MA = Military Authoritarian
*On average, the people of Kosovo are wealthier and better educated than other Albanians.

"INDEPENDENT KOSOVO"
(Separate Albanian state from capital of Priština south and west to Albanian border)

Gv20	PC20	R20	Ec20	EdS20
MA3,2	6	8	1	2

REGIONAL POWERS AND POWER INTEREST INDICATOR CHARTS

ALBANIAN AND SERBIAN WAR OF KOSOVO

	Economic Interests	Historical Interests	Political Interest	Military Interest	Force Generation Potential (off/def*)	Ability to Intervene Politically
Albania	9	9	9	9	2/5	8
Serb/Mtn	8	9	9	8	6/8	8
Albanikos	9	9	9	9	2/3	7
Croatia	7	7	8	4	1	5
Bulgaria	2	7	7	7	1+	4
Turkey	1	8	4	3	2	1
Russia	3	5	6	2	2	8
United States	1	2	5	4	5	7
Germany	3	5	7	5	2	7
Austria	4	6	7	6	1	6
Italy	4	6	7	7	2	7

NOTE: 0 = minimum; 9 = maximum
Serb/Mtn = Serbia and Montenegro
*Kosovo region offense/defense.

"WARS OF YUGOSLAVIAN SUCCESSION": BOSNIAN WAR, SERBO-CROAT WAR, AND SERBO-CROAT-BOSNIAN WAR

	Economic Interests	Historical Interests	Political Interest	Military Interest	Force Generation Potential (off/def*)	Ability to Intervene Politically
Serb/Mtn	9	9	9	9	5/8*	8
Slovenia	9	9	9	9	1−/3	3
Croatia	9	9	9	9	3/6	7
Bosnia	9	9	9	9	1/2	4
Macedon	8	9	8	8	1/3	5
Albania	7	8	9	9	3/7	2
Romania	5	7	8	9	1	4−
Bulgaria	6	8	8	9	1+	4−
Hungary	5	8	8	8	2+	5
Turkey	2	8	7	5	1+	0
Russia	3	8	7	6	4	4
United States	2	4	5	5	5	6
Germany	5	6	7+	7	2	6−
Austria	7	8	8	7	2†	5
Italy	7	8	8	7	4†	6
Britain	4	5	6	6	3	6
France	7	6	7	6	3	7

*Albania has a larger defensive and offensive rating in this war. Reflects Albanian ability to attack into Macedonia and Montenegro as well as Kosovo. Albanian defense factor is inside Albania.

†Austrian and Italian ratings for defense inside Slovenia is 5.

Note on comparative force generation potential among Ex-Yugoslav nations: According to published 1995 figures the Serbs and their militias have over 1,200 tanks (from a few old Soviet T-34s to modern "Yugoslav" M-84 models). The Croats and their militias have around 250 tanks and the Bosnians 50. The Serbs have around 270 combat aircraft, the Croats perhaps 25 (though the Croats have acquired some advanced MiGs). Serb and Serb militias have over 2,800 artillery pieces and heavy mortar; Croats 1,100; Bosnians 400. In manpower Serbia and Montenegro can put 140,000 troops in the field, Bosnian Serbs 80,000, and Krajina Serbs 45,000. Croatia and Bosnian Croats together field 150,000. We estimate Bosnian government troop totals (mostly Muslim) at 115,000. Interestingly, this means a Bosnian-Croatian alliance could theoretically generate as many troops as the Serbs (265,000). However, Serbia does have the manpower, and the old Yugoslav reserve system. With this, Serbia could arm and organize up to 800,000 additional troops. This would be a nation in arms, and a formidable foe for any invader.

MACEDONIAN WAR

	Economic Interests	Historical Interests	Political Interest	Military Interest	Force Generation Potential (off/def*)	Ability to Intervene Politically
Serb/Mtn	9	9	9	9	5/8*	8
Croatia	9	9	9	9	2/7	6
Bosnia	9	9	9	9	1−/2	4
Macedon	9	9	9	9	1/4	5
Albania	7	8	9	9	2	2
Romania	6	7	8	9	1	3
Bulgaria	6	8	8	9	2	4
Greece	8	9	9	9	5	7
Turkey	2	8	6	7	2+	6
Russia	3	5	7	5	4	4
United States	2	4	5	6	5	7
Germany	5	6	7+	7	2	5
Italy	7	8	8	7	2+	4
Britain	4	5	6	6	3−	4
France	7	6	7	6	3−	5

*Split FGP is offense/defense; offensive FGP for Ex-Yugoslav nations is anywhere inside 1990 boundaries of Yugoslavia; defensive FGP is inside new home republic.

PARTICIPANT STRATEGIES AND GOALS

"Kosovo Problem"

Albanikos and other Albanian ethnic dissidents in Kosovo—Keep up the pressure on Belgrade to make Kosovo a republic with strikes, sabotage, threats to Serbs. Goal—a separate republic that would then unite with a "free" Greater Albania.

Albania—Albania may wish to provide political, propaganda, monetary, and perhaps armed support to Albaniko revolutionaries, but given its terrible economic straits its best strategy is to stand up for Kosovo Albanians' human rights and concentrate on getting its own house in order.

Serbia and Montenegro—Curtail Albanian political activity in Kosovo and stop the development of Albanian ethnic terrorist cells. Direct Serbian military and political control of the province brings on repression, but from the Serb point of view it is justified. The increase in Serb "militia" activity means the stage is being set for forced emigration or "ethnic cleansing" of Albanians, at least in the Priština area. A quick war with Albania (the punch in the nose that will give the Albanians in Kosovo an "object lesson") is a long-range option. Serbia wants to retain Kosovo, and especially the Priština area. A division of Kosovo, with Serbia retaining Priština and the northern half, remains a distant but distinct possibility. That still would not satisfy the Albanian population. But "forced emigration" isn't a new concept in the Balkans.

United Nations and various peacemakers—Try to convince Belgrade a war in Kosovo will further isolate Serbia and Montenegro. If war erupts, work to contain the fighting to Kosovo.

"Wars of Yugoslavian Succession"

Serbia and Montenegro—Bosnia should never have existed, according to the Serbs, since it was such an ethnic composite. The Serbs believe the Bosnian state will be inherently unfair to Serbs because it will be run by Muslims. Thus the Serbs' solution: Take the land and control it themselves. Wild historical analogies comparing Serbia with Nazi Germany are inaccurate. Germany in 1936 was a global, industrial power. Serbia is an economic and political dwarf. "New Yugoslavia" is, however, in comparison with its neighbors a regional power with hegemonic ambitions. The Serbs have fought their "creeping war of aggression" brilliantly. They understand how to use the international news media and play on the weaknesses of international bodies like the United Nations. They could apply this understanding to Croatia and Macedonia as well. Croatia has a large Serbian minority that holds a third of Croatia's territory. Serbia and Croatia could agree to carve up Bosnia and make some kind of deal regarding the Serb-held portions of Croatia. The "independent" Serb states in Bosnia and Croatia will merge with Serbia proper to form Greater Serbia. The Bosnian Muslims will be scattered to the winds, forming a new refugee population. New Yugoslavia, however, has economic problems, not all the result of the UN embargo. The 1993 unemployment rate was 60 percent. Some press figures suggest that Serbia's actual 1993 exports were $1 billion, a fifth of the 1990 prewar level. Solving economic woes could curtail the desire to make war. Facing Bosnians or Croats as well supplied with artillery and tanks as Serb units has led the Serbs to seek peace via the 1995 Dayton Accord, but this is a truce, not a peace.

Bosnian Serbs—Play for time. The Bosnian Serbs have their own self-declared statelet. The longer they hold the territory, the more likely it is they will get to keep it. The Bosnian Serbs' dream: Russian ultranationalist (and pro-Serb partisan) Vladimir Zhirinovsky comes to power in Moscow. If that happens, maybe Serbia can retake Slovenia and Croatia as well.

Bosnians—Rescinding the notorious UN arms embargo imposed

upon the Bosnian government and creating a balance of power between Serbia and Bosnia should be central goals. The arms embargo mocks the right to self-defense. At some point the Bosnians must be able to protect themselves. Restoring Bosnia's prewar borders may be a Muslim dream, but as of mid-1995 it is highly unlikely. It would take between 200,000 and 500,000 troops and would risk a major regional war in the Balkans, which would require a million or more troops to suppress. One major issue in a partitioned Bosnia will be access to the various Muslim and Serb "pockets" inside the shrunken state. Bosnian road networks are limited. The Bosnians must also watch the Croats. Croatian President Franjo Tudjman said in mid-1995 that Serbia and Croatia could still divide Bosnia between them.

Are there Islamic radicals in Bosnia? Yes. Will they come to power in a Muslim-dominated Bosnian state? The Muslim moderates must make certain they do not. If an Islamic radical regime settles in Sarajevo, Serbia will suddenly have a lot of friends—and a lot of new tanks and aircraft.

But Islamic radicals already hold sway in Bosnia. Iran is Bosnia's most energetic arms supplier, and Islamic warriors arrive with the weapons. The Bosnians play down the increasingly Islamic coloration of Bosnia's culture. (And the truth is that Europeans both East and West would rather not have a nest of Islamic activists so close to home, thank you.) Turkey could supply arms instead of Iran.

Croatia—The Serbs halted their "creeping war of aggression" against Croatia when the Croats acquired heavy weapons and made Serb war making too costly. A balance of power between Serbs and Croats developed. Croatia is playing a wait-and-see game over Bosnia. Many Bosnian Croats would feel comfortable in a "federal Bosnian state." Many Croats still look upon Bosnia as Croatian territory. The big Croat concern is an energized Serbia that decides to rebuild "Yugoslavia" as a Serbian superstate. The Croats will seek alliances with Hungary and assurances from the West (Austria, Italy, and international organizations) on support for Croat security. Croat ultranationalists still covet Bosnia for Croatia.

Macedonia—The Macedonians are attempting an odd political strategy, at least odd for the Balkans. Skopje is trying to give every ethnic group a voice in the legislature. The Macedonians are allowing ethnic-oriented education. They are assuring the Greeks that they have no intentions of taking the Greek state of Macedonia. The Macedonians are also relying on the United States as an ally. As of mid-1995 the United States had a peacekeeping force in Macedonia, a trip-wire unit to forestall Serb, Greek, Albanian, and Bulgarian aggression.

Slovenia—Sit tight and make money while the other Ex-Yugoslav nations make war. Slovenia seeks mutual defense pacts with Austria and other Western nations. Slovenia had a small trade surplus in 1992, but has since lost access to cheap Serb raw materials. This is a problem. Slovenia also has to navigate border disputes with Croatia. Slovenia has begun to fortify its Croatian border.

United States—The Dayton agreement forced the Muslims into accepting a partition of Bosnia. As of late 1995, the Dayton maps for a "federal Bosnia" had local control delegated to Serb and Croat/Muslim sectors. The idea is that the United States will put the thumb on the Muslims and say: "There is no better deal on the table. We cannot turn the clock back, we cannot raise the dead." Americans understand the larger consequences of genocide, be it directed by Serbs, Croats, or Bosnians, but they have been unwilling to commit troops to stop it. Since the United States has recognized Bosnia, it is committed to assuring some kind of Bosnian state.

Russia—Russia has deep historic ties to the Serbs, but the Balkans have been a graveyard for failed Russian foreign policies. Both czarist and Communist politicians once coveted Yugoslav and Albanian air and naval bases on the Adriatic. Post–cold war Moscow has little need for bases. The current Kremlin has troubles with its own Russian and "pan-Slavic" ultranationalists but must appease them. Russia will always be "pro-Belgrade" but will be a key player in any settlement of the Bosnian war or the other various Ex-Yugoslav conflicts. The Serbs see Russia as a potential military ally.

Great Britain and France—The British and French often view Serbia as an ally who fought in both world wars. Many Europeans argue that Bosnia isn't a survivable nation-state and it was a mistake to recognize Bosnia when it declared its independence in April 1992. They point out that the Yugoslav Republic of Bosnia-Herzegovina was a pizza pie of humanity, with Muslim Bosnians comprising only 40 percent of the population. The French, frankly, don't want a Muslim state in Europe.

The rise of Islamic fundamentalism in North Africa is concern enough for Paris.

Bulgaria—Continues to demand that Macedonia become a province of Greater Bulgaria. Peace and quiet are, however, in Bulgaria's long-term economic interest.

Greece—Short-term goal is to ensure protection of Greek minority in Albania. If a Serbo-Albanian war erupts and Albania gets the worst of it, Athens may attempt to "recover" northern Epirus (southern Albania). Greek eyes are still on Macedonia. Athens may either blunt a Bulgarian grab for Macedonia or make an "arrangement" with Bulgaria to divide Macedonia. (That deal may also be made with the Serbs.) But Greece may be key to achieving a regional political settlement. Greeks and Turks are really making noise about economic cooperation. Athens and Ankara both know that a Balkan war that spreads beyond Bosnia will set them back economically a decade or more. Some Greeks have viciously opposed the new Republic of Macedonia. Until new negotiations, spurred by mutual economic interests, softened the Greek government's policies, Athens imposed an economic embargo on Macedonia. But both the Greeks and Turks fear that a large Balkan war might destabilize Turkey and, should Turkey shake and throw a few foundations, the Kemalists in Ankara could be replaced by a radical Islamic regime. If that happens, the whole of Eastern Europe will go up in flames.

Greek businesses are also interested in investing in Macedonia. Will the Greeks make the connection that their anti-Macedonian policies are precisely the kind of xenophobic foolishness that will bring about the war they fear? The Greek-Macedonia rapprochement is fragile.

Italy—Italy sees the Dalmatian coast, Croatia, and Albania as its logical "sphere of influence" in rebuilding Communist-devastated Eastern Europe.

Hungary—Budapest needs a peaceful southern border; spending on defense would beggar Hungary's economic recovery. But Hungarians will keep a place open for the return of the Hungarian borderlands in Vojvodina. For all that, Hungary is the European nation with the largest number of its ethnic kin outside its borders (mainly in neighboring Romania). This is tinder for another fire.

NATO and UN (international organizations)—Peaceful intervention doesn't bring peace. Peacekeeping in Bosnia failed. Threats of air strikes and economic sanctions fail to halt successful aggressors—that takes deploying troops as combat soldiers, not as notional UN peace-keepers. The international organizations unwilling to use firepower must create diplomatic "firebreaks" outside of the combat zone.

International Islamic radicals—Keep the fires burning in Bosnia and use the issue as a springboard to light other Islamic radical fires in Europe and the West. It's back to the fifteenth century, this time with high-tech weapons.

POTENTIAL OUTCOMES

"Third Balkan War"

The chance through 2001 of the "Third Balkan War" (with all nations involved) is 25 percent. This could ignite from a Serb-Croat, Serb-Albanian, Bulgar-Serb, Greek-Albanian, Greek-Bulgar, Greek-Turk, Romanian-Serb, Bulgar-Romanian, Bulgar-Turk, everybody-over-Macedonia, or you-name-it-combination armed conflict. If this Balkan war erupts, there is a 99 percent chance of bloodbath, with no winners. If everyone gangs up on Serbia and Serbia loses, there is a 50 percent chance of Serbian loss of Kosovo Province.

A 25 percent projection in a four-year time frame is very high for such a major conflict. The outcome could be ignited by any of the potential political and military crises discussed above and the Balkan-area troubles discussed in Chapter 5, on Turkey. How does this "su-peroutcome" work in our game projections? None of these postulated chains of events is discrete. When reading through the potential out-comes, understand that "spillover conflict" is implicit in our analyses of the potential for war in each individual case. Political conflicts may be individually identified but conflicts are rarely isolated. In the Bal-kans, one neighbor's fire is the next guy's fuse.

For example, the 15 percent chance of a Russian invasion of Ro-mania (Outcome 6 of "Second Romanian Civil War") might strike some as high—until one considers the "architecture of instability" in the region. A general Balkan war would drive up Russian blood pressure. The situation in Moldavia becomes a context (or pretext) for action.

The Great Peacekeepers Retreat. The potential also exists for a debacle involving the withdrawal of UN or international peacekeeping forces. This scenario could suddenly draw troops from all over the world, including the United States and Russia, into the Balkan cauldron in an attempt to extract international peacekeepers.

Though we give this a small chance of occurring, this "world strategy" for the Balkans does interest some policy analysts: Peacekeepers and surrounded Muslims would be evacuated from Bosnia. The weapons embargo against Bosnia would be lifted, giving the Bosnians the heavy weapons they need to fight the Serbs on equal footing. Areas of Bosnia and Croatia where fighting has occurred would be "roped off" internationally as an "open combat zone." The whole of Serbia, with the exception of Kosovo, would be included in the "roped off" zone. Macedonia would also be a "no go" zone for combat. If the warring parties crossed the lines—e.g., Serbia attacks in Kosovo—then Belgrade gets bombed and loses its electrical power grid. Inside the "combat zone" the warring Balkan parties would then be allowed to exhaust themselves. A cruel scenario, or one that is coolly realistic?

Kosovo, Albania, and "New Yugoslavia" (Serbia-Montenegro)

1. 55 percent chance through 2001: Occasional riots and infrequent terrorism continue, with growing Albanian ethnic resentment. Belgrade continues to up the economic pressure on Albanians to force emigration, particularly from the Priština region.
2. 40 percent chance through 2001: The same situation described in Outcome 1 except that Albanian resistance is used by Belgrade as a pretext to begin a Bosnian-style "ethnic cleansing" campaign. If this "micro-civil war" occurs, the Serbs have an 80 percent chance of victory with 10 percent chance of stalemate and 10 percent chance of Albanian rebel success in defeating Serbian militias around Priština. If Albanian rebels begin to win, look for inter-

vention by the New Yugoslav Army and counterattack by Albanian Army. That produces a variant of the Serbo-Albanian war.

3. 5 percent through 2001: Serbia, because of economic embargo and reverses in Bosnia, capitulates to ethnic Albanian demand for an Albanian autonomous province in New Yugoslavia.

Albanians in Montenegro and Macedonia request that they be included in this new republic. Look for forced emigrations in this case. If an Albanian republic is created, there's a 10 percent chance that it will remain part of Yugoslavia, a 90 percent chance that it will withdraw from the federation. It obviously isn't in Serbia's interests to make Kosovo an Albanian republic. Chances go to 50 percent either if Albania gains military or if there is a political victory per Outcome 2 of this section.

Wars of Yugoslavian Devolution

Bosnia

1. 50 percent chance through 2001: Bosnia is partitioned. Formulas of partition are very relevant, but the "51-49" (51 percent of prewar Bosnian territory for Bosnia, 49 for Bosnian Serbs, and hence Serbia) is a good possibility. It constitutes a victory for Serbia but Bosnia survives. This outcome goes to 80 percent if Bosnian Croats and Muslims form a successful Bosnian federation.

2. 20 percent chance through 2001: Serbs continue to occupy one half of prewar Bosnia. With no "federal" relationship, de facto Serb state forms (along the lines of the Turkish statelet of northern Cyprus).

3. 20 percent chance through 2001: Bosnian forces receive enough arms to drive Serbs out of all of Bosnia except areas along Serbian border.

4. 10 percent chance through 2001: Yugoslav Army intervenes and takes Sarajevo. Croatia absorbs parts of Herzegovina, and Greater Serbia absorbs the rest.

War for Macedonia

This would be a conflagration drawing in all of Macedonia's neighbors as well as outside powers. If U.S. troops remain in Macedonia, American airpower would participate. It is conceivable, though highly unlikely, that U.S. aircraft could be employed against Greek troops if Greece participated in an invasion of Macedonia.

Analyzing this war is even more highly dependent on alliances and mercurial political relationships than for other Yugoslav wars of devolution. The most likely way an "outside aggressor" could topple the Republic of Macedonia would be through sponsorship of an ethnic guerrilla war. The most likely group to stir up would be the Albanians, but the nation of Albania is the neighbor posing the least threat to Macedonia.

An outright alliance between Macedonia and one of its neighbors, say Bulgaria, would increase tensions with the other neighbors. The Macedonian policy of relying on an outside power for security guarantees (the United States as an example) makes sense. But would the United States come to Macedonia's aid if Serbia invaded, or if Greece and Serbia invaded? What would Russia do if Bulgaria invaded Macedonia? How would Russia respond if U.S. aircraft staged a Desert Storm–type bombing campaign against Serbia?

With these caveats, here's a betting line for Macedonia from 1995 to 2001. Gaming assumes that Russia offers at most rhetorical support for the invading nation (Russia could condemn invaders). Survival means a sovereign Macedon state with capital in Skopje and at least 90 percent of prewar territory.

1. Macedonia invaded by Albania: Odds of survival are 80 percent. Increase to 99.9 percent with U.S. military support.
2. Macedonia invaded by Serbia, or Greece, or Bulgaria (only one, no alliance): Odds of Macedonian survival as a state are 60 percent; 95 percent with U.S. military support.
3. Macedonia invaded by Greek-Bulgar alliance: Odds of Macedonian survival are 50 percent; 95 percent with U.S. military support.

4. Macedonia invaded by Serb-Greek, or Serb-Greek-Bulgar, alliance: Odds of Macedonian survival are 35 percent; 65 percent with U.S. support.

Serbo-Croatian War

The chance that Serbs and Croats will engage in combat between 1995 and 2001 is 100 percent. But will an all-out war of national survival erupt? The odds of this happening are small but extremely dangerous: 15 percent through 2001. As of mid-1995, Croatia was busily buying new, sophisticated weapons. If such a war erupts: 40 percent chance of Serb victory; 40 percent chance of stalemate after Serbia makes some gains along current border; 20 percent chance of Croat victory (i.e., destruction of invading Serb Army).

Peace and Prosperity Outcome. Could the South Slavs decide to beat swords into plowshares? Unlikely, but many of the Ex-Yugoslavs at one time supported the idea of a linked "free trade" zone. (Call it a Yugoslav EEC.) The odds on this occurring through 2001: 25 percent?

COST OF WAR

In the struggle pitting the Albanikos against Belgrade, there have been several hundred dead and wounded, a few thousand imprisoned, and less than $100 million of economic disruption.

In Bosnia, as of mid-1995, at least 60,000 have been killed and around 1.5 million people (Serbs, Croats, and Muslims combined) have fled into various exiles. (Press figures of 200,000 killed in Bosnia are high.) Economic losses to Serbia through 1995 may be as high as $25 billion. Destruction of property and other economic loss in Bosnia is around $20 billion; in Croatia, in the neighborhood of $5 billion.

The potential for enormous loss exists should another Balkan war break out. The Balkan peoples have historically pursued their warfare vigorously. Given the historical trends in Balkan warfare, the cost of a war would be several million dead, many millions more injured. The economic cost of a third Balkan war lasting from four to fourteen months and involving the Ex-Yugoslav nations, Albania, Greece, and Turkey could run as high as $200 billion for property destruction and lost earnings.

Dracula's War

SOURCE OF CONFLICT

There are three lingering conflicts centering on Romania. They are:

1. The Romania-Hungary tussle over the province of Transylvania. A large Hungarian (Magyar) population lives in Transylvania. Though, as of mid-1995, still a province of Romania, Transylvania has been part of Hungary.
2. The brewing trouble between Romania and Russia over Moldavia (the Republic of Moldova). "Moldavia" was part of pre–World War II Romania (Bessarabia), incorporated by Stalin into the Soviet Union.
3. Renewed civil war in Romania, between democratic forces and "new guard" members of former dictator Nicolae Ceauşescu's Securitate secret police and paramilitary forces.

WHO'S INVOLVED

The "Transylvanian War"

Hungary—Hungarians want their kinsmen in Transylvania back.

Romania—We got it; we're going to keep it no matter who lives there.

Hungarian minority in Transylvania—Doesn't want to be a battlefield, but would like to be part of Hungary once more.

Wild Cards (specific to Transylvania)

Austria—The other "half" of the Austro-Hungarian Empire.

Russia—There are troubles at home, but this fight is on Russia's front porch.

Serbia—Hungarian absorption of Transylvania might cause Budapest to look south at Vojvodina, the autonomous province with a large Hungarian minority.

Germany—A reunited Germany returns to the geopolitics of Mitteleuropa.

Moldavia—Romanians-in-waiting.

The Moldavian Crisis

Romania—Wants its kinsmen in Moldova reunited with the motherland.

Russia—Wants to protect the interests of the ethnic Russians living in Moldova; otherwise these people will flee back to a Russia that doesn't want to deal with more refugees.

Russian ultranationalists—Want Russia to regain the missing parts of the Soviet Union. Moldova is one of these missing parts.

Trans-Dniestria Republic—Home of the Fourteenth Army (up to mid-1995 commanded by General Alexander Lebed) and Russians who don't recognize Moldavia. Has become the core of the Moldovan Russians' "Republican Guard" self-defense force.

The Kremlin—Who's in charge, and how the Kremlin manages (or denies) devolution is a big key.

Wild Cards (specific to a Moldavian conflict)

Hungary—If Romania can "recover" Moldova, why can't Hungary have Transylvania back?

Germany—A reunified Germany returns to the old political crises of Mitteleuropa.

NATO—Any military action involving Russia could raise the cold war shield.

The "Second Romanian Civil War"

Securitate factions—The "state within a state" that did not go away when the Communist government fell.

Democratic Romanian dissidents—Want a democratic Romania, not one led by refried Communists.

Hungarian minorities in Transylvania—Want to be part of Hungary.

Wild Cards (specific to Romanian civil war)

Romanian fascist factions—Willing to use force to bring Moldavia back into the fold.

The neighborhood—Hungary, Bulgaria, Serbia, Russia, "Moldavians." All have reasons for getting involved, especially if it looks like there's something to be gained at little risk.

Wild Wild Card

France—The French considered sending troops to aid democratic rebels during the fighting in December 1989.

GEOGRAPHY

Hungary is a horseman's land of rolling plains and valleys edged by low mountains in the northeast and northwest. The total area is 93,000 square kilometers, or about the size of the state of Indiana. The Danube River is a major geographic feature, describing a stretch of the Czech-Hungarian border then hooking south past Budapest and continuing on into Serbia. Lake Balaton, in the middle of western Hungary, is large enough to be considered an inland sea. It is the largest landlocked stretch of water in Europe.

In 1995, Hungary has a population of around 11 million people: 91 percent of the population is ethnic "Magyar" (Hungarian—a combination of the original central Asian Magyars, plus Slavs and anyone else who wandered by). Gypsies and German ethnics account for about 3 percent each. Nearly 70 percent of the people are nominal Roman Catholics. The capital, Budapest (actually two cities, Buda and Pest), with a population of nearly 2.2 million, is the economic and cultural center of the nation. The classic political schism in Hungary pits Budapest (intellectual, cosmopolitan, influential Jewish minority, before communism regarded as wealthy) against "the countryside" (nationalist, stolid, hardworking, common sense, salt of the earth, etc.). An anti-Semitic bias has often cloaked itself in rural opposition to "Budapest elites."

Romania covers nearly 238,000 square kilometers. The country divides into "the Old Kingdom" (the land south of the Transylvanian Alps and east of the Carpathians), the northern region of Transylvania, the disputed province, and Romanian Moldavia in the northeast. The Soviet Socialist Republic of Moldavia, carved by Stalin from Romania, lies to the east. The Carpathian Mountains form a rugged, often wild and beautiful scythe cutting through Romania.

The Danube River describes the southern section of the Romanian-Yugoslav border, then continues east, separating Romania and Bulgaria. East and south of the capital of Bucharest (near Calarasi), the Danube begins to turn north and enter its expansive delta, finally wandering into the Black Sea. The central area of Romania (around Bucharest) is the heart of the old kingdom of Wallachia. The Dobruja is the area between the Danube, as it swings north to its delta, and the Black Sea. In its delta the Danube divides into three arms: the Kiliya, Sulina, and St. George.

In 1995, Romania has a population of 24 million: 87 percent are Romanian, slightly under 10 percent (around 2.3 million) are Hungarian. Most of the Hungarians live in Transylvania. A close-knit community of 200,000 ethnic Germans also live in Romania, as well as

60,000 Serbs, most of them living in Serbian villages along the Serbian border. There are also an estimated 700,000 Gypsies living in Romania. Bucharest, the capital, has around 2 million inhabitants.

The border region between Hungary and Romania—scene of any likely armed confrontation—is predominantly rolling plain. Transylvania possesses three types of country: the mountain ranges, a central plateau, and the plains around the river valleys. The Banat region has plains in the west, as it dips toward the Danube, and mountains in the east (the Szemenik and Orsova extensions of the Transylvanian Alps).

Moldova has a population of 4.5 million people. Sixty-five percent are "Moldavian" Romanian, 13 percent are Ukrainian, 13 percent are Russian. The Turkic Gaugaue people, who live in southern Moldavia, comprise under 3 percent of the population. The "Moldavian language" is a dialect of Romanian. Over 98 percent of the population is Eastern Orthodox Christian.

HISTORY

Transylvania and the Banat

In 1920, 192,000 square kilometers of the kingdom of Hungary (part of the Austro-Hungarian Empire, the big loser in World War I), which began the war with 293,000 square kilometers, was parceled out to Hungary's neighbors. The most grievous losses were Transylvania (or Erdély, as the Hungarians call it) and the Banat, which were ceded to Romania in the Treaty of Trianon (1921).

The Transylvanian region was conquered by the Romans under Trajan in A.D. 106. Between 274 (when the Romans pulled back south of the Danube) and 975, the area was overrun by numerous "barbarians"—Goths, Avars, and "Huns." Magyar (Hungarian) horsemen and the rest of the tribe arrived on the nearby Hungarian plains around 890. Hungarians maintain they first occupied Transylvania in 1009. From 1526 (the Battle of Mohács) to 1699, Transylvania was under Turkish suzerainty (and at times Romanian control, through the principality of Wallachia, a Turkish fief). In 1699 the Treaty of Karlowitz ceded Transylvania to Hungary. During the Hungarian revolution of 1848, the Vlachs (Romanians) of Transylvania failed to support Louis Kossuth and his liberals in their rebellion against the Hapsburgs. The Austrian crown took direct control of Transylvania.

The Banat region, of which Timişoara (Temesvár) is a part, is another "lost" Hungarian territory. One third of the old Banat lies in Vojvodina (in Yugoslavia, running from the present Romanian border to the Danube), the other two thirds in Romania (from the border back to the Transylvanian Alps). The Banat has a large ethnic Hungarian population. The Banat has never been an independent political unit. The Magyar tribe colonized the Banat in the late eleventh century. In 1552 the Turks conquered the Banat. Since 1718 (the Treaty of Passarowitz), the Banat has bounced between Austrian, Hungarian, Romanian, and Serbian control.

When World War I broke out, Romania remained neutral (though it was secretly a member of the Central Powers alliance). In August 1916, Romania entered the war on the side of the Entente (France, England, and Russia) and promptly invaded Transylvania. At first the Romanians made progress. But the German Balkan Army (under Erich von Flakenhayn) struck Romania from Bulgaria. The Germans rolled through Wallachia and pushed the Romanian Army back into Moldavia. Despite French efforts to reconstitute the Romanian Army, by late 1917 Romania was thoroughly demoralized. Romania concluded a peace treaty with Germany in May 1918. The peace treaty allowed for occupation of Bessarabia. Romania bided its time. In November 1918, Romania reentered the war, just in time to enjoy the collapse of the Austro-Hungarian Dual Monarchy and retake Transylvania.

The 1921 Treaty of Trianon shrunk Hungary by two thirds and put one third of Hungary's native population outside Hungarian borders. Border complaints between Hungary and Romania during the years between World Wars I and II were frequent.

The Hungarian community in Transylvania has always feared Romanian assimilation; their cousins across the border support them in their struggle. Ceauşescu's "systemization plan" was perceived as a direct attack on their identity—to "Romanianize" the Hungarian minority. The legacy of Ceauşescu is particularly bitter for the Hungarians. After the 1956 Hungarian revolt against Russia, Communist leader Gheorghiu-Dej (and later Ceauşescu) saw an opportunity. Hungarians could be singled out as both "class and national enemies." In Romanian minds, the Hungarian aristocracy had played a brutal, dominating role in Transylvania over the "landless" Romanian peasants. The Hungarians' 1956 "revolt against socialism" paved the way for "communization in Romanian garb." The Magyar autonomous region of Romania, established in 1950, was reformed and "de-Magyarized" in 1960. After Ceauşescu came to power, "anti-Magyar" policies reinforced his own peculiar brand of hard-line socialism and Romanian nationalism. Ceauşescu denounced "Hungarian revanchism" as a constant threat to both Romania and international socialism.

In the 1980s, Romanian repression of Transylvania's Hungarian community got so bad (1987) there were even rumors of a war between the then still-Communist Hungarians and the Romanians.

One continuing trouble for Hungarians in the post-Ceauşescu world is education. The Hungarians want their own schools with their own language and culture. The Hungarians believe even a post-Ceauşescu Romania is "too primitive" to become a multinational European state. At best, minorities in Romania will receive token concessions, but their rights will be trampled. The establishment of a democratic government in Hungary, formalized in 1990 but really the result of a nearly twenty-year-long Hungarian economic and social exodus from communism, makes unification with Hungary attractive.

For their part, Romanians complain that the Hungarians are arrogant and see themselves as being culturally superior—when, of course, they aren't. There is also a long historical legacy of Hungarian oppression of Romanians when Hungary possessed Transylvania. The Romanians point out Hungarian edicts promoting "Magyarization of the Vlachs" (Romanians) living in Hungarian-ruled Transylvania. Romania also makes extensive historical claims to Transylvania. Romanian histories trace their occupation back to the pre-Roman Empire Dacians and "Daco-Roman" mixed populations of intermarried Dacians and Roman legionaries and settlers. The Romanians claim that the descendants of these people were in Transylvania when the barbarian Magyars arrived on horseback. The Hungarians maintain that "the Vlachs" didn't reach Transylvania until 1175, when they were pushed out of Bulgaria. The Romanians point out that the ancient Russian chronicle ("Nestor's Chronicle") states that after the Hungarians crossed the Carpathians "they began to fight with the Wallachs and Slavs who lived there" (in Transylvania). Romanian histories also point out the existence of an anonymous Hungarian chronicle written in the twelfth century that mentions the Hungarians hearing of a Romanian leader named Gelou who ruled over Romanians and Slavs in a "land renowned for its goodness"—Transylvania. Many historical events dear to Romanian memory occurred in Transylvania.

As a nation, Romania traces its more recent roots to the late medieval principalities of Moldavia and Wallachia. In 1456 the Turks took control of Wallachia, beginning a long period of Turkish domination of the Romanian princes (*voivodes*). The greatest Wallachian prince was Michael the Brave of Wallachia (ruled from 1593 to 1601). He twice defeated the Turks, gaining more autonomy for Wallachia, and also took control of all of Transylvania. The most famous prince of Wallachia was Vlad Tepes (1456–1462, better known as Count Dracula), who impaled his enemies on stakes. Tradition has it that Bran Castle, in Transylvania, was his home. The Moldavian prince, Stephen the Great (1458–1504), stopped three Turk invasions during his reign and at one time tried to organize an alliance of "the Christian nations and Persia" against Turkey. After Stephen's death, however, the Turks forced the Moldavians to submit. From 1714 to 1822 (the Phanariote period), Turkey administered Wallachia and Moldavia through Greeks of the Phanar (lighthouse) Quarter of Constantinople. This Greek "nobility" acted as a tax collector for the Turks.

France became diplomatically active in Romania in the late eighteenth century. In the nineteenth century, Napoleon III favored a "free Romania" as a "Latin" state in the Balkans. In 1859, Alexander Cuza was elected prince by the Moldavian and Wallachian assemblies. He formed the new nation of Romania. Romania didn't gain formal independence from Turkey until May 1877.

Romanian Civil War

Romania was something of a maverick in the old Warsaw Pact camp. Soviet troops pulled out in 1958 and Ceauşescu removed Romania from some of the Warsaw Pact's military commitments. That gave him a political card to play in the West.

Ceauşescu also pursued a radical, go-it-alone economic program. While he and his cohorts lived in luxury (and hid gold in Switzerland), Ceauşescu kept the countryside impoverished by exporting everything of value. Ironically, in the post–cold war ecopolitical environment, Ceauşescu's ruthless program has left Romania with one slight economic advantage—there is little foreign debt. However, there is also little of anything.

In December 1989, Romania caught the revolutionary tide sweeping Eastern Europe. Between December 12 and 17, protests broke out in Timişoara. They seemed to spontaneously spread across the country. Coverage on Serbian and Hungarian television of the troubles in Timişoara appear to have given many Romanians hope that a rebellion could succeed. Ceauşescu reacted and sent the Romanian Army and the Securitate military units into action. Elements in the army balked. Soon combat broke out in all of the major cities. For what are still obscure reasons, the Ceauşescus decided to leave Bucharest. They were captured. On Christmas Day, 1989, the Ceauşescus were tried by a tribunal and executed.

Power in Romania fell into the hands of what appeared to be a broad popular coalition, the National Salvation Front. The NSF included many dissidents, "anti-Ceauşescu" Communists, and a smattering of religious leaders.

Since the fall of Ceauşescu, many Romanian democrats (and many sympathizers in the West) have come to believe that the "revolutionary momentum" created by those first haphazard protests—and those were genuine, democratic protests—was used as an opportunity to execute a long-planned anti-Ceauşescu coup orchestrated by anti-Ceauşescu members of the Securitate. The protests in Timişoara moved up the timetable for the coup and gave the anti-Ceaușescu elements of the secret police a convenient democratic cover.

Many dissident and democratic elements of the NSF left or were forced out of the coalition in the first months of 1990. The "hardline" members of the NSF bused in counterdemonstrators to break up dissident rallies. When democrats asked for laws banning members of the Securitate from running for office for at least ten years, NSF hardliners (many of them suspected Securitate agents) shelved the requests. The 1990 Romanian elections, while nominally open and free, put the NSF in firm control of the Romanian government. Continued protests and work stoppages afflict the government. In October 1990, President Ion Iliescu confirmed that a number of "former" Securitate agents were still running "technical operations" in his government.

From 1991 to 1993, Romania went into a severe economic slide. Roads and other public infrastructure have deteriorated. In the 1992 elections Iliescu won over 60 percent of the vote.

The Moldavian Problem

Moldavia (now Moldova) was formerly the fruit-growing Romanian region of Bessarabia. Bessarabia was part of the Romanian principality of Moldavia. It was taken by Russia in 1812. Parts of the region were returned to Moldavia in 1856, but were given back to Moscow in 1878 at the Congress of Berlin. Out of the chaos of World War I and the collapse of the Russian czar, a democratic Moldavian Republic was founded in 1917 by democratic, anti-Bolshevik Romanians. That led to voluntary union with Romania in April 1918 (though some historians and many Russians question the degree of "volunteerism," given the presence of Romanian Army units in Bessarabia). In 1924 the Bolsheviks established the "Autonomous Moldavian Soviet Socialist Republic" as part of the Ukraine SSR—in part as an objection to incorporating Bessarabia into post–World War I Romania. The "puppet province" was used as a base for propaganda operations and covert activities inside Romania. Russia invaded and annexed the whole of Bessarabia in 1940 and began a process of "Russification." Romania briefly retook the region after the Nazi invasion of the USSR in 1941, but the Red Army returned in 1944 and eventually took the whole of Romania.

In 1990 the name of the main boulevard in Kishinev, the Moldavian capital, was changed from Lenin Street to Stefan (Stephen) the Great Street, memorializing that great Romanian (Moldovan?) leader. In 1991, Moldavia formally withdrew from the Soviet Union and renamed itself Moldova.

In 1992 ethnic Russian agitation led to the creation of the "Trans-Dniestria Republic." This breakaway fragment of Moldova contains most of the Russian ethnics in Moldova. (Russians and Ukrainians comprise over 25 percent of the Moldovan population.) The former Fourteenth Soviet Army, consisting of between 10,000 and 20,000 troops, remained to protect the Russian enclave. Despite orders to withdraw and disband, the Fourteenth Army remained in place (see Local Politics). Some Moldovan (and Romanian) ultranationalists are demanding the return of "Bessarabian areas" ceded to the Ukraine by the Soviet Union.

LOCAL POLITICS

Hungary

Hungarian Democratic Forum (HDF)—Center-right party, regarded as the largest party in Hungary. The nationalist platform plays well outside of Budapest, but the party describes itself as a "European center party" eschewing rabid nationalism. Leader is longtime Hungarian anti-Communist dissident (and participant in the 1956 revolt) Jozsef Antall.

Alliance of Free Democrats—Pro-Western party; core of party is the old Budapest-based dissident movement.

Federation of Young Democrats—Small party allied with Alliance of Free Democrats.

Independent Smallholders party—Hungarian agrarian reform party. A revival of the old Smallholders party, which won 58 percent of the vote in the 1945 election; it was suppressed by the Communists. Advocates returning to the former owners all property confiscated by the Communists.

Christian Democrat party—Center-right party generally supportive of Democratic Forum.

Hungarian Socialist Workers party (HSWP)—Debunked Hungarian Communist party. It reorganized as Hungarian Socialist party (Magyar Szocialista party); took 10 percent of the vote in 1990 elections.

Louis Kossuth—Nineteenth-century Hungarian liberal nationalist (of Sovakian origin); led failed 1848 revolt against Hapsburgs.

Szentkorona orszagai—Lands of the Holy Crown of Saint Stephen. Refers to "historic Hungary" (Hungary minus Croatia and Slavonia) as it existed prior to 1918. He who wears "the Holy Crown of Saint Stephen" is king of Hungary. That crown was worn by the Hapsburgs from 1527 to 1918.

Green Shirts—Storm troopers of Hungarian fascism during the 1930s and 1940s. Wore crossed arrows (the Arrow Cross) instead of a swastika. The Arrow Cross became a leading fascist party.

Hungarian splinter "nativist groups"—National Conservative Thinking Boys, 1956 Anti-Fascist and Anti-Bolshevik Association.

Battle of Nicopolis—Occurred in 1396. Invading Turks defeated King Sigismund of Hungary.

Romania

National Salvation Front (NSF)—Group behind the Council of National Salvation. At first seemingly a broad coalition, one month after the revolt NSF leaders decided to participate in "elections" as a party rather than as a transition government. Now accused of being "neo-Communists." Led by Ion Iliescu, a "former" Communist.

Convention for Democracy—Opposition umbrella organization. Core consists of Liberal and National Peasants party members and Civic Alliance civil rights group.

Union of Democratic Magyars—Ethnic Hungarian opposition party.

Opposition parties—National Peasants party, National Liberal party, Democratic Party of Romania. The Peasants party and National

Liberal party advocate privatization and a free market economy. The Greater Romania party is an anti-Semitic political organization; the splinter Romanian National Unity party operates as an anti-Hungarian party.

Romanian Workers party—Old Romanian Communist party. Its Political Executive Committee was the equivalent of the Politburo.

Ceauşescus—Nicolae and Elena, the old bosses, are dead. Nick was one of the worst dictators on the planet, but when it came to sheer totalitarian cunning, Elena may have had it up on him. Elena served as deputy prime minister and was in charge of party personnel assignments. In the "trial video" made by their executioners, Elena scolds her "children" (the Securitate) for trying them. This leads critics of the National Salvation Front to conclude that the "revolution" really was an inside job. The genetic Ceauşescu kids are still around: son Nicu, playboy and former Communist chief in Sibiu; daughter Zoya, a mathematician; and son Valentin, a physicist.

"Systemization plan"—Ceauşescu's plan for eliminating thousands of Romanian villages and moving their inhabitants to large apartments—his version of modernization and indoctrination. Ceauşescu had targeted eight thousand villages. Hungarians in Transylvania felt the plan was primarily aimed at eradicating their culture. Several villages with buildings dating from the thirteenth century were razed before the December 1989 revolt halted the program.

King Michael—Romanian monarch toppled by Communists in 1947. Exiled in Switzerland; in 1990, wanted to make a comeback.

The Iron Guard—Fascist movement, active in Romania prior to and during World War II. Headquarters was the notorious "Green House" in Bucharest.

Dealul Spirei—Hill in Bucharest where the old national parliament buildings stand.

Transylvania

Hungarian Democratic Union—Represents Hungarians in Romania. In 1990, claimed 650,000 members.

Vatra Romaneascea (Romanian Hearth)—Political group that seeks to defend and protect Romanian culture in Transylvania.

Reverend Lazlo Tokes—Timişoaran Reform Church minister who organized protests against Ceauşescu regime; his courage was instrumental in starting the popular revolt. Tokes is an ethnic Hungarian.

Moldova

Christian Democratic Popular Front—Former Moldavian Popular Front, a coalition front from Moldavian dissident and nationalist groups that took control of Moldavian parliament in 1989; many members support "reunification" with Romania. One of the party's chief aims is to reestablish the Latin alphabet. By the fall of 1990 most of the street and road signs in the major cities were "dual language"— the names were found in both Cyrillic and Latin.

Agrarian Democratic party—Populist nationalist party.

Moldavian language laws—Passed in 1989, they require that Moldavian be written in the Latin alphabet (like Romanian), not in Russian Cyrillic script, and that by 1994 Russian speakers holding leading governmental positions must learn Moldavian or lose their jobs.

Gagauze—Small Turkic-language-speaking minority living in Moldavia.

Trans-Dniestria Republic—Self-proclaimed Russian state in Moldova. Occupied by remnant Fourteenth Army. In early 1996, voted to set up its own parliament and seek membership in Russia's Commonwealth of Independent States.

POLITICAL TREND CHARTS

HUNGARY

Gv95	Gv20	PC95	PC20	R95	R20	Ec95	Ec20	EdS95	EdS20
ED5,5	RD6,7	7	7+	4	4	4	6	6	6

Gv = Government Type
ED = "Evolving" Democracy (effectiveness, 0–9, stability 0–9)
RD = Representative Democracy
PC = Political Cohesiveness (0 = chaos, 9 = maximum)
R = Repression Index (9 = maximum)
Ec = Comparative Economic Status (0–9)
EdS = Relative Education Status (0–9); in this case, urban population only

"GREATER HUNGARY"
(HUNGARY PLUS TRANSYLVANIA)

Gv20	PC20	R20	Ec20	EdS20
AD5,4	4	5	4	5

AD = Authoritarian Democracy

ROMANIA

Gv95	Gv20	PC95	PC20	R95	R20	Ec95	Ec20	EdS95	EdS20
AC3,4	AC4,5	4	4	7	7	3−	3	4	4

AC = Authoritarian Coalition

PARTICIPANT STRATEGIES AND GOALS

Hungary—Hungary's chief strategy is to build a strong economy and shake off the rust and ruin of communism. Hungary has already begun to shrink its army and free up its economy. But ties to Transylvania loom large; Transylvania is a "lost half" of Hungary, and the travails of the Hungarian community in Romania are felt as well as heard. Hungary has reoriented its army to face Romania. A peaceful solution, freedom and democracy in Romania for Romanians as well as Hungarians, is much preferred. In the long term a plebiscite in Transylvania regarding minority rights and even border "adjustments" is a Hungarian goal. Would Hungary go to war over Hungarian ethnic rights in Transylvania? Hungarians point out that they were the only nation that openly revolted against the Russians (1956).

REGIONAL POWERS AND POWER INTEREST INDICATOR CHARTS

TRANSYLVANIA WAR

	Economic Interests	Historical Interests	Political Interest	Military Interest	Force Generation Potential	Ability to Intervene Politically
Hungary	8	9	9	9	5	9
Romania	9	9	9	9	6	9
Russia	3	8	8	9	9	5
United States	3	5	8	7	4	6
Germany	6	8	8	7	2	6
"Yugo"	3	6	8	6	2	2
Serbia	3	8	9	8	2	2

NOTE: 0 = minimum; 9 = maximum

MOLDOVAN WAR

	Economic Interests	Historical Interests	Political Interest	Military Interest	Force Generation Potential	Ability to Intervene Politically
Russia	8	8	9	9	9	9
Romania	9	9	9	9	5−	8
Hungary	5	8	8	8	2−	5
United States	2	3	8	7	4	6
Germany	6	8	9	8	3	7
Poland	4	8	9	7	1−	3

ROMANIAN CIVIL WAR

	Economic Interests	Historical Interests	Political Interest	Military Interest	Force Generation Potential	Ability to Intervene Politically	Interest/ Ability to Promote Economic Development
Hungary	7	9	8	8	2	6	3
Serbia	5	8	8	8	2	2	1
Bulgaria	4	8	9	8	2	3	1
Russia	6	7	8	8	9	6	2
United States	2	3	5	4	4	4	4
Germany	4	6	7	6	2	5	7
France	3	6	6	3	2	5	6

Hungarian community in Transylvania—A new "Magyar Autonomous Region" still politically attached to Romania might work out, *if* Romania becomes a democracy.

Romania—Even in a democratic Romania the debate over "who lost Transylvania" would be traumatizing; the "guilty" party or leaders would be politically (or literally) dead. A totalitarian or authoritarian regime would fan the flames of nationalism by making Transylvania a constant issue. It helps keep the starving populace thinking about something besides their stomachs. Still, under a stable and democratic government some compromise is possible, including a plebiscite.

Romanian dissidents—They don't want to be portrayed as the people responsible for "losing Transylvania," but the core leadership sees "Euro-freedom" as the wave of the future—if the future can only penetrate Romania's borders. The trick is to keep political pressure on the NSF, using appeals to international opinion and acquiring the support of the West. The Convention for Democracy organization is certain the NSF subverted the 1989 revolution and is trying to tell the world.

Russian ultranationalists—Support for Russian populations in "near abroad" regions like Moldova is key to rebuilding the empire.

NATO (Germany and the West)—Economic redevelopment in Eastern Europe requires stability. Irredentism in a key East European nation like Hungary would negatively affect economic recovery and investment.

POTENTIAL OUTCOMES

Transylvania

1. 50 percent chance through 2001: No conflict; Transylvania remains part of Romania. Ethnic fractions continue. Still, the situation is tolerable in comparison with the past.
2. 20 percent chance through 2001: New "Magyar Autonomous Region" inside Romania is established. All but most radical elements of Hungarian ethnics are politically satisfied and turn to economic restructuring.
3. 15 percent chance through 2001: Democratic plebiscite is conducted in Transylvania. Some "border adjustments" occur. Odds increase to 25 percent if Hungarian economy prospers and Hungary can provide economic aid to Romania. Incorporation of parts of Moldavia SSR into Romania also positively affects this outcome.

4. 10 percent chance through 2001: Hard-line elements in Romanian regime crack down on dissidents and democrats. Russian attack on Romania, or chaos caused by civil war, sparks Hungarian occupation of Transylvania to "protect" ethnic Hungarians. Hungary takes Timişoara and border regions and holds them. Negotiations stop war. Border readjustments occur.

5. 5 percent chance through 2001: Romanian civil war occurs and Hungary does not occupy Transylvania. Ethnic tensions in region increase.

Second Romanian Civil War

1. 45 percent chance through 2001: NSF (old Securitate forces) maintains power and becomes increasingly authoritarian. Dissident activity is repressed but not eliminated. Elections are controlled so that the NSF holds majority power.

2. 20 percent chance through 2001: Soft-line leadership in NSF moves Romania toward democracy; repression level drops; economy improves. Successful negotiations with Russia over Moldavian autonomy improve popularity of regime.

3. 15 percent chance through 2001: The Transylvanian war kicks off and the hard-line element of the NSF assumes control. Martial law inside Romania, which conveniently continues after the fighting in Transylvania stops.

4. 10 percent chance through 2001: Fighting between NSF supporters and dissidents provokes new civil war. Romanian Army splits. Old Securitate elements reemerge. If this event occurs and there is no outside intervention, there's a 60 percent chance of hard-liner (totalitarian) victory, 40 percent chance of dissident victory. If outside intervention (in order of likelihood, France, United Nations, Germany/NATO, Russia) occurs, which places foreign troop units in Bucharest, chance of dissident victory jumps to 85 percent.

5. 5 percent chance through 2001: Democratic parties assume power through a free election. "Reforming" Securitate forces accept results. Hard-line hidden Securitate, however, attempts the Sandinista tactic of "rule from below." Democratic government is highly un-

stable. The possible trade-off: no prosecutions of old Communists and Securitate forces for past crimes.

6. 5 percent chance through 2001: War or "war tension" with Russia over Moldova leads to collapse of Romanian government. Civil war erupts. Same odds on civil war as Outcome 4.

Moldova

1. 75 percent chance through 2001: Moldova maintains independence, Russian Army continues to occupy Trans-Dniestria and it functions, quietly, as a separate Russian enclave inside Moldova. War with Russia is avoided. Increased economic cooperation with Romania.

2. 10 percent chance through 2001: Ultranationalists gain control in Moscow. Kremlin acts under pretext of "preserving Russian and Ukrainian rights" in Moldova and invades. After a bitter Chechnya-style fight, Moldovans flee for Romania. A new "Moldavian state" is incorporated as a Russian enclave.

3. 10 percent chance through 2001: Moldova "splits," with the "Russified" area of Moldova (east of Kishinev and along the Dniester River) becoming a Russian statelet and the western half joining Romania.

4. 5 percent chance through 2001: War erupts and pits Russia against Romania. A 90 percent chance that the war ends in negotiated settlement.

KIND AND COST OF WAR

The Romanian revolution of 1989 was partially propelled by lurid stories of thousands of protesters shot dead in the streets. The reality was hundreds of dead. Still grim, but at least demonstrating that people have enough sense to leave the area when someone starts shooting. Neither country has particularly large or lethal armed forces. Poverty and Russian paranoia have kept the local arms holdings modest. Both nations are letting their armed forces waste away so the funds saved can be spent on economic revival. Still, a war between Hungary and Romania would be an ugly affair, no matter how ill-trained, ill-armed, or plain inept most of the troops would be. The death toll, including civilians caught in the crossfire, could easily go into the hundreds of thousands before one side prevailed. Intervention by other European nations to stop the fighting is possible, which would add to the losses. The economic losses would be even more devastating and, worst of all, an attempt at a military solution, no matter what the outcome, would not solve the problem. Only a genocide (not unknown in this part of the world) or a mass population transfer (also a familiar sight) would settle the issue, more or less, in the long term. A war would probably be preceded by some terrorism, and repression, in Transylvania. The losses here would be in the thousands, but that would only get everyone's blood up for a larger war.

Transylvania is not great tank country. Given the rough terrain and forests, war in Transylvania would most likely become a nasty infantry shoving match. The area is better suited for terrorists and guerrillas. There are plenty of places to hide.

QUICK LOOK: Balkan Irredentism; the Third Balkan War

How far does the pie go? Better to ask, how many ways can you cut a peninsula and parts of central Europe. Here are some of the claims and counterclaims on land in the Balkan region. The first and second Balkan wars were fought in 1912 and 1913 over these issues. We've tried to be thorough without becoming trivial.

Bulgaria—Claims parts of Grecian (western) Thrace, Turkish (eastern) Thrace, Grecian Macedonia, and Yugoslavian Macedonia. Bulgaria also believes parts of the southern Romanian coast are more properly placed in Bulgaria.

Greece—Claims parts of southern Albania and some islands in the Adriatic near Albania. There are latent claims to Yugoslav Macedonia; latent claims to a slice of Bulgaria going toward the Black Sea. Greece covets eastern Thrace, and its stifled claims against Turkey outside of the Balkans (but close at hand) are numerous.

Romania—Claims slices of Serbian border area; claims the whole of Moldova and part of the Black Sea coastline south of Moldova. In 1913, Romania and Bulgaria fought over Silistra regarding the Dobruja frontier.

Austria—After a visit to the irredentist dentist, old Hapsburgians look fondly at Slovenia (called Ljubljana Laibach) and Austria's missing seaport, Trieste. Don't raise the question of the Sud Tirol with Italy, but that's getting out of the Balkans.

Italy—Latent claims to Fiume and Spaiato, Italian until 1945, and Dalmatian (Yugoslav) coast based on Venetian control.

Albania—Kosovo Province in Yugoslavia (Serbia). Claims against Montenegro: region around Lake Scutari (Skadarsko); the old port of Ulcinj, which Albanians believe was swiped from them by British and Montenegrin intrigue in the early 1880s.

Hungary—Wants to protect Hungarians in Transylvania and the Banat. Perhaps the best protection is making Transylvania part of a democratic Hungary? Also, latent troubles with Serbia (Yugoslavia) over the Vojvodina (Bachka and that half of the Banat). Ready for a big stretch? Austria received the Bergenland when the Dual Monarchy was cut up, but that's not a picked-over bone anymore, and that really is out of the Balkans, isn't it?

Turkey—Kemal Atatürk forswore irredentism, but . . . well, the Balkans were Ottoman lands . . . Bulgaria, Greece, Albania, the squabbling Yugoslav provinces, and Hungary. And in the seventeenth century Turkish troops marched right up to the walls of Vienna. But that's getting out of the Balkans again.

EX-YUGOSLAV CLAIMS BROKEN DOWN

Serbia and Montenegro—Kosovo Province is the "old core" of Serbia and must remain so; the Vojvodina belongs to Serbia and possibly the old "Baranya" county around the city of Pecs in Hungary (an area of heterogeneous population occupied by Serbia at the end of World War I). Slices of Romania are inhabited by Serbs—border readjustments there. Bosnia, because of "geopolitical realities," is Serbian; if pressed, Serbian nationalists believe all of Macedonia (including the part currently "occupied" by Bulgaria) should be "Yugoslavian" (and later, Serbian). Finally, those troublesome Croats tend to oppress Serbs. Parts of Croatia are more properly Serbian.

Bosnia—Sandzak area of Montenegro (inhabited by Muslims) should not be part of either Serbia or Montenegro.

Slovenia—"Segments of the Istrian coast" (including Trieste?) should belong to Slovenia. If pushed, there's always the subject of Carinthia, the region around Klagenfurt in Austria. That was a biggie issue at the Paris Peace Conference in 1919. Slovenes believe Italy's control of Trieste is not quite proper. U.S. forces had to keep the Yugoslavs and Italians apart after World War II in this area.

Croatia—Bosnia is Croatian. The Montenegrin coastline more properly belongs to Croatia. And the Slovenes are wrong; actually, Trieste belongs to Croatia.

Macedonia—When Macedonia was part of Yugoslavia, Macedonia claimed "parts of Macedonia now in Bulgaria."

EXTENDED LOOK: Greece and Bulgaria

The rather extensive chapter that follows, detailing Turkey and its problems, includes much of the information dealing with a potential "Greco-Bulgarian alliance." This "extended look" provides further background for the material covered in the chapters on Turkey and the Balkans.

GEOGRAPHY

Greece

Greece, at the bottom of the Balkans, is a land of mountains tumbling into the sea. Eighty percent of the nation's 133,000 square-kilometer surface is covered by mountains and rugged hills. Greece also has nearly 2,000 islands, though fewer than 180 of them are inhabited year round. Greece has no navigable rivers, but does boast this interesting bit of geographic trivia: No point in Greece is more than 100 kilometers from the sea. With little arable land, it is no wonder Greeks go to sea. Greece has one of the world's largest merchant navies.

Greece has nine geographic regions. In the north, running from west to east, Epirus, Macedonia, and (Western) Thrace are the Balkan borderlands. Mainland Greece consists of Thessaly, central Greece (Attica), and the Peloponnesian Peninsula. Insular Greece consists of the Ionian Islands in the Adriatic (along the west coast from Albania to the Peloponnesus), the Aegean Islands between Greece and Turkey, and Crete.

Greece has a population of around 10 million people. Over 95 percent of the people are ethnic Greeks. Greeks overwhelmingly belong to the Greek Orthodox Church. There are 40,000 Slavic speakers in Greek Macedonia. In late 1994, Greek estimates put 150,000 Albanian immigrants in Greece.

Bulgaria

Bulgaria covers 110,000 square kilometers. About 75 percent of the land is covered by mountains and rugged hills. There are three comparatively distinct regions: the Danube River "tablelands" in the north along the Romanian border, the Stara Planina Mountains in the middle, and the Thracian Plain and Rhodope and Pirin mountains along the frontier with Turkey and Greece.

Bulgaria has a population of 9 million people. Eighty-five percent are Bulgars, 9 percent are ethnic Turks. Most Bulgars belong to the Bulgarian Orthodox Church.

HISTORY

Greece

Greece, the "cradle of Western civilization," managed to escape the "Ottoman yoke" in 1824 and reestablish itself as an independent nation. Greek memories of Turkish domination are bitter. Turk control

of Constantinople, seat of the patriarch of the Greek (Eastern) Orthodox Church, is, to many Greeks, a fresh wound. Greek city-states
flowered in the fifth and fourth centuries B.C., spotting Greek trading
colonies from the Black Sea to the Pillars of Hercules (Gibraltar). The
height of Greek power, however, was "Hellenized" Byzantium. The
Eastern Roman Empire, with its capital at Constantinople, evolved
into a Greek-speaking, Greek-dominated state.

Recent Greek history centers around the trauma of the army coup
(in cahoots with the EENA, the National Union of Young Officers) in
April 1967 that put in power the notorious "colonels regime," led by
George Papadopoulos. The "colonels" fell in 1974 after Turkey's invasion of Cyprus. To some extent the rampant scandal and theft of
the PASOK government during the 1980s was tolerated because the
socialists were viewed as heroes who stood up to "the colonels." In
the mid-1990s, Greece is heading for an internal political shakeout.
Both the PASOK and New Democracy parties are riddled with corruption and tied to aging economic interests.

Bulgaria

Bulgars first appeared in the Balkans around A.D. 650. In 809 the
Bulgarian Prince Krum besieged Constantinople and ravaged Grecian
lands. In 893, Czar Simeon established the first Bulgarian Empire. Simeon was "Czar of the Bulgarians and Autocrat of the Greeks"; his
empire included much of Serbia. After his death the empire began to
unravel. In 1014, Basil the Bulgar Slayer (Boulgaroktonos) overthrew
Czar Samuel. Byzantium made Bulgaria a Greek dependency. In 1186
the Bulgars rebelled and established a second empire. In 1330 the Bulgars were defeated by the Serbs (Battle of Küstendil) and became a
Serbian principality. Then the Turks started to arrive. In 1393 the
Turks took Trnovo and five centuries of Turkish domination began.

Unlike Russia's other neighbors, Bulgaria looks upon the Musco-
vites as longtime allies and friends. That's because in 1878 (as a result
of the Russo-Turkish War of 1877) the Russians liberated Bulgaria
("the Principality of Bulgaria" and "Eastern Rumelia") from that bit-
terest of enemies, Turkey. Though to be technically accurate, Bulgaria

remained under nominal Turkish suzerainty until October 6, 1908. Like Russian, the written Bulgarian language uses Cyrillic script.

During the twentieth century, Turkey has continued to be a focal point of Bulgarian thinking. The Bulgarians remember the Turks' harsh rule. Many Bulgarian nationalists believe that Thrace (Western and Eastern) is more properly Bulgarian territory, and for short periods during this century (Balkan wars, World War II) Bulgaria has held parts of Thrace with an outlet to the Aegean Sea. During the headier days of the Warsaw Pact, Bulgaria was supposed to be the USSR's jumping-off point for the invasion of Turkey. Forget ideology and pap about "defending socialism"; an invasion of Turkey fit well with Bulgarian historical politics. From 1977 to 1987, Bulgaria spent nearly 7 percent of its meager GNP on defense. The Bulgarian Navy was built to provide amphibious lift for Warsaw Pact forces on assaulting the Turkish Straits. The Black Sea ports of Burgas and Varna were expanded to facilitate rapid "through put" of Soviet troops heading south. Though the Warsaw Pact is militarily bankrupt, these facilities are still in place.

In 1984, Bulgarian Communist leader Tidor Zhikov began an anti-Turkish policy of enforced "Bulgarization." He banned the Turkish language. Turkish names were Slavicized (Mehmet becomes Mikhail).

The Greek state of Macedonia and the Macedonian Republic also loom large in the minds and long memories of those who dream of a Greater Bulgaria.

In the revolutions of 1989, the Bulgarian Communist government of Zhikov collapsed. In December 1989 the anti-Turk policies were renounced by the new government. Still, in January 1990 some ten thousand Bulgars in the city of Kurdjali protested the decision to reverse the discriminatory policies. Bulgarian Communists, unlike those in Hungary, Poland, Czechoslovakia, and East Germany, haven't received as much blame for Bulgaria's economic and political failure. They retained power during free elections in mid-1990.

In 1986, Greece and Bulgaria signed a "declaration of friendship." This has since been expanded. In early 1990, Greece and Bulgaria began to discuss a mutual defense pact. The mutual threat? Turkey. Other contingencies? Macedonia.

Both Greece and Bulgaria, however, have seen good reason to cooperate with Turkey economically. Greece dropped its opposition to Turkey's admission to the EEC customs union. Greek business interests have moderated Greek ultranationalists' policies toward Macedonia. Peace benefits the pocketbook—but in the Balkans, old, dark passions rarely fade.

LOCAL POLITICS

Greece

New Democracy party (Nea Demokratia)—Greek center-right party.

Panhellenic Socialist Movement (Panhellinon Socialistiko Kinima, hence PASOK)—Greek socialist party.

Democratic Initiative party—Formed by ex-PASOK members; advocates a decentralized, mixed economy.

Democratic Center Union—Democratic socialist party.

Democratic Renewal party—Center-right party.

Communist Party of Greece.

Greek National Political Society (EPEN)—Ultra-right-wing organization.

Synaspismos—Leftist, non-Communist "movement"; hopes to build idyllic Greek socialist state.

Megali Idea (the Great Idea)—Greek ultranationalist hope to recover the lands of Greek Byzantium.

Plaka—Nightclub district of Athens; area where (allegedly) the real governmental decisions are made.

Bulgaria

Socialist party—New name for old (and disgraced) Bulgarian Communist party.

Union of Democratic Forces—Coalition group of anti-Stalinist forces; active in toppling Zhivkov regime; now main opposition "party" to Socialist party. Some Bulgarian Turks are active in the party.

Movement for Rights and Freedoms—Bulgarian Turk party.

Podkrepa—"Support," a pre-1989 revolution group of trade unionists loosely modeled after Poland's Solidarity.

Tidor Zhivkov—Stalinist leader who ruled Bulgaria for thirty-five years; overthrown in 1989.

Bulgarian Turks—Approximately 1 million in number; 330,000 Bulgarian Turks went to Turkey during the anti-Turk reparations.

Kozloduy—Decaying nuclear power plant that at one time supplied one third of Bulgaria's electricity.

Saints Cyril and Methodius—Converted the Bulgars to Christianity around A.D. 860. Invented Cyrillic script.

POLITICAL TRENDS CHARTS

GREECE

Gv95	Gv20	PC95	PC20	R95	R20	Ec95	Ec20	EdS95	EdS20
RD4,3	RD5,6	7+	8	4	3−	4+	6*	5+	6

RD = Representative Democracy, but with very authoritarian aspects, especially if PASOK (Greek Socialist party) is in power (effectiveness, 0–9, stability 0–9)

*Assumes no war and government pursues competition-oriented economic policies and gets control of inflation.

"GREATER GREECE"

"Hellenic Greece"—This is your ultra-Greek nationalist fantasy state. It comprises all of Thrace, including Constantinople; parts of Ionia around Smyrna and north to the Dardanelles; Cyprus and all of the Aegean Islands. The likelihood of this state existing in 2001 is virtually nil. The dream, however, exists and the dream is not a joke.

Gv20	PC20	R20	Ec20	EdS20
AD4,3	4−	7*	2−†	6

AD = Authoritarian Democracy (democracy for Greeks, authoritarian for Turks)

*Repression inside former Turkish mainland territory would be an 8+.

†Economy would be beggared by war and military expenditures.

BULGARIA

Gv95	Gv20	PC95	PC20	R95	R20	Ec95	Ec20	EdS95	EdS20
AD3,4	AD4,5	6	6	5	5	3	3+	4	4

AD = Authoritarian Democracy

"GREATER BULGARIA"
(BULGARIA PLUS MACEDONIA)

Gv20	PC20	R20	Ec20	EdS20
AO4,3	3	8	2−	4−

AO = Authoritarian Oligarchy (a Bulgarian grab of Macedonia would lead to militarization and probable martial law in Bulgaria)

QUICK LOOK: European Tribes: The Mosaic of the EEC, the Mosaic of Europe

As this book is written, in 1995, the "economic and political unification" of the European Economic Community (EEC) is well under way. The trend in Western Europe has been toward increasing political, economic, social, and cultural cooperation. Military cooperation within NATO and the now increasingly active Western European Union (WEU), political and economic cooperation within the EEC, and five decades of comparative Western political and economic success have led to a relaxation (and perhaps erasure) of old antagonisms and made for a climate of integration and peace. Mikhail Gorbachev, the last leader of the Soviet Union, spoke of a "common European house" where the integrative trend (and political and economic success) of the EEC ultimately moves east.

But Europe is a quilt of history—the cultural and tribal fabrics are many, and the tribal flags still dot the landscape. The flags may fly over old and rotting castles, but they remain. There are numerous examples of unresolved and historical rivalries in virtually all of the current European states, east and west, north and south. Ethnic and historical realities still have the ability to create a war of words which radicals can turn into a war of bombs, bullets, and civil conflict.

The map of Europe shows central states, but certain populations beg—and sometimes shoot—to differ. This is a dispute that is over two thousand years old; there will never be an end to this.

Local European issues can ignite large European wars. World War I is an ideal example. Ethnic nationalism in the Balkans put the fuse to a Europe primed for armed conflict. Often the local issues that set fire to a region appear to be petty grievances, like demands for use of a language or local autonomy for an ethnic group no one has heard of since the Middle Ages. It leads one to conclude that the Middle Ages are still with us.

They are. Europe, like the rest of the world, is inhabited by tribes, lots of them, some very large (perhaps 150 million Russian Slavs), and some very small (25,000-plus Slavic Wends outside Berlin, for example).

What is a "tribe"? One definition is, ethnic group. Who is a member of an ethnic group? Almost anybody who says he or she is. Ethnic groups identify themselves by:

1. A relationship (usually involving oppression) with another ethnic group that says, "You are different from us."
2. Shared religious beliefs.
3. Shared linguistic heritages (sometimes the same language but different dialects).
4. Historical identification, often involving a "golden age." Almost without exception, each of Europe's unassimilated groups can look back into history and find a gilded era when it was in control of the countryside. History somehow went wrong.

Today some tribes form "nation-states" by reaching a consensus based on geographic, economic, historic, or ethnic considerations. Generally, these tribes finished fighting in so distant a past that everyone has forgotten who killed whose cousin. There is also a second group: those recently at war in which the bloodshed was so bitterly exhausting that the tribal councils are resigned to cooperation. Other tribes form their states—and keep them—with armed force (until 1990, Russia and South Africa were good examples). If the dominant tribe slips up, rebellion results.

Europe's tribes are still trying to sort themselves out politically. This is a dangerous business, especially when Germans get involved. German political reunification, completed in October 1990 when West Germany absorbed East Germany into a new federal republic, is an example of the consolidation and integration. Many people, however, are not overcome with joy at Germany's reunification. Poland, France, the United Kingdom, Holland, and Russia all have reservations. The "German problem" may finally be on the road to some resolution, but don't quite bet on it. The "German problem" has been with us for centuries. German politics—in large measure, the Germans attempt to sort their various states into a German nation—have directly or indirectly been the cause of most European wars since the first century A.D. The Slavs, principally the Russians, have lost over fifty million lives to the various German Reichs. Russian antipathy toward Germany is based on long-standing fears of German *Drang nach Osten,* movement to the east. A lot of folks (and *Volks*) are betting that West Germany's association with the West (i.e., long-time occupation by the United States) has given the Germans a solidifying dose of democracy.

Is it a good bet? Western humanists would like to think that democracies are immune to the various tribal diseases. The idea is that democracies stage planned rebellions, called elections, that seek to reestablish the consensus. This works to some extent, but the demands of ethnic groups are sometimes very difficult to accommodate. The new Germany may succeed, but other European nations, Russia as the extreme example, face stupefying odds.

Sometimes accommodation is possible. Take the United Kingdom, for example. The Celtic tribe of Wales has historic, linguistic, and religious roots that differ from those of the dominant Anglo-Saxons (Germans). Wales today is an occupied country with significant social and economic grievances, but it is pacified by parliamentary representation, not armies. England failed to use that form of pacification with a former colony now called the United States. Remember "taxation without representation"? Both Welsh and Scottish nationalism persist in British politics, but democracy makes for new accommodations.

Not all European tribal demands are so well met. Northern Ireland is still troubled. Corsicans throw bombs; Basques assassinate all kinds of Spaniards; Flemings and Walloons square off in bitter brick-throwing street demonstrations. There are the problems waiting in the wings: Celtic Bretons angry with the central Frankish state in Paris; Tiroleans who, never quite happy with Vienna, look at the South Tirol and wonder if Italy will "Italianize" their southern brethren.

This doesn't begin to address the tribal problems long hidden by the cold war. (See above for a taste of real tribal trouble.) The Russian czars' Slavic state was always an ethnic hodgepodge. Even though the Bolshevik Revolution is finally done with and the Germans have been fended off for a while, the ethnic and nationalistic desires of ethnic minorities still present in a slimmed-down Russia are still boiling.

Not only do European tribal conflicts debilitate their own provinces and destabilize the nation-states the tribes currently inhabit, but in a nuclear-armed Europe, a local tribal demand can demolish everything. Gone are the days when a folk rebel simply burned the other guy's castle and salted the wheat fields.

Yet there are remarkable examples of successful accommodation, even accommodation in places rent by recent and terrible civil wars. Spain provides an example. The Catalans and their relationship with Madrid serve as a remarkable illustration of the dynamics of European tribal politics leading to a moderating situation. Unlike the Basques, the Catalans have controlled their terrorists and struck a working economic and cultural bargain with Spain. But no astute Spanish politician should take the Catalonian stability for granted. (See the 1985 edition of this book for the lowdown on Catalonia.) Catalans do not have the size and power (yet) to create their own nation. However, forming 17 percent of Spain's population, and having 25 percent of the GNP, gives the Catalans the size and power to do a great deal of damage to someone, should they elect to do so.

As tribes go, the Catalans haven't been one of Europe's big winners, at least not for four hundred years, but they certainly cannot be counted among Europe's losers. Catalans have a large measure of wealth and power to complement their sense of ethnic identity.

The Catalans' twentieth-century intrastate quarrel with Madrid doesn't have the same geopolitical implication for Europe that it did five hundred years ago. Geographically, Catalonia isn't situated so that a disturbance in Barcelona could become the Sarajevo of World War III, although the Spanish Civil War (1936–39) did serve as a diplomatic and military test bed for World War II. Catalonia versus Madrid, when compared with other ongoing European intrastate conflicts, is remarkably restrained. Unlike the Basques, the Corsicans, or the IRA in Ulster, the Catalans have their terrorists under control. While anarchist members of the now fractious National Confederation of Labor (NCL) as well as other radical separatists do occasionally extort "revolutionary taxes" from businesses afraid of being bombed, in Catalonia they get sent to prison.

Economically, the Catalans seem to have struck a reasonable bargain with Madrid. Politically, they have a great deal of autonomy. So, what is the problem? Don't you know that Catalonia was never meant to be part of Spain?

Stated simply, the problem is unresolved nationalism. In the larger lens, unresolved nationalism will be the wolf stalking the EEC.

European Ethnic Minorities

Europe was always a continent of many nations. In the last century, many of the ethnic differences have been smoothed out. First, it was done by government decree, with minority languages no longer used in school or for official business. Then came radio and TV, which seized the imagination, and language, of the young. But many ethnic differences remain, and some have shown a revival in the past few decades. There are also eight million Muslim immigrants in Europe, creating a more problematic minority. All nations in Europe are not covered here, primarily to save space. But those nations shown will give you the general idea. Each nation is shown with its total population (in millions), followed by the percentage of the nation's population that the ethnic group comprises.

Great Britain—58.2 million. English 83 percent, Scots 9, Welsh 4.5, Irish 1.8, Muslim 1.7 (mostly Pakistani, Indian, Bangladeshi).

France—58 million. French 68, Occitans 17, Muslim 9 (mostly North African Arab), Bretons 2.1, Germans 1.9, Catalans 0.9, Corsicans 0.7, Basques 0.15, Flemings <.01, Italians <.01.

Germany—81 million. Germans 95, Turks 2.5, Italians 0.7, Poles 0.5, Greeks 0.4, remainder—an increasing number of refugees from war in the Balkans.

Greece—10.6 million. Greeks 96.4, Turkish 1.8, Macedonians 1.1, Romanians 0.5, Albanians 0.2, Bulgarians 0.2.

Italy—58.1 million. Italians 96.5, Sardinians 1.8, Friulians 0.7, Germans 0.5, French 0.4, Romanians <.01, Albanians <.01, Rhaetians <.01, Catalans <.01, Croats <.01, Greeks <.01, Slovenians <.01.

Netherlands—15.4 million. Dutch 97.9, Surinamese 1.3, Frisians 0.7, Indonesians 0.7.

Romania—23.3 million. Romanians 83.9, Hungarians 7.7, Germans 2.7, Bulgarians <.01.

Spain—39.5 million. Spanish 71.4, Catalans 16.2, Galicians 7, Valencianos 4, Basques 1.9.

Switzerland—7 million. Germans 68.8, French 22.1, Italians 10.3, Rhaetians 0.8.

Turkey—63 million. Turkish 90.9, Kurds 3.4, Arabs 0.7, Circassians 0.2, Armenians 0.1, Greeks 0.1, Georgians 0.1, Bulgarians <.01.

Former Yugoslavia—25 million. Serbians 40.1, Croats 22.1, Bosnian Muslims 8.1, Slovenians 8.1, Albanians 6.1, Macedonians 5.9, Montenegrins 2.3, Hungarians 2.2, Italians 1.1, Romanians 0.5, Bulgarians 0.4.

QUICK LOOK: IRA, Urban Guerrillas, and Eternal Wars

In 1994 the British government and the Irish Republican Army (IRA, in this instance the "Provisional Wing") began serious negotiations to end the twenty-five years of violent conflict. Though the action was centered in Northern Ireland, terror and counterterror operations occurred throughout the United Kingdom (UK) and the Republic of Ireland.

The IRA was originally formed in 1916, when yet another rebellion against eight hundred years of British rule flared up. This particular

Irish rebellion succeeded, in part because the Irish compromised and agreed to leave the northern part of the island (Ulster) under British control. Ulster was needed as a refuge for the Protestant Irish. Irish Protestants feared persecution at the hands of the Catholic majority. The population of Ulster is 1.5 million, one third being Catholics, the rest Protestants.

In 1969 the IRA split into mainstream (against violence) and "provisional" (for violence) wings. The "provos" (sometimes called "provies") began a campaign of terror against British control of Northern Ireland.

Throughout the 1970s the IRA waged a terrorist campaign in Ulster. Protestant terrorist organizations (such as the Ulster Defense Forces) then emerged and added to the carnage.

The British strategy was to use superior resources to wear down the IRA. By the 1990s, the IRA leadership, who had been at it for over twenty years, began to tire. The IRA offered to negotiate.

Two conclusions can be derived from the Ulster situation. One is that a government can defeat a terrorist movement, at least temporarily. Victory, however, won't come cheaply or quickly. Over three thousand people died in the twenty-five years of violence and over thirty thousand were injured. IRA strength was never more than a few hundred hard-core terrorists and a few thousand active in the support network. When IRA candidates ran for public office, they never got more than 12 percent of the vote.

The second conclusion: As long as the ethnic tensions remain, there is a certainty that the terrorism will arise once more. These are the wars that will never be won, and will never end.

An unfortunate side effect of organized terrorism is that many of the terrorist groups turn into criminal organizations. That's how the Italian Mafia began, although the "Black Hand" has long since turned into a purely criminal organization. Surviving IRA "provos" may follow a similar path.

QUICK LOOK: Nationalism, Corruption in Italy, and the Return of Fascism

Since the cold war began to end, there has been a marked increase in activity by fascist groups. This should not be surprising. Fascists and fascism never disappeared. With the cold war finished, memories of World War II fascist atrocities grow dimmer, but the nationalistic impulses that fueled fascism remain.

The most successful fascist resurgence has been in Italy, where fascist parties have won a significant number of parliamentary seats. Like the Italian fascists of the 1920s, the Italian fascists of the 1990s ran on a "clean government" platform. Italian governmental corruption has produced a national revulsion and campaigns to "clean up" government and "enforce standards" play well among voters who feel cheated and marginalized.

Fascism puts the state ahead of the individual—well ahead. In the broad sense, fascism is by no means a twentieth-century phenomenon. In this century, and past ones, fascist ideas have opposed democratic and socialist concepts; encouraging racist attitudes and promoting an aggressive military policy are not new notions.

The head of a fascist state was an authoritarian leader who embodied the ideals of the nation. Class divisions were maintained, as were property rights. The fascist state controlled all levels of individual and economic activity, employing secret (and regular) police forces to instill fear and terror as needed.

Fascism, in point of fact, may be considered a twentieth-century version of popular monarchy. When monarchies disappeared wholesale in the nineteenth century, the monarchists didn't disappear. There were still many people who were quite content with a monarchy. The fascists simply updated the technology and titles, but the purpose remained the same.

Modern fascism gained support by promising social justice and "law and order" to the discontented working and middle classes and social order to major corporations and banks. There will be greater appeal for a fascist form of government in a nation that is going through a period of stress, whether it be from economic, moral, or ethnic strife. The ancient Greeks and Romans officially recognized this and made provision for the election of a temporary "dictator" to exert control domestically and overseas until the crises at hand were resolved. Of course, the dictator might not always give up his power, but the ancients recognized that sometimes their democracy was not up to the task of dealing with major emergencies and so made provision for "temporary" dictatorships.

This attitude, that a "strong man" will come along, solve all of the problems, and then fade away, is still with us. Yet history illustrates that supporters of fascism play with fire. As the ancients knew (and made provision for), "power corrupts and absolute power corrupts absolutely." The current European political, economic, and social traumas of Germany's reunification, massive corruption and fiscal crises in Italy, and the trauma of moving from communism to democracy in Russia have all brought the fascists out of the shadows.

We also have the emergence of "fascism with a human face" in countries like Singapore. Actually, this variety might be called "democratic fascism," since new leaders are periodically elected. The leading political party, however, has such a tight control on the society that it is difficult for anyone but the favored (by the ruling party insiders) candidate to win.

One of the complications with fascism is that the word "fascist" is so often used to simply demonize someone who doesn't agree with you. The major Communist leaders of this century, who caused more misery than their fascist counterparts (with the exception of Hitler) came off better in the public relations department because their official line was kinder and gentler. The Communist leaders, however, were fascists in function, if not in form.

Will a fascist government take over in a major, nuclear-armed nation? Possibly. Russia could go fascist, as authoritarian governments in various forms have been the norm there until 1991. Russia's current democratic government is just barely functioning and numerous local "strong men" wait in the political shadows. China could go fascist, as ultranationalist members of the military become increasingly powerful politically.

Economic conditions inside Russia and China are the decisive factor. When people are secure and prosperous (or feel they could be well off), they are less likely to support a dictator or succumb to militant, ultranationalist myths. Yes, Singapore is run by a leader who has enormous power, but not the mandate to make war or ruin the thriving economy Singapore has built.

QUICK LOOK: Migrants and Refugees

Not long after Czechoslovakia split into Slovakia and the Czech Republic, Germany promised the cash-starved Czechs several hundred million marks to "establish and control" the new Czech and Slovak border. The reason for the German largesse? The Germans saw the Czech Republic as a new form of buffer state, one that will help slow the post–cold war human tide sweeping from impoverished East to capitalist West.

Other European nations have tried to use military forces to blunt this human wave. Austria redeployed troops along its Slovenian border. Slovenia in the mid-1990s has become a way station for the war-weary escaping various Balkan bloodbaths.

It is ironic. Though the cold war is over, many Europeans still fear invasion, not by Soviet tank armies but by political refugees and economic immigrants fleeing collapsed Communist dictatorships.

Or are they political immigrants and economic refugees? The distinction blurs as the wave of human dislocation and relocation continues and a new "Fortress Europe," built of border police and tough restrictions on movement, begins to rise.

The "great migration" of the end of the twentieth century also affects Fortress America. In the 1994 elections, Californians passed the controversial Proposition 187, an initiative to deny illegal immigrants certain government services. The Proposition 187 fight demonstrated the emotional heat and high degree of resentment immigration issues ignite in regions suffering economic recession.

There is, however, a global refugee and immigration crisis of staggering dimensions.

According to UN figures, in 1980 there were 7 million refugees worldwide. In 1994 the figure is almost 50 million, with 25 million people forced into other countries and 25 million described as "internally displaced." The *Index on Censorship,* a British human rights publication, believes that 100 million people around the globe "live in countries of which they are not citizens." Other sources estimate that in mid-1995 over 20 million refugees were in the care of international agencies.

Europeans shudder when they read estimates that in the 1995–97 time frame from three to five million people will leave the nations of ex-USSR and go west. Russia also faces its own refugee dilemma, with tens of thousands of Iraqi Kurds and Afghans seeking asylum, as well as millions of ethnic Russians "returning home" after living for decades in Kazakhstan and other ex-Soviet republics.

War, famine, and plague are the traditional forces of migratory apocalypse. Perhaps one million Hutus have left Rwanda for neighboring African nations. The Islamic Sudanese government's war against Christian and animist tribes in southern Sudan has thrown tens of thousands of refugees into Uganda and Ethiopia. Wretched Ethiopia, savaged by civil war and recurrent famine, already has at least one million displaced persons.

Cambodians, who fled the murderous Communist Khmer Rouge in the 1970s, still live in refugee camps inside Thailand. Human rights monitors report that the Cambodians are frequently looted by corrupt authorities, once again underscoring the sad fact that refugees are vulnerable human beings.

While few are so callous as to close a border to someone fleeing death, the scale of human dislocation over the last decade and the speed at which a refugee crisis can occur (with millions swamping a border in a matter of days) have led some in the international community to ask the question, Is the freedom to move a basic human right?

Recall one case where movement was denied: Many European Jews, refused sanctuary in the late 1930s, went back to die in Nazi concentration camps.

The vast number of displaced people, however, overwhelms both rich and poor nations and shreds the international safety net of aid organizations. These refugee and migration crises are the seedbeds of future violence.

LOOK BACK: YUGOSLAVIA

The following editorial, written by author Austin Bay, appeared in the *Dallas Morning News* on November 21, 1991. The editorial is a look back at a moment when it may still have been possible to curb the fighting in Serbia, Croatia, and Bosnia. Was the October to December 1991 time frame the moment combined European political and military action could have prevented the Bosnian war?

> Yugoslavia is dead. Serbs, Croats, Bosnians, and the other tribes once lumped inside Yugoslav borders might ask themselves if indeed the nation ever existed as anything more than a fragile political convenience. Patched from the political fragments of WWI, briefly cemented by fascist threat, Nazi invasion and then the personality and secret police of Josip Broz Tito, with the end of the Cold War the figment of "Yugoslav unity" has disappeared as the old Balkan strifes and troubles return like so many Draculas. Yugoslav disintegration has become a bloodbath that cannot be ignored, for the crisis involves much more than drawing new borders between peoples who have fought one another for centuries. Yugoslav breakdown is an aggressive microcosm of the troubles which haunt post-Cold War European (and for that matter, world) geopolitics: Heterogeneous populations split by ethnic and historical disputes dating back several hundred years, intense religious divisions, and territorial recidivism borne of simple-minded demands for a "Greater Serbia" or "Greater Albania" or "Greater Etcetera," mythical nations that existed in some protean golden age.
>
> Thus Yugoslavia's breakdown has become a political laboratory for Europe and the UN, each bloody day asking The Question: "How do we deal with the historical fragmentation resulting from the end of the Cold War?"
>
> Unending ethnic violence is not the correct answer to the quiz. Since last summer, over a dozen cease-fires brokered between fighting Serb and Croat forces have failed, often within hours of the agreement.
>
> The chief culprit is the former Yugoslav National Army, now thoroughly a creature of Serbia and its ultra-nationalist leader, Slobodan Milosevitch. The Serb Army's strategy is to create a "Greater Serbia" by winning a "creeping" war of aggression. They attack, take a niche of Croatia, halt and wait for the international community's diplomatic rhetoric to subside. Then they attack again.
>
> The Serbs have not confined their assaults to Serb-populated districts. The Serb Army has surrounded and shelled the Croat Adriatic port (and cultural prize) of Dubrovnik, turning a tourist attraction and regional

economic asset into a shooting gallery. Even if the Serbs don't intend to keep Dubrovnik, taking it gives them something to trade for a larger slice of the Croatian coastline.

Until this month [November 1991], the European nations had done little more than kavetch and cajole the Serbs with rhetoric and threats of economic sanctions. Great Britain, France, and Belgium have now asked for UN peacekeeping troops, should the Serbs and Croats agree to yet another cease-fire and allow the UN to intervene.

Economic sanctions could ultimately stop the Serb war machine. The neighbor nations of Romania, Hungary, and Albania, however, given their economic distress, cannot be relied upon to enforce an embargo. Besides, the Serb armed forces may have sufficient fuel and ammunition stocks to continue their calculated attacks for another six months.

Calling for UN-sponsored peace-making troops is the right step, and the UN is the best forum, but action must support rhetoric. Under the umbrella of a Security Council resolution, Western Europeans must be prepared to commit their own armed forces to the peacemaking mission. A dramatic demonstration of willingness to enforce a cease-fire, perhaps breaking the siege of Dubrovnik, would clearly send the message that Europe and the UN stand for evolutionary rather than revolutionary change in the political order. A dozen British, French, and Italian destroyers and minesweepers, protected by their air forces, could relieve Dubrovnik in an afternoon. Such a move is being considered. Elite ground troops, under the UN flag, would then be inserted as Serb and Croat forces disengaged.

The Europeans' goal is not to remake Yugoslavia as it was. Frankly, Slovenia is already essentially a separate nation; the other republics are close behind. The goals are to stop the bloodshed and once more make the case that post–Cold War (New World Order?) geo-political change will not be conducted by wars of aggression. Let the borders of Croatia, Serbia, and Bosnia be redrawn by local plebiscite. The lesson should be this: Democracy works, not war.

A continuing Yugoslav bloodbath could be a prelude to a much larger Balkan war. Unchecked Serbian warmaking encourages pocket fascists in Eastern Europe and the USSR who would use civil war as a means of gaining power. It is time for the members of "next year's superpower," the EEC, to quench through collective political action those terrible ethnic fires which are the threat to peace in the common European home.

Chapter 5

TURKEY—AS EUROPE'S FLANK BEGINS TO FRAY

INTRODUCTION

In 1918 the Ottoman Turk Empire collapsed into chaos. But by the mid-1920s, after a bloody war with Greece (in Anatolia, Thrace, and Ionia) and an extended military and political confrontation with French, British, and Italian occupiers, a new "Republic of Turkey," under the remarkable leadership of Kemal Atatürk (General Mustafa Kemal), regained control of the Turkish heartland. The "Kemalist" republic, using the armed forces as a source of stability, focused on internal Turkish development. The once "Sick Man of Europe" became the Quiet Man of Europe. What was once one of the most powerful and successfully imperialist of nations disengaged from empire, even from its Arabian fiefs. Under the direction of Atatürk, the Islamic superpower of four and a half centuries embarked on a mission into "modernity"—a secular government, Latin written script, women's rights, public education, and a careful program of industrial modernization. A cornerstone of the Turkish republic was "nonrecidivism"—

210

Turkey made no claims on lost provinces. What was over would be over. That has brought Turkey its longest period of peace, nearly seventy years' worth to date.

As the twentieth century draws to a close, the collapse of the Soviet Union has turned Turkey into a regional superpower of military, social, political, and economic import. Yes, Turkey still maintains the second largest army directly committed to NATO and Ankara's fleet and ground forces still guard the critical Turkish Straits (the Bosporus and the Dardanelles).

But the East bloc's demise has placed Turkey in an even hotter political crucible. Turkey, "the flank of NATO," directly confronts the fallout of the Soviet collapse in central Asia, particularly in the emerging Islamic nations. Iran has emerged as a major competitor. Turkey also faces other "old" troubles: a bleeding Kurdish insurgency in its southeastern provinces; internal Islamic fundamentalist revivals and opposition to the "Kemalist" secular state; armed conflict with Iraq's Baathist regime; lurking conflict with Syria and Iraq, old Arab-Turk hatreds renewed by hostility over water resources; loggerheads with the European Economic Community (EEC) which Turkey would love to join; potential war with Greece, over Cyprus and other issues; resentment and suspicion in the Balkans, particularly in Bulgaria; and lingering claims of Ottoman-directed genocide by Armenians.

In late 1995 the Islamist "welfare party" collected the largest percentage of votes cast for any single party in Turkey's parliamentary elections (21 percent). Inside Turkey this has led to negotiations about how to deal with the Islamists political strength. As this book goes to press the internal political situation is fluid. The traditional Kemalist parties may reach a compromise and form a new governing coalition, but the Islamists have made their point.

Change in Turkey won't be easy. New problems are emerging. The old problems have returned. Greece and Turkey are once again sparring over Aegean islets.

SOURCE OF CONFLICT

Turkey is involved in several active, simmering, or latent armed conflicts. The "Kurdish Insurgency" has flared on and off for centuries. When the Turks first entered the area, some of the first people they encountered—and fought—were Kurds. The current insurgency springs from several sources: (1) genuine Kurdish nationalism stemming from Kurdish dreams of an independent Kurdistan (which was supposed to be established after World War I); (2) the remnants of Russian cold war intrigue, using Kurdish radicals to destabilize an important NATO nation; (3) Kurdish activism in Iran, Iraq, and Syria spilling over the border. Turkey has also given refuge to a growing number of Kurdish refugees fleeing Iraq. During the Iran-Iraq War, both combatants made use of Kurdish insurgents. After Iraq launched a series of brutal attacks against the Kurds in 1988, including dousing Kurdish villages with poison gas, the number of Kurdish refugees inside Turkey increased.

The "external troubles" also have deep historical roots. During Ottoman times, Syria and Iraq were both Turkish fiefs. Arab tribes and urban peoples chafed under the Ottoman heel. As the Arabs remember it, Ottoman troops and "high sheriffs" (beys of the Sublime Porte) placed hard taxes and harsher laws on Arab locals. Moreover, the central Asian Turks were ethnically different from the Arabs. The Turks were also united, tough, and successful. The Turks did not hide their disdain for the Arabs. In the Middle East, memories of past cruelty, and success, are, unfortunately, long and abiding.

Many Arabs also resent Turkey's comparative success at modernization. Another group, the religious fundamentalists, which includes Iran's revolutionary mullahs, abhor Ankara's secular state.

The current border between Turkey and Syria is little more than a line drawn in the sand—based roughly on the line Turkish forces withdrew to at the end of World War I. Syria still claims the region around Iskenderun (Alexandretta) and the town of Antakya (Antioch) as part of Greater Syria. Despite their drubbing in the Persian Gulf War, Iraqi Baathists dream of leading the Arab world and becoming the most powerful state in the Middle East. Turkey played a central role in Iraq's 1991 defeat.

While Turkey has spent the last seventy years looking toward Europe, the end of the cold war and rapid political change in the entire southern tier of the ex-Soviet Turkic republics have opened the region to new and intimate Turkish involvement.

Turkey could once again become the region's powerhouse, blunting Iranian revolutionary ambitions, keeping a thumb on Iraq, challenging Russia. But a deeper problem lurks. One cannot drink ambitions. Iraq and Syria's thirst for recognition and power might take a backseat to the more immediate question of water. Turkey has a system of dams on the upper Euphrates. Turkey also controls the sources of the Tigris. Iraq has railed at Syria over its Euphrates water projects and in the last three years has focused even more concern on the Turks. Iraqi access to chemical and nuclear weapons make this problem even more significant. On the flip side, in the aftermath of Iraq's attack on Kuwait, Turkey has demonstrated that the back door to Iraq is the northern Iraq-Turkey border.

Europe is another realm of contest. Turks and Europeans have fought one another in the Balkans for nearly eight hundred years. The Bulgarian Communist government, prior to its fall, conducted a vigorous pogrom against Bulgarian Turks. Three hundred thousand or more fled to Turkey. Though some Bulgarian Turks returned to Bulgaria after the "revolution" of late 1989 and early 1990, the fact remains that the Bulgars despise the Turks (and vice versa); ethnic suspicions are heightened by memories of Ottoman cruelties both real and imagined.

Other Balkan conflicts already involve Turkey. Turkish military units are involved as UN peacekeepers in Bosnia and Croatia. If the Bosnian war spreads, or any of the other dozen-odd lurking Balkan conflicts erupt, Turkey could become involved in an ugly, complicated war in Europe.

Greeks still rankle at the years of Ottoman domination. The fact that Constantinople *is* Istanbul has never been forgiven. Many Greeks talk about their successful revolt against the Ottomans—dating from the 1820s—as if it were recent history. Greece still covets the Ionian coast, at least from Troy to Bodrum (Halicarnassus). The Greco-Turk

War from 1919 to 1922 stirs both Turks and Greeks. All those double names, Smyrna for Izmir, Adrianople for Edirne, Nicaea for Iznik, are a lingual clue. Add the troubles of Cyprus and its still-bleeding conflict between a Greek majority and a Turkish minority—a Turkish minority protected since 1974 by an invading and occupying Turkish army. Add the trouble over exploration for and exploitation of mineral resources on the Aegean shelf. Add the at times vicious squabble over air rights above the Aegean. Still adding? How is it (or how was it) that these two mutually antagonistic nations were ever called allies in NATO? American money and diplomacy, and, indeed, the genuine threat of Russian attack, kept Turks and Greeks from tangling. There may be some good political news from bad economic news, however: Mutual economic troubles may finally begin to temper the conflict between Greek and Turk. For years Turkey has sought to join the European Economic Community (EEC) and the Greeks frustrated that desire. There are signals that many Greeks see regional economic benefit from Turkish economic integration. Finally, enough Greek leaders realize that the Turks have a larger army manned by more ferocious fighters. Threatening war is one thing; actually fighting a war you are pretty sure you will lose big-time is quite another.

Even as the "moderate Islamist" Welfare party scores election victories, Islamic fundamentalists inside Turkey have increased their vocal opposition to the "heretical" Turkish secular state. Likewise, "pan-Turkish" extremists, many with ultraright and outright fascist programs, see the potential reorganization (or collapse) of the Soviet Turkic republics as an opportunity for establishing a new Turkish empire. At the least, it is an opportunity to settle old scores with Russia, a nation Turks identify as a "Western power."

Armenia and Azerbaijan are waging a bitter war. The Armenians are Christian, the Azeris Turkic Muslims. Turkey and Russia could collide if the Azeri-Armenian war spreads. The war could also bring Turkey and Iran into conflict.

Turkey already fights an "old" Armenian war. Armenian radicals scattered throughout the world have turned to terrorism to dramatize their call for recognition of the "Armenian genocide." The Armenians allege that Ottoman troops killed over 600,000 Armenian civilians during World War I. The Turkish government, besides disputing the "genocide" on facts, claims it isn't responsible for what the Ottoman caliphate did or did not do. That only further angers the Armenians, especially those who dream of recovering former Armenian lands for the new post-Soviet nation of Armenia. The 3.5 million Armenians in Armenia would like to be reunited with the 400,000 to a million (depending on who's doing the counting) Armenians across the border in Turkey. This desire is not expressed too publicly, lest the Turks take umbrage.

WHO'S INVOLVED

The Kurdish Insurgency/Struggle for Kurdistan

Turkey—Government in Ankara and "Euro-Turks" of western Turkey.

Kurds—Once labeled by Ankara as "mountain Turks"; unique ethnic group (related to the Iranians, although a separate group for over two thousand years). Some Kurds believe they are the descendants of the ancient Assyrians; others say they are the Carduchi, the tribesmen who harassed Xenophon and the Ten Thousand as they retreated from Persia in the fourth century B.C. (see Local Politics). Others assert they are the "Celts who stayed behind" when the Celtic peoples moved west over three thousand years ago. Whatever the case, the Kurds have been a part of the local ethnic and political landscape for as long as records have been kept.

Iran and Syria—Nations with significant Kurd minorities, and "Kurd troubles" of their own. Iran has 5 million, Syria "several hundred thousand"; perhaps 200,000 Kurds live in Armenia, Azerbaijan, and other former Soviet republics.

Iraq—Iraq has some four million Kurds, some loyal to the Iraqi Baath regime, some influenced by the Turks, some at odds with all non-Kurd regimes.

The Greco-Turk "Balkan" War

Turkey—As far as the Turks are concerned, their quarrels with the Greeks ended in the early 1920s, when a Greek invasion was repulsed and hundreds of thousands of Greeks were expelled from Turkey. That was part of Atatürk's attempt to cut the cycle of unresolved grievances that have long plagued this part of the world. It worked for the Turks, but none of Turkey's neighbors took the pledge. They should have.

Greece—In Greek eyes, Istanbul is Constantinople and Izmir is Smyrna. For Greece, the ancient Byzantine (or Roman) Empire lives on. Aside from the questionable history implicit in this attitude, making any headway against a more populous and combat-ready Turkey is less of a dream than a potential nightmare.

Bulgaria—Hate for Turkey (and Turks) runs deep (as does a desire for Western Thrace, now held by Greece).

Wild Cards

Russia, Macedonia, Yugoslavia (Serbia-Montenegro), United States, Germany, other NATO and EEC nations allied with both Greece and Turkey.

The Cyprus Conflict

Turkey—Its army invaded in 1974 and at least twenty-five thousand troops remain.

Greece—In 1974 the Colonels' military dictatorship in Athens gave Greek Cypriot radicals the go-ahead for *enosis* (unification) of Cyprus with Greece. Unification failed. The Turks invaded. The Colonels fell from power. The Turkish troops are still there and the island is still divided.

Greek and Turk Cypriots—On the same island, but divided by language, religion, and tradition.

UN Forces Cyprus—UNFCYP. Keeps the Greeks and Turks from going at each other, not that either side is eager to raise the conflict beyond the current rhetorical level.

Wild Cards

Great Britain—Remnant of the empire; maintains two "sovereign base areas" on Cyprus, an old protectorate.

European Economic Community (EEC).

The Great Mesopotamian Water War

Turkey—The Tigris and Euphrates rivers begin in Turkey. For years the Turks have wanted to dam the rivers to provide electricity and irrigation to local farms. Now they are doing it, and the Syrians and Iraqis downstream don't like the idea of losing all that water that has come their way for thousands of years.

Syria—the Euphrates River, and the life-giving water it brings, is vulnerable to Turkish dams.

Iraq—The Iraqi leg of the Euphrates is vulnerable to both Turkish and Syrian dams; the Tigris River faces increasing Turkish water demands, also.

Wild Cards

Russia, Israel, the United States.

Wild Wild Cards

Greece, Bulgaria, Kurds, Germany.

The Back Door to Baghdad

Turkey—Until 1918, Mosul and Kirkuk were Turkish (or at least Kurdish) cities. As the borders were rearranged after World War I, Turkey (which sided with the Germans) lost this territory. While Turkey doesn't expect to get the land (and the oil found there) back, it would like some help in containing the Kurdish guerrillas who hide out in northern Iraq among the local Kurdish population.

Iraq—Invaded and looted Kuwait, lost control of the Kurdish lands in northern Iraq to the UN in the aftermath of the war. That was not as bad for Iraq as it sounds. The oil fields in northern Iraq are of no use to Iraq until the oil embargo is lifted. The rambunctious Kurds are now the UN's problem. Of course, there is always the danger that Iraq will not get its northern territories back. But that is unlikely. Once the UN tires of the Iraqi situation, Iraq will send troops and aircraft north once more to bring the restless Kurds into line. Meanwhile, the Kurds fight among themselves and with the Turks.

Saudi Arabia and Arab allies—The Arabs of the Persian Gulf do not want to be threatened by Iraq, but they also see the need for a united Iraq as a buffer against an aggressive Iran. The Gulf Arabs want Iraq weak, but not too weak to hold off the Iranians.

NATO nations—The NATO treaty stipulates that if one member is attacked, all are considered attacked.

United States—Long an ally of Turkey.

Wild Card

The UN.

The "Pan-Turkic" Conflicts

Turkey—The dissolution of the Soviet Union created five new Turkic (and one partly Turkic) nations in its wake (see below for description). For over a century, these Turkic peoples of central Asia had been subjects of the Russian Empire. Turkey had long been fighting the Russians and the Turks of the former Ottoman Turk Empire and the central Asian Turks always had their dislike for Russia to give them common cause. Moreover, Turkey was modern; it had shed the ancient ways while still being Turkic and Muslim. Turkey has no desire to unite the far-flung Turks of central Asia. No one since Genghis, the Great Khan, was able to do that, and that unity did not long outlive Genghis. But Turkey does see the opportunity to play the role of "elder brother" to their kinsmen in central Asia. Turkey can provide experience in modernizing a Turkic people, something for which they have a track record. But, perhaps more important, Turkey can provide mediation services for the many disputes that exist, or wait to break out, among the central Asian Turks.

Russia—Moscow is deeply involved, having kept the peace in central Asia for over a century. Russia fears a dozen other wars like the one in Chechnya. There is more opportunity to ignore wars among the Turkic people in central Asia, but that won't make these conflicts disappear and these battles would eventually spill over into Russia itself.

Iran—Approximately fifteen million Turkic people (mostly Azeris) live in Iran. The Soviets tried to forcibly reunite their Azeris (now an independent nation) with those in Iran right after World War II. The Western nations forced the Soviets to back off. But the Azeri Turks still look favorably on unification. The Iranians do not.

Turkic nations emerging from the former Soviet Union: Azerbaijan, Kazakhstan, Turkmenistan, Uzbekistan, Kyrgyzstan. Tajikistan has a large (about 30 percent) Turkic minority, while the majority Tajiks are related to Iranians. Some 45 million "Turkic peoples" live in the nations of the former USSR. The major Turkic or "Islamic" ethnic groups living in parts of the former Soviet Union are:

Kirghiz—Islamic, Turkic-speaking, with Mongol background. About 2.4 million live in Kyrgyizstan (about 50 percent of the population). A significant minority is still described as "pastoral herders" (a few may indeed be seminomadic), though many Kirghiz work in cotton-related industries and mining. Most of the Kirghiz migrated to "Kirghizia" in the late seventeenth century. They had been Siberian nomads in the Yenisei River region.

Turkomans—Five million central Asian Turks throughout the former Soviet Union. A small minority still live as nomads, relying on camels for transport.

Azeris—Turkic people; 6.5 million in Azerbaijan.

Kazakhs—Related to the Kirghiz. Most are sedentary now. There are 7.2 million living in Kazakhstan.

Tajiks—Not a Turkic tribe but a mingling of Caucasian (as in Caucasus) and Mongol peoples. Over seven million, mostly in mountainous Tajikistan. Their language is related to Persian (Iranian). These Muslim people care for herds of sheep and other animals. Often counted with other Turkic groups in Russia and, because of their proximity, certainly a part of the Turkic bloc in the area.

Tartars—Crimean Tartars were expelled from the Crimea by Stalin in 1944; have been drifting back into the Crimea in the last ten years. There are now only about a million Tartars left.

Uzbeks—Some 18 million live in Uzbekistan but Uzbeks are found throughout "southern" ex-Soviet nations and Russia. There are a million in Afghanistan, 350,000 in Kazakhstan, some 600,000 in Kyrgyzstan, 1.5 million in Tajikistan, and 360,000 in Turkmenistan. There are also about 100,000 scattered through the other parts of the former Soviet Union (many of these are now assimilated into other cultural groups). The Uzbeks are the most numerous Turkic people in central Asia and, as a result, have the most disputes with the other Turkic peoples in the area.

Meskhetian Turks—Small Turk group; many died at the hands of Uzbek Turks during riots in 1989.

"Pan-Turkic" Wild Cards

Bulgaria, Greece, China—Approximately 8 million Turkic people live in China; 2 million in Afghanistan; 900,000 in Bulgaria; 400,000 in Iraq; 200,000 each in Romania, Mongolia, and parts of Yugoslavia; 150,000 in Cyprus; 130,000 in Greece; 100,000 in Syria. There is the potential for a clever and charismatic Turkic politician starting a "Turks United" movement throughout central Asia. It's happened before.

Armenia

The Armenian genocide—Was it genocide, forced emigration, or a tragedy of war? Did it occur in 1915 or continue until 1923?

Turkey—Is "the Republic of Turkey" responsible for what the Ottoman regime did (or did not do) to Armenia?

Armenian "diaspora"—Armenians living around the world, scattered by a history of invasion, forced resettlement, and poverty. Armenia was freed from Persian domination by Alexander the Great (331 B.C.), but history is tough sledding when you're a border state between Greece and Persia, then between Rome/Byzantium and Persia, then between Byzantium and Islamic Arabia, then between Byzantium and Turkic tribes, then between Ottoman Turkey and czarist Russia, then between Turkey and the Soviet Union, then between . . . well, you get the drift. But Armenians have never been assimilated. Armenians retain a strong sense of identity and a creative culture. An influential and wealthy Armenian community lives in the United States (see U.S. Congress, below).

Armenian terrorists—Have conducted numerous attacks on Turkish citizens and Turkish diplomats around the world. This is rather pointless, and is driven by a small group of fanatics pursuing a motive that is nothing more than revenge for ancient grievances.

"International opinion"—The title given to views expressed on CNN's *World News Report*, ABC's *Nightline*, the *MacNeill/Lehrer NewsHour*, and in the *New York Times* and *Wall Street Journal* editorial pages.

Wild card—Armenia. The Armenians have been fighting the Azeris for most of the 1990s and the Turkic Azeris have been getting the worst of it. Emotionally, Turkey sides with the Azeris. But diplomatically and logically, they know there is nothing to be gained from sending Turkish troops into that particular war.

"The Struggle for Turkey's Soul"

"Kemalists"—Will the secular institutions of Kemal Atatürk survive into the twenty-first century?

Islamic fundamentalists—Sunni Muslim activists who believe modern Turkey has lost its Islamic identity and therefore its soul. Many are funded by Iran.

Right- and left-wing extremist organizations (see Local Politics)—Ready to pick up on the chaos.

Turkish Army—Will the army continue to be the Kemalists' "tool of modernity" or will fundamentalists change its outlook? The army has periodically stepped in and taken over the government, either to eliminate corruption or restore order, or both. But the generals have learned, the hard way, that giving orders to well-disciplined troops is a lot easier than running a country. In the 1980s, the army said they were leaving politics for good. . . . Well, at least sort of. The army still sees itself as the shield of the nation. If chaos and civil disorder grow and the politicians appear unable to cope, one could see the troops in the streets and the generals in power again.

GEOGRAPHY

The peninsula of Asia Minor is a geographic bridge between Eastern Europe and the Middle East. Turkey either contains or borders on some of the world's most sensitive geostrategic terrain: Eastern Thrace, the Turkish Straits (the Dardanelles, Sea of Marmara, and the Bosporus), the Aegean Sea, the Black Sea, and the chaotic "southern tier" of nations emerging from the former Soviet Union. Turkey also borders on the volatile nations of Syria, Iraq, and Iran. The entire country covers almost 767,000 square kilometers, slightly bigger than the U.S. state of Texas or roughly double the size of California.

Turkey has a population of 63 million. Turks comprise 78 percent of the population. Kurds account for just under 20 percent of the population (around 12 million), making them a significant ethnic minority. Turkey is overwhelmingly Muslim (98 percent). Of that 98 percent, at least 80 percent are Sunnis and nearly 20 percent are Alawite Muslims. Though comprising only 1 percent of the population, important Jewish and Christian communities exist, most notably in Istanbul (where Jews have thrived for five hundred years). The number of Armenians is also uncertain (figures suggest from 400,000 to perhaps just under 1 million.)

Anatolia (central Turkey) consists of an elevated, fertile plateau ringed by hills and mountains. The Anatolian climate is comparatively moderate. Anatolia was the heart of the Ottoman state and remains the center of contemporary Turkey. The ancient kingdom of Galatia occupied eastern Anatolia. The Galatians of Saint Paul's Epistle were Jewish converts to Christianity living in what is now the Ankara area. The Aegean coastal region (Ionia in particular) is also fertile. The area is dotted with numerous small harbors. Narrow straits separate Turkey from the Greek islands close to the coast.

Eastern Turkey is crisscrossed by rugged mountains and badlands. In the east the mountains rise sharply from the Black Sea coast. Harsh winters characterize the climate of eastern Turkey (for details, see Xenophon's *The Persian Expedition;* ten thousand Greek mercenaries trudged from Persia through eastern Turkey). Lake Van, a 130-kilometer-long inland sea in eastern Turkey, was once a major Armenian area. In general, the Kurds occupy the southeastern corner of the nation. Turkey's most famous mountain is Mount Ararat (5,165 meters), where the Book of Genesis says Noah's Ark docked (permanently). The mountains drop down to the Iraqi frontier. The glacier-fed Tigris River rises in the eastern regions of the Cilo Dat mountains and twists east then south. The Euphrates River rises to the west and flows through Syria and into Iraq. The rivers share a delta, the Shatt-al-Arab, the strategic waterway that was the hub of the Iran-Iraq War of 1980–88.

The border with Syria does not follow a "natural" boundary. Except for the city of Antakya and its immediate environs, the border is more or less the World War I cease-fire line drawn along an old railroad bed then extended into the sand. The city of Antakya (ancient Antioch) lies in the southernmost niche of modern Turkey, the Hatay (formerly the Sanjak of Alexandretta or Iskenderun) between Syria and the Mediterranean. It still has a substantial Arab population, which voted to stay with the Turks in a 1920s referendum.

HISTORY

The peninsula of Asia Minor has been so central to European and Middle Eastern history, indeed, human history, that even a ten-thousand-page account would scarcely do it justice. Troy, on the south side of the Dardanelles, flowered and died at least seven times before the birth of Christ. The Christian New Testament, especially the letters of Paul, are a gazetteer of Asia Minor: Ephesus (Paul's Epistle to the Ephesians), Antioch (modern Antakya), Smyrna (Turkish Izmir), and Tarsus (Paul's hometown) to name a few. The Council of Nicaea (fifth century; Christianity's major statement of faith, the Nicaean Creed) took place in what is modern Turkey's town of Iznik.

In A.D. 330 the Roman emperor Constantine moved his capital to Asia Minor, to his new city of Constantinople. The "eastern empire" evolved into Byzantium, and more or less held out—through invasion from the east and Crusade from the west—until 1453, when Mehmet II and his Turkish army breached the walls.

The Ottoman Empire traces its roots to the Osman Turks. Originally an Oghuz tribe, the original Ottoman, Othman (ruling from 1299–1326), was a tribal leader from the border region between Seljuk Anatolia and Byzantium. The Ottomans were successful *ghazis,* followers of Islam living on the border with "the infidels" who spread the faith as they extended their power into the heathen's territories. Other Turkish tribes and eventually many Arab lands fell under their sway.

Mehmet II (1451–81), Selim I (1512–20, known as Selim the Grim), and Suleyman the Magnificent (1520–66) were the Turkish conquerors who brought the empire to its height. For centuries the Ottoman Empire either ruled or contested southeastern Europe, controlled the Arabian Peninsula, either held suzerainty or exercised strong influence over Persia, and dominated North Africa from Egypt to Morocco. The "Sublime Porte" (the Ottoman court and center of the empire) struggled bitterly with the Russians over control of the Black Sea and domination of central Asia.

The Ottoman Empire began its slow decline in 1683 with the defeat of the invading Turkish forces (under the command of Kara Mustafa Pasha) at the gates of Hapsburg Vienna. The Austrians and their allies counterattacked, reaching into Hungary, Greece, and the Black Sea coast. The Treaty of Karlowitz (1699) marked the first time the Ottoman Empire signed a peace treaty as the defeated party in a major conflict. It was the start of a long downward spiral. By the 1699 treaty, Hungary, Transylvania, and parts of Croatia were ceded to Austria. Podolia was ceded to Poland. From the Treaty of Passarowitz (1718, which ceded the Banat to Austria) to the Treaty of Sèvres (1920, the "cease-fire peace treaty" concluding World War I), the Ottoman Empire slowly, and bloodily, shrank. The Treaty of Lausanne (1923), which ended the Greco-Turk War of 1920–22 (called the War for Independence by the Turks), restored some territories.

The Turks refer to the nineteenth century as "our longest century"—it was a period of retreat and failure. There were several attempts to "Westernize," most notably in 1839 when *tanzemat* (restructuring), a Turkish *perestroika,* was attempted, and largely failed. The rot continued.

The First Balkan War (1912–13) and the Second Balkan War (1913) spelled the end of Turkish power in Europe. These conflicts were kicked off by Austria's grab of Bosnia (1908) and a series of revolts in Albania (1910–12); the linchpin of the Serbian, Montenegrin, Bulgarian, and Greek alliance was hatred for the Turks. In the First Balkan War, the Greeks took several Aegean islands and the Greek Navy bottled up Ottoman reinforcements. Bulgars besieged Istanbul. The Second Balkan War broke out when the Bulgars attacked Greece and Serbia. The Bulgarians felt they had done most of the fighting but hadn't received their share of the spoils. As the rest of the Balkans ganged up on Bulgaria, the Turks retook Eastern Thrace. Their halcyon days in Europe, however, were finished.

Though the Young Turks (1908–18) of the Committee of Union and Progress (CUP) had tried to revitalize and modernize the Ottoman state and Ottoman Army, it was too little too late. The Ottoman Empire was a medieval creature that blundered into modernity, but with its sheer size and remnant armies remained a force to be reckoned with long after its economy, diplomatic creativity, and human energies had fossilized. World War I, and Turkey's decision to side with the Central Powers, finished the Ottomans.

The Treaty of Sèvres (August 1920) carved Turkey into several interesting pieces. Turkey's Arab provinces left the empire and became "mandates" run by Great Britain or France. Greece, after acquiring Western Thrace from Bulgaria, gained Eastern Thrace, to a point forty kilometers from Istanbul (the Catalca Line). Greece gained control of the area around Smyrna (Izmir). After a five-year period, the people of the area, based on a plebiscite, could join the Greek state. Greece also received the Aegean islands. Italy got Rhodes and the rest of the Dodecanese Islands. The Turkish Straits, while under nominal Ottoman control, would actually be administered by an international force; that put France and Britain in de facto control of the straits. The Treaty of Sèvres also contained two other promises. An autonomous Kurdistan was to be organized in eastern Turkey. The Kurds had the right, after a year, to opt for total independence. Likewise, an independent Armenia was to be created. U.S. President Woodrow Wilson would help draw the new Armenian borders. The Ottoman Army was limited to fifty thousand troops.

Prior to the Treaty of Sèvres, fighting had broken out in eastern Turkey as the newly organized Armenian state in the Caucasus (Erivan) sent forces into Anatolia. The Turkish Army counterattacked and Armenia agreed to a peace treaty in December 1920. The Russian Bolsheviks' Red Army attacked the Armenian state shortly thereafter and incorporated it into the forming USSR.

The Greek government, under King Constantine, wasn't satisfied with its slice of Thrace and the region around Smyrna (Izmir) behind the Milne Line. Constantinople had to be retaken, and, if possible, western Anatolia. The Greeks had launched an offensive in June 1920 and had made major gains in central Turkey and Eastern Thrace. Mustafa Kemal, the hero of the Turkish defense against the British Commonwealth assault on Gallipoli in 1915, became the center of Turkish political and military resistance. At the First Battle of Inonu (January 1921), along the Inonu River just north of Kutahya, Turkish forces under the command of Ismet Bey stopped the Greek attack. During 1921 both sides failed to budge the other. In August 1922, the Turks launched the "Great Offensive" that retook Izmir. The Turks, with some supplies and arms provided by the new Soviet regime in Moscow, ignored British and French demands to halt their advance. The Turkish Army reoccupied the straits.

Greek defeat in Asia Minor was near total. The Turks eventually reoccupied Edirne (Adrianople) and claimed Eastern Thrace to the Maritsa River.

The Treaty of Lausanne (July 1923) resulted in forced emigrations of Greeks from Asia Minor and of Turks from most of the Aegean islands (Turkey received Tenedos and Imbros since they control access to the Dardanelles). The Turkish minority in Western Thrace was allowed to remain in Greece; the ancient Greek community in Istanbul was allowed to remain in Turkey. Britain retained its mandate over the oil-rich province of Mosul (Iraq) despite its Turkish and Kurdish populations. No provisions were made for creating an independent Armenia or Kurdistan.

Mustafa Kemal changed his name to Atatürk (Father of Turks); he also wrought, organized, and led one of the most far-reaching—and comparatively successful—social and political engineering feats in human history. The Ottoman Empire was toppled in favor of the new Republic of Turkey (October 29, 1923). Polygamy was outlawed. The fez was banned. Women were given the vote (1930). The Islamic caliphate (religious primate) was abolished (1924) and Turkey became a secular state. The Latin alphabet replaced Arabo-Turkic script.

Atatürk died on November 10, 1938. He was succeeded by Ismet Inonu (Ismet Bey, the victor of the battles of Inonu in the 1922 Greco-Turk War). Meanwhile, the abolition of the caliphate and disestablishment of state Islam has made Turkey the bitter target of Muslim fundamentalists and extremist groups.

In 1939, France, holding the postwar mandate to Syria, ceded the disputed Iskenderun region (the Hatay, where Antakya lies) back to Turkey, much to the dismay of the Syrians. While viewed by some as an opportunistic return to squabbling over borders (despite Atatürkists' claims to renounce "irredentism and recidivism"), the Hatay issue had been left dangling in 1920. France and Britain saw giving the Hatay back to Turkey as a means of assuring Turkish neutrality in the approaching war with Germany (World War II).

Atatürk's Republican People's party ruled Turkey as a rather unique single-party state. The RPP encouraged the development of the opposition Democratic party. Though created in 1946, the Democrats won the election of 1950 and assumed power. The Turkish military has acted as arbiter of Turkish politics and has taken (and released) governmental power three times in the last forty years.

The Kurds rebelled in 1925, protesting the Kemalists disestablishment of the Islamic caliphate. In 1930 a Kurdish insurgency broke out in the Lake Van and Ararat region (the town of Dogubeyazit was destroyed in the fighting). In 1937, Kurds and Turks clashed in the Tunceli area. The Republic of Turkey pursued anti-Kurd policies, referring to them as "mountain Turks," thus playing down the nationalist angle in favor of unruly mountaineers. Many of the eastern provinces were under permanent martial law. Ankara moved thousands of Kurds from the east and settled them in western Turkey. Kurdish nationalists were deeply involved in the leftist agitation of the late 1970s, the political activity that led to the army takeover in 1980.

In 1984 the Kurds began a new series of attacks inside Turkey. The Kurds had been involved in guerrilla activities inside Iran and Iraq, both before and during the recent Iran-Iraq War. Ironically, Turkey has been a haven for many Kurdish refugees fleeing the Iran-Iraq War and Iraqi attacks on Kurdish villages in Iraq. In 1989 and 1990 the Turkish Army and Kurdish guerrillas regularly clashed in the southeastern mountains.

Turkey played a major role in the Persian Gulf War. Though the Turk Army did not engage in direct combat, some twelve Iraqi divisions remained in northern Iraq to defend against a Turk attack. Another three to five Iraqi divisions watched the Kurds. The UN coalition air forces made use of several Turkish air bases, including the huge Turk base at Incirlik. In the aftermath of the Persian Gulf War, Kurds in Iraq rebelled and forces loyal to Iraq's Saddam Hussein stopped the initial rebellion. Displaced Kurds filled refugee camps in Turkey. A massive international relief effort began in April 1991 to relieve starvation among Kurds in northern Iraq. The UN established a no-fly zone above the 36th Parallel in Iraq, which kept the Iraqi Air Force from attacking the Kurds. In effect, a semiautonomous Kurdish state has emerged in this slice of northern Iraq.

Kurds rebelling against Turkey continued to make use of bases in Iraq and in the semiautonomous Kurdish zone. In 1992, Kurdish insurgents inside Turkey launched several new attacks. Turk forces launched attacks against Kurd bases in Iraq in 1992, 1993, and 1994. In 1994 the Turkish Army attacked and burned several villages in southeastern Turkey occupied by supporters of the Kurdish Workers party. Many of the villagers fled to Iraq. In spring 1995, Turkey conducted what amounted to an invasion of northern Iraq. A Turkish Army force of nearly forty thousand troops attacked all along the Iraq-Turkey border and surrounded several Kurdish Workers party enclaves and supply depots in the Atrush and Zakho areas. Ankara announced a new policy of occupying guerrilla base areas (though forces were later withdrawn). Kurdish "internal politics" (actually, interclan politics) are very complicated. The two main Iraqi Kurdish factions, the Kurdish Democratic party and the Patriotic Union of Kurdistan, have been fighting one another in Iraq. Neither of the Iraqi Kurd groups cares much for Turkish Kurds.

Turkish sources estimate that 16,000 to 18,000 people died in the guerrilla wars between 1984 and 1994. Nine hundred Kurdish villages in southeast Turkey have been "evacuated" (which means in some cases destroyed).

Cyprus has been a constant sore in Greek-Turk relations. The alleged birthplace of Aphrodite, the goddess of love, historically Cyprus has been a Greek island, though one ruled by a series of foreign invaders. The Turks took the island in 1570. In 1878, Great Britain took over. By that time a large Turkish minority lived on the island.

During the 1950s, the Greek Cypriots began to press for *enosis*—union with Greece. The Greek Cypriot terrorist organization EOKA (directed by Colonel George Grivas) waged an ugly insurgent war against the British. Britain's stupidity prolonged the conflict. In 1960 an independent Cyprus emerged, with a Greek president (Archbishop Makarios III, Greek Orthodox primate of Cyprus) and a Turk vice president, Rauf Denktash. Britain retained two military bases "in perpetuity." Great Britain and Turkey were to guarantee Cypriot sovereignty. Turkey was allowed to post a small contingent of troops on the island. *Enosis* with Greece was denied.

In 1963 the Cypriot government collapsed. EOKA terrorists attacked Turkish villagers. Battles broke out between Greek and Turk Cypriots. Turkey threatened an invasion. British troops failed to bring calm; UN forces (UNFOCYP) also failed. In 1967, Colonel Grivas formed a new force, EOKA-B, also dedicated to *enosis*. He was supported by the militarist "Colonels' regime" in Athens, which had taken power in Greece.

In 1974, EOKA-B attempted a coup in Cyprus. The Turkish Army invaded to protect the Turkish Cypriot minority. Eventually, the Turkish Army took nearly 40 percent of the island. As of mid-1995 the Turkish Army still occupies (or protects, depending on your point of view) the northeastern third of Cyprus. A Turkish Republic of Northern Cyprus (TRNC, officially named the Turkish Republic of Northern Cyprus in 1983, or Republic of North Kibris)—recognized only by Ankara—claims to be the government in the occupied zone.

Greece and Turkey have made moves to resolve the situation. As of mid-1995, Greek and Turk diplomats were discussing new options regarding elections in Cyprus. Both Turk and Greek Cypriots have called for a new Cypriot federal system of government. Greek Cypriot forces, however, were also in the process of acquiring new medium tanks.

Turkey and Greece have also clashed over air control and air-corridor rights over the Aegean, and exploration for and exploitation of Aegean shelf resources. The Greek community in Turkey has dwindled, the Greeks claim due to Turkish interference. In 1955 there was a series of anti-Greek riots in Istanbul in which over fifteen hundred people died. The Turks claim that Turks living inside Greece (Western Thrace) have had their land stolen and that Turks on the island of Rhodes have been forcibly "Hellenized."

Turkey and Bulgaria have been at bitter odds over Bulgaria's treatment of its Turkish minority. In 1989 over three hundred thousand Bulgarian Turks fled across the border into Turkey. The collapse of the Bulgarian Communist regime has mitigated Bulgar-Turk ethnic friction.

Turkey's often troubled relations with Iraq and Syria have several rotten historical roots. The Iraqi province of Mosul (which includes the town of Kirkuk), an oil-producing region, was once a Turk province with a Turkic majority. Syria's anger over the loss of the Hatay (Iskenderun/Antakya) has already been touched upon. All three nations have trouble with the Kurds and all three have played the "Kurdish card" on one another. During the Iran-Iraq War articles appeared in the Turkish press discussing what Turkey might do if Iraq lost and was "dismembered." Speculation included recovering the "lost Turks" of the Mosul area. The Iraqi invasion of Kuwait, which used a latent Iraqi claim to Kuwait as justification for Baghdad's annexation of the emirate (based on control of Kuwait via the Turkish fief of Basra) raised eyebrows—Turkey's claim to northern Iraq had a better basis in fact than Iraq's claim to Kuwait.

The Southeast Anatolia Project (SAP), a huge water control and dam project on both the Tigris and Euphrates rivers, has become particularly troublesome. Filling the immense reservoir behind the Atatürk Dam (one of twenty-one dams and seventeen hydroelectric projects in the SAP) will require four times the annual flow of the Euphrates. When the SAP is completed (around 2005), Syria's water flow in the Euphrates could shrink from 32 billion cubic meters a year to 20 billion. Iraq's could drop from 30 billion cubic meters a year to less than 11 billion. In 1990 the Syrian government blamed Turkey for a series of electrical outages, allegedly caused by loss of flow in the Euphrates River. The Iraqi invasion of Kuwait and Iraqi threats to use chemical weapons on Israel and Saudi Arabia was also a message for the Turks.

Finally, there's the Armenian problem. In 1915 at least 600,000 Armenians died—that's a rough figure the Turks accept. Armenians claim nearly a million were killed in a "genocide" conducted by the Ottoman armed forces. However, 600,000 seems to be a consistent figure for the number of Armenian dead. The source of all this mayhem was World War I. In 1915 the Russians attacked through eastern Armenia and many Armenians supported the invaders. There is no question that a number of Armenian leaders in Istanbul were rounded up and executed. The historical issue is the deaths of Armenians displaced by the fighting. Were they massacred by Turkish troops in a calculated act of genocide or did the Armenian civilians die from starvation, exposure, and "incidental" fighting? Turks point out that 2 million Muslims (i.e., Turks) died at roughly the same time and call it a reprehensible tragedy all the way around—but not a genocide. The Armenians don't believe it. They point to evidence that the Ottomans gave "permission" to the Kurds to destroy Armenian communities. The Armenians contend that the atrocities continued until 1923 and the Turk-Armenian conflict of 1920 was part of the genocide. They also note that in 1926 Atatürk himself deplored the killings in a press interview.

The political battle continues, as does a terrorist conflict. Armenian extremists began assassinating Turkish diplomats in 1973. Since 1975, ASALA (Armenian Secret Army for the Liberation of Armenia) has been the primary Armenian terrorist organization. ASALA is allegedly connected to several Lebanon-based Arab terrorist organizations. A substantial Armenian community lives in Lebanon and Syria.

Armenia has existed as a separate state on several occasions, most notably in the first century B.C. when Greater Armenia stretched from the Caspian Sea to the Mediterranean (the empire of Tigranes the Great). For the greater part of recorded history, however, Armenia has been a country "in between"—wedged between major regional and/or world powers. Armenia was the first state to accept Christianity as the official religion (A.D. 301). The Armenians' "Christianity in a Muslim sea" helped them keep their identity in conflicts with various Turkic peoples, the Arabs, and the Persians, but the Armenians didn't get along with fellow Christian Georgians or Russians, either. An Armenian state (Eviran) existed briefly in 1920, but was overrun by the Red Army and incorporated into the USSR. At the present time there are at least 4.5 million Armenians in the former USSR. In fact, Armenia is the most ethnically homogeneous nation emerging from the old Soviet Union—nearly 95 percent of the population is Armenian.

LOCAL POLITICS

Turkey

The Meclis—Grand National Assembly; as of 1995, 550 elected members.

7-10—Formula for U.S. military assistance for Turkey. For each ten bucks Turkey receives, Greece gets seven.

True Path party (DYP, the Dogru Yol)—Moderate conservative party, led by Ms. Tansu Ciller (formerly led by Suleyman Demirel); sometimes translated as the "Correct Way party."

Motherland party (ANAP)—Kemalist center-right party. Before his death, was dominated by Turgut Ozal. In 1995, led by Mesut Yilmaz.

Social Democrat Populist party (SHP)—Left-of-center party. Now called Republican People's Party.

Democratic Left party (DLP)—Led by ex-Premier Bulent Ecevit.

Green party—Nascent Turkish environmentalist party.

Welfare party (WP)—Formerly the National Salvation party (NSP); party openly espousing a "moderate" Islamic political philosophy. Took 158 Meclis seats in 1995. Led by Necmettin Erbakan.

Far right parties—National Action party; Nationalist Labor party (neofascist party; formerly the Nationalist Movement party; political home of the Gray Wolves).

Gray Wolves (the Boz Kurt—literally, "ashen wolves")—Fascist Turkish underground terrorist movement; led by Colonel Alpasla Turkes. Memet Ali Agca, the man who tried to assassinate Pope John Paul II in May 1981, was a member. The Gray Wolves may now be involved in the drug trade; allegedly tied to the Bulgarian Communist secret police. The Gray Wolves take their name from Turkish mythology. Out on the steppes of central Asia, the "first Turk" was supposedly suckled by a wolf. (See Roman myth of Romulus and Remus for Latin variant.)

Turkish Socialist party—Maoist-oriented socialists.

Irtica—Turkish word of Arab origin, meaning "religious reaction"—in Turkey's case, Islamic fundamentalist religious reaction.

Pro-Iranian "Islamic" political parties or pressure groups—Hizb al-Islam (Party of Allah); Islamic Jihad; Hizb al-Tahrir (Freedom party).

Alawites—Perhaps 20 percent of the population. This more liberal form of Islam has come under attack by Islamic fundamentalists. Alawites are found in the Turk and Kurdish populations and tend to be better educated and more economically successful.

Tarikats—Militant religious orders with a long history in Turkish culture and politics; basic unit is a *dergah*—a small group of the faithful united around a specific teacher (a *seyh* or *halife*); includes the Nurcu, the Suleymanci, and the Naksibendi. The Naksibendi dates back to the fourteenth century. The Isikcilar is a Naksibendi splinter group that supports the Motherland party.

Dev Sol (Revolutionary Left)—A radical Marxist terrorist group nominally supportive of the Kurds; involved in assassination of several members of the Turkish government. Turkish government actively sought to destroy Dev Sol in 1991 and 1992.

Turkish Army of the Aegean—Turkish armed forces not committed to NATO.

Incirlik—Site of major U.S. Air Force base in south-central Turkey.

European Customs Union—EU's customs zone. Turkey became a member in January 1996.

"Free Kurdistan"

People's Democracy party—Legitimate Kurdish nationalist party in Turkey.

Workers Party of Kurdistan (PKK, for Parti-ye Karkaran-i Kurdistan)—Main Kurdish resistance group active in Turkey; drawn primarily from poorest Kurdish area. Organized by Abdullah Ocalan ("Apo"). Followers of Ocalan are also called Apocus. PKK units are called HRKs (acronym for Kurdish Liberation Brigades). PKK did have troops trained in Lebanon but support bases have now shifted to Iraq.

Receives significant support from Syria. Ocalan is alleged to be living in a safe haven in Syria.

Pesh Merga—The general term for Kurdish resistance but usually applied to Kurdish resistance inside Iraq.

Kurdistan Democratic party (KDP)—Kurdish party inside Iraq.

Kurdish Republican party—Kurdish party inside Iraq.

Illegal Iraqi Kurd parties—Democratic Party of Kurdistan; Socialist Party of Kurdistan; Patriotic Union of Kurdistan.

National Liberationists of Kurdistan (KUK)—Kurd organization often at odds with the PKK.

Massoud Barzani—Kurdish leader seeking total Kurdish autonomy from Iraq.

Saladin—The most famous Kurd; remembered for his successes against the Crusaders. He retook Jerusalem for Islam in 1187.

Yazidi or Yezidi (Peacock Worshipers)—Yazidi Kurds (80,000 to 100,000 in number) who worship the sun; water is also sacred. They are said also to believe that God may ordain what happens on earth, but he lets the devil execute his orders. (Hmmm.) They may be direct descendants of the Assyrians. Viewed by Sunni Turks (and most Sunni Kurds) as extreme heretics.

Treaty of Sèvres—In 1920, this document that divided the Ottoman Empire promised the Kurds autonomy with "fixed frontiers," i.e., their own homeland (Kurdistan). Was replaced by the Treaty of Lausanne (1923).

Cyprus

Democratic Rally party (DISY)—Largest party in Cyprus.

Communist Party of Cyprus (AKEL)—Still strong, despite communism's collapse globally.

Other Greek Cypriot parties—Cypriot Democratic party (DIKO), Cypriot Socialist party (EDEK), Socialist Democratic Renewal party (ADISOK).

Cypriot National Guard—Greek Cypriot army; has 11,000 troops with another 2,000 regulars.

Turkish Republic of Northern Cyprus

National Unity party (UBP)—Major Turk Cypriot party. Led by Rauf Denktash and Dervis Eroglu.

Other Turk Cypriot parties—Republican Turkish party (CTP); Communal Liberation party; New Cyprus party.

Turkish Army—Turkey has two infantry divisions and an armored regiment inside Cyprus (approximately twenty-five thousand soliders).

Armenia (local name: Hayastan)

ASALA—Armenian Secret Army for the Liberation of Armenia; founded by Hagop Hagopian (see History).

Armenian Revolutionary Federation—An "international revolutionary party," which wants to establish a "united Armenia." It would consist of Armenia plus the rest of the region demarcated for an Armenian state by the Sèvres Treaty, plus Nakhichevan and Nagorno-Karabakh autonomous regions of Azerbaijan.

Armenian Apostolic Church—Central Armenian Christian church. Because Mount Ararat was the center of Armenia, many Armenians believe that God chose Armenia as the place to begin humanity anew—after the Flood.

Treaty of Turkmanchai (1828)—Ceded the province of Erivan (Armenia) from Persia to Russia.

Major Armenian political parties—Armenian National Movement; Democratic Party of Armenia.

POLITICAL TREND CHARTS

TURKEY

Gv95	Gv20	PC95	PC20	R95	R20	Ec95	Ec20	EdS95	EdS20
AD6,4	AD7,6	5	6+	5	5−	4+	5	4+	5−

Gv = Government Type

PC = Political Cohesiveness (0 = chaos, 9 = maximum); political cohesiveness excluding Kurdish problem = 7

AD = Authoritarian Democracy (effectiveness, 0–9, stability 0–9)

R = Repression Index (9 maximum)

Ec = Comparative Economic Status (0–9)

EdS = Relative Education Status (0–9)

GREECE

Gv95	Gv20	PC95	PC20	R95	R20	Ec95	Ec20	EdS95	EdS20
RD6,6	RD7,6	8	8	3+	3−	4	6*	5+	6

RD = Representative Democracy, but with very authoritarian aspects, especially if PASOK (Greek Socialist party) is in power (effectiveness, 0–9, stability 0–9)

*Could be significantly higher if Greece enacts open market reforms; Greece is a land of entrepreneurs and could prosper if governmental market obstacles are removed. (A 7?).

ARMENIA

Gv95	Gv20	PC95	PC20	R95	R20	Ec95	Ec20	EdS95	EdS20
ED6,4	AD4,4	7	6	7	7	2	3	3	3

ED = Ethnic Dictatorship

And, for an argument's sake:

"INDEPENDENT CYPRUS"
(COMBINING GREEK AND TURK HALVES)

Gv20	PC20	R20	Ec20	EdS20
RD4,3	2	4	4	4

RD = Representative Democracy, but a curious one; Turks would have to have extensive political guarantees to keep them from being politically victimized by Greek majority

"TURKISH REPUBLIC OF CYPRUS"

Gv20	PC20	R20	Ec20	EdS20
FM6,6	8	6	2	2

FM = Foreign Military, in this case Turk

"KURDISTAN"
(CARVED FROM TURKEY AND IRAQ)

Gv20	PC20	R20	Ec20	EdS20
AC3,2	5	7	1	1−

AC = Authoritarian Coalition

REGIONAL POWERS AND POWER INTEREST INDICATOR CHARTS

TURKEY AND ITS TROUBLES

	Economic Interests	Historical Interests	Political Interest	Military Interest	Force Generation Potential	Ability to Intervene Politically	Interest/ Ability to Promote Economic Development
Russia	4	9	7	8	5−*	5	2
Ukraine	4	9	7	7	2−*	3	1
Greece	3	9	9	9	3	4	3
Syria	2	8	7	8	4	2	2
Iraq	3	6	6	7	1	2	1
Iran	2	4	5	2	1	3	1
Israel	3	3	3	3	1+	1	2
United States	5	4	7	7	4	7	5
Germany	7	6	7	6	1−	5+	6+
Bulgaria	4	8	7	6	1−	2	4
Kurds	6	9	9	8	2	3−	1
"Armenia"	7	9	8	8	1−	1	0

NOTE: 0 = minimum; 9 = maximum
*"All-out" Russian and Ukrainian effort in Black Sea, and eastern Turkey; highly unlikely but Moscow and Kiev together can bring a lot of military power to bear.

GRECO-TURK "BALKAN WAR"

	Economic Interests	Historical Interests	Political Interest	Military Interest	Force Generation Potential*
Greece	8	9	9	9	6
Turkey	9	9	9	9	8
Bulgaria	7	9	8	8	3−
United States†	5	5	8	8	5
Russia†	5	8	8	7	4‡
Serbia†	6	7	8	7	1+‡
Romania†	6	6	7	7	1‡
Germany†	6	6	9−	7	2
France†	6	6	7	6	1

*FGPs for Thrace, southern Bulgaria, and Aegean regions of Turkey and Greece
(†)Actual combat participation unlikely, but forces must be considered
(‡)Russia FGP for D+20 in Bulgaria and European Thrace; Serb and Romanian figures for Bulgaria and Grecian (Western) Thrace

CYPRUS

	Economic Interests	Historical Interests	Political Interest	Military Interest	Force Generation Potential	Ability to Intervene Politically	Interest/ Ability to Promote Economic Development
Turkey	3	8	9	8	9	8	7
Greece	2	8	9	6	3	8	7
United Kingdom	1	7	7	6	3	4	6
United States	1	5	7	6	6	7	4
Israel	2	6	6	7	2	1	4
Syria	2	7	3	6	1	2	0
"UN"	−	7	8	8	1	7	−
GrkCy	9	9	9	9	2	6	9
TurkCy	9	9	9	9	1−	5	9

KURDISH INSURGENCY

	Economic Interests	Historical Interests	Political Interest	Military Interest	Force Generation Potential	Ability to Intervene Politically	Interest/ Ability to Promote Economic Development
Turkey	7	9	9	8	8	8	6
Iran	6	8	7	6	3+	7	6
Iraq	7	8	8	7	1	4	2
Russia	2	6	6	5	2	5	1
United States	1	5	2	2	1	4	4
Syria	2	6	6	6	1−	5	1

MESOPOTAMIAN WATER WAR
(CHART ASSUMES TURKEY, SYRIA, AND IRAQ ARE COMBATANTS)

	Economic Interests	Historical Interests	Political Interest	Military Interest	Force Generation Potential*	Ability to Intervene Politically
Turkey	8	8	9	9	8	−
Syria	9	9	9	9	6	−
Iraq	9	9	9	9	3+	−
Iran	2	8	7	7	3	6
Israel	2	7	7	8	2	2
United States	5	6	7	6	3	7
Russia	4	6	7	7	2	7
Greece	1	4	8+	8	−	2
Bulgaria	1	2	7	6	−	1

*FGPs for southeastern and southern Turkey, Iraq north of Baghdad, and all of Syria. Greece and Bulgaria could exert pressure on Turkey along Aegean and Thracian fronts.

PARTICIPANT STRATEGIES AND GOALS

Turkey—Ankara's first order of business is to improve economic performance; the Turkish government is engaged in a massive attempt to improve public schools and raise education standards. Though their markets have been slow to develop, the Turks perceive the new Turkic and Islamic nations of the former Soviet Union as a potential economic boon. For the first time in five hundred years, Turkey could be an exporter of technology.

The Kurdish problem remains, and is a continuing stain on Turkey's human rights record. The strategy of detribalization of Kurds failed— yes, Kurds moved into the cities, where they stayed poor, angry, and Kurdish. Ankara has tried and will continue to try to destroy PKK guerrillas in the field and to hope that an expanding economy will attract Kurdish moderates. But the Kurdish question will ultimately be solved politically, and all but the most hard-line Turks have come to that conclusion. Even the right-wing Motherland party has begun to support Kurdish education programs and Kurdish television broadcasting, demands moderate Kurds have made for years. The goal is to cut off PKK radicals from moderate Kurds.

Turkey is still wary of Iraq's armed forces. Ankara thinks that Syria and Iraq should trust it not to turn off the water spigot on the Tigris and the Euphrates and has so far let it go at that. The Turks have never had a high opinion of Arab military prowess, although Iraq with nuclear weapons could change that.

The Turks are confident that relations with Greece and Bulgaria will remain stable—perhaps rhetorically nasty at times but no more than that. Turkey wants desperately to join the EEC and resents Greek blockage of its admission. In early 1995 the Greeks agreed to support a Turkish customs union with the EEC. Turkey joined in 1996.

Economic cooperation between Greece and Turkey may make for new accommodations on Cyprus. Turkey's long-range aim in Cyprus was partition, and for nearly two decades Ankara believed that nothing else was practical. That view is changing. Turkey, however, does want to relax Greco-Turk tensions and many mainland Turks would support a "loose" federal Cypriot state that guaranteed Turk Cypriot lives and property. The Greeks would like to see Cyprus admitted to the EEC.

Syria—Damascus has played and could continue to play "the Kurdish card" against Turkey. Right now the issue is control of water. It could once again become Alexandretta and Antioch. Syria is wrapped up in Lebanon and grapples with Israel in a slow, frustrating peace-no-peace process. It cannot really afford to become militarily involved with Turkey. But if Turkey gets into a scrape with the Greeks and Bulgars, and if Syria's share of the Euphrates River water is threatened . . .

Iraq—Baghdad's Baath regime was shocked by Turkey's shutdown of its oil pipeline and military alliance with Saudi Arabia. Iraq is militarily and politically weak, but the Kurd conflict, the damming of the Euphrates River, and control of the Mosul-Kirkuk region remain live issues between Ankara and Baghdad. With nuclear weapons, Iraq could well feel up to confronting the Turks. Among other things, this would boost Iraqi prestige among Arab nations (none of whom ever felt keen about taking on the Turks).

Armenian nationalists—Independent Armenia is a victory. The war over Nagorno-Karabakh with Azerbaijan has depleted Armenia but may have whetted nationalist appetites for recovering other "lost" Armenian territory, such as the Lake Van area in Turkey. Whatever happens, Armenian radicals will continue to be active—with bombs and bullets.

Pan-Turkic radicals—Though small in number, pan-Turkism, the unity of all Turkic peoples, has a grand romantic appeal. The collapse of the USSR gives these groups what they perceive as a unique historical opportunity to return Turkey to its glory.

Muslim fundamentalists inside Turkey—Bemoan "the loss of Turkey's soul" to Western materialism and hope that economic failure will lead to an increase in their political power.

Greece and Bulgaria—These nations are now very interested in economic development. Black Sea economic initiatives have begun to forge new economic links among Bulgaria, Greece, and Turkey. Still, historically, Greece and Bulgaria are the backbones of a grand "anti-Turk" alliance.

244 / A Quick and Dirty Guide to War

Greek Cypriots—Though the prospect of *enosis* grows more remote, there is still some hope for withdrawal of the Turkish Army and a reunification of the island.

Turkish Cypriots—Continue to demand "coequal" status at negotiations with Greek Cypriots.

Potential Outcomes

Kurdistan

1. 55 percent chance through 2001: Turkish Army wins this round of Kurdish conflict inside Turkey and suppresses revolt for a decade or more. Turkey pays an initial political price in Europe, but, alas, Europe soon forgets about the Kurds. Turkish initiatives to politically integrate moderate Kurds begin to pay off.
2. 30 percent chance through 2001: Insurgency continues at late 1980 levels; no resolution. Turkey pays political price in Europe.
3. 4 percent chance through 2001: Kurdish resistance and Turkish political concerns vis-à-vis EEC integration and world opinion lead to an "autonomous Kurdish region" within Turkey. Kurds emigrate into Turkey from Iraq and Iran, exacerbating regional tensions.
4. 3 percent chance before 2001: New Persian Gulf war pits Turkey against Iraq or a Mesopotamian water war becomes a likelihood, and the Kurds ally themselves with Turkey in hopes of backing a winner and gaining Kurdistan. (The Kurds don't forget that Iraq gassed them.)
5. 2 percent chance before 2001: Iraq, Iran, Turkey, and Syria cooperate to defeat the Kurds. (Iraq and Iran commit genocide; Kurds accept Turk conditions in preference to hell of Iran and Iraq. "Kurdish problem" disappears in Turkey for fifty years.)
6. 1 percent chance before 2001: Outcome 4, except Kurds ally with Iraq and/or Syria, in hopes of backing a winner and gaining Kurdistan.

Greco-Turk Balkan War

A minimal 4 percent chance of outright war erupting through 2001. The United States still has a great deal of political sway in Athens and Ankara. "Armed friction" (ships pointing weapons at one another, airplanes buzzing each other) will occur if Greeks block Turk economic integration with Europe.

Who wins if this immensely foolish conflict occurs? The biggest likelihood is a massive and expensive stalemate. An 80 percent chance of a stalemate (border shifts of ten kilometers or less, one or two islands lost or taken; this is largely dependent on Turkish restraint); still, look for several thousand casualties. A 12 percent chance of Turkish victory—Turks gain three or four islands, smash several Greek and Bulgarian regiments and maim the Greek Navy. An 8 percent chance of Greco-Bulgarian victory—the Greeks gain a slice of the Turkish coastline and/or take a Turk island, hold a couple of medium-sized Turkish towns, sink a pair of Turkish destroyers, and bottle up the rest of the Turkish Navy in the straits and Black Sea. The Bulgars shell Turkish Thrace and feel like they've accomplished something.

Cyprus

1. 50 percent chance through 2001: UN- or EEC-brokered treaty leads to Turkish Army pullout. International forces guarantee protection of Turkish minority. Cyprus is reconstituted as a loose federation, but Turkish Cypriots retain a great deal of autonomy in their "canton" (which will be about 33 percent of the island). Call this the Swiss solution.
2. 48 percent chance through 2001: Continued Turkish Army occupation and split into the current (1995) Greek and Turkish zones. (There is a great deal of stability in this situation. The Turkish Cypriot community fears any Turkish Army pullout.)
3. 2 percent chance through 2001: Turkish sector completely separates and forms a new nation. Greek Cypriots finally say "what the

hell" and agree to accept it if "most" of the Turkish Army pulls out. Intermittent violence occurs.

Persian Gulf War Redux: See Chapter 2. If this war reoccurs, expect Turk and NATO forces to invade Iraq from the north.

Great Mesopotamian Water War

There is a 2 percent chance of this conflict occurring in any form through 2001. Not very likely, thank goodness, for this is one of those conflicts that could lead to all kinds of unforeseen sorrow. Here is how one scenario develops: Iraq, believing it is being cheated of its water rights, fails to receive political satisfaction (and more water) from Turkey and/or Syria. Iraq turns to saber rattling and promotes terrorist attacks on the Turkish dams. Iraq could also stir up the Kurds inside Turkey, promising them a "Kurdistan." Tensions mount and war erupts.

If the Balkan, Aegean, or Cyprus fronts don't erupt simultaneously, and especially if the United States (or Israel, for Jews have lived in comparative peace in Turkey for over five hundred years) helps the Turks take out Iraqi rebuilt nuclear and chemical weapon delivery systems, there's a 90 percent chance of a Turkish victory if Turkey and Iraq fight alone; a 70 percent chance of Turkey prevailing against Syria and Iraq. A Turkish-Syrian alliance against Iraq, while unlikely, would best Iraq 95 percent to 5 percent.

The wildest card—An Iraqi, Greek, and Bulgarian alliance.

Armenian Conflicts

The likelihood of a "Greater Armenia" coming into existence, as proposed by Armenian radicals, is near zero. Turkey is too strong and Armenia remains surrounded by Muslims. But trouble and bloodshed on this issue is a sure bet.

KIND AND COST OF WAR

Wars in this part of the world tend to be pretty bloody, especially if Russians or Turks get involved. The Ottoman Turks kept the peace among their restive Arab subjects by sending in the troops with orders to shoot to kill, and kept doing it until the malcontents were cured of their bad habits. The Arabs still remember Turkish military prowess and would only go up against the Turks if they were prepared for some serious fighting, say with nuclear weapons. Deaths would likely run into the hundreds of thousands even for a short war. Aircraft enable the Turks to go after valuable national assets like Iraqi oil fields. Except for the dam project in Turkey, most Turkish assets are spread around or concentrated near Istanbul. Still, none of the nations in the area are very wealthy and a war of any length would cost several tens of billions of dollars of resources no one in the area can afford to lose.

Mountains make for rough infantry combat. There are several key flatlands in which to exercise mechanized forces. Large campaigning areas and the comparative lack of aircraft make it easier for high-performance aircraft with good avionics to attack weakly guarded enemy installations.

Chapter 6

THE RUSSIAN EMPIRE AND THE "NEAR ABROAD"

INTRODUCTION

Russia has reached a historical watershed. The 1917 revolution destroyed the ancient monarchy and simultaneously rejected democracy and the market economy. But the 1917 revolution didn't work. The overbearing and inept czarist aristocracy eventually returned in the form of overbearing and inept Communist party officials and state-appointed industrial managers. The second revolution in 1991 was less bloody than that of 1917. But the huge Communist bureaucracy was not dismissed, only reduced. Unlike the 1917 revolution, 1991 saw the dismemberment of the czarist empire, something even the 1917 Reds were not willing to tolerate. Territories that had been Russia's for centuries, like the Ukraine and Belarus, plus others that had only been conquered in the nineteenth century in central Asia and the Caucasus, were suddenly independent once more. But not completely free—the Russians called their new neighbors the "Near Abroad" and treated them more like prodigal children than sovereign nations. The

New Russia faces serious economic and political problems internally and also on its new borders with these new neighbors. The Near Abroad nations are lurching toward various degrees of armed conflict with themselves and Russia. A series of border wars, and civil wars, are simmering, wars in and among nations with nuclear weapons.

SOURCE OF CONFLICT

Russia was one of the world's last genuine empires. The empire was named the USSR (Union of Soviet Socialist Republics). It contained over a hundred distinct ethnic groups, with eighteen languages spoken by at least one million people. The "real" Russians comprised only about half the population of 290 million. After the USSR collapsed in 1991, the population of the New Russia was 149 million, of which some 82 percent were Russians. Of the remainder, about 4 percent of the population is Tartar, 3 percent Ukrainian, 1 percent Chuvash, and the remaining 10 percent a mélange of ethnic groups. The new nations carved out of the remaining half of the Soviet Union were largely areas that had never been nations before, or had last been independent centuries ago. But these new nations now contained some 25 million Russians. These isolated Russians may seed serious future problems.

After two world wars, one civil war, two revolutions, and several rebellions and border wars, Russia is worse off now, relative to the rest of the industrialized world, than she was before the 1917 revolution. The Russian people are aware of their comparative poverty. While economic reforms and a market economy may improve living standards, the problems of Russia's newly created and unstable neighbors remain. Disorder within Russia, and in the nations of the Near Abroad, are a combination that produces events leading to tragedy.

WHO'S INVOLVED

Russian free marketers—Political freedom is enjoyed by a minority of the world's population, but more and more are getting a taste of economic freedom, the "free market." Given a choice between democracy and prosperity, most people will choose, as the Chinese say, "to get rich." Russians are no different. The free marketers are in favor of free markets, even if it means more economic hardship for Russians in the short term. This is a hard policy to sell to Russia's poverty-stricken population. But the free marketers are also in favor of good relationships with Russia's neighbors, if only to make it easier to do business in areas where Russia has an advantage. This group comprises a minority of the population (perhaps 5 percent), although an able and energetic minority.

Russian democrats—An important minority of Russians, especially among the well educated, who see a functioning democracy as essential to Russia's future. The democrats are inclined to keep hands off the neighbors, if only because they would prefer to see those neighbors ruled by democratic governments.

Russian autocrats—The Communists are still around, even if they don't always call themselves Communists anymore. These Communists think like the Communists of old and, when they can get away with it, act like the autocratic, corrupt, and ruthless Communists who controlled Russia for over seventy years. The Communists have appeal for two reasons: (1) The old people have known nothing but communism all their lives and, in a perverse way, feel more comfortable with it. The economic changes have hurt the elderly pensioners the most, and the Communists promise to revive the old days and their more generous subsidies for the pensioners. (2) The Communists also make headway with the promise of more "order," even if it means the reestablishment of a police state. As social disorder increases, the appeal of the "good old days," warts and all, becomes increasingly compelling. The autocrats tend to make common cause with the Russian nationalists, as a strong Russia is also a nation that can treat its neighbors as vassal states.

Russian nationalists—Russian ultrapatriots, largely rightist and often extremist. There has always been a significant portion of the Russian population that enthusiastically supported making Russia stronger, and larger, and more Russian. The primary motive was the idea that Russians were destined to rule everything in sight. Communism played down the "Russian" aspect of this nationalism in the name of "socialist internationalism." When socialism in its many forms failed, the Russian nationalists popped out of the woodwork again. No single organization has been able to harness that nationalism, yet. Many of the nationalists tend to be older people who remember the USSR's glory days in the afterglow of World War II (or "the Great Patriotic War," as they call it in Russia). Younger Russians, at least the ones who are bright enough to provide leadership, are too busy learning how to operate in a market economy and getting rich. It is, however, only a matter of time before the nationalists get organized, at which point Russian empire-building will once more be a major threat to world peace.

The Baltic States (Lithuania, Latvia, and Estonia)—For the last few centuries, these three nations were either part of Russia or battlegrounds for Russian attempts to control them. What makes the Baltic States so distinct from Russia in the first place is their location (on the Baltic coast) and their trading relationships (with Western and Scandinavian nations). This has made the Baltic States wealthier, better educated, and, in their minds, generally superior to (or at least quite different from) the Russians. A major internal problem is that about 30 percent of the Estonian, 33 percent of the Latvian, and 9 percent of the Lithuanian population is Russian. Russian troops could return to "protect" local Russians now forced to assimilate.

Belarus—Annexed by Russia in the eighteenth century, "White Russia" had never been independent as a nation, but rather always existed as one or more smaller feudal states. Poland and Lithuania had long contended with Russia for control of the area. Belarus became independent in 1991 because of distaste for Communist rule. Many Belarussians want to be part of Russia once more. The 13 percent of the population who are Russian are even more eager for such a merger. The 4 percent of the population who are Polish and 3 percent who are Ukrainian are less so.

The Ukraine—Early on, the Ukraine had a stronger claim as the birthplace of Russia (in Kievan Rus) than the Moscow-centered region to the north. The Ukraine maintained a precarious independence, usually as a collection of uneasy feudal allies, until the seventeenth century. At that point, a better-organized and aggressive "Russia" (with Moscow as its capital) expanded east and west, building what would eventually become the Russian Empire. The Ukraine was one of the first additions, but the Ukrainians never forgot their desire for independence. The Ukrainian language is closely related to Russian. Culturally, the two people are quite similar, although many of the Ukrainians are Roman Catholic, while nearly all religious-minded Russians are Orthodox (and do not recognize the religious supremacy of the pope). Moreover, after three centuries of Russian rule, some 20 percent of the Ukrainian population is ethnic Russian (another 6 percent comprise various other minorities). Like Belarus, there are many Ukrainians who would like to be part of Russia once more, but so far a majority of the population is determined to hang on to independence.

Moldova—Formerly Bessarabia, it was first annexed by Russia in 1815, but has long been claimed by Romania (and reverted to that nation after World War I). With a population of some 4.5 million and 65 percent of the population ethnically related to Romanians, the independence is tenuous. Some 27 percent of the population is Ukrainian and Russian (split 50-50) and neither of these groups are keen to live under Moldovan-Romanian domination.

The new central Asian nations—Five new central Asian nations emerged out of the wreckage of the Soviet Union. None had ever been nations before. While they shared many common characteristics and problems, each had some unique items to distinguish them.

POPULATION AND LAND AREA OF THE NEW CENTRAL ASIAN NATIONS

	Population	Area (sq km)
Kazakhstan	17,400,000	2,717,300
Kyrgyzstan	4,800,000	198,500
Tajikistan	6,100,000	143,100
Turkmenistan	4,100,000	488,100
Uzbekistan	23,000,000	447,400

Kazakhstan—A central Asian region conquered in the late nineteenth century. Only 42 percent of the 17 million inhabitants are Kazakhs (a Turkic people, whose ancestors comprised the Mongol "Golden Horde"). Another 45 percent are European (80 percent Russian, the rest Ukrainian and German). The remaining 13 percent are various other Asian groups. Kazakhstan is the most "Russified" of the central Asian "republics" (as these quasi-autonomous areas were called by the Soviets). The large European minority is needed, as it comprises most of the educated and technically trained people. But the non-Kazakhs are not made to feel welcome and that will be the cause of future problems. This is the only one of the central Asian states to be left with nuclear weapons when the USSR dissolved. One of the conditions of the USSR breakup was that whatever was in one of the new countries when the breakup took effect belonged to the new nation. As a result, a lot of high-tech military equipment ended up in non-Russian hands. Kazakhstan inherited a large number of ICBMs and their nuclear warheads.

Kyrgyzstan—This is one of the smaller central Asian regions; it was overrun by the Russians in the late nineteenth century. In fact, it is one of the last areas so conquered and is hard by the Chinese border (and has many people of the same Turkic background across the border in China). Only 53 percent of the population is Kirghiz, with 20 percent being Russian and the rest other central Asian peoples. A very shaky arrangement. The same old story exists here; The long-time Communist-era bosses are still in charge, running a type of government Stalin would approve of.

Tajikistan—Central Asian region conquered in the late nineteenth century. This area is unique in that it is the only former Soviet Central Asian area that does not consist of Turkic people; the Tajiks are related to the Iranians and speak a similar language. Some 65 percent of the people are Tajiks, with 25 percent Turkic Uzbeks and only 3 percent Russians. Bordering Afghanistan, Tajikistan experiences considerable conflict with antigovernment rebels who maintain bases in Afghanistan and raid across the border. Russian troops are stationed on the border to help maintain security. The former Communist administrators managed to get themselves elected head of the new "democratic" government. These new/old leaders have carried on in the old Soviet style, leading to a fair amount of unrest among the population. Most of the resistance is from Muslim fundamentalists, but the government considers the smaller number of prodemocracy people just as dangerous.

Turkmenistan—Another of the smaller central Asian republics. On the border with Iran, it was conquered by Russia in the 1880s. Population is only four million, with Turkomans (a Turkic people, naturally) comprising nearly 75 percent of the population. Russians account for only 5 percent, and this is steadily falling as Russians, made to feel unwelcome in the newly independent nation, leave. The rest of the people are from various other central Asian areas. There are about a million Turkomans across the border in Iran, a source of potential conflict should the idea arise that all Turkomans should be united. The current Turkmenistan government is run by former Communist officials who, being the only politicians around when the USSR fell, managed to get themselves elected.

Uzbekistan—One of the more populous areas of the former Soviet Central Asia. The population of 23 million is 72 percent Uzbek. Russians account for about 12 percent, and most are leaving when they have the means. As with the other new central Asian nations, the former Communist politicians managed to get themselves elected, there being few other politicians in the country to oppose them. Those who did organize opposition parties have had to deal with Communist-style oppression from the new "democratically elected" leadership.

The Caucasus—As bad as things are in central Asia, they are much worse in the Caucasus. Long a crossroads for ethnic migrations and armies on the march, this mountainous region has always been divided by quite different, and mutually hostile, populations. Some are Christian, some are Muslim. Some are Slav, some are Turk, and some are from ethnic origins lost in the mists of time. There are three new nations in the Caucasus: Armenia, Georgia, and Azerbaijan.

THE CAUCASUS

	Population	Area (sq km)
Armenia	3,600,000	29,800
Georgia	5,700,000	69,700
Azerbaijan	7,700,000	86,600

Armenia is the most ethnically unified of these nations, with nearly 95 percent of the population being Armenian. All would be well were it not for a dispute over an Armenian-populated region (Nagorno-Karabakh) within Azerbaijan. The two nations have been fighting over this issue since 1991, with the Azeris getting the worst of it. The war has wrecked Armenia's economy, but not their resolve to press on. The damage has actually been worse to Azerbaijan, whose population is about 85 percent Azeris (a Turkic people). Despite considerable oil wealth and a larger population, internal political disputes and the war with Armenia have ruined the economy and left the nation in a state of civil disorder. The Muslim Azeris get diplomatic, and some economic, aid from Iran and Turkey, while the Christian Armenians call upon the Russians and Western nations. Physical and psychological exhaustion will eventually bring peace, but not until more damage is done to both nations.

Georgia's population is 70 percent Georgian, an ancient Caucasus people. But 8 percent of the population is Armenian, 6 percent Russian, 5 percent Azeris, 3 percent Ossetians and the remainder various other groups. The Ossetians declared their independence from Georgia and successfully resisted attempts to stop them. Internal bickering also contributed to economic and political chaos. Russia has been called in by one faction or another to help calm things down, with mixed success.

Not all of the Caucasus peoples became independent nations. Chechnya, a small area with a population of about one million, declared independence in 1991, but Russia refused to accept it. An invasion was launched in late 1994, with the fighting lasting well into 1995. Several other small ethnic groups in the Caucasus have tried to separate themselves from Russia, but the experience of the Chechens will likely discourage, for the moment, similar efforts.

Mongolia—Still a bone of contention between Russia and China over who should have the most influence. Mongolia was always an independent nation, sort of. Although the Mongols eventually conquered China in the thirteenth century, they were absorbed by the more numerous Chinese in a century or two. Mongol rule continued in other areas, but Mongolia was never to be a major military power again. In the seventeenth century, yet another northern tribe (the Manchurian Tanguts, or "Manchus") conquered China and proceeded to make sure that none of China's many other neighbors was able to do the same for a while. Mongolia and Tibet were turned into protectorates and considerable influence was exercised in other border areas (Nepal, Cambodia, Vietnam). The Russians were still moving toward the Pacific Ocean while all this was going on, and they wisely avoided antagonizing the powerful Manchus too much. All this changed from 1800 onward as the Manchus began to lose their touch. The Russians moved in, seizing Chinese lands in the Pacific in 1860 that cut China off from the Sea of Japan and gave Russia its "Far Eastern" province (and the port of Vladivostok). By 1900, Mongolia was a Russian-influenced area. Between 1900 and 1921, Mongolia gradually threw off Chinese influence, became nominally independent (as a "Communist republic"), and Russian influence in Mongolia waxed and waned, but never disappeared, right down to the present. After the USSR broke up, Russian troops finally ended their half-century-plus presence in Mongolia. The local Communists managed to get themselves elected to power in the first elections. The population is only 2.5 million (90 percent Mongols). Insignificant in most respects, Mongolia still looms as a bone of contention between China and Russia. Note that there are two "Mongolias." Just south of Mongolia there is the Chinese region known as Inner Mongolia. The population is largely Mongolian, but has been under Chinese control, on and off, for several centuries. The current nation of Mongolia is referred to by the Chinese as Outer Mongolia, and the Chinese would like to unite the two Mongolias under Chinese rule. Eventually. The Chinese are patient, and persistent. And that is what worries the Russians.

Internal dissidents—Before the cold war ended, the dissidents in the Soviet Union were those calling for democracy. In the newly democratic Russia, the dissidents are those calling for a return to some form of totalitarianism. This ranges from the original Communist bureaucracy, to a return to the czarist government or, oddly enough, a Nazi-style fascism. Normally, as in other European democracies, that would be seen as no more than a minor threat. But Russia is new to democracy; it is a nation that has never before experienced this form of government. What Russians are used to is centuries of one form of totalitarian government or another. Haunting Russia is the memory of the German Weimar Republic, the post–World War I democracy that was unable to prevent Adolf Hitler and his Nazis from coming to power. In the 1920s, Germany was also a nation that had never experienced democracy before, and the first attempt at democratic government didn't work.

Eastern Europe—Russia and Eastern Europe need each other. Historically, Eastern Europe has been a buffer—militarily, politically, economically, and culturally—between Russia and the West. Since World War II, this relationship has changed to one where the Eastern European nations were forcibly linked in all ways with Russia. After 1989, all but some of the economic links were severed. Russia is still a viable market for Eastern European products that cannot yet compete in Western markets. And most Eastern European nations obtain much of their energy supplies and some raw materials from Russia. These last economic ties will continue to wither away as Eastern European nations turn increasingly to the West. Eastern Europe has demonstrated the ability to convert their economies to a Western standard faster than Russia. That does not do much for Russia, which will as a consequence find itself increasingly cut off from its best source of many consumer and industrial items that it cannot produce itself. Yet the four decades of Russian domination did produce many links that are worth keeping, and goodwill from Eastern European nations will go a long way toward easing the transition of Russia from its Communist past to whatever the future holds.

Western Europe—Historically, Russia has yearned to be accepted as part of Western Europe instead of being viewed as the unstable (and slightly unsavory) giant to the east. Western Europe, with the exception of Germany, has been allied, or at peace, with Russia for over a century. With Communist dogmatism no longer an issue, there is an eagerness to do some serious business with Russia. Whether this can become a mutually beneficial relationship depends on how well Russia reforms itself politically and economically. Economic reforms in Russia have been coming sporadically and unpredictably. Avoiding war with Communist Russia is proving to be easier than doing business with the New Russia. Western Europe desperately wants to do both, and to that end has been quite generous in terms of economic aid. But the fear of the "Russian Bear" has been kindled anew with Russia's armed suppression of dissent in Chechnya.

United States—Russia is far more affected by its neighbors than by the distant United States (despite the common border between far-off Alaska and Siberia). The biggest impact of the United States on Russia is through U.S. allies and trading partners. But this influence has diminished as Russia went from the status of a common enemy to one of a trading partner. In this respect, America's military allies became economic competitors chasing after the same business opportunities within Russia. While many Russians would prefer to do business primarily with the United States (for a complex mélange of reasons), other closer, more eager, and equally capable trading partners are keen on diminishing opportunities for trade with the United States.

Japan—A demilitarized Japan is seen as a potentially big economic help to Russia and a diplomatic ally against any problems with the Chinese. Should Japan substantially rearm, however, it's a different story, as Japan could make as much of a case for owning Russia's Far Eastern provinces as Russia (or China). The potential for either trade or conflict remains. With Russia possibly slipping into civil disorder, Japan would be faced with opportunities and dangers in dealing with such a situation. There is also the matter of several islands to the north of present-day Japan that were taken by Russia after World War II. The Japanese would like them back, peacefully, if possible. In the fall of 1990 the Kremlin announced that two of the Kurile Islands might be ceded to Japan for certain considerations; this offer was later withdrawn. But the prospect of another round of bidding on this issue remains.

China—Communism also went through some changes in China, and although the changes are not quite the same as those that occurred in Russia, the potential for civil war or disorder is on the same scale. Russia and China cannot do a lot for each other economically, but they can do great damage to each other militarily. There is also little love lost between the populations of both countries, particularly because of the Russian territories on China's northern border whose historical ownership is in dispute.

GEOGRAPHY

Russia is the world's largest nation (it occupies 17.1 million square kilometers, to the United States' 9.4 million). Most of Russia is generally flat, often frozen, and largely unpopulated. Over half the population lives on less than a quarter of the land west of the Ural Mountains (the traditional border between Asia and Europe). Almost all of the country lies as far north as Canada. The climate is as varied as the nation's size, but is generally harsh. Overall, it's a dry and chilly country with relatively little arable land. All of the major ports are blocked by ice for part of the year (yes, even Murmansk gets ice floes). Siberia (Asian Russia), east of the Urals, is covered with vast coniferous forests and tundra. While the bulk of the country is uninhabited, and because of bad climate uninhabitable, there are ample natural resources located in the wilderness areas. Getting these goodies out is a major obstacle, as the rivers generally run north to south, while moving raw materials to where they are needed requires east-west movement. Highland steppes and mountains string along the southern border regions. Geography, like history, has not been kind to Russia.

With the exception of the Baltic States, the border areas that now comprise the Near Abroad are almost all along Russia's southern perimeter. Imperial Russia tended to expand toward warmer weather, with the hope of eventually obtaining an ice-free ocean port. That never happened; the closest Russia came to this goal was the Black Sea ports. But the Black Sea is an inland body of water, with access to the high seas controlled by the Turkish Straits (the Dardanelles). Most of the Near Abroad is territory located on open plains, relatively easy areas to conquer (or reconquer). The Near Abroad states are warmer, although much of the central Asian area is dry or desert. Belarus and the Ukraine are prime real estate; the Caucasus is mountainous and populated by people quite different from the Russians.

HISTORY

At least seven thousand years ago, Indo-European tribes began moving north from the Caucasus Mountains into the largely uninhabited Eurasian plains. Some of these tribes spread north and west and became the "root stock" of all Slavic peoples. Life was tough. Population increase or its flip side, starvation, often forced central Asian tribes to move west. These mounted nomads came wandering—and marauding—across the plains into the lands of these early Slavs. Sometimes the horsemen stayed on and joined the peasantry. Almost always—like all armies—they left babies.

The Slavic people living in the proto-Russian "core region" were also hit from the north by Vikings (A.D. 800–1000). Many Vikings took over as local aristocracy, organizing their lands on a primitive, feudal basis. The "clan"—a collective of sorts—was the center of a peasant's life.

These waves of mounted attacks from the east continued for centuries, culminating with the attack of the Golden Horde (the Mongols) in the thirteenth century. Though Christianity (which Prince Vladimir of Kiev accepted in 988) had a profound, centering influence on Russia's development, and the tentative contact with the West and Byzantium on "Kievan Rus" also left important legacies, the invasions by Orientals made a permanent mark. Russia was neither wholly Western nor Eastern. It would become a cultural, political, and military battleground of West and East.

As early as the twelfth century, Moscow was an important river town and the center of what eventually became the duchy of Muscovy. Prince Dimitri of Moscow finally defeated the Mongols in the fourteenth century. Moscow then proceeded to conquer its Slavic neighbors. By the eighteenth century, Muscovy had become Russia, at least west of the Urals. In the process, Russia had made war on all its neighbors (who, at times, attacked first) and laid the foundation for the modern fear of Russia shared by all of its neighbors. Russian explorers had also been pushing east into the frozen forests and sparsely populated plains of northern Asia. The Russians systematically settled the area (200,000 Russians by 1700; 500,000 by 1800, 8 million by 1900). The Russian march to the east, into Siberia, had a permanent effect on their national outlook. In the seventeenth century, Russian adventurers reached the Pacific Ocean and in the eighteenth century settled Alaska. In the nineteenth century, Russians began moving south from Siberia into the warmer (fewer than 150 days a year of snow) and more populated regions to the south. Russia thus acquired Muslims, as well as disputed borders with Turkey, Iran, and China. In 1900, Russia also occupied Finland, Poland, and portions of China.

In 1905, Japan defeated Russia and threw the Russians out of China. In 1914, Russia entered World War I and, although technically on the winning side, ended the war minus Finland, the Baltic States, and its Polish territories. After the bloody Bolshevik revolution and subsequent civil war, Russia became the world's first Communist state. The next twenty years were filled with death on a scale never before experienced by a large nation. Over fifty million Russians were killed, nearly half of them by the paranoid Communist party and the rest by the invading Germans.

The end of 1945 saw the Russian economy in ruins. The bloody memories of the previous forty years had a searing effect on the survivors. Terrorized and/or in shock, the Russian population hunkered down to rebuild their nation and do whatever was needed to avoid another invasion or civil war.

While the Russians were fearful of what other nations might do to them, their neighbors were equally afraid of Russia. The nations of Eastern Europe, occupied by Russian troops after World War II and forcibly turned into Communist states, resented the arrangement. The Russians dismissed this behavior as ingratitude and the machinations of agents from the capitalist West (especially the United States).

Until the 1960s, there was a goodly amount of idealism among many Russians and Communist party members. Rebuilding shattered farms and factories masked the flaws of the centrally planned Communist economy. Rebuilding the economy was one thing; running it efficiently was beyond the capabilities of a centralized system. This began to show in the 1970s. The senior leadership believed their own press releases and decided to get into an arms race with America. Big mistake: Weapons were becoming more dependent on high technology, an area where Russia was falling behind. Russian scientists could design equipment similar to that found in the West. The problem was that Russian industry was too inefficient to manufacture it in quantity.

Overstepping their technological capabilities was not the only error of ambition Russia made in the 1960s and 1970s. The Western states abandoned their colonies in the 1950s and 1960s, creating scores of new nations. Most of these newly minted countries were initially run by people strongly influenced by Communist or socialist ideas. "Scientific" management and "benevolent" dictatorship had a strong appeal. Russia found its support in demand by numerous new states. Those countries were scattered all over the world, and for the first time in its history, Russian diplomacy went far beyond neighboring states. It was a novel and heady experience for Russian leaders. But these new client states adopted the same inefficient economic policies as their patron. By the 1980s both clients and patron were suffering severe economic problems. Russia could no longer afford to subsidize the demands of its faltering clients. Russia's economic collapse has changed the calculus of international politics. The socialist former colonies had played the United States and Western nations off against Russia in order to obtain aid from both superpowers, or one and then the other. With Russia out of the foreign aid and, to a lesser extent, the foreign affairs game, there is a dramatic shift in how international diplomacy is conducted.

In 1991 the Soviet Union did the unthinkable; it simply dissolved. Faced with popular rebellion and seccession by many of the non-Russian nationalities, the Communist leadership negotiated a series of agreements that shrank "Russia" to its smallest size in several centuries. Not all Russians agreed with these decisions; Russian ultranationalists see the "shrunken" Russia as a Russia sold out by traitors.

Civil wars are usually grounded in economic problems. Since 1991, Russia has had enormous economic problems, the payoff of seventy years of communism. Since 1991 the social and economic chaos has been continuous; if history is any guide, in Russia chaos leads right back to a dictatorship.

Initially, the post-Soviet Russian government faced two major problems. The most immediate was economic: The already weak Communist-controlled economy became even less productive with the end of government subsidies to firms that produced goods or services no one wanted. It wasn't so much that Russians were impoverished when the new market economy was introduced, but that the wealth was redistributed in new ways. Basically, he who hustled got rich. Some of these hustlers were gangsters (*mafiya*), and others were clever Communist-era administrators who quickly grasped the new market-economy opportunities.

The government was in a difficult position. Seventy years of Communist rule had left commercial and government institutions inter-twined. Factory complexes owned and operated the local schools and other government institutions, as well as most of the "commercial" enterprises like food stores and gas stations. These complexes were often one-company towns. Over half the pre-1991 population lived in these collectives, including collective farms. These collective enterprises could not be taken apart overnight. Many were not economically viable, but the government could not abruptly cut off the subsidies without risking civil disorder caused by dire and instant poverty.

Moreover, one sixth of the workforce were government officials of some type, many of whom (e.g., those who ran the central planning bureaus or taught Marxist doctrine) were of no use in a market economy.

Selling off the bulk of the government-owned enterprises was a daunting task. It was made more difficult by the near total lack of people with accounting, marketing, or modern business skills. But there are resourceful Russians. Russia has always had, even during Communist times, entrepreneurs, though until 1991 these hustlers were considered black marketers and criminals. After 1991 many of them remained criminals, but many more went on to become *bizniz-men*. While capitalism was a breath of fresh air for the young and adventurous, it was a disaster for the old and retired. The Communists had allowed workers to retire while still in their fifties. Their meager pensions were viable in a command economy, where basic necessities were subsidized, but with inflation raging and markets setting the prices, the pensioners were in trouble. The medical system, as well as other social services long in decline, broke down completely. The seven decades of Communist rule left a suspicion for bureaucratic authority.

The economic data the Russian government releases is acknowledged to be incomplete, because so much economic activity is now black market. All economic news isn't bleak. By mid-1995 genuine free market enterprises had begun to take root—but the roots are weak.

All the economic commotion and unrealized expectations, however, have left a lot of voters unhappy. With democracy, the rulers of Russia (for the first time in Russian history) have to pay close attention to the mood of the people. The fragmented Russian electorate is frustrated and volatile.

The principal political issues are:

- The economy. All those pensioners and displaced workers can vote, and many vote for the "good old days" of communism. Not everyone is willing to wait for the market to work its magic. They want results now.
- The loss of empire. Russians had taken pride in the old Soviet Union for a number of reasons. The USSR was a superpower, the New Russia is not. Many Russians miss being one of the big boys. Of course, it would likely take a lot of blood and cash to get the old empire back, but few dwell on that. What politicians have done is use foreign adventures to get Russians' minds off the severe problems at home. That is a common gambit and one that could cause much trouble when a major nuclear power starts to push neighboring countries around. The 1995 Chechen rebellion is an example. The Russian Army had some ten thousand casualties; the local civilians suffered three to four times that number.
- The New Russia. Exactly what should the post-Communist Russia be politically and economically? All capitalist countries are not alike. The market economy adapts itself to local conditions and customs. It will be a few years before the shape of the New Russia becomes clear. Getting there is a bumpy ride for the Russians, their neighbors, and many other nations that have a vested interest in a peaceful and prosperous Russia.

LOCAL POLITICS

Since 1991, Russia has gone from no politics to way too much politics. Before 1991, the Communist party took care of everything.

No other political parties were allowed. As of mid-1995 several dozen political parties exist. The body politic is fragmented.

The "one party" collapsed quickly. When Mikhail Gorbachev became leader of the Soviet Union in 1985, he represented a new generation. Gorbachev immediately began to install others of his generation (or way of thinking) into positions of power. His new policy of openness (*glasnost*) was a means of uncovering and discussing problems in Russian society. *Perestroika* (restructuring) was the policy that would mend the flaws.

People outside Russia were surprised at how quickly, and apparently easily, Gorbachev was able to propose and implement one change after another. There was no mystery to it, as dissatisfaction with the older generation of leaders had been growing for over a decade. Many within the Communist party, the *nomenklatura,* and the military were simply waiting for someone to start the process. Apparently the economic crisis and the old guard's glaring political failures in Afghanistan (and the 1983 political battle with NATO over the deployment of intermediate-range missiles) gave the "new thinkers" an opportunity to move.

Gorbachev's personality was a political asset. Russia has a long tradition of respect for the strong, forceful leader. Young taxi drivers had pictures of Stalin, a bloody-minded dictator who died before many of them were born, posted in their cabs. Russians are willing to overlook many character flaws in a strong leader. But the leader must be successful as well as strong. And a lack of success in many areas was what eventually brought Gorbachev down.

A major factor hobbling Russian economic reform was, and is, a widespread distaste for enterprising individuals. Competition was looked down on at all levels of society. Those capitalists who did thrive before the 1917 revolution were members of minority religious communities, foreigners, or the occasional eccentric (and capable) aristocrat. The Communists purged all these groups and preached collectivism as the highest form of social organization. Most of the population took naturally to this attitude and, even now, are not eager to abandon it. "Entrepreneur," "hustler," and "thief" are all interchangeable terms to most Russians. Their idea of a good businessman is an efficient and honest government official running a factory for a modest salary. That does not work if you want to create a Western-style economy.

With *glasnost* and *perestroika*, Gorbachev had unleashed more than he bargained for. Soon he had to accept, at least in principle, the full range of Western-style democratic institutions. This eventually included the heresy that there could be other political parties besides the Communist party. Ironically, what was being played out was similar to what had happened in the 1860s and before World War I. In both cases, reform came. Or at least reform came close before the country fell back into anarchy and repression. The 1905 reforms and the 1917 revolution spawned dozens of political factions that were unable to unite and run the country. The Communists took over with firepower, not ballots. Russians are mindful of their past, and take little comfort in it while contemplating their future. The 1991 "revolution" did involve some fireworks, as the Communist leadership tried to stage a coup against themselves and reinstall an authoritarian government. But the soldiers would not follow orders, and many of the Communist leaders were not nearly as ruthless as their predecessors.

Boris Yeltsin, and a horde of political parties (including a reorganized and now media savvy Communist party), came to power after the Soviet Union dissolved. Yeltsin was the first person in Russian history to be elected to a national office via democratic election. In 1993 and 1995 there were elections for the Duma (legislature). There were 450 seats, and a dozen major parties got them. There are basically three blocs in the Duma. On the right, parties calling for a return to dictatorship (of one form or another Communist or fascist) and state control of the economy; those advocating a free market economy and democracy; the last bloc is a hodgepodge of special interests.

Not all the political power is in the legislature. Russia's new constitution has some checks and balances. But President Boris Yeltsin ruled largely by decree. The Russian government is still run by a vast bureaucracy of officials who grew up in the Communist era. Everyone in the government, and many outside of it, have some political power, but no one is willing to get into a shoving match over who has the ultimate power. The hard-liners in the Duma tried to assert their power in late 1993 and the army backed Yeltsin. The result was hundreds dead and the parliament building shot to pieces. This was a more violent confrontation than in 1991, when the Communists tried to stop the demise of the Soviet Union. The fear is that the next armed confrontation would be even more violent.

The armed forces are a major political power in Russia. Though the army is largely apolitical, if the soldiers do side with one faction or another, the going gets bloody. Traditionally, the Russian armed forces have been quite apolitical. This was the case under the czars as well as the Communists. But this cannot always be depended on. During the Communist years, the military was *the* major part of the government. Over 15 percent of the GNP went to the military, and the officer corps contained over a million troops and was the government's ultimate hedge against internal or external threats to Communist rule. But there were two major flaws in this arrangement. The Soviet-era military contained over four million conscripts. They were average citizens who didn't want to be in uniform and could not be depended upon to shoot their fellow Russians. Worse yet, the creaky Soviet economy could not support this massive force. Things began going downhill in the 1980s, when equipment maintenance and training budgets were gradually eaten into so that the officers' pay and procurement of new weapons could be paid for. After 1991 the money dried up and the conscripts stopped coming. Many of the more enterprising officers left the military and went into business. What was left were the conscripts too patriotic, too dumb, or too afraid to avoid their two years of service. The only officers left were those who really enjoyed the military life, or felt inept to do anything else. To make matters worse, hundreds of thousands of troops were brought back from Eastern Europe and those parts of the old Soviet Union that were no longer Russian. Many of these troops were discharged and their units disbanded. But many of the officers, and their families, were still on duty. Many of them had no place to live, or only shabby quarters. Officers' pay no longer bought what it used to, because the special stores, for officers only, no longer existed to provide luxuries not available to the average civilian. By 1995 nearly a million officers and senior NCOs remained. They had lost respect, livable quarters, and purchasing power. Most of the troops are still conscripts, but increasingly the best-trained and combat-ready units are staffed with people loyal primarily to army commanders. The politicians are aware of these problems and attempt to deal with them by getting more money for the military and, just to be on the safe side, forming their own armed units. The armed forces are the most unlikely, but potentially most decisive, power in Russian politics today. Should they decide to back a candidate for an office such as president (as this book goes to press, General Alexander Lebed, the former commander of the breakaway Fourteenth Army in Moldova, is a possible example), the candidate would have the most effective political organization in Russia.

Russian ultranationalist parties do deserve a special mention. The Liberal Democratic party (headed by Vladimir Zhirinovsky) and a half-dozen other extremist parties draw well in Russian elections by appealing to Russian anger at losing the empire. They also play even older cards: anti-Semitism, fear of Muslims, and fear of the West. These parties play best as part of the opposition. If they had to rule the country, they would likely do worse than Yeltsin. The nationalists are demagogues, not economists, and most of Russia's key problems are economic.

Neither Fish nor Fowl: The Commonwealth of Independent States

In late 1991, several months after the Soviet Union dissolved, a new organization was created called the Commonwealth of Independent States (CIS). The CIS has twelve members: Armenia, Azerbaijan, Belarus, Georgia, Kazakhstan, Kyrgyzstan, Moldova, Russia, Tajikistan, Turkmenistan, Ukraine, and Uzbekistan. To some of its organizers, it was an attempt to preserve the Soviet Union. But that was only a dream. The more pragmatic organizers of the CIS were intent on limiting the damage caused when the centralized economy of the Soviet Union was split among sixteen new nations. This was somewhat successful, although the general lack of experience in dealing with market economies has created chaos in all parts of the former Soviet empire. Getting one's house in order generally takes precedence over cooperation with other CIS states. Attempts to use the CIS as a vehicle for coordinating diplomatic and military activity has also been less successful than originally hoped for. The independent nations comprising the CIS were, by and large, cajoled into joining by Russia, which offered all manner of economic, military, and diplomatic inducements. At the very least, the CIS provided a convenient forum for the new nations to regularly discuss common problems. At worst, the CIS is a reminder that the Soviet Union is indeed gone, and is unlikely to return unless things get quite ugly inside Russia.

And things are ugly. Further bitter political infighting between the presidency and parliament continued from 1993 to 1995. The most serious armed conflict was the Russo-Chechen War or Chechnya War. Irregular Chechen forces in the Caucasus region battled the Russian Army. The struggle for Chechnya's capital of Grozny was particularly slow and brutal. When the Russian Army took the cities and towns, the guerrillas fell back into the hills. Cease-fires were continually broken. Chechen raiders struck Russian cities and took hostages.

Georgia struggled with its Abkhazian secessionists. Tajikistan's ongoing factional war continued into 1996.

In voting for the Russian parliament (Duma) in December 1995, the Communist party took 22 percent of the vote (158 of 450 seats). The ultranationalist Liberal Democratic party's vote (11 percent) was half its 1993 total. The protest vote in Russia shifts from one dictatorial and absolutist bloc to another.

POLITICAL TREND CHART

RUSSIA

Gv95	Gv20	PC95	PC20	R95	R20	Ec95	Ec20	EdS95	EdS20
RD5,3	RD5,5	6−	7	6+	6	3+	5−	6+	7

Gv = Government Type
RD = Representative Democracy, albeit an authoritarian representative democracy
PC = Political Cohesiveness (0 = chaos, 9 = maximum)
R = Repression Index (9 = maximum)
Ec = Comparative Economic Status
EdS = Relative Education Status

Regional Powers and Power Interest Indicator Chart

Civil War in the CIS

	Economic Interests	Historical Interests	Political Interest	Military Interest	Force Generation Potential	Ability to Intervene Politically	Interest/ Ability to Promote Economic Development
Russia	9	9	9	9	9–	8	9
Ukraine	9	9	9	9	7	7	7
Belarus	9	9	9	9	2	2	2
Baltic St.*	9	9	9	9	1	2	5
Caucasus†	9	9	9	9	3+	3	2–
CAR‡	9	9	9	9	4	3	2
United States	5	8	8	9	6	6	4
Germany	8	9	9	9	5	5	5
Poland	8	9	9	9	2	3	3
Hungary	7	8	9	9	1	2	2
China	3	5	8	9	6	4	1–
Japan	6	6	7	8	3	3	5
"EEC"	6	8	8	9	2	5	4
Turkey	7	9	8	9	3+	2	1
Iran	3	5	6	7	1+	1+	0

NOTE: 0 = minimum; 9 = maximum
*Baltic States
†Caucasus Republics
‡Central Asian Republics

PARTICIPANT STRATEGIES AND GOALS

Russian free marketers—Get a market economy functioning in Russia as soon as possible. The free marketers have to overcome three major obstacles. First, most Russians have only a vague idea of what a free market is and few appreciate the more arcane details (long-term investment, commodity futures, distribution, etc.). The people must be educated. But this runs into the second problem, the gangsters. Contemporary Russia has thousands of *mafiya* gangs, and the general shortage of police and enforced business law has allowed them to run rampant. Former Russian Army commandos and paratroopers are in great demand as bodyguards and general antidote to the murderous mobsters. Such rampant criminality is not unusual in some third world countries, but there is no easy solution to the problem and it discourages foreign investment and hobbles local entrepreneurs. The criminality is particularly acute in former Soviet areas because the Communist governments became very corrupt in the last few decades of their existence. There was little personal responsibility and respect for law. The third problem is that the people who ran the economy during the Communist era, by and large, are still there. Although most Russian industry has been privatized, that often resulted in particularly large organizations being "privatized" into the hands of their Communist-era managers. Now some of these fellows are actually good managers, for even the Communists tried to get people who knew what they were doing to run vital industries. But the Communist-era industries were run largely for political purposes, not to make a profit, or even to make economic sense. Many of these "managers" achieved their positions through political skill. After 1991, there were few people qualified to point out which industrial managers were politicians putting on a good act, and which were competent executives trying to run their operations on a businesslike basis. As time went by, even the best politicians could not paper over their management shortcomings. So the politicians in the executive suite went after the Russian government for "loans" (which were not paid back) and outright subsidies. The inept, but politically skillful, managers painted a dire picture of social unrest resulting if these funds were not forthcoming, and their predictions had an element of truth in them. These managers don't want to see their enterprises fail, but they are more skilled and experienced at shifting blame than in solving business problems. These "Red managers" from the Communist era will die out in the next decade, but in the meantime they impede the efforts of the free marketers to put Russia's economy on a rational basis. The best thing the free marketers have going for them is the growth of a middle class. Russians now know that if they hustle, they can earn the money to buy the consumer goodies they have been denied for decades. The people are doing just that.

Russian democrats—The democrats are not just concentrating on bringing democratic practices and honest government to Russia; most of them also understand the need for a more efficient economy. But the democrats have a tall order in front of them. For one thing, most of the population is more concerned with their economic situation than whether the government is democratic or not. The democrats are all too aware that Adolf Hitler got his Nazi party into power in the 1930s by promising, and delivering, an improved economy. Long term, it is democratic practices that allow a strong economy to sustain itself. But short term, too many people are ready to tolerate totalitarianism if it puts bread and meat on the table. The democrats' biggest problem is that there has never been a democracy in Russia, but there has been centuries of totalitarianism. A lot of Russians don't mind dictators as long as there is "order" (another Russian fetish). For decades, Communist propaganda pounded away at the theme that the Western democracies were dangerous, crime-ridden jungles of disorder and personal freedom. The Russian democrats have a hard time convincing Russians that the old Communist propaganda was wrong. For the democratic Russia of today has turned into what the old propaganda described. The democrats also have a problem in getting democratically elected officials to stop acting like the imperious Communist-era (and czarist-era) officials, who behaved like above-the-law aristocrats. Already, only a few years after the Communist bosses were tossed out, the new "democratic" leaders are living it up just as their totalitarian predecessors were and using the same strongarm methods to protect their power and privilege.

Russian autocrats—The stalwarts of the "old ways" (be they czarist or Communist) have a vested interest in democracy and the market economy failing. There was always a substantial minority of the population (20 percent or more) who were leery about "Western ways" and prefer a "strong hand" running government. The autocrats offer order, whether you want it or not. The autocrats' biggest problem is to explain away the economic failures of past autocratic governments. Communism delivered less and less in the 1970s and 1980s. Seventy years of Communist propaganda discredited (somewhat unfairly) the economic policies of the czars. But the grim economic reality of Russia today tends to make the Communist yesterday brighter than it actually was for many people. If the free market parties don't deliver, the autocrats are waiting in the wings with another dictator.

Russian nationalists—The free market and autocratic parties at least stand for something useful (good economics and stable government). The nationalist parties offer only visions of past glories. This is politics at its most visceral. The nationalists also play off the post-1991 disorder in Russia. The line the nationalists must sell is that if Russia were an empire again, and a mighty, saber-rattling military superpower, all the social and economic problems Russia is suffering from would go away. That is dangerous nonsense, but it has been successfully peddled in other places and other times, so one cannot dismiss the nationalists as harmless cranks. If the nationalists gain power, and that is a possibility, it's back to the cold war. Actually, it's worse, for during the cold war Russia was concerned mainly with holding on to what it had. With Russian nationalists in power, the emphasis will be on Russia regaining some, or all, of the former Soviet territories. These new nations, and Eastern Europe, are well aware of this and greatly fear something like this happening. The nationalists may appear like some kind of bad joke to Americans, but to peoples on Russia's borders, the nationalists are a bad memory threatening to return.

The Baltic States—These three nations (Latvia, Lithuania, and Estonia) want to stay independent and integrate their economies and cultures with the West. Fifty years of Russian occupation, and centuries of Russian domination before that, have left their mark (generally negative) on these countries. Each of them has a substantial minority of Russians who, to one degree or another, resist assimilation. The Baltic States deal carefully with Russia, build relationships in the West, and hope for the best. A fascist and anti-Russian resurgence in the Baltic States is possible, particularly in Latvia.

Belarus—An economic and political basket case, the Belorussians are torn between undertaking the tough reforms or just giving up and asking Russia to take them back. Byelorussia had never been independent before and the current situation came about because demagogic local politicians took advantage of the breakup of the Soviet Union to create their own little fiefdom. It didn't work out. The Communist politicians in charge lacked the clout to make the reforms that all former Communist states require in order to survive and lacked the guts to say they were wrong. Different groups of politicians maneuver to either reform or rejoin Russia. The best Belarus can hope for is some kind of accommodation with Russia. Belarus's new parliament has plans for "reintegrating" with Russia.

Ukraine—Aside from solving the same economic problems afflicting Russia, Ukraine also wants to clear up several lingering political problems with Russia. Chief among these is the status of the Crimea. This area, a peninsula in the Black Sea, was conquered from the Tartars (a remnant of the thirteenth-century Mongol invasion) by the Russians early in the eighteenth century. In a purely feel-good gesture, Soviet leader Nikita Khrushchev transferred the Crimea from the Russian Republic to the Ukrainian Republic. Most of the people in the Crimea are Russians, and there is a vocal minority of Tartars. Russia is not sure the Crimea should be Ukrainian, and there is an ongoing dispute over how much of the old Soviet Black Sea Fleet goes to whom. Ukraine also has problems elsewhere in its territory, especially in western Ukraine, where nearly half the population is Russian. Less blessed with natural resources than Russia, Ukraine also lacks a lot of seasoned political talent. Throughout the Soviet period, Ukrainians were always second to Russians when it came to senior leadership positions. Ukraine has to develop solutions and leadership at the same time, and do it quickly before their economy, and social order, collapses.

Moldova—This is another of those new countries that has never been a country before. To make matters worse, Moldova is rent by deep ethnic divisions (Moldovans versus Russians) and has a realistic goal of uniting with Romania (Moldovans are ethnically Romanians) while keeping the local Russians from tearing the place apart. Hanging over all this is Russia itself. A Russian army (the Fourteenth) occupied Moldova for many years, but no one is quite sure whose side the troops were on. The smart money placed the Fourteenth Army behind the local Russians, but no one could be sure. By 1995, Russia was extracting itself from Moldova, downgrading and downsizing the Fourteenth Army.

The new central Asian nations—All of these nations share some common problems and goals. All are ruled by their former Communist-era bosses, who were locals who worked their way through the Soviet bureaucracy to become the caretakers of a part of the Soviet empire they were familiar with. None of these new nations has any experience with democracy or being independent. None has a particularly robust economy, and because they were part of the centrally planned Soviet economy, they lack much of the self-sufficiency expected of independent nations. These nations were, in effect, subsidized by the Soviet Union when they were under Communist rule. With independence, the subsidies disappeared. Per capita income has fallen up to 50 percent by 1995. The Communist leadership is particularly ill equipped to deal with this situation. As all these nations are Islamic, they all are feeling the effects of the Islamic fundamentalism that is spreading through the Muslim world. There are also ethnic differences, even though most of these peoples have a common Turkic heritage. Internecine fighting has already shown up. As a group, or individually, these new nations are not united. There will be more unrest, more poverty, and more trouble in the future from this part of the world. The leaders in all these nations must revive their economies, maintain good relations with Russia, and fend off a growing Islamic fundamentalist movement.

Kazakhstan—The new "democratic" government is the old Communist one, mainly because of the lack of a democratic tradition and the resulting absence of experienced politicians. The "elected" Communists are ruling in the style of the ancient Kazakh chieftains, with the usual armed opposition. It's tribal and clan warfare, after a century or so of truce imposed by the Russians. It is still dependent on Russia, which remains the major trading partner and source of many vital manufactured goods and raw materials.

Tajikistan—The former Communists who got elected rulers of this new country have more than a few stray democrats to worry about because Tajikistan shares a twelve-hundred-kilometer border with Afghanistan. That provides a sanctuary and other support for those Tajiks who want an Islamic government for Tajikistan. Russia has continued to maintain an infantry division on the Afghan border, along with contingents from other central Asian nations. The Tajik-Afghan border is the scene of constant combat as armed groups cross, or try to cross, into Tajikistan. Iran is the principal supporter of the Islamic fundamentalists, which is one reason why Russia is trying to improve its diplomatic and economic relationships with Iran. This, by itself, will not stop the Tajik rebels from operating in Afghanistan, because there is support coming from other Islamic groups and individuals. There is no effective government in Afghanistan, which itself is still embroiled in a civil war. The armed turmoil in Tajikistan will continue.

Kyrgyzstan—The poorest of the new central Asian nations, there are also problems with many minority groups struggling over a shrinking pie. The government (of former Communist leaders) has problems with Islamic fundamentalists (thus they support the use of Russian troops in Tajikistan) and large-scale illegal drug activity (manufacture and shipping). The drug situation is particularly worrisome, because the local officials are often content to be bought off and move on to their other problems. The principal solution to the pressing economic problems is aid and trade with neighboring nations (particularly Russia). Prospects are grim, with the likely future being increased poverty and civil disorder.

Turkmenistan—The major problems to solve here are economic. With natural gas and oil plus a large amount of irrigated land, Turkmenistan is the wealthiest of the new central Asian nations. Its Communist rulers are cautiously working toward a market economy. But there are major ecological problems. Decades of intensive irrigation have created a looming ecological catastrophe of large proportions. The Aral Sea is shrinking because of all the water diverted to farmland.

Inefficient Soviet-era irrigation methods are ruining the land that is cultivated with the water that may soon be unavailable. The shrinking Aral Sea is expanding the desert area, and Turkmenistan was always primarily desert, good for little more than grazing. The Communist rulers appear incapable of making the politically unpopular, and technically difficult, decisions needed to deal with the ecological problems. The prognosis is not good.

Uzbekistan—One of the more successful of the new central Asian countries, Uzbekistan has done the most to develop a market economy. Along with Belarus, Armenia, Kazakhstan and Tajikistan, Uzbekistan initially linked its currency with Russia by using the ruble. The Uzbeks have also sent troops to Tajikistan to help the Russian 201st Infantry Division deal with Islamic fundamentalist raids from Afghanistan. The largest and most populated of the central Asian nations, it is also the poorest, despite abundant natural resources. The adjacent Aral Sea has shrunk due to a mismanaged Soviet-era irrigation scheme, causing major ecological and economic problems. Pollution from Soviet-era industrial projects also burden the economy and public health. The Communist leaders who still run the country as elected officials have to deal with all this, as well as a growing population and fending off true democrats and Islamic fundamentalists.

Mongolia—The Mongolians are poor and led by their (now elected) Communist-era leaders. In many ways, Mongolia's situation is similar to that of the new central Asian nations. Mongolia is, however, 90 percent Mongolian and was a satellite, not a part, of the Soviet Union. However, when the Soviet Union still existed, it provided subsidies that amounted to 30 percent of Mongolia's GDP. The subsidies are gone and the inefficient Soviet-style economy still exists. The 2.5 million Mongolians are poor and their leadership does not have the skills or financial means to change the situation. The major religion is Buddhism, so they don't have to worry about Islamic fundamentalism. But Mongolia is still a diplomatic pawn in the ongoing struggle between China and Russia. Mongolia's rulers try to exploit this to obtain foreign aid and continued independence. The Chinese, remember, consider independent Mongolia a "lost" part of China, and have long occupied Mongolian-populated "Inner Mongolia" (and call the current state of Mongolia "Outer Mongolia").

Internal dissidents—Russia's dissidents are numerous and vocal. There is a lot of noise, but not much result because of the abundance of agendas. The most worrisome aspect of this, to Russians and non-Russians alike, is that no one seems to be in charge. For Russians, accustomed to centuries of authoritarian rule, this lack of a strong hand at "the center" becomes an explanation for all the bad things that are happening in post-Soviet Russia. In this the Russians are right, up to a point. Foreigners see another problem with the constant squabbling and lack of decisiveness in Russia, and that is the absence of legal institutions that are the bedrock of democracies and, especially, successful market economies. Russia has never had this kind of "law and order." Under the czars, you could always use influence with some aristocrat or another to circumvent the courts. Under the Communists, the legal system became more of a sham. Most of the current crop of dissidents know they want order and prosperity (among other things), but few comprehend how important a rational legal code, honest law enforcement, and an independent court system are to a brighter future. Some of the dissident groups are advocating the adoption of these foreign concepts, but they are at a disadvantage against those groups that preach going back to the "strong man" era of the czar or Communist commissar. For the truth of the matter is that the Communists merely continued the autocratic rule of the czars, but in a more brutal fashion. While the dissidents fiddle, Russia burns, and foreigners fear the fire will get out of control and spread outside Russia's borders.

Eastern Europe—Perhaps better than many Russians, the Eastern Europeans understand what the Russians are going through and what must be done to reform Russia without triggering a catastrophe. Having been forced to endure a Russian-style economic and political system since the late 1940s, yet being basically Western European in outlook, the Eastern Europeans may appear uncommonly accommodating to Russia now that Eastern Europe is free. What the Eastern Europeans are trying to do is ensure that Russia doesn't turn about toward despotism again and take Eastern Europe back into Russian bondage. Eastern European nations, except those that get waylaid by their own internal problems, will assist Russia diplomatically, encouraging the liberals and free marketers while acting as a bridge between the West and Russia. The goal of all this is to discourage the Russians from once more turning Eastern Europe into satellite nations. The issue of Eastern European nations joining NATO is a vexing one. The Eastern Europeans want to do this to add a measure of protection against Russian aggression (and squabbles among themselves over ancient territorial disputes that were kept underground by the cold war). Many Russians see Eastern Europeans joining NATO as a Western plot to surround Russia. That is absurd, but it plays well in Russia when used by Russian nationalists.

Western Europe—The changes in Eastern Europe and Russia are seen as a great boon for Western Europe. The threat of Russian invasion has greatly diminished and with it have come opportunities to reduce defense spending. Moreover, Eastern Europe and Russia are now open to Western companies. The potential benefits are great, but only if Russia avoids slipping into disorder, or worse. More so than the United States, Western Europe is eager to do whatever they can to ease Russia's transition from communism to whatever else works and doesn't threaten the security or economic stability of Europe.

United States—Being much farther away from Russia, both historically and geographically, than Russia's numerous neighbors, the United States is more circumspect in dealing with the rapidly changing situation in Russia. For decades, the primary role of the United States in world affairs was to "contain" Russian expansion and to block any Russian attempt at nuclear (or other kinds of) blackmail. This task remains, but the role as leader of the Western nations against Russia's attempt to spread communism has disappeared. The United States doesn't know quite what to do with itself in its dealings with the remnants of the Soviet Union. Russia would prefer economic assistance, free trade, and cooperation in dealing with lesser world troublemakers. With the end of the cold war, and the diminution of Russia's superpower status, Russia is still, ironically, calling the shots. America worries about "what Russia will do next" and can only be ready to respond. Russia has more neighbors who are concerned about both Russia's future and how to influence it. Europe, especially Eastern Europe, still worries about Russian domination. Russia sits in the middle of a volatile collection of new and old nations that are ripe for new wars large and small. Russia is the likely nation to "do something" about these wars, or potential wars, on its new borders. If

America is too aggressive in telling Russia how to deal with these situations, the Russians get upset about "interference with Russian affairs." There is some truth to that, as Russia is better prepared to deal with problems in new countries that were once part of the Soviet Union. Americans aren't really keen on risking anything on obscure conflicts in central Asia; Russia is. So, even with the end of the cold war and America's status as the sole superpower, everyone still dances to Russia's tune.

Japan—Eager to develop new markets, Japan also wants to recover the Kurile Islands, and several other minor ones, lost to Russia after World War II. While these islands are of no great economic value, their recovery becomes an emotional, and political, issue in Japan. A deal could be struck, as the Russians had, in the last century, traded the Kurile Islands to Japan in return for Sakhalin. Russia needs Japanese technology more than it needs another chilly island off its coasts. Economic cooperation has stalled over Russia's refusal to even discuss the matter. Meanwhile, Japanese companies pursue investment opportunities in Russia's Far Eastern region. This involves far less money than if Japan were dealing with Moscow, but given the unsettled legal situation in Russia, the Japanese do not seem upset by this. No one is eager to put a lot of money into Russia just yet. What the Japanese are doing is establishing a presence in the event that Russia comes apart. Japan would then already be there, ready to do business with whoever ended up in control of the Russian Far East. This might be China.

China—As neighbors, there is some opportunity for trade and this activity has been steadily increasing, although the long distances between each nation's major industrial and population centers limits economic exchanges. There are still disputes, such as China's claim on Russia's Pacific provinces. But the Chinese see recovery of these territories as an inevitable eventuality. The Chinese take the long view in these matters. Of more immediate import is the political turmoil caused by Russia abandoning dictatorship while China tries to hang on to it. Both nations are working hard not to inflame matters in the other country. If either nation fell into civil disorder, it would probably have an effect, possibly grave, on the other.

Other neighbors—Russia's numerous other neighbors nervously

watch events unfold. To the north, Finland sees its decades of subservience to Russia paying off. Finland now stands to reap large economic rewards when, and if, the Russian economy recovers. To the south, Turkey and Iran see Russia as less of a threat, for the moment. Russia's other Muslim neighbors, Afghanistan and Pakistan, go about their own affairs with less potential for Russian intervention.

Third world clients—This group is hit hardest by the changes in Russia and has few options. One remaining tie these nations have with Russia is debt. Russia has sold (on very generous credit terms) over $100 billion worth of goods to its various third world clients. Most of this debt is unlikely to be recovered, especially now that an economically strapped Russia can no longer threaten to withhold future shipments. Russia's fall from diplomatic power has also caused unrest in many third world client states that had copied Russia's Communist government and economic policies. Without Russia to play off against the United States, the foreign aid game just became a much less remunerative undertaking. Many poor nations will continue to depend on Russia, if they can find hard currency to pay for the cheaper Russian goods.

POTENTIAL OUTCOMES

RUSSIA

1. 45 percent chance through 2001: Russia stabilizes its economy; democracy survives. Minimal number of military operations in the Near Abroad (peacekeeping missions really are sent to keep the peace, not intervene on behalf of Moscow). If this occurs, there is an 85 percent chance that a de facto Russia-Belarus-Ukraine-Kazakh federation develops, based on mutual defense treaties. This federation functions as an economic trading zone, with Russia supplying natural resources, heavy industry, and defense; Ukraine food and industry; Kazakhstan oil; and Belarus wondering why it ever left Russia to begin with. (See the Preface, page v, for more.)
2. 25 percent chance through 2001: Chaos and instability continue

with little improvement in the economic or political situation. The overall economic situation, however, does not become disastrous. Ultranationalists are catered to politically with some more aggressive intervention in the Near Abroad. The warfare along the periphery leads to long-term gains in political power for the military. Democracy, however, remains.

3. 20 percent chance through 2001: Economic and political conditions decline. Chaos spreads in the Near Abroad. Russian politicians look for something to distract the people from internal problems, and generals and politicians seek to carve out new empires in the Near Abroad. These "new Russian duchies" become the source of larger conflicts with Iran, Turkey, and China. The military and the ultranationalists effectively call the shots politically. Russia once more becomes an authoritarian state.

4. 10 percent chance through 2001: Russia loses it—civil disorder, economic collapse, perhaps even civil war. The worst case that everyone will strive to avoid the closer it gets. There have been several civil wars in Russian history, and yet another one is not out of the question. Perhaps a one-third chance that nuclear weapons would be used. It's hard to say, as there has not yet been a civil war in a nation armed with nukes. If actual civil war occurs, 90 percent chance of war breaking out between Russian forces and one (or several) of these nations: Ukraine, Turkey, Iran, Kazakhstan, Georgia, Azerbaijan; 5 percent chance of war breaking out with Poland and/or Lithuania over the Russian Kaliningrad (Königsberg) Oblast.

COST AND KINDS OF WAR

The last round of civil disorder and reform (1917–38) killed off nearly 20 percent of the population. Russia has a strong incentive to manage change with less bloodshed this time. Even so, the casualty list has grown through the 1990s. The Communist attempt to shut down the legislature in 1991 and the right-wing coup attempt in 1993 were accompanied by very low casualties (a few hundred dead). The war in Chechnya killed over 50,000 people (mostly Chechens) through

1995, but the Russian Army suffered over 5,000 dead. But the excess deaths due to the failing economy are even greater. Poor medical care and low living standards have led to an acknowledged decline in life expectancy during the 1980s, which has continued into the 1990s. That pushes the losses to over 100,000 dead and fuels the discontent that causes the armed conflict. A major civil war could easily kill millions, even without someone using a nuclear weapon. Large-scale civil unrest could push the death rate way into the tens of thousands. Along with any of these disorder situations would come economic damage that would cost billions of dollars to repair.

Russia has many freelance fighters armed with cold war surplus AK-47s. Sloppy administration and endemic pilferage have allowed hundreds of thousands of Red Army weapons to reach civilians since World War II. During periods of civil disorder, as in the Caucasus and central Asia in the late 1980s and early 1990s, even more weapons were taken (or sold by the ill-paid troops) and used in ethnic clashes. Millions of small arms, and hundreds of thousands of heavier weapons, are stored in hundreds of poorly guarded warehouses throughout the country. Those warehouses belonged to over a hundred reserve divisions of the old Soviet Army. Most of the troops assigned to those divisions (as little as 10 percent of the divisions' full personnel strength) were young conscripts who were paid only a few dollars a month. Slipping an AK-47, or some other weapon, out the back door for a few bottles of vodka was so common that officers spent more effort papering over the thefts than trying to stop them. Commanders also engaged in large-scale private arms sales. As a result of this leakage of weapons, several of the non-Russian nations soon had private militias operating. Some of these outfits—the Chechens, for example—consist of thousands of armed and organized fighters.

The "Mingle" Factor, and the Cost of "Unmingling"

While the numerous different ethnic groups in Russia prefer to live among their own kind, there is a fair amount of intermingling. In particular, many (about twenty-five million) Russians live outside of the Russian area of the old Soviet Union. The Baltic States population is over a quarter Russian and even the central Asian republics are about 20 percent Russian. Because of geography and similarities in culture, there is a lot of population mingling among Russia, the Ukraine, and Belarus. Once the Soviet Union dissolved, there was a lot of pressure on people (gentler in some areas than in others) to "go back where they came from." This had already happened in the Caucasus during the late 1980s, resulting in several hundred thousand Russian refugees wandering about Russia. In the wake of the Soviet Union's breakup, over ten million people were displaced. Russia also obtained a lot of "refugees" with the removal of half a million of their troops (and the officers' families) from Eastern Europe. There was no housing for those people in the Soviet Union and many ended up living in tents, shacks, and railroad boxcars. This movement of populations in a nation notoriously short of housing was a major problem that could still reach catastrophic proportions as the numbers involved increase.

Well, What About the Nuclear Weapons?

Russia has over twenty thousand nuclear weapons. Most have always been stored within the Russian part of the Soviet Union. After the ethnic disturbances of the late 1980s, those few thousand that were outside Russia were removed from the Caucasus, Baltic States, etc., and brought "home." Even so, there are over a hundred locations where these weapons are stored and, even though they are guarded (and controlled until released for use) by the KGB (and its successor organizations), it doesn't take much imagination to see how easily the wrong people could get their hands on some nukes if civil disorder broke out in the Soviet Union. Even without civil disorder, the nukes are liable to fall into the hands of foreigners with a lot of dollars.

Just having a nuke is not enough; you have to know how to use it. So it's more than just having a mob liberate a few nuclear weapons, or the guards selling one. You have to have someone with experience in operating them. Usually, only officers are entrusted with the details of getting a nuclear weapon into action. There are plenty of active and retired officers with nuclear weapons experience (probably nearly one hundred thousand). Of course, there are many different types of nuclear weapons, so an officer who was in charge of naval nuclear weapons might have a difficult, if not impossible, time working with a nuclear artillery shell.

The possibility of uncontrolled use of nuclear weapons is real in Russia, but it is not as likely as it might appear on the surface.

The Red Army Turns White

In five years, from its peak strength in 1989 to 1995, the mighty Red Army turned white from loss of strength and the disappearance of its Marxist core. The term "Red" Army arose during the Russian civil war (1917–22). Red was the color of revolution. The royalist Russian troops were called Whites. The Reds won, the Whites lost, and Russia became a Communist state for the next sixty or so years. The Whites lost because the czar and his nobles were corrupt and out of touch with the people. The Reds lost sixty years later for the same reason. But the Red Army is another matter. All of the Communist-era institutions survived, to one degree or another, the collapse of the Soviet Union. The Soviet armed forces, the Red Army, survived with many of its Communist-era symbols and customs intact. The red star still appears on equipment and uniforms. Traditions and customs of the Soviet era still survive in the armed forces of the Russian Federation (as the Red Army is now called). But in one important respect, the Red Army has changed dramatically.

DECLINE IN STRENGTH OF THE RED ARMY

	1989	1994
Divisions	214	79
Troops (mill.)	3.8	1.7
AFV*	132,000	56,000
Aircraft	11,500	5,200

*AFV are tanks and other armored vehicles.

In 1989 the Red Army was the most powerful in the world, at least on paper. Even in the late 1980s, there were questions about the quality of the Soviet forces. But, as the founder of the Soviet Union (Vladimir Lenin) put it, "quantity has a quality of its own." Yet by 1994, the quantity was gone and quality of any sort was demonstrably missing. Between the disarmament treaties of the late 1980s and the dissolution of the Soviet Union in 1991, most of the Red Army was either demobilized or became the armed forces of the new nations created from the fragments of the Soviet Union. The Red Army had been in decay since the 1950s. As the World War II veterans died or retired, their places were taken by careerists more interested in material benefits than combat readiness. This was noted during those few times the Red Army was used. Invasions of Hungary (1956) and Czechoslovakia (1968) revealed that all was not well as far as combat capability went. The Afghanistan war of the 1980s confirmed what many had long suspected. It should not have been surprising that, as the Red Army grew larger after the early 1960s, its quality suffered. This is common with most armed forces in peacetime, and particularly with the Russians.

During the late 1980s, an increasing percentage of conscripts (who comprised 75 percent of the manpower) evaded service. After 1991, the number of evaders exceeded 50 percent of those called. There was never much of an NCO (noncommissioned officers, or sergeants) corps to speak of in the Red Army, and many of the more able officers got out in the early 1990s, eager to pursue more lucrative opportunities in the market economy. What was left was about 60 percent conscripts and 40 percent officers (and some career NCOs). Not an efficient mix. While more than half the military equipment of 1989 was disposed of, what was left was more modern, and more difficult to maintain. There wasn't much money for anything, the defense budget had been slashed by nearly two thirds. Training funds were virtually nonexistent, so units rarely exercised. Attempts were made to maintain equipment, but there was still more gear in hand than the troops available could handle.

Desperate to maintain some combat capability, about 10 percent of the armed forces (paratroopers, commandos, etc.) were given the pick of the recruits and a larger allotment of funds for training. Money was made available to form "contract" battalions. These *contractski* troops received several hundred dollars a month, over a hundred times what conscripts received. The officers were often from former KGB divisions (the units that existed to assure the loyalty of the army). Russia still has a dozen or so regular combat divisions it can depend on. The rest, with only 20–50 percent of their troop strength, would require a national emergency, several months, and a lot of resources (fuel, ammunition, and so on) to get into shape.

The air force and navy did about as poorly as the ground forces. There's no money to buy the fuel to allow pilots to practice flying. The same situation exists with the navy; the ships rot next to a pier, with no funds for maintenance, much less steaming about on the high seas.

It's a rare, but not unknown, event in history for a mighty military host to suddenly collapse and melt away in peacetime. The demise of the Red Army was simply one of the more dramatic examples of this.

What does the future hold for the much diminished Red Army? Many of the officers want to emulate Western practice and form a wholly professional armed forces. At the moment, that is too expensive, and would result in an even smaller armed forces. Russia is reluctant to reduce its forces too much, as it still has enormous borders to protect, and a lot of potentially hostile neighbors. The war in Chechnya strengthened the hand of the reformers. You can't fight well, if at all, with recently mobilized conscripts. You need trained troops to actually do anything.

Despite the shortage of money, an NCO corps is being built up and competitive wages offered to those conscripts who are qualified, and willing, to be professional sergeants. Officers are doing a lot of technical work that, in Western nations, would be performed by enlisted troops. But Russia has always used officers for jobs that "had to be done right" and could not, it was thought, be trusted to enlisted conscripts. In any event, Russian officers generally make much less than Western enlisted soldiers, so at least the Russians are getting their money's worth.

While the U.S. defense budget (for 1.5 million troops and over half a million civilians) still runs to about $250 billion a year, Russia is able to spend only about a third of that. Lower pay scales give the

Russians about half the purchasing power of the U.S. budget, but it still isn't enough to maintain all the equipment and keep the troops trained. Russia still has a vast defense industry, but little is being produced anymore. Money still goes into developing new generations of weapons, in the hope that funds will be forthcoming in the next five or ten years to mass-produce this stuff. But one of the painful legacies of the Arab-Israeli wars and the 1991 Persian Gulf War was the poor performance of Russian equipment against Western material. Russia is having a hard (but not impossible) time selling its best weapons to foreign customers. The Russians have to offer extremely low prices, often as low as one tenth what an equivalent (on paper, anyway) system would cost from America or Western Europe. The Russians have plenty of modern equipment to sell. They either sell it or watch it slowly waste away.

In times like these, the Russian Army has to draw upon its long tradition of pulling through periods of adversity. Much was made, in Moscow, of the fiftieth anniversary of VE Day. The defeat of the German Wehrmacht in World War II was, and is, the crowning glory of the Russian armed forces. Over many centuries of fighting, the Germans had pummeled the Russians often. In 1945 the Russians finally turned the tables. The current Russian officer corps has many very professional soldiers. They know they have to solve numerous material and morale problems to forge an effective post-Soviet armed forces. Barring a civil war, they will probably do so in the next ten years.

Part 3
AFRICA

The African continent houses the planet's widest variety of languages and cultures. It is also the home of the greatest number of outright wars and ethnic, religious, tribal, and other armed conflicts. Added to this extreme in warfare there is a depth of poverty matched nowhere else on the planet.

Chapter 7

THE MAGHREB AFLAME: ALGERIA AND THE GREAT WAR OF THE WESTERN SAHARA

The Arabs called it Djaziret al Maghreb, the Island of the Sunset, the land west of the Nile. Indeed, North Africa's central and western reaches were something of an island, cut off from central Africa and the Middle East by the sand sea of the Sahara.

But the Maghreb also has fine ports along the southern Mediterranean littoral and, from northwestern Libya to Morocco's northern coast, a comparatively well-watered coastal strip protected from the Sahara by rugged mountains. This string of port cities became the Arabs' invasion route to Spain and, ultimately, France.

Today the Maghreb consists of Algeria, Tunisia, Morocco, Libya, and the disputed territory (or nation) of the Western Sahara. The region's spectrum of political, economic, ethnic, and religious troubles brings the boiling pot of the Middle East to Europe's door.

Source of Conflict

In the Maghreb the conflict between political Islamic fundamentalism and national development following "Western European" models
is brutally evident.

European nations, primarily France, Spain, and Italy, have wielded
great cultural, economic, and political influence in the Maghreb region. That is understandable, given the proximity of Europe—and its
economic, military, and political might. The Strait of Gibraltar is narrow, only thirteen kilometers in width between Gibraltar, in Europe,
and Ceuta, in Morocco.

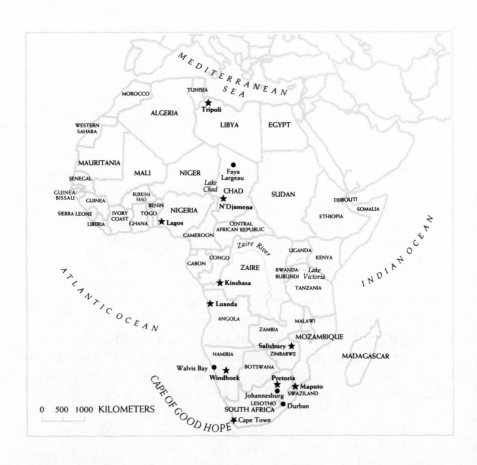

In fact, the Maghreb is a grand cultural collision. When the Mediterranean Sea was a Roman lake, the Roman provinces of the North African coast were vital elements of the empire. The West is an intimate part of its heritage.

The Algerian civil war is the most dangerous of the Maghreb's current conflicts. Ancient ethnic disputes, old colonial strife, and the modern theological-ideological struggles (imported from the Persian Gulf and the Middle East) feed the conflict, but the chief source of friction is the failed promise of an early twentieth-century revolution.

France had made Algeria a province. The French natives of Algeria, the *pieds-noirs,* had a century and a half of grapes in the ground. The Arab and Arab-Berbers, however, chafed under French domination. World War II weakened France as a colonial power in Africa and Asia. Several Algerian resistance groups began fighting the French in the 1950s. By the late 1950s, France was involved in an ugly, full-scale guerrilla war in Algeria. In 1962, Charles de Gaulle's government withdrew from Algeria.

The Algerian revolutionaries imposed a one-party, socialist state. Oil revenues kept Algeria's "socialist experiment" afloat, for a while, anyway. However, democratic aspirations, whetted by the revolution, were never fulfilled. The Algerian revolutionaries, with their power centered on the military, became new elites. As in the centuries before the French colonial rule, these Arab elites are more concerned with keeping their wealth and power than they are with supporting either democracy or socialism. What is being played out in Algeria is something new for North African potentates: The great democratic wave that began sweeping the world with the American and French revolutions two centuries ago has finally arrived. Although the Islamic fundamentalists represent a form of totalitarian rule themselves, they preach, and use, the democratic aspirations of the people.

The decline in oil revenues and governmental corruption alienated much of the population. With democracy stymied, religion became a haven for dissent, and a fertile ground for Iranian-style political Islam. Berber ethnic demands, rapid population growth, the role of France in Algerian politics, and foreign-trained and -supplied (Iranian and Sudanese) terrorists complicate the political turmoil. The war could ultimately involve European forces.

The war in the Western Sahara pits Morocco against the "native" Polisario movement. At one time Algeria backed the Polisario. In some ways the war in the Western Sahara is a cold war hangover. Polisario is structured and operated like literally hundreds of other "Soviet-backed" cold-war-era liberation groups. Sympathetic Algerian socialists in cahoots with the KGB provided the network to organize the various desert tribes.

But the Polisario propaganda has a basis in truth. On the part of Morocco the war is a classic imperialist war. When Spain withdrew from its West African colony, Morocco filled the power vacuum and moved in—the vast phosphate deposits were an economic prize. The war is an "imperialist war" that predates European colonialism: It is the war of the urban coastal dweller versus the desert tribes of the interior.

Libya—Ah yes, Libya. Libya, under the direction of the mercurial Colonel Mu'ammar Qaddafi, still keeps its armed tentacles in a dozen unstable nations and destabilizing situations, in Africa (Burkina Faso, the Sudan, and Liberia), in Europe (Bosnia), and in the Middle East. The 1985 edition of *A Quick and Dirty Guide* gave a full explication, which this chapter in the 1995 edition will summarize. Since 1985, Qaddafi has had his grandiose presumptions frustrated by U.S. air attacks, his military plans sacked by Chadian tribesmen, his petro-dollar purse picked by the collapse of oil prices, and his arms purchases pinched by UN sanctions. And the collapse of the Soviet Union hurt the guy as well. Without a superpower backer, he's exposed as the armed gadfly he is. The source of Libya's conflicts? Qaddafi tells us he is a great leader who simply needs a great country to lead. This militant ego, backed by billions of oil dollars, can lead to a thicket of troubles.

WHO'S INVOLVED

Algerian Civil War

Algerian government, FLN, and the Algerian Army—The military-controlled and "socialist" Algerian government finds itself in an odd position. The core supporters of the government were those who led the revolt against the French and established Algerian independence, the FLN (Front de Libération Nationale, i.e., National Liberation Front). The FLN regime, in power since 1962, didn't produce the economic and social benefits it promised and became increasingly corrupt. There developed a fair amount of corruption and self-serving politics among the old revolutionaries. That is nothing unique, but it comes with a price. Eventually the people the revolutionaries were supposed to serve, but now exploit, get fed up and agitate for a change. Now the old revolutionaries find they have more in common with Paris than with Algeria's political Islamic radicals.

Islamic Salvation Front (FIS)—This collection of religiously motivated opposition forces might have won the open election in 1992, but radicals in the FIS made noises that an FIS victory would be a "final victory for Islam"—i.e., the vote would be Algeria's first and last democratic vote. The FIS, however, is something of an enigma.

Armed Islamic Group (GIA)—More radical than the FIS and more militant, nothing short of an Iranian-type theocratic dictatorship may satisfy the GIA.

Berbers and other ethnics—The Berbers resisted the initial Arab invasions and have maintained their own ethnic identity. They prefer their own customs and own brand of (much more liberal) Islam. They also comprise up to 30 percent of the population, depending on who's counting.

France—The former colonial power in Tunisia, Algeria, and Morocco (French West Africa), France reconciled itself to the loss of Algeria. However, Arab immigration into France, French economic interests, French relationships with the Algerian armed forces, and French cultural connections put Paris deep into this ugly battle.

Wild Cards

European Economic Community (EEC)—Italy also has major economic interests in Algeria. All EEC members have interests in stopping the spread of anti-Western political Islamic regimes.

Iran and Sudan—Both radical Islamic nations are interested in stirring the pot, and perhaps adding another "Islamic republic" to the UN.

Libya—An aging and sidelined Colonel Qaddafi is always interested in spreading his own influence.

The War of the Western Sahara

Morocco—After Spain quit the region, Morocco occupied the Western Sahara and attempted to absorb it—then fought a slow and brutal war to keep it. Morocco's monarchy isn't stable politically.

Popular Front for the Liberation of the Saguia el Hamra and Rio de Oro (Polisario)—Backed by Algeria, this umbrella guerrilla organization was formed in 1969 to combat Spain. Polisario put together a tough and resilient insurgent combat force based in Algeria's Tindouf region. Formally created a government-in-exile in 1976, the Sahrawi Arab Democratic Republic (SADR).

Wild Cards

Spain—The former colonial power in the Western Sahara has interests in containing and resolving the Moroccan-Polisario conflict. But old conflicts between "Christian" Spain and the "Muslim" Moors (and Algerians) remain. The Strait of Gibraltar is narrow and waves of immigrants have crossed it seeking a better life in Europe. Spain's

Canary Islands sit off the Moroccan coast. Two Spanish enclaves remain on the Moroccan coast.

United Nations—The UN has tried to construct an acceptable framework for a vote to resolve the war.

Algeria—Algerian sponsorship for the Polisario has diminished as troubles in Algeria increase. Would a radical political Islamic government renew the war in hopes of toppling Morocco's monarchy?

The Libyan Intrigues

Qaddafi's Libya—The oil revenues have fallen off, UN sanctions hurt, and memories of the U.S. attack in 1986 inhibit Colonel Qaddafi's style. But he is still linked to international terrorism and harbors land claims against his neighbors.

Libyan exiles—Haphazardly financed by the United States, Egypt, and Italy.

Tunisia and Egypt—Both remain interested in Qaddafi's fall, as long as he isn't replaced by an Iranian-type political Islamic dictatorship.

United States, Italy, and Great Britain—These Western powers could move against Qaddafi, though with the end of the cold war he is viewed as more of a pest.

Wild Cards

Chad and France—Libya's southern neighbor, with the backing of its former colonial master, France, dealt Qaddafi's dreams of empire a harsh blow in 1987 when Chad's tribal rebels destroyed Libya's army in Chad.

Burkina Faso—Qaddafi helped put this tiny nation's current regime in power.

International oil companies—Still interested in doing business in Libya.

GEOGRAPHY

The Sahara Desert dominates North Africa and the Maghreb, but the Maghreb is by no means all desert. The Arabs named Algeria Barr al Djazir, the Land of the Islands. The rocky islands along the Mediterranean coast were a threat to navigation. The islands also harbored pirates.

But 80 percent of Algeria's 2,380,000 square kilometers (about three and a half times the size of Texas) is desert. Algeria has many political borders: Morocco to the west; Mauritania and the disputed territory of the Western Sahara to the southwest; Mali and Niger to the south; Tunisia and Libya to the east; Spain and Spain's Balearic Islands not too far across the Mediterranean Sea. Less than 20 percent of Algeria's land is arable and most of the arable land lies along the narrow Mediterranean coastal plain. Because of limited agricultural resources and a burgeoning population, Algeria imports over 50 percent of its food.

The Atlas Mountains separate the temperate and comparatively moist coastal plain from the interior plateaus and the Sahara Desert. The interior is tough country for military operations. A wide, semiarid plateau divides the Tell Atlas from the southern Saharan Atlas range. South of the Saharan Atlas lies the desert. The Sahara is a vast region of dry sirocco winds, sand dunes (ergs), rugged mountains (jebels), gravel flats, occasional palm oases, and high, barren massifs. The temperature in the desert ranges from −10 degrees C to 50 degrees C (123 degrees F). The massifs and plateaus are cut by seasonal streams (wadis). Shallow salt lakes (chotts) rim the desert and are also found in the plateau region. Algeria's major oil and gas fields lie in the north-central Sahara region and to the east along the Sahara border with Libya.

Algeria's 1995 population was some 28 million, with 2 million living in the capital of Algiers. More than 92 percent of the population lives in the north near the coastal strip. Ninety-nine percent of the population is Sunni Muslim. The birth rate is extremely high; 72 percent of the population is under the age of twenty-four. Despite a GDP per capita of over $3,000 (1995), the national unemployment rate is high (over 20 percent) and is much higher among younger Algerians. This has increased political disaffection.

Arabs and Berbers constitute Algeria's two main ethnic groups. The French population, which reached 10 percent in the colonial era, is now 1 percent. A million Algerians live abroad, and most of them in France. Eighty-two percent of the population speaks Arabic, and French is widely understood, particularly in the cities.

Precise statistics are not available, but perhaps 20–30 percent of the Algerian population may speak a Berber dialect as their primary language. That has political consequences both for the government and the Islamic radicals. In Kabylia (east of Algiers) government efforts to "Arabize" the Berbers provoked resistance. The Shawia (who live in the Aures Mountains), the Mozabites in the city of Ghardaia, and Tuareg nomads speak their own dialects.

Algeria has the world's fourth largest proven natural gas reserves as well as significant oil deposits. It exports approximately 1.1 million barrels of oil a day and 20 billion cubic meters of natural gas per year, most of it to Europe. Mercury, phosphates, zinc, and iron ore are also found. Petroleum and natural gas provide 97 percent of Algeria's export earnings.

The kingdom of Morocco (Arabic name: Al-Maghreb) has beach-front property on both the Atlantic Ocean and Mediterranean Sea. With 446,550 square kilometers, the nation is slightly larger than California. Spain's Canary Islands (under Spanish control since 1479) lie 100 kilometers west of Morocco in the Atlantic. The 13-kilometer-wide Strait of Gibraltar connects the Atlantic and Mediterranean and separates Morocco from Spain and the British colony of Gibraltar. A 30- to 50-kilometer-wide temperate coastal plain runs down the western Atlantic coast.

The Rif Mountain range runs along the Mediterranean coast. The Moroccan interior consists of mountains (Atlas Mountains) and plateaus. Rain is plentiful in the mountains (up to 1,000 millimeters or 40 inches per year). Plateaus east of the Atlas range gradually meld into the Sahara Desert.

Morocco's 1994 population was twenty-nine million. The birth rate is high, and 70 percent of the population is under the age of thirty.

Arabs and Arab-Berbers make up nearly 65 percent of the population; Berbers make up the rest, giving Morocco the largest Berber minority in the Maghreb. Most of the Berbers live in the mountains. The Berbers are the ancient "Mauritanians" who bedeviled the Carthaginian and Roman rulers for many centuries.

Arabic is the official language, but various Berber dialects continue to be spoken. According to U.S. State Department sources, the three main Berber dialects are not mutually intelligible. French is still widely used, especially in government and business. Islam is the official religion, to which almost 99 percent of the inhabitants adhere. About ten thousand Jews still live in Morocco.

About half of Morocco's labor force is engaged in agriculture. Morocco controls 75 percent of the world's known phosphate reserves (including those in Western Sahara) and has deposits of copper, petroleum, iron ore, and coal.

Morocco has many land disputes with Spain. Spain maintains two fortified cities (military garrisons, according to Moroccans) on the Moroccan coast. Ceuta (population 71,000) lies on the southern side of the Strait of Gibraltar. Mount Hacho, located in Ceuta, is the southern Pillar of Hercules (the other being the Rock of Gibraltar). Ceuta was founded by the Phoenicians. Spain has held it since 1580. Melilla (population 54,000) is located on the Mediterranean coast east of Ceuta.

Melilla was founded by the Phoenicians and held at various times by the Carthaginians, Romans, Byzantines, and Moors. Spain took control in 1497.

Morocco also disputes Spanish control of the small islands of Peñón de Alhucemas, Peñón de Vélez de la Gomera, and Islas Chafarinas.

After ten years of fighting a very low-level war with Morocco, in 1969 Spain ceded control of the fifteen-hundred-square-kilometer Ifni region (in southwestern Morocco along the Atlantic Ocean). The Spanish settled along the desert Ifni coast in 1476 and held it until 1524, then reclaimed it in 1860. Ifni is now part of Morocco's Agadir Province.

South of Morocco, north of Mauritania, and west of Algeria lies the former Spanish colony of the Spanish Sahara. Now known as the Western Sahara, with an area of 266,000 square kilometers, it is slightly smaller than Colorado. The mineral-rich region was a land of nomads. When Spain withdrew in 1975, Morocco claimed the northern two thirds of the Western Sahara, and Mauritania the southern third. In 1979 the Polisario forced Mauritania to withdraw its claim, and Morocco occupied the whole of the territory.

The Republic of Tunisia lies between Algeria and Libya and is only 150 kilometers from Sicily. With a land area of 163,610 square kilometers, it is slightly smaller than Missouri.

Tunisia divides into three distinct regions: the northern mountains, the hot and dry central plain, and a semiarid south, which merges into the Sahara Desert. The Atlas Mountains run from Algeria into northern Tunisia, where they form two chains, the Northern Tell and the High Tell. Northern Tunisia has a Mediterranean climate.

More than half of Tunisia's 8.8 million people live in urban areas. Tunisia has a serious unemployment problem aggravated by a high rate of population growth. In 1992, 38 percent of the population was under the age of fifteen.

Tunisia's native Berber population rapidly "Arabized" after the Arab conquest in the seventh century. Large numbers of Spanish Arabs, fleeing mainland Spain, settled in northern Tunisia in the sixteenth century. Italian and French colonists settled in the 1850s. A small Jewish community remains in Tunisia.

Virtually 100 percent of the population speaks Arabic, though French is the language of commerce and government. Berber-speaking people, who form less than 1 percent of the population, live in small isolated villages in southern Tunisia. Ninety-eight percent of the people are Sunni Muslim. Tourism is Tunisia's largest single source of income. An estimated five hundred thousand Tunisians work abroad, about half of them in France.

Libya is not always thought of as being part of the Maghreb, but the nation is a key player in North African politics. With 1,760,000 square kilometers of territory, it is slightly larger than Alaska. Libya also has three distinct physical regions: the northwest coast, the northeast coast, and the huge Sahara Desert southern region that covers more than 90 percent of the nation. The northwest coastal region (the old Roman province of Tripolitania) consists of the narrow coastal plain and the Jaffara Plain. The northeastern Libyan coastal region (roughly the old Roman province of Cyrenaica) lies to the east of the Gulf of Sidra. Interesting note: Libya has no perennial rivers.

Some 85 percent of Libya's 5.1 million people live along the coast. About 5 percent of the population remains nomadic. About 90 percent of Libya's population are Arabic-speakers of mixed Arab-Berber ancestry. Berbers who retain the language and way of life comprise only 4 percent and most of these people live in small villages in western Libya. Other minorities include the Arabic-speaking Harratin, of negroid and West African ancestry, who live in the southern desert oases and make up 3 percent of the population. The Berber-related Tuareg and Tebu also live in the south and comprise less than 1 percent of the population. According to Libyan statistics nearly 100 percent of the population speak Arabic, though Italian and English are often spoken in the cities. Ninety-seven percent of the people are Sunni Muslims.

Oil was discovered in Libya in 1959. A member of OPEC, in 1991 Libya ranked twelfth among international oil producers. Petro dollars finance large-scale social programs and support a well-equipped, though poorly led, military.

HISTORY

Historical Overview of the Western Maghreb

Until the sixteenth century, the western Maghreb (Algeria, Tunisia, and Morocco) were, in terms of history, closely linked. Berbers inhabited the North African coast west of Egypt, and Berber and other ethnic nomads traipsed across the Saharan interior. By the twelfth century B.C., Phoenician sailors were making regular stops along the Maghreb coast. The Phoenicians built the city of Carthage, near the present-day city of Tunis in Tunisia. Eventually, Carthage controlled the entire western Mediterranean. In the mid-fifth century B.C. the Carthaginians colonized the north Moroccan coast and named it Barbary because of the Berber inhabitants. An expanding imperial power,

Rome, encountered Carthage. The First Punic War (264–241 B.C.) ended with the Roman defeat of Carthage.

The Algerian coast came under the control of Rome after the 105 B.C. defeat of the Numidians. Rome dominated the Maghreb coast. The Carthage region (Tunisia) became Rome's province of Africa. Berber tribes continued to roam the interior and harass the Roman settlements. Africa's western Mediterranean coast became vital Roman territory. After Emperor Constantine, Christianity flourished in northern Africa. The theologian Saint Augustine (A.D. 354–430) was bishop of Hippo (now Annaba in Algeria).

The Vandal invasion ended Roman rule in the fifth century. In the early sixth century the Byzantines carved out a duchy in the area around present-day Algiers. The Arab invasions in the seventh and eighth centuries A.D. threw the Byzantines out of North Africa. The Arabs pushed into Europe and took Spain. The Maghreb Berbers converted to Islam, but the interior Berber tribes resisted total Arab dominance. Between the eleventh and thirteenth centuries Arab-Berber dynasties of Almoravids and Almohads ruled both the western Maghreb and Spain.

Algeria: Sixteenth Century to Present

In 1492, Spain destroyed the last Muslim state on the Iberian Peninsula. Spanish fleets also attacked and captured several North African Muslim ports. The Muslims appealed to Ottoman Turkey for assistance and Turkish fleets forced the Spaniards to withdraw. In 1518, Algiers and its surrounding region became part of the Ottoman Empire, but the local sovereigns retained political autonomy.

Muslim pirates based along the Maghreb coast plundered foreign shipping. That led to British and American intervention in the early nineteenth century. In 1830, France, under the pretext of thwarting piracy, invaded and deposed the bey of Algiers. France began colonizing Algeria in the 1830s, but the military campaign in Algeria took decades. Resistance in the Algerian Saharan regions continued into the early twentieth century.

The French *pieds-noirs* colonists thrived. Algerian Muslims, however, had few francs and fewer political rights. Several Algerian nationalist organizations formed after World War I. The radical Messali Hadj advocated complete independence. Moderate "assimilationists" like Ferhat Abbas demanded that France fulfill its stated assimilationist goals and make Algeria's Arab-Berbers full citizens.

After the fall of France in 1940 and the Allied invasion of North Africa in World War II, French North African units played an important role in the creation of Free French military units. During the war Algerian nationalists began to lay the political groundwork for independence. However, a nationalist rally in Setif in 1945 led to the deaths of ninety Frenchmen and a bloody round of French military reprisals. The French government was caught between the increasingly radicalized Algerian nationalists and French colonists opposed to any deal.

Tension mounted. The Algerian National Liberation Front (FLN) declared war in 1954. FLN operatives launched terrorist attacks in France, making Europe part of the battleground. In the 1990s this tactic has been repeated by the Islamic Salvation Front and Armed Islamic Group. The Algerian War was terribly divisive in France—the colonists had tremendous political sympathy, particularly inside the French Army. Divisions over the war toppled France's Fourth Republic (1958). In July 1962, French President Charles de Gaulle declared Algeria independent. Multiparty elections were held.

Ahmed Ben Bella, an ardent nationalist and socialist, became Algeria's first president in 1963. The radical Ben Bella began sponsoring liberation groups throughout the Maghreb. The FLN effectively became the sole political party in Algeria. In 1965, Ben Bella was deposed by Houari Boumedienne. Boumedienne supported the Polisario resistance to Spain in the Spanish Sahara and in 1971 nationalized French petroleum concessions.

Chadli Benjedid became president in 1979. During the 1980s, Algeria's economic and social fabric began to tatter. Massive unemployment, high inflation, and charges of government corruption and theft led to demonstrations in 1988. In 1989 the government agreed to constitutional reforms and the end of the FLN's one-party state.

In local multiparty elections held in June 1990, Islamic fundamentalists in the Islamic Salvation Front (FIS) won over 60 percent of the popular vote. The Algerian military, still controlled by old FLN elites, began a campaign to limit the power of the FIS. A violent splinter faction of the FIS initiated a series of terrorist attacks, which led to an official state of siege from June to September 1991.

In December 1991 the FIS won the first round of national legislative elections. The old revolutionaries were not about to be replaced by democratically elected Islamic fundamentalists. In January 1992, Benjedid was forced to quit as president and the Algerian Army took power. Runoff elections were canceled and the FIS outlawed. The army's position: Better a military dictatorship than an Islamic fundamentalist dictatorship.

Since 1992 the unrest has continued—as the economy continues to slide (paying foreign debt in the mid-1990s absorbed 80 percent of the annual petroleum earnings). Islamic radicals have assassinated many foreign workers (especially European Christians), pro-Western Algerians, intellectuals, journalists and, interestingly, Algerian women who wear "Western dress." Islamic radicals (the GIA in the main) established "Islamic enclaves" in villages on the Mitidja Plain outside of Algiers. The army began a "dirty war" involving death squads aimed at the Islamists. Counterinsurgency operations against armed Islamic guerrilla groups have been conducted. In 1993, Algeria broke diplomatic relations with Iran. In 1994 the army declared the beginning of a "national dialogue" and a three-year transition period that would lead to democratic rule. (Presidents may come and go but the Algerian Army and the security services remain the real powers). Rifts have developed in the Islamic fundamentalist opposition. The Armed Islamic Group (GIA) had pressed a vicious terror campaign, which has been denounced by the FIS. In early 1995 the GIA succeeded in kidnapping and decapitating a member of the FLN's central committee.

In early 1995 members of the FLN, the FIS, and the Front for Socialist Forces hammered out an agreement that called for a "credible truce" and an end to the Islamic militants' attacks on Algerian secularists. The three parties would then form a government of national unity. Islamic militants in the GIA and the Islamic Salvation Army rejected the agreement. Politicians identified with the Algerian Army's "eradicationist" wing called it unworkable. A national vote in late 1995 reelected the FLN government, though many observers believed the vote was a vote to end the violence.

The vicious circle of Algerian politics remains: Most Algerians are afraid of the Islamic radicals and do not want a theocratic state. At the same time, they are tired of the FLN's long-term one-party rule and corruption.

Morocco

Spain and Portugal began to acquire Moroccan territory in the fifteenth century and several small wars between the Iberians and Morocco's Arab-Berbers occurred in the sixteenth and seventeenth centuries. Morocco's Alawite (an Islamic sect) dynasty came to power in 1666, but the Alawite sultans controlled the coastal cities—and little else. Spain controlled the port of Ceuta. European competition for control of North Africa resulted in the Moroccan crises of 1905 and 1911–12. Imperial Germany attempted to frustrate France's attempts to gain control of Morocco, but in 1911, Berlin recognized French authority in Morocco. In 1912 most of Morocco became a French protectorate. The Treaty of Fez made Tangier an international zone.

Spain, which had controlled the port of Tangier on and off since the beginning of the sixteenth century, became the de facto sovereign of Tangier. During World War II, Spain occupied the international zone.

After World War II, Alawite Sultan Mohammed V led an anti-French Moroccan nationalist movement. The French colonial government sent the sultan into exile. He returned to the throne in 1956 when Morocco became independent. Upon independence, Tangier was returned to Moroccan control. Upon Mohammed V's death in 1961, his son, Hassan II, became king. Since 1961 Hassan has survived at least three coup attempts. He is regarded as a pro-Western Moroccan nationalist.

In 1969, Spain ceded its Ifni enclave to Morocco. In 1975, Spain decided to quit the Spanish Sahara (now the Western Sahara). Morocco and Mauritania laid claim to the region. The war has been popular with Moroccan nationalists. The fact that Algeria supported the Polisario further stoked Moroccan resentment of Algiers.

Historical Focus: The Western Sahara

In 1884, Spain established the colony of Spanish Sahara with the capital at El Aaiun. It was a barren, dismal colony of little interest to anyone until 1963 when large, and very valuable, phosphate deposits were discovered.

As other European powers left Africa, Morocco and Mauritania began pressuring Madrid to give up the Spanish Sahara. Algeria, and later Libya, helped back the Polisario, a Sahrawi (Western Sahara natives) anti-Spanish independence organization. A low-level insurgency began in 1969.

In 1975 the World Court ruled that the Spanish Sahara should be granted self-determination. But before a plebiscite could be conducted, Morocco invaded—in a rather unusual way. In what became known as the Green March, Morocco's King Hassan sent a half-million unarmed Moroccans into the territory. Madrid withdrew, ceding the northern two thirds of the colony to Morocco and the rest to Mauritania.

The Polisario went back to war. In 1979, Mauritania renounced its claim to the Western Sahara. Morocco responded by annexing the entire region. Rather than face the wily Polisario out in the desert, the Moroccan Army constructed a long wall and string of fortifications around the Western Sahara's population centers and mines. Many Moroccan settlers were moved into the protected zone.

In 1988, Morocco and the Polisario agreed in principle to a UN-sponsored referendum. The sticking point: Who is a Sahrawi and who gets to vote? Further negotiations (and Algerian pressure on the Polisario) led to a cease-fire in 1990, but the UN referendum has been repeatedly postponed. The Western Sahara increasingly functions as part of Morocco. In fact, many Western Saharans voted in Morocco's 1993 elections.

Tunisia

The Turkish Ottoman Empire conquered Tunisia in 1574. Tunis continued to be a center of Mediterranean piracy. During the nineteenth century, Tunisia fell into political and economic chaos. France established a protectorate in 1881, which lasted until 1956.

The 1952 assassination of Ferhat Hached renewed the Tunisian nationalist surge. France, bogged down in Algeria, had no need of further trouble. In 1957, Tunisia became an independent republic. Nationalist Habib Bourguiba became president. In 1975 Bourguiba was elected president for life. Economic troubles in the early 1980s led to increased Islamic fundamentalist agitation.

In 1987, Prime Minister Zine el-Abidine Ben Ali seized power from Bourguiba. Ben Ali promoted private investment and liberalized the Tunisian economy. He was reelected president (without opposition) in 1989 and 1994.

Tunisia began cracking down on political Islamic fundamentalists in the mid-1980s. In 1992 several hundred members of the Ennahda political Islamic group were arrested for plotting to overthrow the government. The government continues to combat the radicals. In late 1994, Tunisia held over two thousand Islamic fundamentalists in prison. Tunisia also has a problem with Algerian migrants fleeing the violence in Algeria.

Libya

Arab armies overran Libya in the seventh century, driving the Berber tribes away from the coast and deeper into the desert. The Turks exercised nominal control over Libya from the sixteenth through the early twentieth centuries. "Nominal" scarcely describes the situation. Muslim pirates operated from the Libyan coast, and Sanusi tribes and religious sects controlled the oases in the interior.

In the early twentieth century, Italy wrested control of Libya from the Turks. The Italians had grand designs, which included settling large numbers of Italian immigrants along the coast. Mussolini's visions of a new Roman Empire (similar to Qaddafi's visions of a new Arab empire) gave the Libyan project additional impetus, but then his failure in World War II lost Libya entirely.

Significant oil reserves were discovered in 1959. King Idris, leader of the Libyan resistance to Italian colonialism and head of a postwar constitutional monarchy, was deposed by military coup in 1969. Colonel Mu'ammar Qaddafi assumed power as "leader of the Revolution" and ruled through his army-dominated Revolutionary Command Council.

Qaddafi had bankrolled coups, assassinations, and revolts in at least a dozen countries. His only success seems to be in Burkina Faso (the nation formerly known as Upper Volta). He has, at various times, tried to merge Libya with Morocco, Tunisia, and Egypt. Qaddafi has provided arms and military training to various terrorist and guerrilla groups, including supplying everyone from Bosnian Muslims to Tuareg nomads in a war against Mali. This has brought him into direct conflict with the United States, France, Great Britain, and the United Nations. In 1986 the United States launched air attacks on Libya in retaliation for Qaddafi's support of terrorist attacks on U.S. facilities in Germany.

In 1978 the Egyptians beat Libya badly in their short border war. The Tanzanian Army routed Qaddafi's two-thousand-man Libyan Legion in 1979 fighting in Uganda. Qaddafi has survived coup attempts in 1970, 1975, 1984, 1993, and 1994. In April 1992 the UN put Libya under an arms embargo and banned airline flights to Libya. The UN imposed the sanctions because Qaddafi refused to turn over two Libyan intelligence agents the British determined were directly involved in the 1988 terrorist bombing of Pan Am Flight 103, which blew up over Scotland.

LOCAL POLITICS

The Arab Maghreb Union, formed in 1989 by Algeria, Morocco, Tunisia, Libya, and Mauritania, is a trade organization intended to further regional economic cooperation.

Algeria

National Liberation Front (FLN)—The party of the revolution against France became the front for a corrupt one-party state.

Islamic Salvation Front (FIS)—Exists in several factions; would have won the 1992 elections but was banned by the military.

Armed Islamic Group (GIA)—Led by Afghan war veterans; allied with the Islamic Salvation Army, splinter radical Islamic faction.

Socialist Front Forces—Berber-based socialist party; important "swing" political constituency between the Islamists and the army.

Organization of Free Young Algerians—Anti-FIS terrorist group.

Rally of Culture and Democracy—Secular democratic opposition group.

Algerian Army—Divides into the accommodationists (who try to get along with the fundamentalists) and the eradicationists (who try to kill, or otherwise suppress, the fundamentalists). Eradicationists include top generals, police chiefs, and defense ministers. (See Participant Strategies.)

Le Pouvoir Occulte (The Hidden Power)—Algeria's military and security service elites who seek to maintain governmental control no matter who is in charge.

Ninjas—Masked (to prevent retaliation against them or their families) antiterrorist forces.

Berber Cultural Movement—Once a nonpolitical group devoted to protecting Berber languages and customs. Advocates teaching Berber along with Arabic in schools.

Sonatrach—State-run energy corporation.

Morocco

Moroccan progovernment parties—Popular Movement (MP); Constitutional Union party (UC); National Democratic party (PND).

Moroccan opposition parties—Socialist Union of Popular Forces (USFP); Istiqlal party (IP: an old guard Moroccan nationalist party);

Justice and Charity ("Islamist" political fundamentalist group, led by Abdessalem Yassine).

Major independent parties—National Rally of Independents (RNI); Democracy and Istiqlal party (PDI); Non-Obedience Candidates party (SAP).

Ceuta and Melilla—Spanish enclaves along Morocco's North African coast. Ceuta is opposite Gibraltar, the other Pillar of Hercules.

Libya

Colonel Mu'ammar Qaddafi—Has no official title; he's referred to as Leader of the Revolution.

Green Revolution—Qaddafi's name for the 1969 revolt. Hence, *The Green Book,* Qaddafi's revolutionary manifesto, commingling Islam, romance, Marxist jargon, and the colonel's insights into life.

Jamajiriyya—Republic of the Masses, in Arabic. Qaddafi's name for his government.

National Front for the Salvation of Libya—Umbrella organization for anti-Qaddafi dissidents. Includes over a dozen different organizations.

Great Man-made River—Qaddafi's superproject designed to bring water from the Saharan aquifers to Libya's coastal cities. (Considered a technically flawed boondoggle; billions have already been spent on it.)

Tunisia

Constitutional Democratic party (RCD)—Founded as Habib Bourguiba's neo-Destour party; was renamed Destourian Socialist party (PSD) in 1964 and became the RCD in 1988. By far Tunisia's dominant political party. Think of it as an FLN that knew how to begin to accommodate change, and did so.

Other Tunisian political parties—Movement of Democratic Socialists (MDS); Socialist Progressive party (RSP); Popular Unity party

(PUP); Democratic Unionist party (UDU); Social Liberal party (PSP); Renewal party (former Communist party).

Ennahda (The Awakening, or Renaissance Party)—Banned Tunisian political Islamic organization.

General Union of Tunisian Workers (UGTT)—Labor union, no longer the political and social force it was before Bourguiba's crackdowns in 1978, 1984, and 1985, but still a major political factor in Tunisia.

Personal Status Code—Adopted in 1956. Prohibits polygamy. Functions as a very limited "bill of rights."

POLITICAL TREND CHARTS

ALGERIA

Gv95	Gv20	PC95	PC20	R95	R20	Ec95	Ec20	EdS95	EdS20
MD4,2	AO3,3	3	5	8	7	4-	4	3-	3-

Gv = Government type
MD = Military Dictatorship
AO = Authoritarian Oligarchy
PC = Political Cohesiveness (0 = chaos, 9 = maximum)
R = Repression Index (9 maximum)
Ec = Comparative Economic Status (0–9)
EdS = Relative Education Status (0–9)

MOROCCO

Gv95	Gv20	PC95	PC20	R95	R20	Ec95	Ec20	EdS95	EdS20
AM6,5	AM5,4	7	7	6	6	3+	3	3+	3+

AM = Authoritarian Monarchy

TUNISIA

Gv95	Gv20	PC95	PC20	R95	R20	Ec95	Ec20	EdS95	EdS20
AO5,4	AO5,3	6	5	6+	6	3+	3+	4+	4+

LIBYA

Gv95	Gv20	PC95	PC20	R95	R20	Ec95	Ec20	EdS95	EdS20
MD4,2	AO3,3	4	5	8	7	4+	4	5−	4+

"INDEPENDENT WESTERN SAHARA"

Gv20	PC20	R20	Ec20	EdS20
AO3,2	2	5	1+	1

FRANCE

Gv95	Gv20	PC95	PC20	R95	R20	Ec95	Ec20	EdS95	EdS20
RD8,7+	RD8,8	8+	8+	2+	2	8−	8	9−	9−

RD = Representative Democracy

Regional Powers and Power Interest Indicator Charts

Algerian Civil War

	Economic Interests	Historical Interests	Political Interest	Military Interest	Force Generation Potential	Ability to Intervene Politically
Algerian people	9	9	9	9	2−	6
Alger Army	9	9	9	9	6	7
Alger Islam	9	9	9	9	4	8
France	8	8	7	8+	3+	6
Morocco	7	9	9	9	2	2
Tunisia	8	9	9	9	1+	3
Libya	2	2	5	2	1−	2
Spain	7	7	8	9	2+	3
Italy	6	6	7	8	2+	2
United States	5	6	7	8	4	2
Iran	1	2	8	1	0	5
Other "EEC"	6	5	7	7	2	4

Note: 0 = minimum; 9 = maximum

Western Sahara

	Economic Interests	Historical Interests	Political Interest	Military Interest	Force Generation Potential	Ability to Intervene Politically
Morocco	8	8	9	9	7	7
Polisario	9	9	9	9	3	8
Algeria	4	6	6	6	4	7
Spain	7	7	6	5	2	5
Mauritania	8	9	8	7	1−	4
United States	2	1	3	3	8	6
France	6	5	5	5	2	5

SEVERAL LIBYAN WARS
(VS. EGYPT, CHAD, TUNISIA, UNITED STATES, EEC)

	Economic Interests	Historical Interests	Political Interest	Military Interest	Force Generation Potential (def/off*)	Ability to Intervene Politically
Libya (Q)†	9	9	9	9	4	9
LibyaDis‡	9	9	9	9	1−	4
Egypt	7	8	8	8	8/7	5
United States	6	4	5	5	6	2
Chad	9	9	9	9	5/1+	1
Tunisia	9	9	9	9	4/1	3
Italy	8	8	8	9	4	5
"EEC"	7	7	8	7	3+	6
Russia	1	2	1	1	2−	5

*FGP in defense in own country/FGP on offense
†Qaddafi
‡Libyan anti-Qaddafi dissidents

SPANISH-MOROCCAN WAR/FRENCH-ALGERIAN WAR/
EUROPEAN INTERVENTIONS

	Economic Interests	Historical Interests	Political Interest	Military Interest	Force Generation Potential	Ability to Intervene Politically
Spain	8	9	9	9	3/8	7
Morocco	9	9	9	9	4/2+	8
Algeria	9	9	9	9	5/4	7
Britain	7	7	7	6	2+	6
France	8	8	9	9	4	7
United States	6	6	7	6	6	3
Iran	1	4	9	8	1−	7

PARTICIPANT STRATEGIES AND GOALS

Algeria

Algerian government—For all practical purposes the Algerian government is the Algerian Army and the old FLN elite. The Algerian Army has its factions: the accommodationists, who seek to find some political agreement with the more moderate elements of the FIS; and the "eradicationists," who seek to totally destroy the Islamic fundamentalist movement. The eradicationists (or *eradicateurs*) prefer death squads, torture, and extrajudicial arrests. They loathe Islamic revivalism. The accommodationists are trying to hammer out an agreement with Islamic moderates. The army is pursuing a "two-faced strategy," fighting militants while conducting talks. The political problem the FLN and the army constantly face remains Algeria's "trapped majority": Overwhelmingly, the majority of Algerians are afraid of Islamic radicals but tired of the FLN's long-term one-party rule and corruption. The FLN may have waited too long to change.

Emerging Islamic moderates—These elements in the FIS would make peace with the army in exchange for open elections and power sharing. They are, however, increasingly outflanked by the GIA.

Algerian Islamic radicals—The radical GIA (Armed Islamic Group) wants to convince the population that it can hit the army blow for blow. Hijacking aircraft to France gets headlines and shocks the French colonialists. Blowing up the natural gas pipeline to Italy would get even more. The radicals have begun attacking economic targets, which is a certain way to weaken the FLN and the army. The political Islamists see themselves as riding the wave of the future, i.e., revival of a glorious Arab-Islamic past. They aim to establish *sharia* (Koranic) law and have shown they will use violence to compel compliance. The GIA has also threatened to widen the conflict. GIA communiqués have focused on France as the real enemy—which leads to speculation of a far wider war pitting Christian France against the new political Islam.

Such a strategy might win converts. Bringing France into a broad conflict could easily backfire against the Islamic radicals, with French covert operations teams attacking GIA support centers in the Sudan or
even Iran.

Berbers and other ethnics—The Front for Socialist Forces advocates
the formation of a transitional government and new elections. The
Berbers do not want a radical Islamic state, which would impinge on
their autonomy. The Berbers also dislike the generals. The Berbers still
carry on the notion of detaching the Kabylia region (where two thirds
of the Berbers live) from the rest of Algeria and forming a Berber state.

France—Paris is key to any settlement in Algeria. Political Islamist
radicals—the GIA in particular—understand France's support of the
FLN-Army dominated government as a formalized French-FLN alliance. That means that in the eyes of the GIA, France is a belligerent.
Paris doesn't want it that way. But France has its own "Islam problem." About four to five million Muslims, most of them Arab immigrants and a third of them Algerian, live in France. In 1970, France
had two dozen mosques. In 1994 there were around a thousand
mosques in France. Some of the most hard-line anti-immigrant activists
in France are former French Algerian colonists. They refer to the new
immigrants as "Islamic colonizers." Twenty-five thousand Frenchmen
are registered as living in Algeria (fifty thousand people have dual
citizenship). The French in Algeria are prime targets for the GIA.

GIA terrorism led France to try cutting air and sea links to Algeria.
France then cracked down on Algerian militants living in France. But
get-tough and verbal support for the FLN hasn't been France's only
strategy. France has tried to encourage the Algerian Army's accommodationists by criticizing the eradicationists. France has explored a
European-sponsored peace conference on Algeria in hopes of bringing
international pressure on both the Algerian Army hard-liners and the
FIS. A political solution in Algeria that protects French economic interests is the Parisian dream. France relies to a great degree on Algerian
natural gas.

France's interests, however, do not lie with a radical Islamic fundamentalist regime. What happens if the Algerian Army and FLN's
fortunes begin to rapidly decline? The French have prepared plans for

the evacuation of foreign nationals from Algiers and Oran. Two major Western European Union (WEU) defense exercises conducted in 1994 included practice mass evacuations.

France can put some very capable forces into North Africa very quickly. The French Rapid Reaction Force (FAR) is an excellent intervention force. It consists of two light armored divisions, a paratroop infantry division, an airmobile division, some special operations units, and a logistics brigade. An alpine light infantry division was formerly part of the FAR and could be brought in as a reinforcing unit.

Other European nations and organizations—The European Union is pushing for a negotiated solution. EEC is interested in a steady supply of natural gas and regional economic development.

Tunisia—Scared of spillover from war and a rise in Islamic fundamentalism. In early 1995, Algerian Islamic fundamentalists raided a Tunisian border post.

Western Sahara

Morocco—Morocco wants to structure the UN plebiscite so that its control of the Western Sahara is legitimated in an international forum. How? Morocco wants the Moroccan immigrants who have settled in the region since 1976 eligible to vote, but the Polisario and the UN have insisted on a residency requirement, i.e., residency when Spain left the Western Sahara.

Morocco's military strategy has been quite successful. Isolating the towns and mines behind a long string of fortifications and launching interdiction ground and air strikes at Polisario supply routes and forward bases was a long-term winner.

Polisario—With Algerian backing waning, the Polisario will be on their own. The Polisario could win an open election for an independent Western Sahara but they are no longer militarily strong enough to contest Morocco for the region. Other options include forming alliances with Moroccan Islamic dissidents.

Libya

Qaddafi—Wants to stay in power and keep the game going as long as possible. Qaddafi has finally realized his revolution will not spread.

Anti-Qaddafi militants—Hope for a military coup or a war with Egypt as a result of which Egypt installs a new government, or an invasion by Western allies. . . . Or they will wait until he dies of old age.

POTENTIAL OUTCOMES

Algerian Civil War

1. 45 percent chance through 2001: Military accommodationists, Berbers, and FIS moderates form transitional government of national unity. New elections are held. Military checks its extremists. GIA and other political Islamic extremists, however, continue to wage a guerrilla war. The Islamic extremists become increasingly isolated politically.
2. 35 percent chance through 2001: FLN and army "eradicationists" continue to pursue aggressive "dirty war" against Islamic radicals. Promised elections are continually delayed. Economy continues to slide. Violence and anarchy reign.
3. 15 percent chance through 2001: FLN and army hard-liners factionalize. GIA and Islamic radicals supplant FIS as main opposition political force. Mass armed uprising occurs and FLN elites flee country. An Islamic republic along Iranian lines is established.
4. 5 percent chance through 2001: The "dirty war" succeeds. Algerian Army eradicationists destroy all GIA terror cells. Elections are held under tight FLN control. FIS allowed to exist as token opposition party.

Western Sahara

1. 55 percent chance through 2001: Western Sahara incorporated into
   Morocco, either by UN plebiscite (with the vote rigged by Morocco) or by agreement with Polisario factions no longer interested
   in fighting. Morocco wins renewed guerrilla war with weakened
   Polisario militant factions.
2. 35 percent chance through 2001: Polisario wins open plebiscite.
   Western Sahara becomes an independent nation.
3. 10 percent chance through 2001: Plebiscite fails to occur or neither
   party accepts the results. Warfare renews. Morocco attacks and
   destroys Polisario bases inside Algeria. Low-level guerrilla war
   continues with weakened Polisario raiding Western Sahara and
   southern Morocco. Western Sahara incorporated into Morocco but
   annexation is not recognized by international community.

The Libyan intrigues. A 35 percent chance before 2001 that a military revolt topples Qaddafi. Exiled Libyan dissidents are themselves
in disarray and though many have democratic aspirations, the economic and political husk of Libya will be slow to revive. If Qaddafi is
toppled, there's an 85 percent chance of a new military regime taking
power. Islamic fundamentalists will slip from Qaddafi's jails and Libya
could become another Algeria.

Spanish-Moroccan war. This is highly unlikely. We give it a 2 percent chance before 2001, unless King Hassan II falls from power. Then
shooting between Moroccan nationalists and Spanish forces defending
Ceuta and Melilla becomes a possibility (50 percent). If political Islamists become a real factor in Morocco, trouble between Spain and
Morocco becomes a likelihood. Potential outcome: Spain is prepared
for this. Their armed forces are designed for intervention in North
Africa. Spain would win the conventional battles. The terror war that
the Islamists would take to Europe, however, would be long and
bloody.

*French-Algerian war of 2001 ("Defense of Islam, Defense of Chris-
tendom").* This war is also a distant prospect. It may also be misnamed

since a new Franco-Algerian conflict could turn into a series of wars across North Africa, pitting Europeans, Arab secularists, Islamic radicals, and various minority ethnic groups in a swirl of military and political contention. Give it a 3 percent chance before 2001 unless the Armed Islamic Group comes to power and decides to rid Algeria of all Western influence. If the GIA takes power the possibility jumps to 25 percent; in other words, very high.

COST AND KINDS OF WAR

By early 1995, several Western press sources suggested 1,000 lives a week were being lost in Algeria's internal war. Total killed as of mid-1995 may be 35,000 people. Cost to the fragile Algerian GDP 1992–95 is $25–$35 billion. That's about 16 percent of GDP each year.

The Western Sahara is a sideshow but one that has cost Morocco up to $1 billion a year to prosecute. Estimates on lives lost varies widely, from 1,500 to 4,000 over a fifteen-year period. How much has Colonel Qaddafi squandered on buying weapons his military cannot use and wasted on senseless military escapades? Figures vary widely, but until the UN sanctions started to bite, some Western sources put the figure at $22 billion between 1971 and 1992, or a little over a billion dollars a year.

The Algerian civil war is being fought as a "dirty war" by the Algerian Army, similar to Argentina's war against leftist guerrillas in the 1970s. It's also similar to the war fought by France against Algerians in the 1960s. Murder, terror, and torture are the means. It has been, and will likely continue to be, urban combat. The GIA and radicals in the FIS have also attempted larger operations, using hundreds of armed irregulars. But this escalation of the fighting has not been successful so far, and has led to some disastrous defeats. But the radicals must be able to, eventually, beat the army at its own game if they want to take over the country. The fundamentalists depend on urban areas for protection and sustenance, so whatever heavy combat there might be will occur in the urban areas (either the cities or the villages and towns in the suburbs). The Berbers are primarily outside the cities,

322 / A Quick and Dirty Guide to War

and are either progovernment or simply hostile to the fundamentalists. That further constrains any fundamentalist military action outside the cities. Fighting in urban areas is bloody and difficult to defeat. But such combat on a large scale is also quite destructive of lives and property. Most areas of the cities are medieval in their layout, with mile after mile of narrow streets that most armored vehicles cannot navigate. The government troops tend to cede these constricted areas to the fundamentalists. The broad, French-built boulevards and their adjacent buildings belong to the police and government troops. But everything else belongs to the fundamentalists. The government also controls the water and electricity, as well as access to the fundamentalist areas. If the fundamentalists decide to increase the tempo of combat, it is their followers who would suffer the most. Thus the fundamentalists pursue a low-level war of terrorism, hoping to demoralize the government forces to the point where they will simply collapse. That worked against the French in the 1960s. But the French could go home; the government forces are fighting for them. It's going to be a bloody battle for as long as it lasts.

War of the Western Sahara. There has been some conventional combat but most of the fight is desert hit-and-run. The Moroccan Air Force has conducted some air strikes and the Moroccan Army sites its artillery in "firebase"-type arrangements to support the Moroccan fortifications and "great desert wall." Guerrillas move in jeeps, trucks, and on foot, with supplies in trucks. There are reports that the Polisario have some Soviet-type light armor, but maintenance is a problem. The Moroccan Army has proven itself superior at desert warfare. With air superiority and better logistics, the Polisario has opted for the ballot. A resumption of the fighting would likely go badly for the Polisario.

Chapter 8

THE GRAND SAHEL:
BAD ECOLOGY, BAD POLITICS,
BAD TIMES

The Sahel is a semidesert "weather zone" cutting across Africa just south of the Sahara Desert. Technically, "the Sahel" proper, a savanna land, only exists in the western half of Africa. However, the ecological and, sadly, the political conditions characteristic of this "desertifying" region now extend as a band ("the Grand Sahel") across the continent, from Mauritania on the Atlantic coast through Chad in central Africa to Somalia and the Red Sea in the east. Rainfall varies from 8 to 16 inches a year. Compare this with the 30 to 50 inches a year the United States west of the Mississippi gets.

This huge belt-land serves as the rough and rugged border between Arab Africa in the north and black Africa in the south. For the last one hundred years, the entire region has been increasingly plagued by severe, periodic droughts, which, because of growing human populations and the destruction of vegetation, have led to "desertification,"

323

the encroachment of the Sahara and the transformation of pastoral and sparse crop land into so much dust.

In the popular Western imagination, mentioning the Sahel conjures up TV pictures of emaciated refugees, bankrupt countries, ruthless banditry, and desperate international appeals for food. The nations in the sub-Saharan strip—Mauritania, Senegal and Gambia (erstwhile Senegambia), Niger, Mali, Chad, the Sudan, Ethiopia, Somalia, and Djibouti—are desperate and struggling by any definition. The dire economic conditions in these nations, exacerbated by ancient animosities among tribes, races, and religions; by the legacy of European and Arab colonialism; and, in the case of Ethiopia, by the final breakdown of an ancient empire, have produced a relentless cycle of armed conflict and death wrought by combat and starvation. In the Sahel starvation has become both a weapon in and a cause of war.

SOURCE OF CONFLICT

Rapid population growth, the departure of colonial governments that failed to prepare their colonies for independence, and the establishment of corrupt homegrown regimes in the 1960s produced political and economic collapse. Intermittent warfare, cyclic famine, millions of refugees, and other woes now characterize the region. In this century, population has more than quadrupled, far outstripping local food supplies and other natural resources.

The periodic famines and endemic ethnic conflicts have intensified traditional tribal rivalries and plunged the region into a constant state of conflict. The warfare is basically fought with small arms; occasionally, heavier weapons and aircraft are used when any of these poor nations can beg, borrow, or steal them from wealthier benefactors or opponents. Nearly all the warfare is internal, among different ethnic, political, and/or religious groups within the same nation. The individual suffering is new, but at times the form of warfare is almost ancient; camels and horses are used for supply and troop transport almost as often as Toyota Land Cruisers, heavy trucks, and armored personnel carriers. Sometimes prisoners are literally enslaved.

Aiding and often encouraging the strife are several major outside groups. Many Arab nations give support to their Arab kinsmen and fellow Muslims in these nations. On occasion, Colonel Mu'ammar Qaddafi of Libya sends in troops. In particular, Chad and the Sudan have been Libyan stomping grounds, though Libya has allegedly armed and politically supported "rebels" in Mauritania and Senegal as well. Libya has been very low-key about this support since U.S. aircraft attacked Libya in 1986, and UN economic sanctions were invoked against Libya in 1992. This last action was in response to Libya's refusal to surrender several suspects in terrorist bombings.

Iran, in an effort to export its political "Islamist" fundamentalism, has backed the Islamist faction in Sudan. While Libya keeps a low profile, Sudan now serves as the main base for Iranian-sponsored terrorists in the region. (Some of the money also comes from other wealthy Persian Gulf–area fundamentalists.) As a result, Sudan has become the source of all sorts of mischief for its neighbors, and anyone else reachable by the terrorists now based in the Sudan.

During the cold war, the Soviet Union sold weapons and trained terrorists for "friendly" states. The Grand Sahel's fragile nations were the perfect spot to "wage war on the periphery"; by exploiting old colonial antagonisms, the Kremlin figured to gain allies and victories on the cheap. But the end of the cold war, and the end of the Soviet Union in 1991, caused this support to evaporate. For the Russians, these African adventures were dismal enterprises. Victories were few, losses added up, nothing was cheap.

Western nations have also supported various groups and governments in the Sahel, partially to counterbalance Soviet interference and partially to maintain influence in their former colonies. France in particular is a major player in the region. Djibouti, while nominally sovereign, is still essentially a French Foreign Legion post and navy base covering the critical Horn of Africa.

Ethiopia, with its long-running wars, is in many ways an intense example of the entire region's troubles. Essentially, Ethiopia as it exists today is the remnant of an empire at least twenty-five hundred years old. Overrun by Italy in the 1930s in specific, and overrun by the twentieth century in general, with the fall of Emperor Haile Selassie ("the Lion of Judah") in 1974, the Ethiopian empire centered in Addis Ababa has finally shattered. In its place there appeared a Communist dictatorship backed by Soviet money and Cuban soldiers. The long-subjected Tigre and Omoroan peoples fought in league with rebellious Eritrea Province (formerly an Italian colony) and, in 1991, overthrew the Ethiopian Communists. Eritrea became an independent nation and the Tigre rebels took over the central government. Ethiopia remains disorganized and unsettled, though its agricultural sector is recovering.

Somalia went through a meltdown similar to neighboring Ethiopia's. Originally a pro-Soviet state, Somalia was dumped by the Russians in favor of newly Marxist (and much larger) Ethiopia in 1977. Western aid was sought, but was not as lavish (nor did it consist of much weaponry). The dictator Barre, whom Soviet money, arms and advisers had propped up until 1977, held on until 1991. Then he lost control and fled. Somalia fell apart; the pictures of the subsequent famine and bloodletting got onto Western TV screens. The result was a United States–led UN military intervention. After much "peacekeeping" and some bloodshed, the U.S. force withdrew in 1994 and the remaining UN troops in 1995.

WHO'S INVOLVED

General note: Many Arab states provide legitimate economic and humanitarian aid and assistance to their fellow Arabs and Muslims in the northern portions of most Sahel states. The United States and many other Western nations have provided considerable food and economic assistance to these nations.

Ethiopia

Central Ethiopian government—The former Marxist government fell in 1991, partially as a result of the cutoff of Soviet aid, but more because of internal resistance to harsh Communist rule. The new government, while nominally democratic, has been barely able to maintain itself in power. The new government is largely composed of men, and troops, from the former Tigre rebels. The Tigreans comprise less than

10 percent of the Ethiopian population and many other factions in the country feel cut out of the government.

Eritrea—A part of Ethiopia since 1952; but constant resistance to Ethiopia rule led to independence in 1993. Primarily the old Italian colony of Eritrea, and the area that had long been settled by a mixture of Arab and Ethiopian peoples.

Somalia—Claims the Ogaden region.

Wild Cards

Israel—The "return" of Ethiopian "black Hebrews" to Israel has been dependent on the flow of Israeli advice and Israeli arms, and, after 1991, technical aid and trade relations. All (or at least the vast majority of) the Ethiopian Jews are in Israel now, but Israel still maintains a close relationship with Ethiopia (the only Christian nation in otherwise Muslim North Africa).

Iran—The Islamic revolutionary government provides moral and material support for the like-minded Islamic government in the Sudan. Iran spends over $100 million a year to support Islamic fundamentalism. A large chunk of that goes to the Sudan.

France—Maintains a garrison in Djibouti (on the northern border of Somalia).

The Sudan

Muslim and Arab north—Maintains traditional dominance over black Africans. Provides bases for international terrorism.

Black tribal groups—Christian and animist, in the south, fighting for independence.

Wild Cards

Egypt—Interested in "stability" along the upper Nile.
Libya—Supports several rebel groups, but very quietly.

United States—Wants peace and stability. With the cold war over, there's nothing much else to aspire to.

Chad

Anti-Libyan political and tribal groups.
Pro-Libyan political and tribal groups—Note that the pro- and anti-Libyan groups will sometimes switch allegiance if it suits their immediate purpose.
Libya—Extend its power, and perhaps pick up valuable territory.
France—French troops and arms still stand by to intervene. Paris has remained involved in its former colonies in the area from Senegal to Chad.

Wild Cards

Nigeria—A large army next door. Though caught up in its own internal problems, the "Brazil" of Africa sees itself as the local "superpower" and the one that should intervene to keep the peace.
United States—Provided some military aid to Chad in an effort to counter Libyan invasion. Has tried to keep a low profile.

The Mauritanian-Senegalese Emigration War

These nations spar over their citizens who live on, and have long wandered across, their common border.
Mauritania—Representing the Arab north.
Senegal—Representing the black south.
Gambia—Essentially a part of Senegal.

GEOGRAPHY

The Sahel is the semiarid fringe of the Sahara Desert. For thousands of years its grassy plains and slender rainfall (marginally heavier—up to 16 inches a year—than the under 10 inches a year on the Sahara) kept the desert at bay. The Sahel's annual rainfall is similar to that of the U.S. high plains from Wyoming to New Mexico. Every ten years or so, drought hits the Sahel, population growth either stops or declines, then, belatedly, the rains return. Sometimes the droughts last several years. Deaths occur and migration begins.

The Sahel starts as coastal grassland near the Senegal River. Ecologically, Gambia, located along the Gambia River in the middle of Senegal, is not in the Sahel, but political events in Senegal resonate in Gambia. Four hundred miles from the coast the land rises several thousand feet to an equally semiarid plateau that extends nearly 3,000 miles eastward (broken only by some hills in the southwestern Sudan) to the Ethiopian highlands (over 6,000 feet higher). Nearly 500 miles farther east the land drops again to the Somali Plateau and then the Red Sea coast.

The Sahel served as the natural buffer zone between the arid wastes of the Sahara and the tropical rain forests of central Africa. The people living in the Sahel lived largely off their herds of cattle, goats, or sheep. With herds, the people could move to find water when drought occurred. But once much of the population settled down, a dry growing season spelled starvation.

Nearly five thousand years ago, this flat corridor allowed the dark-skinned Nilo-Saharan and Cushite people of the west coast to spread east. They bumped up against the Negro peoples in the Niger River area three thousand years ago. Eleven hundred years ago, the camel was introduced on a large scale, making it practical to trade regularly with the Arab states to the north (along the Mediterranean coast). Three hundred years ago the population of the area stood at about ten million, largely at the east and west extremes. The twenty-five-hundred-mile region in the middle was largely for nomadic grazing and travel. Currently the population of the Sahel region is over seventy million. The agricultural infrastructure has not kept pace with the growth. The Sahel cannot support that many people on a continual basis. Only imports of food prevent massive die-offs when the droughts arrive.

Life was always hard in the Sahel, with population increasing during years of good rainfall and declining as periodic droughts ravaged the region, with famine and disease killing off children and the elderly. Colonial government in the nineteenth and twentieth centuries brought improved medical care, sanitation, and better organization in general. By the middle of the twentieth century, it was also possible to quickly bring in large quantities of food, and use trucks and motorized boats to quickly distribute it to the starving population. Population increased dramatically. Better able to survive the regular droughts, the population now began to overgraze the land. Resources were gobbled up by enlarged herds. That led to a steady spread of the Sahara Desert and a reduction in grazing land.

The biggest factor influencing population, however, was not the overgrazing and expansion of the desert (though those are of course significant), but the periodic breakdown in government administration, which prevented food movements into famine areas. Man's action, not nature, was now the biggest cause of death. Politics increased the impact of ecological damage.

Senegal and Mauritania are at the western end of the Sahel. The most severely desertified portion of the western Sahel in this area lies in Mauritania.

Mali, Niger, and Chad form the core of the Sahel. The northern portion of Mali is Sahara Desert and Sahel. The lower portion is better watered and more suitable for farming or more intensive grazing. Niger is much the same as Mali, desert in the north, moister land in the south (particularly along the Niger River). Chad is the inland "keystone" to central Africa. It borders Libya to the north, the Sudan to the east, the Central African Republic to the south, Niger to the west, and Cameroon and Nigeria to the southwest. Mountains cover the northwestern corner of the country and the area south of Abeche. Lake Chad divides Chad from Nigeria. Lake Chad is a vital water source, for most of the country is desert or arid pasture land.

Sudan is also largely desert or savanna. But Sudan also has the Nile River, along whose banks agriculture is possible. The southern Sudan is south of the Sahel and thus capable of some farming and intensive grazing.

Ethiopia has highlands with better water resources. As a result, the country has always supported a larger population than surrounding areas, which are mainly desert or semiarid.

Somalia for the most part is coastal desert, receiving about as much rainfall as the Sahara. Somalia is, in effect, a southeastern parcel of the Sahara Desert. Were the Ethiopian highlands not in the way, the Sahara would stretch unimpeded from the Somali coast to Mauritania on the Atlantic. As it is, the Sahara Desert climate skips across the Nile River Valley right to the Red Sea coast and then down around the Horn of Africa.

HISTORY

In the beginning, eight to nine thousand years ago, the lush plains of the Sahara region began to dry out and turn into a desert. The only water that remained was the vast underground aquifers, which still exist and pour forth in places to form oases. The Sahel is still drying out, as the Sahara continues to inch southward. Some five thousand years ago, there were five major ethnic groups in sub-Saharan Africa. Along the west coast from Senegal to Nigeria were the ancestors of the Negro peoples. Near the center, below Egypt, were the Nilo-Saharans, a dark-skinned, but non-Negro group. On the east there were the Cushites, also dark-skinned, the ancestors of the Ethiopians, Somalis, and other related peoples. In central Africa were the Pygmies and to the south the Bushmen (or "Click language" speakers). North of the Sahara was a subgroup of the Middle Eastern Semites (including the ancient Egyptians and Berbers). Note that Africa has greater ethnic diversity than any other continent.

Some two thousand years ago, the Bantu peoples (a Negro ethnic group) moved east and south, overwhelming the Pygmies and Bushmen with greater numbers, better organization (formal military units), and superior technology (metal weapons). The Nilo-Saharans went west along the Sahel corridor, as did some of the Cushites. In the east, a 500 B.C. invasion of Semitic tribes into Eritrea and south into the heart of Ethiopia transformed the local Cushite tribes into what we now consider Ethiopians and Somali (dark-skinned people with some non-Negro features, speaking Semitic languages).

With the exception of Christians (and, until recently, some Jews) in Ethiopia, most of the Sahel peoples became (officially, at least) Muslim about a thousand years ago. Pockets of paganism (animism) persist to the present day and many pagan religious practices continue to coexist with Muslim customs.

The savanna lands have never been peaceful, but are too poor and thinly populated to support many major wars, or attract big-time conquerors. Most of the population is nomadic, so raiding (for horses, camels, livestock, slaves) is the predominant form of conflict. The Negro peoples to the south were not eager to advance out of their familiar forests toward the drier north. The North African Arabs and Berbers, confronted with the vastness of the Sahara Desert, were slow to move down into the Sahel, but gradually groups of them did just that when the camel was used on a wide scale in the eighth century (camels first appeared in the area in the final century, when the area was part of the Roman Empire). Eventually, the more numerous, better-organized, and more warlike Arabs and Berbers to the north overcame the difficulty of getting across the Sahara Desert in large numbers. Thus most of the Sahel became populated with a mixture of Negro and North African peoples, who all adopted a pastoral lifestyle, moving their herds toward what little water fell on this semiarid area. The Arab-influenced people also tended to form the leadership in the areas where they lived and led the kingdoms and empires that formed (and fell) from time to time.

On the west coast, the Sahel savanna was dominated as early as the eighth century by the kingdom of Ghana, which controlled Arab access to large gold mines to the south. But eventually, the Arabs worked their way down the west coast of Africa and began converting blacks to Islam. The Berbers (fair-skinned, blue-eyed locals who long preceeded everyone else in North Africa) took control of modern Mauritania by A.D. 1000, advancing down the coast and from the mountains of the interior they had long dominated. Eventually, Ghana declined in the eleventh century, only to make a comeback a century later as blacks reacted violently against Arabs and Islam (a pattern that continues to reappear). In the thirteenth century, one of Ghana's vassal states (Mali) grew enormously, forming the largest black kingdom in history. Greater Mali controlled a large tract between Chad and the Atlantic (although not the coast itself). The Mali kingdom eventually shrank and was replaced by the even larger, Arab-dominated, Songhay empire, which eventually succumbed to Arab conquerers from Morocco to the north and became the fabled kingdom of Timbuktu.

From the ninth to the sixteenth centuries, the Sao tribes controlled most of Chad, Niger, and parts of the Sudan. The black Sao central African kingdom was under constant pressure from Arabs and black Islamic converts to the north. By the seventeenth century the Arabs were in nominal control of Chad.

The Arabs and Berbers usually came out on top when contending with the black peoples simply because the Arabs had a wider area (the entire Islamic and Christian world) in which to acquire new technology and ideas. The blacks lacked similar access. To the west was the Atlantic Ocean; to the east and south was jungle and more equally isolated Bantu and other black African peoples. A similar situation occurred over a thousand years earlier in Europe, when the Germanic tribes began pressing up against the Roman Empire. For centuries, the Germans got the worst of it from the better-organized and technologically superior Romans. Eventually the Germans adopted many Roman techniques and prevailed. Something similar occurred in sub-Saharan Africa once camel caravans began to cross the desert on a regular basis. Trade created access to critical ideas and technology. Cultures mixed. Many of the Sahel's "blacks" became somewhat "Arabized" and by the time the Europeans arrived by sea (from the fifteenth centry on), the Sahel's Arabized black kingdoms were able to deal on more equal terms with the Europeans.

Adjacent to Chad is the Sudan. This region is a desert centered on the upper portion of the Nile. The Sudan has long been populated by the dark-skinned Nilo-Saharans, many of whom migrated across the Sahel thousands of years ago. The Sudanese have traditionally been caught between the advance of Egyptians from downriver and the Cushite people pressing out from the Ethiopian highlands.

Egyptians have always been concerned with the Sudan. The threat of direct attack on Egypt from the south was somewhat mitigated by the fact that portions of the upper Nile are long rapids and were unusable by boats. The geography also works the other way. Water flowed down the Nile to Egypt, but the Egyptians could not sail up the Nile to the Sudan. Marching upriver to the Sudan was a long and expensive process. The Sudan always contained a multiplicity of ethnic groups, most of whom did not get along very well. Even today, there are over 150 languages spoken in the Sudan. Fortunately for the Egyptians, the upper Nile does not contain the fertile flood plains of the lower Nile. Thus Egyptians always had an enormous population advantage over the Sudanese tribes and kingdoms.

While the threat from Egypt was infrequent, the threat posed by Sudanese tribes against one another was constant. The herding Sudanese tribes were nomadic, their cattle following the availability of grassland, and raiding the more settled groups along the Nile for food, gold, slaves, and cattle became an accepted part of life's routine.

There were a number of cities that grew up along the Sudanese tributaries of the Nile, and they became centers for a succession of kingdoms and empires. These entities were usually feudal and quite loose in organization. Their primary purpose was mutual protection, to keep the Egyptians and other strangers out of the Sudan. Fortunately, the Egyptians had more lucrative potential conquests to the northeast and west. The only Egyptian armies to march up the Nile were usually punitive expeditions, to keep raiders from the Sudan in check, or deliver some revenge raids of their own.

Arab tribes began to predominate in the arid Sudanese north, while black farmers predominated in the south. The Arabs eventually became Muslim; the blacks became, and tended to remain, Christian or pagan.

Except for a short period during the fourteenth century, the Egyptians (and Arabs) were kept from controlling the Sudan. That did not keep a lot of individual Egyptians and Arabs from coming into the country to settle or trade. This was tolerated. It wasn't until 1811 that Egypt, using European weapons training and tactics, again conquered the Sudan. However, this turned out to be a disastrous undertaking. The expense eventually bankrupted the Egyptian government (and was one of the reasons the British managed to take control of Egypt).

Egyptian control gave the disparate Sudanese tribes and factions a common enemy. Warfare sputtered in the hinterland for nearly seven decades. In 1881 an all-out rebellion, linked to religious revivalism, broke out. Zealous religious warriors supporting "the Mahdi" went on a rampage that sent the Egyptians back down the river. In 1896 the new rulers of Egypt, the British, marched up the Nile and exorcised the Mahdists with machine-gun fire. This put the Sudan under foreign (British) control until 1956. In the east, the Abyssinians (as the Ethiopians were called until recently) held forth in the relatively well-watered mountain highlands. That area possessed the only good farmland in the Sahel region. Surrounding the Abyssinian highlands were deserts and arid grasslands. Many Ethiopians were converted to Christianity in the fourth century and, until driven from the Eritrean coast by Muslim Arabs in the eighth century, they were one of the more potent kingdoms in the region.

The eighteenth and nineteenth centuries witnessed the arrival of European colonialism. While the Arabs had been mixing genes, religion, and dynasties in the western Sahel, the Europeans had been building big ships, big guns and big ideas about empire.

The Portuguese had been trading down the West African coast since the fifteenth century. Other European nations followed. For several hundred years all that Portugal (or other European powers) wanted was gold or slaves (the same commodities that had attracted the Arabs). The Europeans would control a port area and barter with the coastal and interior tribes. Some trading posts were set up in the interior, but their direct colonial administration was for the most part nonexistent. For example, the French had established trading forts on the Senegal River in the seventeenth century. During this period, the area was governed by a number of Fulani (Negro Muslim) city-states, which would occasionally be united under one strong ruler or another. Disease, and lack of enthusiasm in Paris, kept the Senegal adventure small.

But in the mid-nineteenth century actual colonies became "practical"; with a colony structure, all the goodies fell under direct control.

In 1830, France took over administration of part of Senegal. Once the French decided to go into the colony business big-time in the 1870s, the Senegal River area was already covered by a number of French forts and trading posts. By 1890, French control had crept several hundred miles inland along the Sahel corridor. By 1900, nearly all of West Africa between the Senegal River and modern Nigeria had become the colony of French West Africa. Senegal was the first French colony in Africa; it was also one of the first European colonies in tropical Africa. Senegal was the first of the many colonial ventures that, between 1860 and 1880, saw European nations carve up all of Africa into colonies or "spheres of influence." Only Ethiopia, the old Abyssinian empire, and Liberia (under American protection) avoided colonization.

Two events propelled increasing colonial extension. First, there was the discovery, in the 1840s, that a daily dose of quinine would keep malaria from killing off most Europeans trying to live in the tropical areas of Africa. Next came the French defeat by Germany in the 1871 Franco-Prussian War. This led to an uncharacteristically long (forty-three years) period of peace in Europe. Without each other to fight, Europeans looked for something else to conquer. America was off limits, Asia was already taken. Africa, however, had been overlooked till now because of the disease problem. So, with modern weapons, quinine, and bureaucrats in tow, Europeans began a mad scramble to stake out real or imagined claims to African territory. At the Berlin Conference of 1885, the European nations with colonies in Africa agreed on how they would divide up the continent. The plan was to "civilize" (by European standards) these colonies and, more important, make the colonies economically viable, and valuable, for the ruling nation.

All of this came as a bit of a surprise to the Africans. While much of interior Africa was not "governed" in the traditional sense (except by thousands of independent tribal organizations), the coastal areas and the Sahel corridor were largely covered by a changing mosaic of feudal-type kingdoms and principalities. However, these local entities were several centuries behind the Europeans in technology. The European bureaucrats, industrialists, and soldiers proved an overwhelming combination.

By the late 1880s the French also had nominal control of the area to the north of the Senegal River (Mauritania). But this was a largely desert area populated by Arab rather than black tribes. There was little of immediate exploitative worth in this portion of the Sahel, and the nomadic tribes saw any French interlopers as just another source of loot and pillage. This attitude (disdainful) of the Arab tribes toward blacks and Europeans south of the Senegal River continues. After the area became independent, the Senegal River provided a clear boundary between the Arab north and the Negro lands south of the river.

By 1914, France had nominal control of all the western Sahel as far as modern Sudan. The British controlled the rest, except independent Ethiopia and the Eritrean coast, which was controlled by Italy.

The major impact of colonialism was an uncharacteristic spell of law and order, imposed with the help of machine guns (many) and a European-style civil service (small). Most of the population was left to pursue their customary lifestyles. One major change was the suppression of slavery, which persisted in Africa after it had died out in Europe. A small minority of the local population was exposed to European-style education, and European ideas. Thus when colonial rule ended in the 1950s and 1960s, the Sahel people were left with a new set of borders and an upper class who were often more European than African in their manners and ideas.

While African leaders often complain of the "artificial" borders forced on them during the creation of the colonies, those borders that now serve as the frontiers of the current African states have since been regarded as inviolate by their inhabitants. The borders are the first system of national frontiers to be established throughout the entire continent. While the borders were imposed by outsiders, and Africans constantly complain about it, everyone is scared of the increased conflict border changes would surely bring.

Historical Impact of Ethnicity and Religion

Africa's European colonial period did not erase the historic enmity between Muslim and non-Muslim and between Arab and Negro. There were also other reasons for internal division. The hundreds of languages spoken in the Sahel further fragmented new "national" populations. The numerous empires and kingdoms that had preceded the colonial states also had to contend with the multiplicity of ethnic groups. The European powers simply exerted power in a more systematic fashion, thanks to modern technology (telegraph, radio, railroad, trucks, aircraft, etc.).

Ethnicity has always been a key factor in the Sahel. Chad alone has over one hundred different languages spoken within its borders, as does the Sudan. Beyond that, there are over two hundred different ethnic groups in Chad and over fifty in the Sudan. Most other Sahel nations have fewer than ten distinct ethnic groups, but that's more than enough to keep domestic politics on the wild side. Before the Europeans came along with their colonial governments, local strongmen would cobble together kingdoms at sword point and several of these lasted far longer than any of the European colonies. What the Europeans left behind was the technology for a local politician or soldier to gather together sundry ethnic groups into a tightly controlled entity. Power was maintained using the weapons and communications technology the Europeans left behind.

Well before European military empires were created in the Sahel, soldiers on horseback could quickly get around in the flatland and keep the locals in line. The threat of a few hundred, or few thousand, armed horsemen descending on a herder's pastures ensured some degree of "loyalty" to a distant king.

Many of the Sahel empires were further cemented by fear of Arab raiders crossing the Saharan wastelands. The Sahara was not entirely a sandy wilderness. Much of it contained some vegetation, and there were numerous well-known waterholes. Some of them were large enough to form an oasis capable of supporting a small settlement. There were three major, semidesert corridors from the north. Against an undefended Sahel, raiders would travel these routes. But strong Sahel kingdoms would force the Arabs to come as traders and merchants instead of soldiers.

The Sahel economy had herds of animals, some agriculture, plus gold and slaves from the south. The Arabs brought cloth and technology. It was from the north that the Sahel and the rest of Africa obtained the technology to work iron. From the Arabs, the Sahel also received Islam, although the Muslim religion met more opposition than the techniques for making iron weapons. Although many blacks became Muslims, there was still a great deal of animosity between the lighter-skinned Arabs and the darker-skinned Sahel natives.

Chad became a particularly striking example of ethnic animosity. In the sixteenth century, a major movement of Negro nomads from the Niger River area collided with a similar Arab nomad movement from the east in what is now Chad. The result: over two hundred ethnic groups speaking over one hundred distinct languages, all within a population of six million people.

The Arab-Negro animosity was more than the Arabs thinking themselves more "civilized." There was also the slavery issue. Slavery was an ancient custom in the area. Slavery is less an enduring problem when people of the same appearance enslave one another. Europeans enslaving other Europeans only died out some four hundred years ago and was quickly forgotten by slaves and owners. The former slaves easily slipped into the culture that enslaved them. But for centuries, Arabs would take several thousand blacks north each year, where dark skin became another sign of a people considered inferior. That many of the slaves were captured by black Saheleans from Negro tribes farther south did nothing to ameliorate the feelings. Blacks enslaved other blacks. But the way the Arabs carried on was much more bothersome. Moreover, as of 1995, some Arab slaving allegedly continues (with local buyers, and foreign markets in the UAE and Oman). Reports of Muslim slaving in the southern Sudan surface regularly.

All of the Sahel's wars have, at their root, vicious animosities between Arabs and blacks that continually fuel the area's conflicts.

In the west, Arab Mauritanian merchants dominate retail trade in Senegal and treat the Negro Senegalese with disdain. In Chad, Libyan Arabs set one group of black Chadians against another to further Libyan attempts to annex portions of Chad. In the Sudan, Arabs from the north of the country raid and enslave blacks from the south. Ethiopian blacks battle Arab-supported Somalis.

Local Histories After Independence

Senegal and Mauritania

Mauritania and Senegal were both French colonies that achieved independence in 1960. Mauritania aligns itself with the Arabs, although only a third of the population is Arab (another 40 percent are mixed Arab/Negro while the remainder are Negro, largely from Senegal tribes). Senegal has a much more stable government, which as of 1995 was one of the few functioning democracies in Africa. However, the 1988 and 1993 elections were widely thought to be tainted and internal disorder continues. Corruption charges plague the government.

Mauritania has gone through the usual string of coups and military takeovers associated with single-party rule. Mauritania had a rough time of it in the 1970s, as it was caught in the middle of the war between Morocco and Algeria over the disputed territory of the Western Sahara. A small portion of that territory was claimed by Mauritania. Thus part of the irregular warfare was directed at Mauritania. This wrecked much of Mauritania's fragile export economy. In 1975, Mauritania renounced its claims on the Western Sahara, thus becoming friendly with Algeria and hostile to Morocco. The local Mauritanian strongman, Colonel Maouiya Ould Sidi, declared the nation an Islamic republic in 1991, and held elections in 1992 that were, according to most observers, rigged.

While most inhabitants of both nations are Muslim, the Senegalese are largely Negro and the Mauritanians are either Arab (30 percent) or mixed Arab (Berber)/Negro (40 percent, and identify with the Arabs). Islamic fundamentalism does not play as well among Negro Muslims as it does among Arabs, and that is the chief political dispute between the two nations.

Despite years of relative peace, war between Senegal and Mauritania became more probable after a small border incident in April 1989 rekindled old animosities. More armed skirmishes followed. Ancient resentments in Senegal increased to the point that mobs attacked the resident Arab minority. Most of these Mauritanian Arabs were merchants, who dominated the retail trade. This forced the emergency evacuation of over sixty thousand Arabs, most of whom were Mauritanians. Both countries expelled each other's ambassador. Additional troops were sent to the border.

The ill will between the two nations has economic and ethnic origins. Mauritanian farmers want access to pasture in Senegal, particularly the rich "bottom land" in dispute along the Senegal River Valley. A four-hundred-mile-long stretch of the Senegal River forms the border. Only one major road crosses this border, and that's near the coast.

The river is fordable in many places and there are a few small bridges. There is a lot of traffic across the river, as it is the most productive part of Mauritania and one of the more fertile parts of Senegal.

During the 1989 crisis, Iraq flew over thirty tons of weapons into Mauritania (Iraq wanted to set up a long-range-missile test site there). Both nations have inadequate stocks of ammunition and could not afford to purchase more in a hurry. Both use mostly French equipment. France would likely supply Senegal, and various Arab states would supply Mauritania. Actual territorial conquest is highly unlikely. France would not allow Mauritania to hold any significant Senegalese territory for very long, and Senegal has no interest in acquiring Mauritanian desert property. Even so, there are some minor border disagreements caused by periodic changes in the course of the river, causing considerable tension.

Mali

Mali, with its capital at Timbuktu, had been one of the key African kingdoms until smashed by a Moroccan army in 1590. The Moroccans couldn't put the empire back together and the French eventually turned it into "French Sudan" by 1898. In 1960, Mali became independent. The initial socialist government was soon (1963) overthrown by a coup. Severe droughts and famine followed in the 1970s and 1980s. The group that was in power since the 1968 coup were themselves overthrown in 1991. Elections were held in 1992 and Alpha Omar Konare became president in what appeared to be a reasonably honest ballot. Aside from drought, overpopulation, and a 25 percent literacy rate, the major bit of unrest has been the continued armed resistance of the local Berbers (or Tuaregs, 5 percent of the population). Long accustomed to raiding the sedentary Africans, and generally doing as they please, the Tuaregs have not taken well to a government run by blacks. There are not enough Tuaregs to overthrow the government, and none of the nearby Arab nations will give them much in the way of support. Before the French came along, the Tuaregs held many of the local blacks as slaves. No one in Mali has forgotten this, but the Tuaregs simply don't have the numbers, or weapons, to bring back the past.

Niger

Niger achieved independence in 1960. A constitutional democratic government existed until 1974, when Lieutenant Colonel Seyni Kountche took power in a bloodless coup. Kountche later promoted himself to general, but his ruling cabinet included many civilians. Kountche died in 1987. The new government under Ali Saibou promotes policies encouraging private enterprise and public education. This government was overthrown in 1991 (peacefully) by a national conference. In 1993 elections were held and Mahamane Ousmane was elected president.

Aside from the usual problems with drought, famine, and over-population, Libya claims the northeastern corner of Niger and has backed Tuareg desert tribesmen (about 8 percent of the population) in attacks on several towns in Niger. France keeps a small military garrison near the capital, Niamey. There is a French expatriate community of over four thousand people.

Chad

Chad was a part of French Equatorial Africa (FEA) until the FEA was disbanded in 1959. In 1975 a military coup toppled the fifteen-year-old regime of Ngarta Tombalbaye. Fighting broke out between the new junta and various rebel groups, the strongest group led by Muslim rebel leader Hissene Habre. A coalition government with former junta leader Felix Malloum and Habre sharing power proved to be unstable.

Nigerian mediation arranged a new truce in 1979 and Goukouni Oueddei was installed as a compromise leader. Religious rioting and the massacre of southern Muslims shook Goukouni's government. Nigeria once again tried to mediate but in 1980 the cease-fire broke down again. Habre finally overthrew Goukouni in 1980.

One of the major reasons for the overthrow of Goukouni's regime was the Libyan report of January 6, 1981, that Goukouni and Colonel Mu'ammar Qaddafi, the Libyan dictator, had decided to merge the countries of Libya and Chad. This, combined with Libya's interest in the potentially mineral-rich (uranium) Aozou Strip, added to a series of internal disagreements that ended in the overthrow of Goukouni by Habre and a coalition of southern tribes. Sudan and Egypt supported Habre during the final stages of the civil war.

What followed in the next few years was complex and almost comic opera in its execution. Between December 1986 and September 1987, the decade of warfare concludes. The "Toyota War" begins as French aircraft sweep Libyan planes from the air. In January, anti-Libyan Chadian forces (Habre) move north. Their fast-moving columns contained a large number of Toyota Land Cruisers and pickup trucks. In the back of the trucks were Chadian soldiers armed with machine guns and antitank weapons (MILAN antitank missiles, recoilless rifles, RPGs). The tactics are reminiscent of traditional attacks by nomadic horseman: rapid movement to the battlefield, a quick jab at the Libyan column or fortified position, a rapid breakthrough and attack from the rear. The "Toyota tactics" proved hugely successful. By March, several battles with Libyan forces left Chadian forces in control of most of their country. In August, the Libyans were driven from the disputed Aozou Strip on the Libyan border. This small sliver of desert had been the main cause of the Libyan-Chad conflict in the first place. The Libyans counterattacked and retook one of their Aozou bases. The Chadians responded by crossing the Libyan border and destroying a large Libyan air base. A cease-fire was then declared. Libya had lost over seven thousand dead and nearly $2 billion worth of equipment. The Chadians lost less than a tenth of that.

In 1989, Libya and Chad agreed in August to end their state of war. Then several tribal factions once more switched sides and military activity started up again on Chad's northern borders. In 1990, Chad announced free elections. Meanwhile, the Libyan-backed "Islamic Legion," led by Idriss Deby, captured the towns of Tine and Baha on Chad's eastern border with Sudan. Eventually, Deby, originally Libya's man, took control (as much as anyone could) of the country. Habre fled to Cameroon.

In 1995 the elections were held and their honesty hotly debated. Several tribes were not impressed with the fairness or purpose of "democracy."

Chad's conflicts are typical of the long struggle between the Arabs in the north and the blacks in the south. In Chad, however, Arabs and blacks not only collided from the north and south, but also Arabs moving in from the east met blacks from the west.

Colonel Qaddafi's direct meddling, in the name of Arab/Muslim interests, stirred up an already volatile situation. The political situation in France seems to favor a continued military involvement in Chad, especially as long as Libya remains an antagonist. Even if the Libyans are completely shut out of Chad, the locals will continue to struggle with each other for supremacy.

Unfortunately, Chad can be expected to experience low-level warfare well into the next century.

The Sudan

Formal independence from colonial rule came in 1956. That also meant an end to Egyptian influence, as the British considered their administration a joint enterprise with the Egyptians. One could send the Arabic (Egyptian) bureaucrats back down the Nile River, but you couldn't dispense with the fact that most of the population in northern Sudan was Arab and Muslim while most of the population in southern Sudan was not.

The year prior to independence witnessed serious riots in the south and a major army mutiny of black troops. That mutiny was put down with some difficulty. In 1958, the worst fears of the southern blacks were realized when the Arab-dominated armed forces staged a coup against the civilian politicians the British had installed. The new junta immediately began to persecute the (largely black) Christians in the south.

By the early 1960s, a black rebel movement sprang up and for the next ten years waged incessant war against the better-trained and -armed Arab northerners. Nearly half a million people, largely civilians caught in the crossfire, perished.

In 1969 there was another coup, and the new military man in charge, Jaafar Nimeiri, turned out to be surprisingly statesmanlike. In 1972 he made considerable concessions to the southerners in order to stop the rebellion. The more numerous minor tribal players in the civil war were not as willing to settle down, but most parties accepted the need for peace.

This "peace" did not solve Sudan's problems. The economy was mismanaged, Libya encouraged Muslim fundamentalists, and the non-Muslim blacks in the south still felt put upon by the Arabs in the north. In 1983 the civil war began again. This renewed revolt was led by John Garang, a college-educated (in the United States) Christian from the large Dinka tribe. Immediate survival of Dinka populations was at issue: One of the Sahel's periodic droughts had created famine. The Arab-dominated Sudanese government had not done much to save the drought victims, so the blacks saw it as a struggle for survival. The Sudanese Peoples Liberation Army (SPLA) became the umbrella organization for the southern resistance groups.

In 1985, Nimeiri was overthrown by a great-grandson of the nineteenth-century Mahdi (military-religious leader who forced the Egyptians out). Saddiq el-Mahdi, the new ruler, came to power preaching more Arab and Muslim privilege in the country as well as an even harder line on the black rebels. Thus, as the drought got worse, food (or lack of it) was used against the rebels and the civilians who could, or did, support them.

El-Mahdi was overthrown by an impatient military in 1989. The new leader, General Omar Hassan al-Bashir, continued the trend toward establishing an Islamic state. In 1993, al-Bashir assumed the title of president and intensified the war against black Christians and animists in the south. He kept out UN relief for the hundreds of thousands of refugees in southern Sudan and has become a client of Iran. Sudan now serves as one of the few refuges for international terrorists. Yet Sudan has not become a puppet for Iran, Iraq, Libya, or any other benefactor.

Sudan's liberation from British colonial rule in 1956 has still left it at risk with respect to its traditional enemy, Egypt, and internal rancor between the Arab and black inhabitants of Sudan (yes, inhabitants, not citizens, as Sudan has always had a fragile concept of unity). What now constitutes Sudan was historically a constantly changing mosaic of large and small "nations" held together by the successful conqueror of the moment. Modern technology and the concept of nation-states (as opposed to feudal entities) have provided a larger entity (Sudan) for the hundred-plus ethnic groups to fight over. The only likely change in this situation is a split-up of Sudan into two states: a predominantly Arab one in the north and a largely black, and Christian, one in the south. As of late 1995, a bitter low-level war, featuring slaving and starvation, continues. Uganda now backs the SPLA.

Ethiopia

Aside from brief Italian occupation during the 1930s and World War II, Ethiopia has not known any prolonged colonialization. Alone among the many nations covered in this chapter, Ethiopia does not have a recent "independence" from colonial rule to mark its current period. Since the 1960s, Ethiopia has experienced four wars. Until 1991 over half the population of 44 million was in rebellion (4 million Eritreans, 5 million Tigreans, and 15 million Oromoans).

In 1991 the Marxist government was overthrown and Eritrea became independent. The provinces of Tigre and Oromo were given a larger degree of self-rule.

Somalia, the nation at the tip of the Horn, still wants the Ethiopian province of Ogaden, a desert area largely populated by Somalis. However, Somalia has its own internal problems (dictatorship and rebellion).

Eritrea is the coastal area closest to the traditional highland homeland of the Christian Amhara (Ethiopian) people. But ever since the upsurge of Islam in the seventh century, Eritrea has been increasingly populated by Arabs and Arabic-speaking peoples. Those Arabs had strong ties with other Arabs in the Red Sea area and thus Muslim Eritrea was strong enough to dominate adjacent Christian populations. Although occasionally a strong Ethiopian leader could occupy Eritrea, the Arabs would quickly take it back. Eritrea became an Ethiopian province only after World War II. That was done unilaterally by the Western Allies as a form of guilt payment for having abandoned Ethiopia to Italian aggression in the 1930s.

When the Ethiopian government in Addis Ababa made this annexation permanent in 1962, the halting Eritrean rebellion went forward in earnest. At first, the Ethiopians simply marshaled their forces and marched into Eritrea to smash the rebels and reestablish central government control at any cost. This tactic failed, as the rebels were backed by other Arab nations and Russia. But in 1974, a military coup in Ethiopia brought a Marxist government to power. The Russians did a little arithmetic and promptly switched their support to the Ethiopian Communists. Backed by generous Russian arms shipments, Red Army advisers, and finally Cuban troops, the Ethiopians reversed the situation in Eritrea. They were, however, unable to completely suppress the rebellion.

Meanwhile, a Christian Eritrean rebel movement usurped the Arab movement and continued the rebellion from the interior hill country. The Eritreans were determined to maintain their independence. The military-age population headed for the bush to take up guerrilla warfare. Many Ethiopian conscripts were not keen on a war of conquest among these alien Eritreans and had no stomach for the fighting. The Eritreans gradually built up a string of battlefield successes, and piles of captured Ethiopian weapons.

In 1989, Russia, increasingly wound up in its own internal problems, tired of the apparently futile exercise and began cutting back support. The Eritreans shifted from guerrilla strikes and began mainforce attacks on Ethiopian positions and cities. By mid-1990 they controlled almost all of Eritrea and had troops pressing south toward Addis Ababa. In 1991 the Eritrean rebels were among those who took over Ethiopia. The price of Eritrean cooperation was Eritrean independence. The bill was promptly paid, and Eritrea became independent since then. Eritrea has made great economic strides.

Adjacent to Eritrea is the province of Tigre. Ethnically close to the Amharic people of the Ethiopian heartland, Tigre has been (with a few breaks) part of Ethiopia for centuries. About a third of the Tigreans are Muslim and several Ethiopian emperors came from Tigre. A famine in 1972–73 saw over a hundred thousand Tigreans starve to death, largely through the incompetence of the Ethiopian government. While the military took over in Ethiopia, the Tigreans rebelled for greater self-determination and an end to the central government incompetence that had caused so much Tigrean grief in the past. With Russian and Cuban help, Ethiopia held on to the major towns and ravaged the countryside. When the rebels took over in 1991, the Tigreans managed to get most of the key positions in the new government.

Oromo (also known as Galla) is the largest and most fertile of Ethiopia's provinces. While ethnically related to the traditional Ethiopian Amharic people, the Galla people are not Christian and speak a different language. From time to time, a strong Ethiopian emperor would conquer and hold Oromo for a while. Ethiopia has held on to Galla for the last century. The Oromo revolution began in the wake of the 1974 coup and was largely supported by the small urban, and educated, population. The 90 percent of the people living in the countryside are less involved and as a consequence this rebellion was less intense than the others. However, the Ethiopian Marxists were not inclined to make any concessions. For one thing, the Marxist Ethiopian leader, Mengistu, was a Galla. The Oromos found themselves outmaneuvered by the Tigreans when the Marxist government fell in 1991. Thus, to a certain extent, the Oromo unrest continues.

The new government held elections in 1995, but many groups with a grudge against the government refused to participate. This, in spite of the offer by the government to allow the different regions the power to vote themselves a great deal of autonomy. Democracy is new, and novel, for Ethiopia. Most Ethiopians are seeped in the ancient all-or-nothing school of politics and are having a hard time adapting to the give-and-take required in a democracy. Unrest and civil strife is likely to continue in Ethiopia for some time yet.

Somalia

Somalia juts out from Africa like an elbow pointing toward the Arabian Sea. Oil tanker traffic to and from the Persian Gulf, as well as access to the Red Sea and the Suez Canal, make Somalia, the French protectorate of Djibouti, and Ethiopia the flip side of South Yemen. Air and naval bases in the African Horn can be used to support forces in the Arabian Peninsula—or to close the entire region to merchant traffic.

In 1964 and 1977–78, Ethiopia and Somalia fought over the Ogaden. In both 1964 and 1978, the Somalis were defeated by superior Ethiopian forces. (Cuban troops fighting in a mechanized brigade group were used by the Ethiopians in 1978.) Through the 1980s, constant military pressure by the Somalis kept the Ethiopians (who were distracted by their other rebellions) on the defensive. Somalia also has similar disputes with Kenya and Djibouti. The Barre government of Somalia (after 1969) was a rather nasty dictatorship that maintained power through terror, and the fact that Somalia has a rather homogeneous population compared with most other nations in the area. There are differences based on affiliation to different Somali tribes, and, for example, Ethiopia has supported members of the Isaaq tribe against Barre's power base in the Marehan tribe.

In 1991, Barre lost control of the government. The Somali National Movement took control of northern Somalia (old British Somalia) in the wake of the 1991 collapse of the central government, and proclaimed independence as the Somaliland Republic. The situation in the north wasn't much better than in the rest of Somalia, with rival factions fighting each other for whatever could be found to fight over. But the spotlight of media attention never fixed on northern Somalia, but rather focused on the more lively action in the south.

Things got so rough in the capital of Mogadishu that in January 1991 foreign embassies were evacuated. On January 27, ninety-one rebels entered the city and drove Siad Barre out. Clan warfare and looting ensued. On January 29 the United Somali Congress, headed by Ali Mahid Mohammed, found itself fighting one of its factions, led by Mohammed Farah Aidid.

On May 15, several clans attempted to organize a peace conference, but the northern Somali National Movement seceded and founded the Somaliland Republic.

In August, UNICEF relief personnel returned to Mogadishu, but other UN agencies stayed away. In September, fighting between Ali Mahid and Aidid ended after several days of talks with clan elders. But in November, fighting between rival clans began again (for the third time in 1991). By the end of 1991, thirty thousand people had died in the fighting.

In March 1992, Aidid and Ali Mahid signed a cease-fire but failed to agree on how to monitor it. That April, Siad Barre fled southern Somalia to Kenya and then went into exile in Nigeria.

In May 1992, UN food shipments began to arrive, but some air-shipped foodstuffs were looted. That summer, five hundred armed Pakistani troops were deployed and new U.S., French, Belgian, and German food airlifts began. In late August, two UN observers were wounded as the port of Mogadishu was attacked by clan warriors (led by two tanks) and three hundred tons of food were stolen. The warring clans saw the food aid as a means to maintain their power. Whoever had food could feed their gunmen and their followers. Stealing food from the UN relief shipments denied food to rival clans. The clans would not cooperate, lest another clan obtain an advantage.

Foreign TV crews regularly filmed hundreds of thousands of starving Somali refugees. On November 25 the United States offered the UN thirty thousand troops to aid in landing and distributing relief supplies. On December 3, 1992, the UN voted to approve military intervention.

In December 1992, the U.S. troops began to arrive. These included U.S. Army troops from the 10th Mountain Division (two infantry battalions and a lot of support troops). The Marines contributed the 1st Marine Expeditionary Force (MEF).

Though the food got through, the political situation in Mogadishu went from bad to worse. The breaking point came in October 1993, when U.S. troops, searching for Aidid (whose men had already killed dozens of UN troops) got caught in a firefight. U.S. forces suffered 14 dead and nearly 100 wounded. The Somalis suffered over 300 dead and over 700 wounded. (One source estimates as many as 600 of Aidid's fighters may have been killed.) Various news media, however, played it as a U.S. defeat and that turned U.S. public opinion against the peacekeeping operation.

U.S. troops were withdrawn in early 1994; the remaining UN troops were pulled out in 1995. The Somali clans continue to wage war on one another. Late in 1995, UN relief agencies returned, nervously.

The nations that donated food, and peacekeeping troops, were justifiably bitter with their experience in Somalia. The Somalis were told that they could not expect another international effort and were, for all practical purposes, on their own. Ironically, some of the more desperate Somalis even suggested a temporary return to colonialism, feeling (with some justification) that colonial administrators would bring a large measure of stability to the area. But the international community was having none of it. Colonialism was found to be a bad economic and political deal. The end of the cold war had also made the Horn of Africa a less vital pawn of international diplomacy. Somalia was an object lesson in the limitations of peacekeeping.

Djibouti is a special case. Some 60 percent of the population of 430,000 are from various Somali clans. But about 40 percent are from the Afar people (related to Somalis, but native to Djibouti). France still controls the nominally independent area by playing on the Afar fear of what the Somali majority might do. A French military garrison provides a guarantee that the Afars will stay in control, under French "guidance." Internal ethnic tensions, however, have increased.

LOCAL POLITICS

Senegal

Senegal is one of the few functioning democracies in Africa, largely because there are two strong, major parties.

The Socialist party (PS)—Led by Abdou Diouf. Has been in power since the early 1980s. Controls 70 percent of the seats in the parliament.

Senegalese Democratic party (PDS)—The principal opposition party, controlling about a quarter of the parliament.

Brotherhoods—Islamic sects; also active in economic development in Senegal. The various brotherhoods are led by *marabouts* ("spiritual guides"). The Mouride Brotherhood has over 650,000 members.

Senegambia Confederation—Dates from February 1982, officially dissolved in 1989. Senegal has promoted a unification of Senegal and Gambia. Gambia isn't so sure, but the two neighbors do cooperate politically and economically. Confederation is largely a facade because Gambia refuses to be absorbed by Senegal. Now known as the Gambia, with a population of about one million.

Gambian parties—Progressive People's party controls about 58 percent of the seats in the parliament; Gambia People's party; National Convention party.

Kunte Kinte—Alex Haley's ancestor (*Roots*) hailed from Juffure in Gambia. The eighteenth-century slavers worked this area over rather well.

Mauritania

Mauritania has political parties, officially and unofficially, that tend to be tribally based. In fact, the country is an Islamic republic run by the army. The first coup was in 1978, with another group in the army taking over in a bloodless coup in 1984. There were elections in 1994, which didn't change much, because the colonels got themselves elected. Officially, the nation is an Islamic republic.

Niger

Until 1993 political parties were banned in Niger. The nation was ruled by a Supreme Military Council. Elections were held in 1993, after a national referendum in 1992. No party obtained a majority. The top three finishers (with their number of the eighty-three seats in parliament) were:

National Movement of the Development Society—Twenty-nine seats. The head of this party, Mahamane Ousmane, is the chief of state. He refuses to let other parties participate in the government, however.

Democratic and Social Convention—Twenty-two seats.

Nigerian Party for Democracy and Socialism—Thirteen seats.

Nigerian Alliance for Democracy and Progress—Eleven seats.

Organization of Armed Resistance—Tuareg (Berber) resistance to government. Burkina Faso, France, and Algeria are trying to mediate this, and there have been some cease-fires and negotiations. About 8 percent of the population is Berber.

Mali

Association for Democracy—Major party in Mali.

The Tuaregs (Berber clans)—About 10 percent of the population and not well organized, but always opposed to black African domination. The less tribal, and more Arab, of this group tend to control a lot of the business activity.

Timbuktu—In Mali. Heart of one of the many Arab desert kingdoms.

Chad

Union for Democracy and Republic—Moderates, and usually the opposition. Have shown some skill in organizing elections and gaining power.

Chadian League of Human Rights—Observes, and gets away with, reporting political corruption.

Patriotic Salvation Front—Party of longtime strongman Idriss Deby.

National Union for Independence and Revolution (UNIR)—Hissein Habre's coalition.

GUNT—Formerly pro-Libyan; several GUNT units switched sides in 1987.

Sudan

Sudanese Army—There are a large number of political parties in Sudan, but only one counts, and that is the one that really doesn't see itself as a political party. It's the army, and even when the army is not directly running things, its influence hangs heavily on those civilians who think they are. Two years after independence in 1956 there was a military coup. In 1964 a civilian rebellion installed a civilian government, but in 1969 the army took over again. In 1985 another uprising installed a civilian government, which was overthrown by yet another army coup in 1989. The government was officially "civilianized" in 1993, but the same army officers were still in charge.

Government Revolutionary Command Council—No longer officially exists; was the army's political front. Chairman and Prime Minister Brigadier General Umar Hasan Ahmad al-Bashir was still in charge in 1995. The council still exists, insofar as the army still dominates the government.

National Islamic Front (Muslim Brotherhood)—Actually right-wing and Islamic fundamentalist. The only other "northern" party. Controls domestic and foreign policies, in return for not turning on the army.

Sharia law—Islamic law; what the Sudanese Muslim radicals want established throughout the Sudan.

Southern (non-Arab) parties—Sudan African Congress; Southern Sudanese Political Association.

Southern rebel movements—SPLA (Sudan People's Liberation Army) drawn largely from the Dinka tribe and the Anya Nya (literally, "snake poison") of the Nuer tribe. The SPLA is headed by Colonel John Garang, an American-educated Christian Dinka. He has a Ph.D. in economics. The SPLA is well organized and disciplined, but was rent by internal disputes in the early 1990s. Reports in late 1995 suggest that Ugandan involvement with the SPLA may help resolve some of the SPLA's internal troubles.

(Note: Like everything else in Sudan, the political parties in the north are largely Arab and Muslim while those in the south are Negro and animist or Christian.)

Ethiopia

Ethiopian People's Revolutionary Democratic Front (EPRDF)— Evolved from the Tigre People's Liberation Front (TPLF, five million, largely Christian) and managed to gain control of the central government when the Communists fled in 1991.

Oromo People's Democratic Organization (OPDO).

Oromo Liberation Front (OLF)—The eighteen million Muslim, Christian, and animist Oromo live in Ethiopia's largest province. The OLF represented the Oromo during the rebellion that led to the collapse of the Communist government. However, the OLF did not spread much beyond the tenth of the local population that is educated and lives in urban areas. The OPDO evolved from the OLF after 1991.

Ethiopian People's Revolutionary Party (EPRP).

Other groups—Numerous small, ethnic-based groups have formed since the Communist government collapsed in 1991. There are also several Islamic militant groups active in Muslim areas.

The Amhara—People who have historically formed the core of the

Ethiopian empire; eleven million, largely Christian. Tainted by their support of the Communist government. Now supplanted by the Tigreans, the Amhara still consider themselves the traditional ruling group of Ethiopia.

Somalia

Somali politics center on the individual clan and relationships between clan alliances. This is not unusual in many parts of the world, but in Somalia it gets particularly convoluted and nasty. The Dir, Daarood, Isaaq, and Hawiye clans, which make up the Samaal group of clans, comprise about 75 percent of the population. The Samaal population live largely off their herds and are dispersed all over the country. In the last few generations, a growing minority of Samaal settled down to raise crops. The Digil and Rahanwayn clans make up about 20 percent of the population. These clans settled in the river valleys of southern Somalia and rely on both crops and cattle and camel herds. There are hundreds of subclans. Out of the clan affiliations grew several political movements around which armed men gathered once the central government was gone.

Somali Salvation Democratic Front—Organization of Daarood and Majeerteen clans; operates in the south.

United Somali Congress—Hawiye clan organization. Operates around the capital of Mogadishu. At one time it included both Ali Mahid Mohammed and Mohammed Farah Aidid. Both of these split over who was to be in charge. Aidid had more firepower; Ali Mahid Mohammed had more prestige and tenacity. As of 1995, Aidid was winning the struggle. Somalis tend to prefer guns to diplomacy.

Somali National Movement—Isaaq clan organization in the north. The clans established their own Somaliland Republic. Mohammed Farah Aidid favored cooperation with this group.

Somali Patriotic Movement—The Ogaden clan organization (over a million people), driven into exile by the victorious Ethiopians as a result of the Ogaden war.

Somali Democratic Movement—Rahanwayn clan (and others) organization.

Political Trend Charts

Mauritania

Gv95	Gv20	PC95	PC20	R95	R20	Ec95	Ec20	EdS95	EdS20
MA5,3	MA4,2	5	6	4	4	1	1	1	1+

MA = Military Authoritarian (effectiveness 0–9, stability 0–9)

Senegal

Gv95	Gv20	PC95	PC20	R95	R20	Ec95	Ec20	EdS95	EdS20
RD5,3	RD6,3	4	5	8	7	3	3+	2+	3−

RD = Representative Democracy

Niger

Gv95	Gv20	PC95	PC20	R95	R20	Ec95	Ec20	EdS95	EdS20
MA4,5*	MA5,5	4	5	5	4	2+	3	1+	2

*A curious military government, however. Legacy of Seyni Kountche lives on.

Chad

Gv95	Gv20	PC95	PC20	R95	R20	Ec95	Ec20	EdS95	EdS20
MA3,4	MA4,5	5	5	4	4	2−	2−	1	1

Sudan

Gv95	Gv20	PC95	PC20	R95	R20	Ec95	Ec20	EdS95	EdS20
MA3,6	MA4,5	2	3	8	7	2−	1+	1	1

"INDEPENDENT SOUTH SUDAN"

Gv20	PC20	R20	Ec20	EdS20
MA3,5	6	5+	1	2

ETHIOPIA

Gv95	Gv20	PC95	PC20	R95	R20	Ec95	Ec20	EdS95	EdS20
MA3,3	MA4,3	3	4	8	6	2−	2+	2−	2−

SOMALIA

Gv95	Gv20	PC95	PC20	R95	R20	Ec95	Ec20	EdS95	EdS20
MA2,2	MA3,4	1+	3	7	7	1	2	1	1

ERITREA

Gv95	Gv20	PC95	PC20	R95	R20	Ec95	Ec20	EdS95	EdS20
MA7,6	AD5,6	8	7	6	5	2	3−	3	3+

AD = Authoritarian Democracy

"GREATER SOMALIA"
(SOMALIA PLUS OGADEN AND DJIBOUTI)

Gv20	PC20	R20	Ec20	EdS20
MA4,4	3	7+	2+	2

DJIBOUTI

Gv95	Gv20	PC95	PC20	R95	R20	Ec95	Ec20	EdS95	EdS20
AD6,4*	AD6,6	4	6–	4	4	3+	4	3–	3

*French Foreign Legion helps keep the peace and also keeps out Somalia, though Djibouti Afars and Somalis are set for a civil war.

REGIONAL POWERS AND POWER INTEREST INDICATOR CHARTS

CHAD

	Economic Interests	Historical Interests	Political Interest	Military Interest	Force Generation Potential	Ability to Intervene Politically	Interest/ Ability to Promote Economic Development
Libya	7	8	9	8	2+/4*	7	1
Chad-Gv†	9	9	9	9	3+	7	–
Chad-Rbs‡	7	8	9	9	2	7	–
France	4	6	6	6	4	7	6
United States	2	2	5	6§	4–	5	3
Nigeria	2	3	5	6	3–	1	1
Japan	1‖	0	1	0	0	1–	4

NOTE: 0 = minimum; 9 = maximum

*Inside Chad/inside Aozou Strip and Libya. A logistically weak and poorly led army, but 4 FGP is there.

†Chad government.

‡Chad rebels.

§United States is always concerned when Qaddafi's Libya is involved.

‖Advertisement for Toyotas.

NOTE: French, United States, and Nigerian FGPs based on 180-day buildup; French 1995 force power in Chad is 1.

MAURITANIA-SENEGAL

	Economic Interests	Historical Interests	Political Interest	Military Interest	Force Generation Potential	Ability to Intervene Politically	Interest/ Ability to Promote Economic Development
Mauritania	9	9	9	9	1	6	–
Senegal	8	8	9	9	2+	7	–
France	4	5	5	4	4	8	5
United States	2	2	3	3	4	5	3
Libya	0	1	2	1	1–	2–	1
Iraq	1	2	2	1	1–	5*	1

*In Mauritania.

SUDAN

	Economic Interests	Historical Interests	Political Interest	Military Interest	Force Generation Potential	Ability to Intervene Politically	Interest/ Ability to Promote Economic Development
Egypt	7	8	7	7	6	6	3
United States	2	3	4	3	2	4	2
Libya	1	2	6	6	1	3	1
Saudi Arabia	2	4	6	4	0	5	4
Chad*	1	4	6	7	1+	1	0

*Rebels in Chad used bases in Sudan. The Chadian government, with its abundant supply of captured Libyan weapons, could prop up anti-Sudanese government rebels.

Participant Strategies and Goals

The conflicts in this region have fundamentally different situations and, consequently, different strategies.

Mauritania-Senegal

Mauritania—Even after Mauritania extracted itself from this conflict in 1980, economic conditions did not appreciably improve. The droughts that periodically punish the Sahel were particularly hard in the early 1980s. Mauritania needs more than peace; it needs a new climate. Large-scale birth control will help, but the population pressures loom large. That's why the Senegal expulsions are a large problem.

Senegal—Senegal's primary aim is to maintain its stable democracy and keep the economy growing. As with most black African nations, there are always nervous glances northward at the historically dominant Arabs. Senegal wants to maintain "the French connection," which assures French aid in its confrontation with Mauritania.

Chad

Central government—With over a hundred distinct (different customs and language) ethnic groups in a nation of five million, it's a major goal just to maintain some form of national unity. It will continue to rely on French and Western support as a prop against Libya and Libyan-backed rebels.

Libya—Libya wants the Aozou Strip. It always has, and it always will, as long as there is hope that vast mineral wealth might be found there. While the uranium thought to be there is not as valuable as it was during the cold war, it's still a marketable commodity to nations wanting to build nuclear weapons. Libya will continue to back guerrilla groups in Chad until a government to its liking takes power and cedes the Aozou.

Colonel Qaddafi—Thinks he's a great leader and that fighting his many "enemies" shows his prowess. His defeats in Chad still haven't sunk in.

Sudan

There are fifty-six ethnic groups in Sudan, and over five hundred different tribes. Which tribe you belong to still means something in Sudan. The basic political dispute is between the Arab-dominated north (only 40 percent of the population are Arab, while 70 percent are Muslim) and the largely Negro south. The south wants some autonomy and, while many Arabs and Muslims would just as soon grant it, there is a strong Islamic faction that would prefer that all Sudanese were Muslims and that the nation conformed to Islamic law. Without the religious issue, Negroes and Arabs would probably get along. But religion is present in a big way and the strife continues.

While many Arab Sudanese would prefer to grant the black Sudanese the autonomy they have so long fought for, the Islamic fundamentalists and Arab supremacists hold the upper hand. The fighting and economic disruption have killed nearly half a million people to date, plus created over two million refugees. This is in addition to nearly half a million dead from the earlier civil war that ended in the early 1970s. The Arab northerners have also grown weary of the fighting, and have largely withdrawn the army from the south. Instead, Arab tribesmen have been given automatic weapons and the freedom to raid into the south as they have done for centuries. Those raids result in most of the male victims being killed and many of the women being taken into slavery.

With half the population in the south, even after over 5 percent of the population was killed in the last twenty-five years, the Arabs cannot realistically hope to prevail. But as long as the Arabs and Islamic fundamentalists persist in their traditional domination of the south Sudan, the fighting will continue. Eventually the south will, in effect, break away or autonomy will be achieved.

Ethiopia

Ethiopia is trying to recover from the political and economic damage inflicted by nearly two decades of Communist rule. It won't be easy, or gentle.

Somalia

The world tried to help Somalia, and the Somalis responded with gunfire and armed robbery. Some things never change. A turn-of-the-century British colonial administrator concluded that the only way to deal with Somalis was to "shoot on sight, shoot first, shoot often, shoot to kill." Note that UN peacekeeping in the Balkans has encountered a situation similar to what they ran into with Somalia. Which is one reason why the UN peacekeepers in the Balkans tend to keep their heads down. The Somalis will continue to fight each other. Northern Somalia, the self-proclaimed Republic of Somaliland, suffers from less civil strife, and will try to remain independent, at least until things settle down in Somalia proper.

POTENTIAL OUTCOMES

No one has any burning interest in making a substantial effort in settling these Sahel wars.

Chad

France backed away from her long involvement with Chad and expends little more than soothing words regarding the Mauritanian-Senegal conflict. Libya is seen as a threat, not in the Sahel, but in North Africa and the Middle East (not to mention as a base for worldwide terrorism). So Chad will be allowed to lurch along to whatever political/military solution it is capable of.

Mauritania-Senegal

Mauritania-Senegal will be largely ignored by the rest of the world and will probably never amount to much of a war because the Mauritanians are too weak to get what they want from the Senegalese and there is nothing in Mauritania that the Senegalese want.

Sudan

Sudan is a similar situation. There is nothing there that grabs the world's attention, except the millions of starving refugees and victims of the fighting, and then only on a very slow news day. The government, desperate to obtain aid in fighting the southern rebels, and anxious to forestall Muslim fundamentalists, has become an Islamic republic and allowed Iran to use the country as a base for Islamic terrorists.

Ethiopia

Ethiopia gets marginally more attention because the fighting occurs close to major shipping lanes for Western oil.

Eritrea

Peace could lead to economic improvement—and a move to democracy.

Somalia

The shooting will go on until everyone gets tired of it. That's what happened in Lebanon, where it took fifteen years for all concerned to lose their enthusiasm for the killing. It could take as long, if not longer, in Somalia.

QUICK LOOK: The Berber Question

In the first surviving accounts of warfare, recorded by the ancient Egyptians, one of the contingents mentioned were Berber (or Numidian) horsemen from the "western desert." These people call themselves the Amazigh and they have lived in North Africa (west of Egypt) for thousands of years. They speak a language similar to that of ancient Egypt (Coptic, still spoken by the Christian minority in Egypt). Today, there are 20–25 million Berbers. This is an estimate; no one has ever been able to conduct a census. They are large minorities in Morocco (about 40 percent of the population), Algeria (as much as 30 percent), Libya, Mali, Tunisia, Egypt, Niger, and Mauritania (this last nation derives its name from what the ancient Romans called the Berbers). Many Berbers are in various stages of assimilation. It's common for them to be bilingual (in Arabic and Berber). There has always been some intermarriage with non-Berbers, but often the non-Berber spouse (especially if a wife) becomes a Berber culturally.

No one has ever been able to actually conquer the Berbers. Even the first Muslim Arab armies, flush with victory and moving west out of Egypt, were initially defeated by the Berbers (who, at that point, were Christian, Jewish, or pagan, depending on the tribe). The Muslims cut a deal with the Berbers ("Join us in conquest, we can discuss religion later"). And so they did, although over the next century or two, most Berbers became Muslim.

The Berbers have always been independent to a fault, but willing to do business with anyone who would respect their culture and freedom of movement. Like the Bedouins to the east of Egypt, the Berbers were largely nomads, driving their herds over the sparsely watered grasslands of North Africa. Unlike the Bedouins, the Berbers are not Semites. Fair-skinned and often blue-eyed, their language and culture are ancient, related to that of ancient Egypt.

Berber warriors, and generals, led the Arab Muslim invasion of Spain and France in the eighth century. Berbers were often the hired swords who provided the muscle to put new strongmen on the thrones of North Africa during the centuries after Islam erupted out of the Arabian desert. All the other people conquered in North Africa by the Arabs eventually switched to speaking Arabic, except the Berbers. For the centuries of warfare between Spaniards and Muslims, the "moors" were Berbers (or "Mauritanians").

When France and Spain moved into North Africa to establish colonies in the nineteenth century, they faced the most resistance when they pushed south into the mountains and desert wastes. The Berbers resisted. They continued to resist until the colonial period ended in the 1960s. The Berbers lost battles, but to their way of thinking, they never lost a war. In a way, however, the Berbers did lose big-time. In the Sahel states the French controlled, the social relationships between Berber and black ("master and slave") were broken. After these Sahel regions became independent nations, the blacks were no longer subservient to their former Berber overlords.

Unlike the Kurds, the other stateless ethnic group we hear so much about, there has never been a major movement among the Berbers for the establishment of a Berber state. Part of this has to do with the multiplicity of dialects and cultural variations among the many Berber tribes. The Berbers have always been willing to work out a deal, as long as their culture and nomadic proclivities were not molested. Arab states, based on long experience, have generally agreed to this. The black African states are another matter. For there the Berbers have usually been a minority group dominating the black majority. The "Arab" warriors that gradually fought their way into the areas of the Sahel were usually Berbers. Mauritania, Mali, Niger, and Chad have long been areas with Berber minorities lording it over the black Africans. In the postcolonial area, the blacks have asserted their power with greater numbers and the apparatus of modern government (including black-dominated armed forces equipped with heavy weapons).

This has not stopped Berber minorities from agitating, and often fighting, for Berber rights. The most nomadic Berbers tend to be those who resist most vociferously, though they are ill equipped to confront modern weapons. Out in the Sahel countryside, however, the Berber warrior is still a powerful foe.

Chapter 9

THE HEART OF DARKNESS: ZAIRE AND SUB-SAHARAN AFRICA

INTRODUCTION

South of the Sahara Desert and the Sahel lie the vast plains and rain forests of Africa. In the middle of this region is Zaire, a nation that, given its chaos and conflict, is truly the Heart of Darkness. Poor in agricultural resources, and rich in typically abundant tropical diseases, the area at best supports its large populations on a precarious and debilitated subsistence basis. The endemic diseases blind and cripple large numbers of the adult population, and kill off many of the children and anyone lucky enough to make it past age fifty. Added to this arduous life is a persistent state, or threat, of war.

Zaire and its neighbors in sub-Saharan Africa each fight several wars. There are the internal ones, fought among the country's elites over who will be in power. There are the endemic tribal conflicts, often seen as the battles between the separate provinces that for colonialism would be different tribal entities. Border disputes are another source of war; most of sub-Saharan Africa's nations have at least one ongoing border dispute with a neighbor. Religious and ethnic animosities flare up continually. Finally, there's the war with the International Monetary Fund (IMF), the world body that tries to cycle cash from the relatively wealthy to the definitely poverty-stricken. Zaire is losing this war in a big way, and dragging the banks of its "allies" to the brink.

Almost every nation in "middle Africa" suffers from similar problems, the only difference being in degree.

SOURCE OF CONFLICT

Zaire's problems are classic examples of a form of government endemic to Africa since the departure of the colonial governments in the 1960s. This uniquely African form of one-man rule resulted in a steady decline in economic performance and increase in violence. The economic decline has been severe. Economic growth has declined several percentage points a year through the 1980s. Most Africans find themselves much worse off in 1995 than in 1980.

One of the primary causes of the prevalence of dictatorships had been the colonial legacy. Borders were drawn in European parlors on the basis of who had explorers and troops where and/or who was currently in political hock to whom. Tribal areas, cultural development, language, etc., were given little consideration. The colonial powers thought the natives were all "savages" anyway, and besides, if things go bad the empire's troops will bring order out of the chaos. But the colonial empires broke up, and the world wars accelerated the process. The Belgians tried to keep their Congo (Zaire) after World War II and succeeded for fifteen postwar years or so, but controlling tens of millions of people living in central Africa is a big task. Sub-Saharan Africans have trouble doing it and they live there. Zaire has over two hundred different ethnic groups. But even before the colonial borders came along, the multitude of ethnic groups were at each other's throats on a regular basis. Back then there were no TV camera crews recording it all, but that doesn't eliminate the mass graves of ancient vintage that are uncovered from time to time.

The gist of the problem: When the colonial power leaves there's an inevitable power vacuum, no matter how seemingly well prepared the

colony was for independence. Colonial "cadres" of physicians, engineers, and other skilled personnel often leave with the colonial army, and if no locals have been trained to take their place, economic and political disruption was not only likely, but precisely what happened everywhere.

In 1960, Zaire (then the Belgian Congo) had three native medical doctors. The colonial powers either made weak attempts (Great Britain) or no attempts (Belgium) to leave their former colonies with a sense of national identity or with the technical means to run a country and an economy. This has been a cause of great suffering, although the task of bringing African populations up to anything near European levels of education and technical competence would have been an immense one. When there is no effort, or desire, on the part of the newly independent to re-sort the country into nations along tribal lines, the real bickering starts. Most tribes try to dominate the others, and make few efforts to work out compromises on local powers. This situation is exacerbated even further if the tribes were divided across national boundaries (like the Somalis, many of whom live in Ethiopia and Kenya). Zaire, compared with other former middle African colonies, had a diversified economy when it achieved independence, but the seven years of warfare from decolonization in 1960 to 1967 stymied development. The Shaba invasion of 1977 began another series of internal and external conflicts.

The precolonial form of government in Africa came in as many flavors, as would be expected from an area with a thousand distinct ethnic groups. But one common thread was a form of cooperative tribalism. Africans organized themselves for work and play. The tribes had chiefs, but those chiefs were selected by various forms of election. An old African saying sums it up best: No people, no chief. In other words, a bad chief would find his people wandering off until there was no tribe to oppress. The African concept of nationhood was based on the allegiance of the people, not occupation of a lot of real estate. This is the most ancient form of government, and one that Europe had emerged from only in the past thousand years. The Europeans brought into Africa their more modern concepts of territorial entities and control over large numbers of people. Colonial administrators tended to appoint chiefs and ignore pleas for the removal of bad ones. Many of the postcolonial African nations became private enterprises for those who managed to grab control of the central government as the colonial rulers left. By controlling the bank accounts and the army, Africa was left with a perversion of its ancient tribal system. For one downside of the cooperative tribal system was that it represented cooperation only within the tribe. Everyone else was an outsider and fair game for exploitation.

After over three decades of watching Africans run their own affairs, and receiving more foreign aid per capita than any other region in the world, it became apparent to the aid donors that there were certain uniquely African elements at work. The most successful dictators were the ones who combined the technology of the West with the traditional tribal control mechanisms of Africa. So the longest surviving African dictator, Joseph Mobutu, set up a communications and propaganda system, and spent much of his time visiting small villages throughout Zaire dressed as a traditional chief. These images were constantly in circulation throughout the nation. Mobutu professed to be the only man capable of holding Zaire together. Mobutu's less successful peers in other African nations soon found themselves dead or in exile as many of their own people began to grope, often with AK-47 in hand, for a better, or at least less painful, form of government.

Imaginary Economies

While technology was skillfully used to dominate large populations, it was also misapplied to the economy. Africans had never been well off before the Europeans showed up. When the fourteenth-century Renaissance brought investment banking and modern accounting, and the nineteenth-century Industrial Revolution brought mass production to Europe, the Europeans became immensely wealthy. While the Europeans who invented these things had a century or more to ease into them, the Africans only had a generation to absorb all this technique and technology. It didn't stick. Blinded by the elusive promises of Soviet-style socialism, the new African nations at first sought to apply strict controls to their economies. The first crop of African leaders were, for the most part, well educated in European universities. Unfortunately, their generation of students was indoctrinated with all this socialist theory and there were no African elder statesmen to rein in ambitious, but ill-conceived, economic programs. Moreover, the former colonial masters were willing to provide loans and grants to assist their erstwhile colonies. This enabled the new nations to ruin their economies while putting off the day of reckoning by living off the foreign aid. It got worse. The Soviet-style central planning was never implemented as firmly as the Russians had done it simply because there were not enough trained administrators to do so. The net result: Money was poured into inefficient manufacturing plants, and food was imported and sold at prices that drove local farmers out of business. As agriculture, except for inefficient subsistence farming, declined, people moved to the urban areas for increasingly scarce factory jobs. The government tried to deal with the resulting unemployment, and potential urban unrest, by creating many government jobs. But the new bureaucrats and clerks had little to do except make life miserable for those engaged in private enterprise.

It wasn't until the 1980s that everyone realized what an economic dead end they had entered. The collapse of the European Communist economies in the late 1980s merely confirmed what many Africans already believed.

It has not been an easy task for poor nations to backtrack and revive market economies. Firing excess government workers has proven unpopular; so has laying off workers in unproductive factories. Lifting price, and other, regulations from farmers has cut back on the need for food imports and given the farmers hope. But many of those who already moved to the cities don't want to go back to farming. Most African nations are stuck with large urban populations and high unemployment rates. The availability of television and VCRs has made it clear that Africans are missing out on the worldwide economic boom. The people are broke, unhappy, and more inclined to violent solutions to their seemingly hopeless plight.

Our Gang

Easily overlooked by non-Africans is the "tribal" issue. There are over a thousand different ethnic groups in Africa, at least in terms of groups having a distinct language and customs. Many nations have over a hundred of these ethnic groups within their borders. No other region on the planet has such a density of ethnic groups. This plethora of ethnic groups is a severe obstacle to nation building. Combined with Africa's other handicaps, the poor economic development and endemic conflict should not be surprising. The half-dozen "tribes" of Yugoslavia were enough to foment a vicious civil war, and several dozen factions in Lebanon caused a civil war from 1975 to 1990. With over a thousand ethnic factions, Africa is condemned to a future of rancor and bloodshed.

The traditional African social order placed great emphasis on mutual support and communal ownership of land and other assets. Everyone was expected to share with their family, clan, and village. If one person made it big in politics or commerce, he (and it was usually a he in male-dominated Africa) was expected to take care of everyone in his family, village, and tribe (in that order). This is an ancient tradition that is found in many other parts of the world. This attitude changed in Europe with the rise of capitalism. In Europe, great concentrations of wealth were amassed and used to fund economic growth. Local and national governments taxed this wealth to provide the social services that had formerly come from family and clan members. It took a century or so for the Europeans to make the transition from private social security to state supported services.

In Africa, the traditional methods of spreading the wealth are still strong, and the ability of the state to substitute for the traditional approach minimal. People are more comfortable relying on family members and few African governments have demonstrated any ability to provide a meaningful substitute. The new, postcolonial leaders of Africa knew of the European methods. But the power of family obligation was greater than the theoretical duty of government officials to govern in an honest and even-handed manner. Family, village, and tribe came first. That's where much of the foreign aid went. The people running the government knew they could trust members of their tribe, and it made sense to spread the government's wealth around within the tribe to maintain loyalty. But that meant that the other tribes, and the country as a whole, lost out. This problem still bedevils Africa, and will for some time to come.

Another economic curse of tribalism is the difficulty in raising capital. African entrepreneurs now, at least, openly complain of the difficulty in raising capital in the face of constant demands for aid from family or tribe members. To refuse such requests risks social ostracism, and even violence. If an African entrepreneur manages to get a small business going, profits are constantly eroded by demands from less well off family members for aid. Loans for business expansion can also be plundered by social demands for financial aid. Of course, profitability is a key requirement before loans can be made and too many African enterprises cannot achieve high profitability because of the communal customs. Even foreign firms setting up enterprises in Africa find themselves being "adopted" by the dominant tribe and subsequently being nickeled and dimed to death with pleas for special treatment. Refusal to address these pleas can lead to unrest and a surly workforce.

The problem of capital formation is being overcome as African entrepreneurs learn to creatively say no to demands from kinsmen that they share the wealth. African custom holds that generosity to one's family, village, or clan comes before something as mundane as accumulating capital for business expansion. More and more African entrepreneurs realize that they can never compete if they cannot accumulate capital. To do that they must adopt the foreign custom of deferring consumption in order to build up capital for investment in the future. This is not the first time capitalism has run afoul of tribal communalism. But like every such encounter, the tribal peoples must accept the concept of saving money and building up capital for investment.

Foreign companies are learning how to introduce Western business customs to Africa without starting a riot. All of this is helped, somewhat, by the mass movement of people from their rural villages to the urban areas. This migration is usually by individuals and it weakens the tribal ties. Tribalism is still strong in African cities, but in urban areas it is easier to break free from all the social obligations that hobble economic development.

The Colonial Legacy

Shaky government is not new to Africa. Before the European colonial administrations arrived, most of Africa was a patchwork of largely independent ethnic entities. The poor communications in most of Africa made nation (or, more often, empire) building a daunting task. Those empires that were occasionally built up rarely survived long. Long-term, stable national governments are a relatively recent development. Africa had not got that far by the nineteenth century, and Europe itself was pretty new to it at that point.

The colonial experience left bitter memories in Africa. The Europeans were foreign, and they took over. Colonial rule was not gentle, and Europeans were, to put it mildly, condescending in their relationships with Africans. As a result of the bad feelings, there was a tendency to blame the colonial period for all that went wrong in the new nations that had formerly been colonies.

But Ethiopia and Liberia had escaped the colonial experience, and proved no different from their colonized brethren after the Europeans left Africa. The basic fact was that most of Africa was not as well equipped to move into the industrial age as other parts of the world were. There's no mystery about this. Lacking literacy, mechanization, strong agricultural resources, and ample natural transport routes, what happened in Africa is not surprising. Moreover, there were positive aspects of the colonial period. Slavery was suppressed and peace was maintained. Before colonies were established, the tribes were frequently fighting each other. Colonial troops, often comprised of native soldiers, put an end to that. Roads, ports, and other infrastructure improvements were made. The bottom line was that the population increased immensely during the colonial period. Africans didn't like the treatment they were afforded by colonial overlords, but they often benefited from it. Yet the colonies were not established to benefit Africans, but to reap profits for the nations establishing them. After World War II it became clear that the profits were not all that great. This was one of the primary reasons that Europeans made such haste to abandon their colonies in the 1950s and 1960s. Nation building is expensive and the Europeans didn't want to be bothered with the responsibility and expense.

Zaire is little different from its neighbors in nearly all respects. A study of Zaire is a study of the bulk of sub-Saharan Africa.

WHO'S INVOLVED

Zaire—Government in Kinshasa. The personal fiefdom of Mr. Mobutu. The central government no longer controls the nation. Each region either rules itself or is ruled by no one. The central government has an army, drawn from the smaller tribes to assure their loyalty, and this force acts as a band of mercenaries for those on Mobutu's payroll.

Zairian ethnic and religious groups—With over two hundred such groups spread among the population, they aren't a typical "unified" player in the political game, but the existence of their immense divisions leaves Zaire open to constant internal disputes; the government's game is to play the groups off of one another. Mobutu's policies of "national homogeneity" are mostly for show. Most of the "ethnic groups" are of Bantu origin. The four largest tribes—the Mongo, Luba, Kongo (all Bantu), and the Mangbetu-Azande (Hamitic)—make up nearly half of the population.

Opposition parties—In the afterglow of falling dictatorships (particularly Communist ones), even Mobutu has had to pay some attention to local demands for a more pluralistic form of government. He proposed that an official opposition be set up, for the purpose of creating a new, "democratic" government. This proved to be an interesting process, as nearly everyone in Zaire who is anyone (in terms of education and skills) was on Mobutu's payroll, or lists of people he has done favors for. The opposition parties that emerged from this process were a combination of groups truly opposed to Mobutu and others that simply wanted to get rich the way Mobutu did, by looting the country. From 1991 through 1995, there have been a series of political actions without substance. The opposition has issued demands and tried to pass laws, while Mobutu forms numerous "opposition" parties of his own and checkmates the real opposition at every turn. There is a transitional government and a transitional parliament, both of which Mobutu either controls, or short-circuits, behind the scenes. Mobutu still possesses vast wealth (over $10 billion in offshore accounts), and an enormous number of Zairians are on his payroll, or are otherwise beholden to him. When money and influence fail, there is the occasional murder of a prominent foe of Mobutu.

Opposition groups—Each of the two hundred African ethnic groups could form an opposition group—and several have. Mobutu has made strenuous efforts to prevent anyone from using these tribal groupings into a power base. As half the population is Roman Catholic (another 20 percent are Protestant; plus 10 percent, Kimbanguist; 10 percent, Muslim; and the remainder hold traditional beliefs), control of the

Catholic clergy has always been high on his list. The most worrisome source of opposition is from the urban population. Overall, about half the male population is literate (and a third of the females). There is more literacy in the urban areas, which contain about a third of the population. Although 75 percent of the labor force is in agriculture, 10–15 percent are wage earners. This includes most of the educated classes, the people with the means to get the urban population stirred up.

Wild Cards

France—Zaire is a member of the French "union" of former colonies, and so Mobutu, or his potential opposition, has some call on the use of French economic and diplomatic muscle, not to mention the ever-ready French 11th Airborne Division and Foreign Legion.

CIA—America's intelligence agency has had several major operations in Zaire and cannot help getting mixed up in local affairs. The United States wants Mobutu out, and the CIA has the only covert means to assist in this effort.

GEOGRAPHY

The Congo River (named after the Bakongo people who live along much of its length) has been renamed the Zaire River; that should clear up any lingering discrepancies. Zaire remains the same equatorial land of 2.3 million square kilometers (one-fourth the size of the United States). Terrain varies from grasslands and savannas to mountains to tropical rain forests: basically, a vast central basin that is a low-lying plateau. There are mountains in the east. Some 80 percent of the country is forest and woodland, including a dense tropical rain forest in the central part of the country and eastern highlands with periodic droughts in the south. The climate is tropical. Hot and humid along the Zaire River. Cooler and drier in the southern highlands. Cooler and wetter in the eastern highlands.

The population is over 43 million, with a third of the people living in cities. Kinshasa has a population of over 4 million. Over 50 percent of the people are Christian; the remaining half are members of syncretic and animist sects.

Zaire borders Angola, Zambia, Tanzania, Burundi, Rwanda, Uganda, Sudan, Central African Republic, and the Congo (on the other side of the "Congo" River). It has large deposits of copper and cobalt as well as deposits of zinc, manganese, gold, and other minerals. The Shaba region, especially the mining area of Kolwezi, is particularly rich in mineral deposits. Shaba, formerly called Katanga, borders on Angola.

Some statisticians estimate that Zaire alone has 13 percent of the entire world's potential hydroelectric power. Zaire's land and climate make it a potential African breadbasket, but so far agricultural development has not kept pace with expanding domestic food needs.

HISTORY

Migrating from Nigeria, Bantu tribes entered the Congo Basin around A.D. 700, driving the more primitive Bushmen inhabitants south and east. The Portuguese explorer Diego Cão surveyed the Congo River's estuary in 1482. This was the heartland of the Bakongo kingdom. Given the thick jungle, endemic diseases Europeans had no resistance to, and native tales of wild interior tribes, few Europeans attempted to penetrate beyond the coast. Besides, the Bakongos proved to be reasonable trading partners, supplying the Europeans with slaves and ivory. The hinterland remained relatively unexplored by Europeans until Henry Morton Stanley ("Dr. Livingston, I presume?") passed through present-day Zaire in the 1870s. Belgium's King Leopold II, after hiring Stanley as an explorer and adviser, claimed the Congo area at the Berlin Conference of 1885.

The Congo was Belgium's great colony, but the Belgians did little to provide for an improvement in native education or living standards. Their primary interest was in extracting Zaire's plentiful natural resources and shipping them to resource-poor Belgium. There were several native anticolonial movements, most of them religion-centered. These included Kimbanguism and the Kitawala sect.

French African decolonization made Belgium's already shaky post–World War II hold on Zaire completely untenable. Zaire (then still called the Congo) became independent on June 30, 1960. Patrice Lumumba became prime minister and Joseph Kasavubu president. Peace lasted less than a week. The army mutinied, Belgian troops acted to protect Belgians living in Zaire, and Katanga Province (now Shaba), under the leadership of Moise Tshombe, seceded from the new republic. UN peacekeeping forces showed up, but Lumumba demanded they be placed under his direct control. The UN commander refused on the grounds that that was not part of his mandate. Lumumba then startled the world by requesting direct Russian aid.

This was too much. Exercising his powers as president, Kasavubu tried to fire Lumumba, but Lumumba refused to leave the government. He tried to remove Kasavubu. Colonel Joseph Mobutu (as in the current president) led a military coup that toppled the unmanageable government. Mobutu threw all East bloc diplomats and advisers out, put Lumumba in prison, then returned Kasavubu to power. Meanwhile, Lumumba died from "mysterious causes"; in all likelihood he was assassinated by his rivals.

In 1961, Zaire was in shambles. The reborn Kasavubu government faced a half-dozen dissident groups, the chief ones being a "pro-Lumumba people's government" in Kisangani, run by ex-vice premier and Lumumba loyalist Antoine Gizenga, Tshombe down in Katanga, and a Baluba tribe separatist rebellion in Kasai. Confusion, combat, negotiations, and UN troops brought the Baluba rebellion and Gizenga back into the government, but Katanga held out until 1963.

Katanga's reintegration and the UN withdrawal in 1964 didn't stop the internal instability. A tribal rebellion erupted in Kwilu Province, directed by former Lumumba ally Pierre Mulele. Another broke out in Kivu Province, led by another Lumumba faction. In July 1964 Tshombe was named head of the central government. He directed a counterattack on rebel strongholds and got strong support from Belgium.

In late 1965, further political infighting among the elites led to a toppling of the Tshombe regime. Mobutu, by now a lieutenant general, led another military coup. He installed himself as president, a position he still holds. In July 1966, white mercenaries and Katangan rebels, many of them former members of the national army and police forces, launched another drive on the central government. Combat ensued and was renewed a year later. By late 1967 the insurgency had been defeated and the Katangans withdrew into Angola.

They returned in 1977 with a fast-paced invasion that overran Shaba (Katanga Province with a new name). Mobutu asked for French and Belgian assistance. He was provided with a regiment of the Moroccan Army, which pushed the rebels back into Angola. The rebels fought a series of holding actions, avoiding pitched battles with the Moroccan forces. In May 1978 the rebels launched another offensive, this time directed at the mining town of Kolwezi. This was a most calculated invasion, one designed to strike at Zaire's economy. When they took Kolwezi, the rebels machine-gunned Belgian and French technical advisers and mining personnel. They also proceeded to slaughter Zairian civilians. The rebels may have killed as many as 200 foreigners and 5,000 Zairians. France responded by sending the Foreign Legion. The Legionnaires and the Zairian Army routed the rebels and drove them from Shaba. Belgium provided a paratroop battalion.

Since 1978, the Zairian government has been racked with economic difficulties that have compounded some of the internal tribal contentions. The French used the situation as an opportunity to draw Zaire into the successful "union" it had established with its former colonies to the north since independence in 1960.

The overt war is in a quiet phase. Katangan separatist groups become stronger as the power of the central government declines. There is some bandit activity around Lake Tanganyika and in other scattered areas. Muttering in the urban areas about the need for multiparty democracy and other heresies grow in response to the fall of dictatorships in Europe, Latin America, and Asia.

The more serious conflict is on the economic front. Accurate figures for Zaire's IMF war are hard to produce, but sources cite an inflation rate of nearly 100 percent. International debt is over $7 billion. That compares with a 1987 GNP of slightly more than $5 billion. By 1990, GDP was up to $6.6 billion, but for the rest of the 1990s, Zaire's economy disintegrated. The national currency no longer had any value, commerce is done with foreign currency and barter. In many respects, Zaire's economic situation is typical of sub-Saharan Africa (less South Africa). Consider the grim statistics for this region. While world economic activity increased several percentage points a year through the 1980s, sub-Saharan Africa's *fell* over 2 percent a year through the decade. Africa's share of world trade is now about 1 percent; in 1960 it was 3 percent. Return on investment in the area is under 5 percent, versus 30 percent in 1960. This is the major reason for the reluctance to invest in Africa. Not that a lot of money doesn't flow into the area. Africa receives more aid per capita than any other region in the world. Despite all the aid, the region's external debt equals its GNP. It costs a lot more to do business in Africa (over 50 percent more than in Asia) and, with many other underdeveloped nations clamoring for new investment, Africa comes up dead last in the investment potential department. Zaire is one of the worst examples of this syndrome.

Internal development is at a standstill despite Mobutu's policy of "national homogenization." That policy is an attempt to forge a national identity for Zaire. The actual policy is to spread as many economic goodies as possible around among the tribes while keeping the elites in the federal district of Kinshasa supplied with new Mercedeses. That works when copper prices are high. When they aren't, the country's "consensus" begins to break down. In the 1990s, the effects of decades of waste and corruption, as well as weak copper prices, have brought Zaire's economy about as low as it can go.

Mobutu did feel confident enough about the internal and external situation that he has lent Chad and France two thousand troops for duty in Chad during the late 1980s. But then he also owed France a thank-you for the Foreign Legion in 1978. Chad also provided Mobutu's troops with an opportunity to train and gain field experience. Perhaps Mobutu's strongest form of insurance was to strike a deal with the American CIA to provide logistical bases for U.S. support of Angolan rebels during the 1980s. These CIA bases were the largest U.S. intelligence presence on the continent and form the source for many other intelligence-gathering operations in surrounding states. As a result, the CIA had a strong interest in keeping Mobutu in power. Most of this CIA and American support disappeared when foreign forces withdrew from Angola in the early 1990s. But Mobutu further cemented his position by maintaining good relations with South Africa, before and after the black-dominated African National Congress party took over in South Africa. He managed that feat because he always positioned himself as a leader in the fight against apartheid and the promoter of anti-Communist rebellions in Africa. The events of 1989 in the Communist world have shown Mobutu's policies to be wise (or just lucky). The many African nations that threw in with the Russians are now out of luck (and foreign aid). Mobutu's gamble with maintaining good relations with the West paid off. All of this external support was needed in the 1990s when meaningful opposition developed within Zaire. No Western nation called for armed intervention in Zaire, despite Mobutu's known record of theft and tyranny. Mobutu was calling in favors and getting away with robbery, and murder.

A half-dozen rebellions of army units occurred between 1991 and 1995 (including an aborted rebellion by the so-called parachute brigade in Kinshasa). Mobutu either put the rebellions down easily or mollified the leaders by promising political change. When the war in Angola picked up again in 1992, UNITA (Angolan rebels) soldiers moved into Zaire's diamond mining region and set up shop. That lucrative operation went on until 1994, when the Zairian Army finally moved in and evicted the UNITA troops. Meanwhile, the so-called Zairian "transitional government" of 1993 proved to be a sham. As of 1995, Mobutu is still in tenuous control. The slaughter in Rwanda provides a glimpse of a possible future for Zaire, and no one in the UN, or anywhere else, appears eager to send troops into the Heart of Darkness.

LOCAL POLITICS

Zaire—Nominally a federal republic, but actually a strongman-type dictatorship backed by the army and a consensus of tribal leaders.

Mobutu Sese Seko—President of Zaire, referred to as "the Guide," essentially a strongman dictator backed by the army; still appears to be the only consensus leader.

High Council of the Republic Transition Parliament—Faced with revolution, Mobutu set up this organization, staffed by leaders of parties in the new Republic Transition Parliament. Years of dickering, dithering, and deal making have produced much rhetoric but little meaningful transition to a government not dominated by Mobutu.

Progressive Convention—Moderate opposition party (i.e., many members beholden to Mobutu).

Political Forces of the Conclave—Replaces the Popular Movement of the Revolution (MPR), which was, until the early 1990s, the only legal political party, and a Mobutu front.

Union for Democracy and Social Progress—Radical opposition to Mobutu.

Other parties and groups form and unform as Mobutu keeps the pot boiling in order to deflect attention from removing Mobutu.

The Kongo (plural, Bakongo)—Largest ethnic group, with over three million members; only 10 percent of population, which illustrates the ethnic diversity of the country; a Bantu tribe.

Baluba, Balunda, Mongos—Other major Zairian Bantu tribes. The Mongo, Luba, Kongo (all Bantu), and the Mangbetu-Azande make up about 45 percent of Zaire's population.

Manbetu-Azande—Major Zairian Hamitic tribe (related to the Ethiopians and Somalis).

Lingala—A Zairian patois; the language used by the Zairian Army and closest thing to a national Zairian language; government "nationalization policies" encourage its use. Zaire may have as many as 650 local languages and dialects. The plethora of languages and ethnic groups makes it difficult for someone without an army, aircraft, and radio stations to oppose someone (Mobutu) who has.

Kimbanguism—Syncretic tribal religion; full name the Church of Christ on Earth by the Prophet Simon Kimbangu; 3–4 million members.

CIA—Their logistical bases and large number of operatives, plus the implicit obligation of the U.S. government for this hospitality, long made additional U.S. support in time of internal crises a major asset for Mobutu and his followers. At the very least, the CIA gave Mobutu an assured exit from Zaire to comfortable exile should things get too hot. The end of the cold war and the departure of most of the CIA staff diminished Mobutu's support from the U.S. government. Moreover, increasing media attention on the mess Mobutu had made in Zaire caused the American government to officially oppose him. But the United States is unlikely to support any legal action against Mobutu, in power or in exile, for economic and other crimes committed while he was in charge. Mobutu knows too much about CIA operations.

POLITICAL TREND CHART

ZAIRE

Gv95	Gv20	PC95	PC20	R95	R20	Ec95	Ec20	EdS95	EdS20
MD4,2	MD2,1	2−	1	7	6	1+	1−	0+	0+

MD = Military Dictatorship (albeit a strange one) (effectiveness, stability)

REGIONAL POWERS AND POWER INTEREST INDICATOR CHART

"ZAIREAN CIVIL DISINTEGRATION"

	Economic Interests	Historical Interests	Political Interest	Military Interest	Force Generation Potential	Ability to Intervene Politically	Interest/ Ability to Promote Economic Development
United States	7	4	6	3	6	5	6
S. Africa	9	9	9	9	3	6	5
"Arabs"	4	9	7	3	2	4	3
France	6	7	7	3	7	7	6
Russia	2	1	4	3	1	2	1
Belgium	6	7	5	2	1+	3	5
Nigeria	3	2	4	4	2−	1	1

NOTE: 0 = minimum; 9 = maximum

PARTICIPANT STRATEGIES AND GOALS

Zaire's central government—Continues to play the internal payoff game and hope the IMF doesn't close the bank. Currently, the IMF, and other foreign donors, have cut off Zaire's aid. Growing demands by the urban population for real democracy are a major political problem. Economic decline caused by lower prices for export goods and rampant corruption exacerbate the situation. Potential problems in Shaba (formerly Katanga) Province shrink by comparison. But the government must ensure that Shaba is adequately defended in order to forestall another invasion. Shaba is economically vital to Zaire's existence and everyone knows it. While 75 percent of the population produce 30 percent of the GNP scratching a living out of subsistence farming, the raw materials industries generate the majority of the GNP using most of the remaining people. As for internal politics, the program of increasing use of Lingala as well as educational development programs are crucial to national survival, but this will take a long time and a lot of political stability.

Mobutu opposition—Outfoxed at every turn, their best hope seems to be waiting for the elderly (born in 1919) Mobutu to die, of natural causes or otherwise.

France—Is increasingly keen on getting competent leadership in the French Union states. For over twenty years France has been tolerant of unsuccessful African attempts to reinvent some form of state socialism. France's economic and monetary ties to the French Union states is getting expensive. Patience is running out. The French Foreign Legion and 11th Airborne Division may become a means of political reform in more nations.

United States—With South Africa democratic, the focus has shifted to the more depressing situations in the rest of Africa. The Heart of Darkness dictators have been getting away with murder (on a vast scale) and plunder (big-time) while the Western media spotlighted South Africa's problems. Now that these thugs get more attention, the United States will either feel compelled to twist some arms or, quite likely, continue to ignore the mess. The CIA may become the major cause of U.S. involvement here, as the U.S. military and intelligence agencies are looking for something to justify their large budgets now that the cold war is over. "Saving Africa," has a nice ring to it, especially if you're a general or CIA honcho about to have your budget torn to ribbons. Somalia and Rwanda have taken some of the enthusiasm out of this option, however.

POTENTIAL OUTCOMES

Zaire

1. 60 percent chance through 2001: Same old suffering with increased agitation for more power sharing. Look for increasing corruption in an already corrupt kleptocracy.
2. 30 percent chance through 2001: Utter disintegration into separate "nations" and tribal areas. (Katanga becomes a viable independent country.)
3. 10 percent chance through 2001: Successful tribal federation system established. Goes to 40 percent if Mobutu dies and is not succeeded by someone like him.

COST AND KINDS OF WAR

Since independence (1960 for most nations), the region has suffered over 3 million deaths directly attributable to warfare, rebellion, and other forms of civil strife. This out of a population of some 150 million people. That's about 1 person in 50. For the United States, that would mean over 5 million dead in some thirty years. America suffered about one-tenth that number of deaths from gunshot wounds in that period. The collateral damage to Africa was more significant, as the fragile economies involved were further weakened and this is the primary cause of local life expectancy being five to six years lower than in India (a country with a lower per capita GNP, but also a lower level of violence).

The most prominent of these conflicts were: Zaire's civil wars (1960–65, 110,000 dead); Angola's rebellion against Portugal (1961–75, 120,000 dead) and subsequent civil war (1975–present, 160,000); Uganda's civil disorder (1966–present, 700,000); in Burundi, Tutsi and Hutu massacres of each other (1972, 210,000; 1988, 33,000; 1994–95, 800,000); Liberia's civil war (1986–95, 200,000); Sierra Leone's civil war (1991–present, 20,000).

In most of these conflicts small groups of lightly armed irregulars shoot at each other or butcher unarmed civilians. While there are over a thousand armored vehicles in the region, most of them are not maintained effectively and even those that are running well don't have many places to go. The Heart of Darkness is also the heart of the African rain forest. In addition to the jungles, there are numerous swampy spots (not all of which announce themselves to the unwary tank driver). The flat, dry areas are filled with rocky outcroppings and gullies. While there is some good tank terrain, there's nothing there for tanks to fight over. In a word, this is not the best terrain for mechanized warfare. This is infantry country: geographically, psychologically, and culturally. The population is spread out in thousands of small settlements. The people (armed or not) respond well to a disciplined platoon of heavily armed infantry. Not that anyone fighting a war in this region would want to do it in the bush anyway. All that's worth having is concentrated in a few urban areas or industrial sites. Light armored vehicles and infantry also work best in these areas. Countries in these regions tend to keep their heavy vehicles in the built-up areas, the better to use them most effectively against unruly urban citizens and to avoid mechanical (or loyalty) breakdowns.

QUICK LOOK: South Africa

In 1990 the African National Congress (ANC) was legalized and its leader, Nelson Mandela, released after serving twenty-six years in an apartheid prison. 1991, South Africa's Land Acts and the other "pillars of apartheid" were rescinded. After two years of give-and-take, which led to a new constitution being approved in December 1993, in April 1994 the apartheid state run by white South Africans ended with a free election. In May 1994, Nelson Mandela became president of a very new Republic of South Africa.

Apartheid is finished. South Africa now faces a freer but harsh new world. South Africa has many first world attributes. It had a 1994 GDP of $111 billion. It has first-class industries and universities.

The nation also has many problems that could throw it back toward third world status. Meeting the expectations of the long-oppressed black majority is one. How the new government improves the lives of the black majority without razing Africa's strongest and richest economy is the central issue in this period of change and transition.

A telling statistic current as of 1995: In South Africa, 5 percent of the population (almost all of that 5 percent being white) own 88 percent of the wealth. To get some perspective on the statistic, it is nearly twice the concentration of wealth among an elite in the ten wealthiest Western nations.

Land is a particularly tough issue. Under apartheid laws blacks could only own land in the "tribal homelands" (see below). Between 1960 and 1980 the apartheid government forcibly relocated nearly 3.5 million people, moving them from their homes to one of the *bantustans*. Several Western press sources have noted the anomaly between the ANC's and Pan-Africanist Congress's (PAC) land redistribution political positions in the 1994 campaign and the new South African constitution's promise of protecting private ownership of property and guaranteeing compensation for expropriated land. (The Pan-Africanist Congress utilized the slogan *Izwe lethu!*—"the land is ours!")

The Reconstruction and Development Plan (RDP) is the centerpiece of the Mandela government's attempt to re-create South Africa. The RDP has five goals: (1) to provide jobs, land, and housing for the very poor; (2) to develop education and training programs to raise skill levels; (3) to promote economic growth; (4) to complete the democratization process; (5) to change or create the governmental structure to implement the RDP's aims.

The RDP has been slow to take effect. The ANC promised during the 1994 elections to build a million houses in five years. (In May 1995, *The New York Times* reported that in its first year in office the ANC-led government had only built one thousand houses for the poor.)

There is also this worrisome sign: South Africa's new governmental elite are pulling very large salaries. Lavish salaries create a bureaucratic bourgeoisie—and have been a bane to sound development in Africa. They also have a tendency to self-perpetuate and, in order to keep their privileges, dispense with democracy. (The *London Review of Books* reports that Mandela is paid as much as the President of the United States and that both of Mandela's vice presidents make more than the U.S. veep.)

The bonds of tribal kinship remain strong. Tribal strife in South Africa has killed many more blacks than apartheid. White and nonwhite South Africans have much to be fearful of if their future offers the dictatorial rule so common in the rest of Africa. (In the first thirty years of independence from colonial rule, less than 2 percent of the 150-plus African rulers left office voluntarily.)

What are the prospects for trouble? Political trouble and occasional tribal violence are guaranteed. There are many black groups that want change but not at their expense. Tribal concerns continually conflict with national political objectives.

The possibility of a civil war remains in the background. As of mid-1995 right-wing white violence had been confined to demonstrations and minor sabotage. The rural Boer army militias, however, are well trained and well supplied with weapons. The Boers can field several hundred thousand soldiers very quickly. The Zulus are also well armed and Zulu radicals highly motivated. Zulu radicals completely reject the Xhosa-dominated ANC.

There are many black radicals ready to exact revenge on the Boers and on their traditional tribal enemies. Elements in the ANC remain hard-line "socialist revolutionaries" who think they should control all land and the entire economy. They are waiting for the ANC's moderates to fail. Some black organizations still want to establish their own state. (That would be fine with the Boers as long as the Boers get choice tribal lands.)

Political killings, which began to rise dramatically in 1990 (to nearly four thousand that year), have only moderated since the election. Unemployment hovers between 35 and 40 percent. The new democratic government of post-apartheid South Africa faces many complex challenges. Street demonstrations are much easier to run than democratic, pluralistic governments.

A GAZETTEER OF SOUTH AFRICAN POLITICS

Nelson Mandela—Now he's president and the most important man in the entire process. In some ways he always was. Held in prison since the 1960s, he was finally released in 1990 and resumed his leading position in the ANC leadership. Now in his seventies, Mandela is still vigorous. How long he remains on the scene to direct postapartheid South Africa is a key question.

African National Congress (ANC)—Nelson Mandela's umbrella political organization. Originally formed in 1912 as a nonviolent, democratic organization for the advancement of blacks, it became the leading militant organization against apartheid. The ANC is still going through a transition from being a clandestine revolutionary movement to becoming an open democratic party, and it's a tough transition. The ANC, under Mandela's guidance, is attempting to move from a "socialist" organization to a democratic party supporting free markets. But the ANC could splinter, especially if Mandela were to leave the scene. The ANC has grown into a very broad organization but still retains a solid base in the various Bantu tribes (especially the Xhosa tribe) of South Africa. The ANC has several political wings. The most troublesome at the moment is "the Spear of the Nation" (Umkhonto we Sizwe, referred to by the initials MK), the ANC's old military arm. This crowd is not eager to turn in their weapons and join the SANDF.

Pan-Africanist Congress (PAC—also called Pan-Africanist Congress of Azania)—Banned splinter faction of the ANC; advocates black-controlled government. The PAC became a refuge for disenchanted ANC members who don't agree with the ANC's conciliatory approach.

The Comrades—With so many unemployed adolescents and young men in the black urban areas, nature and politics took its usual course. The youths organized into gangs the better to keep the revolution going. Many were kept under control by ANC leaders, but many more became a force unto themselves. Calling themselves "the Comrades," they used vigilante-style justice to punish real or imagined transgressions against the movement. The Comrades are becoming more difficult to control. Boycotting school and becoming more unemployable, many Comrade groups are turning to crime against the very people they profess to liberate from oppression. Nelson Mandela's former wife and radical activist, Winnie Mandela, is the patron saint of the Comrades and their cohorts. Winnie Mandela suggests that the ANC has become a pawn of the old white establishment.

Inkatha (also called the Inkatha Freedom party [IFP])—Zulu-based organization led by Zulu chief Mangosuthu Buthelezi. Inkatha is the ANC's main African opposition. No tribe in southern Africa arouses the fear, envy, and respect aroused by the Zulus. Inkatha wants to make sure that historically dominant Zulus are not subordinated to other (i.e., Bantu) tribes. Inkatha has many Boer extremist allies. Buthelezi, a hereditary Zulu ruler, has assumed a characteristically Zulu approach to the situation. While the Zulus have had their battles with the Boers, they also feel a certain kinship with them. For example, when scholars looked into the genealogy of Boers, it was discovered that most had blacks in their ancestry. A common Boer response was, "Well, that's probably true, but it's *Zulu* blood." The Boers and Zulus have both suffered oppression from the British. Boers and Zulus are feared by other blacks because of past conquests. Boers and Zulus keep their combative traditions alive, much to the distress of other South African ethnic groups. Buthelezi, a university-trained leader with considerable speaking and administrative skills (and a substantial ego), regularly points out that the Boers have firepower and would not hesitate to use it against blacks if it came to a fight. The Zulus are at odds with the ANC government. Zulu and ANC supporters regularly clash in black-populated areas. The Zulus thus represent a more conservative black attitude to the ANC program for political reform. No one is sure if Buthelezi is simply being a Zulu statesman or is a proponent of past Zulu hegemony in South Africa. The ANC largely represents the Bantu peoples, who have been kicked around in the past by both Zulus and whites and feel that, this time, it's going to be different. The Zulus are South Africa's largest single tribe group, with nearly 7.5 million of South Africa's 40 million people.

Boers—The Afrikaners, South Africa's white tribe. Descendants of

Dutch farmers who reached the Cape of Good Hope in the seventeenth century, they are a minority within the white minority. There are approximately 3.3 million Boers.

Broederbond—"Secret" Afrikaner society dedicated to Afrikaner cultural and political control. Probably a participant in the increasing number of terrorist actions against blacks.

Dutch Reformed Church—In South Africa, the cultural as well as religious heart of the Boers; extreme Calvinism (a very narrow interpretation unfair to John Calvin) concerning predestination of "God's elect" was used to justify apartheid.

National party—Afrikaner party of former President F. W. de Klerk. The NP created the apartheid system, and its moderates, under De Klerk, took it apart. The moderates are now a majority.

Afrikaner Resistance Movement (AWB)—Radical Boer extremist organization, fascist and even neo-Nazi in its political program. Completely against Mandela and De Klerk. Closely aligned with the Herstigte Nationale party (Reconstituted National Party), a far right-wing splinter of the National party that formed well before apartheid ended. These Boer groups are religiously oriented, Calvinist, and advocate a separate Boer state (and apartheid in that state).

Conservative Party of South Africa—Formed in 1982, another National party splinter group. During the last days of apartheid, it was the main opposition to the National party. It has now grown in strength and advocates the creation of an Afrikaner *Volkstaat* (separate state). Afrikaner Volksunie is a splinter group of the conservatives that wants confederation of "regional" (tribal?) states.

Anglo South Africans—Primarily British in origin. Around two million strong.

Other parties, and ethnic and special interest groups—There are many mid-sized and minor players in the South African political arena. Some operate in coalitions. Some have merged and then splintered once again. Here are a few of the smorgasbord:

Indian National Conference of South Africa—Indian- and colored-based political party.

New Republic party—Advocates a new federal republic with each racial group self-governing.

Progressive Federal party—Advocates a democratic federal system.

Was a mainline antiapartheid party with many South African English members.

Black People's Convention—Now no longer as active as it was during the apartheid days, the BPC advocated black organization outside of "white racist political regime." It was very influential among urban blacks and was part of the Black Consciousness Movement.

South African Black Alliance—Black and colored coalition. Advocated nonviolent, democratic change during apartheid. Many members have gravitated to moderate ANC candidates.

Colored Labor party—Asian and mixed-race party.

Colored Federal party—Asian and mixed-race party.

The Minority Front party—Main theme is protection of minority rights, particularly Indians in Natal.

Workers Rights party—Champions feminist and socialist causes.

African Christian Democratic party (ACDP)—Platform: "It's time to do it God's way."

The Africa Muslim party—Platform: "Enjoining good and prohibiting evil."

Soccer party—Run by a Rastafarian with long dreadlocks. Platform: "A sports organization for collective contribution to equal rights."

OTHER SOUTH AFRICAN ORGANIZATIONS

Xhosa—Major Bantu tribe.

South African National Defense Force (SANDF)—The new postapartheid South African military.

South African Police Union (SAPU)—"Conservative" police organization formed in late 1994. Intended to protect the rights of right-wing police personnel.

"Tribal homelands"—The concept behind these states is that if black tribes are recognized as being citizens of a nation other than South Africa, their disenfranchisement from South African politics is made legitimate. Also called *bantustans*. The ANC made campaign promises that all civil servants in the tribal homelands would retain their jobs even after the homelands were abolished. That puts a lot of unnecessary people on stretched government payrolls.

Desmond Tutu—Anglican bishop, South African moderate, and member of the Xhosa tribe; major figure in national effort of reconciliation between black tribes and Boers. Here's a Tutu quote to consider: "Had Nelson Mandela and all these others not been willing to forgive, we would not have even reached first base" (in the effort to end apartheid peacefully). And here's another one with resonance: "For the Church to retreat from politics is nothing short of heresy. Christianity is political or it is not Christianity."

De Beers—Giant South African mining consortium; monopolizes, with Russia, the world's diamond business. In 1990 it paid Russia $1 billion just for marketing rights to a Russian diamond horde. The Russians needed the dollars; only De Beers could unload that many diamonds and pay up front in cash.

COSATU—Congress of South African Trade Unions. COSATU is a mainly black organization that was a key antiapartheid political organization. Its leader, Jay Naidoo, became a minister without portfolio in Mandela's first government. Labor, especially cheap black labor, enabled the old apartheid South Africa to continue economic growth despite foreign economic sanctions. White workers in South Africa get paid on a Western scale; most black workers, on a third world scale (one-fifth to one-tenth as much as whites). A job in the urban cash economy is seen as far superior to subsistence farming, and despite strenuous government controls, young blacks continue coming into the cities looking for work. COSATU became a potent force when it threatened to upset the economic apple cart. COSATU faces a formidable task in postapartheid South Africa. Only a portion of black workers will be able to get jobs in the cash economy, and COSATU may find itself deciding who will join the cash economy and who will remain in third world poverty. In performing this function, COSATU will acquire considerable political power and find itself in the position of defending white-dominated industry. The only alternative is the destruction of South Africa's Western-style economy—and the loss of COSATU's *raison d'être*.

Rand Monetary Area/South African Customs Union—South African–run economic group that includes Botswana, Swaziland, Lesotho, and Namibia. The rand is the basic South African currency.

SASOL—South African Coal, Oil, and Gas Corporation; has been instrumental in developing coal gasification and liquefaction processes to produce oil from coal.

Executive Outcomes—Private company organized by former SADF officers. It is now reorganizing several African armies—for cash. (As of early 1996, Executive Outcomes was "managing" the Sierra Leonean Army.)

A TIME LINE OF SOUTH AFRICAN HISTORY

1652	Dutch traders and settlers arrive at the Cape of Good Hope.
1779	Dutch and other European settlements extend throughout the Cape region.
1795	British forces take control of Capetown area.
1815	Chaka (1787–1828), the supreme Zulu chief, begins to build a Zulu empire, at the expense of the Zulus' tribal neighbors.
1828	Chaka assassinated; replaced by his half-brother Dingane.
1836	Boer farmers begin "the Great Trek" to the hinterland to escape British control.
1838	The Battle of Blood River. Zulus and Boer "Voortrekkers" collide in battle. Boers defeat Dingane and his Zulus.
1852–54	Independent Boer republics of the Transvaal and Orange Free State are formed.
1879	Zulus defeat British Army at the Battle of Isandhlwana, but are delayed at Rourke's Drift and fail to attack Durban. British counteroffensive defeats Zulus.
1880–81	Anglo-Boer War.

1899–1902   British defeat Boers in Boer War.

1910   Union of South Africa created.

1912   South Africa Native National Congress (predecessor of ANC) forms.

1913   Land Act segregates whites and blacks.

1948   National party takes power and institutes apartheid.

1960   Sharpeville revolt. ANC is banned.

1964   ANC leader Nelson Mandela jailed.

1976   Major Soweto uprising.

1983   Parliament chambers created for Indians and coloreds.

1989   F. W. de Klerk becomes president.

1990   Nelson Mandela released from jail. ANC no longer banned.

1994   In national democratic elections, Mandela is elected president.

POTENTIAL OUTCOMES

1. 75 percent chance through 2004: South Africa's new moderate democratic government continues to work. Consensus rules. The whites continue to control the wealth but economic overcomes revenge. White skills and capital stay, black employment (and pay) climbs, and the South African economy booms. Still, look for the political parties to retain tribal bases. (Wild card factor: Nelson Mandela remains alive.)

2. 15 percent chance through 2004: The new multiracial and multi-tribal South African government encounters severe economic difficulties. (Wild card factor: Nelson Mandela dies suddenly, from natural causes.) Various factions (especially well-armed and -organized Boer radicals) wage terror and guerrilla war against new government. The tribally based political parties fail to reach democratic compromises. Street trouble continues but civil war does not erupt.

3. 10 percent chance through 2004: Civil war erupts in South Af-

rica—ANC, Inkatha, Boer, and other groups go at it with whatever weapons are available. (Wild card factor: Nelson Mandela is assassinated by opposition forces.) If this occurs, 75 percent chance of a division of South Africa into "tribal enclaves"—microstates organized by race and tribe. South Africa is functionally renamed "South Lebanon."

QUICK LOOK: Other Central and Sub-Saharan African Conflicts

All the nations of Africa suffer from the same problems of multiculturalism, tribalism, low literacy, poor education, insufficient infrastructure, corruption, inept administration, civil disorder, and a tendency to blame everyone but themselves for their problems. Many Africans are beginning to recognize that something must be done. When the rulers and the people agree on this, some progress is made. But often the ruling groups prefer to go more slowly with reforms than the people. This causes, and will cause, more civil strife and warfare.

Angola—The 1991 cease-fire agreement between the ruling Popular Movement for the Liberation of Angola (MPLA) and Jonas Savimibi's UNITA (National Union for the Total Independence of Angola) broke down after UNITA refused to recognize the MPLA's October 1992 national election victory. The years 1993 and 1994 witnessed a new round of fighting. As of mid-1995 both sides are exhausted. New negotiations on ending twenty-five years of war began. Population growth, desertification, and a war-devastated economy mean that peace will continue to be hell. Nearly 1 percent of the population has been killed or wounded by the millions of mines planted during the war.

Benin—With forty-two different ethnic groups, and nearly as many political parties, Benin manages to make some progress in building its economy.

Burkina Faso—A Libyan-backed government remains in power.

Cameroon—Decades of corruption have brought the economy to the brink of collapse. No one is eager to start a war, as the only one with a steady paycheck is the military.

Côte d'Ivoire (Ivory Coast)—Tried democracy, but the elected politicians are now jiggering the constitution and playing ethnic politics so that they can make their jobs permanent. Corruption and government inefficiency continue.

Congo—This was the part of the "Greater Zaire" that the French snatched. Belgium took the rest of the Congo River basin. Official name: The People's Republic of the Congo. Socialist illusions were kept alive by large oil revenues, the majority of the people (75 percent) tending their subsistence farms out in the bush in physical and political isolation from the urban and better-educated minority living off the foreign exchange. Weak oil prices and ill-conceived and -executed development projects have piled up the foreign debt and domestic discontent. While the Congo looks like a paradise compared with its neighbor Zaire, there is trouble brewing in paradise. A member of the French Union.

CAR—The Central African Republic was once the Central African Empire. This short-lived imperium spent much of one year's GNP on the coronation of the emperor, who was later run out of the country on charges of embezzlement, child abuse, and cannibalism. As the Central African Republic, the nation is not doing much better. Three ethnic groups comprise 75 percent of the small population. With 20 percent literacy, 30 percent unemployment, massive trade deficit, and foreign debt, it remains a sad case. A member of the French Union.

Equatorial Guinea—A one-party country firmly ruled (and largely owned) by government officials. The soldiers are paid well, and on time.

Gabon—Economic problems caused a mass deportation of Mali migrants. That has strained relations with Mali, but internal Gabon politics and social unrest made the attacks on foreigners seem like the lesser of two evils.

Ghana—One military coup too many has brought the population to the brink of civil war.

Guinea—A democracy as of 1993, but still mired in the poverty and bad administration of the past.

Guinea-Bissau—Border skirmishes with Senegal in 1995. Senegal attacked villages in Guinea-Bissau thought to be bases for Senegal rebels.

Kenya—Long a bright spot in Africa, Kenya became a British colony in 1886. Kenya long benefited from trade with Arabs and was anxious to obtain its freedom. A guerrilla movement (the mau-mau) in the 1950s caused the British to free the area in 1963. The first president, Jomo Kenyatta, was one of the great African leaders who produced a golden age of political and economic freedom in Kenya. Kenyatta died in 1978 and was succeeded by Daniel ap Moi, who was more of a standard-issue African head of state. One-party politics, dictatorship, corruption, and economic decline followed. This has made Kenya a likely candidate for civil war. Expect increasing instability.

Liberia—Liberia has an odd political and historical heritage. It was founded by freed American slaves. In 1816, the American Colonization Society was chartered by the U.S. government to help freed slaves return to Africa. The first freed slaves landed at the site of present-day Monrovia in 1822. In 1838 the settlers formed the Commonwealth of Liberia, and in 1847 Liberia became Africa's first independent republic. Liberia eventually claimed 111,000 square kilometers of land. The freed slaves, through the "True Whig" party, became the upper, ruling class in Liberia. Though only 5 percent of the population, the freed slaves' descendants (Americo-Liberians) thoroughly controlled the "tribal" Liberians—until 1980 when Master Sergeant Samuel K. Doe overthrew the government of President William R. Tolbert. Tolbert was executed in a bloody spectacle.

Doe proceeded to dominate the government in much the same manner as the Americo-Liberians. He did this with the support of his tribe, the Krahn. (The Krahn are one of Liberia's smaller tribes.) Since Doe's government favored the Krahn, other tribes began to resent Doe. Doe put many Krahn in important positions in the Armed Forces of Liberia (AFL). Tribal tensions and historical hatreds powered a general dislike of President Doe's corrupt regime and led to rebellion. Civil war broke out in December 1989 when rebel forces (the National Patriotic Front of Liberia, or NPFL) entered Liberia from the Ivory Coast. The NPFL forces, loyal to former Doe aide Charles Taylor, originally consisted of a guerrilla band of only sixty soldiers. Taylor's forces attracted several hundred recruits.

Doe responded by slaughtering tribespeople loyal to Taylor. Liberia collapsed into anarchy. In the summer of 1990, Taylor's forces began to besiege Monrovia. In late July 1990 the NPFL suddenly split apart. Prince Yealu Johnson and 400 soldiers broke away from the NPFL and took over part of Monrovia. Taylor's attempts to take the city, however, were frustrated by the introduction of a 3,500-man peace-keeping force sponsored by the 16-member Economic Community of West African States (acronym ECOWAS). In September 1990, Doe's government fell when he was captured, tortured, and murdered by Prince Yealu Johnson. The war came to a chaotic halt of sorts in 1995. Around 200,000 people were slaughtered in the conflict.

Doe's regime clearly favored his Krahn tribe. Both Johnson's and Taylor's rebel groups (at one time in an alliance) drew strength from the Gio and Mano tribes. (There are fourteen major tribal groups in Liberia, which has made political settlement very difficult. Several have formed their own "rebel militia" to defend themselves. The tribes are: the Kpelle, Bassa, Gio, Kru, Grebo, Mano, Krahn, Gola, Gbandi, Loma, Kissi, Vai, Mandingo, and Belle.)

ECOWAS's Liberian peacekeeping venture may have set an example for future mutual security action in Africa. Though ECOWAS peacekeepers did not create a peace, they did prevent total chaos. For the most part, ECOWAS forces occupied Monrovia, denied Taylor victory, and even installed their own interim Liberian president, Amos Sawyer. In June 1991 a new guerrilla group led by Alhaji Kromach, the United Liberation Movement for Democracy in Liberia (ULIMO), declared war on Sawyer. In 1992, ULIMO split into two factions. The ECOWAS contingent eventually grew a ten-thousand-man army, with Nigeria effectively entering the war as a combatant against Taylor's forces. As of late 1995 seven thousand ECOWAS troops remain. Ethnic hatreds could reignite the war at any moment. This trouble won't go away.

Madagascar—A very poor, and very ethnically mixed (African, Indonesian, and Arab), nation already suffering political unrest and some violence.

Malawi—Another 1990s democracy, but landlocked and very poor.

Mozambique—Nearly two decades of war have made this nation very war-weary. Things should be quiet here for a decade or more as everyone tries to rebuild their shattered lives.

Namibia—Another country at peace largely because the guerrilla war is over. The Namibians are making strenuous efforts to overcome the ethnic differences that typically cause wars and unrest in Africa.

Nigeria—The most populous nation in Africa (around 100 million people as of 1995), Nigeria sees itself as a potential African superpower. Alluding to Brazil, a nation that casts a similar large shadow in South America, Nigerians like to see themselves as the "Brazil of Africa." Such has not been the case. Despite considerable oil wealth, the large population and above-average (for Africa) literacy, Nigeria never took off economically. Corruption and tribal and religious rivalries crippled efforts to build a robust economy and stable society. As was often the case in other African nations, the military took over several times when it became obvious that the elected politicians were ineffective and corrupt. But, again, as has happened elsewhere, the soldiers were no better at running the country. In 1993 popular demands for a return to democracy were turned down by the generals, touching off a political crisis that has not, as of mid-1995, been resolved. Nigeria suffers from the same problems as the rest of Africa and has not been able, thus far, to escape the consequences. But Nigeria already has had one major civil war, when the Ibo people tried to secede and form the Biafran republic (1967–70). What many fear is that the current situation will lead to civil war once more, but on a larger scale.

Rwanda/Burundi—These two nations have much in common. Both lie in the fertile highlands surrounding Lake Victoria. Both are populated largely with Hutu people with a significant Tutsi minority. In the sixteenth century the Tutsi (plural, Watutsi) moved south from their original home in the Sahel. With a different complexion (an important point for the Tutsi) and a foot taller than the local Hutu, it did not take long for the Tutsi to take over and install their own brand of apartheid. The area eventually evolved into two Tutsi-ruled empires, each roughly covering the territory of modern Burundi and Rwanda. In 1899 the Germans moved in and made both areas colonies. The British replaced the Germans in 1916 and passed the area over to the Belgians in the 1920s. It was assumed that when the areas became independent nations, the Hutu (over 80 percent of the population) would run the place. The more aggressive and warlike Tutsi had other ideas, and the Hutu knew it. In 1959 the Hutu of Rwanda rose up against the Tutsi (who held most positions of local power), slaughtered thousands of them, and drove several hundred thousand into exile (mainly in Uganda). Several thousand of these exiles formed an army and attempted a comeback in 1990. This comeback waxed and waned until the Hutu of Rwanda struck back in 1994, slaughtering nearly a million people (Tutsi and Hutus who sympathized with the Tutsi). The Tutsi rebels, better organized and trained than the Hutu, dominated the Rwandan Army, eventually took control of the government as much of the Hutu population fled to refugee camps in Zaire and other neighboring countries.

After 1959, the Tutsi in Burundi took the hint and were successful in repressing the Hutu rebellion that occurred in 1965. With 14 percent of the Burundi population (contrasted with only 9 percent in Rwanda), the Tutsi were numerous, and savage, enough to hold on to their power. Periodic massacres of the Hutu kept that majority people out of power for years. But the ballot, and Hutu numbers, eventually prevailed. By the 1980s, Hutus occupied most senior government positions. But the Hutu-Tutsi animosity remained, and was intensified by the mass murder that took place in neighboring Rwanda in 1994. The Rwanda killings were organized by the Hutu-dominated Rwanda government, and the Tutsi in Burundi fear the same thing might happen to them. The Burundi Hutu saw what happened in Rwanda and are not encouraged. As of late 1995 Burundi remains a nervous standoff with the Tutsi army ready to foil Hutu militants. Several press sources indicate that from 80,000 to 100,000 people died in fighting (or forced starvation) in Burundi in the 1994–95 time frame. Burundi will be a bloodbath before 2001.

Sierra Leone—In 1991 a rebellion by some disgruntled soldiers touched a nerve among many people in this small country adjacent to Liberia. The rebellion could not be put down, partly because the rebels fled into the bush, and partly because other Sierra Leone soldiers were sympathetic to the rebels' demands for "just government." Another military coup in 1992 didn't help matters much and the rebellion grew. By 1995 the entire country was affected. Over 20 percent of the population were refugees and over twenty thousand were dead. The rebels received aid from Libya and Burkina Faso, and other former Sierra

Leone politicians in exile began forming their own armies. Now the Revolutionary United Front (RUF) has joined the war. The RUF doesn't have much of a revolutionary agenda other than eliminating government authority. Sierra Leone's urban elites have gotten rich while the tribes in "the outback" have received few benefits. This, for want of any better theory, explains why yet another nation has fallen into armed anarchy.

Tanzania—More typical of sub-Saharan Africa than Zaire, Tanzania is a one-party state run by the "Revolutionary party." The party, in this case, is superior in legal and de facto power to the government. Not that it matters much, as 90 percent of the population fights a losing battle trying to scrape a living out of an arid landscape. Twenty years of poorly implemented socialism caused the ruling party to loosen things up economically in 1986. That proved an immediate success, although the rate of improvement was so small that it will take a decade or more to make a significant difference. Over a hundred different ethnic groups live in the country; only 1 percent (these being mainly Arab) is not black African. A third of the population is Muslim, mainly near the coast where Arabs have long traded. A third are various Christian denominations and the remainder have traditional (animist, etc.) beliefs. Literacy is high, nearly 80 percent. This, coupled with the government's new economic policies and a growing demand for multiparty democracy, may make the next century a better time for the country.

Tanzania—The new democracy is now faced with politicians playing the ethnic and tribal angles to consolidate power.

Togo—A functioning democracy in 1995, but just barely, as the elected politicians argued over who should have which job and not much legislation got passed. Meanwhile, another military coup is always a possibility.

Uganda—Uganda's long post–Idi Amin civil war has ended. The national government of reconstruction (Yoweri Museveni's National Resistance Movement) is trying to rebuild what was once one of Africa's wealthier exporting economies, but GDP is still below the levels of the early 1970s. Tribalism and trouble between Christians and Muslims remain big problems.

Zambia—Another one-party "democracy" with a failing economy

404 / A QUICK AND DIRTY GUIDE TO WAR

and over sixty different ethnic groups. The price of copper fell through most of the 1980s and local mismanagement did the rest. Democratic elections brought a wave of privatizations (the government owned most major industries) that plunged the economy into chaos (the government-owned industries had been systematically looted).

Zimbabwe—Since 1979, the black majority has ruled over a white minority that still controls most of the economy. A precursor of black rule in South Africa, the outcome has been mixed. While the whites have been allowed to take care of business, the government has turned into a one-party affair with a "president for life." South Africans nervously look on, seeing their future in Zimbabwe's present.

QUICK LOOK: Tribalism and Colonialism

Africa was not a blank slate when the Europeans began showing up four centuries ago. For nearly three thousand years there had been extensive intercourse (economic, cultural, and otherwise) between Caucasians (Arabs and Berbers) in North Africa and the Negro, Nilo-Saharan, and Cushite peoples in the Sahel and farther south. The Arabs were more advanced technologically and that led to various forms of domination over the sub-Saharan peoples. For thousands of years the Arabs have been sending technology, trade goods, and armies south and bringing gold, slaves, and mercenaries back north with them. The black Africans were apt students and, because they always outnumbered the Arabs south of the Sahara, the empires and kingdoms that developed were often run by blacks who had adapted Arab technology and, later, religion (Islam). Out of this developed an antagonism between Arabs and blacks that persists to the present. It was this mélange of Arab and sub-Saharan cultures that greeted the Europeans when they first ventured into Africa. At first, the best the Europeans could do was establish trading posts down the west coast of Africa. The Arabs controlled the east coast and North Africa. It wasn't until European nations conquered the Arab states in North Africa in the nineteenth century that large-scale colonization of Africa took place.

A century earlier the largest European commercial venture in Africa was the cross-Atlantic slave trade. The Arabs had been slaving in sub-Saharan Africa for thousands of years, but because they largely used land routes, only a few thousand blacks were sent north in chains each year. The Western Hemisphere plantations (mostly in the Caribbean and Brazil) were able to take over one hundred thousand slaves a year. The Arab and black kingdoms on the west coast of Africa saw this as a great opportunity. While wars in this area were frequent, and slaves were usually taken (although some tribes, like the Ashanti, used some of their captives for human sacrifices), there was never before a market like the Europeans with their huge sailing ships full of trade goods to exchange for all the slaves the stronger kingdoms could capture. So for over a century the west coast of Africa was in turmoil as the strong tribes raided the weak ones for slaves. Many tribes fled the area for points south, causing ethnic rearrangements that persist to this day.

The Europeans suppressed the slave trade in the early nineteenth century, bringing on a period of prolonged economic depression to the area. This coincided with the European conquest of the Arab states in North Africa and the realization by the Europeans that the only continent left to conquer was Africa. Advances in medicine had now made Africa less lethal for Europeans, so they moved in full-time and in significant numbers. Prior to the better medical care of the nineteenth century, most Europeans would not survive more than a year among the ample tropical diseases of sub-Saharan Africa. Now, with a measure of medical protection, large numbers of Europeans ventured into the heart of Africa.

What they found was the most complex patchwork of tribes, kingdoms, and empires that has ever existed on the planet. Over seven hundred separate languages are spoken in Africa, and over a thousand different ethnic groups exist. In all of Europe at that time there were fewer than a hundred ethnic groups, and most were concentrated in less than a dozen highly organized nation-states. As the British discovered in India, such a multiplicity of different, and often mutually hostile, ethnic groups makes it easier to divide and conquer. Superior weapons helped also. Skin color helped too, as the Arabs were lighter skinned and better armed and had put the fear of pale-faced warriors (with better weapons and organization) into the black Africans. To many black Africans, the Europeans were just another form of Arab.

With few exceptions (the Ashantis and Zulus, for example) the black Africans were unable to put up much meaningful resistance to the European inroads. The European invasion was much more rapid and thorough than the Arab one. In less than a century, most of Africa had been carved up by European colonizers.

Twentieth-century population growth combining with fifteenth-century tribal politics and a veneer of European technology and customs had a strange effect on Africa. Colonialism brought many things, such as education for small numbers of the locals and some infrastructure. Medicines, disease control, and suppression of warfare enabled population to grow rapidly. Similar progress was not made in agriculture or the economy in general. But the most lasting contribution was borders. African kingdoms had existed for thousands of years, but they had always been very temporary affairs. Poor communications in the continent is the main reason for the thousand or so ethnic groups, and the most an able conqueror could expect to do was hold a large area of antagonistic tribes by force of arms for a few decades, or as much as a century if there were a string of good leaders (which was quite rare). The tribes themselves were wont to move around when the action became too uncomfortable, so there was little consciousness that "this land is our land" and all that it entails. The European colonial administrators changed all that. They had surveyors, maps, intrepid explorers, engineers, steamboats, roads, and railroads. The Europeans drew borders on maps, and after they left, the one thing the Africans did not trifle with was those borders, even when they split ethnic groups (which they often did). Naturally, this left several dozen African nations to divide those thousand ethnic groups among themselves. This presents a daunting problem for the Africans. Ethnic antagonisms afflict many nations. Canada, most of Latin America, Russia, India, and Ireland are only some of the examples that pop up in the news frequently. Even the United States, a veritable melting pot compared with most other polyglot countries, is constantly struggling with ethnic disputes. Most African nations have barely begun dealing with the problem. Ironically, South Africa is much farther down the road of planned ethnic accommodation than most other African nations. But, then, South Africa has relatively fewer ethnic groups than most other African nations.

For African nations to move their populations out of medieval economic conditions, they will require technology. After trying, and failing, to adopt a socialist (Russian) -type economy in the last twenty-five years, Africa is now back to the Western model. But this implies a well-educated population, free market economies, efficient government, and a stable political atmosphere. Few of these conditions are present in most African nations. All they have from the colonial experience is a small, educated elite and borders.

QUICK LOOK: The French "Union"

Most of the nations on Africa's west coast, from Senegal to Zaire (plus Djibouti, north of Somalia), are part of a loose economic, commercial, diplomatic, and military union with France. Until 1960 most of these nations were French colonies. Unlike Great Britain, the other big colonizer in Africa, France did not abandon all its many ties to its former colonies. The French were unique in their efforts to integrate the educated elites of these nations into French culture, politics, and commerce. In the 1950s several of these French Africans even served in the French government (by virtue of the colonies electing representatives to the French national legislature). At least among these elites, there was a confidence resulting from French university education and participation in French government that enabled them to eagerly enter into a mesh of treaties and agreements before and after the colonies became independent nations. In addition to some one hundred thousand French citizens continuing to work in the former colonies (in government, military, and commercial sectors), these African nations link their currencies with the French franc and use the French central bank with their own. There is free trade between France and the former colonies as well as a web of commercial arrangements. Since 1960, French troops have intervened more than a dozen times to stymie local coups, rebellions, and, in Chad, foreign invasions. While only 10–20 percent of the people in these nations speak French to any degree, the top 5 percent of the population that comprise the national leadership are thoroughly Francofied. In many cases there are third- and fourth-generation Africans who have grown up speaking French from an early age and obtaining the same education and indoctrination available to the middle and upper classes in France. Some nations that were reluctant to join this French union in 1960 later did so because of the obvious benefits.

The strong French ties with the former colonies have not solved most of the problems these nations, like most others in Africa, have been afflicted with. But there has been a greater degree of political and economic stability. Ironically, Zaire came to the union only in the 1970s. That was because Zaire was a former Belgian colony and France had its hands full initially with its own former colonies. But other nations that were not French colonies are edging toward joining. These relationships with France are not panaceas, but they do provide these still struggling nations with another resource to get them over the numerous problems they continue to encounter.

Zaire signed a military assistance agreement with France in 1974 (as have fifteen other African nations). Six African nations have defense agreements with France (seen as insurance policies by the African heads of state). Mobutu might like such as agreement, but the French would like to see what develops after Mobutu dies or is otherwise removed from the scene.

QUICK LOOK: AIDS in Africa

AIDS may or may not be of African origin. However, tropical areas are the source of more diseases than temperate or arctic areas simply because it's easier for more life-forms to proliferate without the annual onset of freezing weather. For that reason, arctic people (Eskimos, etc.) often find the common cold lethal. The cold germ rarely survives in areas where winter is the longest season. Diseases similar to AIDS began showing up (to Western medical personnel) in the 1960s. That AIDS first spread widely in the West was due largely to a mobile, sexually active homosexual population. AIDS may have existed in parts of Africa for centuries, but was unable to spread because so many isolated populations had no way to pass it on. But things changed in Africa after World War II. Many roads, albeit primitive ones, were built and truck traffic became much more widespread and intense. Fewer Africans lived in total isolation. Globe-trotting Westerners, or equally mobile African elites, may have moved the disease from Africa into the West. Whatever the case, the wildfire spread of AIDS in Africa can be traced to sectors of the population that move around a lot (truck drivers and the small middle class).

Prostitution is widespread and most of these women quickly become infected. Attitudes toward casual sex are different in Africa than in the West, and poor medical care and hygiene, plus certain sexual practices, make it easier for AIDS to spread via heterosexual contact. AIDS is spreading virtually unchecked in Africa, and until recently most African governments had a policy of denying the existence of AIDS within their borders. Huge die-offs in some regions have gotten the attention of the local governments, but there are few resources to treat the disease or its spread.

In the 1990s, AIDS is expected to become a major killer on this continent long noted for its multitude of lethal and disabling diseases. Estimates of over 10 percent infection on the continent and eventual loss of an even higher portion of the population are not unreasonable. AIDS is a relatively silent killer, even though it kills a disproportionate number of relatively affluent people in their prime. Outsiders discover the epidemic in rural African areas only after someone notices the empty villages and untilled fields. Endemic warfare and economic collapse may get most of the attention in Africa, but it's quite likely that AIDS will have the biggest impact for this decade and into the next century. Even if a cure is discovered soon, getting it to the widely dispersed population will not be easy. Some nations will suffer more than others. The nations covered in this chapter are the most affected. South Africa has taken measures to keep the disease out and to control it when it is found within its borders. But South Africa has more resources than the rest of sub-Saharan Africa. For the Heart of Darkness, AIDS may be the ultimate burden.

Part 4
ASIA

With half the planet's population, Asia contains more than half the potential for new wars of unprecedented savagery. Nuclear weapons, massive armies, civil discord, ethnic rivalries, and dynamic economic growth make for an explosive mixture.

Chapter 10

CHINA—WAITING FOR CHANGE, WAITING FOR THE NEXT EXPLOSION

INTRODUCTION

China has awakened quickly. A creaky, sleepy (large and Communist) molehill in the mid-1970s, by the mid-1990s China has become a political and economic volcano (large and authoritarian) in the throes of grand eruption. What finished the dormant state? In the mid-1980s, the government relaxed the economic chains of central planning and control and let loose a chain reaction of development. That brought forth annual double-digit economic growth. Relaxed economic chains (and new prosperity) also brought forth calls for democracy. Wealth also whetted the Chinese military's taste for power.

The Communist party has resisted demands that it share governmental power. But the aging and infirm central party apparatus is increasingly unable to control the spurting economy. The Chinese succession crisis—moving from the aged Long March leaders to a younger generation—may be the world's biggest international relations issue in the 1996–2001 era. If the change goes smoothly, other

413

crises will have the headlines. If change goes badly, the entire world could go tilt.

China's military is also changing. The Fourth Modernization, military modernization, is under way. Beijing is building new missiles. Aircraft carriers may be on the buy list. As China's military power expands, so does its need for world respect. The South China Sea and the Spratly Islands are now in China's "sphere of influence." Taiwan's independence movement presents a special challenge. Ultra-nationalists (many in the military) see an independent Taiwan as prelude to further Chinese political fragmentation. War over Taiwan is possible, especially if Beijing practices armed intimidation. However, Beijing's and Taipei's many mutual, profitable economic interests reduce the likelihood.

Internal migration presents Beijing with another colossal problem. As the economy grows, many Chinese are moving from the countryside to the cities. More than 100 million peasants, between 1990 and 1995, left China's interior and moved to the prosperous coastal cities. Mega-cities like Shanghai and Canton are rapidly becoming twenty-first century economic giants. Economic power may increase their taste for local political power.

As far as Beijing is concerned (particularly the military), lurking in the shadows of regional differences in economic growth is the specter of increasing regionalism. In the past, regions going their separate ways meant warlords. And warlords, in Chinese history, meant "more time of troubles."

SOURCE OF CONFLICT

China is on the verge of another revolution, this one caused by a failed Communist regime's inability to transform itself into a more accommodating system that can satisfy (and shape) China's growing economic and political needs. This would be China's third revolution in the twentieth century (not counting minor revolts, invasions, and sundry purges). In 1900, China was ruled by a feudal nobility; a "republican" (Kuomintang) dictatorship had nominal rule through World

War II and the 1940s; and a Communist dictatorship, with varying degrees of Marxist orthodoxy but an invariant reliance on military control, has ruled the mainland since 1949.

The Chinese road to more responsive and democratic government has been a story of many opportunities and many failures. In 1919 students marched through the capital calling for "democracy and science." In 1989 the students marched again, this time in ill-fated Tiananmen Square, appealing for just democracy. Contemporary China has wrenched itself out of the seventeenth century as far as science and technology goes. But the people must still kowtow to the officials as their ancestors have done for thousands of years. The statist system of government in China has not changed, despite republican revolutionaries and Communists, but the attitudes and desires of many of the Chinese people have.

While the Chinese economy was growing at unheard-of rates in the 1980s and 1990s, Russia's was slipping further into terminal decline. In 1985, the Soviet (i.e., Russian) Communist party installed a reform government, which promptly called for greater openness, democracy, and, more important, restructuring of the economy. But where the Chinese had radically changed their economy by allowing entrepreneurs and free enterprise, the Russians merely wanted to make the centrally planned economy work more efficiently.

The differences between the Russian and Chinese approach to reviving their societies had a greater (and much more positive) economic effect on the Chinese. In less than twenty years, China has made astounding economic progress. The number of people living in absolute poverty (bare subsistence, i.e., scarcely able to feed themselves) has fallen from over 200 million to under 100 million. Nearly 100 million people, mainly in the urban areas, have entered the consumer economy, able to buy household appliances, electronic gadgets, fast food, and, for nearly 300,000 of them, automobiles. On the downside, the privatization of some state industries and the increased productivity of agriculture have created as many as 100 million unemployed. Many of these have moved to the urban areas looking for work. Some have found it; others, the government fears, may resort to violent protest to get attention.

While the Chinese enjoyed the benefits of their growing, free enterprise economy, many people also sought to transfer these free enterprise concepts to the way the country was governed. They wanted democracy, which they saw the Russian people getting in the form of free elections. This was more in line with historical precedent. In the past, kings and emperors first allowed economic freedom and then had to grant political freedom to the newly enriched entrepreneurial groups.

Russia has always looked westward. The Chinese, particularly the leadership, tended to look to themselves. It was the "Middle Kingdom syndrome"—China as the center of the world. Democracy was an alien concept that interfered with the smooth flow of government control from top to bottom. The Chinese people increasingly saw that they had thrown off one set of nobles for another. The new Communist rulers were becoming as corrupt and inefficient as the old order.

China's overwhelmingly rural and agrarian society added another difficulty. The revolutions usually began in the cities and among the ruling and/or educated classes. The twentieth century had brought with it the need for universities to educate the millions of highly trained Chinese experts needed to run a modern, technological economy. But these students learned more than technical skills. They learned about power, and how to get it. Students were the vanguard of the first revolution earlier in the century. That revolution was led by individuals who had received Western-style university educations. They wanted democracy, or at least more freedom to pursue their own economic goals.

The students did not have guns, but they did have stature among the people. The Chinese had long respected education, as it had always been a way for even the humblest peasant child, at least in theory, to move into the aristocratic Mandarin civil service. The modern students were more numerous and saw themselves as heirs to this meritocracy tradition. Moreover, the chaos of the Red Guard revolution of the 1960s had virtually shut down the universities and eliminated a generation of college graduates. The students of the 1980s knew they were China's future, and they wanted a say in it now.

But the students in 1989 also knew, or at least some of them did, that the masses of Chinese people rarely rise up in rebellion, although when they do the result is catastrophe. Changes usually come when factions of the ruling classes reorganize themselves and play a complex political game the Chinese play so well. The 1989 student and urban worker demonstrations persuaded some of the Chinese leadership that democracy might be worth trying, or that they might eventually have little choice but to go democratic. But the majority of the Communist aristocracy was not persuaded. For a combination of reasons both personal (losing their power) and ideological (some still believed in the current version of socialism), the government replied with guns and violence.

The suppression of the 1989 uprisings merely laid the foundation for the next round of unrest. And there will be a next round. Any student of Chinese history can see the familiar pattern. As if to play into this ancient pattern, the Communist government cracked down on economic freedom after 1989, thus threatening the recent well-being of many farmers and rural entrepreneurs. These people remained neutral in 1989, as they so often do when the students erupt. In 1990 the government backed down on their suppression of economic reforms. They knew that the next round of unrest could include rural people. The bulk of the conscript troops are from outside the cities. Their loyalty was touch and go in 1989, and it was difficult finding soldiers who would do the dirty work. Military support could evaporate the next time around.

The next round of conflict could easily bring to the fore the regional differences within China. The wealthiest cities of China's coast could end up fighting with the peasants of China's still-impoverished interior. Although most Chinese are of the same ethnic group (Han Chinese), they speak several different (and mutually incomprehensible) versions of Chinese. Local customs, and loyalties, vary considerably from one region to another. Civil war could reoccur. Many of the warlords of the millennium will have access to nuclear weapons, and all will possess large quantities of conventional arms.

The 1989 unrest gave pause to the younger reformers. They realized that the old revolutionaries, while elderly, intended to fight for power.

WHO'S INVOLVED

Mainland China—Not just the Communist regime in Beijing. Mainland China divides into geographic regions and economic interest groups. Each province has its own local Communist party, army, and commercial (state-owned firms) bureaucracy. The provinces (or groups of provinces) are increasingly deviating from Beijing's lead.

Old guard Communist leadership—Deng Xiaoping and the other Long Marchers (who made the legendary six-thousand-mile retreat that saved the Chinese Communists in 1934) are finally fading. Their legacy of hard authoritarian leadership remains.

Chinese economic technocrats—Many of the new breed long ago

forsook ideology for capitalism. They are fast becoming the new power brokers in China's economically progressive regions. Many of these have university and/or technical training. They see the progress other Asian nations have made and don't want China to lose out. This is the generation of university graduates that came out of school in the late 1970s, after the universities had been closed because of Mao's Cultural Revolution. They have seen the dark side of communism and revolution, and don't want to see it again.

Chinese armed forces—Some 2.6 million troops; half are professionals, the rest conscripts. The leadership is finally getting its new weapons. It is also making money. The nightclub in Shanghai is built on army-owned land (and speculation has it the club is actually owned by senior military officers). NORINCO (Northern Chinese Industries), the Chinese arms manufacturer, is essentially controlled by the army. The armed forces may own as many as twenty thousand different companies. Estimated profit in 1993: $5 billion. The frosting on the cake: From 1992 to 1994, China's military spending increased by an average of 17 percent a year.

Overseas Chinese—For centuries, Chinese have gone abroad to seek a better life. In most cases, they did not adopt the language and culture of their new country. They spoke the local language as a second language. They still looked upon China as their nation. One of the few exceptions to this was the United States. There are over 50 million overseas Chinese, although by Chinese reckoning, there are fewer than 25 million. (The official Beijing count assumes that Taiwan and Hong Kong are part of China proper.) The overseas Chinese can be a source of international friction. Overseas Chinese are often highly successful economically and invite resentment from the non-Chinese local national majority. That is particularly true in Malaysia; there the ethnic antagonism is exacerbated by the fact that until the mid-1980s the Malays were battling a Chinese-backed Communist insurgency. China could act to protect overseas Chinese communities in Asia. Aside from several million Chinese scattered in many other nations, the principal concentrations of overseas Chinese are Taiwan (22 million), Thailand (8 million), Hong Kong (6 million), Malaysia (6 million), Indonesia (3 million), Singapore (2 million), Vietnam (2 million), U.S. (2 million), Philippines (1 million).

Taiwan—Taiwan has often been outside the mainland's control. Despite economic "convergence" with China, many Taiwanese now see themselves as "different"—and democratic. This riles Beijing's nationalists, who may seek "reunification" via arms. Taiwan, however, has a solid military and, as of 1995, $90 billion in currency reserves—enough to buy its own nuke, perhaps?

Vietnam—At times, Vietnam has been a province of China, but more often Vietnam simply acknowledged China as its "elder brother" and maintained its independence. There has always been a significant ethnic Chinese minority in Vietnam. These Chinese are often merchants and just as often resented by the Vietnamese. Many of these Chinese were expelled from Vietnam in the late 1970s (the first "boat people"). Relations with China continue to be tense.

The Koreas—Like Vietnam, Korea has long been a vassal state of China. The Koreans have historically been more successful at keeping the Chinese out, or at least at arm's length. That is largely because Korea is between China and Japan, and these two nations have been threatening each other for several centuries.

Hong Kong—A relic of the nineteenth-century European incursions into China, the prosperous British colony reverts to Chinese control in 1997. That is a mixed blessing. The British ran the four-hundred-square-mile, six-million-population colony like an economic enterprise. There was no democracy, but there was ample economic freedom and access to world markets.

Russia—Although technically they are friendly neighbors, and, after the collapse of the Soviet Union, more energetic trading partners, relations between Russia and China continue to be tense—and could be violent.

India and Pakistan—The border with India is an obscure and out-of-the-way frontier. This did not prevent a minor war between India and China in the early 1960s (see Extended Look: India). The disputed Sino-Indian territory is also part of the province of Kashmir, which has been (and is) one of the causes of several wars between Pakistan and India. This ongoing Kashmir dispute was a major cause of India becoming an ally and trading partner of Russia and Pakistan allying itself with China. But that's not all. The Chinese province bordering on India in Kashmir is largely Muslim, and the Chinese-dominated

Muslims have always been restive, putting Muslim Pakistan on the spot if their fellow Muslims in China call upon other Muslim nations for aid. China won the border war with India in 1962 and continues to occupy the disputed territory.

Tibet—Invaded by China in 1950 (as happened several times in past centuries) and increasingly restive. Tibet further complicates relations with India. India opposed the Chinese occupation of Tibet in the 1950s and India still supports the Tibetan rebels.

GEOGRAPHY

China is a large country (9.6 million square kilometers), slightly larger than the United States. It is the third largest country in the world in land area (after Russia and Canada). China shares 24,000 kilometers of border with North Korea, Russia, Kazakhstan, Afghanistan, Pakistan, India, Nepal, Bhutan, Myanmar, Laos, and Vietnam. Around 90 percent of the people live in eastern China. Coastal regions contain some of the most productive farmland in the world. Most of northeast China is flat farmland, producing various grains. The southeast portion is more rugged, with its highland farms producing rice on terraces. Most of western China is either desert (in the north) or mountainous Tibet (in the south, and the mountains in Tibet are the Himalayas). Yunan and Guangxi provinces (by Vietnam) reach into the tropical zone.

It's a geopolitical reality: China is held together by three great river systems that travel from west to east and empty into the Yellow Sea (the Yellow River), and the East China Sea (Yangtze and Yu Hsi rivers). Each of these rivers supports enormous populations along their banks, in the river valleys, and, near the coast, on the river flood plains. Climate in the north is similar to the New England region of the United States. Southern China is subtropical (similar to Florida). Western China has mountains, arid plains, and several local climates that are unique. In general, China has a collection of local climates quite similar to the United States.

China had a 1995 population of 1.3 billion—by far the world's largest. Ninety-three percent of the population is Han Chinese. The remaining 7 percent includes some 18 million Zhuangs, 9 million Huis, 8 million Uygurs, 7 million Yu, 7 million Miao, 5 million Manchus, 4.5 million Tibetans, 4 million Mongols, 2 million Koreans, and dozens of other small ethnic groups. Standard Chinese or Mandarin (*putonhua,* based on the Beijing dialect) is the national language. Language, however, is a cause of division. While the Chinese written language can be read by all literate Chinese, the differences among regional dialects (spoken Chinese) are enormous. Major dialects include Yue (Cantonese), Minbei (Fuzhou), Minnan (Hokkien-Taiwanese), Xiang, Gan, and Hakka. Most government officials, especially senior officials, can speak Mandarin. Many others can speak some Mandarin, but many Chinese in rural areas speak a dialect that is mutually incomprehensible with Mandarin. Bottom line: China does not share a common language.

Taoism and various forms of Buddhism are practiced by a large majority of the Chinese (90-plus percent)—even by many Communists. Approximately 3 percent of the Chinese population is Muslim and 1 percent Christian. Confucianism (strictly speaking, not a religion but a system of family and social values) is practiced by nearly all Chinese. Long condemned (unsuccessfully) by the Communists, Confucian values are now praised by the aging Communist leadership. That is not surprising, as Confucius preached respect for one's elders and rulers.

HISTORY

China possesses one of the world's oldest civilizations, and—with few arguments—perhaps the longest "continuous human civilization" on the planet. While suffering several major invasions, China has managed to absorb (demographically, culturally, linguistically) its invaders, suffering few permanent changes in the process.

What is now thought of as "Chinese civilization" began to evolve in northern China over five thousand years ago and slowly spread among the nearby Oriental peoples. Only geographic and climactic extremes "contained" Chinese influence: the frozen wilderness to the north, deserts to the west, and jungle, and disease, to the south. Within those confines, what we know as modern China coalesced long before Rome ever got the notion of an empire.

From antiquity, China developed a feudal society directed by the usual gang of powerful nobles. What made a huge difference in the strength and resiliency of Chinese feudalism was the institutionalization of a highly educated civil service. The civil service was open to the sons of the poorest peasants—as long as they were intellectually gifted. As the system evolved, the rigorous civil service tests focused on the nuances of Chinese poetry and aesthetics—the deep traditions of Chinese arts. This system, the "Mandarin system," provided efficient, consistent, and remarkably capable government over the centuries. Unfortunately, it was also a very static system, focused on maintaining an imperial center, rooted in Confucian (mutual obligation, respect for authority and tradition) doctrine. Innovation came slowly, although often efficiently. When the Europeans began to develop numerous technological innovations, and apply them on a large scale, China found itself unable to cope with the speed and power of the European challenge.

In 1644 the Manchus overthrew the Ming dynasty. They established the Ch'ing (or Qing) dynasty and made their capital in Beijing. Competition from the technologically superior West, however, was fierce and even the militarily capable Manchus were ill prepared.

China's encounter with Western civilization was a humiliating experience for the Middle Kingdom. (For the Chinese have always maintained, and largely still do, that their culture is the central one on the planet: a Middle Kingdom surrounded by lesser realms.)

By the nineteenth century, the Europeans arrived with their big ships, big guns, and big ideas about trade and began picking China apart. But even industrialized, and well-armed, Europeans were unable, and unwilling, to try conquering a nation as vast and populous as China. They would, however, snip off parts. The Opium War (1840–42) gave Great Britain and other Western nations special rights in five treaty ports along the Chinese coast.

A mid-nineteenth-century revolution, the Tai-Ping Rebellion, led by a low-born Chinese claiming to be the brother of Jesus Christ, weakened China more than all of that era's Western military activity. The failed Tai-Ping Rebellion killed nearly twenty million Chinese and left the traditional Chinese empire ripe for a more far-reaching revolution in the twentieth century.

The brief war with the technologically superior Japanese (1894–95) brought further social and psychological devastation. Then the so-called Boxer Rebellion (1900) brought imperial China to a low point, when a coalition of foreign forces entered Beijing and put down an anti-Western, anti-Christian rebellion by Chinese secret societies.

In 1911, China's "liberal democratic" revolution occurred, led by Western-educated Chinese intellectuals. Their ideas were not really so liberal and democratic as much as based on introducing modern technological and social reforms. The intellectuals saw themselves as modern Mandarins, leading the Chinese masses to a future where China would again be strong and once more the Middle Kingdom, now on a worldwide scale.

But China fell prey to another common pattern in its history: civil war and regions falling under the control of independent warlords. As united as China has been through the centuries, the unity was maintained largely through Mandarins backed up by effective armies (which military-minded Mandarins would sometimes lead). In the twentieth century, power once again devolved to the different regions.

Two major forces emerged as the optimistic 1920s lurched into the worldwide depression of the 1930s. The original 1911 revolutionary party, the Kuomintang (KMT), now led by the young, able, resourceful, and ruthless Chiang Kai-shek, ran into another revolutionary movement—the Communists.

Russia went Communist after World War I. By the early 1920s the false liberalism and genuine militancy of communism was catching on with ardent young Chinese students, in particular a young librarian and poet named Mao Tse-tung. The Communists saw the KMT as the party of revolution from above. The Communists wanted revolution from below. The KMT sought to win over the most powerful groups in China, including the landowners and commercial magnates. The Communists wanted to kill the rich and rebuild China from scratch. Chinese peasants, however, were not as revolutionary in their thinking as the Communist elites. The KMT was on its way toward eradicating the Communists when, in the early 1930s, Japan began a series of invasions, taking the Rising Sun ever deeper into China.

The Japanese attempt to conquer China, piece by piece, eventually brought the United States into World War II. In 1945 both Japan and China lay in ruins from the ravages of the war. The Chinese claim that thirty-five million of their people died during the Japanese invasion. The Communists had grown strong on their promise (and occasional action) to fight the Japanese. By 1949, the Communists had defeated the KMT and driven them to Taiwan. Russian willingness to aid the Chinese Communists was decisive in the 1945–49 civil war. The Chinese repaid the debt when they sent millions of troops to Korea to fight the Americans after a Russian-inspired invasion of U.S.-backed South Korea failed. The Chinese suffered a million casualties.

Mao Tse-tung and his Communist government faced two major problems in the 1950s. First, there was the need to get the economy going. Second, there were the Russians. The problem with Russia was that it was a neighbor of China and had participated, with the other European powers, in the nineteenth-century plundering of China. Russia had even annexed large tracts of Chinese territory. The Russian (Communist or non-Communist) government saw no reason to return the Chinese territory the czarist Russian government had seized. The Russians were also Occidentals, and despite the cries of universal brotherhood, they still looked down upon Orientals in general, and made no exception for their Chinese "brothers." In the same spirit, the Chinese looked down on all Occidentals, and especially the Russians.

The Chinese resented the Russians and were suspicious of Russian motives. By 1959, the two nations broke their economic ties. That was a high price for the Chinese to pay, but Mao convinced his cohorts that there was no other way. China would go it alone, as it always had. China would succeed. China would once more become the Middle Kingdom, but with the Mandate of Marx instead of the Mandate of Heaven.

Mao's cruel techniques for building a new China failed. An estimated sixty million Chinese died as a result of various Communist schemes. Mao's frustration culminated in the Cultural Revolution of 1966–75. Mao intended to use the "revolution" to destroy all vestiges of China's cultural past. If China was to be modern, then everything must change. He unleashed millions of students in an orgy of destruction and civil unrest. Eventually, Mao ran out of support. Teenagers can wreck a country, but they can't fix it or run it. By 1970 the Cultural Revolution was in eclipse and by 1975 it was just one more bitter memory of failure. In 1976, Mao died, and a new set of "pragmatic" leaders took over.

While the Communists succeeded in eliminating non-Communist parties in the late 1940s, they found themselves divided over what to do about Russia and its technical aid. There had always been pro- and anti-Russian factions in the Chinese Communist party. The anti-Russian group was stronger and eventually had their way in the late 1950s. That dispute out of the way, the Communists then divided over how to modernize China. The radicals (led by party leader Mao Tse-tung himself) wanted to totally transform Chinese society. The pragmatists (supported by the bulk of the leadership) wanted more flexibility. Mao had his way for a while, made a mess of things, and in the 1970s, the pragmatists took over. Then came the split between the economic pragmatists and the political pragmatists. The latter group realized that the political process in the nation had to be opened up as well as the economic process. This problem was made worse when democracy broke out in Russia and Eastern Europe.

Democracy has few roots in China. A culture that stressed obedience to authority and the long existence of an efficient governing civil service made it more difficult for the current Communist party authorities to give up their power.

While 80 percent of China's people still lived in farming communities, the remaining 260 million were urban and they wanted no part of the Mandarin past. Even if imperfectly understood, the urban population wanted democracy, or at least more personal freedom, and the rural population was not against it. But it is very important to remember that the rural population puts economic issues far ahead of political ones. The farmers are pragmatic, very conservative, and not at all swayed by slogans.

The economic reforms begun in the late 1970s have shaken every institution in China to its very foundations. While the increase in prosperity has been striking, so has the social cost. With some 600 million workers, unemployment and large disparities in wealth threaten to unravel Chinese society. Some 60 percent of the workforce is still on the farm and their income has stagnated since 1985. After an initial jump in productivity, farm income leveled off because there wasn't much more efficiency to be extracted from an agricultural system that still depended on large numbers of workers, small plots, and often marginal land. Capital investment in infrastructure and machinery has also fallen, from 6 percent of national investments in 1981 to 1 percent in 1993. Putting this money into urban industrial enterprises has been more attractive and the farmers have suffered for it. But the farmers have not suffered in silence. Still beset by a bureaucracy often as venial, corrupt, and oppressive as that of the landlords the Communists destroyed in the 1940s, rebellion has become more common in the countryside. In the mid-1990s, there were reports in the Chinese press of nearly a thousand uprisings (often just mob attacks) a year, each involving at least 500 people. A few percent of these involved thousands of desperate farmers—not a great deal of ruckus for a rural population of over 800 million people, but indicative of brewing trouble in the countryside. The Communist party bureaucrats lost much of their power and access to wealth when the farmers were allowed to own their land and work it as they pleased. Many (over 100 million) farmers have voted with their feet and drifted into the urban areas looking for work. That has taken a lot of heat off the rural officials and transferred the problem to the cities.

Switching from state-owned enterprises to private ownership of companies caused another problem often encountered when converting a Communist economy to a free market. Not all the state-run activities can be changed quickly. The most productive state companies switch rapidly to private ownership; the government continues to subsidize the most uncompetitive ones. By the early 1990s there were still over 100 million workers in some 100,000 state-owned firms. By 1995 a third were still losing money. To cover losses, more than half of the cash available for investment was gobbled up in subsidies. Not wanting to simply print more money, and cause a lot of inflation that would upset the entire population, the government sought investment capital from overseas. That brought more foreign money into the country, but also more foreigners and foreign ideas. The government was reluctant to shut down the remaining state enterprises. Unemployment was becoming an increasing problem, and dumping tens of millions more workers on the street was considered political suicide. The Communist rulers of China have pinned their hopes on the growing private sector, hoping that these firms can create enough jobs and tax revenue to solve the investment capital and unemployment problems before those problems get out of hand. But the private sector firms, and the local governments that they work closely with, want more independence from central control. Thus the Communists have to struggle with economic and political problems as the new business class becomes more aware of their power, and how to use it.

Further complicating domestic politics are the regional loyalties. These have become a problem despite strenuous efforts by the nationwide Communist party membership. As the original revolutionary cadres got older, more comfortable, and more corrupt, the local officials began to form regional associations. New, local economic opportunities hastened this process. (The Communist party is a recent development; regional loyalties and local commerce go back thousands of years. Regional loyalties are more attractive, profitable, and real.) Against their better judgment, the Communist party leadership used regional differences to put down the workers and students during the 1989 Beijing demonstrations. The Beijing-based troops refused to fire on the students. Troops from other regions were brought in to do the deed. That solved the immediate problem, but at the cost of regional antipathy. Regional tensions have torn China apart in the past, and the strife often began when troops from one region were brought in to control the inhabitants of another region.

The Chinese Communists have consistently used the regional differences to keep non-Chinese portions of China in line. The major examples have been Tibet and the Muslim areas of the western portions of the country. The Tibetans and Muslims have not responded well to this oppression, and the ethnic Chinese won't either.

The regional loyalties have been exploited by the army, which divides the nation into seven military regions and twenty-eight military districts, which roughly correlate with the province boundaries. While the provincial governors have money, the region commanders have money, from their own business and corruption enterprises, and guns. If it ever comes down to a dispute between provincial and central authority, the governors will have to ally with the regional military commander to survive.

In the years after Mao's death, communism, at least in many parts of the economy, was replaced with free enterprise. Deng led the economic reorganization. The economy began to boom, particularly in the countryside where 80 percent of China's population still lived and worked. But in the 1990s, growth has shifted from the rural areas to the cities. And at least half of the rural population were too poor or out of the way to benefit from the initial economic liberalization. The rapid growth of the Chinese economy has created haves and have-nots. The latter comprise about two thirds of the population and are a potential source of social unrest.

China's support for North Vietnamese Communists in the Vietnam War was its last major attempt to spread the Communist creed by force of arms. In 1979, China and a united Vietnam fought each other (China suffered twenty thousand casualties in the three-week brawl). During the 1980s, peace was made with everyone, including the Russians. Diplomatic relations had been resumed with America in 1972, partially to provide some additional protection against the Russians. China seemed on its way to a bright future when, unexpectedly, democracy struck.

Economic liberalization has not translated into political liberalization. The prodemocracy demonstrations of 1989 were brutally suppressed and for a while the economic liberalization was reined in. But the grumbling of poor Chinese led to a loosening of economic controls once more in 1990, and most Chinese settled in to wait for the old-time revolutionaries to die before trying once more for democracy, or at least a Chinese interpretation of this alien practice. What worries many inside and outside of China is that the new leaders will be as reluctant to share power with the people as hundreds of previous generations have been.

LOCAL POLITICS

The Chinese Communist party—Survived hardships at the hands of the nationalists and Japanese in the 1920s and 1930s. Grew stronger during World War II and, with Russian assistance, defeated the Nationalists by 1949. Over sixty million real or imagined opponents (or simply people who got in the way) died while the party consolidated its rule. Party leader since the 1920s, Mao Tse-tung ordered several disastrous policies in an attempt to industrialize, culminating in the Red Guard movement of the late 1960s. In this last operation, the several million key Communist party members (the "cadres") were often the victims. In 1976, Mao died, but many of the original leaders were now back in control and determined to keep control in the future. In doing so, the majority of the people began to resent what appeared to be the development of a privileged class that was bent on making itself hereditary.

The democracy movement—A loose term for a growing number of Chinese desiring a democratic form of government. Largely from the educated classes and the urban workers. The movement is slowly spreading into the countryside as the farmers realize that their economic gains of the 1980s can easily be taken away by unelected Communist bureaucrats. This is not a "democracy" movement in the Western sense, as most Chinese have only a vague idea of what the rights and obligations of democracy entail. China has never been a democracy and most Chinese are more intent on economic freedom than political opportunity.

The "princes"—The children of the senior Communist officials who abused (or simply used) their privileged position at the heart of government power, often in an embarrassingly public fashion. Not a large group in numbers, and many of these people used their advantages to good effect. But those who abused their position caused a great deal of dissatisfaction and are used as a symbol of the need for change. The situation has become increasingly acute as China's economy, liberated from central control and state ownership, but not supported by an adequate legal or regulatory system, provides ample opportunity for those with connections at the highest levels to sell their access to the few people who can make binding decisions in the government. When their parents' generation passes from the scene, these "princes" will lose much of their power, but not all of it, and none of their desire to keep what they have.

The farmers—The largest constituency in the country, as 80 percent of the population still lives in the countryside and most of them are engaged in farming. About half the farmers did very well because of the policies of the 1980s that allowed farmers to operate their land as a business enterprise. However, many of these farmers have lost ground in the 1990s as economic activity has been increasingly concentrated in the urban areas. But all of these farmers now have something to lose. In learning to operate independently, they weakened the control and influence of the local Communist party cadres. The farmers who did not improve their lot provide a growing mass of unemployed or desperate Chinese. If nothing else, the farmers have the numbers, and a common culture grounded in hundreds of generations tilling the soil.

The *nomenklatura*—This is a Russian term for the list of key officials; those who hold crucial positions, wield considerable power, and are rewarded with many privileges. The Chinese Communists took this concept over from the Russians, although the Chinese version was influenced by the memories of the ancient Chinese Mandarin civil service. This *nomenklatura* "officialdom" is nearly as old as China. But many of the current officials have their jobs more for their doctrinal purity than for their professional skills. The ancient Mandarin system, where only one in a hundred of those taking civil service examinations would pass, was suppressed by the Communists. Many people currently holding key positions do so because of their loyalty to the Communist party, and its current leaders, and not because of how well they discharge their duties. These officials have become increasingly corrupt. This is ironic, as the Communists initially won popular support in the 1930s and 1940s by offering honest administration of government functions.

The urban workers—Oddly enough, these workers (blue-collar and white-collar) are generally supporters of democracy, or at least more personal opportunities, even though they have suffered from the loosening of the Communist controls on the economy during the 1980s. Unlike the farmers, the urban workers initially had few opportunities to participate in a free market, except to buy more abundant, and more expensive, goods. This the urban workers must do on fixed, and relatively low, salaries. However, the workers are finding new, and better, employment opportunities at the increasing number of privately owned firms. Moreover, there are many urban entrepreneurs, most of whom came from the ranks of the urban workers. Note that, unlike the United States, only a few percent of eighteen-year-olds get into a university. Many bright and capable potential students go straight to the workforce. Many of them apparently feel their economic prospects would brighten under a democratic government. These workers are aware of the greater opportunities available to people their age in neighboring nations like Singapore, Taiwan, Japan, and South Korea. While the farmers in the poor portions of the countryside see little cause for optimism, the urban population sees plenty of examples all around them, and the more energetic of their number take advantage of these opportunities. This group also has the numbers in the urban centers, where a large demonstration can have enormous impact.

People's Liberation Army (PLA)—Official name of the army and armed forces. The final arbiter of political disputes and a growing industrial force, the PLA runs its own system of factories and other enterprises. The core of the armed forces, which is largely the army, is about half a million officers and NCOs. About half the troops are conscripts. The professional officers and NCOs see themselves as a class apart, as soldiers have always seen themselves in China. The rest of the People's Liberation Army, however, is a bit different. Unlike all previous Chinese armies, the PLA is touted as one that identifies more with the people than the national, or regional, leadership. It was this philosophy that caused so much trouble during the disturbances in 1989. As these political actions involved hundreds of thousands of "people," it was difficult to get the troops of the PLA to act. Eventually, troops were found (PAP troops, see below, from outside the Beijing region) who were willing to shoot demonstrators in Beijing. The morale and loyalty problems arising from this action continue to trouble the leadership and troops of the People's Army, and the national leadership. The army has sought to solve these problems by going into business, turning many troops into employees of commercial enterprises or using army clout and resources to set up factories and other money-making firms. Thus, while the troops may not have an emotional attachment to their officers, they do have a financial one. In China, more people want to get rich than want to die for democracy. Dollars and yuan also speak to the generals. The People's Armed

Police (PAP) has special security divisions of politically reliable troops used to control any popular unrest. Two PAP divisions now occupy Beijing. Only the PLA can counter the PAP if the police lose control. The Second Artillery Corps is China's strategic missile force (the folks controlling China's nuclear-armed missiles). Whoever controls this group controls more than China.

The overseas Chinese—The overseas Chinese maintain commercial as well as cultural contacts with the old country. The overseas Chinese are a potential source of skills and capital. (For the last twenty years, the overseas Chinese have been a key element in rebuilding a market economy in China.) While mainland China was Communist from the 1940s through the 1980s, most overseas Chinese were staunchly capitalist. But before communism came to China, it was first picked up by overseas Chinese studying in European universities. Overseas Chinese have long been the messengers who brought foreign ideas to the Middle Kingdom.

The provinces—While China has maintained its unity as a nation over the centuries, the various provinces have still retained distinct customs and languages. In the north, Mandarin is spoken, while in the south, several versions of Cantonese are used. In the west, the central Asian peoples speak a variety of non-Chinese languages. On all border areas there are also a number of non-Chinese languages spoken. These provincial differences become important during times of civil disorder, when some provinces attempt to become independent. Northern China has long been the center of the Chinese Middle Kingdom and the emperors who ruled from there. But for all that time, Chinese subjects outside of northern China were fond of saying, "The mountains are high and the emperor is far away," to justify ignoring unwelcome commands from the central government.

PARTICIPANT STRATEGIES AND GOALS

The Chinese Communist party—State socialism doesn't work for the economy and, as events in the late 1980s demonstrated, doesn't hold the people in line either. But not all Communist parties were willing to concede these points and the Chinese Communist party was one of them. The Chinese Communists do have the advantage of an ancient Chinese tradition of autocratic rule. But this is unable to keep a modern economy going (which was why modern democracy developed in the first place). The Party is faced with an almost impossible situation. Unless they can placate the groups (students, entrepreneurs, etc.) needed to get the economy going, conditions will deteriorate and unrest will continue to grow. Using deadly force to clear demonstrators out of Beijing made it difficult, although not impossible, to achieve some form of compromise. Note that most of the executions in the wake of the 1989 crackdown were of workers, not students. Workers don't become future leaders, students do. The Party can also rely on another Chinese trait, nonviolent compromise and change of government. This occurred in the wake of Mao Tse-tung's demise and could happen again. Many of the young democracy enthusiasts of 1989 freely admit that they took one look at the army's savage repression and decided they could wait for some political freedom. During the 1980s, and especially after the events of 1989, the Communists began to rehabilitate the memory of Confucius. This was in marked contrast to policy under Mao and especially during the Cultural Revolution. The philosophy of Confucius stressed the duties of leaders and followers and the need to "listen to the people." The Communists also showered praise on the capitalistic, and authoritarian, government of Singapore. All this in apparent recognition that it is unlikely that the current Communist party will continue in power to the degree it did in the past. The last of the original Chinese Communists are about to die off. These men have tenaciously held on to power, if not the Communist ideology of their youth, as they grew into their dotage. But the next generation knows that their hold on power depends on how well they can emulate their predecessors in maintaining a Communist party monopoly on power. What appears to be happening is a replay of an ancient Chinese practice, where a foreign ideology is absorbed by China and turned into something more Chinese than foreign. This was done with foreign conquerors (Mongols, Manchus) and religions (Buddhism and Christianity) and is now happening with communism. The uniquely Chinese Confucian traditions have once more conquered the foreign invader. If this were all that was going on, there would be little problem. But the Communists have also grown corrupt, and that is more of a problem than failed attempts at state socialism. The Communist party has turned to nationalism to maintain its power, proclaiming that an economically and militarily strong China is its goal. The Communists have, as nationalists are prone to do, picked fights with their neighbors in order to maintain unity at home.

The democracy movement—This group consists of very visible academics and students who want something approximating Western-style democracy. But there are also many democracy advocates in the Communist party, and not all were purged in 1989. As happened in Eastern Europe (and in China in the 1970s), a new government could easily evolve with the Communist "liberals" convincing the Party hard-liners that retirement was preferable to civil war, but that did not develop after the crackdown in 1989. What comes next could be very interesting. Lacking any tradition of democracy, China will have to invent something suitable to its needs. India did it, and India is much more ethnically diverse than China. While India also had over a century of British administration, the British were not there to create a democracy, but to run commercial colonies. The Indians learned about democracy by study, observation, and experimentation. Many Chinese fear, however, that democracy will spiral into anarchy.

The children of privilege—Many, if not most, of this generation have sided with their less well-connected peers. Those who fell into the good life too enthusiastically will be swept away by larger events. Those who play their relationships correctly will survive and prosper. This is their strategy and goal and those who go with the democrats will probably achieve it.

The farmers—This is the bedrock of the Chinese economy and culture. Long oppressed, they have tasted freedom and prosperity in the 1970s and 1980s and could prove a formidable opponent to any group that attempts to turn the clock back. The Party now deals warily with the farmers and the democracy crowd has to cope with what will be the largest voting bloc in an elected government. After the first round of democracy, the farmers' vote will fragment between those farmers who have done well and the majority who are still mired in poverty on less arable and more crowded lands. How to deal with the less fortunate farmers will be the major medium and long-term problem for any democratic Chinese government. The farmers want prosperity, but many would settle for protection from starvation and utter poverty. Most ominous of all is the simple fact that, in a democracy, the farmers would hold 80 percent of the votes. If democracy is achieved, the farmers' voice will be loud, their veto decisive, and their demands impossible to ignore.

The *nomenklatura*—The civil service in any Communist country is noted for the emphasis placed on the party loyalty of the bureaucrats. Competence at the job they are in is quite secondary. This is politics at its worst and these people are in big trouble in the best of times. The nomenklatura officials are well connected and are adept at putting a good face on things. But after several decades of this, the economic results were catastrophic. These officials have everything to lose if the system changes. Yet their very incompetence prevents them from doing very much to hold back change. The bureaucrats in the military can turn their weapons on the people, but this is useful for only a while. Actually, the most effective bureaucrats are usually those in the secret police. To keep the Party in power, they maintain a close and accurate eye on the pulse of the nation. The pattern has been that eventually the counsel of the secret police is ignored, as it becomes more and more grim and unappetizing. Despite their relative competence, the secret police are generally among the most hated Party operatives and receive particularly brutal treatment from the people when a violent change in government occurs. The example of other formerly Communist countries indicates that the Chinese nomenklatura will most likely work diligently to find themselves a place in any new (non-Communist) government. Their political experience and connections will probably result in a lot of Communist bureaucrats becoming, overnight, democratic bureaucrats. The more able Communist officials have taken advantage of the new economic climate to become rich. Some do it by engaging in commerce; many others simply engage in corrupt practices like extortion and bribe taking. Communist China never had laws to regulate a market economy, so many key decisions about who may do what in a business deal are left up to a senior government official. Of course, another senior official can come along and change an earlier ruling, unless another bribe was paid first. What struggle there is among the nomenklatura is between the factions that want to establish a system of law for commercial transactions, and those who prefer things as they are, and the wealth that comes to those who run such a corrupt system. If the Communists can clean up their own corruption and establish a workable system of business laws, they will be able to establish themselves as a major power in a democratic China. Otherwise, the Communists will face a much bleaker future.

The urban workers—These comprise about 15 percent of the population and are perhaps the most oppressed people in China. Drawn largely from the ranks of the poorest farmers, the urban workers found their way to the cities and a variety of industrial jobs. The work did not pay much, but there was the vaunted "iron rice bowl." That is, there would always be something to eat. Periodic starvation from droughts or floods was no longer a major concern for farmers turned into industrial workers. The economic liberalization of the 1970s and 1980s helped workers the least. Yet the urban workers have not become fans or defenders of the Communist party. To the surprise of Party officials and students alike, the urban workers joined the 1989 student-inspired demonstrations in Beijing and elsewhere. For a variety of reasons, many of the urban workers are willing, at great personal risk, to go up against the Party. They expect to obtain a better life. If the Chinese economy can be opened to further growth and liberalization, this would be the urban workers' reward.

The army—The army is a strange cross between nomenklatura and urban worker, with a little of the Party mentality thrown in. Naturally, the strength of the army lies in its weapons. These weapons are bought by the labor of the entire population and operated largely by the sons of farmers and workers. The officers are largely Party members and often members of the nomenklatura. What keeps these two disparate groups in step with each other is the traditional role of the army as the final defender of the public peace from enemies within and without China. There are no significant external enemies at the moment, so the weapons are generally turned toward other Chinese. This is not a situation that inspires loyalty among the troops. The officers know this. The army wants peace within China. War with the Chinese people could easily turn into civil war. The old-timers remember how brutal and self-destructive that could be. The government has bought off the army for the moment. In addition to massive funding from the government, the army has been allowed to go into business for itself.

Since the army owns most of the Chinese arms factories, they have been energetic in selling weapons overseas. By the mid-1990s, China was the fourth largest exporter of arms in the world (over $1 billion a year, exceeded only by the United States, Russia, and Great Britain). This has caused some diplomatic problems, as the Chinese arms cannot compete on the basis of quality, so they offer low prices and a willingness to sell to anyone. Many officers have become rich, and all but the most thick-headed officers have seen to it that their troops also enjoy some of this new prosperity. The army is also hedging its bets by spotlighting, and preparing for, potential clashes with China's neighbors. Squabbles with neighboring nations over ownership of islands in the China Sea are one example, as are rumblings directed toward India over Chinese control of Tibet. There is the over-forty-year dispute with Taiwan that won't go away. Even Russia is being used as a distraction as disputes again arise over border disagreements. The army is certain it will survive any change of government and is keen on making sure that the current officer corps survives with it. The army would become the new government.

The provinces—The major differences among the twenty-three provinces, five regions, and three autonomous cities (Beijing, Shanghai, and Taijin), aside from language and culture, involve wealth and resources. Some of the coastal provinces and all of the autonomous cities have done quite well economically during the 1980s. Several of the interior provinces have done much less well. Population and military forces are not distributed in the same proportions as wealth. The well-off provinces are going to try to hang on to their advantaged position while the less affluent provinces will be looking for ways to catch up. The poor provinces have always been poor and the problems of restructuring these areas is an ancient one in China. The Party can gain some small advantage by playing the poor provinces against the not so poor ones. But that merely increases tensions at a time when the Party wants to keep things quiet. Any new government, particularly a democratic one, will find the votes of the poor provinces in conflict with the wealthier provinces over how the national wealth should be spent. The wealthier provinces will want to expand their flourishing economies while the less wealthy provinces will want investments and subsidies. The poor provinces have more people than the rich ones and, in any democratic setup, would have to be catered to by the wealthier areas.

The overseas Chinese—Possessed of substantial commercial capabilities, the overseas Chinese are too spread out and too involved in trade to become dominated by any one political doctrine. During the economic revitalization on the mainland in the 1980s, the overseas Chinese became a prime source of monetary and technical assistance. Although not all the overseas Chinese practice perfect democracy in areas they control (Taiwan, Singapore), they are partial to more democracy for the mainland. The overseas Chinese have allied themselves with a wide variety of groups in China. Their principal allies have been Chinese government officials who have backed, and participated in, new economic activity. The overseas Chinese have substantial investment in the coastal provinces of China. Should a political crisis come to China, the overseas Chinese will follow their investments and ally themselves with whatever governments establish themselves in the coastal provinces. The Chinese government may abhor Taiwan, but they view the authoritarian, and economically successful, government of Singapore as a model worth emulating.

Taiwan is something of a special case. The largest, and most economically successful, of the overseas Chinese groups, the Taiwanese are technically at war with the Chinese Communist government. As the last survivors of the losing side in the Chinese civil war that "ended" in 1949, the Taiwanese (the Republic of China, or ROC) government still asserts its right to govern all of China. The mainland (People's Republic of China, or PRC) considers Taiwan the twenty-third province. Taiwan has been protected from Communist conquest by their own powerful armed forces, the U.S. Navy, and the PRC's unwillingness to go to all that trouble to bring Taiwan to heel. The Communists always felt that time was on their side and that eventually Taiwan would resume its status as a province with a minimum of fuss. This no longer appears to be the case and the PRC has rattled the propaganda saber and made moves toward a military conquest of Taiwan. The PRC has stated that if Taiwan were to declare itself an independent nation, then there would be an invasion. While the United States no longer has a public commitment to defending Taiwan, there is no guarantee that American warships would *not* intervene. In any event, the Taiwanese armed forces are still quite strong. In 1995, Taiwan installed missiles (with a range of 170 kilometers) on islands 50 kilometers off the coast of China. At the same time, the PRC has been building up its armed forces on that same coast. Meanwhile, the Taiwanese who came from the mainland in 1949 have been losing their control of Taiwan to democracy and the larger numbers of native Taiwanese (Chinese who came to the island before 1949). Taiwan wants to be an independent nation; China wants Taiwan as part of China. As long as the living standard on Taiwan is so much higher than in China, there will never be any agreement on this issue. But business is business, and Taiwanese firms carry on a lively commerce with the mainland via middlemen in Hong Kong. This trade route will change when China takes over Hong Kong in 1997. By 2000, the situation between China and Taiwan may be very ugly, or solved.

Vietnam—For over a thousand years, the primary objective of Vietnamese foreign policy was to keep the Chinese out. Today, nothing has changed in this respect. Although the Vietnamese Communists are going through their own struggles with local democrats and economic reformers, they are having less trouble with these two groups than the Chinese. Should the Chinese Army cross the Vietnamese again as they did in 1979, they would find all Vietnamese united against them. Vietnam will avoid direct involvement in a Chinese civil war. Hanoi, however, will see the war as a business opportunity.

Hong Kong—The workers and business owners in Hong Kong are at the mercy of events beyond their control. They can either flee—which many are doing—or hope that a more congenial government comes into power before 1997. It would be in everyone's best interest that the commercial community in Hong Kong be left alone. Hong Kong is already physically part of China and populated largely by Chinese, although nearly half are refugees from Communist China. Overseas Chinese have numerous personal and commercial ties with Hong Kong residents. All these commercial relationships would be lost or severely damaged should Hong Kong's economy be trashed by Communist party mismanagement. The 20 percent of the Hong Kong population wealthy enough, or sufficiently well connected, can get out to Great Britain or another non-Communist nation. Another 20 percent have access to foreign passports and could also flee legally. Most of the population is stuck, and they have not been silent about that prospect. China stands to inherit a well-trained and -educated Hong Kong population that will swell the ranks of the democrats in the Chinese social system. Should provincial separatism arise in China, Hong Kong would find itself the prisoner of its many economic links to neighboring Guangdong Province. The other provinces in southern China would also see Hong Kong as a natural ally.

Russia—A civil war in China would be costly to Russia, as it would quite likely spill over into Russian territories, particularly those bordering the Pacific Ocean. At the very least, there would be refugees. If a Chinese civil war went nuclear, the Russians would have even greater problems, particularly dealing with the option of throwing a few of their own nukes into China to eliminate Chinese nuclear weapons. It is in Russia's interest to keep things on an even keel in China. The Russians really don't care who runs the country as long as they respect Russian borders. To this end, in 1992 the Russians confirmed a 1991 agreement with China that returned six square miles of territory that had been in dispute for decades. In the long run, China wants several nearby Russian territories back. But in the short run, Russia just wants a peaceful transition from China in the present to whatever China in the future will be. To achieve this, Russia will back whichever faction appears best able to keep the peace.

"MOST LIKELY" POLITICAL TREND CHARTS

"MAINLAND" CHINA

Gv95	Gv20	PC95	PC20	R95	R20	Ec95	Ec20	EdS95	EdS20
ST7,7	NMD7,5	6+	6	7+	7−	6	7−	4	4+

Gv = Government Type
ST = Socialist Totalitarian (effectiveness, stability)
NMD = Nationalist-Military Dictatorship
PC = Political Cohesiveness (0 = chaos, 9 = maximum)
R = Repression Index (9 = maximum)
Ec = Comparative Economic Status
EdS = Relative Education Status

TAIWAN ("REPUBLIC OF CHINA")

Gv95	Gv20	PC95	PC20	R95	R20	Ec95	Ec20	EdS95	EdS20
AD7,6	AD7,6	7	7	6+	5	7	7+	5	5+

AD = Authoritarian Democracy

REGIONAL POWERS AND POWER INTEREST INDICATOR CHARTS

CHINESE INTERNAL STRUGGLE

	Economic Interests	Historical Interests	Political Interest	Military Interest	Force Generation Potential	Ability to Intervene Politically	Interest/ Ability to Promote Economic Development
Russia	3	4	7	7	6+	2	1–
Japan	7	7	8	8	1	4	7
Vietnam	2	7	7	8	3+	1	0
United States	4	4	6	4	3	5	3
India	1	2	4	3	2+	1	0
Taiwan	9	9	9	9	3	3	7

NOTE: 0 = minimum; 9 = maximum

Russo-Chinese Border War

	Economic Interests	Historical Interests	Political Interest	Military Interest	Force Generation Potential	Ability to Intervene Politically
China	6	8	9	9	8	6
Russia	7	8	9	9	9	7
Japan	7	7	6	6	1−	7
Vietnam	1	3	7	8	3	2
United States	4	2	7	7	2+	8

War in Tibet

	Economic Interests	Historical Interests	Political Interest	Military Interest	Force Generation Potential	Ability to Intervene Politically	Interest/ Ability to Promote Economic Development
China	3	6	7	8	9	8	4
Russia	0	2	3	2	3	3	0
India	3	7	8	8	7	8	1
Pakistan	3	6	7	7	2	4	0
United States	1	2	5	2	1	5	3

Potential Outcomes

As of late 1995, an aging Communist leadership was attempting to hold on to power, keep the economy moving, and clamp down on democratic political reform. But things could change—rapidly and with global repercussions. There are several ways the situation can go, especially if the military gains more political power. Note that some of these outcomes are not mutually exclusive.

1. 40 percent chance through 2001, 30 percent chance after that: China remains a "stable" dictatorship. The Party is not without its adherents and there is a younger generation of Party functionaries eager to continue Communist party rule into the next century. There is also the army. Moreover, the bulk of the population couldn't care less who runs the country as long as there is peace and prosperity. Okay, it isn't really socialism—it's a nationalist military dictatorship with Communist trappings.

2. 35 percent chance through 2001 rising to 60 percent chance by 2010: China goes democratic. While there are still Communists willing to carry on, and most of the population don't really care who's in charge, the key people in the modern sectors of the economy, plus most of the urban population, do want more shared power. History is on their side, as the growth of democracy in Europe, and India, was a result of a larger number of educated people getting involved in an increasingly complex decision-making process. The odds, and history, favor the democrats.

3. 20 percent chance through 2001: Chinese civil war (nonnuclear). The Communists have already demonstrated that they are not willing to go without a fight. Civil war tore the country apart earlier in this century and could do so again.

4. 5 percent chance through 2001: Chinese civil war (nuclear). While a civil war is possible, nuclear civil war is less likely. While particularly rabid individuals might want to resort to nuclear weapons, it's unlikely that any organized group would. After all, who wants to run a China dotted with radioactive wreckage and hundreds of millions of corpses. But the nuclear weapons do exist, and someone could use them.

We'll also add this separate projection:

10 percent chance through 2001: China gets involved in a major war with one or more of its neighbors. This more than doubles if there is civil war in China. After 1989, the army was rewarded, for its suppression of the democracy demonstrators in Beijing, with a larger chunk of the national budget and a free hand in modern-

izing China's armed forces. Once you have larger and more capable armed forces, you feel a need to do something with them (like intimidate Taiwan). Aside from beefing up the contingents on the border with Russia and the coast facing Taiwan, the newly modernized and enlarged fleet was sent out into the South China Sea to lay claim to small islands that secure rights to potentially huge oil fields in the area. Late model Chinese warplanes and warships are now frequently seen in the area defending these tiny islands against claims from nearby Indonesia, the Philippines, and Vietnam.

COST AND KINDS OF WAR

Civil wars in China are noted for their high casualty rates. The Tai-Ping Rebellion of the 1850s, fought with primitive weapons in a rather disorganized fashion, killed over twenty million. The civil wars between the 1911 rebellion and the consolidation of Communist party power in the 1950s killed many more than that. A nonnuclear civil war today might be over quickly because of the speed of communication and the intervention (diplomatically, at least) of superpowers. That, plus the threat of nuclear weapons being used, might limit casualties. However, if one faction or another obtains, and uses, nuclear weapons, then the losses could easily exceed a hundred million, if not several hundred million, dead. As the various factions would be based on what forces major military leaders control, there would be many nuclear weapons available.

The fighting in China from the mid-1920s to 1949 ranged from pitched battles with the full panoply of modern weapons (rare) to banditry, terrorism, and guerrilla warfare in general (more common). In classic Chinese fashion, there was much movement and just as much avoidance of major combat. A major civil war in the future would no doubt follow the same pattern, with the regular army even more reluctant to test their troops' loyalty by exposing them to the stress and danger of combat. A major difference in a future civil war would be the presence of several thousand nuclear weapons. Most of these are stored in remote areas and guarded by specially selected (for loyalty and reliability) troops. But they are there and any faction possessing nukes would feel compelled to use, or threaten to use, the "nuclear option."

In the late 1960s there was a different kind of war in China, the Cultural Revolution. It was basically an officially sanctioned rampage by largely adolescent Communist zealots who were urged to "purify" Chinese culture by suppressing all the "old ways." Many cultural treasures were destroyed, and tens of thousands were killed and many more exiled and imprisoned. This was not a unique campaign in China, but much rarer than the usual civil disorder and outright war.

In the late 1980s, technology became a factor in the struggle for power. Faxes, electronic mail, and all other forms of communications technology soared beyond government control. Despite energetic measures in the early 1990s, the government has not been able to bring all these technologies under control. If civil disorder and war breaks out, it will be preceded and driven by electronic communications. These technologies will not themselves kill, but they will drive the men behind the weapons, and rifles and bombs will be as deadly at the end of the twentieth century as they were throughout that blood-soaked hundred years of Chinese history.

QUICK LOOK: Chinese Boxes: An Introduction to Internal Administration in Shanghai

Even on paper, China's internal governmental structure is a puzzle. For many foreign businessmen, learning who is responsible for what, and when, has been a bankrupting experience. Decision making in mainland China is still closely intertwined with the Communist party. There is no commercial code and supreme court that one can appeal to. That is the major difference between Hong Kong, where commerce flourishes, and China, where commerce walks through a minefield of capricious decisions by inept, and often corrupt, bureaucrats. For investors, timely and accurate answers to questions have been hard to come by.

At the top, in Beijing's central government, are the various ministries. Below the ministry, in a province or major municipality like Shanghai, is the "bureau." Below the bureau level several organizations suddenly sprout like a Kafkaesque castle: vice-bureaus, divisions, departments or "offices." On the bottom rung is a governmental group.

The Ministry of Public Security has a great deal of power in China. It also gets into some unusual and (by Western standards) mundane activities for a "police" ministry. The Ministry of Public Security controls both the Gong An (the police) and the Wu Jin (the armed security police). The Gong An in a major city like Shanghai (working through the Shanghai Public Security Bureau, or SPSB) are responsible for most standard police functions: traffic, criminal investigation, patrol, and surveillance. The Gong An do not carry weapons. The Wu Jin do carry arms. The fire department operates as a vice-bureau of the Shanghai Public Security Bureau.

The traffic "division" of the SPSB also functions as a public works agency for traffic signals. They design, repair, and install road signs and pavement markings. But the traffic division has an even larger job, and one that has grown as Shanghai's economy has taken off: The traffic division also has the authority to review and approve building site plans—a function that, in many other nations, is normally controlled by planning or public works administrations, not the police.

Provincial and city bosses (for want of a better term for the senior officials) can set up their own legal and administrative systems for free market enterprises. Those areas that have (as in southern China and Shanghai), prosper. In other areas, the bosses get rich from bribes and commerce suffers.

QUICK LOOK: Indonesia: The Straits-Jacket: East Timor, the Moluccans, Irian Jaya

Indonesia's government in Jakarta has been waging a quiet, ugly war in the ex-Portuguese colony of East Timor (on Timor Island, eastern Indonesia). East Timor experienced several upheavals, including one led by a short-lived leftist rebel front; Indonesia invaded in 1975, claiming that (1) East Timor was Indonesian all along and (2) pro-Communist control in East Timor would not be tolerated.

The East Timorese liberation front, Freitilin, fights a very low-level guerrilla war—with little success. The Roman Catholic East Timorese have no allies, little opportunity to acquire weapons, and don't have a public relations firm trying to interest the Western press in their cause. Estimates vary widely: anywhere from 80,000 to 200,000 people have been killed in East Timor since the Indonesians invaded. The Indonesian government admits 30,000 have died—5,000 in fighting, 25,000 from hunger. East Timor has a population of around 800,000. Until the mid-1990s, when demonstrations by Timorese in the capital of Dili finally attracted international attention, Indonesia's war in East Timor had been a silent massacre, with a higher proportion of the population dying in East Timor than during the 1970s Khmer Rouge terror in Cambodia. The Indonesians hold the Freitilin leader, Xanana Gusmao, in custody. In 1994 the Indonesian government began a political offensive, including press censorship, against domestic and foreign critics of its policies in East Timor. As of early 1995 the Indonesian Army kept 6,000 soldiers in East Timor.

The South Moluccans, at least those exiled in Holland, do understand media attention. Hijacking Dutch trains, blowing up Dutch school buildings, threatening the assassination of Indonesian ambassadors, the South Moluccans know how to grab headlines in the West. But they have not been successful at creating an active guerrilla movement in the islands to challenge the Indonesians. Press reports in 1984 had the Moluccans looking to the East bloc for support. That support never developed. Now the East bloc has dissipated.

The Moluccans believe they were promised an independent Moluccan state when the Dutch turned loose the Dutch East Indies. Decolonization of the Indies, however, was not a planned or calculated Dutch policy. It was brought about by a Japanese invasion; and post–World War II Holland, with its own home country shattered by the Germans, was in no mood to properly oversee the division of its old Far Eastern island empire. Javanese and Sumatran imperialists (the Moluccan names for the Indonesian government) took advantage of a power vacuum and assumed control. Forty-five years later the Moluccans remain angry.

The Indonesian government also has a low-level war going on in Irian Jaya, the former colony of Dutch New Guinea. Jakarta formally annexed Irian Jaya in 1963. There was little consultation with the inhabitants, a collection of near–Stone Age tribes and a few fishing villages. Some of the tribes in the mountain jungles, according to missionary sources, still occasionally practice ritual cannibalism. Now and then—the stories go—a little headhunting still occurs. But bows and arrows and spears and a few submachine guns are no match for Indonesian troops armed with automatic rifles and helicopters. The Free Papua Movement has failed. Support from Papua New Guinea, the other half of the island of New Guinea, is now virtually nonexistent.

WHITHER INDONESIA?

In 1995, Indonesia had a population of slightly over 200 million people. The cultural and economic spectrum of Indonesia runs from the ultra high-tech of the Indonesian petroleum industry to the Stone Age technology (circa 25,000 B.C.) of mountain tribes on Irian Jaya.

The political spine of Indonesia runs through the islands of Java and Sumatra. The island of Java has nearly 110 million inhabitants. Jakarta, the capital, is one of the world's most densely populated cities.

Over three hundred ethnic groups populate an island chain of 2 million square kilometers and thirteen thousand-plus islands, which run from the Straits of Malacca and Malaya nearly to Australia, a distance of over 5,500 kilometers. Eighty-seven percent of the people of Indonesia are Sunni Muslim, 9 percent Christian. The island of Bali is Hindu, a holdover from the days when the whole of Indonesia was either Hindu or Buddhist. The South Moluccans (island of Ambon) are primarily Dutch Calvinist. Religious differences exacerbate the problems between the South Moluccans and the rest of Indonesia.

Indonesia has an awakening Islamic fundamentalist movement. The military-sponsored regime tends to be Western-oriented and is open to fundamentalist charges of "co-option" by Western influences. There are also tensions between the Javanese and the ethnic Chinese who make up a large portion of the merchant class and run many banking institutions.

Indonesia has experienced a dramatic improvement in its standard of living. The economy continues to expand (the average annual growth the last twenty years being near 6 percent) but political tranquility is not at hand. Democratic aspirations are also awakening. As aging President Suharto nears the end of his sixth term (1996), this awakening affects the military and its "New Order" control over the country. Government censorship of the press has increased. The experiment in "controlled democracy" (which allowed the creation of the Islamic PPP and nationalist Christian PDI parties) has left the military uncomfortable and the new parties dissatisfied.

The Indonesian military claims to serve "two functions"—to defend against external and internal threats and to take a leading role in promoting internal political life and development. Through a system of *korems* and *korams* (essentially military districts), the Indonesian military elites often do more than merely encourage development projects and economic activity, but direct it as well. Charges of corruption are rife but proof hazy. Still, even the army has complained that President Suharto's immediate family has benefited from influence peddling—which they have by acquiring large stakes in new business ventures. That has led to friction in the military. The years 1996 and 1997 may be difficult ones in Jakarta as the military seeks to navigate a time of transition to new—and possibly "more civilian"—leadership.

QUICK LOOK: The Philippines: The Recovering Man of ASEAN

The Philippines were the first Asian nation to be deeply influenced by Western culture and economics. A Spanish colony taken by the United States in the Spanish-American War, the country was once one of Asia's most progressive and educated societies, possessing a strong foundation for the expansion of democratic institutions.

In February 1986 those democratic roots and aspirations were powerful enough to topple dictator Ferdinand Marcos. Marcos attempted to deny Corazón Aquino, widow of slain opposition leader Benigno Aquino, a victory at the ballot box. With aid from the United States and world opinion, Mrs. Aquino essentially overthrew Marcos in a democratic coup reinforced by armies of voters.

Still, the basic political and economic afflictions that the Marcos regime exacerbated remain. Democracy is fragile; poverty and corruption are persistent, though the new administration under President Fidel Ramos has begun to make real economic strides.

The Philippines are still involved in the low-budget but high-risk military and political controversy over the Spratly Islands. Potential oil deposits, political one-upmanship, and old suspicions drive this dispute over a scattered South China Sea archipelago. The Spratlys (an archipelago spread over 80,000 square kilometers of sea) are one of two island chains in the region in dispute, and the Philippines are in the thick of it.

Vietnam and China have fought small naval battles over the disputed Paracel Islands off the Vietnam coast. Malaysia, Taiwan, China, Vietnam, the sultanate of Brunei, and the Philippines dispute the Spratlys. Some islets occupied by the Filipinos are almost inundated at high tide. With the exception of Brunei, all of the nations have garrisoned some of the islands and islets. The Chinese believe the South China Sea is clearly in their "great power" sphere of influence. For decades Chinese aspirations in the Spratlys were checked by the presence of the U.S. Navy. The U.S. Navy, however, has returned its Subic Bay naval base to the Philippines. The U.S. Air Force also returned Clark Field, which, unfortunately, was ruined by the 1991 eruption of Mount Pinatubo.

In mid-1995 the Filipinos and the Chinese faced off over Mischief Reef. The confrontation plays well in both Filipino and Chinese domestic politics by striking nationalist sparks—and deflecting attention from both Filipino and Chinese domestic ills. However, given China's "uncertainties" (economic and political transition and the new generation of Chinese leaders), a confrontation in the Spratlys could get out of hand and escalate into a far larger Southeast Asian war. It could be a free-for-all. In 1995, Vietnam charged that Taiwanese troops stationed on the island of Taiping (the largest of the Spratlys) had fired on Vietnamese transport ships.

But the Philippines' internal problems are more pressing. The Communist New People's Army insurgency still lingers. Communist remnants often unite with other radicals in antigovernment protests. However, with the closure of the U.S. military bases, the old anti-American card doesn't inflame as it once did.

Several ethnic groups, most notably the Muslim Moros, fight a guerrilla war in the bush. The Philippine Moro (Muslim) insurgency is centered in western Mindanao. Mindanao and Sulu are essentially occupied by the Philippine Army, which gives the Moro militants lots of targets. Since the mid-1950s up to fifty thousand people have been killed in this war. Attacking the army, however, makes Moro villages and barrios vulnerable to reprisal. Muslim Indonesia has not been very helpful to the Moros, fearing Philippine "stimulation" of Indonesia's many ethnic antagonisms.

The Moro National Liberation Front (MNLF) is the key resistance group (though some of its key leadership is in exile in Libya). The Abu Sayyuf Islamist terrorist organization has also been active in the Philippines and has been linked to Iran. The Abu Sayyuf carried out several attacks in 1995. But Moro activists must fight more than the Manila government. The *datu* system—the old Moro "headman" system—originally a flexible means of allowing a man with natural leadership abilities to become a tribal leader, has over the years evolved into a rigid hereditary system. The Moro "tribal" organization has been helpful in keeping the insurgency going but has been a dismal failure in establishing a political framework that can challenge Manila.

Despite the rise of democracy, there has as yet been no broad-based power sharing among the Philippines' many ethnic and economic groups. A small number of wealthy families still control the destiny of the nation and have been slow to share power. During the late 1990s the economic reforms of the early 1990s may finally get the Philippines on the way to a better future. The old American naval base at Subic Bay was turned into a special economic zone and competent administration installed. Several multinational corporations moved in and prosperity returned to the area. If war over the Spratlys is avoided, the Philippines may finally begin to get a handle on its foreign debt and make significant economic gains.

QUICK LOOK: Cambodia and the Great Indochina War

The twentieth century's "Great Indochina War" continues to sputter on—with tragic consequences—in the sad confines of Cambodia.

Cambodian nationalist forces and the resilient Khmer Rouge tangle over the corpse of a country.

The Khmer Rouge, orchestrators of one of this century's most grievous genocides, refuse to fade away. They are still propped up, at least with arms and ammunition, by "interested parties" who will sell to anyone for hard currency. The Khmer Rouge have gone into business in the backwoods areas they still control, selling mineral and lumber rights to foreigners, bribing Thai officials to allow access and spending the money to keep their cause going.

The Western powers have flip-flopped through a series of promises to back then not to back the Sihanoukist nationalists. The Cambodian nationalists (centered on the revived monarchy led by Norodom Sihanouk) remain weak "in the field." Their combat forces are largely ineffectual. Even massive Western support might accomplish little. Vietnam keeps troops at the door. Elections have been held, the UN supervises the enterprise, and yet, Cambodia is still not at peace.

The Great Indochina War, which began as resistance against the French colonial masters in the 1930s, has been a hell for all participants. What the United States thinks of as the Vietnam War was only one particularly awful twelve-year slice of what is now six decades of combat. An agreement to end the struggle in Cambodia will be a step toward more peace and less war, but few believe the members of the "psychotic wing" of the Khmer Rouge will ever put their arms down.

EXTENDED LOOK: India: Local Superpower or Troubled Empire?

The Indian subcontinent, with nuclear arms stashed in the saber-rattling states of India and Pakistan, is one of the more likely sites for the next use of nuclear weapons. India has had nuclear weapons since the 1970s; if Pakistan doesn't officially possess nuclear arms, then trust that Islamabad is but a few short steps from assembling an atomic weapon.

A constant state of tension between these two regional powers, the atomic weapons, and the region's chronic ethnic and religious turmoil makes the area a potential post–cold war thermonuclear combat zone.

More troubling is the political situation in India. The nation sees itself, in the post–cold-war world, as a local superpower and, if it plays its cards right, an international superpower in the near future. Meanwhile, there are serious internal problems, arising from the raucous mixture of cultures, religions, and languages within India itself.

India is less a nation and more a teeming near-continent of many different ethnic states loosely united as the world's largest functioning, though creaky, democracy. When Great Britain's Indian empire was granted independence in 1947, Burma, Sri Lanka and Muslim Pakistan, separated by Hindu India into East and West Pakistan, also became independent. All four parts of the former British Indian territories have continued to suffer discord because of their complex ethnic and religious makeups.

The simplest facts illustrate the polyglot culture: Contemporary India has sixteen major languages and hundreds of minor ones. The

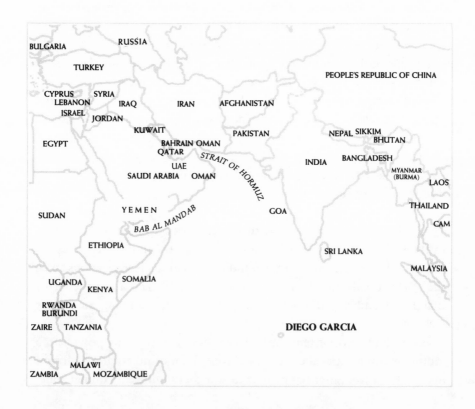

major language, Hindi, is spoken, or understood, by about half the population. English, a colonial leftover from the years of British domination, is spoken or at least partially understood by 15 to 25 percent of the population, particularly the commercial, administrative, and educated classes. English, to pun, serves India's interior commerce as a lingua franca. India is second, only to the United States, in the number of English speakers. Subcontinent English has now developed into a unique Indian dialect. Interestingly, English has become one of the elements that holds India together. There is an ethnic plus: As a language not native to India, its use does not displace one local language in favor of another. Yet English also carries a political downside: English is the language of the (sometimes) despised former rulers.

Religion is one of the most divisive elements in the region. Most people are Hindu, but the next largest group is Muslim. Islam came to India at sword point as several waves of Muslim invaders swept across the Indus River in the northwest. The last major incursion, by central Asian tribes under Babur in the sixteenth century, established the Mughul empire. Islam ruled across northern India. When the British took over, they left religion out of it. While there were some Christian missionaries, and there had been centuries before the British arrived, religion never became an issue for the British.

Hinduism is a native Indian religion that developed over a thousand years before Christianity. Buddhism began twenty-five hundred years ago as a "protestant" form of Hinduism. These two religions still hold the devotion of over 80 percent of the people living in India. But 11 percent are Muslim, 3 percent Christian, and over 2 percent Sikh. In India, like China, small percentages add up. That's why "over 2 percent" of 930 million people amounts to nearly 20 million Sikhs. That's a larger population than many of the world's nations.

Pakistan and Bangladesh are both over 90 percent Muslim, and Sri Lanka 70 percent Buddhist. Although Muslims within India are loyal citizens, India's chief rival in the area is Muslim Pakistan, and this creates yet another flashpoint between the two communities.

With a total area of 3.3 million square kilometers, India is approximately one-third the size of the United States (with over three times the population). Most of the land is suitable for farming, with intensive rice farming predominant along the coasts and into the upland plateau.

Wheat and similar crops are grown in the north. In the northwest, particularly along the Pakistan border, the land is drier, and more primitive agriculture and grazing is predominant. In the far south, and on much of Sri Lanka, large-scale plantation farming is common.

India's estimated 1995 population was 930 million, with 40 percent of these people either starving or on the borderline. The population is dense everywhere, but particularly in the rice farming and river valley areas. That is because India is the southernmost recipient of the huge quantities of moisture that blow in off the Pacific onto the east coast of Asia (from Korea southwest to Sri Lanka). As a consequence, the huge eastern coast of Asia is better supplied with water than the eastern part of the United States. This enables intensive agriculture to flourish in this largely tropical and semitropical area. The result has been a degree of intensive, although relatively unmechanized, farming that supports over half the world's population, including India.

Language is also an important aspect of the geography. There are three major language groups in the area: Indic (Indo-European), Dravidian, and Asiatic. The Indic group is the source of most European languages. The principal one here is Hindi (and a closely related dialect, Urdu). It is spoken across northern India, east of the Indus River valley. A quarter of India's population speaks Hindi, and the majority now at least understands it due to the showing of Hindu-language movies on TV throughout the nation. The Indus River valley, and much of Pakistan, speak other Indic languages, such as Punjabi and several other related tongues. Due south of Pakistan, Rajasthani is widely spoken. In the east, largely in Bangladesh, Bengali, a close relative of Hindi, is spoken. Another similar tongue, Marathi, is spoken across much of central India. Nepali is spoken in Nepal and a half-dozen other related languages are spoken across northern India. Sinhalese, an Indic language, is spoken only in Sri Lanka. A telling statistic about India's diversity of languages: twenty-four different languages are each spoken by at least one million people.

The western portions of Pakistan speak a number of Indo-European languages related to Farsi (or Persian, the language of Iran). Chief among these are Pushtu (language of the Pathans of Afghanistan) and Baluchi.

Southern India speaks a non–Indo-European language: Dravidian (the original language of India before the Indo-Europeans arrived). It is actually a number of separate languages, the principal ones being Telugu (central India along the east coast), Tamil (far south and Sri Lanka), Kannada (south-central India), Malayalam (southwest coast), and several other variants.

Various "Asian" languages are spoken along the northern border and in scattered interior areas (inhabited by invaders and colonists who retained their language and customs). The principal one is Sino-Tibetan, the language of Tibet that is similar to Chinese.

India alone contains a number of competing ethnic and social groups. For example:

Hindus—These comprise over 80 percent of India's population. Nearly a third speak Hindi (or Urdu, a closely related tongue), the principal language of India. The Hindu religion is probably the strongest unifying force in the country. Religious intolerance among many Hindus is also what is pulling the nation apart.

The Indo-Aryans—Northern Indians of light complexion.

The Dravidians—These are the darker-skinned inhabitants of southern India. Descended from the original inhabitants of India, they were gradually pushed south by the waves of lighter-skinned Aryan invaders.

The upper castes—The caste system, originally part of the Hindu religion, is technically outlawed. But in practice it still survives. The caste you were born into is usually the one you stay in. The upper three castes comprise about 150 million people (the lowest castes comprise about the same number; everyone else is in between).

The untouchables—Technically, the lowest caste. About 15 percent of the population. The outcasts in this "out caste" are the people who do the most unappealing work having to do with blood, feces, and dead bodies. The lower castes in general, and the untouchables in particular, are a constant source of (quite justified) agitation for social justice. Just one more vexing problem for India's leaders to contend with.

Indian middle class—A recent phenomenon. Taken as a whole, India has an enormous economy and nearly two hundred million people operate the bulk of it and get most of the advantages.

The Indian Army—India has long had a strong military tradition.

Hindus have a caste for soldiers and the profession is seen as a respectable one. On top of this was laid the British military tradition, which stressed a high degree of professionalism, subservience to civilian control, and technical proficiency. The Indian Army fields several first-rate divisions that soldier for soldier are the equal of most other powers around the globe.

The Indian government bureaucracy—Originally modeled after the efficient British bureaucracy, the Indian version soon became immobilized by politics. Unlike the military, the civil service quickly became corrupted by political patronage and, to a lesser extent, graft. Part of this was due to a typical third world condition: low civil service salaries. Worst of all, the bureaucracy became obstructionist and self-serving. Nationalist and socialist attitudes encouraged growth in the bureaucracy as a means of exerting better control over the economy. That had the result of crippling the economy with reams of red tape. Over ten million civil servants are still a political, economic, and social force to be recognized.

Muslims—There are nearly 400 million Muslims in the region. The largest number, some 130 million, are in Pakistan. Another 128 million are in Bangladesh. Despite the millions of Muslims who fled from India to neighboring Islamic areas, 11 percent of the population of India is still Muslim. That will add up to over 100 million Muslims by the end of the century. But the Indian Muslims exist in, in their words, "a sea of Hindus." Although most of the Muslims are in northern India, a large number of Muslims are still found distributed around the nation, with the largest clumps normally being all-Muslim villages near cities or all-Muslim neighborhoods in urban areas. The Indian National Conference party, which is an arm of the Congress party, has many Muslims in its hierarchy.

Sikhs—Sikhism is a religion founded in the fifteenth century as something of a cross between Islam and Hinduism. It eliminates the caste system and promotes individual effort and fierce defense of their religion. Every Sikh is considered a warrior and the common name each male assumes, Singh, means "lion." A very tough, unified group, the Sikhs eventually in the early nineteenth century controlled the northwestern Indian province of Punjab, where Sikhism first developed. Their discipline and military prowess made them popular with

British administrators and generals. There are only about twenty million Sikhs, most of whom are in Punjab, where they are a majority.

Kashmir and Kashmiris—India's two thirds of the old state is called the State of Jammu and Kashmir; Pakistan refers to its portion of Kashmir as Azad Kashmir, or Independent (or Free) Kashmir. Indians call the Pakistani third Pak-Occupied Kashmir. The State of Jammu and Kashmir is an Indian province on the Pakistani border with the state capital in Srinagar. Kashmir is the only state in India with a Muslim majority (65 percent are Muslim). Most of the Muslims live in the Kashmir Valley. Many Buddhists live in the Ladakh region (northeastern quarter). In 1947, Jammu and Kashmir became part of India, rather than Pakistan, because of "larger political considerations," not due to the desires of the population. The political consideration? Pakistan's abortive invasion in 1948, launched after Indian troops moved into Kashmir to suppress a Muslim-led revolt against the local Hindu maharaja. When India gained its independence in 1947, those provinces ruled by Indian nobles (and controlled by the British) had the option to remain independent or, if they were in an area between Hindu and Muslim regions, to go with one nation or the other. Once the Indians were in control, they did not allow any of the nobles to stay in power. Most of the aristocrats complied when they got the word; a few required the threat or use of military force. One special case was Kashmir, a wealthy province between Pakistan and India. Kashmir's population was, and still is, mostly Muslim, with a sizable Hindu minority in the eastern Jammu region. The maharaja was Hindu, and he thought he could get away with the independence option. It didn't work. Islamic irregular troops started moving in from Pakistan; Indian troops then entered, then regular Pakistani troops. The war was brief, and most of Kashmir became Indian, complete with a Muslim majority. Pakistan has been attempting to rectify the situation ever since. The fight left a jagged cease-fire line cutting the province, and has sparked two more wars. Interestingly, the leader of the 1940s Muslim guerrilla force was Mohammed Abdul Qayyum Khan, who in 1990 was the president of Pakistani Kashmir. From 1992 to 1995 tension in Kashmir increased—and so did the presence of Indian troops. Muslim guerrilla activity led to a reinforcement of Indian forces in the state (by early 1995, 250,000 soldiers). The Jammu and

460 / A Quick and Dirty Guide to War

Kashmir Liberation Front is the largely Muslim organization that creates most of the local mayhem, and is now pushing for complete independence. That makes it difficult for either India or Pakistan to come to terms with the rebels.

Border tribes and border states—India is a triangle, with two sides bordering on ocean. But the third side is covered with a jumble of ethnic groups that are antagonistic to India for one reason or another. Starting in the east there is Pakistan. Next there are the Chinese forces in Chinese-occupied Tibet (and other Chinese-Indian border disputes). Next there is Nepal, over which India exercises considerable influence and with which India has always had uncomfortable relations. To the east of Bangladesh lies a large territory, connected to India only by a thin strip of territory north of Bangladesh, populated by a mélange of tribes, and India's only domestic source of oil. For years these tribes lived in relative isolation from each other and the teeming Indian populations to the west. But since World War II, population pressures in India have sent millions of Indians into these sparsely populated territories (over twenty million inhabitants) in search of living space. The tribes were not happy with this, and the warfare resulting, while low level, has been persistent and intractable. Some of the rebellions were settled, or at least died down, in the late 1980s. But in the 1990s the unrest fired up once more. The largest movements, in Assam and Nagaland, continue to grow larger. (New weapons keep ending up in Naga hands. Some of the weapons may be supplied by Pakistan.) These groups make use of bases in Burma and Bangladesh.

Pakistan—Although poverty-stricken and rent with ethnic strife, Pakistan is one of the largest, and possibly the strongest, Muslim nations in the world. It is the one Muslim nation closest to having nuclear weapons, and may already have them. The peoples occupying Pakistan have, over the ages, periodically invaded, and often conquered, India. There are several current border disputes and no love lost between the two nations. But Pakistan is also rent by political movements at odds over Islamic fundamentalism and patronage. Corruption and an intelligence agency (ISI) and armed forces that are both in business for themselves further complicates the situation. Many Pakistanis, especially many running the government, truly believe that India is out to absorb Pakistan. Thus Pakistan's decades-long program to build nuclear weapons. The Pakistani armed forces are designed to fight the only kind of war it can possibly win against India: a short, violent conflict backed up by nuclear weapons.

Pakistani tribes—Pakistan is largely populated by Punjabis. But these comprise only two thirds of the population. Other major groups are Sinds (13 percent, related to Punjabis), Pushtuns (9 percent, the major group in Afghanistan and related to the Iranians), Baluchis (3 percent), and a few others. The Baluchis are the biggest problem, as these people are scattered across three nations (including Iran and Afghanistan), do not have their own country, and would like one. The other groups are less of a problem as they have someplace to go to.

Other Players in the Region

Sri Lanka—Sri Lanka's civil war began in the early 1980s and has, to date, killed nearly forty thousand people. In the early 1990s steps were made to resolve the war politically. However, as of mid-1995 renewed terror campaigns by the Tamil guerrillas indicate that the struggle in Sri Lanka will continue. India has put troops at the disposal of the Sri Lankan government before and the Indian Navy has interdicted supplies for the rebel "Tamil Tigers." The rebels are drawn from the 10 percent of the Sri Lankan population whose ancestors came from the Tamil-populated areas of southern India over the past two centuries. The majority Sinhalese are similar in appearance to northern Indians, but practice Buddhism, rather than the Hinduism of the Tamils. The majority of Sinhalese cannot agree on whether to seek a compromise with the Tamils, or try to wipe them out.

Russia—After the Indian border war with China in the 1960s, India became quite cozy with Russia. All this can be considered just good power politics. Russia and China had nuclear weapons in the 1960s; India did not. Russia's relations with China were strained. Russia was willing to sell inexpensive, but fairly modern, weapons to India. Getting close to Russia increased India's stature among third world nations (at least until Afghanistan). Today Russia has made a diplomatic comeback by offering even more generous arms deals to India, and by taking a gentler line with Pakistan.

China—In the 1950s, China occupied Tibet—as it had done so many times in the past centuries. A vaguely drawn border in the mountain wilderness separating China and India became the subject of a dispute that escalated to combat. The Indians lost. Since the 1960s, diplomatic relations with China have been relatively frosty. Pakistan, in turn, has become an ally of China. Until the Russian invasion of Afghanistan in 1979, Pakistan was also cool to the United States, because of American support of Israel. China continues to supply Pakistan with cheap but reliable arms and is always a threat to move on India.

United States—Despite the area's need for economic aid from the United States, a number of local conditions have caused America to maintain a low profile in the region since World War II. India's alignment with Russia in the 1960s and India's desire to be regarded as the leader of the third world nations created an antagonistic attitude toward the United States. Pakistan has been generally lukewarm toward the United States because of America's support for Israel. Yet in the 1971 Indo-Pakistani War, the United States tilted toward Pakistan—and sent a carrier-led task force into the area. With the end of the Afghan and cold wars, American-Pakistani relations stumble only over the issue of nuclear weapons. The United States does not want Pakistan to have them, and Pakistan refuses to renounce nukes. Since India began to open up its economy to foreign investment in the 1990s, American relations with India have become friendlier.

Great Britain—Despite Indian suspicions of the former colonial power, Great Britain continues to maintain good diplomatic and commercial ties with former colonies in the region.

India has a complex political landscape. The major players are:

The Congress party (also, the Congress (I) party—the "I" standing for India)—Politically, India's democracy has been dominated by the Congress party since independence. It is the party that grew out of the nonviolent independence activities of Mohandas Gandhi, the spiritual father of modern India. In 1969 the Congress party split into the New Congress and Old Congress parties.

The Congress party has maintained its hold on power, and maintenance of national unity, by using its vast patronage power to dole out jobs and favors to key people in the thirty-one states and territories. Jobs are given out to maximize their political effect, not to obtain the greatest efficiency. The Dravida Munnetra Kazgham (DMK) party in the southern state of Tamil Nadu (near Sri Lanka) is an example of an ethnic, state-based party. The DMK has participated in the National Front coalition. The Akali Dal (also called the United Akali Dal) is a Sikh party confined to Punjab. V. P. Singh's Janata Dal operates in several states, but is a ragtag collection of local parties.

Bharatiya Janata (Janata means "people's") party (BJP)—"Hindu First party"; a Hindu-based party. Has been a coalition member with Janata Dal. BJP now leads the official opposition, because it has the second largest number of seats in parliament. Through the 1990s, one can expect Hindi speakers to launch additional drives to make Hindi the national language.

Communist and "socialist" parties—The Communist Party of India (CPI) is still active. The Communist Party—Marxist (CPM), however, is still powerful in the states of West Bengal and Kerala and behaves more like a "state" party. The local Communists maintain themselves by providing relatively corruption-free government and, of course, talk the talk of "socialist economic equality."

The overriding goal of the Indian government is to maintain itself as the central government of India, and the decisive power in the region. India has superpower ambitions. Part of this strategy has India acting as "the region's policeman." To that end, between 1985 and 1995, India bought over $20 billion worth of weapons, making it one of the world's leading buyers of conventional arms. Tanks, artillery, jet aircraft, aircraft carriers, and nuclear subs "leased" from Russia are included in the weapons mix. Call it Indian gunboat diplomacy. The spending on the Indian Navy gives India the ability to "intervene" anywhere in the Indian Ocean, from Singapore to Madagascar. That has made India's neighbors understandably nervous.

India is also a nuclear power. With the end of the cold war, India has sought to play the lead role in negotiations between third world nations and the industrialized countries.

India and Pakistan have fought three wars to date, minor ones in 1948 and 1965, and a major conflict in 1971 that resulted in the loss of Pakistan's eastern portion, which became the nation of Bangladesh.

Serious disagreements remain between Pakistan and India over who will control the Indian state of Kashmir, which is largely Muslim.

In 1974, India exploded a nuclear weapon. India's nuclear arsenal has probably grown since then, even though no further nuclear explosions have been detected. Pakistan has redoubled its own efforts to manufacture nuclear weapons. Intelligence estimates published in 1995 suggested that Pakistan was very close to producing a nuclear device.

Normally, a war between India and Pakistan is a pretty uneven contest with India the likely winner, Pakistan the loser. Pakistan's first-line forces, however, are excellent and a short, minor war is a more even-up affair. India's huge arms buildup in the late 1980s may have shifted the power balance so strongly in India's favor that New Delhi would most certainly prevail in a long, major conventional war. When both sides have nuclear weapons and become locked into a desperate border battle, however, nuclear warfare looms likely—especially if one side (Pakistan?) begins to feel hard-pressed. It looks as if even more bitter, brutal, and destructive Indo-Pakistani wars are in the offing.

India also has a long-running conflict with another regional power, and one that is definitely nuclear: China. In 1962 a dispute over a Chinese-built road running through a slice of territory claimed by India set off a series of border clashes between the Chinese and Indian armies. China attacked Indian positions in Arunachal Pradesh (northeastern India, near the Burmese border) and also seized some territory in the Ladakh region of Kashmir near the Kongka Pass. After a month of combat, China won its objectives and declared a unilateral cease-fire. In 1967 the Sino-Indian conflict erupted once again, this time in the Nathu La Pass on the Sikkim-Tibetan border. In 1986, India accused China of sending troops into Indian valleys in Arunachal Pradesh.

A major new political and diplomatic development occurred in 1991, when India decided to dismantle its socialist economy and move full speed to a more open market economy. The 1991 Persian Gulf War gave impetus to this decision. That conflict sent thousands of well-paid Indian workers home from the Middle East, most of them with only the clothes on their backs. Those workers had been a major source of foreign exchange, via earnings remitted to their families in

India. Foreign exchange was always in short supply in India, which had followed a projectionist, socialist economic policy since 1947. The loss of the hard currency from these expatriate Indians created financial crisis.

The 1991 hard currency shortage, the success of China's experiments with the market economy in the 1980s, and the economic and political collapse of the Soviet Union finally gave Indian free market reformers the political clout they needed to overcome the vested interests in India's socialist economy. The effects were remarkable, not only economically, but also politically and diplomatically. The economy began to boom and the middle class began to grow. The need for good commercial relations with the West made it necessary to patch up diplomatic relations. The new middle class was more concerned with economic issues than with ethnic or religious disputes. The new 1991 government, formed in the wake of Prime Minister Rajiv Gandhi's assassination by Sri Lankan (Tamil) assassins, went forward with the new policies.

With a newly robust economy and good relations with all the planet's major powers, India sees itself on the brink of something big. Namely, India sees itself about to become a global power. This aspiration, however, could be short-circuited by a nuclear war with Pakistan, or internal disorder getting out of control.

INDIA AS A "THIRD WORLD COMMON MARKET"

An interesting way to look at India's internal organization (or disorganization, as the case may be) is to consider the Republic of India as a sort of third world common market comprising all the parts of India. Hundreds of millions of people operate in one vast economy, under more or less one overall "economic government" that sets the pace for thirty-one, or more, "local nations." Oddly enough, one of the old customs that India has not been able to eliminate is the continued use of custom tolls charged on goods moved from province to province. In this respect, the European Economic Union is more of a unified economy than India's. In some ways, if compared with the situation inside India in 1947, the "results" produced by this arrangement look encouraging. Despite a meager 36 percent literacy rate and steadily growing population, India's economy grew stronger and India began to feed itself. Both of these accomplishments are rare in third world countries. Note, however, that 64 percent of the population remains illiterate; this forms a large pool of people who rely solely on radio and TV (or other forms of mass rumor and hearsay) for their political information and thus may be swayed by whoever controls the radio and TV media. This is especially true with radio, which is accessible to nearly everyone in India. Even television is found in remote areas, and large numbers of people will see important events on those isolated receivers.

By other comparative slide rules, however, the Indian Common Market has done poorly. In 1950, India accounted for 2 percent of total world exports and 6 percent of exports generated by third world countries. In 1980, India's share in each category had shrunk to .4 percent and 1.4 percent. In 1955, India was the world's tenth-ranked industrial power; in 1975 it ranked twentieth. China, even hobbled by Maoism, produced a 5.2 percent growth in real GNP per person between 1965 and 1987. India's real per capita GNP growth during the same time frame was 1.8 percent. Why? The New Delhi–led bureaucracy that runs the whole show. Inefficiency percolates through the system. India is an economic "success" partially because it has avoided doing as badly as many experts expected. All this changed in 1991, with a capitalist-minded prime minister in power. By 1995, India had an economic growth rate of 5.5 percent a year and it was still growing. The savings rate, at over 20 percent, was the same as in the highly successful Asian nations of Japan, South Korea, Taiwan, and Singapore. Exports increased and it was all done without the government taking on billions in foreign debt. The giant of south Asia is stirring, and foreign investment is flowing in. That is perhaps the most convincing evidence to support Indian assumption that they will soon be a superpower in every sense of the word. That may be too optimistic for the moment, but in a generation or two, who knows?

WHERE WILL IT ALL END?

Here are some estimates.

Pakistan-India

1. 30 percent chance through 2001: A short, minor Indo-Pakistani war occurs. A clash of two divisions per side or less on the primary front with gains or losses of territory measured in a couple of dozen kilometers or less. Time of actual fighting is a week or less. Limited air strikes on military targets near cities, lots of shooting in the mountains. Fighting sputters out as UN brokers negotiations. In this scenario, 50 percent chance Pakistan slightly improves political and military situation in Kashmir, 40 percent India does, 10 percent no change. (There may be several of these clashes.)

2. 25 percent chance through 2001: Call it the "hesitant peace"; continuing ethnic troubles in Kashmir and saber rattling by New Delhi and Islamabad. Shooting on the Siachen Glacier. Increases to 40 percent chance if Indian Army suppresses Punjab or if New Delhi annexes Sri Lanka.

3. 20 percent chance through 2001: Major war. An all-out conventional slugfest stopped only by the explicit threat of one side, probably Pakistan, to use nuclear weapons or one side suing for peace. Could last from days to months. 70 percent chance of relative Indian victory (India makes significant geographic gains in Kashmir area).

4. 15 percent chance through 2001: Nuclear war. Yes, this book's most aggressive projection. A "super-major" war; both sides use nukes and both sides experience heavy civilian casualties. (Both sides move their economic development back thirty years.) No real winner, but if the nuclear war does occur, there's a 75 percent chance Indian forces will occupy a significant part of radioactive Pakistani Kashmir if India is the first to use nuclear weapons (so

the Indians claim a "glowing" victory—of a most cruel and terrible sort).

5. 10 percent or less chance through 2001: A "negotiated solution" to the Kashmir problem. Kashmir is either made "autonomous" along the lines of Punjab autonomy (see Potential Outcomes, Punjab) or joins Pakistan through plebiscite. A projectable outcome— but don't even bet the ant farm on it.

Sri Lanka

1. 50 percent chance through 2001: Continuation of civil strife. The Tigers rise and fall. No resolution, no new accommodations.
2. 20 percent chance through 2001: Military suppression of Tamil separatists. The Sinhalese have the numbers, the growing hatred of the terrorists, and, increasingly, the military capability. The 1987 Indian intervention was caused largely by Sinhalese ruthlessness, and success, at cornering large numbers of rebels. The Tamils of India were outraged and put pressure on the government to allow aid to get through the Sri Lankan blockade. Now the Sinhalese are even more bitter, and with greater numbers and resolve, they could put down the Tamil rebellion. The cost, however, would be great, and the aftermath would likely lay the groundwork for yet another rebellion in the future. Outcomes 1 and 2 reflect the likelihood of some type of military-authoritarian government taking power in Sri Lanka (see "Most Likely" Political Trend Chart). Goes up to 30 percent if there is a major Indo-Pakistani war. Indian military attention would then be almost completely drawn to Pakistan. If India won, significant Indian forces would be engaged in occupying territory taken from Pakistan.
3. 20 percent chance through 2001: Political partition of Sri Lanka. This would involve setting up part of the country for the exclusive use of Tamils. Similar to partition that took place between India and Pakistan in 1947. Will involve a great deal of intense and immediate violence.
4. 7 percent chance through 2001: Annexation by India. Actually,

India does not want to try this for several reasons. For one thing, they discovered how difficult it was to deal with this sort of conflict when they sent troops into Sri Lanka in 1987, and withdrew them two years later, without having achieved much success. There is also the world opinion of India as a peaceful state in warlike world. India cherishes this image, which is increasingly tarnished by Indian military operations. Annexation, however, is always a possibility and a difficult one to estimate.

5. 3 percent chance through 2001: Expulsion of Tamils. An increasing number of Sinhalese see this as a viable option. It really isn't, for the simple reason that there is no nation out there willing to take three million Tamils. The Tamils of Tamil Nadu have grown impatient with the war their kin are waging in Sri Lanka. Support in Tamil Nadu is gradually evaporating, and even the thousands of Sri Lankan Tamils who have fled to India are being made to feel uncomfortable. Tamil Nadu is no longer willing to provide training bases and supplies for the Tamil rebels of Sri Lanka. However, if the level of violence becomes high enough, and the Indian government maintains its reluctance to get involved once more, a major evacuation of Tamils from Sri Lanka remains a distant possibility.

Pakistan: Internal Situation

1. 72 percent chance through 2001: No significant change from rickety status quo, despite war with India.
2. 15 percent chance through 2001: Civil war sparked by war with India or rebellions on Afghan border. Islamabad eventually gets control. Minor border adjustments result. Pakistan is greatly weakened vis-à-vis India. Jumps to 40 percent if Indo-Pakistani war goes nuclear.
3. 11 percent chance through 2001: Partition, brought about either by war with India, by civil war, or (less likely) by vote in Kashmir that produces an autonomous Kashmir.
4. 2 percent chance through 2001: Total annexation by India, as a result of India's internal situation.

India: Internal Situation

There is a fair chance that a civil war will break out in India by 2006, sparked by either a war with Pakistan or one of the inevitable local squabbles. The language issue could set it off, if Hindi radicals try to get rid of English. Yet the Congress party is resourceful and resilient—and adept at diffusing these issues. A good case in point is how the fanatical Sikh separatists in the Punjab were handled. Violence grew in the early 1980s, culminating in the 1984 storming of the major Sikh temple in 1984. From 1985 to 1990, the killings escalated. In 1985 only 6 or 7 people a month were killed. This number went up tenfold in 1986 and then more than doubled again in 1987. By 1988, over 150 people a month were being killed in the Punjab by terrorist action (although over a third were terrorists themselves).

The Indian government has blamed Pakistan (and the U.S. CIA) for supporting the Sikh rebels, and there may indeed be some Pakistani support. But the primary cause is a fanatical core of Sikhs who want independence and revenge (in no particular order at this point). The state of Punjab did not turn into another Lebanon, as there was no multiplicity of militias. Most of the Sikhs and nearly all of the local Hindus wanted no part of the violence. Eventually, more adroit provincial leadership persuaded the majority of the Sikhs to turn against the terrorists (still led by a number of Sikh holy men). But the nationwide damage was already done. Many of the local Hindus moved out of the Punjab as the Indian Army and Punjabi police intensified their antiterrorism efforts. Hindu resentment of terrorists killing Hindus caused anti-Sikh riots in other parts of India, causing some Sikhs to move back to the Punjab. All of this played into the terrorists' hands, but not sufficiently to create an independent Sikh state. Although things have settled down for the moment, Punjab could become a pawn in some future India-Pakistan war, as the Pakistanis have already made noises about their willingness to recognize an independent Sikh state. This is somewhat far-fetched, as Punjab is well integrated into the Indian economy and has substantial non-Sikh minorities (mainly Hindus).

Still, for purposes of argument, let's say there is a 10 percent chance of an extensive armed civil conflict erupting inside India (excluding Punjab and Kashmir and the ongoing troubles with the Naga). This is, admittedly, a rather high figure, but India has a lot of factions that could radicalize on the drop of a rupee. For further argument, the possibility of civil war rises to 30 percent if a nuclear war erupts and extremist factions see the resulting chaos and fear as their best opportunity.

India and China

There exists a slight chance that India and China will come to blows through 2001. China might well shake sabers if Pakistan and India got into a major war that lasted over a couple of weeks.

COST AND KINDS OF WAR

The wars between Pakistan and India were relatively bloodless as major wars go. The 1965 war killed about 20,000 people; the 1971 war killed another 12,000. The 1962 war between China and India caused 5,000 deaths. The formal wars have not been the chief cause of death by violence, but the civil unrest that sometimes leads to war. The massacres began with the million killed during the partition that accompanied independence in 1948. The 1971 Pakistani civil war killed over 300,000. Left-wing rebellions in Sri Lanka during the 1970s killed as many as 3,000. The Tamil separatist activity during the 1980s has killed nearly 20,000 through 1990 and nearly as many again in the 1990s. Over 20,000 died in the Punjab before the terrorism was put down in the early 1990s. The fighting in the tribal areas has caused over a thousand deaths since the 1970s. Several thousand have died in Kashmir since 1989—and in Kashmir the terror and killing continue.

But the biggest death toll could occur during a future war between India and Pakistan if either nation used its nuclear weapons. While Pakistan may not have operational nuclear weapons yet, they could get their hands on chemical weapons and they could be nearly as deadly. The casualty toll in a nuclear or chemical war would easily be in the hundreds of thousands and could go into the millions if things got out of hand.

India has fought several large conventional wars, with masses of tanks and aircraft slugging it out amid large infantry forces. Those battles are usually fought in the open plains of northern India, which favors mechanized operations. But that is the exception. The more common form of armed violence is small-scale, violent terrorism: Small bands of rebels walk into a village, or stop a bus, and slaughter as many unarmed civilians as they can. The rebels then depart, returning either to camps deep in the forest or to their own civilian identities. The security forces often reply by doing a little slaughtering of their own. The usual victims: civilians caught between the terrorists and the army.

QUICK LOOK: Myanmar: Burma's Bitter Road

The idea was horrifyingly simple: Burmese society, in order to realize socialist perfection, would "internalize development," curl upon itself like a political lotus, a "Marxist-Buddha" rejecting the virus of bourgeois values, the disease of capitalism, the legacy of "western imperialism"—and the grim reality of its own ethnically fractured and poverty-stricken hinterland. But for decades Burma—recast by General Ne Win's brutal regime as "Myanmar" (Union of Myanma, a transliteration of the name in Burmese), a name intended to exorcise any lingering British imperial ghosts—has been less of an Asian Albania and more of an anguished battlefield, a hushed battlefield outside the focus of network video cams and the concerns of the "external" world.

Burma is the basket case of catchphrases describing a national state of self-inflicted economic destruction, political oppression, military corruption, social degradation, and ethnic partisanship. What was in the mid-1950s a rice-exporting nation and a comparatively literate society (an adult rate of 80 percent by some estimates) has become a net rice importer, a land of jails for intellectuals, and one of the earth's more devastated economies, though in 1994 the military junta began a campaign to open up the economy—as long as the generals got a cut of the action.

The long-running military regime (which initially espoused a curious concoction of socialism and Buddhism) stifled private markets, shut down foreign trade, and produced the appalling economic catastrophe. Ironically, the isolationist policies, intended to promote independent economic development and reinforce political neutrality, made the country even more dependent on foreign aid. To this potent mix add a host of failed promises to historically antagonistic indigenous ethnic groups, creeping environmental destruction in the jungle, a never-ending drug war for control of the opium trade, and the looming strategic interests of two nuclear-armed and mutually suspicious "super" regional powers, China and India.

There are several small, bitter wars: a continuing Burmese civil war pitting the military against democrats (which took on new force when the military junta quashed the results of the 1990 election); an "opium war" for control of the lucrative heroin trade; various ethnic conflicts, which pit the Myanmar military against tribes never quite brought to heel; and various "economic wars" including the "Teak War" involving logging rights and ecological destruction.

The democracy war pits the military (in various guises, which include the National Unity party and the State Law and Order Restoration Council [SLORC]) against the National League for Democracy (NLD). The NLD is a "spectrum" party of democratic dissidents who managed to win a solid majority of the seats in the open election held in May 1990. The NLD is led by dissident General Ti Oo and Nobel Peace Prize winner Daw Aung San Suu Kyi, daughter of Burmese World War II revolutionary hero Au Maung. Daw Aung has been held under house arrest for years.

The opium war is news that's the same old news. The "drug war" has dragged on for more or less fifty years. (Before that it was something of a smugglers' war, with opium being one of the more important contraband items. The opening of U.S. and European heroin markets led the smugglers to concentrate on what brought in the most cash.)

Opium trading has long been a way of life in Burma's rural "Golden Triangle" region. Growing poppies is easy, moving the narcotic "base" is relatively simple, and the payoff is huge. The Golden Triangle region is mountainous, jungle-covered, and isolated. The opium conflict also has strong political overtones, especially among the Shan peoples. Forces involved in the opium war include the Burmese Communist party (BCP), Chinese Nationalist Kuomintang (KMT) Opium Army, Laotian Royalists who fled the Communist Pathet Lao takeover in Vientiane, some Pathet Lao forces, and of course a sprinkling of just plain mountain bandits. The best-known drug lord, Khun Sa, controls his own well-equipped army in eastern Burma. His headquarters is the town of Ho Mong. Khun Sa is half-Chinese and half-Shan. As this book goes to press, several intelligence sources report that Khun Sa has negotiated an "amnesty" agreement with the Burmese government. There is more to this than mere surrender: Khun Sa will stop his insurgency but stay in the drug business. Odds are good he will have some new business partners, some well-placed officers in the Burmese Army. The U.S. Drug Enforcement Agency (DEA) estimated in 1994 that Burma harvested 2,400 tons of opium.

The opium war illustrates how once-politically motivated guerrilla groups can degenerate into totally bandit operations. The BCP is no longer a major political player in Burmese politics; its five thousand armed troops control many of the Shan State poppy fields. The Kuomintang Opium Army (also called Chinese Irregular Forces) are now a rather ill-defined group broken into at least two major subarmies, the Third Chinese Irregular Forces and the Fifth Chinese Irregular Forces. (The Fifth has a sub-subgroup called the Yang hwe-kang Group, named for its leader.) These troops are the descendants of remnants of various Yunan (Province) Nationalist Chinese forces and the Ninety-third Chinese Nationalist Army. After the Maoist victory in 1949, the Nationalists fled China and entered the Shan State. They went into the opium business. In 1953 and again in the early 1960s, several thousand were evacuated to Taiwan. But several thousand stayed. The dope business was lucrative. The KMT Opium Army suffered a major defeat in 1975 when the Burmese Army attacked their headquarters and disrupted their drug operation; it may now be considered something of an "ethnopolitical" group, with up to four thousand troops. At one time the KMT was allied with the Shan United Revolutionary Army, which has two thousand troops.

Another Shan outfit, the Shan United Army (SUA), still operates under the propaganda guise of Shan nationalism but was in fact a drug cartel at one time. The SUA had six thousand troops, though in 1995 this organization was reported to have been severely damaged in fighting the Burmese Army.

Geographic note: Burma covers 676,500 square kilometers, Texaslike in size. Administratively, Burma is carved into seven "minority peoples" districts, called states (e.g., Shan State), and seven "divisions" where ethnic Burmese predominate.

Burma's "ethnic conflicts" pit several armed separatist movements against the central military government, and often against each other. In 1991 around thirty "armies" were operating in Burma. Estimates for total troops in all of these ethnic armies range from 35,000 to 55,000. The lower figure seems more likely. Burma's 1994 population was 45 million. Burmese comprised 68 percent of the population, Shan 9 percent, Karen 7 percent, Rakhine 4 percent, Chinese 3 percent, Mon 2 percent, Indian 2 percent, and others (including Wa, Lahu, and Paluang) 5 percent.

The "economic wars" are a hodgepodge of conflicts, some of which are little more than battles for control of smuggling specific goods or acquiring development concessions. One worth noting is the so-called Teak War, the name applied to the battle over hardwood logging in Karen State's jungles and forests. The demand for hardwoods (largely from Japan) has produced a "smuggling" war with the Karen people caught in the middle. Industrial and military "interests" in neighboring Thailand have a finger in this conflict. Thai and Burmese army interests don't care much about the jungle and "the ecology." There is a very real risk of irreversible damage to the forests.

The War for Democracy gets most of the international press. Daw Aung San Suu Kyi, the NLD's key civilian leader, is the daughter of Aung San (Burmese independence leader assassinated in 1947). She was raised in England and is married to an Oxford professor of Tibetan studies. She returned to Burma in 1988. She has two political handicaps: She is a woman in a male-dominated culture and she has lived most of her life as an expatriate.

In 1992 the SLORC (Burmese military government) brokered a cease-fire with the Karens. In 1993 five other ethnic groups signed cease-

476 / A QUICK AND DIRTY GUIDE TO WAR

fire agreements. The SLORC, however, proceeded to break the cease-fire with the Karens in late 1994. The military also fought significant battles with the Kachin and Mon in 1994.

ASEAN nations have become increasingly interested in establishing trade links with Burma, and the military junta has used this to increase its political prestige. In 1994 the SLORC proposed a new Burmese constitution that would essentially entrench the military's political power.

In the mid-1990s, China took a renewed interest in Burma, to include new weapons for the military. China may also be operating naval intelligence facilities in Burma along the Bay of Bengal and the Andaman Sea.

Chapter 11

KOREA—THE STRANGE KINGDOM

INTRODUCTION

For the better part of the last millennium, Korea has been a vassal state of either China or Japan. The aftermath of World War II left Korea divided: the north a curious Stalinist kingdom, the south an authoritarian state in the Western bloc.

The unsuccessful 1950 North Korean Communist military invasion of the south produced the current stalemate. Seventy million Koreans are separated by an armistice line and old cold war complexities. Both Koreas want reunification, but on their own particular terms. The radically different political systems make this very difficult, even in the post–cold war environment.

Until his death in 1994, Kim Il Sung, North Korea's dictator, was obsessed with Korean reunification via military force and subversion. Economic prosperity in the more populous South made subversion difficult; a second all-out invasion was a dangerous gamble. Kim Il Sung—correctly—treated the United States and Japan as antagonists.

To level the playing field he began a nuclear weapons programs, one that has borne an evil fruit: As of mid-1995, intelligence estimates gave North Korea as many as a half-dozen nuclear bombs. Attach a nuclear warhead to one of the North Korea's improved SCUD-type theater ballistic missiles, then suddenly Guam, parts of Hawaii, and Alaska are in range, to say nothing of Japan and northern China.

The death of Kim Il Sung has left numerous unanswered questions. Kim Il Sung had dynastic ambitions. His son, Kim Jong Il, has been groomed to rule the North.

SOURCE OF CONFLICT

The Korean War (1950–53) ended in a stalemate, leaving two heavily armed and very determined adversaries confronting one another across a fortified armistice line. As this chapter is written in mid-1995, North and South Korea continue to make further preliminary moves toward reunification. This cannot take place, however, until the Communist government in the North undergoes substantial change.

Most Koreans desire reunification. To this end there have been on-again, off-again talks between the two Koreas.

America stands staunchly behind South Korea, while Russia has ceased to support its neighbor North Korea. The Kremlin, just before the Soviet Union disappeared, told North Korea to "reform" economically and politically. China waits and watches, still officially and publicly an ally of its fellow Communist state. Japan worries.

Some commentators speculate that the economically strong South will eventually "absorb" the North, mimicking West Germany's absorption of the ex-Communist East. That is a distinct possibility, especially as South Korea continues to forge strong economic links with China (See Potential Outcomes, this chapter). Perhaps we'll see it occur by 2005, if the Chinese succession comes off peacefully and North Korea begins to open a window to the world. As this chapter is being written, however, there are just too many guns and the immediate memory of fratricidal war. With two generations of government-programmed hate (in both the North and South) and the presence of large armies, the situation could easily degenerate into open war.

North Korea's isolation increases the complexity. North Korea has been one of the most, if not the most, isolated of the Communist dictatorships. Heavily militarized and closely supervised, the North's population and their controllers might react in unpleasant and/or very surprising ways to a change in their government.

The huge disparity in living standards, and political freedom, between North Korea and South Korea increases potential instability in the North. The North's economy, along with other Communist economies, declined over the years. As of mid-1995 economic shortages are rampant. After a flood, North Korea accepted some "emergency food aid" from international donors, which included the South. This could have been a diplomatic opening; more likely, it was a sign of extreme economic deprivation.

Militarily, an armed struggle between the two Koreas would be similar to World War I. Both sides still adhere to a doctrine of frontal assault until the objective is taken or the attacker is demolished. The front (the DMZ, or demilitarized zone) is 240 kilometers of mostly mountainous terrain. The largest open area is the 100-kilometer front only 24 kilometers north of the South Korean capital of Seoul. Both sides concentrate their best forces on this front.

Even the Koreans realize that a battlefield decision would be difficult to achieve if either side relied solely upon their conventional forces. Therefore, the North Koreans have organized commando forces numbering some 100,000 men. These troops are trained to move by air and sea into South Korea's interior. There the North Korean forces would attack logistical and other essential support installations. South Korea has responded by organizing its own Special Forces, on the U.S. model, who will return the favor. In addition, both sides have large militias distributed throughout their territories. Over 1 million men are so equipped in North Korea and nearly 5 million in South Korea.

Starting in the mid-1970s, North Korea began a program to develop and produce chemical weapons. Buying equipment from Japan (for the manufacture of insecticide, etc.) and weapons technology from Russia, by the 1980s the North Koreans had chemical weapons. South Korea did not. South Korea did have nuclear weapons, at least nuclear weapons belonging to U.S. units in South Korea. What North Korea expected to gain by using chemical weapons is difficult to fathom. Perhaps they assumed that U.S. forces would not use nuclear weapons if only South Korean troops were hit with chemical weapons. Perhaps the North Korean leaders had taken leave of their senses. It simply added to the general fear that North Korea would do something self-destructive, and harmful to South Korea in the bargain.

The Japanese are very concerned about North Korean nuclear weapons. The "nuclear card" has led the Japanese to support developing antiballistic missile (ABM) defense systems.

WHO'S INVOLVED

North Korean "hereditary Communist" regime—Kim Jong Il, son of Kim Il Sung, and the military dynasty in P'yongyang.

South Korea—South Korea is a military-authoritarian nation getting rich and, increasingly, evolving into a democracy. South Korea's capital, Seoul, has 20 percent of the population and produces nearly half the nation's economic wealth. It is also within artillery range of North Korea.

United States—The guarantor of South Korean independence and a major trade partner. South Korea's Korean War generation remembers the sacrifices and generosity of Americans and remains grateful. The younger generations have known only peace and prosperity and tend to attribute that to Korean virtues rather than any contributions from unwanted foreigners. They often blame the United States for Korea's division and militarization.

Russia—Former patron of North Korean Communist regime. Russia, because it shares a border with North Korea and is wary of China's influence, still plays a role. North Korea sorely misses "Soviet" economic and military aid. The loss of the Soviet Union as a major diplomatic and military ally hurt even more. Some Russian ultranationalists still admire North Korea's militancy.

United Nations—Still technically involved in overseeing the armistice.

China—North Korea's rescuer in 1950, and still ultimate guarantor of North Korean independence.

Japan—Although generally disliked by Koreans, a major trading partner and economic influence in North and South. Also shares many military concerns with the South, particularly potential aggressive moves by North Korea. Japan is also allied with the United States.

GEOGRAPHY

The Korean Peninsula is 966 kilometers long and 217 kilometers wide. North Korea has 120,500 square kilometers (about the size of Mississippi); South Korea has around 98,500 (approximately the size of Indiana). The eastern half of the peninsula is covered with a rugged, comparatively underpopulated mountain range. On the west coast lies a coastal plain containing most of the agriculture and population. (For example, the South Korean capital of Seoul and its immediate environs contain 20 percent of South Korea's population of 45 million. North Korea has around 25 million people.)

The northern slice of the peninsula has more natural resources, including coal and iron. The south is the breadbasket, with 22 percent of the land being arable and farmed intensively.

In military terms, Korea is infantry country—and at that, country for infantry with very strong legs. The dominant features are very steep hills in the form of parallel ridge lines. From the infantry perspective that is one ridge line right after another. This is an ideal situation for defensive warfare. In the last thirty years the South Koreans have built up their road network; the North Koreans have not. The North Koreans utilize the bare minimum of roads necessary to keep their agriculture and mining economy functioning.

There are very few good ports on the east coast. The west and south coasts are much better off, supporting a large fishing industry.

Both Koreas are, ethnically, almost 100 percent Korean. A small Chinese minority (twenty thousand or so) live in South Korea. South Korea is quickly becoming a predominantly Christian nation. According to 1992 estimates, 48 percent of the people of South Korea called themselves Christian; 47 percent were Buddhist; 3 percent were Confucian. Communist and officially atheist North Korea remains Confucian and Buddhist. A very tiny minority in both Koreas practice the syncretic Chondogyo faith (the Religion of the Heavenly Way).

A unique feature of Korean landscape is the DMZ (demilitarized zone) that marks the front line positions of UN and Chinese troops when the cease-fire went into effect in 1953. Each side withdrew 2 kilometers, leaving a 2.5-mile-wide neutral zone. This zone stretches some 240 kilometers from one side of the peninsula to the other. Within the DMZ, nothing but the wreckage of war (as of 1953) and wildlife remain. The DMZ contains many old minefields as well as other military debris. That includes a few skeletons of troops who died there and whose bodies were not found by the time both armies withdrew. The wildlife in the DMZ flourishes, including many of the few remaining specimens of the Korean tiger. The grass grows wild and over two feet high, along with sundry brush and some trees. Both sides occasionally burn off the brush to make it more difficult for infiltrators to get through.

Some 500–1,000 meters from the north and south edge of the DMZ is a barbed-wire fence, electrified in many places, with a ten-meter cleared area on either side of it. Some sectors of the fence have other sensors nearby and the entire fence is covered by a series of small bunkers (for two or three men). These are usually only occupied at night or when the political situation heats up. Sometimes the bunkers are connected to each other by a trench, but they are there mainly for observation. Nothing larger than a machine gun is used in them.

About 300 meters behind the fence line bunkers is a double barbed-wire fence, another cleared zone, and platoon-size bunker systems (each individual concrete bunker can hold four to six men) connected along the length of the DMZ by trenches and tunnels. Where appropriate, there are also antitank obstacles, in the form of thick concrete pillars or 10- to 30-foot earth-and-stone walls. Also found in this area are concrete artillery positions, underground ammo dumps, command centers, and so on. In effect, a fortified line stretching across the peninsula. Each kilometer of DMZ frontage is held by 100–200 troops in peacetime, with several hundred more behind the lines and over 1,000 men per kilometer for wartime deployment.

Nearly a million acres of Korean real estate (nearly 1 percent of both countries) is taken up by the DMZ and adjacent military areas.

Unlike the Berlin Wall (and the border between East and West Germany), the DMZ is heavily fortified and manned on both sides. Moreover, the North Koreans have been digging tunnels under the DMZ for years and regularly send infiltrators across. The DMZ is an active zone of military operations, just waiting for a spark to set it off. The DMZ is the Eastern European Iron Curtain writ very large.

The climate of Korea, from both the infantry and meteorological perspective, consists of sweltering summers and bitterly cold (and relatively dry) winters. A rainy season occurs in early summer.

HISTORY

Many Koreans trace their ancestry to Mongol and other similar central Asian invaders (a few Korean academics also claim ethnic bonds with the Turkic peoples). Around the sixth century, Korea became a united kingdom. For centuries Korea was an isolated kingdom, walking a wary path among the local superpowers (China, Japan, and, since the nineteenth century, Russia). The Koreans tried to follow a strict isolationist policy.

Japan annexed Korea in 1910, as a result of Russia's defeat in the Russo-Japanese War of 1904–5. Japan tried to eradicate the Korean language and culture and turn the Koreans into second-class Japanese. Japanese attempts to delete Korean culture merely created a vehement dislike of the Japanese by the Koreans, which persists to this day.

World War II ended the Japanese occupation. Because the USSR bordered Korea, Russian troops replaced Japanese forces in the northern part of the country, while American forces landed and took the southern half. A "temporary" administration was set up in the North. That administration was quickly turned over to a Russian-trained Korean Communist named Kim Il Sung. The United States wanted to replace its occupation forces with a democratic Korean administration. Elections were held under UN auspices in 1948, but the Russians wouldn't let the UN election commission into the North. Syngman Rhee, a longtime champion of an independent Korea, was elected president in the South. The UN proclaimed Rhee to be the president of the provisional Republic of Korea. Kim Il Sung and the Russians denounced Rhee's election. In June 1949 the United States withdrew all but a small contingent of advisers.

China has always had a significant Korean population. Many Koreans joined the Communist forces during the Chinese civil war. When the Chinese civil war ended in 1949, many of these soldiers returned to North Korea and joined the North Korean Army. That gave the North an army with a cadre of combat veterans.

Communism appealed to many Koreans in the North and South; everyone had suffered severe economic deprivation under the Japanese occupation. It had been two generations since Korea had governed itself and much had changed in the world. The Communists had succeeded in Russia and China. For the young and the visionary, it seemed the way of the future. Moreover, the government in South Korea was riddled with Koreans who had served in the despised Japanese colonial government. In North Korea, only those who had been dedicated Communists were allowed to hold government posts.

Although there were many Chinese and Russian military advisers in the North, at least they could be seen as "neighbors." In the South, the American advisers were from a quite alien culture. The Americans preached this strange concept called democracy. While communism was equally strange to Korean life, "the Party" still had the familiar Confucian hierarchy of officials and bureaucrats.

Korea had had one major Western influence: German missionaries. Those missionaries were not expelled by the Japanese during World War II because of the alliance with Hitler. The good works of the missionaries produced an affection for things German, ranging from industrial efficiency to baked goods, beer, Goethe, and Beethoven.

In 1950 the Communists in North Korea saw that the Americans had withdrawn all but token advisory forces. The United States also made a severe political blunder by implying that the U.S. Asian defense line did not include Korea (an error repeated with Iraq and Kuwait in 1990—so much for the lessons of history). A Communist-inspired insurgency in South Korea was going well, but was taking too long. In June 1950, with the nod from Russia's Stalin, the North Korean Army crossed the border to hasten the revolutionary process.

America responded, and three years later the Chinese (who soon came in to save North Korea) and the North Koreans agreed to an armistice. The battle line remained.

In the North, a Communist bureaucracy took over, eliminating absolute privation, but spreading poverty—except among the senior bureaucrats and the members of the armed forces. These "cadres" lived a better life than the "people." A classic military dictatorship under Kim Il Sung was taking shape. Abortive coups by various factions were put down in the late 1950s. In the South, eight years of generally corrupt and ineffective civilian government were followed by military dictatorship in the early 1960s. Unlike the North, the South Korean military did not try to take over everything. The takeover was largely in revulsion to the corruption of the civilian government. Thus the military enforced clean, by regional standards, government.

Aided by an admirable work ethic, a desire for education, American loans, and a proximity to the flourishing Japanese economy, the Korean economy began to take off in the 1960s. The results of this economic expansion will most influence the immediate future of both Koreas.

Consider the current contrasts. North Korea occupies 55 percent of the peninsula but has only one third of the population and about one tenth of the GDP. South Korean military spending is more than twice that of North Korea. North Korea keeps conscripts in uniform twice as long as South Korea. The North has about 20 percent more men in uniform, but the South has superior weaponry.

Koreans tend to be courageous and diligent fighters. The Korean people are very keen on physical fitness, careful preparation, and unquestioning respect for authority. As demonstrated in the Korean and Vietnam wars, Korean soldiers make formidable adversaries.

Koreans of all levels are hardworking and persistent. The South Koreans save money as diligently as the Japanese, thus giving their government and industrial leaders the capital and support required to lift South Korea from poverty in the 1960s to a major industrial state in the 1980s.

In the North, the same Korean qualities brought about the world's most successful dictatorship. That, apparently, was a wasted effort and all Koreans simply wait for the fall of the Communist government and reunification.

North Korea has 12 percent of the working male population assigned to the military. The minimum conscription period is five years.
The economy is controlled by the state and the state is controlled by
the Kim dynasty (Kim Il Sung, and now his son, Kim Jong Il) and its
personal security apparatus, which includes the secret police and domination of the army. In typical police state fashion, all material and
social benefits flow from enthusiastic participation in following the
regime. In truth the North Korean government is the army; as long as
Kim Jong Il controls the army, he controls North Korea. To keep the
army in line, Kim has an extensive network of informants and a powerful secret police. The army can be picked apart by the secret police,
but not replaced by it. The army is not organized to go after the secret
police, as the army officers are never sure who works for the secret
police and who is just another soldier. The economy has been slowly
declining through the 1980s and into the 1990s. More important politically is North Korea's ability to keep foreign media out.

The prosperity in South Korea, however, has not gone unnoticed
by the northerners. South Korean propaganda has seen to that. Desire
for unification and an increase in the standard of living are an ever
present danger to the North Korean government.

In the South, there is enough prosperity to keep everyone happy, or
at least busy. While student activists and opponents of the government
make a lot of noise, they have little impact on the population as a
whole. A basic conservatism, traditional subservience to authority, and
economic prosperity make the population content with the current
semidemocratic government. The only previous experiences with democracy, in the 1950s, were not favorable (corruption and economic
stagnation). Before that there had always been a king. A king by any
other name is an armed strongman who takes over and rules successfully. The post-1953 southern "king" did (and then retired to a mon-
astery); the northern "king," with his alien doctrine, has not. So the
northern dictator cannot even use the South's lack of democracy for
propaganda anymore. The northerners do make much of the foreigners (Americans) in the country. The North is pure, only Koreans, and
this form of xenophobia plays well on both sides of the DMZ. The
poverty in the North is a growing shadow on North Korea's remnant
prestige as a "pure Korean" government.

The return of democracy to the South in the late 1980s changed the political scene significantly. There were three principal changes.

1. Most noticeable was the reduction in agitation for the overthrow of the government. The first elected government was put together by a disciplined collection of officials who had served in the previous military-dominated regimes. This came about because the opposition was too splintered to put up a majority coalition. The new government then joined with one of the opposition groups to form an overwhelming majority. The opposition parties left out made loud and long protests, but they could not deny that it was done democratically. In the next round of elections, the opposition got into power, but that first transition government was helpful, if not essential, in making the move from military dictatorship to democracy without a lot of violence.

2. A more troublesome development of evolving democracy was a decline in the labor discipline that had allowed South Korea to be a major "low-cost producer" of manufactured goods. Workers were no longer willing to defer economic gains for the sake of a strong export economy. Koreans are not like the Japanese in this respect. Koreans are much more individualistic and suspicious of authority than the Japanese. South Korea still had a trade surplus going into the 1990s, but it was obvious that the earlier "labor cost" advantage was disappearing. Once labor costs get out of hand, export sales decline, the economy can go into recession, and another source of political discontent emerges. But the Korean discipline and boldness appear to be preventing this. Although wages shot ahead of productivity in 1989, demands were scaled back in the 1990s and, so far, the economy has continued to prosper.

3. Regional and class antagonisms are no longer hidden by authoritarian control. The crises of World War II, the Korean War, reconstruction, and the military government suppressed regional competition (southern versus central, rural versus urban). Also put aside were the class (economic and cultural) differences between the educated and professional workers and the laborers. Both of these "industrial" groups have been at odds with the farmers. With

everyone now having a more meaningful vote, politicians are not reluctant to exploit these differences in order to gain votes.

These three changes have altered the political landscape in South Korea. These changes affect the relationship between North and South Korea and also U.S.-South Korea relations. The increase in democracy in South Korea has improved relations with the United States and made it harder for the North Korean government to view the South as just another military dictatorship. The shakeup in South Korea's economy has also calmed U.S. calls for trade restrictions. The South's increasingly powerful economy stands in stark contrast to the continuing economic decline in the North. Should the two Koreas unite, the regional and class differences will be major problems.

As of 1995 the North Korean military dictatorship was under increasing international pressure and the South's democracy was strong enough to begin to weed out corrupt politicians. For over two decades (until the late 1980s), South Korea had been an economic success story but had a dismal human rights record. That's changing. The North's economic performance has been dismal and its human rights record worse. Now North Korea appeals to South Korea and Japan for food aid, but keeps its army ready. Despite the starvation and economic failure, North Korea's military dictatorship in Communist trappings slowly turns into a hereditary autocracy in Communist trappings.

LOCAL POLITICS

North Korea

The Kim family—Kim Il Sung was an exiled Korean Communist most of his life until he was plucked out of relative obscurity in 1945 (at age thirty-four) to lead the new Communist state of North Korea. Kim quickly made the most of his opportunities, first suppressing all potential opposition and then surviving the disastrous Korean War (1950–53). Kim groomed his son to inherit the regime. Growing old none too gracefully, he ordered a terror campaign against South Korea and its rulers from the 1960s on. This included commando raids, assassinations, and subversion in general. Kim ran a tight ship, so tight that there were very few challenges to his rule. He was a world-class dictator, but even Kim was shaken by the events of 1989 in the Communist world. After the elder Kim died in 1994, his son, Kim Jong Il, came to power. He has two younger brothers (Kim Pyong Il and Kim Yong Ju) born to his father's second wife. Kim Jong Il is not as able a leader as his father.

The *nomenklatura*—Just like every other Communist state, a new royalty has been created from those demonstrating sufficient loyalty to the Party and especially to the Kim regime. North Korea's bureaucrats are armed bureaucrats: All positions of authority are filled with military-trained personnel (which makes North Korea an army with a country attached).

The Inmun Gun—This is the North Korean Army, in which nearly every adult male serves at least five years. With about 800,000 troops, over 3,000 tanks, 3,000 other AFV, nearly 8,000 artillery pieces (including 2,000 rocket launchers). Two armored divisions, twelve motorized infantry and twenty-three "leg" infantry divisions (for occupying the DMZ positions).

Juche—Modern dictatorships usually come with some kind of new political philosophy to explain and justify the tyranny. Kim Il Sung's particular secular religion was uniquely Korean and is called Juche. What makes it so "Korean" is its emphasis on the uniqueness of the Korean character and a particular emphasis on the need to unite Korea under the Juche banner. Combining nationalism, collectivism, and shards of several Asian and Western philosophies, Kim made Juche the state religion, or philosophy anyway. Some believe it, but hardly anyone dares criticize it. Kim's son has not disowned it.

The silent majority—North Korea's isolated proletarians and peasants (see Participant Strategies, this chapter).

South Korea

Military-industrial complex—Although officially a free market, capitalist economy, Korea's enormous economic growth since the 1960s is the result of government support for a few huge corporations. While not a state-controlled economy—the megacorporations (*chaebol*) are quite competitive—the economy is very much state influenced. This group comprises several percent of the population, up to 5 percent if you include loyal retainers and followers.

NSPA—National Security Planning Agency. This outfit was, until the democrats took over, the Korean Central Intelligence Agency (KCIA) and is, on the surface, the Korean version of the U.S. CIA (although in Korea that includes the large military intelligence agencies). The NSPA is more than that, as it does most of its work inside the country, while the U.S. CIA is barred by law from conducting operations in the United States. Until the 1980s, the KCIA was a potent political power. Originally set up to deal with the rabidly aggressive clandestine operations of the North Koreans (and North Korean operations in general), the KCIA operatives worked their way into every aspect of South Korean life. While the military was the primary kingmaker from the 1950s, the KCIA held a veto by virtue of their huge amount of information, including embarrassing details of most presidential candidates' social and business affairs. Still a power to be reckoned with, the NSPA has been tamed somewhat as democracy became more of a reality through the late 1980s. The NSPA is not a large organization, unless you count the informants and other part-timers. In that case, you have several hundred thousand people involved.

Democrats—The newly emerging democrats are South Korea's hope for the future. Democracy is a new phenomenon. Until the Japanese took over in 1905, Korea had always been a monarchy. After the Japanese left in 1945, the North went Communist (as did many people in the South until the 1950 war). The U.S. occupiers wanted the South to become a democracy. But a series of dictatorships by the military-industrial politicians left democracy on hold until the 1980s when increasing agitation and instability made democracy preferable to revolt (and poverty). The former democratic "dissidents" came into their own. Unfortunately, the democratic-minded folks take their freedom of speech and expression too literally, fragmenting into contending parties instead of uniting to take power. The Democratic Justice party (DJP) was run by ex-General Roh (pronounced Noh) Tae Woo, who became the president of the country. Opposition parties are led by the "three Kims": Kim Dae Jung (Peace and Democracy party—PPD), Kim Young Sam (Korean Reunification Democratic party—RPD), and Kim Jong Pil (New Democratic Republican party—NDRP). Kim Young Sam won the next presidential elections and took office in early 1993. That was the first democratic transfer of power from one elected president to another in Korean history. Korean democrats are finding themselves split by long-suppressed regional and class differences. Overall, however, at least 80 percent of the population is in favor of some form of democracy.

Radical nationalists—Largely, but not exclusively, composed of wild-eyed students, this group tends toward radical proposals put forward in a radical fashion (riots, fire bombs, and general disorder). These people are not just for radical solutions (some socialist, some otherwise), but also hold Korean nationalism as their primary purpose. Reunification as soon as possible is a big issue, and will remain so until the unification takes place. Small in numbers—under ten thousand activists, with over ten times that number willing to turn out for a demonstration—they look more formidable when rioting.

Labor unions—A large number of the *chaebol* (megacorporations) workers are unionized. Overall, only about two million union members nationwide. Originally, there were to be Japanese-style unions, subservient to the needs of the company. But the workers eventually thought otherwise and now the labor unions are an increasingly independent force to be reckoned with. They are largely interested only in labor-related issues, particularly higher pay and improved working conditions. They also tend to focus the discontent of those who do not own land or their own homes (60 percent of the population) and thus have not benefited from the sharp increase in real estate values in the 1980s. Unlike the Japanese, Koreans do not tolerate well large inequities in income. Although the portion of families living in poverty has declined from 53 percent in 1965 to 23 percent in 1990, there are now a lot more very wealthy people riding around in fancy cars and generally living it up. That is a source of social strife that the growing labor movement exploits.

Farmers—South Korea always was, and to a large extent still is, an agricultural country. Some 20 percent of the workforce of 17 million are farming. This is a conservative group that has prospered with the growing economy. In fact, most farmers have tended to do better than any other group because of the vast increase in land values as the national trade surplus turned positive in the late 1980s.

United Nations—Because of the resolutions of 1950, the UN is still a participant in defense of South Korea. Given the demise of the cold war and a closer relationship among the superpowers, any aggressive actions by North Korea could expect a cohesive UN opposition. United Nations/U.S. forces in South Korea were sent under a UN mandate, and remnants of that mandate remain in the form of various inspection and monitoring organizations. In the 1990s the UN's activities in the control of nuclear weapons proliferation became more popular. Now that the world has only one superpower, nearly all nations are quite keen on limiting the spread of nuclear weapons technology. The 1991 Persian Gulf War put a scare into most governments when it was discovered how close Iraq was to building nuclear weapons, and how likely Iraq was to use them.

North Korea was known to be keen on acquiring nuclear weapons and the UN nuclear inspectors turned their attention toward North Korea. The Nuclear Non-Proliferation Treaty (NPT), a UN-sponsored affair that was signed by most of the world's nations, was monitored by the IAEA (International Atomic Energy Agency). All nations that signed the NPT were supposed to allow IAEA inspectors access to any of their real, or suspected, nuclear facilities. Inspections in Iraq had to be done under threat of military force. North Korean inspections required a lot of diplomacy. The UN was also taking advantage of its newly acquired influence, a side benefit of the disappearance of the struggle between the superpowers. Every nation, if only for show, now supported UN peacekeeping activities. There was immense pressure on North Korea to go along with IAEA inspections and cease efforts to build nuclear weapons. A deal was worked out in 1994 whereby North Korea would stop work on nuclear weapons in return for economic aid (including new nuclear power plants) from America. Negotiations went on through 1995, as North Korea resisted having South Korea provide the nuclear technology. No other nation was willing to provide the several billion dollars of nuclear technology, and

North Korea was reluctant to receive same from the South. For decades, northern propaganda to North Koreans had pictured South Korea as a poverty-stricken, backward puppet of the United States. To receive state-of-the-art nuclear power technology from South Korea would discredit those decades of propaganda and could lead to unrest. North Korea has little choice. China now prefers to sell food (no more credit) and the North has had to go begging for handouts from nations like Japan.

China—Provided manpower to produce stalemate during the 1950–53 war. Traditional patron state of Korea. A firm backer of North Korea, but more in need of South Korea's economic muscle. The closer China gets to South Korea, the more isolated North Korea is. Once the Communist party loses its control of China, North Korea (if it still exists) will have lost its major ally and supporter.

PARTICIPANT STRATEGIES AND GOALS

North Korea

The Kim Family—While Kim Jong Il and his family officially adhere to a modern (Communist) philosophy, in practice they are traditional monarchists. Take away the Marxist cant and you have a very traditional Korean aristocrat surrounded by courtiers and loyal generals, and espousing a xenophobic and nationalistic line (Juche). Kim has seen what has happened to his fellow Communist dictators and it's uncertain if he has developed a plan to avoid a similar fate or is simply reacting to each new shock. Kim has two choices: a German solution (allow free elections for unification as in East Germany, with a likely similar result) or a Romanian solution (a little bit of coup and civil war, with possible South Korean intervention and a large chance of Kim's violent death). There is no precedent for a Communist dictator hanging on indefinitely, and it's not likely to happen. Moreover, Kim Jong Il is not as powerful a leader as his father was, in the ways of orthodox communism. There's a much better chance that the younger Kim will cut a reunification deal with the South than his father. But first Kim has to convince the other members of his ruling circle, and the younger Kim is not as skillful in these matters as his father.

The *nomenklatura*—As the years went by, key jobs in the economy were given out more for loyalty to Kim than for ability to make things work. Starting in the 1970s, things began to unravel and the economy is in such a sorry state now that few of the nomenklatura bureaucrats can expect to keep their positions if unification (or even a change in government) occurs. Some of these bureaucrats see the writing on the wall and would welcome a change, even if it meant their jobs. But too many of these party hacks are still looking out for number one and can be expected to make whatever inept moves they are capable of to stifle reform, unification, or a change in government. That is particularly true of the security forces, who have made a lot of enemies over the years. That said, since the 1980s there has been increasing contact between senior officials in the North and South. The persistent rumors have been that deals are being made to, in effect, buy out the northern leadership when the time is right (that is, when northern officials can make a move without getting a bullet in the back of the head).

The Inmun Gun (armed forces)—Despite the praise the North Korean Army receives from their opposite numbers in the West (a form of professional courtesy), the generals are not much more able than their counterparts in the nomenklatura. However, the generals have guns, and some troops that will follow them. However, most of the troops are conscripts and, despite years of indoctrination, many of these young men can be expected to catch whatever political fever the general population contracts. Most soldiers would be quite happy to dispense with military service. The professional officers need some kind of economic inducement, as they saw how promptly their opposite numbers in the East German Army were unemployed after unification.

The silent majority—With the fall of Ceauşescu's Romanian dictatorship as an example of an isolated and "hereditary" Communist regime collapsing, one can argue that the smallest disruption in North Korea could lead to a national revolt. But who knows—the lid in North Korea is screwed on tightly. The biggest spur to a popular uprising is the increasingly shabby state of the economy. Despite the emphasis on agriculture, North Korea still has to import a lot of food.

The economy has sunk to the level where even that is no longer a sure thing because of a lack of hard currency or credit. As the Russians (and the French) are fond of pointing out, when there are food short-ages, unrest and revolution are usually not far behind.

South Korea

Military-industrial complex—There are already murmurs about a "peace dividend" in South Korea. Although the economy continues to grow, the popular move toward pay increases and shorter work weeks is putting a damper on that growth. The military still gets 3–4 percent of GNP, which is high for a developing country. But the percentage has been coming down since the end of the cold war, even as GNP growth continues at an above-average rate (5–8 percent a year). As North Korea's military threat shrinks, all Koreans look for relief from the defense burdens they have supported for nearly fifty years. The discredited generals on both sides of the DMZ can do little to stem this attitude. The energetic industrialists in South Korea have gained most of their success from nonmilitary manufacturing. The prospects of more customers, and workers, in the North is appealing. Certainly, another war could severely damage much of the industry concentrated in the northern part of South Korea. The industrialists want peace, reunification, and subservient labor unions. They also want more workers, and that's what unification would provide. The North has chronic unemployment and a workforce that would see wages less than half of what southerners make as a fortune beyond imagining.

NSPA—Despite unsavory, and often illegal, involvement in political matters, the intelligence crowd has managed to escape massive public wrath. The NSPA has mixed feelings about reunification, as it would eliminate one of their chief sources of work. The major objective of the NSPA (like their "big brother," the CIA, in the United States) is to transform themselves into something more acceptable to a post–cold war world. For the moment, however, the NSPA serves a vital purpose in keeping an eye on developments in the North, and their impact on the South. Whether it's an invasion by the North Korean Army, or a civil war up there, the NSPA is supposed to give some warning. Information is vital in a situation where things could get real bad real fast.

Democrats—Aside from obtaining free elections, the democrats want elections to mean something. Old habits die hard and many of the generals, bureaucrats, and industrialists would restore their dictatorial control of the government if they thought they could get away with it. But once the democratic genie is out of the bottle, it is difficult to get it back in. The other major problem facing the democrats is the pluralistic nature of the democratic process. Korea has never had a tradition of coalition politics; it has generally been "winner take all." As the various regional, economic, ideological, and other interest groups sort themselves out, the democrats have to continually struggle to work out Korean methods to move forward without need of a traditional strongman. Many use contemporary Japan as a model.

Radical nationalists—For the moment, this is a fringe group. Once reunification is achieved, there will be a lot more Juche-indoctrinated nationalists from the North. If the German experience is any guide, one can expect to see an increase in socialist-minded voters from the North (strange as it may seem, but decades of indoctrination have their effect). While getting U.S. military forces out of the country is not a particularly odious goal for the Koreans or Americans, Radical nationalists have more troublesome items on their agenda, such as "purifying" the Western "pollution" out of Korean society and playing a hard line on international trade issues. This could create big problems, but probably not until the next decade.

Labor unions—Unlike the more cooperative Japanese unions, the South Korean labor leaders find themselves edging into politics. That would have disruptive effects on a nation not accustomed to dealing with factionalism.

Farmers—As in Japan, the farmers find themselves fighting a losing battle. Korean farmers cannot grow enough food to support the population, yet the nation does not want to completely abandon its increasingly uncompetitive agriculture heritage, which, until the last few decades, was the occupation of most of the population. If the farmers get sufficiently organized (especially after reunification) and manage to make an effective appeal to the general population's longings for their agricultural past, there would be created a major trade problem with agricultural exporters, particularly the United States. But, then, more of the farmers might just leave their fields and get jobs in the cities, as most of them have done in the past thirty years. Farming, particularly rice farming, is a hard life.

United States—Primary objective here is the demise of North Korea, a military and diplomatic thorn in America's side since the late 1940s. The North Korean nuclear threat and the end of the cold war have moved Korea to near the top of America's list of diplomatic priorities. Getting the expensive U.S. forces out of South Korea would be a bonus. Meanwhile, the job of containing North Korean military moves remains.

Russia—In the past, it was thought that Russia would not willingly give up a vassal state like North Korea. But the events of 1989 and 1991 have made Russia much less keen about maintaining the dictatorship in North Korea. The flagrant terrorism practiced by North Korea, as well as its eagerness to acquire chemical, or even nuclear, weapons is seen as the kind of mischief Russia could do without. Moreover, Russia would be better off with a Korea on its borders similar to the economic powerhouse found in South Korea. Russia's former Eastern European satellites see things the same way, and have been increasing economic and political relations with South Korea.

United Nations—A peaceful reunification of Korea (and settlement of the only major war the UN participated directly in) would be real nice.

China—The Chinese remain a unexpected source of support, despite closer economic ties with South Korea. If China chooses to oppose reunification, it is not likely to happen. An active economic and diplomatic effort by America and South Korea has tried to ensure that China will not interfere to prevent unification of the two Koreas. China experienced diplomatic isolation after 1989's unrest. Chinese distaste for the way they are treated by the rest of the (increasingly democratic) world makes them more tolerant of the North Korean government. Diplomatic allies are few and pariahs tend to cling together for mutual support. Even so, China has growing economic links to South Korea, and ultimately needs South Korea's economic cooperation more than it needs North Korea's diplomatic succor. North Korea, however, could ally with China against Taiwan.

Japan—A stable economic, military, and political ally in the neighborhood is always welcome. Would a reunified Korea be that kind of ally? Many Japanese wonder. Although Japan has warmed up to North Korea over the years, little serious can come of it because of the sorry state of North Korea's economy and ideology. South Korea is already a valued neighbor. Despite the centuries-old animosity between Japanese and Koreans, the Pax Americana has provided both nations with an atmosphere in which they could learn to get along. No one seems unhappy with this development. In 1995, Japan approached North Korea with an offer of diplomatic recognition and generous economic aid—actually a polite way of giving North Korea the same monetary reparations earlier given to South Korea.

"MOST LIKELY" POLITICAL TREND CHARTS

SOUTH KOREA

Gv95	Gv20	PC95	PC20	R95	R20	Ec95	Ec20	EdS95	EdS20
AD6,5	RD7,5	7	7	5	4+	8−	8−	6	6+

AD = Authoritarian Democracy
RD = Representative Democracy (effectiveness, stability)

NORTH KOREA

Gv95	Gv20	PC95	PC20	R95	R20	Ec95	Ec20	EdS95	EdS20
ST5,4	ST5,3	7	3	9	9	2−	2−	2+	2

ST = Socialist Totalitarian (effectiveness, stability)

"UNITED KOREA"

Gv20	PC20	R20	Ec20	EdS20
RD5,4	5	5	4	6−

REGIONAL POWERS AND POWER INTEREST INDICATOR CHART

SECOND KOREAN WAR
RELATIVE

	Economic Interests	Historical Interests	Political Interest	Military Interest	Force Generation Potential	Ability to Intervene Politically
N. Korea	9	9	9	9	8+	7
S. Korea	9	9	9	9	8	8
United States	5	8	8	8	7	7
Russia	3	7	6	8	5	6
China	6	8	9	8+	7	7
Japan	7	8	9	9	3	5

A united Korea would be the third strongest nation, economically and militarily, in the region, after China and Japan. Note that a united Korea has about the same population as Vietnam, but over ten times the economic power.

POTENTIAL OUTCOMES

Since Kim Il Sung died in 1994 and the new regime under Kim Jong Il has not established a track record, our analysis had to account for and explore several different strategic options. We concluded that during the 1995–96 time frame, the new regime will simply be getting its feet wet. We used a ten-year (1996–2005) window for the analysis in this chapter.

1. 35 percent chance through 2005: Peaceful reunification of the Koreas. It's East and West Germany all over again. A scenario: By

2005, China will be under new leadership. The South Korean economy will continue to expand; the northern economy will continue to perform miserably. This outcome assumes that the diplomatic tussle over North Korea's nuclear weapons increasingly brings North Korea into the world arena. Other issues of interest, such as electrical power and markets for North Korean natural resources, slowly open the North Korean leadership. What does the deal entail? Amnesty for the North Korean leadership and strict, nonnuclear neutrality from the newly united Korea.

2. 30 percent chance through 2005: Continuation of the status quo. Even with the possible instabilities associated with changes in the North Korean regime, the odds are that the current stalemate will continue. The cost, in lives and material, of trying to change things quickly, and violently, is far too high.

3. 25 percent chance through 2005: Political breakdown in North Korea. This leads to a dangerous civil war in the North, a "Korean Lebanon." Southern forces eventually intervene. Korea is reunified.

4. 4 percent chance through 2005: As in Outcome 3, political breakdown in North Korea leads to civil war; however, the presence of North Korean nuclear weapons causes the South to hesitate. The North Korean Army remains loyal to the Communist government. A Communist government, with or without the Kim dynasty, remains in power. Return to status quo (Outcome 2).

5. 2.5 percent chance through 2005: North Korea launches an invasion of the South. The invasion fails. The subsequent South Korean counteroffensive reunifies the country. (But China will demand that united Korea, if it wants to continue to exist, be neutral.)

6. 1.5 percent chance through 2005: Outcome 5 with a different twist. North Korea launches an invasion of the South. The invasion bogs down and fails. China and the United States force the Koreas to return to the post–Korean War DMZ. Reunification is now decades away.

7. 1.5 percent chance through 2005: Successful North Korean military invasion of South Korea. China gives Pyongyang its tacit support. The South Korean government falls. This outcome is highly un-

likely. South Korea would have to weaken considerably in military strength. The U.S.–South Korean relation would have to deteriorate significantly. But as long as the North can keep its huge military together, this remains a small possibility.

8. 0.5 percent chance through 2005: Just a smidgen, but a terrible smidgen. North Korea launches a nuclear attack on South Korea and destroys Seoul. North Asia and east Asia go tilt. The United States, Japan, and China, in an odd coalition, counterattack Pyongyang. The Korean Peninsula is devastated.

COST AND KINDS OF WAR

The Korean War of 1950–53 killed over two million people and injured three million more. The cost of that war was hundreds of billions of dollars. Another war would be at least as destructive economically, although less deadly in human terms if the Chinese do not intervene. The prospect of such a war precipitating a larger war between America and China increases the potential costs more than tenfold.

For nearly forty years the Communist and UN armies have fought, or been ready to fight, two kinds of war. On the relatively flat plain there is the mobile war with armored vehicles. Most of Korea, however, is hills and mountains and that is where the infantry war is fought; call it trench warfare in the mountains. Climatic extremes complete the terrible experience. Muggy, torrid summers are followed by harsh winters; although snowfall is not particularly heavy, it is quite cold.

Before Korea is united, there may be another kind of war, a disorderly war in the cities and urban areas of North Korea. That would be a war of civil disorder brought about by the fall of the Kim dynasty. The son, the longtime heir apparent, apparently does not have all his father's talents. The generals and senior bureaucrats have been seen to maneuver for positions of strength after the elder Kim's death. The succession question could be ultimately settled with words, or pistols in meeting rooms, or with heavy weapons in the streets as the northern population riots. A "Korean Lebanon" could ensue, with the use of nuclear weapons a frightening possibility. South Korea may feel constrained to move north to keep the peace and facilitate reunification. There is great potential for violence in Korea in the 1990s.

Part 5
THE AMERICAS

Long a bastion of little wars, and bereft of larger conflicts, this pattern persists. Dominated, economically, militarily, and diplomatically, by the United States, the Americas keep the peace partially because it's obvious that if anyone gets too rambunctious, the "Colossus of the North" will, as it has often done in the past, intervene.

Chapter 12

BORDER WARS AND COCAINE COWBOYS: PERU, ECUADOR, AND COLOMBIA

INTRODUCTION

The ancient Incan Empire ran up and down the spine of the high Andes Mountain range. Pizarro came seeking gold, and he found it. He destroyed the Incan Empire in the process, but did not destroy the Incas. Subsequent Spanish settlers set up their own empires, with Indians supplying the workers.

Over time the Spaniards' separate empires began to squabble. Peru and Ecuador are an example. They share a long, mountainous, and ill-defined border. The population of the region—where there is any—consists of Indians living in small, isolated villages. The simmering border conflict between Ecuador and Peru, which so far has featured infantry skirmishes and strikes by armed aircraft, isn't solely driven by Ecuadorian national pride. There are strong indications that the border area sits on significant gold reserves and possibly a pool of oil.

The Indians don't particularly care for the mestizo (mixed race) and white soldiers of either side.

Enter Sendero Luminoso, the Shining Path. Founded by extreme leftist intellectuals in Lima, in the early 1980s Sendero Luminoso began a brutal series of terror attacks against the Peruvian government. The intent was to forment an Indian revolt. The intellectuals even called on the power of old Inca legends that say "sleeping" Inca kings will rise out of the Andes to kill the Spanish invaders. Naturally, the

Leninists want the Indians to conclude that the Shining Path is that Incan resurrection. To the Indians, leftist intellectuals from Lima are just central-government Spaniards spouting a different verse of the old saw, You be like us, or else.

Added to this mix of ethnicity, politics, and border conflict is the cocaine war. Financed by the U.S. dope-buying public (not the U.S. government), that war started in the foothills of the Andes Mountains, in the backcountry of Colombia, Bolivia, and Peru.

The soldiers in this war are the gunmen of the criminal cartels, trained mercenaries, and leftist guerrillas, all formed into a working cohort of violence. The cocaine war follows the route of drug distribution, down into the urban areas of Colombia, up through Central America and the Caribbean, and into the United States. The war is over the control of the cocaine trade, the thousands of square miles of hill country where the coca leaf is grown, and finally the streets of urban America where most of the drug is sold. Nearly a million South American farmers, technicians, gunmen, pilots, sailors, soldiers, policemen, and accountants comprise the drug producers' forces. In North America, over ten million cocaine users pay out over $50 billion a year for the drug.

SOURCE OF CONFLICT

Old conflicting land claims, national pride, and greed, in the conquistador tradition, lie behind the border disputes among Peru and Ecuador, and Colombia and Venezuela.

Indian wars are an element of the conflict. Ideological wars among the Spanish and mestizo elite often amount to a fight over control of the Indians. The still-armed-and-Marxist Sendero Luminoso movement hasn't been very successful at organizing the Indians. The governments of Ecuador and Peru have both followed a policy of neglect that cannot be characterized as benign. The Indians lack basic medical care; their agricultural methods remain primitive. But the Indian peasants also want to be left alone. They are classic mountaineers.

The cocaine war is all about money, control of the coca-growing lands, and—occasionally—politics. In Colombia, where the per capita

1993 GNP was about $5,500, most farming families in the hinterland still made less than $1,000 a year. Thus cocaine can be the quick road to riches. Each acre of coca plants can produce 800–900 pounds of leaves a year. These the farmer sells to one of the cocaine cartels for anywhere from fifteen cents to several dollars a pound, depending on market conditions. The price is now on the low side, because so many farmers are cultivating coca leaves. But the farmers are still able to get up to $200 an acre from a plant that requires relatively little effort to grow and harvest. And the farmers don't have to worry about lack of transportation to get their crops out. The drug lords take care of all details—and pay cash. With 300–500 tons of cocaine coming into the United States each year, farmers in the backcountry of Colombia, Bolivia, and Peru are producing up to 250,000 tons of coca leaves. That's over 650 square miles of coca plants and over $80 million flowing into the farmers' pockets. Each 500 pounds of coca leaves ends up as 1 pound of cocaine, which can sell for over $10,000 in the United States. Lots of profit to be made between buying $100 worth of coca leaves in the bush, performing a few chemical operations on them, and getting the resulting pound of cocaine into the United States and the cash out. The Colombian cartels that control most of the business thus garner over $10 billion a year from the cocaine trade. That is about a third of the total GNP of Colombia, and a 1984 cartel offer to pay off Colombia's $9 billion national debt in return for amnesty, while possibly not serious, was certainly within the cartel's means.

With such large sums of cash at stake, the cartel spares no expense in offering "gold or lead" to all who oppose them. If opponents can't be bought off, they are killed off. Thousands of Colombian police and soldiers have died, as well as dozens of judges and prosecutors. No one is safe, not even senior members of the government.

WHO'S INVOLVED

The Peru-Ecuador Border War

Peru—The "regional military power."
Ecuador—National pride was wounded by the loss of most of the Oriente in 1941; also, access to the Amazon River is at stake.

Wild Cards

United States—Chief guarantor of the Rio Protocols of 1942.
Brazil—Concerned about any border squabbles in the Andes, and an old ally of Peru.
Argentina, Colombia, and Israel—All three have sold arms to Ecuador (and perhaps to Peru).
Sendero Luminoso and drug cartels—Revolutionaries and *bandidos* are interested in seeing the governments fight; it takes the pressure off them.

Another Sendero Luminoso "War of Liberation"

Peruvian government—For now curbing the rebellion.
Sendero Luminoso—The leadership is either dead or in jail but the terror cells remain.
Tupac Amaru—Other guerrilla groups oppose the "Spanish" Peruvian government.

Wild Card

Drug cartels—A government involved with guerrillas has fewer resources to commit to the drug war.

The Cocaine War

Colombian government
Peruvian government
Drug cartels—The demand for drugs attracts armed entrepreneurs.
U.S. government—Includes Coast Guard, Customs Agency, Border Patrol, and U.S. Southern Command (SOUTHCOM).

Wild Cards

Drug demand in the United States
Latin American revolutionary movements—E.g., Tupac Amaru revolutionary organizations. There are at least two or three in every Latin American nation.
Mafia (organized crime in United States and worldwide).

Colombian-Venezuelan Border War

Drug cartels and former leftist revolutionaries—The border war distracts federal attention from their activities.

GEOGRAPHY

The Pacific coast to the west, the long spine of the Andes Mountains, and the eastern Andean foothills dropping into the Amazonian jungles are the dominating geographic features of Peru and Ecuador.

Peru has an area of 1,285,000 square kilometers, which makes it slightly smaller than Alaska. The population in 1994 was twenty-four million. Peru is bordered to the north by Ecuador and Colombia, on the east by Brazil and Bolivia, and by Chile to the south.

Peru divides into three distinct geographic regions: the Pacific coastal lowlands (the Costa), where nearly half the population resides;

the Andes Mountains (the Sierra), where around 40 percent of the population resides; and the eastern jungle region (the Selva). More than half of Peru's land area is in the Selva. The high jungle region on the Andes' eastern slopes is called the Montaña. The disputed zone between Peru and Ecuador is in a particularly rugged part of the Montaña.

Lima, Peru's capital, lies in the dry coastal zone. Rivers have cut deep longitudinal valleys into the plateau of the mineral-rich Andean Sierra. Lake Titicaca, a major geographic feature, is located in the southeastern Sierra astride the Bolivian border.

Rivers plunging eastward from the Andes have dissected the Montaña, often forming a tortuous, jungle-clad terrain. The Amazon River basin is a jungle plain where average annual rainfall exceeds 100 inches (2,500 millimeters).

Indians make up 54 percent of Peru's population; mestizo, 31 percent; and Europeans, 12 percent. Blacks and Asians account for the remaining 2 percent. The nation is 98 percent Roman Catholic. Half of the population speaks Quechua, the Incan language. Quechua is Peru's official second language. Most of the Quechua speakers live in the Sierra. Aymara, another Indian dialect, is also widely spoken.

Ecuador is bordered on the north by Colombia and on the east and south by Peru. It has an area of 284,000 square kilometers, about the size of Nevada. Ecuador, like Peru, has three distinct regions, its tropical Costa, its Sierra, and its Amazonian region, the Oriente. The ecologically unique Galápagos Islands, off the Pacific Coast, are also part of Ecuador. The port of Guayaquil, Ecuador's largest city (1.5 million inhabitants) is the hub of the Costa. Quito, the national capital, lies in the Sierra. The Oriente constitutes over half of Ecuador's total area.

Ecuador has a population of around twelve million and is very ethnically mixed. Forty percent of the population is mestizo and 40 percent Indian. Europeans and mulattos are about 10 percent each. While the Costa has a very heterogeneous population mix, the Oriente is almost solely inhabited by Indians. Spanish is the official language. Several Indian dialects, including Quechua, are also spoken. Over 90 percent of the population is Roman Catholic.

Ecuador has large petroleum deposits located in the Oriente. A pipeline crosses the Andes and brings the oil to the coast. In 1990, Ecuador was the third largest petroleum exporter in Latin America, behind Mexico and Venezuela. Until the development of the oil fields, the large landowners of the Sierra region and the military were the most powerful political forces in Ecuador.

Colombia is bordered by Ecuador and Peru on the south, Brazil and Venezuela on the east, and Panama on the north. It has long Pacific and Atlantic (Caribbean) coastlines. Colombia has an area of 1,140,000 square kilometers (the size of Texas, New Mexico, and Arkansas combined). Three Andean ranges cut the nation from southwest to northeast and separate Colombia into three regions—the highland core, the coastal lowlands, and the eastern plains. Two large rivers, the Magdalena and the Cauca, run through the valleys on either side of the Cordillera Central. The Cundinamarca region, where the capital of Bogotá (population 5 million) is located, lies in the Magdalena Valley. To the west of the Magdalena are two of Colombia's most important cities, Manizales and Medellín. Colombia's richest farmland lies in the Cauca Valley, where Cali is located.

Coffee remains Colombia's key legal agricultural export, though recent oil discoveries (such as the Cuisana fields) have given the nation large reserves (three billion barrels). Colombia has the largest coal deposits in Latin America and is South America's leading gold producer. Ninety-five percent of the world's emeralds come from Colombia. The drug trade, as in cocaine, may be as large as the coffee trade and oil business combined.

Colombia has a population of nearly thirty-six million. Seventy-five percent are mestizo; 20 percent Europeans; 4 percent blacks; and 1 percent Indians. Europeans dominate the economic and social strata. Most people speak Spanish, and 95 percent of the population is Roman Catholic.

Venezuela borders on Colombia, Brazil, and Guyana. Venezuela has a total area of 912,000 square kilometers and a population of twenty-one million. Venezuela is rich in oil and mineral resources, with the Orinoco River basin being prime oil property. Nearly 88 percent of Venezuela's population is either mestizo or white, with blacks comprising 10 percent and Indians 2 percent. Immigration and a high birth rate have led to rapid population growth. Most of Venezuela's Indian population lives in the tropical and savanna region south of the Orinoco River known as the Guayana.

HISTORY

Incan Empire

Both Peru and Ecuador were part of the Incan Empire at the time of the Spanish Conquest in the 1530s—an Incan empire in the midst of a civil war. This precolonial Incan conflict still has mythic—and therefore real political—resonance for Peruvians and Ecuadorians in the twentieth century.

The Incan state was originally one of several regional tribal groups in the Andean Costa and Sierra regions of Peru. From a homeland centered on Cuzco, the Incas began to enlarge their empire sometime in the fourteenth century. In the fifteenth century the Incas expanded rapidly, defeating the Chanca Confederation north of Cuzco and reaching the coast. Incan Emperor Pachacutec (approximately 1438–71) gave the state an imperial structure. The empire, known as Tahuantinsuyu (Land of Four Quarters), was split into four provinces and the provinces into subdivisions. The Incas used the *mita* system of tribute (i.e., forced) labor to build their cities and roads. A similar system had long been common in Europe and other parts of the world. It was very effective; it was the system used to build the pyramids. Ultimately, the Incas extended their power to modern-day Chile and Argentina. They never quite subdued the more primitive tribes of the Montaña, the difficult terrain proving to be an obstacle to central state control.

The Incas demanded absolute submission to the emperor and his imperial officials. Tribal revolts were punished by execution and mass reprisal. The Incas did try to use local leaders to co-opt subjugated tribes.

When Huayna Capac (Incan emperor from 1493 to 1527) died, the divided empire was split by his two sons, Atahualpa and Huascar. The half brothers quarreled. Atahualpa's power base was in the north, in Quito, and he was popular with the northern Incan Army. In the minds of many modern Ecuadorians, Atahualpa was the first Ecuadorian. Huascar, the favorite of the Incan nobility, controlled the Incan capital in Cuzco, in modern-day Peru. The civil war lasted five years. Atahualpa emerged victorious. Meanwhile, Spanish vessels had been sailing along the Peruvian coast—vessels manned by conquistadors, warriors hardened by generations of war with the Muslims and each other.

Francisco Pizarro sought gold and silver in what is modern-day Colombia in 1524 and reached Ecuador in 1526. The Incan civil war greatly weakened the empire so that when Pizarro arrived in Peru in 1531, he was able to lead a small expedition deep into the Incan heartland. In November 1532, Pizarro's small force of 106 foot soldiers and 62 horsemen arrived at Cajamarca. Atahualpa massed 30,000 Incan soldiers. The Incas planned on capturing then slaughtering the Spaniards. Pizarro, with typical conquistador bravado and subterfuge, trapped Atahualpa and imprisoned him. After receiving a ransom, Pizarro, under uncertain circumstances, had Atahualpa executed. Pizarro took Cuzco in 1533 and installed a puppet Inca emperor, Manco Inca. The Spaniards now controlled the vast Incan Empire. In 1535, Pizarro founded Lima.

The Spaniards (the Pizarro family and the Almagros) fought several internecine conflicts over control of the new colony. Eventually, Eurasian diseases (borne by Europeans coming to the New World) ravaged the indigenous populations (they lacked resistance). Before the Incas could learn how to deal with the Spaniards using European technology and methods, many of the Inca people were dead from smallpox, measles, and other pathogens.

Peru

In 1544, Lima became the capital of the viceroyalty of Peru. This "megaviceroyalty" controlled all Spanish territory in South America, with the exception of parts of Venezuela, until the creation of the viceroyalty of New Granada in 1717 and the viceroyalty of La Plata in 1776. Lima was Spanish South America's political and economic hub. As such, Spanish influence remained strong.

Francisco de Toledo y Figueroa, viceroy from 1569 to 1580, brought order to the colony. But "Indian problems" remained. The Spaniards established *reducciones* (protected settlements in easily controlled areas) where the Indians were "Christianized." Toledo also adapted the Incan system of using local chiefs to extend Spanish control in the hinterland. A "rump" Incan state existed in Vilcabamba until 1571.

The viceroyalty was divided into *audenicas* (court jurisdictions). As in other Spanish colonies, *encomienda* was practiced. *Encomienda* gave individual colonists total civil (to include taxation) and religious control over Indians living in areas deeded to the colonists by the crown. During 1781–82 the Spaniards battled a major Indian revolt led by Tupac Amaru II, who claimed descent from the Inca emperors. By this time, the Incan population had recovered some of its numbers lost earlier to disease. But the Spanish had meanwhile obtained two centuries of time in which to solidify their empire. The Incan revolts were bloody, but they never threatened Spanish power.

Conflict between the native colonial elites, the *criollos,* and representatives of the crown in Spain (the *peninsulares*) set the stage for revolt against Spain throughout Latin America. In the first decade of the nineteenth century, when Napoleon toppled Spain's King Charles IV, the South Americans revolted.

The Argentine revolutionary José de San Martín took Lima in July 1821 and proclaimed Peru's independence from Spain. San Martín, however, withdrew his troops in 1822. Units under the Colombian revolutionary leader Simón Bolívar completed Peru's liberation by defeating the Spaniards in the Battles of Junin (August 1824) and Ayacucho (December 1824). Bolívar, an intellectual as well as political and military leader, was the central figure in the struggle against Spanish authority in Venezuela, Colombia, Ecuador, Peru, and Bolivia (the "Bolivarian" countries).

Liberty did not bring peace or prosperity to Peru. The geographical bounds of free Peru were poorly defined. In fact, from 1836 to 1839, Peru and Bolivia, known as Upper Peru, were reunited. The revolutionary wars had spawned numerous private armies that still controlled the backcountry. Military governments ruled until 1845, when a civil war between military factions abated and Ramon Castilla became president.

Castilla was a political and economic reformer, who served two terms as president in 1845–51 and then in 1855–62. But Castilla's retirement was followed by an era of political chaos and corruption.

Spain never quite gave up designs of recovering Peru. Fighting broke out between Spain and Peru in 1864. In 1866, Peru, with the help of Chile (and supported by Ecuador and Bolivia), defeated a Spanish invasion, ostensibly initiated because of Peru's debt. In the 1879 peace treaty Spain recognized Peru's independence for the first time.

During the 1870s, Peru agreed to a secret defense pact with Bolivia against Chile. This alliance led to Peru's participation (1879–83) in the War of the Pacific, which turned out to be a Peruvian catastrophe. The Chileans captured Lima in 1881 and occupied it for three years. Peru lost control of valuable nitrate deposits in the Costa. The lengthy Tacna-Arica border dispute was another outcome of the war.

Peruvian politics in the twentieth century have vacillated from near dictatorial control by civilian presidents (such as Bernardino Leguia y Salcedo, who was deposed in 1930) to military regimes taking power by coup d'état. Economic troubles, brought on by mismanagement, "mercantilist" economic policies where companies controlled by the wealthy are protected by the state, fluctuations in world metal and other commodity prices, and social turmoil caused by poverty have plagued even the most reform-minded civilian and military regimes.

Peru and Ecuador fought a war over disputed territory in 1941 (see Ecuador, 1995 War of the Andes).

In 1968 the military toppled Belaunde Terry's civilian government. The junta nationalized several industries (including oil) and began a land-distribution program based on farm cooperatives. In the mid-1970s inflation crippled Peru and the amount of money owed to foreign lenders skyrocketed. In 1975 a new military junta took power and tried to address the economic disaster.

In July 1980 the junta dissolved. Belaunde Terry formed a new civilian government in Lima. Belaunde confronted another round of economic troubles and inflation. Then, in 1981, the Sendero Luminoso began a nationwide terror campaign.

The Sendero Luminoso: The Shining Path

Shining Path's founder, Abimael Guzman Reynosa, a Lima intellectual, proclaimed himself to be "the fourth sword of Marxism," an apocalyptic complement to Marx, Lenin, and Mao. Unlike other South American guerrilla groups, the Shining Path did not rely on outside advisers or arms shipments. Guzman built an internal network of terror cells led by former students and leftists attracted to his cause. He attempted to radicalize the Indians. The aim was to destroy the Peruvian state and take power amid the debris. In 1983 the government declared a state of emergency. In 1985 the socialist-leaning Alan Garcia Perez and his Popular Revolutionary Alliance (APRA) won the election. Garcia Perez's mixed bag of programs failed to stabilize the economy. In the summer of 1984, Peruvian government estimates put Sendero's strength at 2,000 to 7,000 guerrillas. Recruitment and economic failure (highlight the latter) increased Senderista appeal.

But by the late 1980s the war with the Sendero Luminoso was no longer the only armed conflict confronting Peru. Cocaine traffickers set up operations in several Sierran valleys, carving virtual fiefdoms out of the nation. (See Colombia, Cocaine War.)

Both wars intensified. The collapse of communism in Eastern Europe and the impoverishment of Castro's Cuban regime had little effect on the Marxist Senderistas. The Senderistas hated Moscow as intensely as they hate Washington. The Shining Path's central clique maintained that they were the only ones who really knew how to make Marxism work. The Russians' failure was a subject of scorn. By 1990, Shining Path had from 25,000 to 35,000 guerrillas in the field fighting the Peruvian Army.

In 1990, Alberto Fujimori became president. In April 1992, Fujimori led what became known as "the auto coup." Essentially, Fujimori toppled his own government. He disbanded the legislature, suspended the constitution, and installed himself as an "absolute president" until the 1995 elections (which he won). In September 1992, Peruvian forces captured Guzman. Guzman's image of invincibility was shattered. Guzman urged Senderistas to lay down their arms. Between 1992 and 1995 the Peruvian Army made great gains in the field against Sendero

Luminoso and the police and intelligence forces whittled away at the Senderistas' urban infrastructure. Estimated Sendero guerrillas in the field in mid-1995 were less than fifteen hundred. Many of them may have gone to work for local coca growers in the high Sierra valleys, the Huallaga Valley in particular. But Sendero Luminoso isn't totally finished. In February 1995, after counterinsurgent infantry battalions were withdrawn from the Huallaga and sent north to fight Ecuador, Sendero Luminoso forces under the command of former Guzman aide Oscar Ramirez Duran launched a series of guerrilla raids in rural areas and terrorist bomb attacks in Lima.

Ecuador

Ecuador was part of the Spanish viceroyalty of Peru (except for a brief period) until 1739, when it joined the newly created viceroyalty of New Granada. In May 1822, Simon Bolívar's lieutenant, General Antonio José de Sucre, defeated the Spanish at Pichinicha and freed Ecuador. Ecuador became a province of the new republic of Gran Colombia (consisting of Panama, Venezuela, Colombia, and Ecuador) and Bolívar was made president.

The federation dissolved in 1830 and Ecuador became an independent republic. Dictators and "strongmen" (*caudillos*) dominated Ecuadorian politics until 1895 when Eloy Alfaro (1864–1912) led the Liberal Revolution. Alfaro advocated liberal economic policies. He was assassinated, but the Liberals remained a powerful force in Ecuador until 1944. During the twentieth century, military and civilian governments have swapped control with virtually no change in social and economic policies. Ecuador had fourteen presidents between 1931 and 1940. (The popular José María Velasco Ibarra did bring some stability to Ecuadorian politics in the late 1940s and 1950s.)

Military regimes controlled Ecuador in the 1960s and 1970s. In 1979 a civilian government returned to power. Sixto Duran Ballen was elected president in 1992. His regime had to face the consequences of the global slump in oil prices and Ecuador's mounting foreign debt.

The Peru-Ecuador War: The 1995 War of the Andes

The Council of the Indies in 1779 attempted to draw a more definite boundary between the Spanish viceroyalties of Peru and New Granada; the isolated, jungle-clad expanse of the Maranon and Amazon rivers and their northern tributaries, however, gave the geographers fits. The "guesstimated" 1779 borders were incorporated into the royal patent of 1802, which addressed the border issue.

Local disputes erupted in 1829, spawned by the ill-defined Spanish boundaries. In 1832, Peru and Ecuador signed the Accord of Friendship and Alliance (also called the Pando-Novoa Accord), which recognized Peru's possession of the Mayans, Jaen, and Tumbes regions. Ecuador still claimed large tracts of the Amazon beyond the Oriente.

For over one hundred years the border remained disputed, with Peru enlarging its settlements in the Amazon. In the 1936 Act of Lima both Peru and Ecuador agreed to maintain the status quo.

Armed border incidents, allegedly provoked by Ecuador, occurred in 1938, 1939, and 1940. In July 1941, Peru attacked and occupied Ecuador's Provincia del Oro. (Peru had 15,000 troops, Ecuador 3,000.) Peru dropped airborne troops on Puerto Bolívar in Ecuador— the first use of parachute soldiers in combat in the Western Hemisphere.

The Rio Protocols of January 29, 1942, confirmed Peru's victory and ceded to Peru's control nearly 200,000 square kilometers of Amazon lands claimed by Ecuador. Chile, Argentina, Brazil, and the United States guaranteed the treaty.

Subsequently, Ecuadorians claimed that the guarantors (i.e., the United States) forced them to sign the treaty because of more immediate U.S. concerns (like World War II). Ecuador cited Peruvian documents acknowledging that the settlement gave Peru nearly 30,000 square kilometers of land more than it had ever claimed.

Vague Amazonian geography continued to plague the Rio Protocols. Eighty kilometers of border territory between the Zamora and Santiago rivers north of the Maranon River were identified as a "watershed," which does not exist. Instead, U.S. Air Force mappers in 1947 discovered an extension of the Cenepa River, a Maranon tributary, on the Cordillera del Condor region, which rendered the language in the Rio Protocol meaningless—at least as far as Ecuador was concerned.

In 1960, Ecuadorian President Velasco Ibarra declared the treaty to be null and unenforceable in the Cordillera del Condor region, an area of mountains and jungle. Ecuador demands an adjustment in the eighty-kilometer disputed zone in the Cordillera del Condor.

War broke out anew in mid-January 1995. While deposits of gold and oil may lie in the disputed area, wounded Ecuadorian national pride and Ecuadorian demands for direct access to the Amazon are the key issues as far is Quito is concerned. Retaining as much land as possible near Ecuador's oil reserves—or perhaps taking Ecuador's oil fields in a new Oriente battle—interest Peru.

Fighting in January through March 1995 was confined to the disputed zone. Most of the conflict pitted jungle infantry and special forces units against one another in jungle and mountain valley combat. Fighting centered on the Tiwintza, Base Sur, and Cueva de los Tallos outposts in the Cordillera del Condor region. Peru attempted air strikes and lost at least four jets and two helicopters. The Ecuadorians used mountain artillery effectively, winning a limited victory in the Cordillera.

Early indications were that Ecuador may have provoked this round of fighting (see Participant Strategies). Ecuador did try to buy new arms and military supplies from Argentina and Colombia early in 1995. Ecuador also attempted to buy arms and ammunition from Bulgaria and may have bought spare parts from Israel and private international military arms and supply companies. (In late 1995, Ecuador tried to buy a half-dozen jet fighters from Israel.)

The crisis abated as Peru massed its light armored forces around the Tumbes salient on the coast and sent its superior navy off the Ecuadorian coast, suggesting that Peru might attempt to impose a sea blockade.

The war has most affected the Shuar and Achuar Indians living in the isolated Cordillera del Condor. Fifty thousand Shuar and Achuars reside on the Ecuadorian side, 12,000 on the Peruvian. Indians have served as scouts and guides for both armies. Ecuador's Iwia Battalion, which was involved in the early 1995 fighting, is almost entirely manned by Indians.

Colombia

In November 1509, Alonso de Ojeda sailed into modern-day Colombia's Bay of Cartagena. Bogotá was established in 1538 near the Chicha Indian town of Bacata. Initially an *audencia* of Peru, Colombia became part of the colony of New Granada in 1717.

Simon Bolívar won a major victory over Spanish forces in Colombia at the Battle of Boyaca on August 7, 1819. That same year he convened the Angostura Congress to found Gran Colombia (a federation of present-day Venezuela, Colombia, Panama, and Ecuador). Bolívar became president. This action was formalized at Cucuta in July 1821. Bolívar's chief lieutenant was General Francisco de Paula Santander.

By 1830, as the result of factional fighting, Gran Colombia disintegrated, and Colombia (with Panama as a province), Ecuador, and Venezuela separated.

In the 1830s, Bolívar's followers, who favored a strong central government and an alliance with the Catholic Church, founded the Conservative party. Santander's followers founded the Liberal political party, advocating broadened voters' rights and decentralized government. Throughout the nineteenth century the intense (and armed) rivalry between the two parties blighted Colombian politics. The internecine struggles culminated in civil war, the War of a Thousand Days (1899–1902). The province of Panama rebelled and, with the aid of the United States, became independent. Over one hundred thousand people died in the civil war. Colombian ultranationalists still consider Panama to be part of Colombia.

Conflict between the Liberals and Conservatives continued. A second civil war, prolonged and ugly, referred to as La Violencia (the Violence) occurred from 1948 to 1957. Three hundred thousand died in La Violencia (slightly more than the number of Americans killed in World War II). In 1953, General Gustavo Rojas Pinilla engineered a military coup and became dictator.

In 1957 the military overthrew Pinilla. The Liberals and Conservatives agreed in the Declaration of Sitges to form a joint National Front government. The National Front officially ended in 1974 but de facto power sharing continued.

In the late 1970s, Marxist guerrilla and terrorist activity began throughout Colombia. A state of siege was declared in 1984. Guerrillas (perhaps with the connivance of newly formed drug cartels) seized the National Court Building in 1985, and one hundred people were killed when government troops counterattacked.

In 1986, President Virgilio Barco Vargas (of the Liberal party) declared war on the drug cartels. (The Barco government marked the end of collaborative government.) In 1990 three presidential candidates were assassinated. Drug cartel leaders were held responsible. Liberal Cesar Gaviria Trujillo was elected president on a platform of *apertura* (political opening, i.e., constitutional reform). In 1991 a new constitution replaced the constitution of 1886. Several of the guerrilla organizations laid down their arms.

In 1992 former guerrilla groups (like M-19) and Indian-based political parties also entered the new democratic system.

But drug-related violence continued unabated. Colombia entered a period of "New Violence." The government increased counterdrug efforts and encouraged drug traffickers to give themselves up in return for lenient sentences. Pablo Escobar, the head of the Medellín cartel, accepted these terms and until his murder in 1993 lived in his mansion under house arrest.

By 1993, however, the Cali cartel had taken control of most of the Colombian drug trade. Governmental corruption increased. The Cali leaders bought off Indian revolutionaries and paid former M-19 guerrilla groups to watch and protect their cocaine business. In 1994, Colombia decriminalized the personal use of drugs, including cocaine.

The Cocaine War

Until the late 1970s, the cocaine trade from South America to North America was relatively insignificant and divided among dozens of small operators. But then demand in Yankeeland skyrocketed; new "cartels" started to build "field to street" businesses, paying farmers to grow coca leaves, building processing labs, and creating large transportation systems to move ever-larger quantities of "coke" to Uncle Sam's apparently insatiable market. In the early 1980s an attempt by leftist guerrillas to cash in on the trade by kidnapping members of the drug rings backfired. The drug producers in Colombia united to fight the guerrillas, and succeeded. The drug lords were better terrorists than the revolutionaries. And money proved to be a better goal than revolution. The new "drug lord-revolutionary" combines decided to stay together.

Thus were born the Colombian cocaine cartels. By the late 1980s, the cartels had increased cocaine production and distribution more than ten times 1970s' volume.

Bolivia and Peru are also deeply involved in this complex war of "narco-terror" and dollars. Bolivia, by one 1995 estimate, has around 180,000 acres producing coca leaf (about 25 percent of the world's production, much of it in the Chapare region). In Peru, 200,000 peasant (*campesino*) farmers grow coca on over 400,000 acres of land (around 55 percent of the world's crop). This makes Peru the world's largest coca leaf producer. (Most Peruvian cultivation and production occurs in the Huallaga and Aguaytia areas in the central region and in the Apurimac region in south-central Peru.) Drug eradication programs anger the Indian farmers. Peruvian Indians began supporting the Shining Path (whom many Indians despise) when the government began pressing coca eradication programs in the Uchiza area. The eradication programs were halted and Indian support for Sendero waned.

Peruvian and Bolivian coca, in paste form, moves north to Colombia for further refinement. The refinement process requires laboratories and large amounts of HCL. The laboratory result: cocaine.

While the Peruvian government wages an antidrug war where politics and drugs often meld, it is in Colombia that the new "narco-political" struggle becomes truly grim geopolitical reality. Old political conflicts become drug wars. Colombia has suffered periods of endemic violence (La Violencia). In Colombia in the late 1980s, the annual deaths from shootouts, assassinations, banditry, and the like reached over 20,000. An equivalent number of deaths in the United States would be 150,000. The Colombian death rate from such violence is over five times what it is in the United States.

In Colombia the cocaine war has led to large-scale social breakdown and the formation of private protective forces and armies. Three thousand Colombian police and thirty-three judges were killed between 1984 and 1994. Rival cartels and guerrilla factions fight each other as well as the government.

The Latin American nations are wary of accepting direct military aid or intervention from the United States. With $10 to $12 billion a year in drug cash flowing into Colombia's coffers, there is a lot of reason to ignore Washington.

Venezuela

Columbus first sailed off the Venezuelan coast in 1498. Venezuela, with no precious metals and few natives, failed to attract large-scale Spanish settlement. Governed either from Santo Domingo (now the Dominican Republic) or by the viceroyalty of New Granada, Venezuela was a secondary Spanish colonial concern.

On July 5, 1811, Venezuela declared independence. When Gran Colombia dissolved in 1830, Venezuela became an independent nation. Venezuela remained an impoverished backwater throughout the nineteenth and early twentieth centuries, a backwater controlled by dictatorial oligarchs. Venezuela did occasionally enter regional politics. Misbehavior by the Venezuelan dictator Cipriano Castro (1899–1908) led to a combined German and British naval blockade of the Orinoco River and Venezuelan coast in 1902.

The oil business—and new prosperity—came to Venezuela in 1914 when the first commercial well was drilled on Lake Maracaibo. By 1930, Venezuela was an oil exporter. (Venezuela nationalized the iron industry in 1975 and the oil industry in 1976. Venezuela is an OPEC member.)

Prosperity led Venezuela from dictatorship to a constitutional democracy. In 1958 a new democratic Venezuela emerged in the wake of the Punto Fijo Agreement to create a coalition democratic government.

The economic difficulties of the 1980s severely tested Venezuela's democracy. As unemployment rose, governmental corruption increased, and human rights abuses by the police and army occurred.

Venezuela has tasted Colombia's brand of internal violence. In 1992 two coup attempts against President Carlos Andres Perez occurred. In 1993, Perez was impeached for corruption and bribes, allegedly paid by drug cartels. The level of violence increased in 1994. Caracas witnessed two hundred killings a month in 1994.

Venezuela claims vast chunks of neighboring Guyana. Venezuela and Colombia also have two boundary disputes, which have been arbitrated but continue to cause some nationalist resentment. Colombia claims certain territorial waters in the Gulf of Venezuela that may contain oil. The border near the Gold River and an area south of the Meta River, while demarcated in the 1930s, still cause friction. The most likely cause of trouble between Venezuela and Colombia is "misunderstandings" over smuggling, over migrants, and the continual guerrilla warfare. In 1995, Colombian guerrillas killed eight Venezuelan marines in the Meta River region. The guerrillas, from the ELN, are suspected of trying to start a war between Colombia and Venezuela.

LOCAL POLITICS

Peru

Major political parties—Popular Action party (AP) and Popular Christian party (PPC) are center-right and right parties; American Popular Revolutionary Alliance (APRA) is center-left; Democratic Left Movement (MDI) is left-wing.

Alberto Fujimori—President; reelected for five-year term in 1995; Peruvian of Japanese descent.

Sendero Luminoso—The Shining Path; draws its name from Incan myth; ultra-Marxist terrorist and guerrilla movement (see History, Peru).

Tupac Amaru—The MRTA-MIR Insurgent Group (Movement of the Revolutionary Left); Marxist guerrillas who tried to lead an Indian revolt; group is now destroyed.

Repentance law—Law encouraged guerrillas to surrender and receive lenient treatment.

Upper Huallaga Valley—Referred to also as the Huallaga Front; Andean valley that is a major zone of both anti-Sendero warfare and counterdrug operations.

Colina Group—Name of suspected Peruvian Army "death squad"; may have carried out Cantuta killings in July 1992 where ten people from La Cantuta University were kidnapped and killed in counter-Sendero violence.

Garua—Heavy winter fog in the Costa's desert region.

Ecuador

Major political parties—Republican Unity party (PUR); Conservative party (PCE); Social Christian party (PSC); Democratic Left (ID). Ecuador has fifteen legal political parties, none of which dominate the political process. (Note: The PSC, PUR, and the Roldosist party all believe that Ecuador's territorial interests have been repeatedly sold out to Peru.)

Sixto Duran Ballen—Ecuadorian president in 1995; member of Republican Unity party.

Amazonian Affairs Committee—Ecuadorian irredentist group advocating recovery of all territory "lost to Peru" as the result of the Rio Protocols of 1942.

Puk Iti—Left-wing subversive group; base is leftist intellectuals in Quito.

Indigenismo—Social and political philosophy advocating integration of Indian traditions into a new national culture.

Tribes of the Ecuadorian Oriente—Auchuars, Jivaros, Shuars, Yumbos, and Zaparos.

Colombia

Major political parties—Liberal party, Social Conservative party, Patriotic Union (UP).

Democratic Alliance/M-19 (AD/M-19)—Political party emerging from former Marxist M-19 guerrilla group; M-19 started as an urban-proletariat-oriented revolutionary group. Allegedly, many former M-19 members are now in the cocaine business.

Cali drug cartel—As of 1995 major Colombian drug cartel based in the city of Cali. Cali has used its wealth to penetrate government institutions through bribes and payoffs. Medellín cartel is based in the city of Medellín.

DEA—U.S. Drug Enforcement Administration.

FARC (Revolutionary Armed Forces of Colombia)—Marxist guerrilla movement. Many of its members now operate as "narco-guerrillas" and work for drug cartels.

ELN (National Liberation Army)—Active guerrilla group; known to blow up oil pipelines.

El Libertador—Simón Bolívar.

Money laundering—Cleaning and recycling drug money continues to be big white-collar business in Colombia and neighboring Panama.

Traquetos—Uzi-submachine-gun-toting cartel underlings.

Concordata—Signed in 1887, exempts the Catholic Church from taxes and makes religious instruction mandatory. Is at odds with the 1991 constitution.

Panama—Considered by many Colombians to be a missing province.

Venezuela

Major political parties—Democratic Action (AD); Social Christian (COPEI); Convergencia (coalition party); the Radical Cause (Causa R); and Movimiento al Socialismo (MAS) are all left-wing.

Crillo—Pure-bred white born in the New World.

Adecos—Members of the Democratic Action party.

PDVZA—Petroleos de Venezuela, the national oil company.

FAC—Armed Forces of Cooperation (Venezuelan national guard tasked with internal security).

Sembrando el petroleo—Policy of economic diversification from dependence on oil revenues ("sowing the petroleum").

POLITICAL TREND CHARTS

PERU

Gv95	Gv20	PC95	PC20	R95	R20	Ec95	Ec20	EdS95	EdS20
AD7,6	AD7,7	6	7	6	6	4+	5	4	4

Gv = Government Type
AD = Authoritarian Democracy
PC = Political Cohesiveness (0 = chaos, 9 = maximum)
R = Repression Index (9 = maximum)
Ec = Comparative Economic Status (0–9)
EdS = Relative Education Status (0–9); in this case, urban population only

ECUADOR

Gv95	Gv20	PC95	PC20	R95	R20	Ec95	Ec20	EdS95	EdS20
AD5,6	AD6,6	7	7	5	5	4–	4–	3–	3

COLOMBIA

Gv95	Gv20	PC95	PC20	R95	R20	Ec95	Ec20	EdS95	EdS20
AD3,3	MD4,3	3	5	7	6	5	5	4+	4+

MD = Military Dictatorship

VENEZUELA

Gv95	Gv20	PC95	PC20	R95	R20	Ec95	Ec20	EdS95	EdS20
AD4,4	AO3,3	5	4	5	6	5	5−	5−	5−

AO = Authoritarian Oligarchy (masked as an Authoritarian Democracy)

BOLIVIA

Gv95	Gv20	PC95	PC20	R95	R20	Ec95	Ec20	EdS95	EdS20
AO4,3	AO4,3	5	4	6	6	1+	1+	1−	1−

REGIONAL POWERS AND POWER INTEREST INDICATOR CHARTS

PERU-ECUADOR "WAR OF THE ANDES"

	Economic Interests	Historical Interests	Political Interest	Military Interest	Force Generation Potential	Ability to Intervene Politically
Peru	5	7	7	7	6+	9
Ecuador	8	9	8	8	4	8
Colombia	4	6	6	3	2	5
Chile	2	2	5	3	5	5
Brazil	3	6	8	6	5	7
Bolivia	1	1	2	1	0	2
United States	4	3	7	1	5	8
Sendero	1	1	9	3−	1	1
Drug Cartels	7	0	7	8	1	1

A finer lens:

Power Interest Indicators take an overall strategic look at particular conflicts. Here's a look at "operational" force generation capabilities in specific zones. This should illustrate why Ecuador wants to keep the war confined to the Oriente.

Peru's FGP for attack along the Ecuadorian coast	7
Ecuador's defensive FGP along the coast	4
Peru's FGP in Cordillera del Condor	2+
Ecuador's FGP in Cordillera del Condor	2

"SENDERO LUMINOSO REVOLT"

	Economic Interests	Historical Interests	Political Interest	Military Interest	Force Generation Potential	Ability to Intervene Politically
Peru	9	9	9	9	8	8
Sendero	9	9	9	9	1	9
Drug Cartels	9	1	8	7	1	5
United States	5	5	7	2	4	4
Ecuador	6	6	8	8	1	5

COLOMBIAN COCAINE WAR

	Economic Interests	Historical Interests	Political Interest	Military Interest	Force Generation Potential	Ability to Intervene Politically
Colombia	9	9	9	9	7	7
Peru	8	7	8	8	5	5
Drug Cartels	9	9	9	9	4	9
U.S. Milit.*	2	3	5	8	5	3
U.S. Cntr.Dr.*	9	9	9	9	2	4

*Reflects divided U.S. counterdrug efforts. Combine FGPs for potential total.

COLOMBIA-VENEZUELAN BORDER WAR

	Economic Interests	Historical Interests	Political Interest	Military Interest	Force Generation Potential	Ability to Intervene Politically
Colombia	6	7	6	7	4	9
Venezuela	7	7	7	8	4	8
United States	5	3	6	3	6	8
Drug Cartels	7	2	3	2	1+	8
Brazil	4	6	6	5	2	7
Holland	3	6	5	6	1	5

PARTICIPANT STRATEGIES AND GOALS

Peru

War of the Andes—Resolving the border dispute is in Peru's long-term economic and political interest. Peru's President Alberto Fujimori, however, clearly used the flare-up in early 1995 to burnish his credentials as a Peruvian patriot. He was reelected by an overwhelming majority; Peru's case of war fever was his political gain.

The Peruvians know that they have the advantage in a one-on-one military conflict against Ecuador. Peru has a larger, better-trained navy and air force. Peru's navy could blockade Ecuador's major port, Guayaquil. While both armies have low equipment "operational readiness" rates, Peru has more tanks, better-trained soldiers, and several crack airborne special forces battalions.

The Cordillera del Condor would not be Peru's choice of battlefields. Peru's light armor could drive north into Ecuador along the narrow coastal strip between the Andes and the Pacific. However, a deep attack toward Guayaquil, 125 miles up the coast, would be very difficult. The Peruvians would have to bridge nearly a dozen rivers, though if the Peruvian Air Force controls the skies the Peruvians might be tempted to push the offensive.

The Peruvians might simply take a "bite" out of Ecuadorian territory and hold it. Still, when the shooting stopped, Peru would in all probability control vital Ecuadorian territory. Unless Ecuadorian diplomats could convince the international community otherwise, Peru would be in a position to dictate terms to Ecuador.

The Sendero Luminoso war—In some ways Sendero has been to Peru what the narco-terror and narco-guerrilla wars have been to Colombia. President Fujimori's suspension of democracy gave the military and police the edge against the Senderistas. It also resulted in large numbers of human rights abuses and more Indian killing. Peru chose to fight "a dirty war" against the Senderistas. As long as poverty remains endemic, particularly among the Indians of the Sierra and Montaña, some sort of guerrilla activity will continue.

Ecuador—Local politics always plays a major part in border conflicts. No doubt Ecuadorian politicians improve their political standing by rattling sabers at Peru and playing upon Ecuadorian nationalism. Likewise, the Ecuadorian Army, facing some budget cuts, would welcome the opportunity to demonstrate a reason to keep the budget "fully funded." But the War of the Andes 1995 flare-up may have had a very Machiavellian source—in Quito. Ecuador may have pursued a high-risk, high-payoff strategy linked to U.S. hopes for hemispheric cooperation. In a one-on-one confrontation with Peru, Ecuador is outclassed and the Ecuadorians know it. Ecuador, however, benefits greatly if the conflict is resolved in the international arena. Ecuador has been a major player in the Summit of the Americas process and OAS (Organization of American States) political initiatives; Peru, especially after President Fujimori's suspension of democracy, was on the outs. That gave Ecuador somewhat better political leverage than Peru. But leverage doesn't last. Ecuador apparently calculated that early 1995 was the best time to try to build the framework for an internationally directed resolution of the border dispute.

At the Summit of the Americas in Miami in December 1994, the United States took the position that an era of peace (brought on by the end of the cold war) had come to the Americas. Now was a time for new economic, political, and social cooperation. Ecuador proceeded to leverage Washington's aspirations for hemispheric peace by saying, You want peace? Then help us resolve this conflict. Ecuador ordered arms and equipment, got its small air force and navy in shape, then started shooting in the jungle. Ecuador had just enough conventional forces deployed along the coast to leave some doubt in Peru's mind about the results of a deep attack into Ecuador. And Ecuador made certain Peru knew there would be a huge political price paid for any kind of Peruvian invasion of Ecuador. As for countering a Peruvian deep attack? The Ecuadorians have been working on a war plan for over fifty years and may believe they have a surprise or two that can trap and defeat a reckless Peruvian deep offensive.

Colombia—The cocaine wars: Colombia needs peace and stability to develop and prosper. If the chaos and corruption continue, the country could split into a half-dozen subcountries. Bogotá would remain the nominal capital, but army, drug cartel, narco-guerrilla, and even Indian forces would effectively rule small "duchies" inside Colombia. The Colombian people, and to a certain extent the Colombian government, want the terror to end. A "national strategy" by Colombia alone won't crimp the power of the drug cartels. Colombia needs regional cooperation and help from the United States. But corruption in Colombia is deep and at the highest levels of government. What would hurt the cartels the most? Curbing demand for drugs in the United States and Canada.

Venezuela—The oil-dependent economy has been boom and bust. Venezuela is attempting to broaden its economy. But the insidious combination of drug cash and poverty has begun to weaken Venezuela's democratic traditions. Corruption is spreading. A border war with Colombia would be a short-lived political boost for Venezuelan nationalists, until the bills came due.

United States—The United States knows the strategic axis has shifted. The cold war's strategic axis ran east-west, from Russia through Europe to Asia. Post–cold war realities suggest a larger compass, a compass that also has a north-south azimuth magnetized by economic and political affiliations. Economic ties bind North and South America. The United States hopes peace, security, and economic liberalization will lead to hemispheric prosperity. This was the United States' platform for the December 1994 Summit of the Americas.

Then up pops the Peru-Ecuador spat. As one of the guarantors of the Rio Protocols, the United States was immediately involved in "internationalizing" the dispute. Indeed, the United States is committed to trade liberalization and diplomatically "fixing" Latin American historical disputes as part of that process.

The cocaine war, however, is another beast. Drug wars are fought daily on U.S. soil. Washington has tried to stop the flow of drugs by employing Pentagon and CIA assets throughout Latin America. U.S. electronic warfare aircraft track drug-carrying aircraft from Peru to the U.S. border. The Coast Guard regularly shakes down ships for drugs. The United States has devoted billions to helping Peru, Colombia, and Bolivia fight drug cartels on the battlefield and in the banking system. But the most effective strategy is curbing American demand for drugs. That means addressing social problems in the United States. Another possible strategy: legalizing cocaine, heroin, and other now illegal narcotics. This option may become increasingly attractive, though it too entails social, political, and medical costs.

Brazil—Tries to exercise political muscle to resolve border disputes among its neighbors. Brazil wants to stop the spread of Colombian-style chaos to Venezuela—and to Brazil.

POTENTIAL OUTCOMES

War of the Andes

1. 50 percent chance through 2001: Border dispute diplomatically resolved. If this occurs, 80 percent chance of Ecuador receiving a "better deal," which means direct access to the Maranon River (the Amazon's chief tributary).
2. 35 percent chance through 2001: No diplomatic resolution. Warfare in the Cordillera del Condor continues to sputter along at the light-infantry level, with infantry squads, platoons, and companies fighting one another.

3. 15 percent chance through 2001: Large-scale conventional war erupts. Peru attacks north into Ecuador. If Peru takes only a 25- to 30-kilometer-deep "bite" out of Ecuador, 85 percent chance of Peruvian "victory." Look for the shooting to stop quickly but for the diplomatic negotiations to take months, perhaps years. Eventually, Peru would withdraw, but would dictate terms, to include forcing Ecuador to accept Peru's borders for the Oriente. If Peru attempts to take Guayaquil or even Quito, 60 percent chance of Peruvian victory. Peru would be an international pariah but might then occupy Ecuador's oil fields.

Sendero Luminoso

1. 90 percent chance through 2001: Sendero Luminoso totally defeated by Peruvian government. Leftist and Maoist leadership of Sendero destroyed. Good-bye Marxism and Maoism.
2. 99 percent chance through 2001: Continued low-grade counter Indian/guerrilla/narco-guerrilla war in the Andean Sierra. Hello usual Indian wars.

The Cocaine War

1. 65 percent chance through 2001: Internal situation in Colombia continues to decline. Corruption worsens. If this occurs, 75 percent chance of breakdown of Colombia into a half-dozen "duchies," each one controlled by either army generals or various drug cartels.
2. 20 percent chance through 2001: "Citizens revolt" occurs. Elections throw corrupt politicians out of office en masse. Reformist military officers and politicians purge police forces and military, then attack and destroy drug cartels and narco-guerrillas in vicious civil war.
3. 15 percent chance through 2001: Narcotics legalized in the United States. Some drug lords "go straight," but the price of cocaine drops to that of coffee. Internal war in Colombia begins to fizzle.

Kind of Conflict

Amazonian Border Wars

Squabbles over territory and those who live there have long plagued South America. In the Amazon and in the jungle-covered Andean Montaña regions, the terrain is often a tougher opponent than enemy soldiers. Light infantry units armed with automatic rifles, light machine-guns, and light mortars (60 to 82 millimeters) have done most of the fighting in the Peruvian and Ecuadorian Amazon. These infantry, guerrilla, and commando units are supported by occasional air strikes. Ecuador has placed medium and heavy artillery in the mountains to support its border posts, and the mountains and jungle have protected the guns from Peruvian air strikes. If the Andean war turned to all-out war, however, large-scale conventional combat would occur on the coast, pitting Peruvian divisions (5,000 to 8,000 troops) against Ecuadorian brigades (3,000 to 4,000 troops). Peru would have a decided advantage in personnel and equipment. Ecuador, however, has invested in new antiaircraft systems, including advanced Soviet-type shoulder-fired antiaircraft missiles (SA-14, SA-16) and radar-directed antiaircraft artillery. Both sides would soon discover that the jungle is as formidable a foe as any human one. Disease and heat exhaustion would soon bring down more troops than enemy firepower.

The Cocaine War and "War of Internal Disorder"

This type of internal-bandit-guerrilla-smuggling war has been going on in the "Golden Triangle" of Thailand and Burma since the late 1940s. Unless Colombia can resolve the issue of governmental corruption (the political "buying power" of drug cash), the conflict will linger and the killing will continue. There is always a danger that the small-scale fighting could accelerate. A drug lord could decide he wants to be the national political leader, and if he cannot buy his way into power, he might try to build an army big enough to shoot his way into power.

COST OF WAR

Every one of the "minor conflicts" analyzed in this chapter is very expensive in economic terms. Peru estimates that the Sendero war cost it $25 billion between 1987 and 1993. The violence in Colombia may have caused as much as $6 to $8 billion in damage to the economy between 1990 and 1992. This figure does not begin to address the value of human lives and the damage done to governmental and social institutions. The U.S. drug war cost $64 billion from 1989 to 1995. But America has a $6 trillion economy; Peru's GNP is more like $25 billion, in a good year. (What kind of chaos would the United States endure if it lost a trillion dollars a year in GDP for six years in a row?)

The border conflict in spring 1995 may have cost Ecuador $2 billion in direct outlays for weapons, military operations, and support costs.

QUICK LOOK: Bolivia, Chile, and Peru: The Lingering War of the Pacific

During the War of the Pacific (1878–84), Bolivia lost to Chile the port of Arica, its outlet to the sea. Over 110 years later, Bolivia and Chile still have not resolved that loss, and it remains a potentially troublesome issue of the 1990s. The economic performance of all of these countries can either resolve or exacerbate the situation. The lack of a seaport provides Bolivia, or at least Bolivian military regimes, with a "legitimate" external excuse for poor economic performance— "it's not our fault." Bolivian calls for negotiations have been, for the most part, ignored and certainly have been rebuffed. Even Chile's new democratic government prefers to ignore this issue. But the argument over access to the sea through a national port isn't simply an issue of hurt national pride, and it isn't about an insignificant area (like Chile and Argentina's old dispute over islands in the Beagle Channel, which as of 1995 appears to have been resolved). When it comes to trade and tariffs, Chile and neighboring Peru have a geostrategic choke hold on Bolivia. The result: a brew for renewed conflict in a poor and suffering corner of the world.

QUICK LOOK: Brazil

THE BRAZILIAN MILITARY

While Brazil's army, in the main, consists of politicized generals and units chiefly designed for policing Brazil, it is capable of waging an offensive war beyond its borders. The army has 220,000 troops (145,000 conscripts) but is expanding to 260,000. Those troops man eight infantry divisions and approximately twenty-five "brigade groups" that include armor, jungle infantry, and mountain warfare units. The Brazilian airborne brigade, which includes a special forces battalion, is highly trained. Brazil equips its light armored formations with the "homemade" Urutu and Cascavel armored personnel carriers and recon vehicles, vehicles ideally suited for combat in South America. The Brazilian Army is increasingly tasked with strengthening Amazon border defenses.

The Brazilian Navy has nearly fifty thousand sailors and marines. The navy isn't strictly a coastal force. It deploys a small antisubmarine aircraft carrier, seven submarines, ten destroyers, and fifteen frigates and corvettes. Several of the ships are armed with modern ship-to-ship missiles. Brazil also maintains a large river (Amazon) warfare force. The navy has flirted with the idea of buying or producing a nuclear submarine.

The air force has over fifty thousand personnel manning nearly 250 combat aircraft. Air force technical capabilities are good—Brazilians know how to service their aircraft. Front-line fighters are aging French Mirage IIIs and U.S. F-5s. Their counterinsurgency squadrons operate the locally produced (by Embraer) Xavante aircraft. The air force wants to acquire long-range tanker and transport aircraft. An increase in range means an increase in the strategic reach of Brazil's airpower.

BRAZILIAN STRATEGIC SITUATION: SOURCES OF CONFLICT

Regional: Land and Border Claims

1. Brazil is concerned that the border war between Ecuador and Peru will reignite other South American land disputes. Brazil is particularly concerned about the Amazon, which comprises 60 percent of Brazil's territory. (See Geostrategic Goal 3.)
2. Brazil and Uruguay have several small border disputes.
3. Brazil claims a "zone of interest" in Antarctica; Brazil's claim has a regional feature—it is a counterbalance to Chilean and Argentine claims on the Antarctic continent.
4. Brazil and hapless Paraguay have a lingering boundary dispute in the Piranhas River area.

International

Economic—The overall Brazilian foreign debt in 1993 was over $119 billion. The debt service was estimated at close to $20 billion a year. International Monetary Fund (IMF) belt tightening does not and will not sell in party-mad Brazil. In fact, the Brazilians aren't too worried about the debt. They view it as being unpayable. When asked about their foreign debt, Brazilians point a finger at the massive U.S. debt and shrug. Besides, since a Brazilian default could initiate a worldwide economic collapse, the Brazilians feel certain that the United States and its other Western lenders won't let that happen. Nevertheless, the potential remains. Brazil's first priority goal is debt restructuring and repayment. All developmental projects hinge on successfully resolving the foreign debt load.

Increasing Brazilian military and economic power—With 8.5 million square kilometers of landmass and a population of 160 million, resource-rich Brazil has the makings of a superpower. (After all, Brazil has 10 million more people than Russia, and a better climate.) Venezuela and Argentina oppose Brazil's attempt to assume the mantle of Latin American leader (see Geostrategic Goal 6) though new trade relationships seem to be modifying the "traditional" Brazilian-Argentine antipathy. Brazil has maintained a long and strong influence within the Chilean and Bolivian military. In the fall of 1990, Brazil's civilian government confirmed that past military governments had begun a program intended to build a nuclear weapon. The civilian government says it has killed the program.

Arms industry fiascos—Supplying Libya, Iraq, Iran, and a host of other volatile nations with weapons and munitions may make money but it also invites a whole host of risks, including terrorist retribution and economic sanctions.

Brazil has one of the largest arms industries in the developing world. Its light armored vehicles, attack aircraft, trucks, munitions, and—now—missiles provide jobs and foreign exchange. Brazil has astutely specialized in producing what they call "sellable vanilla": tough, relatively unsophisticated but functional weapons that don't require a lot of detailed maintenance or a highly educated crew. In competing with inexpensive Russian equipment, Brazilian arms salesmen can point out that their stuff is "Western" and not that shabby stuff the Russians peddle. But basically the Brazilians sell on the basis of price and availability. Brazil has few, if any, qualms about selling weapons to any nation. Brazil supplied both sides in the Iran-Iraq War.

Political Trend Charts

Brazil

Gv95	Gv20	PC95	PC20	R95	R20	Ec95	Ec20	EdS95	EdS20
AD5,3	AD6,4	6+	7	6	5	5−	6	4−	4

AD = Authoritarian Democracy

ARGENTINA

Gv95	Gv20	PC95	PC20	R95	R20	Ec95	Ec20	EdS95	EdS20
AD5,4	AD5,4	6	6+	6+	5	5	6−	6	6

BRAZILIAN GEOSTRATEGIC GOALS

Goal 1: Resolving economic problems—The debt issue won't go away. Likewise, poverty is a tremendous issue, particularly urban poverty. The *favelas* (slums) of São Paulo and Rio de Janeiro breed gangs, crime, and political turmoil. An overvalued currency (the new *real*) and rising imports may be leading Brazil to a Mexicolike economic meltdown.

Goal 2: Curbing crime and corruption in Brazil—This is closely linked to the economic issue. Corruption in Brazilian politics has inhibited economic development. In 1992, President Fernando Collor de Mello was deposed for corruption. In 1994 the state elections in Rio de Janeiro were annulled due to massive fraud.

Goal 3: Defend and control the Amazon—Brazil has eleven thousand kilometers of Amazonian border facing seven different countries. Various military journals have reported that Brazil is constructing an "advanced military belt" in Amazon regions facing Colombia, Guyana, Venezuela, and Bolivia. Governmental control in many of these regions is weak. Drug traffickers, gold miners, landowners, and criminal organizations operate outside of Brazilian law. The SIVAM (Amazon surveillance system) ground- and air-based radar and reconnaissance system has been added to the 1985 North Path (Calha Norte) frontier fortification project. Brazil intends to exert control of Amazonian resources. Interestingly, some Brazilians fear that the United Nations intends to "internationalize" control of the Amazon, in order to protect rain forests, defend indigenous peoples, and regulate the exploitation of mineral resources.

Goal 5: Stabilizing governments in the Western Hemisphere—This used to mean controlling Castroite insurgents, but the economic failure of Cuba and the 1989 Communist collapse in Eastern Europe has eliminated Fidel's appeal. Still, Brazil's military remembers the situation in 1964 and they put a great deal of the blame on "Castroites." Ethnic and cultlike terror and guerrilla organizations, such as the Sendero Luminoso (Shining Path) guerrilla movement in Peru are viewed with alarm. The link between former leftists and the new gangs in the slums (such as the Red Command or Red Falange) may be a new source of insurgency. Government failure to redress atrocities committed in the Amazon against indigenous tribes by groups like the *garimpeiros* (nomad gold and diamond miners) on the Yanomamo in Brazil's Roraima State also fuel new insurgency activity. Just treatment of Amazon tribes by South American governments (and giving the tribes a political voice) will strengthen democracy and decrease political instability.

Goal 6: Becoming the leader of Latin America—The Brazilians have one of the best-trained and most sophisticated diplomatic corps in Latin America. Given their nation's size, power, and savoir faire, they believe they are the natural regional coordinators of policy. The creation of the Southern Common Market (MERCOSUR, also MERCOSUL in Portuguese) in 1995, which consists of Brazil, Argentina, Paraguay, and Uruguay, has made Brazil the leading foreign investor in Argentina. Peru may also join.

Goal 7: Forging the Industrialized Third World Co-Prosperity Sphere—This might be a more subtle title for the long-range goal outlined below. As the Brazilians see it, with their nascent space program, strong arms industry, multiracial democracy (although there are plenty of racial tensions), and burgeoning population, their nation is a natural leader in a tier of nations including South Korea, Taiwan, South Africa, and perhaps Egypt. This loose collection conveniently ignores India. Supporting this upper tier would be another group of third world nations that would be "happier" trading their resources for goods produced by other third world nations, rather than goods produced by the "old" imperialists (Japan, Great Britain, France, etc.).

Long-range Goal: The Brazilian route to world power—Call this reestablishing the "axis of Portuguese influence" around the globe, this time under the direction of Brazil. Brazil would dearly love to have a direct (and directing) relationship with Angola and Mozambique, reestablishing to a degree the "band of the Portuguese" that once stretched from Guinea-Bissau to Formosa.

This new "band" through Africa is a geostrategic means of becoming a world power, similar to the French strategy of "overseas departments," and might be accurately described as an economic-based form of neocolonialism. (But please don't use that word in front of the Angolans.)

Brazilians assert that the cultural and linguistic frameworks are already in place. We all came from Portugal, the Brazilians say. Perhaps the United Kingdom's "commonwealth" approach best describes this Brazilian aspiration: a loose confederation of former Portuguese colonies with the leadership supplied by Brazil. Heavens, even Portugal could join, as long as it was clearly third or fourth fiddle.

In the meantime, Brazil must contend with an economy that still has a lot of problems, a divisive ethnic mix, hidden agendas by various groups (the military was discovered, in 1990, to be secretly developing nuclear weapons and not telling the government about it), and several other problems that might just make Brazil one of those perpetual "future superpowers."

EXTENDED LOOK: Indian Wars: Central America

SOURCE OF CONFLICT

Central America, Spain's colonial backwater, long avoided the twentieth century's tides of social, economic, and political change. Dualistic market (markets seriously restricted by political access) and barter economies, the *patrón* (pah-trone) system of land ownership (vesting all authority, including life-and-death legalities, in the large-estate landowner), submission to outside economic interests (such as U.S. fruit companies), and governmental failure to integrate the hinterlands into the national economic and political fabric produced countries needing not one but several revolutions. Yet revolutionary slogans and firepower cannot solve problems created by 450 years of neglect. Solutions require education, capital, and stability. All of these take peace and time. In Central America, peace has been in short supply.

With the end of the cold war the basic political situation in Central America remains unchanged. With Belize and Costa Rica excepted, the short story of Central America has been the sad fact that the genuine social revolutions have been co-opted by outside interests that have little real commitment to the betterment of the people. These revolutions were long overdue. Inequitable distribution of wealth, lack of social and economic opportunity for all but the elite, and inhumane military regimes created a social and political climate where rapid, revolutionary action was inevitable. Cuba's armed revolution, in the overt name of "new socialism," produced a new form of mass, endemic poverty. The Sandinista revolt produced a new class of the privileged—the Sandinista bureaucratic functionaries and the Sandinista army. The democracy that replaced the Sandinistas has creaked along, exhibiting the social and political divisions of old. Central America's unanswered question remains: What kind of revolution could make change stick? After the revolutionaries toss out the government, they are the government. Now the real problems begin. The old revolutionary vanguard becomes the new elite. Commissars become *patrones*.

The isthmus between the North and South American continents really is the strategic neck of the Western Hemisphere. That's the geographic fact that drove the superpowers' cold war contest in the region.

Where are those who would deal with the fundamental human problems that fed the covert war between the superpowers and continue to provide the background for future armed disputes? Moderates—and there are many who want change without bloodshed—get shot by right-wing death squads or assassinated by left-wing terrorists. The old oligarch elites run to Miami.

The peasant who spilled his blood for the revolution sees his new farm taken over by "the state." Back in the woods the Indians continue to starve. In fact, in Guatemala, the government continues to fight an Indian war now four centuries old. In future wars between the elites, the Indians will continue to suffer.

WHO'S INVOLVED

United States

The Colossus of the North is involved in every Central American country. Washington used to support whoever claimed to be anti-Communist and provided local stability. Now it tries to promote "democratic change"—in the interest of local stability—and a "drug free" body politic. Promotion efforts can include military invasion—witness Panama, December 1989.

Guatemala

Guatemalan government—Always armed; at times it's even civilian.
Guatemalan military—A power unto itself.
Left-wing Guatemalan revolutionaries—What's left of them.
"Guatemalan" (Mayan) Indians—With increasing access to the international media, they are fighting for their human rights.

Nicaragua

The "new democratic" Nicaragua (see Local Politics)—A fractured collection of moderate democrats, socialists, and anti-Sandinista leftists and revolutionaries who united against Sandinista subversion of the anti-Somoza revolt.

Nicaraguan Sandinistas—The remaining "revolutionary vanguard" and "militarized" political elites of the anti-Somoza revolution.

U.S.-backed anti-Sandinista groups—Remnants of the overt "covert army" backed by the CIA. Now allegedly disarmed.

Miskito Indians—Creole and native American peoples living in eastern Nicaragua.

El Salvador

El Salvador government—Right-wing but says it is "reformed."

Left-wing El Salvadoran guerrillas and terrorists—Many were trained by Havana. They have now entered politics but don't do well in the elections.

Panama

"Elected" Panamanian government, underground elements of "old" (Torrijos/Noriega) Panamanian National Guard tied to drug running, former Castroites, and—yes—former CIA operators.

Wild Cards

Costa Rica—In the area, comparatively rich and comparatively defenseless.

Colombian, Central American, and U.S. drug cartels—Bad guys with lots of money, guns, and lawyers.

Catholic Church—Split between an old guard wing and a Marxist-influenced, social activist "liberation theology" wing.

"Insurgent" Protestant evangelical organizations—Especially active in Guatemala; represent a challenge to several traditional Latin American means of social control (i.e., the Catholic Church, militarism, and, for that matter, Marxism). The message is self-help.

Belize—Guatemala has moved toward renouncing its long-term claim to Belize, but a Guatemalan military dictatorship, suddenly in need of a foreign enemy that could deflect domestic discontent, might find the claim to Belize worth resurrecting. Much like the Argentine junta of 1982, they would make a Falklands mistake and involve a wild wild card—Great Britain, which keeps a troop training base in Belize.

GEOGRAPHY

Central America may be seen as a mountain range dividing two coastal plains. The Caribbean coastal lowlands form the eastern margin. Flat, swampy, and largely covered by tropical forest, the region's hurricanes, poor soils, and insects discourage settlement. It tends to get left to the Indians and the poor.

The Pacific coastal plain is narrower than its Caribbean cousin. Weather patterns give it a tropical wet-dry climate. There are more deciduous forests and some open grasslands. The western plain is widest around the Gulf of Fonseca.

The mountains sweep down the isthmus in a long arc of parallel ridges. The western range is volcanically active. The eastern range, especially in Honduras and Guatemala, is also rugged. The backcountry tends to remain culturally and economically isolated. Mayan Indians in the Guatemalan highlands remained relatively untouched by the dominant Spanish society well into the twentieth century. The isolated mountain regions and the relatively empty wetlands provide excellent rebel staging areas.

The people of El Salvador and Honduras tend to cluster in the *tierra templada,* a temperate and less-disease-ridden zone that runs from roughly 800 to 1,800 meters above sea level. This also holds true for Guatemala and Costa Rica.

The mountains break around Nicaragua's lake district. Nicaragua's largest population centers lie along the shores of Lake Managua and Lake Nicaragua. Guatemala has an area of 109,000 square kilometers. Nicaragua is the largest Central American country, with 148,000 square kilometers. Honduras covers 109,500 square kilometers and tiny El Salvador nearly 21,500. Costa Rica covers 51,000 square kilometers; Panama, 77,300; and Belize, 23,000, roughly the size of Massachusetts.

Coffee is the region's primary export crop. Bananas and other agricultural products follow in importance. Dependence on these crops makes national economies highly vulnerable to price fluctuations. Even a shift of fifteen to twenty-five cents in export coffee prices can have a major effect. Only in Costa Rica is industrial activity a larger portion of the GDP than agriculture.

Some 26 million people live in Central America; a large minority are Indians, of various tribes that were there when the Spanish first entered the area five hundred years ago.

El Salvador has a population of 5.8 million. Mestizos comprise 94 percent of that, with 5 percent Indians and 1 percent white. Roman Catholicism is on the decline, although 75 percent of the people are still nominally Catholic. The other quarter of the population are Protestant, and nearly a million of those are evangelicals.

Guatemala has a population of 10.7 million, 55 percent *ladino* (Westernized Indians and mestizos) and 44 percent Mayan Indian. Some sources dispute these figures, suggesting that Indians may make up as much as 60 percent of the Guatemalan population. Many of the Mayan Indians in the mountains do not understand Spanish. Fundamentalist Protestantism has swept through Guatemala. Some estimates put the percentage of Protestants in the country as high as 35 percent, extraordinary for "Catholic" Latin America. Guatemala has the biggest economy and largest population on the American isthmus.

Over 90 percent of Honduras's 5.3 million people are mestizo—of mixed Indian and European ancestry. El Salvador has some 5.8 million people. Mestizos account for 94 percent of its population, Indians 5 percent, and European whites 1 percent. Some 1.5 million people live in the capital, San Salvador.

Nicaragua has 4.1 million people. Mestizos make up 69 percent of its population; 17 percent are white European; 9 percent, Caribbean black; and 5 percent, Indian. Ninety-five percent of Nicaragua's people are Roman Catholic.

Costa Rica has a population of 3.5 million, 96 percent of European origin, the majority of whom trace their ancestry to Spain. Ninety-five percent of the people are Roman Catholic. The relative homogeneity of Costa Rica's population, combined with a higher level of education and health, is a major factor in Costa Rica's comparative stability. Cynics say Costa Rica is stable because they killed off most of the Indians. That overstates the case, but not by much. There are twenty thousand Indians in Costa Rica, roughly the same number inhabiting Costa Rica in 1525.

Belize, on the other hand, is highly heterogeneous, though the population is small. In a population of only 210,000, 37 percent are Creole blacks of Caribbean origin (most in Belize City and the coastal area), 12 percent are Mayan Indian, and 43 percent are mestizo. The British military support unit stationed in Belize gives the nation a lot of local stability and political confidence. English is the official language of Belize, though Spanish is widely spoken, especially along the Mexican and Guatemalan borders.

Panama has a population of 2.6 million people, 70 percent mestizo, 14 percent Caribbean/West Indian, 10 percent white European, and 6 percent Indian. Spanish is the official language, but 15 percent of the population speaks English as their native language.

In all of these countries, with Belize as something of an exception, the "Europeans" tend to control the political processes and the economy.

Rapid population growth gives another dimension to the region's problems. The regional rate of increase is over 3.2 percent per year. Honduras sports a whopping 3.6-percent-plus growth rate. That gives already struggling Honduras another 125,000 or so mouths to feed every twelve months. Decline in infant mortality rates, due to improved nutrition and health for children, has helped produce these high growth rates. The powerful Catholic Church opposes birth control programs.

Population growth is also a problem for land reformers. More and more peasants must be settled on smaller and smaller farms. This problem is already apparent in El Salvador, which has the highest population density in all of Latin America. If the birth rate isn't controlled, revolutions of any flavor simply won't make any difference in terms of solving the problem of poverty. Another ten years at the present birth rate will make any productivity increases or revolutionary redistribution of wealth meaningless.

HISTORY

Regional Overview

Spain conquered Central America between 1502 and 1540. The conquistadors didn't find much gold in Nicaragua, El Salvador, and Honduras, but they did take the best agricultural lands and establish large private landholdings for the Spanish overseers. In Panama (for years a province of Colombia), at the isthmus, they found a route that opened up the west coast of South America. The Indians either retreated into the hills, became slaves, or died off.

Guatemala, Nicaragua, Costa Rica, El Salvador, and Honduras were provinces under the Captaincy General of Guatemala. In 1821 they broke with Spain during the Latin American revolt.

At first Mexico tried to keep all of the Central American provinces in one large union, but El Salvador insisted on Central American autonomy. Mexican forces invaded El Salvador in 1823. Mexican imperialism is not a foreign notion in Central America. El Salvador, looking for an ally, asked the U.S. government to make it a state. The United States was cool to the idea, but a revolution in Mexico led to a Mexican withdrawal. Later that year the five Central American provinces of El Salvador, Nicaragua, Honduras, Costa Rica, and Guatemala formed the Federal Republic of Central America. The union dissolved in 1838, with much mutual bickering and recrimination. Honduras seemed to be the only nation interested in continuing the arrangement. In fact, until 1922, the reestablishment of the Central American Federation was a major feature of Honduran policy. There have been several union proposals made since the breakup, but they have failed to arouse much enthusiasm.

British and German investments in the 1850s, primarily in coffee plantations, did return some capital to the region, but they also tied the local economies to one or two crops. In the twentieth century large U.S. firms began to acquire banana and coffee plantations in the area.

Native businessmen and politicians tended to become the local representatives of foreign investment interests.

One of the major historical factors, U.S. Central American policy, could be summed up as unqualified support for any pro-U.S. regime. As long as foreign powers stayed away, as long as U.S. citizens weren't threatened, as long as American business interests weren't complaining, and as long as national borders weren't violated, Washington could have cared less.

The Countries

El Salvador

El Salvador's history is one of frequent revolutions. Since the 1930s all but two governments have been led by the military. In 1979 a civilian-military group overthrew President Carlos Humberto Romero. Young officers and Christian Democrat allies formed a new junta in early 1980 and began a series of economic reforms that included expropriating all estates larger than 1,250 acres, nationalization of export marketing, and nationalization of the banks. The right wing objected and many wealthy landowners left the country. The left-wing opposition refused to join the government. Members of the radical Popular Liberation Forces, already waging a low-level war in the countryside, saw the splintering of its center and right opposition as an opportunity. The civil war was on.

Centrist socialist José Napoleon Duarte tried to forge a moderate political center in the midst of the turmoil. He was foiled by radicals of the Left and Right and his own failing health. In 1989, Alfredo Cristiani of the right-wing Arena party was elected president. The leftist FMLN guerrillas launched a "final" offensive on November 11, 1989. The assault marked a new phase in the war; for the first time in the conflict the left-wing guerrillas tried to seize and hold territory. The strategy was to tie down army units with attacks on headquarters and economic sites, then hit political targets. After eleven days the offensive sputtered. The guerrillas withdrew, leaving some 460 dead

(5 percent of their total strength). While the assault was, from a military perspective, a defeat for the guerrillas, the FMLN did score on the political front. They shredded the El Salvadoran government's claims that the rebels could no longer mass forces.

The El Salvadoran civil war officially ended in early 1992, after some 70,000 deaths (one in 83 people) and $4.5 billion in U.S. aid. In January 1993 the El Salvadoran government had 63,000 troops under arms. The peace accord required the government to shrink the force to 31,000 by May 1994. Reports in late 1994 suggested the El Salvadoran Army had been reduced to around 35,000. In the same period guerrilla strength shrank from 7,000 to perhaps 1,000.

The UN-brokered peace accord set up the Truth Commission to monitor compliance with the accords and monitor human rights violations. The peace agreement called for the creation of a new 6,000-man National Civil Police, an independent civilian police force to replace the military-run National Police. Both former guerrillas and National Police officers would serve in the National Civil Police.

Yet in 1993 several FMLN candidates were murdered, an indication that the death squads had not disappeared. Likewise, the May 1993 discovery of an alleged FMLN arms cache in Nicaragua suggested the guerrillas had not disappeared, either. Other arms dumps turned up in El Salvador and Honduras. On the other hand, the "purge" of rightist officers in the military did not meet the UN deadline.

Arena's candidate, Armando Calderon Sol, was elected president in 1994. Left-wing parties took only 25 percent of the seats in the National Assembly. With the end of the cold war and the loss of Communist support, the Salvadoran Left appeared to be in disarray. The People's Revolutionary Army (ERP), an FMLN faction, even explored alliances with business interests.

The war may have ended but kidnappings for ransom have increased. Calderon Sol began a probe of criminal links with the army.

Nicaragua

In the seventeenth, eighteenth, and nineteenth centuries, Spaniards in Nicaragua fought a number of battles with the Miskito Indians of the Caribbean coast. Great Britain supported the Miskitos and even controlled a small strip of the eastern coast until the late nineteenth century.

After the breakup of the Central American federation, Nicaragua experienced nearly one hundred years of instability. American adventurers, the notorious William Walker being the most prominent, fueled the ongoing disputes between polarized liberal democrats and supporters of the old patriarchal elite.

The United States intervened on a number of occasions. U.S. Marines were in and out of Nicaragua between 1912 and 1933. President Franklin Roosevelt finally withdrew the Marines as part of his Good Neighbor Policy. (The Great Depression of the 1930s also played a role. With economic woes at home, the United States cut back on economic operations.)

Before the Marines left, they placed Anastasio Somoza Garcia into power. The Somozas controlled the country until 1979 when Anastasio Somoza Debayle was overthrown by the Sandinistas. The 1979 revolution was a popular revolution. Businessmen, church groups, peasants, the middle class, and ideological opponents banded together to topple the Somoza regime.

The Sandinista junta became increasingly militant and anti-U.S. East bloc military advisers entered the country, along with a flood of small arms and antiquated tanks and helicopters. The Sandinistas doubled, then tripled, the size of their armed forces. The reason given was to thwart a U.S. invasion. The Sandinistas frightened Honduras and shook Costa Rica's complacent worldview. CIA-sponsored *contras*, anti-Sandinista forces, operated from bases in Honduras and from camps inside Nicaragua.

In the mid-1980s several Sandinista revolutionaries broke with the regime and had their own guerrilla groups operating from inside Nicaragua and from Costa Rica. Worse, ham-handed and ideological Sandinista attempts to control the Miskito Indians of the Caribbean coast backfired and produced an Indian revolt—and outright war in 1981. The Sandinistas and Miskitos fought until 1987 when an "autonomy law" was drafted by Managua that essentially left the Indians alone and made the eastern Miskito area a near autonomous Miskito nation. The law required the central government to consult with the Miskitos over use of natural resources in Miskito lands. In the western cities, however, the Sandinista junta beefed up the secret police, imposed press censorship, and shut down the offices of human rights groups that have objected to Sandinista junta policies. That led to further defections from the anti-Somoza ranks.

The Sandinistas, however, expanded the governmental bureaucracy and stuffed it with Sandinista supporters. They confiscated opposition goods and real estate and redistributed it to their guys and gals.

In late 1989 outside pressure and economic decline forced the Sandinsta junta to agree to open, internationally monitored elections.

In one of the more surprising electoral results ever to come out of Central America, Mrs. Violeta Chamorro and her UNO party defeated the Sandinistas in February 1990. The war-weariness of the populace (thirty thousand Nicaraguans killed) was a major factor in her election as well as popular disenchantment with the Sandinistas. Disaffection with the Sandinistas ran deep. Even Masaya, the first town of any size to rise against Somoza and long considered hard-core Sandinista territory, spurned the FSLN in favor of the National Opposition Union (UNO). Two thousand foreign observers witnessed the election and kept them reasonably honest.

Mrs. Chamorro was inaugurated in April 1990—after the Sandinistas had rammed through legislation exempting them from prosecution for theft and other crimes. In what was viewed as a troubling compromise on Chamorro's part, Sandinista Humberto Ortega remained in charge of the EPS (Ejercito Popular Sandinista, Sandinista People's Army). Contra forces returned to Nicaragua and began a slow process of disarmament.

The rebels' demobilization gave Mrs. Chamorro the political opportunity to slice up the EPS. The Chamorro government planned to first shrink the army to less than 40,000 troops, end the bitterly divisive Sandinista military draft, then turn the force into an even smaller, professional border guard of 15,000.

This struck at the heart of Sandinista power. The question in Nicaragua remains who in the military is loyal to what and to whom. Old Sandinista military officials retained control of the military.

Nicaraguan politics from 1991 through 1994 remained chaotic. The National Assembly effectively ceased to function from 1992 through 1994 when conservatives launched a boycott in order to protest political corruption. In 1993 both Sandinista rebels and *re-contra* rebels shot up towns in the hinterland. Led by Pedrito the Honduran, an ex-army major, the Sandinista rebels shot up the city of Estelí. Other embarrassments: Documents turned up in Managua exposing an international kidnapping ring run out of Nicaragua by Latin American leftists and the Spanish Basque terrorist group, ETA. The real problem: In 1993 unemployment and underemployment affected 60 percent of the workforce. Poverty breeds more trouble. In 1995 the "war of the constitutions" began as the legislature tried to weaken the executive branch. Among the hottest points of contention were rules limiting presidential terms and prohibiting succession by a relative. Dynastic (or clan) rule has been the custom in Nicaragua and many democrats argue that it must be prohibited if real democracy is to take root.

Trouble reoccurred along the Miskito coast with the Miskitos fighting fishing boats illegally fishing in their waters. The war-hardened Miskitos attacked the fishing boats (from "unidentified Central and South American nations") with rocket-propelled grenades.

Honduras

During the twentieth century's first six decades Honduras experienced over a hundred internal revolts and governmental changes, turmoil even more marked by the fact that the Andino administration ruled from 1932 to 1948 and provided a relative source of calm and stability. Honduras received a visit from the U.S. Marines in 1912 and the partisan political clashes typical of the region continue unabated into the present. In Honduras, oddly enough, those clashes have never produced the polarization found in Guatemala, El Salvador, and Nicaragua. Though plagued by military coups, Honduras has enjoyed periods of national cooperation. Ever since their highly successful national strike in 1954, Honduran labor unions have held a great deal of political power. The military, however, is still the central political player in the nation, and increasingly controls large businesses (see Local Politics).

Guerrilla activity in Honduras has been minimal, though spillover fighting along guerrilla infiltration routes around the Gulf of Fonseca (between El Salvador and Nicaragua) occurred. The end of the Nicaraguan civil war and the removal of the ten-thousand-man contra force from Honduras has been a major relief to the entire nation.

The 1969 Soccer War between El Salvador and Honduras didn't officially end until 1980 when the two countries finally agreed to settle lingering border differences. Rivalry over a series of soccer matches sparked the brief five-day fight. The real issue was, from the Salvadoran perspective, Honduran "mistreatment" of Salvadoran migrants. From the Honduran perspective, it was illegal Salvadoran immigration.

Poor economic performance, rapid population growth, corruption, and low productivity remain Honduras's chief problems. Formal unemployment is 45 percent and foreign debt is growing. The issue of corruption in the Honduran Army will become a more open—and more explosive—political problem.

Belize

Belize is increasingly recognized as a major zone of early Mayan Indian development. With sites excavated at Altun Ha, Xunantunich ("Maid of the Rock," near the Guatemalan border), and El Pilar, archaeologists have begun to focus on the area's importance as a pre-Columbian center of Mayan civilization. Columbus passed the Belizean coastline on his fourth voyage (1502), but the first European settlements were begun in 1638—by shipwrecked Englishmen.

The area around Belize City was a perfect haven for pirates—shallow-water approaches discouraged deep draft men-of-war from chasing the smaller and swifter pirate craft, and if the soldiers did land, there was lots of jungle in which to slink. Over the next 150 years the area attracted runaway slaves, adventurers, thieves, and loggers. Mahogany hauled out of the swamps paid for a trek into that moist hinterland.

Foreign powers exerted little control over the area. Great Britain "officially" recognized Spanish dominion during the eighteenth century. With the collapse of Spain's continental empire, the area was up for grabs. Still, Britain didn't formally establish British Honduras as a colony until 1840. Guatemala's on-again, off-again claim to Belize is based on eighteenth-century treaties between Spain and Britain.

In June 1973 the colony changed its name to Belize. It became independent in September 1981. Belize has one of the finest barrier reefs in the world. The government hopes to use the reefs as a means of attracting more tourists. There may also be significant oil fields in the area.

Since the 1980s the British Army garrison has been significantly reduced in size. Belize has also become a haven for migrants escaping Central America's many wars, most notably Guatemala. Drug trafficking through Belize has also increased, disrupting what had been a quiet Creole life.

Guatemala

With the great city of Tikal as archaeological testament, Guatemala was the center of Mayan civilization. Parts of Guatemala came under Spanish control in 1524 after the defeat of the Mayas by the conquistador Pedro de Alvarado. Guatemala seceded from Spain in 1821, at first as part of Mexico, then as a chief architect (in an attempt to maintain the Captaincy General of Guatemala) of the ill-fated Central American Federation. After the federation collapsed, the cycle of Guatemalan internal politics was bitterly established: long periods of military dictatorship infrequently interrupted by brief, unstable democratic governments.

In 1944 "the October revolutionaries" overthrew General Jorge Ubico's dictatorship. A period of attempts at social change were begun by President Juan José Arevalo (1945–50).

In 1952, Colonel Jacobo Arbenz, Arevalo's successor as president, gave the underground Communist-run Guatemalan Labor party (PGT, see Local Politics) legal status. By 1954 the PGT controlled several labor organizations and key posts in the government. The red flag went up in Washington. The Arbenz government was toppled by a CIA-aided army coup.

Guatemala was governed by a series of military juntas or military-"sponsored" civilian governments until 1985, when a civilian president, Vinicio Cerezo Arevalo, was elected. One of the more interesting military governments was headed by General Efrain Rios Montt. Rios Montt took power in March 1982 and ruled for sixteen months. Rios

Montt denounced death squad activity and set in place a number of "populist" programs, the majority of which, however, were designed to gain Indian help in fighting leftist guerrillas. Rios Montt belonged to a fundamentalist Protestant Church sect and was viewed with suspicion by the influential hierarchy of the Catholic Church. His regime was characterized by bitter "anti-Communist" repression. Rios Montt was toppled in October 1983.

As of mid-1995 the Guatemalan Army's thirty-five-year-old war against the Mayans and the now shrunken Guatemalan Revolutionary National Unity movement (URNG) forces continues. URNG has also occasionally waged a terror war against the Mayans, in order to extract "taxes" from the Indians, but URNG's attacks are insignificant compared with the Guatemalan Army's. Even some Guatemalan government sources admit that the government is responsible for at least 80 percent of the human rights violations. In February 1993, 700 Mayans fled to Mexico to escape an army "counterguerrilla" operation. URNG, which had nearly 10,000 guerrillas in the field in the early 1980s, now has around 700. A weapons cache discovered in Nicaragua in 1993, however, had enough weapons to supply a battalion earmarked for URNG.

The year 1993 also saw turmoil in the nominally constitutional democratic government when President José Serrano, allegedly fed up with corrupt politics, attempted to shut down the congress. Serrano was opposed, and then deposed, by the military. Serrano was replaced by Ramiro de Leon Carpio, who supported an anticorruption drive and political reforms. Corruption, however, continues, as do political killings. Army officers continue to run many businesses.

There are allegations of U.S. CIA involvement with Guatemalan Army death squads. Guatemalan Colonel Julio Roberto Alpirez, the alleged perpetrator in the killing of Efrain Bamaca Velasquez, a guerrilla leader, may have been a paid CIA source.

The actual naming of army officers allegedly involved in death squads deeply shook the Guatemalan Army. As of spring 1995, several press sources report that the "CIA revelations" have left the Guatemalan Army in turmoil. There are many reasons. First of all, the army, used to operating beyond the reach of law, is suddenly under intense international scrutiny. There is also a morale issue: The troops were told in the 1970s and 1980s (when the United States diminished then finally cut off military aid) that the United States was not a friend of Guatemala. In 1995 the troops learned that their leaders were taking cash from the Yankee enemy.

The issue of corruption also deeply divides the military, and the divisions are starting to show. Press sources report that when a senior member of the Defense Ministry was accused by a leftist guerrilla organization of drug trafficking and running car theft rackets, the information was supplied by sources inside Guatemalan military intelligence.

Over 100,000 people have been killed in the long Guatemalan "Indian war." According to press and human rights organization sources, 400 Guatemalan Mayan Indian villages have been destroyed. The Guatemalan government itself says the war has produced over 40,000 widows and 150,000 orphans. Guatemala continues to be a highly polarized society.

Costa Rica

Columbus landed in the Costa Rican region in 1502. The Spaniards began to settle the area in 1522. Despite its name ("Rich Coast"), Costa Rica wasn't a land of mineral wealth; it had no gold, no gems, and an Indian population adept at escaping Spanish slavers.

Costa Rica seceded from Spain in 1821. In the midst of the turmoil associated with the Central American federation, Costa Rica took its Guanacaste Province from neighboring Nicaragua. This is still remembered by the Nicaraguans. When the Sandinistas made noises about chasing Eden Pastora's ARDE guerrilla group into its Costa Rican sanctuaries, the fact that Guanacaste had been Nicaraguan territory was an unspoken justification.

Costa Rica held its first free election in 1889. Since that time Costa Rican democracy has proved quite resilient. Only two events mar the record: the short-lived dictatorship of Federico Tinoco (1917–18) and the disputed 1948 presidential election. Two thousand people died in 1948 when the army allied with a Communist-led guerrilla force and attempted a coup. José Figueres Ferrer (known affectionately as Don Pepe), leader of the revolt against the coup, established an interim

regime that wrote a new constitution that guaranteed universal suf-
frage and abolished the army. He served three terms as president.

Costa Rica's Civil Guard is essentially a police force trained for
border surveillance and patrol in the urban areas. The Rural Guard
polices the backcountry. Total force is around four thousand men.
During the height of the Sandinista tensions, the Civil Guard clashed
with Nicaraguan forces along the border. Costa Rica relies on the
Organization of American States to defend its borders. That means
Costa Rica's borders are guaranteed by the armed forces of the United
States, but because of the so-called sensitivities of small nation politics,
no one is supposed to say that out loud.

Panama

The first European explorers reached Panama in 1501. In 1513,
Vasco Núñez de Balboa crossed the isthmus and encountered the
"Southern Sea" (Pacific Ocean). From that point on, geography made
Panama a strategic asset for any power wishing to operate in both the
Pacific and Atlantic oceans.

The Spaniards transshipped Incan gold and silver from their Pacific
coast mines and ports, across Panama, and to their Iberia-bound treasure galleons. The Spaniards dreamed of a canal across the isthmus—
gold-humping mule trains and Indian slaves were slow and a pain to
maintain.

Panama seceded from Spain in 1821 and joined the new Republic
of Greater Colombia. Three times during the nineteenth century, Panamanians attempted to secede from Colombia. In 1903, after Colombia refused a U.S. bid to build a canal across the isthmus, the United
States bankrolled and protected a Panamanian secessionist movement.
The Panamanians declared independence and Colombia decided it
didn't want to fight the U.S. Navy.

In 1914 the United States completed the 83-kilometer-long canal in
the 16-kilometer-wide U.S. Canal Zone. The Canal Zone was Panamanian territory but was completely administered by Washington.

From 1903 to 1968, an often less-than-more democratic government
ruled in Panama. Local trading and business families actually controlled

most of the politics. Still, all Panamanians resented U.S. control of the canal and Canal Zone. Demonstrations against U.S. control became more frequent and more heated.

In 1968, Brigadier General Omar Torrijos Herrera overthrew the newly elected president. From that time on, until the U.S. invasion in December 1989, the Panamanian National Guard (later renamed the Panamanian Defense Forces—PDF) was the arbiter of power, even under the guise of civilian rule. Constitutional democracy was supposedly restored in 1984. But in Panama, 1984 really was an Orwellian 1984—the military dictatorship was increasingly entrenched.

In February 1988, the head of the PDF, General Manuel Antonio Noriega, was indicted by a U.S. grand jury on drug smuggling charges. The civilian president of Panama, Eric Arturo Delvalle, attempted to remove Noriega from command. Noriega took over the government. Noriega conducted a bizarre anti-U.S. campaign that included hobnobbing with the Sandinistas and Fidel Castro. He stifled the May 1989 elections. "Dignity battalions"—a streetwise force of brutal thugs paid off by Noriega and the PDF (and suggested by Fidel Castro)—beat opposition political leaders. In the fall of 1989, Noriega foiled an attempted coup by lower-ranking PDF officers.

Noriega believed himself invincible. In early December, harassment of U.S. personnel in Panama increased. After a U.S. Marine lieutenant was murdered, the United States struck.

In an operation code-named Just Cause, U.S. airborne rangers hit the Panamanian control points and airfields as mechanized infantry and attack helicopters assaulted PDF headquarters. U.S. special operations forces hit houses where intelligence sources suspected Noriega had been hiding. AC-130 Specter gunships pinned down PDF forces. A total of twenty-four thousand U.S. troops took part. In less than eight hours the PDF was destroyed.

Noriega eluded capture for several days and eventually sought asylum in the Vatican embassy. A car sent by the papal nuncio picked up Noriega outside of a Dairy Queen ice cream shop. U.S. troops bombarded the embassy compound with amplified heavy-metal rock and roll. The young soldiers and local Panamanian kids loved the music; the Vatican protested to Washington. The Vatican "urged" Noriega to turn himself over to the United States for trial as a drug smuggler. Noriega was tried and convicted in a U.S. court. As of mid-1995 he remained in jail.

However, Noriega's former political party, the Democratic Revolutionary party (PRD), returned to power in 1994 when Ernesto Perez Balladares was elected president of Panama. Balladares declared December 20, 1994 (the anniversary of the U.S. invasion), a day of national mourning.

U.S. Southern Command (SOUTHCOM) announced in 1995 it would move its headquarters from Quarry Heights, Panama, to Miami, Florida.

LOCAL POLITICS

Belize

People's United party (PUP) and the United Democratic party (UDP) are the main parties in Belize. There are three smaller parties: the Toledo Progressive party, the Belize Popular party, and the Christian Democratic party.

Costa Rica

National Liberation party (PLN) and Social Christian Unity party (PUSC) are the major parties. The PLN is a member of the Socialist International. Other parties include the Costa Rican Socialist party, the Costa Rican People's party, and the Popular Vanguard party.

El Salvador

Truth Commission—Organization set up to observe compliance with UN-brokered Salvadoran peace accords.
FMLN—Farabundo Martí Revolutionary Front for National Lib-

eration; guerrilla alliance; chief group is Salvadoran Communist party. Three other members, the Popular Liberation Forces (PLF, a group with a Maoist orientation), the People's Revolutionary Army, and the Armed Forces of National Resistance, are splinter groups of the Communist party. A fifth guerrilla group is the Central American Revolutionary Workers party. In mid-1983 an even more radical group, the Clara Elizabeth Ramirez Front, split from the PLF. FMLN fractured even more in the aftermath of the Sandinistas' defeat in the February 1990 Nicaraguan elections and the 1994 elections in El Salvador. Chief combat leaders were Joaquin Villalobos and Gustavo Anaya.

Arena party—Nationalist Republican Alliance, right-wing. The Salvadoran Authentic Institutional party is another right-wing group.

Major Roberto D'Aubuisson—Now dead; suspected death squad ringleader.

Christian Democratic party—Moderates.

Salvadoran Army (Fuerza Armada)—Main source of political power in the country; the air force is armed with US-supplied A-37 Dragonfly light attack jets.

Association of Demobilized Veterans (ADEFAES)—New military association that may serve as a front for old El Salvadoran Army units.

Death squads—Name usually applied to right-wing terror groups that seek to enforce their aims by "making examples" of those who oppose them. Estimates vary, but death squads may have murdered as many as ten thousand people since 1980. The leftists had their own death squads, but they never caught as much media attention.

Pipil Indians—Indigenous group caught in the crossfire between El Salvador's Right and Left.

ISTA—Salvadoran Institute for Agrarian Transformation; government bureau tasked with administering land reform.

Guatemala

Christian Democratic party (DCG)—As of 1990 the largest and most powerful party, though ultimate control lies with the army.

Guatemalan Republican Front—Emerging right-wing "umbrella" political party.

Union of the National Center (UCN)—Is also called the National Centrist Union.

Other parties—National Liberation Movement; Nationalist Authentic Center (Authentic Nationalist party); Democratic Institutional party; Democratic Party of National Cooperation; National Renewal party; Social Democratic party. The Revolutionary party (PR) is actually a moderate party.

Army of Guatemala—Main source of power in the nation; thirty-five thousand total troops. When the U.S. military arms embargo started to bite into the army's capabilities, its senior officers turned to the international arms market for spares and simultaneously began to develop indigenous light weapons repair capabilities. As many of the rebels were now better armed, the army sought to capture weapons from them. Elite forces have allegedly been trained by the Israelis. In 1988 the army also took command of the Treasury Police and National Police.

Outlawed party—Guatemalan Labor party (PGT); the Communist party of Guatemala.

Guatemalan Revolutionary National Unity (URNG)—"Unified" organization of three former left-wing guerrilla groups, the Guerrilla Army of the Poor (EGP), the Revolutionary Organization of the Armed People (ORPA), and the Rebel Armed Forces (FAR); now includes the Guatemalan Labor party and its small armed contingents.

Secret Anti-Communist Army (ESA)—Guatemalan death squad organization; allegedly run by high-ranking regular army officers.

Rigoberta Menchú—Guatemalan Indian awarded Nobel Peace Prize in 1992 for her defense of indigenous peoples' rights.

The White Hand—Right-wing terrorist force.

Cronica—Leftist guerrilla group. Accused of assassinating several dozen opponents. Efrain Bamaca, slain husband of a U.S. citizen, was a leader in this organization.

Alfredo Tay Tocoy—Became education minister in 1993. He is a Quiche Indian and first "indigenous" (nonmestizo or non-European) cabinet member in Guatemala's history.

Alvaro Arzu—Former mayor of Guatemala City. Advocate of democracy and more liberal economy.

National Interagency Coordinating Office (Coordinadora Inter-

Institucional Nacional)—Advisory bodies set up in each Guatemalan province. The officers and advisers on the boards report directly to the regional military commander. They are tasked with coordinating all civilian agencies operating in the province. These boards are how the military keeps its thumb on all aspects of the government.

Panzos—Site of 1978 army massacre of Indian population.

Drug producers—In 1989, Guatemala became the world's sixth largest producer of opium poppies.

"Bullets and beans" (actually, guns and beans—*fusiles y frijoles*)— General Efrain Rios Montt's strategy of providing food, shelter, and protection for villages that would turn against leftist guerrillas. Rios Montt, a Protestant evangelical, ran the military dictatorship in the early 1980s.

The Kaibiles: Elite army counterinsurgency unit linked to the destruction of Indian villages.

Canjobal Indians: Filed suit in U.S. federal court against former Guatemalan Defense Minister General Hector Gramajo and were awarded $47.5 million in damages. The suit alleged that forces under Gramajo tortured an American nun, destroyed the Canjobals' village, and killed their relatives.

Honduras

Army of Honduras—Twenty-four thousand troops; most powerful political force in Honduras.

Military Pensions Institute (IPM)—Established to provide retirement pensions to officers. In 1995 the IPM was run by General Luis Alonso Discua, the head of the Honduran armed forces. The IPM has tremendous economic clout. Allegedly, the military chooses the managers of IPM businesses. Allegedly, military-owned businesses include Honduras's largest cement plant, a funeral home, cattle ranches, and radio stations. IPM's Honduran investments tend to do very well. The tradition of mixing business and guns continues.

The National party (PNH) and the Liberal party (PLH) are the country's largest and strongest parties. The National party leans more toward the right; the Liberal, left. The National party has two factions, the Monarca and the Oswaldista. The Liberal party exists in three main factions, the Rodista, FUL, and ALIPO. Two other parties both attract approximately 5 percent of the electorate: the National Innovation and Unity party (PINU) and the Honduran Christian Democratic party (PDCH).

"Unregistered" parties—Include Communist Party of Honduras (PCH), Socialist Party of Honduras (PASO).

Other political groups—Association of Honduran Campesinos (ANACH); Honduran Council of Private Enterprise (COHEP); Confederation of Honduran Workers (CTH); United Federation of Honduran Workers (FUTH). The Association for the Progress of Honduras was a right-wing political group.

316 Battalion—Antiguerrilla "intelligence unit" set up in early 1980s to kill left-wing activists. Members of the unit are accused by human rights organizations of torture and corruption.

General Francisco Morazan—Historical national hero of Honduras; tried to keep Central American Federation together.

Potential guerrilla force—Morazan Liberation Front; at one time a Sandinista puppet; now a "Marxist" rebel splinter group.

Nicaragua

National Assembly—Quit functioning in 1992 when conservative parties began a boycott in protest of political corruption in Chamorro regime. In 1994 it began to meet again.

UNO—National Opposition Union. The fourteen-party-bloc umbrella organization of opposition to the Sandinista junta that elected Violeta Chamorro president in 1990. Began to fracture after the election victory. It covered the spectrum of politics from right to left, including: National Conservative party, Conservative Popular Alliance, Conservative National Action party (a splinter group of Conservative Democratic Movement), Democratic Party of National Confidence, Independent Liberal party, Liberal party, Liberal Constitutionalist party, National Action party, Nicaraguan Democratic Movement (MDN), Nicaraguan Socialist party (formerly a pro-Moscow Communist party, now social democratic), Communist party of Nicaragua (splinter group of Nicaraguan Socialist party), Popular Social Christian party, Central American Integrationist party, and the Social Democratic party (which includes key Chamorro advisers Alfredo Cesar and Pedro Joaquin Chamorro, her son).

Former Sandinista junta—Headed by former president Daniel Ortega Saavedra; includes his brother, Humberto Ortega, and head of the secret police, Tomas Borges.

FSLN—Sandinista Front for National Liberation; original umbrella group for opposition to Somoza; as the moderates left in disgust or fright, became increasingly Marxist and anti-U.S.

Nicaraguan Army—As of mid-1995 still under the control of the Sandinistas despite February 1995 amendment to the constitution to place the army under direct civilian control. The army now allegedly controls several businesses (as in Honduras and Nicaragua) and acts as an independent economic force.

Civilista movement—Political group that seeks complete abolition of the Nicaraguan Army.

DGSE—General Directorate for State Security; Nicaraguan intelligence service; transferred by Sandinistas from the Interior Ministry to the army so they could retain control.

Commando 3-80—Re-contra guerrilla group, organized to fight the current government because of the continued presence of Sandinista influence in the government.

National Dignity Command—Sandinista rebel guerrilla group active in 1993.

Estelí—Site of July 1993 "Sandinista rebel" revolt. Rebels robbed banks and took over the city. The army put down the rebellion. Some critics contend the rebellion was staged so that the Sandinista-controlled army could appear to be acting evenhandedly. However, up to sixty people died in the fighting.

National Employees Union—Sandinista-controlled union of government civil service workers.

Turbas—Pro-Sandinista street mobs used to terrorize opponents.

Contras and re-contras—Former anti-Sandinista guerrillas; main group was Nicaraguan Democratic Force; total force in the field at the time of the February 1990 elections was sixteen thousand. As of mid-1995 perhaps three hundred re-contras were in the hills. Important

568 / A QUICK AND DIRTY GUIDE TO WAR

commanders included Commander Rueben and Commander Franklin. Re-contras under the command of José Angel Talavera fought a series of battles with the Nicaraguan Army in January 1993 near the town of Quilali, one hundred miles northeast of Managua.

Misurasata—Miskito, Sumo, and Rama Indian organization; leader is Stedman Fagoth Muller; Miskitos still can field an army of three thousand guerrillas; associated with Yatama, another Miskito organization.

Yapti Taspa—Miskito name for their nation.

Mikupia (Miskito Heart)—Well-armed Miskito ecological protection group.

La Prensa—Nicaraguan opposition newspaper owned by the Chamorro family; was frequently shut down by Somoza, frequently shut down by the Sandinista junta.

Chamorro clan—Violeta Barrios de Chamorro (Doña Violeta) is the widow of Pedro Joaquin Chamorro Cardenal, the publisher of *La Prensa* who was murdered by order of Somoza in 1978. Two of her four children, Pedro Joaquin Chamorro and Cristiana Chamorro, joined her in UNO. Her other two children, Carlos Fernando Chamorro and Claudia Chamorro, were militant, high-ranking Sandinistas. Carlos edited the Sandinista newspaper, *Barricada.*

Eden Pastora—His nom de guerre was Commander Zero; the Che Guevara of the anti-Somoza revolution who led the assault on Somoza's private bunker. He revolted against the Sandinistas. Though personally popular, he was regarded by the Left, Right, and Center as an unpredictable, and therefore dangerous, romantic.

Democratic Revolutionary Alliance (ARDE)—Anti-Sandinista guerrilla group once led by revolutionary socialist Eden Pastora; was based in Costa Rica; faded from scene after 1987.

General Augusto César Sandino—Nicaraguan national hero; fought U.S. Marines to a stalemate in 1920s and 1930s. When the Marines left in 1933, he left the backcountry and made peace with the new government. Was murdered during dinner with President Bautista by National Guardsmen under the command of Anastasio Somoza. The Sandinistas take their name from Sandino.

Sandinistas' foreign supporters—Often nicknamed "Sandalistas"; a legion of "leftish" groups and small political organizations in the

United States and Western Europe attracted by the Sandinistas' revolutionary aura and romantic rhetoric. They enjoyed protesting in front of the American embassy and spoke of being in "internationalist solidarity" with the Sandinistas. Groups included Bikes Not Bombs, Nicaragua Network, Witness for Peace, and dozens more. Many Sandalistas expressed "utter shock" and "disorientation" at the results of the February 1990 Nicaraguan election.

Panama

Authentic Panamenista party (PPA); Christian Democratic party (PDC); Labor party (PALA); Republican party (PR); Nationalist Republican Liberal party (MOLIRENA).

Democratic Revolutionary party (PRD)—Former party of General Noriega.

Panamanian Defense Forces (PDF)—New name of the Noriega-led National Guard. Its organization was destroyed by U.S. forces in the December 1989 invasion.

Panama Canal Treaty—Signed on September 7, 1977, by U.S. President Jimmy Carter and the Panamanian dictator, General Omar Torrijos. Treaty went into effect in October 1979. The treaty governed the operation and defense of the canal and guaranteed its neutrality. Panama would take over full operation of the canal in December 2001.

Panama Canal Commission—U.S. government agency tasked with running the Panama Canal and training Panamanians for takeover of canal operations in 2001.

Canal Alternative Study Commission—Established by the United States, Japan, and Panama. Is studying the feasibility of a new sea-level canal through the Panamanian isthmus.

Rabi-blanco ("white tails," or "white ass")—Nickname for Panama's elites, who control the economy and government. Panama splits along racial as well as class lines; the predominant blacks are called "black ass."

Answer to the Canal Trivia Question—The Pacific (Balboa) end of the canal is actually east of the Atlantic (Colón) end. The canal is cut northwest to southeast, from Atlantic to Pacific.

EXTENDED CENTRAL AMERICAN LOCAL POLITICS

CACM (MERCOMUN)—Central American Common Market; established in 1960 by Guatemala, Honduras, El Salvador, Nicaragua, and Costa Rica (though Costa Rica didn't formally join until 1963). A good idea but a failed venture. Was designed to promote Central American trade and develop local industries. What happened was that industry ended up being concentrated in countries with the lowest wage rates. Honduras withdrew in 1971. Now nonoperative.

The School of the Americas—Once located in Panama, now located at Fort Benning, Georgia, and run by the U.S. Army. Training institution for many Latin American soldiers. Called by critics School for Assassins. The U.S. Army maintains that of approximately 59,000 students who have gone through the school since it opened in 1946, only 300 have been named as human rights violators. Those named include Roberto D'Aubuisson (El Salvador death squads), Colonel Julio Roberto Alpirez (Guatemalan accused of murdering political opponents), and General Manuel Noriega (Panamanian dictator and drug kingpin). Considering the heavy dose of civil affairs instruction (with emphasis on not committing atrocities) the students get, the School of the Americas can't help but discourage such behavior among officers who come from a tradition of heavy-handed dealings with civilians.

U.S. Congress, U.S. public opinion, American newspapers, and TV networks—Considered by many participants to be the most important political battleground in Central America.

POTENTIAL OUTCOMES

Nicaragua

1. 35 percent chance through 2001: Severe instability wracks democratically elected government; UNO-coalition fragments; an "au-

thoritarian democratic" but non-Sandinista regime comes to power. (Contingent factor is foreign economic aid. See Outcome 3.)

2. 35 percent chance through 2001: UNO coalition stabilizes; Sandinista Army is demobilized and new army formed as a "border guard"; new Nicaraguan constitution instituted using Costa Rica as a model. Note: Increases to overall 75 percent chance if massive economic aid arrives in 1995–99 time frame. (Massive is defined as $400 million or more. It would be unfair to assume the United States should foot the bill, given the aid promised to the Sandinistas by Western European governments.)

3. 25 percent chance through 2001: Sandinistas regain power through elections and/or "military leverage" (i.e., threats and intimidation); if that happens, 70 percent chance of a new Indian and contra insurgency.

4. 5 percent chance through 2001: U.S. invasion of Nicaragua provoked by a Sandinista power-grab. A Sandinista-inspired insurgency begins in the hinterland.

El Salvador

1. 65 percent chance through 2001: Moderates and conservatives succeed in controlling right-wing death squad elements; left wing remains part of political process. Reconstruction begins in a war-weary nation. Increases to 80 percent if effective U.S. economic aid materializes ($200 million in direct economic assistance). In order to be effective, aid must be coupled with controls limiting effects of local corruption. Note: A major political indicator for this outcome: successful prosecution of death squad members for murder and terror activities.

2. 25 percent chance through 2001: Left renounces political participation and guerrilla war erupts. No-win war between Left and Right develops. History repeats itself.

3. 10 percent chance through 2001: Extreme Right stages successful military coup and takes power. Probability goes up to 33 percent if Sandinistas regain power in Nicaragua. (Extremists of Left and Right benefit by Sandinistas holding power in Managua.)

Guatemala

1. 75 percent chance through 2001: Want a safe projection anyone can make? The recurrent cycle of bloodshed, poverty, low-grade guerrilla war, army coup d'état, the taking of Indian lands in the mountains.
2. 24 percent chance through 2001: Incremental progress made on integrating Indians into the nation and addressing chronic problems of poverty and health.
3. Small chance through 2001: The Guatemalan Army is abolished.
4. Less than small chance through 2001: The Guatemalans attack Belize; the resulting Belizean-British victory could lead to the abolition of the Guatemalan Army.

Honduras

15 percent chance of army coup d'état by 2001; 85 percent chance of stability of present regime.

Panama

5 percent chance through 2001: Reemergence of a military-backed, anti-U.S. strongman; if that results, 80 percent chance of another U.S. invasion.

Side bet: Pressure in the United States increases for the renegotiation of defense aspects of the Panama Canal Treaty; might entail a "new" U.S.-Panamanian regional defense treaty.

KIND AND COST OF WAR

Central American wars have followed a familiar pattern: small groups of infantry chasing each other through the bush. Military assistance from superpowers (usually the United States, sometimes Russia) has provided some major league gear, but the addition of tanks, heavy artillery, and jets is usually overdoing it. Central America is light infantry country, particularly when the locals are fighting each other. It almost always is locals versus locals, so warfare remains a relatively low-key, but still quite bloody, process.

War has savaged economic growth in Central America. Nicaragua's per capita income in 1981 was $1,396; in 1992 it was $425. Honduras's figures were $1,056 in 1981 and $1,050 in 1992—stagnation. El Salvador's were similar: $1,070 in 1981 and $1,010 in 1992.

Central America is poor to begin with, so the accountants won't come up with large numbers from the war damages. The human cost is higher, as most of the wars have degenerated into endemic banditry and lawlessness.

QUICK LOOK: Cuba: ¡*Viva Fidel!* The Last Days of the Castro Regime

For years Fidel Castro reveled in his role as a thorn in the side of U.S. policy. Castro provided Cuban troops to third world "struggles for liberation." He touted the USSR as "the natural ally" of the third world. He supported Marxist insurgencies throughout the hemisphere, from Bolivia and Brazil to Nicaragua and El Salvador. He gloated on the toasts of the American Left.

But the end of the cold war has left El Jefe Máximo (the Supreme Leader) rotting on the dictatorial vine. His old left-wing buddies shun his repressive junta. The Cuban economy is kaput. Fidel has allowed some private ownership of small businesses. Foreigners can also buy some investment properties through carefully controlled investment combines.

But the self-declared Period of Emergency finds Cuba moving from tractors to oxen, from buses to bicycles. And the Cuban Army (reminiscent of Guatemala?) has become a larger presence in the economy.

Castro had been reselling discounted Russian oil elsewhere on the world market, earning hard currency. The Russian oil spigot is closed. The Castro regime began in late 1990 to cut back on railroad operations and bought a million bicycles. Bikes don't need gasoline, just legs fueled by carbohydrates. Loss of Russian economic aid has meant loss of Russian military backing. Castro's sole means of "offensive action" has been to send migrants from Cuba to Florida, creating political problems in the United States.

Fidel has kept a firm lid on political opposition. There is no Communist successor to Castro. Fearing competitors, Fidel has done his best to eliminate potential successors. He occasionally tests the United States, offering to trade some degree of political reform for the elimination of the U.S. economic embargo against Cuba. There are political circumstances where such a deal could occur before 2001.

Finally, Fidel is getting old. Combat fatigues don't hide the paunch; his face sags; he doesn't look like the future. Still, Castro styles himself as the true believer in communism. More likely, he is the last romantic Communist revolutionary, faithful despite the ugly reality of national poverty and fascist repression, his own handiwork. A great irony lurks, however. He may ultimately model himself after Spain's fascist dictator, Francisco Franco, and allow a small internal opposition to form.

POTENTIAL OUTCOMES

1. 40 percent chance through 2001: Castro regime is replaced by more-than-less "peaceful means"; representative democracy nurtured by Cuban exiles returning from the United States is established; chance goes to 90 percent if Fidel dies a "natural death" before 2001. So, how might this occur? "Natural death" is the obvious scenario (in Fidel's case, that includes anything from lung cancer to "a Nelson Rockefeller" demise via overexertion with a mistress). There are several other interesting cases. One is "the Alzheimer's scenario." Fidel gets old fast. He is replaced in a "bloodless" Cuban Army coup and progressives in the army liberalize the system. The doddering Castro is put out to a well-foddered, and well-policed, pasture. Another scenario: Fidel risks a "Nicaraguan election" (or a democratic referendum like the one that removed Chile's General Pinochet), which is internationally monitored and allows all Cubans to vote freely. Then Castro gets surprised just

like the Sandinistas. Not too likely an outcome, but possible; what might bring an "open election" about is that there's a decent chance that Fidel would win the presidency, making for an interesting clash of values with a democratic legislature.

2. 30 percent chance through 2001: ¡*Viva Fidel!* El Jefe lives. Fidel stuffs all coup attempts and continues to strut his anti-Yankee line, though the third world is now more interested in yen and Eurodollars. The Cuban Communist regime continues to ossify. Under this scenario, repression level in 2001 is an 8-plus.

3. 15 percent chance through 2001: Castro is assassinated or replaced by members of the secret police or disgruntled army troops in a coup. (A more-than-less bloody replacement.) A *menshevik* military dictatorship comes to power, possibly with strong drug cartel ties.

4. 15 percent chance through 2001: Coup attempt against Castro fails, but Castro cannot suppress the rebels. Civil war breaks out on the island. If that occurs, 60 percent chance of U.S. military intervention on the anti-Castro side, especially in Guantánamo Bay area.

Chapter 13

¡VIVA NAFTA! ¡VIVA ZAPATISTA! MEXICO, OR THE BIG DOMINO

INTRODUCTION

Mexico is a nation with vast human and natural resources. It is the most populous Spanish-speaking country in the world, a should-be international economic and political powerhouse.

From 1910 to 1924, Mexico experienced one of the twentieth century's great revolutions. The issues were complex: historical class inequities, ethnic divisions, land distribution, labor and industrialization policies, the role of religious institutions in politics, and the creation of a modern democratic political structure out of a complicated feudal culture with Spanish colonial and (to an extent) native oligarchic origins.

The Institutional Revolutionary party (PRI) emerged from the revolution as a catch-all political bag for the terribly fragmented Mexican society. Mexico remains a complex stew of feudal and colonial authoritarianism and emerging democratic capitalism; a developing nation with a composite high-tech, low-tech, and tortilla economy. But

576

the people were tired of war, and the PRI seemed a reasonable alternative to more decades of violence.

In the 1980s, regional and global economic, political, and social change began to split the PRI. The veneer of political accommodation began to peel. In the 1990s new economic pressures and opportunities, such as NAFTA (North American Free Trade Agreement), great popular dissatisfaction with corrupt politicians, and old ethnic predicaments, such as unassimilated Indian groups, generated fierce political—and sometimes violent—confrontation within Mexico.

SOURCE OF CONFLICT

The list of problems affecting Mexico is lengthy and involved. The "unfinished revolution," disaffected and oppressed Indian populations, government corruption, land struggles, a tradition of oligarchic control and nearly seven decades of single-party rule, urban capitalism versus a rural farm tradition, a history of political violence and assassination reasserting itself, all are part of a dynamic puzzle.

The volatile concoction of population growth, scarce land, increased urbanization, and endemic poverty are ready sparks for severe political trouble and—quite possibly—civil war.

Frustrated expectations are also key to the disaffection. For years the PRI has touted Mexico's economic progress and pointed to the growth of an educated and able middle class. But political control remains vested in an authoritarian system where a decreasingly strong president manages the hodgepodge of the PRI. Genuine competing interests and ideas are often excluded, though these interests are increasingly making themselves heard. Traditions of corruption and bribery (diseases of the old Spanish colonial administration) frustrate open, democratic politics.

Global, post–cold war economic changes have shaken the PRI's hold on business and banking. New information outlets, such as satellite TV, have allowed the PRI's opponents to change the debate. When Subcommandante Marcos's Zapatistas launched their war in Chiapas on January 1, 1994 (the first day of the implementation of the North American Free Trade Agreement), the public-relations-savvy

Zapatistas had faxes ready and sound bites prepared. Yet the PRI's *dinosaurios* remain strong and embedded in the bureaucracy, business, labor unions, and the military.

Were it located anywhere else, Mexico would be regarded as a major regional power. Mexico, however, for better and worse, borders the Colossus of the North, the world's only superpower, the United States. Historically, Mexico's proximity to the United States has been both a blessing and a disaster. In 1847, after the Mexican War, the United States annexed Mexico's northern provinces. The United States has been both bully and banker. The huge U.S. economy and lax immigration policies along the southern U.S. border have succored Mexican economic growth, bailed out economic mistakes, and provided Mexico's political elites with a safety valve. The disaffected can pick up and head north. New U.S. immigration policies may shut the valve, but historically they have not done so.

WHO'S INVOLVED

Mexican government—Call it highly bureaucratized and centralized; in fact, call it the Institutional Revolutionary party (PRI), which has exercised near-absolute control for some seven decades. The National Congress has two houses: the Chamber of Deputies (500 members) and the Senate (128 senators). The president is elected by direct popular vote and serves only one 6-year term. Despite these strict term limitations, the president possesses extraordinary executive power.

Mexican people—Looking for a better deal economically and a real political democracy. Mexico is a country of socioeconomic levels as well as regions, and "the better economic deal" many people want conflicts with other groups' concepts of "the better deal." However, a consensus is nearing on the need for genuine democracy.

Mexican rebels—From disgruntled free marketers in PAN (National Action party) to the Zapatistas to various Indian groups, leftists, and labor organizations, and even *norteño* separationists, they all want change. Some talk of change with guns.

Mexican Army—The elite infantry brigades that make up the strongest element of the army are loyal to the central government. The

other units are divided among military districts—which could ultimately lead to divided loyalties.

Mexican industrialists and superrich—Mexico is home to some of
the world's wealthiest people. They have held and exercised power
since the conquistadors took control. Twenty-six new Mexican billionaires emerged during the Salinas administration.

United States—The Colossus of the North.

NAFTA (North American Free Trade Agreement)—The "common
market" of the United States, Canada, and Mexico.

U.S. Border Patrol and Immigration and Naturalization Service—
Sometimes they operate as powers unto themselves.

International Monetary Fund, Wall Street investors, and Wall Street
sharks—"Externally controlled" capital.

Wild Cards

Local politics in California and Texas—The most populous and
second most populous states in the United States have a lot of political
clout in Washington. They also have borders with Mexico.

California Proposition 187—Ballot referendum passed in California
in November 1994, which would deny most public aid to illegal immigrants. Mexicans saw the law as xenophobic legislation aimed
primarily at stemming illegal Mexican immigrants. The Mexican government has used immigration as a means of deflating political tensions and economic reform inside Mexico. The United States has relied
on cheap Mexican labor to pick crops.

Drug barons—Profits from illegal narcotics are high. There's a lot
of cash to spread around to buy Mexican and U.S. politicians. There's
also cash to support security forces—and rebels.

GEOGRAPHY

Mexico (proper name: United Mexican States) borders on the
United States, Guatemala, and Belize. Mexico borders on the U.S.
states of Texas, New Mexico, Arizona, and California. With an area

of 1.98 million square kilometers it is approximately three times the size of the state of Texas (which is one reason Mexicans are still steamed over the Texas revolution). The nation is divided into thirty-one states and one federal district (around the capital, Mexico City).

Mexico is the southern flank of North America. Its topography varies from coastal jungle to rugged mountains and high, dry plateaus. The central Mexican Plateau lies between two major mountain chains: the Sierra Madre Occidental in the west and the Sierra Madre Oriental in the east. The Sierra Zacatecas divides the Mexican Plateau into the dry Northern Mesa and the populous Central Mesa.

To the west lies the Pacific Ocean. Baja California (the rest of California was lost to the United States in 1847), the desert peninsula south of the U.S. state of California, is separated from the Mexican mainland by the Gulf of California. To the east the Yucatán Peninsula projects northward from the Isthmus of Tehuantepec into the Gulf of Mexico.

While much of northern Mexico is semiarid or desert, tropical rain forest occurs in southeastern Mexico (especially in the states of Chiapas, Campeche, and Tabasco) as well as on the southeastern end of the Yucatán Peninsula. These areas receive over 75 inches of rain per annum.

The hottest and most humid regions (*tierra caliente*) are along the southern coasts, in the Balsas River basin, and in the southern Chiapas Valley. The Chiapas Highlands can be seasonally cool, with elevations reaching nine thousand feet. The Mexican Plateau, however, is temperate.

Mexico City (altitude 7,350 feet) lies in a huge interior basin surrounded by mountains. With a 1992 population of 23–24 million, Mexico City may be the most populous city on the planet.

Mexico had a population of 94 million in 1995. With an annual population increase of over 2.2 percent, Mexico could have 110 million people by the year 2001. (One source suggests that the 1994 population figures may be grossly understated and Mexico's actual 1994 population was already 100–110 million.)

Under any circumstances Mexico's population bomb has already exploded. In 1900, Mexico had a population of around 14 million.

By 1960 the population had reached 35 million. By 1980 it had doubled to 70 million. The population has risen in Chiapas (site of the Zapatista rebellion) by 3.6 percent a year since 1975. In the Zapatista district of Ocosingo, the growth rate is 6.4 percent.

In the mid-1970s the government introduced rigorous family-planning policies and rates of increase have declined. Still, as of mid-1995, Mexico has a very young population, with over half under the age of twenty-one. Migration from rural to urban areas continues. Mexico is now an urbanized nation, with 70 percent of the population living in cities, towns, and suburbs.

The Mexican government last officially collected racial data in the 1920s, but U.S. State Department figures suggest the Mexican population is 60 percent mestizo, 30 percent Indian, 9 percent European, and 1 percent other. Ninety percent are Roman Catholics, 5 percent Protestant, 5 percent other. Many of the Indians and rural Mexicans practice a "syncretic" form of Catholic Christianity, which incorporates indigenous (Mayan, Aztec, etc.) religious concepts.

Some 96 percent of the people speak Spanish. Still, at least 6.5 million Mexicans can speak an Indian language on a daily basis (the number could be as high as 10 million). That means that for 7 to 9 percent of the Mexican population, Spanish is either a second language or foreign language. The most widely spoken Indian language groups are Mayan, spoken in Chiapas and in the Yucatán; Nahuatl, in east central Mexico; Zapotec and Mixtec, in the southern state of Oaxaca; and Otomi, spoken in the states of Veracruz and Puebla.

Mexico has oil—lots of it, especially along the coastal plain skirting the Gulf of Mexico. Mid-1995 estimates give Mexico between 55 and 65 billion barrels of recoverable crude oil. The Reforma field of Chiapas and Tabasco states, in production since 1972, and offshore deposits in the Gulf of Campeche (developed in the 1970s and 1980s) make Mexico the world's fifth-leading oil exporter. Oil earned Mexico around $10 billion in 1990. Exploration and production are controlled by the state-owned oil combine, PEMEX (Petroleos Mexicanos). Mexico is also the world's leading exporter of silver.

Tourism is the second largest source of foreign exchange, after oil. Since 1990 tourism has annually brought between $4 and $5 billion into Mexico.

HISTORY

The Olmecs carved out the first important Mexican empire. Based in what are now the states of Tabasco and Veracruz, Olmec culture flourished from approximately 1,200 to 500 B.C. Between A.D. 100 and 200 the first Mayan city-states emerged in Guatemala's Petén region (east and south of Chiapas). The Mayans went through several phases of expansion and decline and by A.D. 1,200 their empire had fragmented.

Emerging sometime in the first century, the city-state of Teotihuacán, located in the central Mexican valley not far from present-day Mexico City, was a regional power until A.D. 700. Teotihuacán, however, had a long and lasting effect on the subsequent Toltec civilization (900?–1200) and the Aztecs (or Mexicas).

The Aztecs, who mythically trace their origin to the land of Aztlan, located somewhere in northwestern Mexico, entered the central valley in the late thirteenth or early fourteenth century. After encountering a mystical omen, an eagle roosting on a cactus while holding a snake in its hooked beak, the tribe settled on islands in the middle of Lake Texcoco. The eagle-cactus-snake would later become Mexico's national emblem. The Aztecs began to build an empire with Tenochtitlán (which became Mexico City) as their capital. The empire eventually included all of central and southern Mexico and stretched into present-day Guatemala and El Salvador. At its height the Aztec Empire had nearly eight million inhabitants. This was the northernmost of the pre-Columbian American "civilizations." To the north there was basically a thinly populated Stone Age culture. Some of these North American groups, like the Navaho (belonging to the last of three waves of North Asian migrants to the Americas) and the "mound people" (defunct when Columbus arrived) of the Mississippi Valley did urbanize.

In 1502, Moctezuma became the Aztec emperor. In 1519 Hernán Cortés of Spain arrived off Veracruz with five hundred men and sixteen horses. The Aztecs, thinking Cortés might be the god Quetzalcoatl returned to earth, sent gifts of gold and silver. Their appetites for treasure whetted, the Spaniards headed for Tenochtitlán. Cortés battled various tribes and also picked up allies who resented Aztec power. Cortés entered Tenochtitlán as a guest. Subsequently, he arrested Moctezuma. Moctezuma died trying to calm an uprising caused by a Spanish atrocity. Eventually the Spaniards abandoned the city and fled east. In May 1521 the Spaniards attacked Tenochtitlán again. The Aztecs' new emperor, Cuauhtemoc, beat back the initial assault. The Spaniards then besieged the city and took it in August 1521. New Spain, consisting of Mexico and Central America, was born. The Spaniards' advantage was one of greed, technology, religious fervor, a flair for bureaucracy, centuries of experience battling the Muslims, and a reckless spirit of adventure. Europeans achieved similar success in Asia and Africa against similar odds. But in the Americas, the Europeans had another advantage: the Eurasian disease pool, to which the inhabitants of the Americas had no resistance.

Disease and warfare ravaged the Indian populations. Indians continued to fight each other, as well as the Spaniards. But the big killer was disease; the native Americans died by the millions from Eurasian diseases like measles, smallpox, and other afflictions. In the mid-seventeenth century, Mexico's population had declined to around three million. Many Indians continued to live traditional indigenous lifestyles. They spoke their own languages. If they practiced Christian Catholicism it was a syncretic Catholicism identifying the old Aztec and Mayan gods with Christian saints. The Virgin of Guadalupe, Mexico's patroness, appeared on December 12, 1531, on the Hill of Tepeyac outside of Mexico City—the site of a temple sanctuary of the Aztec goddess Tonantzin.

Peninsulares (Spaniards from Spain) kept political control in the name of the king, but native European elites, *criollos,* carved out large private estates and amassed great wealth. The Mexican War of Independence, like many of the other Latin American revolutionary movements of the early nineteenth century, was a struggle between the *peninsulares* and *criollos,* though the first organized revolt (1810) was led by a Catholic priest (Father Miguel Hidalgo) in the name of the oppressed Indians and mestizos. Another failed liberal revolt was led by Father José Maria Morelos. The Spanish executed Hidalgo in 1811 and Morelos in 1815.

In 1821, however, a weakened Spain capitulated to forces under

Agustin de Iturbide. Iturbide was backed by Mexican elites seeking political independence but interested in preserving their economic status quo. In 1822, Iturbide was crowned emperor. General Antonio Lopez de Santa Anna led a coup in 1823. A republic was established in 1824.

Mexico had fifty governments during its first thirty chaotic years of existence. Santa Anna led eleven of them. Santa Anna fancied himself the Napoleon of the West. He was a terrible general but a very clever politician and *caudillo* (strongman).

In 1835 the former Spanish colony of Texas revolted against Santa Anna's government. The "Texicans" defeated Santa Anna at the Battle of San Jacinto in April 1836. Santa Anna signed the Treaty of Velasco, which promised recognition of Texas's independence and stated that Mexican troops would remain south of the Rio Grande.

The Mexican War (1846–47) still looms large in how many Mexicans think about the Colossus of the North, the United States. What caused the Mexican War? Theories conflict. Once back in Mexico City, Santa Anna appeared to change his mind about Texas independence. The Mexican government objected to the U.S. annexation (1845) of Texas. Revisionist historians—and many Mexicans—argue that the United States provoked the war by annexing Texas and by deploying a large army at the mouth of the Rio Grande, with Washington's ultimate objective seizure of California and the Southwest.

Mexico, however, launched the first military blows. On April 25, 1846, Mexican units attacked U.S. troops along the Rio Grande. The United States counterattacked with land campaigns directed at Monterey and Mexico City and an amphibious landing at Veracruz. The war ended when U.S. General Winfield Scott occupied Mexico City on September 14, 1847. The Treaty of Guadalupe Hidalgo, which officially concluded the conflict, was signed on February 2, 1848. The treaty sliced off three fifths of "Greater Mexico" (3.1 million square kilometers). The region became the U.S. states of California, New Mexico, and Arizona.

The Mexican War still has resonance in current Mexican domestic politics. In 1846 *criollos* living in the Yucatán armed a large force of Mayan Indians. The Mayan army was supposed to fight the invading Yankees. Instead, the Mayans turned on the Mexican oligarchs. The

Indians wanted to recover communal lands that had been incorporated into haciendas. The Mayan rebellion, called the War of the Castes, lasted until 1849, when army units loyal to the Mexican central government drove the last organized Indian forces into the jungle. One source estimates that half of the Yucatán's Mayans were killed.

One of the more bizarre eras in Mexican history was the reign of Emperor Maxmilian. The Mexican Conservative party schemed with France's Napoleon III to establish a Hapsburg throne in Mexico. A French expeditionary force defeated Republican Mexican forces in the Battle of Puebla (May 5, 1862, the Cinco de Mayo). When Napoleon III withdrew French forces to confront the Prussians, the weak Maxmilian fell. He was executed in 1867.

A former vice president, Benito Juarez, became president. Juarez was a full-blooded Zapotec Indian, an avowed political and social liberal, and the leader of the republican resistance against the French. Juarez favored economic development and reorganized public education. He died in 1872. In 1876, General Porfirio Diaz led a rebellion against President Sebastian Lerdo. In a new vote Diaz was elected president. Diaz served as president from 1877 to 1880 and 1880 to 1911. He was a dictator, not a democrat. Diaz satisfied the rich and the military, co-opted the Catholic Church, and censored the press. His government appropriated Indian communal lands, suppressed the growing labor movement, and controlled banditry (as well as rebellion) with his three-thousand-man federal police force known as the *rurales*. Still, the Porfiriato, the name given his long-running dictatorship, was a time of comparative domestic peace and development.

In 1909, an aging and weakening Diaz declared he would reinstate democracy. In 1910, however, Diaz arrested his rival, Francisco Madero, leader of the Anti-Reeleccionista party. In all likelihood the popular Madero won the 1910 election. Released from prison, but outraged at the rigged election, Madero formulated the Plan of San Luis Potosi, which called for revolt against Diaz's dictatorship. Madero kicked off the revolt in November 1910 but his revolt collapsed. Rebel units at Ciudad Juarez, however, under the command of Francisco "Pancho" Villa and Pascual Orozco, defeated Diaz's government forces. Disgruntled army units began to defect to the rebels, and Madero, backed by the rebel army, toppled Diaz in May 1911.

The Mexican Revolution, however, was far from over. Once in power, Madero, the democratic idealist, seemed to be overwhelmed by the chaos the revolt unleashed. Emiliano Zapata accused Madero of betraying the revolution. Zapata's chief grievance: Madero had failed to restore the old Indian communal land system (*ejidos*).

In 1909, Zapata, the son of prosperous middle-class mestizo (mixed Spanish-Indian) parents from the state of Morelos, had defended his village against land claims made by the owner of a large hacienda. Zapata occupied the disputed land. Suddenly he was the leader of a spreading peasant rights movement. In 1911, Zapata drew up the Plan of Ayala, which called for Mexican agrarian reform under the slogan Land and Liberty. In February 1913, Madero was overthrown in a military coup led by General Victoriano Huerta. Madero was subsequently murdered.

War flared across Mexico. Zapata rebelled against Huerta's dictatorship. Troops loyal to Pancho Villa (whom Huerta had jailed) joined Venustiano Carranza in a revolt against Huerta. Huerta angered Washington, and U.S. Marines landed in Veracruz. Huerta was overthrown in July 1914 and Carranza became president. Zapata and Villa formed an alliance against Carranza and occupied Mexico City. Defeated in battles at Celaya and Leon in 1915 by Carranza loyalist Alvaro Obregon, Villa withdrew to Chihuahua. Retaliating against U.S. recognition of Carranza's government, Villa attacked Columbus, New Mexico. As a result of this, in 1916 the United States launched the Pershing Punitive Expedition against Villa. Villa eluded U.S. forces.

In 1917, Carranza defeated Villa and forced Zapata to withdraw to Morelos. Zapata continued to fight as a guerrilla until he was tricked by the feigned defection of an army unit loyal to Carranza and assassinated. Carranza was killed in 1920 in the Agua Prieta rebellion. Villa received amnesty but was assassinated in 1923 by Obregon partisans.

Obregon, replacing a provisional post-Carranza government, became president of Mexico. Obregon supported agrarian and labor reform. After fending off a rebellion involving military commanders in Veracruz, Jalisco, and Oaxaca, Obregon purged the Mexican Army. He left office in 1924. Reelected president in 1928, Obregon was assassinated before he took office. His assassin was a Catholic religious radical.

Plutarco Elias Calles served as president from 1924 to 1928. Calles, like Obregon, was cut from the *caudillo* mold. He was also an anticlerical radical antagonized by the Catholic Church's longtime support of the Diaz dictatorship. Calles enforced the anticlerical provisions of the constitution of 1917. In 1926 peasants (the Cristeros) in several western states, led by conservative priests, launched a guerrilla war. The army ruthlessly suppressed the revolt.

When Obregon was murdered in 1928, Calles stepped down as president but he did not lose his grip on power. From 1928 until 1935, when General Lazaro Cardenas became president, Calles ran Mexico from his mansion in Cuernavaca. He also created the National Revolutionary party (PNR), the forerunner of the PRI. Calles intended to halt Mexico's political fragmentation and the resulting chaos and violence. The PNR was founded as an incorporative Mexican national political organization. Everyone in the government was made a member. Liberals, socialists, and intellectuals were absorbed in an expanded bureaucracy.

Cardenas actually began to carry out land reform and redistribution. He formed the National Peasant Confederation (CNC) within the PNR. He also strengthened PNR control over labor unions. Cardenas formed the party into four sectors: labor, peasant, popular, and military. The military wing was eliminated in 1940. He created the "strong presidency" and turned the PNR into an effective political machine. The PNR became the Party of the Mexican Revolution in 1938. It was officially named the PRI in 1946.

Current Economic and Political Issues

From 1930 to 1988 the Institutional Revolutionary Party (PRI) completely controlled Mexican national politics. The PRI's brand of "authoritarian inclusivism" held the nation together, but in the late 1980s the PRI's control began to waver.

The promises of the Mexican revolution have not been realized.

Since the revolution many *ejidos* (small farms) have been given to the peasants (a whopping 250 million acres to 28,000 ejidos worked by 2.8 million peasant farmers). However, the ejido system is extremely unproductive and uncompetitive in an era of international economic integration. In 1991, Mexico abolished the constitutional protections of the ejidos and ended the ejido system (thereby favoring larger, more productive farms). This was a major shift in Mexican policy—the Mexican state was no longer obligated to give land to the landless. The changes would allow companies to own farmland (an option previously denied to corporations).

Economic crises have plagued Mexico since the early 1980s. The exchange rate in 1980 was 23 pesos to the dollar. In 1992 it reached 3,000. In late 1994 and early 1995 the "new peso" (1NP equals 1,000 old pesos) also tumbled to over 7 pesos to the dollar (i.e., 7,000 1980 pesos). An estimated 45 percent of the workforce was unemployed or underemployed in 1994.

The Mexican economy is no longer insular. Mexico's expanding oil business has put it near the top of the list of petroleum exporters. The U.S.-Mexico Border Industries Program (started in 1965) has created over seventeen hundred new *maquiladora* factories in Mexico's border cities. (*Maquiladora* comes from the term for the portion of the grain retained by a miller when he grinds corn. Mexico retains part of the factories' profits by providing labor and space.)

The PRI's process of choosing new presidents is also unraveling. The PRI's share of the national vote fell from 93.6 percent in 1976 to 50.7 percent in 1988. And the 1988 electoral results were disputed (with good reason) by PRD candidate Cuauhtemoc Cardenas. In 1991 disputed election results led to a "negotiated" PAN victory in Guanajuato State. In 1995, PAN won outright in Guanajuato. PAN won a major victory in 1992 when its candidate became governor of the state of Chihuahua (the largest state in Mexico). In 1993, PRD supporters clashed with government security forces while protesting PRI electoral fraud in elections in the states of Michoacán and Oaxaca. Assassination has returned to presidential politics. Former President Carlos Salinas de Gortari chose Luis Donaldo Colosio Murrieta in November 1993 to be the party's candidate in the August 1994 presidential elections. Colosio was assassinated on March 23, 1994. A "murky" investigation named a lone gunman but everyone in Mexico suspected involvement of PRI-istas who were against Salinas's liberal economic policies.

Ernesto Zedillo Ponce de León became the new PRI candidate and was elected president, defeating the PAN's Diego Fernandez and the PRD's Cuauhtemoc Cardenas. (Cardenas is the son of former president Lazaro Cardenas.)

Violence continued to plague the new Zedillo regime. In the fall of 1994, José Francisco Ruiz Massieu, secretary general of the PRI, was murdered. Subsequently, President Salinas, his family, and other PRI officials were implicated as being involved with the murder or in obstructing the murder investigation. Salinas's brother Raul was charged with committing the crime. The main point: Corruption reaches into the highest levels of Mexican government. There is also little dispute that the drug money of *narcotraficantes* is creating a new dimension of corruption.

The New Zapatista Rebellion

New Year's Day, 1994, the first day of NAFTA, began not with new prosperity but with an Indian war—or was it? In the early hours of 1994 an odd series of attacks took place in the Mexican state of Chiapas in and near the vast Lancandon jungle. Led by a mystery man in a mask with the nom de guerre of Subcommandante Marcos, the Zapatista National Liberation Army (EZLN) catapulted from obscurity onto the international political stage.

In four days of fighting in Chiapas, over 150 people were killed, mostly EZLN guerrillas. The rebels, who numbered from 300 to 500, captured six towns then abandoned them as the Mexican Army arrived on the scene. Some of the rebels were well armed and well trained, but most were armed with wooden sticks carved to look like guns with knives taped on the end of the barrels.

The Mexican Army formed a special army corps (Task Force Rainbow) and sealed off the jungle area and instituted a policy of containment. Marcos proved to be a first-rate television-age propagandist, wearing a ski mask to hide his identity, spouting sound bites and puffing on a pipe. He used international press attention to promote the often vague Zapatista agenda. Press attention also kept the Mexican Army under a human rights spotlight. In fact, the "war" was a propaganda vehicle. Marcos told several journalists: "We did not go to war on January first to kill or have them kill us. We went to make ourselves heard."

From February through March 1994, Marcos conducted negotiations with a Mexican "peace commission" and repeatedly demanded sweeping political and social reform in Chiapas. In June 1994 the EZLN rejected a government peace proposal. In August 1994, Marcos held a "national convention for progressive activists" and then publicly supported the PRD candidate for governor of Chiapas.

In December 1994 the EZLN stated they were contemplating further military action and demanded the withdrawal of the Mexican Army. Negotiations began again. In late January, Mexican police discovered arms caches in Mexico City and Veracruz. Whether they were connected to the EZLN was not certain but in early February 1995, the Mexican Army acted. The EZLN also fractured and several members began to talk to the government. Marcos was identified as Professor Rafael Sebastian Guillen Vicente. The Mexican Army moved into the EZLN's jungle territory with twenty thousand troops backed by tanks and helicopters and the Zapatista forces evaporated. They still existed as a political force, however. Talks began again, with an eye to addressing some of the Mayans' basic economic concerns. The EZLN might disappear, but Indian poverty remains.

Chiapas is Mexico's poorest state. PRI rule in Chiapas is little different than Spanish colonial rule; i.e., it's corrupt and feudal. Exacerbating the problem is population. Besides the high birth rate, Chiapas has been hit hard by immigration. Mayan peasants from the Guatemalan highlands fled Guatemala's ugly civil war and took refuge in Mexico.

One thing Marcos made very clear was that the Indians fear that NAFTA would further widen the gap between Mexico's relatively prosperous north and the impoverished southern Mexican states. Once more, Marcos argued, Mexico's Indians were being left out and cut off.

The origins of the EZLN may lie in Grupo Torreon, a group formed by revolutionaries and leftist Catholic priests in 1974. Guillen was from an upper-middle-class Mexican family, had studied in Jesuit schools in Tampico, and allegedly had been active in Nicaragua in the mid-1980s, using the nom de guerre El Mexicano. The Mexican government maintained that this showed the EZLN was "neither a popular movement nor Indian nor from Chiapas."

The Zapatistas did spur Mexican opposition parties to launch a more serious challenge to the PRI in the 1994 elections. Racism lurks behind many Indian confrontations in Mexico. Though the Mexican mestizos claim to respect their Indian ancestry, economic success is much more difficult for those with browner skins. Being an *indio* is regarded as being low-class. This racism only fuels the Indians' resentment.

Other Mexican Insurgencies and the Mexican Army

Mexico has actually been fighting several low-level insurgencies (officially identified by the government as "bandits") since the late 1960s. Perhaps the best known was a small leftist guerrilla band that operated in the state of Guerrero. Led by Lucio Cabanas and Genaro Vazquez Rojas, the group was destroyed when the army killed Cabanas in 1974.

Mexico has around 175,000 troops. Mexico spends less than 0.5 percent of its GNP on defense. Reorganized in the 1940s, the army has an elite cadre of from three to five well-equipped infantry brigades, which were modernized in the 1980s. The army is divided among thirty-seven military regions or zones, with particular interest paid to protecting the Federal District and Mexico City as well as Yucatán oil fields. Each military region will have a handful of infantry battalions and a "cavalry" (wheeled) unit of some sort. The Mexican Army's central mission is maintaining internal order; naturally, dissidents and many Indians say that means oppressing the populace.

The Mexican Army assumes a low profile in politics. Local military commanders, however, are closely tied to the police and government. Knowledgeable police sources suggest that regional military commanders are tied into the *mordida* ("little bite," or bribery) system of corruption and payoff. The Mexican Army is also active in counterdrug operations throughout Mexico. Several sources also suggest the Mexican Army cooperates with the *narcotraficantes*.

NAFTA

Nationalized industries and high tariffs had played a large political and social role in Mexico; high tariffs kept the United States out of Mexico's economy; nationalization meant Yankees didn't own Mexico—at least the PRI said so.

The push to create a North American trade zone began in Mexico and in the U.S. states bordering Mexico. The oil price collapse of the early 1980s demonstrated the need to diversify and open Mexico's closed economy. Mexico joined the General Agreement on Trades and Tariffs (GATT) and lowered import tariffs. Economists and some social progressives, particularly those who believed endemic political corruption meant Mexico's political system would never change, saw economic integration with the United States and Canada as a means of moving Mexico into the twenty-first century's global market. Some Mexicans saw NAFTA as a move toward hemispheric free trade.

Economic nationalists in the United States, Canada, and Mexico still oppose the treaty. Integrating economies with very different standards of living is difficult. Many Mexican opponents oppose NAFTA on the grounds of "cultural imperialism."

Mexico is slowly changing and NAFTA is part of that change. More and more Mexicans reject the one-party, corrupt paternalism of the PRI. The question time will answer: Will the adjustments be peaceful or will a new Mexican revolution occur with factional fighting, new Indian revolts, and regional warlords?

LOCAL POLITICS

Institutional Revolutionary party (PRI; Partido Revolucionario Institucional)—Ideology is less at issue among PRI factions than who owes whom in political chits and cash. Three sectors are: farm (with the communal peasant farmers), labor (urban, industrial workers), popular (professionals, small farm owners, small business, civil servants). The PRI sectors are no longer of equal weight. Business and government dominate the others. Labor is a "diminishing pillar" in the PRI. The farmers (*campesinos*) have been all but abandoned.

Dinosaurios—Hard-line PRI faction opposed to political reform, especially anticorruption reforms. Many *dinosaurios* are nationalist-corporatists, the very wealthy closely allied with ruling elites in Mexico City. They buy privatized banks and "denationalized" companies at fire sale prices. They don't want to lose their political entree. The low-level *dinosaurios* are the *funcionarios*, the local political ward heeler types who can (for a slight grease of the palm) grant *permisos*. If the PRI changes or collapses, they are out on the street and out of cash.

Congress of Mexican Workers (CTM)—PRI-run union; bastion of official unionism and home of many *dinosaurios*. As of mid-1995, still run by Fidel Velasquez ("Don Fidel"). Don Fidel (in 1995, aged ninety-five) took control of the CTM in 1941.

PRI revolutionaries—Include former Mexico City mayor Manuel Camacho, a negotiator in Chiapas.

National Action party (PAN; Partido Acción Nacional))—Conservative and center-conservative democratic party advocating liberalized economy and democracy. Antonio Lozano, a PAN member, was appointed attorney general by President Zedillo.

Revolutionary Democratic Party (PRD; Partido de la Revolución Democratica)—Leftist. Led in 1994 by Cuauhtemoc Cardenas. Cardenas makes the case that he was elected president in 1988 and was defrauded by the PRI. Many up-and-coming young left-wingers quit the PRI and joined Cardenas.

Other parties—Popular Socialist party (PPS); Authentic Party of the Mexican Revolution (PARM); Party of the Cardenist Front of National Reconstruction (PFCRN); Labor party (PT; Partido del Trabajo); Mexican Green Ecology party (PVEM); Democratic Party of Mexico (PDM).

EZLN—Zapatista Liberation Army; military wing of so-called Indigenous Revolutionary Clandestine Committee.

Another evolving opposition group—Authentic Workers Front.

May Fifth (Cinco de Mayo)—May 5 (Cinco de Mayo) is the anniversary of the Battle of Puebla in 1862 when the Mexican Army and militias fought a French occupation army.

Tecnicos—Name give to U.S.-trained Mexican economists and businesspeople who favor economic expansion and free trade.

Tesobonos—Mexican bonds denominated in dollars. The need to pay back the principal on these, and the possible lack of dollars in government coffers to do so, triggered the financial crises in 1994.

Barzonistas—Members of El Barzon, a dissident group of some 250,000. Started by farmers in northern Mexico. The name comes from a leather strap used to yoke an ox to a plow.

Petroleos Mexicanos (PEMEX)—Mexican national oil company.

Federales—Mexican national police (federal judicial police). Considered by many to be very corrupt. They can also field local paramilitary security forces. Some of these forces include *madrinas*—civilian thugs who work for the *federales*.

Mexican Institute of Social Security (IMSS)—Established in 1931; Mexican social security and health program—a social safety net and a large PRI bureaucracy.

Ejidatarios—Communal peasant farmers.

Narcotraficantes—From five to eight major Mexican "narco-cartels" wheel and deal. Their economic and political power is difficult to estimate, but most sources say their power is large and growing.

POLITICAL TREND CHARTS

MEXICO

Gv95	Gv20	PC95	PC20	R95	R20	Ec95	Ec20	EdS95	EdS20
AD6,5	AD4,3	5	4	6	6−	5	5+	4	4+

AD = Authoritarian Democracy

UNITED STATES

Gv95	Gv20	PC95	PC20	R95	R20	Ec95	Ec20	EdS95	EdS20
RD8,9	RD8,9	9	9	1+	1+	8+	9−	8−	8

RD = Representative Democracy

CANADA

Gv95	Gv20	PC95	PC20	R95	R20	Ec95	Ec20	EdS95	EdS20
RD8,7	RD8,8	7−	7	1+	1+	8	8	8	8+

REGIONAL POWERS AND POWER INTEREST INDICATOR CHARTS

WAR OF CHIAPAS

	Economic Interests	Historical Interests	Political Interest	Military Interest	Force Generation Potential	Ability to Intervene Politically	Interest/ Ability to Promote Economic Development
MexicoGvt	4	4	8	2	8	8	8
EZLN	9	6	9	9	0+	5	1
Maya	9	9	9	9	3	4	2
United States	3	2	6	2	9	7	8
Guatemala	6	6	7	5	1+	3	2

DRUG WAR

	Economic Interests	Historical Interests	Political Interest	Military Interest	Force Generation Potential	Ability to Intervene Politically	Interest/ Ability to Promote Economic Development
United States	7	7	8	8	9	8	6
Mexico	3	5	6	3	3	4	1
Drug Cartel	9	1	3	1	2	4	1

NOTE: 0 = minimum; 9 = maximum

Mexican Civil War
(Mexican Internal Breakdown)

NOTE: This analytic chart is organized differently from others in this book. Various potential factions in a civil conflict are rated for political power, military power, economic power, and propaganda (information) power. Ratings are based on a 0 minimum–100 maximum scale. The rating for the Mexican Army zonal commands is for an "average" command (there are 37 such commands). The MexArmyFed rating is for forces protecting the Federal District and selected elite Army strike forces drawn from the military regions. Each state has a state police (Judiciales) as well as assigned Federales. Baja California Norte and Chihuahua are included as examples of economically strong northern states. They have high propaganda values because of proximity to the United States.

	Political	Military	Economic	Propaganda
CentMexicoGvt	50	18	75	48
PRI	65	22	51	78
PAN	44	10	50	58
PRD	36	15	35	50
MexArmyFedDist	15	80	20	25
EZLN	5	2	0	50
BajaNorte	12	3	22	45
Chihuahua	10	2	20	40
Yaqui	2	5	4	3
MayanChiapas	6	7	4	15
MayanYucatan	8	3	7	5
PEMEX	20	15	45	40
Federales (combined)	20	20	5	8
MexArmyZone (ea zone)	5	10	5	4
Judiciales* (ea state)	2	1	1	1

*In this case state police and security units.

PARTICIPANT STRATEGIES AND GOALS

PRI—The world is changing but the PRI is the grand chameleon of world politics. If civil war erupted, how loyal is the Mexican Army and other security forces to the PRI? Big goal: Keep power.

PAN and other center to right opposition elements—The PAN has been behind economic liberalization and expansion from the beginning. Ultimately, this may be Mexico's only path to peaceful change. It will be difficult. The anticorruption campaign, however, has galvanized the PAN. Attacking the PRI's corruption is PAN's strongest card. The north is important to PAN; Chihuahua and Jalisco states are vital to its power base. PAN also supports dual-citizenship proposals that would let Mexicans living outside of Mexico (like those in the United States) become citizens of the nation they live in but retain Mexican citizenship and the right to vote in Mexican elections. The Panistas see Mexicans living in the United States as a potent force for evolutionary political change and economic liberalization.

PRD and other left opposition elements—NAFTA could become the fall guy for Mexican failure. That would place the PRD in excellent position to take the elections in the year 2000. The anticorruption drive also appeals to the PRD's leftist idealists. With the "farm" (*campesino*) sector of the PRI now ignored by the PRI, what is happening in the southern states (such as Tabasco and Chiapas) is of vital concern to the PRD. Labor unions are a source of future PRD strength.

Mexican superrich—Have owned the country and pulled the strings behind the PRI. That trick is getting harder to execute. Mexico's billionaires stash their capital outside of Mexico.

EZLN and other radicals—The leftists still dream of a free, socialist Mexico. Maybe socialism didn't work in Cuba and Nicaragua but perhaps this time "they'll" get it right. . . .

Mayans and other Indians—These unassimilated ethnic groups are at the bottom of the economic and social pile. Some Mayans dream of a free Mayan homeland encompassing parts of the Yucatán, Chiapas, and Guatemala's Petén region. Should large-scale civil war break out, it is possible the southern Indian tribes and possibly the Yaqui in the northwest might try to establish "autonomous zones."

Norteños—Many inhabitants of northern Mexican states feel victimized by the central government's high taxes and bad politics. Some residents of Baja California Norte (another state where PAN has won victories) have already talked of secession.

Mexicans in the United States—As many as 2 million Mexicans live and work illegally in the United States. They send home between $2 and $3 billion a year.

United States—It's a fact often ignored: Mexico is the United States' most important foreign relationship. NAFTA and the immigration debate in the United States reflect an increasing awareness of the importance of the U.S.-Mexican relationship. The United States is very interested in Mexico maintaining stability, getting its population growth under control, and creating a solid, modern economy.

The United States will continue to bail out Mexican economic stumbles. In 1994 and 1995 the United States provided nearly $50 billion to support the peso. Would the United States intervene if another Mexican civil war erupted? At a minimum U.S. troops would try to control the flood of political and economic refugees who would head north.

Guatemala—The new Indian insurgencies in Mexico could bring Mexico and Guatemala much closer, though historically Guatemalans say, "Mexico is to Guatemala what the USA is to Mexico" (i.e., an imperialist giant). Guatemala has been fighting its own ugly brand of Indian wars for decades. Trade perks and military cooperation with Mexico would help the Guatemalan government.

POTENTIAL OUTCOMES

Zapatista War

A 99.9 percent chance of Mexican Army victory through 2001 if the EZLN and Mexican Army actually fight. The Zapatistas' only strength is propaganda appeal.

Indian wars, however, will continue to plague Mexico. The army occupies Mayan territory and the central government controls and taxes the Indians. As long as the Indians remain at the bottom rung of the economic ladder, other uprisings will occur.

Second Mexican revolution (second Mexican civil war)—Odds on this occurring through 2001 are low, say, 5 percent. However, if Mexico blows, expect a flood of genuine political refugees to head north.

Is "Soviet-style" political devolution possible? Mexico may be seen as three separate nations: the "Panista" north, the traditional Mexico of Mexico City and the central states, and the Indian south. Let's say the PRD takes control of several southern states and the northern states become dominated by the PAN. What keeps Mexico together if the southern states discover they have much more in common with the rest of Central America? Odds on this happening through 2004 are slight. We'll give it 1 percent (and that is high) but the regional divisions are rapidly increasing and if a second Mexican civil war erupts, three or four new nations is a possible result. All of Mexico's northern border states would become "North Mexico." The center becomes "Mexico." The south becomes—apologies to the Middle East—"Mayastan." The fourth nation? Baja California.

WHAT KIND OF CONFLICT

Low-level guerrilla conflict with fighting by former leftists, New Age rebels, and various impoverished Indian tribes. This kind of war has been fought for decades in other parts of Latin America. Some urban terrorism; in the rural areas it sometimes looks like banditry, and often is.

A second civil war, however, could become a major conventional war. Weapons are stockpiled around the nation. The air force is small, but some factions would have artillery and tanks. These would be the chief offensive arms on the battlefield.

COST OF WAR

The guerrilla war, as waged by the EZLN in 1994 and early 1995, cost Mexico very little in terms of lives and cash. A second civil war, however, if fought with the ferocity of the first, would be a megadisaster. Waves of refugees, economic and political, would head north to the United States to escape the fighting. In an all-out Mexican civil war lasting one year, the damage to infrastructure and population, and lost income, could easily amount to $150 billion for Mexico. It would cost the United States as much as $100 billion in trade, costs of dealing with refugees, etc.

QUICK LOOK: The United States and Canada: Controlled Anarchy on the North American "Island of Stability"

In parts of southern Missouri, Jesse James is still regarded as a hero. That's a kind of clue—the United States has always been an easy place in which to stage a riot or rob the stage or bomb a federal building in Oklahoma City. Yet it's damned hard to overthrow the U.S. government—because democracy provides a way to at least give the appearance of toppling the government every few years. Being rich also helps. Wealth keeps a lot of potential troublemakers occupied with commerce and high living.

One of the biggest reasons for U.S. (and Canadian) democratic success is that they do sit on a big island. The Mexicans to the south aren't the Germans. There aren't any Hapsburg empresses building armies next door in Greenland; no Russians lie across the river. No one has ever heard of Attila the Eskimo (or, to be ethnically specific, Attila the Inuit). All of the "local barbarians" (i.e., the Native Americans) were either destroyed by Eurasian diseases or, after being starved, hounded into large desert relocation camps (often in desert wastelands) euphemistically called Indian reservations. The fact is, even the toughest of North American tribes, the Comanches, just could never get an all-out invasion together like the Goths could. Comanche warriors were the world's greatest light cavalry; the best they could manage was an extended cavalry raid, with a little looting, burning, and scalping.

Yet even in the latter days of the twentieth century, "Indian troubles" continue. Many Native American organizations have strong claims to land now "owned" by others. Those claims involve billions of dollars and many are in litigation. Thus if you can't burn the settlers' wagons, wait a few generations and get a good trial lawyer. Other Indian groups in the United States are pressing environmental degradation lawsuits against opponents.

Low-grade "Indian war" occasionally breaks out in the United States and Canada. Shooting incidents involving Mohawks (some with obviously legitimate claims against the governments, others a criminal element engaged in drug running and smuggling operations) have erupted in both upstate New York and Quebec.

Still, these fights are far less violent than the many civil rights riots that erupted in the United States in the 1960s and 1970s. The potential for extended "guerrilla conflicts" waged by far-right-wing paramilitary militias is also quite small, just as it was for earlier left-wing extremist groups.

The North American system is designed to let the steam out of polarized positions by allowing for loud political debate and occasional riots. This is then followed by a period of muddling compromise. Historically, the United States and Canada have had time to muddle through because there isn't a Hun at the doorstep. One can see the geographic analogy—the Atlantic and Pacific oceans serve as rather large English Channels. For the most part, the potent cold war threat of nuclear bombardment by ICBM barely affected this myopic perception of isolation.

Even the portending breakup of Canada has all of the features of muddling compromise. Initially, Quebec's separatist Parti Quebecois began to falter as soon as the French Canadians saw that all the English (and American) companies leaving Montreal for Toronto and Burlington meant a "Free Quebec" could get a nasty case of third world poverty. Yet Quebecois still toy with the romantic notion of separatism, though the economic price argues against it.

Some governmental theoreticians argue that the Canadian parliamentary system is too weak for continental rule. Other observers argue that the U.S.-Canada Free Trade Pact and NAFTA will effectively counter political fracturing of Canada.

Even if new political arrangements are reached, the argument goes, the pressing reality of economic cooperation will ultimately force separatists to cooperate with their former countrymen. If disunion comes about, it will scarcely matter since none of the new "nations" or political entities will present a military threat to one another. Still, the 1995 Quebec referendum where federalists barely defeated separatists means that Canada's political geography could change drastically.

What might an "altered" Canada look like? We'll go with what we wrote in the 1991 edition. Quebec is in many aspects a genuine European nation-state—a "people" with cultural, linguistic, religious, and historical identity. The irony haunting the French Quebecois' claims is that their Mohawk minority is as equally "unique" in contrast to French culture as the Quebecois claim to be in contrast to the rest of "English" Canada. The Quebecers show no signs of wanting to grant the Mohawks the same recognition they demand. *Ironique?*

British Columbia, interestingly, has most of the assets required to make it as a separate nation: access to the sea, strong industrial and educational bases, raw materials, a well-educated populace with linguistic integration.

Oil-producing Alberta might be interested in joining the United States, and would immediately find common ground with Alaska, Louisiana, Texas, Oklahoma, and California. The impoverished Canadian Atlantic provinces would be the best bets for joining the United States and extending the New England coastline. The remains of Canada might stick together, with Manitoba and Saskatchewan wary of being adjuncts to a "Greater Ontario." Ontario is still the home of the Royal American Regiment. Tories fleeing the American Revolution (and choosing to remain loyal to King George) put a mild but still-present anti-U.S. disposition on Ontarian politics.

The wild card? If Canada breaks up, watch for Newfoundland to petition the United Kingdom to be taken over as a colony.

Chapter 14

AMERICA AND THE NEW AGE OF LITTLE WARS

INTRODUCTION

As the cold war fades, a batch of "new" conflicts has suddenly emerged. Indeed, the world has entered yet another age of "little wars." These conflicts, many in anarchic "failed states," seed larger conflicts. The "stable world," however, isn't quite sure how to react. These conflicts seem so sordid. Even as the number of small military contingencies increases, America, the globe's strongest military power, but a power with isolationist tendencies, is "downsizing" its forces.

Lapsing superpower conflict often leads to a period of small wars (usually ancient wars rekindled). Usually the major powers attempt to maintain a semblance of world order through suppression of smaller conflicts in the planet's flaring hot spots. When superpowers are dueling one another, a lot of small conflicts succumb to superpower muscle, money, or intrigue. When superpower fights stop, lots of weapons remain. The cold war left lots of weapons. This means this phase of little wars will be nasty. The United States and "the stable world"

603

have to respond in some fashion. Usually the response is called "peace-keeping."

Many "little wars" are quite complex and are tough to police. The combatants may consist of tens, or hundreds, of thousands of troops armed with nothing heavier than machine guns or mortars. There might be a few secondhand tanks and artillery pieces, but basically we're talking about a lot of people with little training, wearing civilian clothes and divided into many (dozens or more) different factions. The only thing that often unites them is the arrival of peacekeepers. The locals fight the peacekeepers—and they know the terrain. Okay, if the peacekeepers are light infantry, they can at least get down to the enemy's level and fight him on somewhat equal terms. But with the fighters and local civilians dressed alike, and TV cameras in attendance, it's not long before military operations get broadcast as atrocities and the peacekeepers turned into the heavies. Negotiating a way out of these low-tech conflicts is not much of an option either. The disputes are very local, and often have ancient and arcane origins. In most parts of the world, disputes that began centuries before are still considered worth fighting for. Many little wars can be settled with light infantry firepower, but only if the peacekeepers are willing to kill a lot of people. Peacekeepers are not allowed to do that. In the past, before television, "peacekeepers" could "create a desert and call it peace." That is no longer acceptable. Often peacekeepers can, at best, let the little-war combatants kill each other until they get tired of it. That is how the Lebanese civil war (1975–90) was finally resolved. Peacekeepers were sent into Lebanon several times, to little effect. The war didn't end until the Lebanese decided they were tired of mutual slaughter.

Some of the little wars don't stay that way. Border wars in regions important to great powers can expand. The 1990–91 Persian Gulf War was one such example. A possible war in Korea is another, and a future conflict in the Persian Gulf region would generate as much interest as the last one. But most little wars are rather more modest affairs, and involve issues that mean little to those nations wealthy enough to get involved as peacekeepers.

Since World War II it has been the custom to avoid little wars so as not to "waste" resources needed for the major war that was always just around the corner. Well, the corner was turned and there was nothing there. Little wars are the only wars the military has got, and so little wars are going to be the only game in town until a larger threat shows up. The question is, how well can America, and the other major military powers, deal with little wars? Do they even want to? Does anyone anywhere want to? Possibly not. There are more pressing problems. According to the World Health Organization, infectious diseases and parasites kill over sixteen million people a year. Another six million die from cancer. Some three million children a year die from diarrhea and over the two million adults die from tuberculosis. While a million deaths a year from warfare seem enormous, they pale in comparison to disease deaths. And many, in some years most, of the war deaths are actually disease deaths, brought about as refugees are thrown out of their homes, often in times of bad weather and no food.

SOURCE OF CONFLICT

In the last two centuries there have been over four hundred wars worldwide, and many conflicts that, while violent, did not quite qualify. You have to draw the line somewhere. Most of these wars were either territorial disputes, and most of the remainder revolutions. There have been four megawars in this period (the Napoleonic Wars, the Tai-Ping Rebellion, and World Wars I and II) that accounted for three quarters of the two hundred million war dead. The remaining deaths, and wars, were, to varying degrees, "little wars." With the introduction of nuclear weapons after 1945, and the acquisition by most major powers of these weapons of mass destruction, the major powers have, for the first time in history, been extremely reluctant to engage each other in war. While there have been periods in the past when the major powers refrained from conflict with each other for a few decades, the period of major power peace since World War II has been unprecedented in its length. And despite the ominous noises coming from China and Russia, the peace continues.

Rather than fight each other during the cold war, and risk a nuclear holocaust, the superpowers encouraged smaller nations with grievances to fight as proxies. Most of the wars fought since 1945 have had at least a bit of that superpower conflict, and support, in them.

But now the cold war is over and Russia is unwilling, and increasingly unable, to get involved in distant little wars. That doesn't stop the Russians from getting involved with the many wars on its borders. But this is nothing new, or unusual. Those wars are a result of the breakup of the Soviet Union. The creation of nations where none had ever existed before, or had not existed for a long time, was bound to cause problems. Russia intervenes in these partly out of habit, partly out of self-defense. These "domestic" problems, and a large degree of self-sufficiency, make it easy for Russia to avoid any international police work.

America's situation is quite the opposite. The United States is a maritime and trading nation. American firms do business all over the world, as do America's major allies. What goes wrong in numerous obscure parts of the globe can have a significant impact on these trading nations. While the United States is the strongest militarily, many other trading nations have the capability to "peace keep" in little wars. Yet America is not the only trading nation reluctant to send troops overseas to keep the peace. The United Nations has, since 1991, stepped up its efforts "to coordinate" peacekeeping. It has a tough job. (See Quick Look, this chapter.)

To further complicate matters, there is the issue of using force to prevent nations from building nuclear weapons. That is a rather new development in the little-wars department. Nuclear proliferation means a "little war" could produce huge casualties.

In the wake of the experience with little wars in the Balkans, Somalia, Rwanda, and several other conflicts in new nations formed from parts of the former Soviet Union, few nations are much interested in getting involved. The little wars will be there, but most nations, unless dragged in, will not be eager to jump in just to keep the peace.

WHO'S INVOLVED

United States Groups

The United States Congress and the President—While these are separate branches of government, in an electronic democracy they are under the same pressure of opinion polls and media coverage given to foreign wars. By law, the President handles foreign affairs, but the Congress controls the purse strings and, in the wake of the Vietnam War, has the War Powers Act to stop a President from sending U.S. troops overseas. The War Powers Act has proven, in practice, unable to stop the President, though it slows him down. The War Powers Act was first used in 1983, by a Democratic Congress against a Republican president, and didn't have much effect. But if the War Powers Act is not a major impediment to presidential action, public opinion is. Presidents and members of Congress are propelled more by the attitudes of their constituents than by personal beliefs. Public opinion is driven largely by whatever foreign catastrophe catches the attention of the media. This is a somewhat random selection from the many foreign wars that are going on at any one time. If American citizens or military forces are threatened overseas, that usually makes the news right away. If the electronic media piles on (they tend to follow each other after a story) then that war becomes an "issue." Calls are soon made for the United States to "do something." These wars usually involve considerable suffering among civilians, so the TV images of dead, wounded, or starving women and children drive public opinion. But the American public generally draws the line at sending in U.S. troops. Foreign allies may want American help over there, and they usually place pressure on the American President. Unless clear-cut American interests are at stake (lives of U.S. citizens or U.S. economic interests), the bulk of public opinion is against intervention. The Iraqi invasion of Kuwait in 1990 was one of the few examples where Americans got behind an overseas war. America needed the oil from the Persian Gulf, the American public recognized this, thus it was possible for the President to mobilize public opinion behind an armed intervention. But unless another Kuwait comes along, American public opinion will not support sending U.S. troops overseas. The memory of Vietnam, where U.S. troops were drawn in bit by bit until America was in deep, and eventually over its head, still lingers. Smaller operations, like Panama or Grenada, are still possible. But they are usually ordered by a President secretly, the idea being that they will be successful and over before public opinion and Congress can do any damage to the President. The President is charged with conducting foreign affairs for the common good. But for the most part, President and Congress conduct foreign affairs under the direction of public opinion and what the media considers hot news at the moment. The President and Congress try to shape public opinion, but so do many lobbyists, working for special interest groups.

The United States State Department—It's not that the State Department diplomats are warmongers, but they are charged with dealing with foreign affairs on a day-to-day basis, and State Department employees will be the first to run up against little wars when they break out. The U.S. Central Intelligence Agency (CIA) works closely with the State Department people (and the U.S. President) in dealing with real or potential little wars. But it is the State Department that is in theory, and in practice, the lead U.S. agency in the little-wars department. Of course, the State Department works for the U.S. President and if the President says keep a lid on things, or stir things up, that is what the diplomats and CIA operatives try to do. Note also that the vast majority of the CIA employees are gathering and collecting information. The State Department has far more people in contact with foreigners (although some of these diplomats are actually CIA employees). Put simply, the State Department and CIA keep an eye on things, report back to the President, the President makes decisions, and the State Department tries to carry out the new policy. If diplomatic means fail, the military comes in. The State Department is your first line of defense in stopping little wars, or at least spotting them before they blow up.

The United States Navy and Marine Corps—Of all the U.S. armed forces, the Navy has traditionally maintained the most contacts with foreigners. From its inception, the U.S. Navy has ranged far beyond American coastal waters. The United States has always depended on foreign trade, and the Navy was always out there to protect it from pirates and unfriendly foreigners in general. Over the years, especially in this century, the Navy's Marine Corps steadily grew with the increasing need for troops to be landed quickly on foreign shores. Before World War II, the U.S. Marines were often referred to as "State Department troops" because the Marines were the most readily available force when U.S. military action was needed. The ending of the cold war brings with it a reduction of U.S. overseas bases. While the Navy will lose some facilities, they can still maintain substantial combat power off a foreign shore where the Army and Air Force cannot.

The United States Army—Until World War II, the Army had few overseas responsibilities. At the outbreak of World War II, the largest Army presence overseas was in the Philippines, and that was scheduled to end before the end of the 1940s. Since 1945, the largest overseas Army commitments have been Europe (the Seventh Army, with peak strength of 250,000 troops, in 1995 about 100,000) and South Korea (the Eighth Army, in 1995 25,000 troops). The end of the cold war makes both of these situations increasingly untenable. Having had a taste of foreign adventure, the Army is reluctant to give it up. Basically, the Army has been encroaching on the Marines' traditional turf, and a major interservice brawl has developed since the end of the cold war as the Army attempts to carve out a permanent piece of the "foreign intervention" market. The Army has opted for a strategy that combines high technology (to "overmatch" any opponent) with high-quality troops and training. The U.S. Army's development of the National Training Center (NTC) has made it a world leader in thorough, realistic preparation for combat. A principal political tool for maintaining Army strength is the "two-war policy." Developed after the cold war and the Persian Gulf War, this official goal stipulates that forces be maintained to fight two "major" wars "near" simultaneously. (That is, two wars of roughly the same size as the 1990–91 Persian Gulf War.) It is a mythical goal, considering the cuts that have been made in all services. Yet, at least at the news release level of reality, the goal is clung to, as if it had some magical power to ward off future cuts. The magic is highly questionable. The fact is, the American public is unlikely to tolerate two wars at once. Still, if the Persian Gulf were threatened once again, and U.S. forces in Korea attacked, it could happen. U.S. forces would be hard-pressed to respond.

The United States Air Force—The Air Force did not exist as a separate service until shortly after the end of World War II. Since then, the Air Force has followed the Army to the same foreign stations. Like the Army, the Air Force is in danger of losing its overseas bases. Unlike the Army, the Air Force has a better chance of keeping a piece of the foreign intervention business. Unlike the Army, with all its heavy equipment, the Air Force can rapidly fly hundreds of combat aircraft and their support units to most distant trouble spots. Although the Navy has its own large air force, most of the naval aviation flies from aircraft carriers. The Air Force can, in many instances, get their aircraft to a distant location faster than the Navy. But it's troops on the ground that settle these affairs, so the Air Force in most little wars is condemned to play a supporting role.

Other Nations

Great Britain—Long the ruler of a worldwide empire, Britain has seen the empire disappear in the past fifty years, but not all the military responsibilities associated with it. Small British garrisons still dot the globe in out-of-the-way places like South America and Asia. Great Britain, like the United States, is a trading nation. The British have "solved" more than a few nasty commercial problems with armed force.

France—While never possessed of as large a worldwide empire as the British, the French were even more keen on maintaining a well-rounded approach to diplomacy. In other words, the French maintain, and use, several regiments of light infantry for intervention in distant places. This is particularly true in Africa, where France keeps closer ties with its former colonies than has any other colonial power.

Other EEC (European Economic Community) countries—Several other European nations also maintain "intervention forces" for either diplomatic (foreign trade) or nostalgic (former colonies) reasons. Belgium and the Netherlands are two examples. Also new European countries like Ukraine, that are willing to contribute troops for UN peacekeeping in nearby areas like the Balkans. Poland and Hungary have long been willing to contribute contingents for peacekeeping operations.

Russia—The 1960s and 1970s were something of a golden age for Russian diplomacy. As the leader of the "world Communist revolution," Russia had diplomats, military advisers, and arms salesmen everywhere. But the Russians were never cut out for this sort of thing, and going into the 1980s it all began to fall apart. Communism and its economic system turned out to be more of a liability than an asset, while dealing with revolution-minded foreigners was clearly demonstrated to be something Russian (or any other) diplomats were never going to become particularly good at. Russia is still stuck with a lot of these diplomatic remnants (as in Cuba), and there is always national pride to consider. Failure can always be fogged over with an unwillingness to completely abandon poor diplomatic efforts. But Russia can no longer afford to play the game big-time. Diplomacy is expensive and Russia needs the money for more important matters at home. Yet Russia is still a large and powerful nation with long and substantial diplomatic ties with its many neighbors. With those neighbors, at least, Russia is still a potent diplomatic force. The Chechen war (1994–95) illustrated how the Russian Army has sunk since its halcyon cold war days. Despite their economic straits, Russia is attempting to modernize the professional core of its army.

China—Traditionally even more insular than the Russians, the Chinese have historically felt that if foreigners wanted to deal with them, they could come to China and present themselves. Attempts at diplomacy on foreign lands were not successful. The end of the cold war and vast improvements in China's economic health have made China more aggressive in its foreign relations. China continues to maintain a keen interest in relations with its many neighbors, and with any interests it has in the region. The Fourth Modernization (of China's armed forces) has begun and China is building a force capable of limited intervention in the South China Sea and into nations bordering China.

The United Nations—The most active participant in dealing with little wars. The UN has no armed forces of its own, but must convince member nations to contribute troops. Thus there is great variation in troop quality. The UN is also very reluctant to get involved in an actual shooting war. Thus, UN peacekeepers tend to serve as armed targets for the local combatants.

Third world "little warriors"—Like Russia and China, many large third world nations must maintain complex relations with their neighbors. Examples are India, Indonesia, Brazil, Nigeria, and so on. These "regional superpowers" often intervene in local conflicts, although usually only after being invited.

The outcasts—Several nations have become diplomatic outcasts in the past forty years. Those nations maintain a very active diplomacy simply to better survive this pariah status. Chief examples are South Africa (now off the list), Israel (working its way off the list), Taiwan (not on the list for the best of reasons), Iraq (on the list for good reason), North Korea (ditto), Cuba (which now has little offensive military capability), Libya, Iran, and a few others. These nations tend to sell anything to anyone for both the diplomatic and the commercial access this provides. The most dangerous of these nations are the ones who are, or are suspected of, developing nuclear weapons. Iran is also on the list of major supporters of international terrorism. Libya and Sudan provide support for rebellions, coups, and general mayhem in neighboring nations.

GEOGRAPHY

The three most crucial elements of little-war geography are ports, air bases (military and commercial), and money. Put another way, the "geography" of little wars consists of time and money. Little wars tend to occur in the most out-of-the-way places and the quickest way in is usually a local airport. The commercial air bases are often preferable to military ones, as the commercial airport is often better equipped to handle heavy freighter aircraft. The United States has set a goal of being able to move 48 million ton miles of air freight a day during a crisis. Thus if the trouble spot were 10,000 miles from the United States, that means 4,800 tons of freight can be moved a day. But a port, preferably with its docking facilities intact, is required if the little war is going to involve more than paratroopers and light infantry. While marines are theoretically capable of moving in big-time without ports, there are few marine forces that can do this and only one, the U.S. Marine Corps, that can do it on a large scale (a division or more of troops). Moreover, even the U.S. Marines have as their first objective the capture of a port so that they can better supply themselves. Moving goods by sea is a lot cheaper than by air, and in warfare, money is often a crucial factor.

There are nearly a hundred nations that are likely to involve little wars. For most of those nations, the wars loom large, local, and at a greater cost than they can afford. These are usually conflicts with neighbors, like Iraq's invasion of Kuwait in 1990 (which was mainly about money) or the mass murder in Rwanda in 1994 (which was mainly about real estate). Others involve forces moving a few hundred miles to join in a regional conflict, as happened in Saudi Arabia and Liberia in 1990. In most cases these little wars are small because it's so expensive to send armed forces any distance. It's more expensive still to actually use them at that distance and keep them supplied. Sending armed forces large distances is more expensive still. Even light infantry forces are expensive to move as the cost is ultimately more than just a round trip by aircraft. "Light troops" have a certain amount of heavy equipment (light vehicles and heavy weapons).

And all this stuff is generally moved by air freight, an expensive proposition when large air-freight planes cost $40,000–$60,000 a day to operate and can be used ten to twelve hours a day. But that comes to about 30 cents per mile each ton is carried. Since each soldier in a little war requires at least a hundred pounds of supply a day, the costs add up. Even a light-infantry–type troop will require up to a ton of air freight capacity to get him, his equipment, and supplies to the battlefield. If the combat area is 10,000 miles away, it's going to cost $3,000 just to get him there. Each day the soldier is there will cost another $30 just for air freight. If the soldier gets killed, it will cost about $60 just to ship the body back. If the soldier is wounded and has to be evacuated out of the area, the air freight bill goes to several hundred dollars. Thus air freighting 5,000 troops to a distant (10,000 miles away) hot spot will cost over $15 million and another $150,000 per day (over $4 million a month) just to fly the supplies in. After about a month, you can establish supply lines by sea, which costs only a small percentage as much as air freight. But it can take twenty to forty-five days to travel 10,000 miles by sea depending on what type of ship you use (fast ones cost more to operate) and which continents you have to sail around. But by the time seaborne supply has been established, the little war has been around for a while and is on its way to becoming a not-so-little war.

Aside from the cost of shipping the troops somewhere far away, there is the fact that not all the soldiers you send will actually be fighting. Even with our hypothetical force of 5,000 light infantry, no more than half of them will actually be out there with weapons ready. The remainder (and they are usually the majority) are there for the ever-increasing number of support jobs, including taking care of all the supplies coming in by air and sea.

In terms of more traditional geography, little wars tend to be fought in places where the geographical conditions are, well, difficult. Little wars are often found in less developed nations where nature has not yet been tamed. There are relatively fewer roads, and relatively more disease, bad water, and conditions that require more medical person- nel and other support troops (engineers in particular).

HISTORY

The last major period of little wars ran from the U.S. Civil War (1865) and the Franco-Prussian War (1871) all the way to World War I (1914). However, since World War II (1945), in the absence of any major-power war, there have already been a string of small wars that have waxed and waned while the heavily armed superpowers glared at each other across the Iron Curtain in Europe. The size of a war is a matter of perception. The perceptions are changing as we move sev- eral generations away from the bloodbaths of World Wars I and II (plus the slaughters that took place just before World War I and be- tween the world wars). To put it in clearer perspective, from 1900 to 1945, an average of over two million people a year died in wars. From 1945 to 1990, the average annual deaths has been half that (a million dead a year). When you adjust for the enormous population growth since World War II, we find that the annual death rate from wars was three times higher in the first half of the century than in the second half. Yet, one cannot avoid the fact that the past four decades have been full of little wars. The superpowers simply didn't concentrate on them. Instead they put most of their effort into the World War III that never came off and is now acknowledged to be a dead issue.

With a major war less likely, the military is now keen to pay close attention to the kinds of wars they usually fight. Those are the dirty little wars that often lack support back home and frequently have ambiguous endings. America has had more of these than it likes to remember. Before Vietnam there was Korea, the Philippine insurrection, and several major operations in Latin America. But now these wars are the only wars the military has, and without war, or the prospect of war, the public will perceive less need for armed forces. So, motivated by a combination of common sense and institutional self-preservation, the military has gone back to the little wars.

This most recent return to little wars, however, is different. The world has changed. Little wars always existed, but never before was there an international media providing quick transmission of words and pictures. In the past, little wars could be ignored, or safely viewed from a large distance of time and space, a distance that brought events to the public's attention long after they happened, and usually long after anyone could do anything about it. Now, not only do we have man-made and natural disasters shoved in our faces instantly via radio and TV, but we also have thousands of nongovernment organizations (NGOs) that will take action in some foreign disaster even if no government will.

The NGOs have been around for a while, since the early nineteenth century. Some are quite famous, like the Red Cross and CARE. Most, however, came into being after World War II. Indeed, these organizations have proliferated tremendously since the 1960s. There are now thousands of them. Some of the names are recognizable to anyone who follows the news: Feed the Children, OXFAM, Doctors Without Frontiers, Amnesty International, and so on. The NGOs raise some of their money from the public, but an increasing amount comes from governments. Some NGOs are influenced by governments, but usually it's the other way around. More and more, NGOs are hired by governments to apply foreign aid. This has become increasingly popular as it has been realized that much foreign aid gets stolen if given to foreign governments. Currently, over a third of U.S. foreign aid is disbursed via NGOs. Other nations take the same tack. NGOs also assure that some of the foreign aid money comes back to the donor country in the form of salaries for NGO employees and goods purchased in the donor nation.

The NGOs are largely from the industrialized nations, where there is a large pool of educated people, with the right skills, who can be hired and sent to foreign lands to do good works. The populations of industrialized nations are also generous in making donations to NGOs, as are the governments the NGO members come from. But NGOs are emphatically not staffed and run by government employees. And therein lies the rub.

While many NGOs are lobbying organizations for one cause or another, the ones that practice charity in dangerous places are somewhat different. While charity is the goal of these NGOs, they tend to believe in their missions so strongly that they vigorously plead for governments to support the NGO effort with government resources on an official level. When one NGO goes into a foreign nation to relieve famine or treat the casualties of some civil disorder, pressure is put on other governments to get involved. What has developed is a symbiotic relationship among the media, NGOs, and governments. Media brings attention, often distorted, to some foreign disaster. Governments are usually somewhat cautious in getting involved in foreign disasters that involve gunfire, but NGOs go anywhere people are suffering. The media knows a good story when it sees one, namely the daring and selfless NGOs going into harm's way to succor the starving and injured. The NGOs either ask for protection from their governments, or simply state their case on TV and let the politicians take the heat. Thus were foreign troops pulled into Somalia, Haiti, Liberia, the Balkans, Rwanda (just to mention the more recent cases), and many other places. It doesn't always work, and when it does it usually doesn't make much difference and, arguably, makes the situation worse. Moreover, there are a lot of places (Sudan, Indonesia, New Guinea, etc.) where the NGO/media combo never gets rolling and foreign governments are not pulled in.

LOCAL POLITICS

There are three areas where little wars are most likely to occur, and have done so over the centuries. These are Africa, the Middle East, and East Asia.

The most war-torn area is Africa, but these are not only little wars but also inconsequential wars as far as the more heavily armed industrialized nations are concerned. Over the past two centuries (through the end of the cold war), 22 percent of the wars have been in Africa, but only 2 percent of the deaths have occurred there. Since World War II, the loss rate has gone up, but these wars are still generally ignored.

The Middle East has been the next most violent area in the past two centuries, with 20 percent of the wars and only 2 percent of the deaths. Again, the death rate has gone up since World War II, but not as much as in Africa because civilians are less likely to be victims of large-scale massacre in Middle Eastern conflicts. The industrialized powers do take an interest in these little wars, mainly because of the oil in the region and also because of the Suez Canal and, until recently, the area's proximity to Russia.

East Asia has had 16 percent of the wars in the last two centuries, and 44 percent of the war dead. This is a densely populated area and includes China, Japan, and Vietnam, three nations long noted for their warlike proclivities.

Two of these three areas are of interest to the industrialized nations.

The Middle East, especially the Persian Gulf, contains most of the exportable oil in the world. The industrialized nations need that oil and will fight to retain access to it at an affordable price. The oil money that has poured into the region has bought huge amounts of arms and inspired even more ambitious plans for national conquest among the normally factious groups occupying the region. The region now attracts attention from the industrialized nations because several local despots are well on their way toward possessing chemical weapons, atom bombs, and long-range missiles in their arsenals.

East Asia contains China and Japan, plus several other rapidly industrializing nations (Taiwan, South Korea, Singapore, etc.). All of these nations are important to the maintenance of a stable world economy. America also has treaty obligations with Japan, South Korea, and several other nations in the region. The region also contains several unstable nations, China being the most worrisome. Civil war in China would likely mean a number of little wars rather than one large conflict between two clearly defined groups. North Korea is another unstable country that could slip into civil war, or simply civil disorder.

When it comes to little wars, Africa is indeed the sad continent. There is an overabundance of little wars going on, but no particularly pressing interest on the part of the industrialized nations to get involved. The world's major military powers would like to see things calm down, if only to reduce the waste of economic aid. Currently this aid is either blown away on a hundred battlefields or stolen and deposited in hundreds of foreign bank accounts. As long as conditions are so chaotic, and nonvital to outside interests, the African little wars will be of interest largely to those few journalists who happen to pass through.

POWER INTEREST INDICATOR CHARTS

A slight twist: Here we look at the various "expeditionary powers" areas of interest.

UNITED STATES*

	Economic Interests	Historical Interests	Political Interest	Military Interest	Force Generation Potential	Ability to Intervene Politically	Interest/ Ability to Promote Economic Development
Americas	8	8	9	9	9	7	8
Europe	8	8	9	9	7	6	6
Mid East	8	5	8	8	6	4	2
Africa	2	2	4	2	5	4	5
S. Asia	3	4	5	4	5	3	4
E. Asia	7+	7	8+	8	7	6	5

*This chart shows the degree to which the U.S. government, and Americans in general, are inclined to get involved in the little wars of the world's regions.

FRANCE

	Economic Interests	Historical Interests	Political Interest	Military Interest	Force Generation Potential	Ability to Intervene Politically	Interest/ Ability to Promote Economic Development
Americas	2	3	5	2	2	3	2
Europe	9	9	9	9	6	7	7
Mid East	7	8	8	7	3	5	4
Africa	8	8	7	7	5	7	8
S. Asia	3	5	7	2	1	4	1
E. Asia	6	3	6	2	1−	2	1

UNITED KINGDOM

	Economic Interests	Historical Interests	Political Interest	Military Interest	Force Generation Potential	Ability to Intervene Politically	Interest/ Ability to Promote Economic Development
Americas	4	8	7	2	2	4	2
Europe	8	8	9	9	4+	6	6
Mid East	8	8	8	8	3	6	3
Africa	7	7	6	6	3	7	4
S. Asia	3	4	6	2	2	5	1
E. Asia	5	3	6	2	1	3	1

RUSSIA

	Economic Interests	Historical Interests	Political Interest	Military Interest	Force Generation Potential	Ability to Intervene Politically	Interest/ Ability to Promote Economic Development
Americas	1–	2	4	4	2+	2	0
Europe	9	7	9	9	8+	7	2
Mid East	3	2	5	6	7	6	1
Africa	0	2	3	1	2	4	0
S. Asia	2	2	5	2	3	4	1
E. Asia	5	6	8	8	7+	4	3

PARTICIPANT STRATEGIES AND GOALS

United States Groups

The United States Congress and the President—Both the President and Congress have become more adept at reading public opinion correctly, and then trying to "spin" the media to change that opinion. In the last twenty years, as electronic media became more pervasive, and persuasive, all politicians and government officials have learned to play the media to shape public opinion. Sometimes this is done in self-defense, to repair damage to themselves done by the media (either accidentally or on purpose). Dealing with the media fallout from foreign wars is particularly difficult. The images of the suffering are shown enthusiastically by electronic media. Video violence sells, but it also disturbs the audience and leads to calls for "someone" to "do something." Sometimes the President or members of Congress will propose something, and promptly be shot down by the public's aversion to do anything that might endanger American lives, or cost the taxpayers too much.

The United States State Department—The United States has traditionally been isolationist. That came about partially because the United States is geographically isolated from the rest of the world and partially because many U.S. residents have an immigrant attitude of wanting to leave the "old country's" strife and mayhem behind them. But the United States is part of a world economy, and as the Persian Gulf crisis of 1990 demonstrated, America simply cannot ignore some of the ruckus overseas. Usually, the State Department prefers to settle all foreign disputes with diplomacy, which makes sense coming from diplomats. Besides, once the military gets called in, the State Department takes a very distant second place in the chain of command. Military solutions find more support among members of any U.S. President's staff and, after all, the State Department works for the President, not the other way around. While the State Department is under the direct control of the President, it does have its institutional biases and customs. The secretary of state and his deputies, as well as many ambassadors, may be appointed by the President, but most of the staff are career people.

State Department professionals tend to take the long view and often develop an expertise in one area of the world or another. These "area experts" are often at odds with the current President and his staff when it comes to making foreign policy. The President, being an elected official, tends to represent the attitudes of the electorate. That is, presidential policies tend to be isolationist. The area experts in the State Department have to persuade the President, as well as the voters, that a policy of more involvement in some distant area is in the country's interest. This tugging match between the elected officials (including Congress) and the State Department is a constant fixture on the American political scene. The "interventionists" of the State Department are aided, sometimes more than they would like, by the electronic media, which makes the voters instant experts and equally instant advocates for "doing something." The State Department is one of the few U.S. government agencies that has benefited from the cutbacks after the end of the cold war. During the cold war, many "diplomatic" agencies were set up outside the State Department. Now, in the name of saving money, those agencies are either being disbanded or reduced and made a part of the State Department.

The United States Navy and Marine Corps—The Navy is a large organization that, like any large organization, will not go cheerfully, or willingly, through a downsizing. The Navy's position is that with at least a dozen carrier task forces (down from the current fourteen to fifteen) and three Marine divisions (a level mandated by law), it would provide the "State Department troops" numerous enough to take care of any conceivable little war. Perhaps a little backup from the Army and Air Force, but those two services are there, preferably in skeletal form, to mobilize for the rare occasion when a little war grows into a big one. This is a major departure from the traditional missions of the Navy (to protect American access to the high seas) and the Marines (to secure forward bases for the fleet). Even during World War II, the main function of the Marines was to secure those bases. But starting with Korea, and thence into Vietnam (and many smaller places), the Marines have chalked up a reputation for doing what has to be done, anywhere, anytime. From the turn of the century right up to World War II, the Marines demonstrated a flexibility that made them quite capable at dealing with little-war situations. This attitude and capability is their major asset in keeping the Marine Corps employed for the post–cold war world.

The United States Army—As recently as 1940, the U.S. Army had only 150,000 troops (fewer than the post–World War II Marine Corps). The cold war changed all that, but with the cold war over, the Army faces a lot of pressure to shrink back to its 1940 size (or something close to it). With the Navy reasserting its traditional monopoly on little wars, the Army is in big trouble. Since World War II, the Army has built up substantial little-war forces. These include one parachute division, one air assault division, two light infantry divisions, and a division worth of Ranger and Special Forces (commando) troops. These forces exceed the strength of the Marine Corps, but as events in the Persian Gulf demonstrated, there are situations where little-war forces are not enough. In the Persian Gulf War, a tank-heavy mechanized army was needed, which pleased the Army no end and put the Marines on the defensive. But most of the little wars do not involve a lot of tanks. Most little wars are low-tech infantry operations. The "enemy" often consists of many different groups of armed civilians. The Army's heavy-metal approach to combat is at a distinct disadvantage in these murky situations (though the Army's heavy units remain critical in larger wars). The Army also has thousands of "special operations" troops (Rangers and Special Forces) as well as paratroopers and light infantry. These lighter forces are able to deal with the messy little wars the Marines have proven so adept at handling. The Army's new "force projection" approach, however, combined with the Army's proven logistics capabilities, may give it new leverage in the budget wars. Finally, Army "light cavalry" units, integrating armed wheeled vehicles, helicopters, light armor, and high-tech intelligence systems, may prove to be very useful.

The United States Air Force—The "blue suit" crowd is pushing their ability to rapidly deploy substantial firepower on short notice. This concept is also being used to support the long-range B-2 bomber, and new transport aircraft such as the C-17 and 747-type cargo aircraft (ostensibly to move Army units, but also capable of moving support units for Air Force combat aircraft). As a prime exponent of high-tech warfare, the Air Force is also promoting more (and quite expensive) research on new sensors, the better to spot little-war adversaries hiding in the bush or whatever. Not as well positioned as the Navy, but better off than the Army. At least the Air Force can offer more tank-killing capability faster for the Marines.

Great Britain—With acceptance of the decline of their empire and increasing budget problems at home, Britain does not want to increase its involvement in little wars. If it can get away with it, it will allow the United States to take the lead and send token contingents when asked.

France—More for *la gloire* than real national interest, with the exception of action in Africa, France continues to maintain and use "intervention forces." Largely light infantry backed up by airpower.

Other EEC (European Economic Community) countries—These nations will follow the lead of whoever jumps in first, as long as there is enough public support for another foreign adventure.

United Nations—It's a long story; see Quick Look on the UN at the end of this chapter.

Russia—With an abundance of domestic problems, the Russians

have neither the desire nor the resources to engage in military operations far from their borders. Although the Russians still maintain a large array of armed forces, they are having severe personnel problems. Financial problems at home make overseas adventures prohibitively expensive and there are increasing problems just maintaining all the equipment still in the inventory. Russia may offer contributions of light forces for UN interventions, but that's about it. Where Russian troops will see a lot of action outside the country is just over its borders in the former Soviet areas Russia calls the "Near Abroad." Russia is already militarily involved in many of these areas and their local conflicts. That will continue.

China—Like Russia, China has a multitude of internal problems and a traditional dislike of foreign adventures. Since the 1950s, China's foreign military involvements have been restricted to aid and advisers. Economic and political problems limited even these operations. Operations against bumptious neighbors are still a possibility. Since the 1980s, China began to modernize its armed forces. That was worrisome to its neighbors because much of this effort was concentrated on long-range warships and modern aircraft. China has been asserting its territorial rights in the South China Sea, and these new ships and aircraft have been seen hundreds of miles from China for the first time in centuries. To compound this adventuresome new attitude, China continues to seek new customers for its growing arms business. China cares little whom it sells to, as long as the weapons are paid for. These arms sales are not, as in the past, partly driven by diplomatic considerations, but are principally a means for the military, which owns the weapons plants, to make more money for Chinese armed forces modernization. In the age of little wars, China is generally part of the problem, not the solution.

Third world "little warriors"—The passing of the cold war also eliminated the ability of major third world nations to play one superpower off against another and extract tribute from both. Without this aid, local military adventures become prohibitively expensive. Well, not always, but impoverished third world military adventures will first have to check with the Ministry of Finance more so than in the past. While this has restrained the larger third world nations, smaller countries have readily fallen into a state best described as civil disorder.

Somalia, Rwanda, and the Balkans are current examples. In these wars, expense is not a factor because the participants are fighting with whatever they've got. In the case of Rwanda, this meant a lot of machetes. With these primitive weapons, hundreds of thousands were killed.

The outcasts—With so many nations now cut off from access to free weapons or easy credit the cold war provided, the outcasts have more markets open to them. The outcasts tend to provide "technical advisers" with their weapons. While this does not mean you will encounter Israeli or Taiwanese troops in some little war, you are likely to find troops trained (and often well trained) by outcast advisers. This growing problem is producing some strange diplomatic side effects.

POTENTIAL OUTCOMES

1. 50 percent chance through 2001: United States continues to build up large intervention force, and engages in only one or two expeditionary missions in the 1996–2001 time frame.
2. 25 percent chance through 2001: United States builds up a large intervention force, and engages in three or more expeditionary missions in the 1996–2001 time frame.
3. 15 percent chance through 2001: United States maintains large intervention force and does not use it in the 1996–2001 time frame.
4. 10 percent chance through 2001: United States cuts back its forces and does not engage in a major expeditionary campaign in the 1996–2001 time frame.

COST OF WAR

At a minimum, several hundred thousand people are killed each year in the sundry little wars being fought around the world. Over a million are wounded or injured, and several times that number have their lives disrupted or even become refugees. On average, since 1945, the deaths from sundry wars has been about a million a year. That includes situations where nations make war on their own people

(China, Cambodia, Rwanda, Argentina, etc.). Some of those situations are civil wars, others are simply cases of the government du jour deciding to kill a lot of its own citizens for one reason or another. These internal wars have proven to be more deadly than those pitting one nation against another.

WHAT KIND OF WAR

War is still shooting and killing. There is still the need to obtain traditional military victories, which means convincing the other fellow to surrender. Ever since Vietnam, more effort has gone into winning the "hearts and minds" of the other side's people (and soldiers, if possible). While this policy didn't bring victory in Vietnam, it did have some success. And in other post–World War II conflicts, it was decisive. For small wars, often civil wars, this approach shows promise. It also would be cheaper to win wars with these techniques, generally referred to as psychological warfare. But it doesn't always work; in fact, it rarely works in a big way. But "psywar" does help. And if the limitations of psywar are kept in mind, it can help. Psywar helped demoralize Iraqi troops in 1990, before the shooting war began in earnest. It also helped to prevent widespread violence in the 1994 Haiti operation. But in most other conflicts, psywar has had much less success. Nevertheless, these small wars, considered an extension of day-to-day diplomacy, will see more use of psywar. After all, standing aside, deciding whether or not to get deeply involved, *is* a form of psywar.

Another form of psywar (sort of) is the use of nonlethal weapons. This springs from the aversion to seeing all that mayhem on the evening news. "Phasers on stun" and all that. Police have been using nonlethal weapons for several decades, with mixed success. It's unlikely it would work very well on some little-war battlefield. The police typically use nonlethal weapons on deranged individuals, not large groups of heavily armed opponents. Stun guns, rubber bullets, tear gas, and more exotic devices have some use in crowd control. But mobs are not war. Armchair generals love to dream up these things, especially if they are senior government officials without any responsibility for what happens on the battlefield. But nonlethal weapons have caught the fancy of many governments and will keep showing up until a lot of someone's soldiers get killed trying to use them in a hostile environment.

The conventional wisdom is that most little wars will be infantry affairs. In many cases that is true, but as the Persian Gulf War of 1991 demonstrated, there are still times when a lot of tanks are needed. When you do run into a heavily armed, mechanized opponent, you have to match such force with an adequate array of tanks and artillery.

The current size of the U.S. tank force was originally determined by the need to possibly face Russia and the Warsaw Pact in a post–World War II standoff between the Communist and Western democratic nations. But the Warsaw Pact disappeared in 1990, with East Germany and its three thousand tanks disappearing altogether. At the same time, negotiations in Vienna further reduced tank holdings in Europe and North America. Thus it is immediately apparent that fewer U.S. tanks will be needed. The question is, how many will be needed in the 1990s?

That depends on how many other tank battalions you might have to fight. There are about 100,000 tanks in the world (as of 1995). Two powers (Russia and the United States) own a third of those vehicles. Of the twenty or so nations with 2,000 or more tanks, four could be considered potential battlefield opponents (plus a fifth that is diligently building up its tank strength). Most of these potential foes are countered by nearby U.S. allies who have large tank parks of their own. Thus Syria would have to deal with Israel, Libya faces Egypt, North Korea must contend with South Korea, and Iran has Iraq and the Gulf states to deal with. To face this threat, the United States has five active-duty "tank-heavy divisions" (one armored, four mechanized) containing about 1,400 tanks. Another 10,000 tanks are used in "tank-light" divisions (including the three Marine divisions), and Reserve/National Guard units, or are held as replacements, or to form new tank units, or in a few independent tank units. Some 7,000 of these are the most modern M-1 model.

NATIONAL TANK HOLDINGS OF POTENTIAL AGGRESSORS (1995)

Iraq	2,500
Syria	3,000
Libya	3,000
North Korea	3,000
Iran	1,600

Each of the above nations has local enemies with as many, or more, tanks.

The key question is, How much is enough? It is increasingly difficult to get defense budgets through Congress, so you have to carefully make your pitch for force levels. Assuming the Russian threat is gone, at least for the moment, then we are faced with all those other nations possessing tanks. How to deal with them? History, and any tank commander, will tell you that the best antitank weapon is another tank. That is often true, even though tanks are not always responsible for most of the other fellow's tank losses. The tank was not invented to fight other tanks but to spearhead the ground forces in the face of the strongest opposition. Sometimes that means other tanks, sometimes not. Whatever the case, the tank can move a lot of firepower around quickly and take care of itself in the bargain. This makes tanks useful even when the other fellow has not got a lot of them.

But tanks are heavy beasts and difficult to move anywhere in a hurry. Moreover, there is an abundance of other weapons that can destroy, or at least immobilize, a tank. Aircraft carry a wide array of weapons, including several types of mines. Mines are a favorite and cheap antitank weapon. The most numerous is the small (two- to five-pound) "trackbuster" mine, which immobilizes a tank by damaging, but not destroying, the track-laying mechanism. It can take several hours to a day or more to get a "trackbusted" tank moving again. Missiles are also a favorite weapon and most nations have more anti-tank missiles than they have tanks.

Thus we are faced with two primary questions. First, what is the most effective and economical way to neutralize enemy tanks? And second, how many of our own tanks do we need for wars in the 1990s? As events in the Persian Gulf demonstrated, the first U.S. antitank weapons to arrive on the scene were carried by U.S. ground attack aircraft. Next came the antitank missiles (with trucks and helicopters to carry them) of the light infantry and Marines. Last came (by ship) the tanks. Without a month's warning, there is no practical way to get enough tanks to any faraway battlefield. You can get aircraft and light infantry there within a few days.

You do eventually need sufficient tanks if you want to go on the offensive. This saves a lot of lives among your own troops and generally speeds up any offensive operations. In the 1991 war, despite a vigorous coalition air war against Iraqi tanks, many enemy tanks escaped the air attacks and had to be destroyed by American M-1 tanks. This was what ended the war, U.S. tanks rolling over those last Iraqi positions.

Most of the world's existing tanks are poorly maintained, have ill-trained crews, and are much less capable than those held by America and its allies. This is a very substantial advantage, as was shown in the 1991 Gulf War where nearly five hundred Iraqi tanks were destroyed in ground combat and fewer than a hundred U.S. tanks were even hit (and only a handful disabled).

Given the lineup of potential opponents, America needs fewer than half the tanks it now has. It could use more antitank missiles and mines. There are more effective mines in the works. A true "light tank" would also come in handy to speed up offensive operations without waiting for the heavy tanks to be shipped in.

There, that was simple, wasn't it?

Light Infantry Forces

Even before the end of the cold war, many nations began to pay more attention to light infantry forces. Vietnam had proved that light infantry had a place in modern warfare, but those lessons had largely been ignored immediately after American forces withdrew, and the focus of U.S. military effort turned back to Europe. Then, the Russians' experience in the 1980s Afghan war made the case for light infantry again, and this time it stuck. The United States had formed four light infantry divisions by the late 1980s. Two of them disappeared in the overall reduction of the Army's size after the cold war. But the proportion of Army strength that comprised light infantry went up. The airborne and airmobile division remained, as did the Ranger battalions and Special Forces groups. These latter two comprise the bulk of the 18,000 SOF (Special Operations Forces) troops America maintains. Including the two light infantry divisions, the airborne and airmobile division, and the three Marine divisions, there are some 120,000 light infantry available for rapid deployment to places where the bad guys don't have a lot of armored vehicles.

Real light infantry is anything but a featherweight combat force, at least in terms of effectiveness. As has been demonstrated on many third world battlefields, well-trained, well-equipped, and well-led light infantry can handle just about anything it encounters. Light infantry equipped with modern antitank missiles and supported by airpower can even stop a mechanized force. However, there are many limitations in throwing light infantry against a mechanized foe. It can be done, but at great cost to your light troops. Even against foes who are largely infantry, friendly losses will be rather high. Light infantry means that there are not a lot of armored vehicles to protect the troops, nor massive artillery to do most of the killing. Light infantry combat means getting in close to do the dirty work.

It's costly to send light infantry against irregulars engaged in some little war in an out-of-the-way place. Somalia was a good example of that. So is the ongoing conflict in the Balkans as well as the earlier civil war in Lebanon. Russia's campaign to pacify Chechnya in 1995 shows how traditional mechanized forces can fail to achieve a quick win. The Russians only made progress when they brought in their elite light infantry forces. And even then it was a bloody process, made more painful by all the negative media attention.

But light infantry is not a panacea. These units are "light" only compared with mechanized units. Light infantry divisions have over a thousand trucks and other vehicles. To keep the casualty rate down, light units use a lot of helicopters and air support. Artillery and mortars need a lot of ammunition; otherwise your light infantry melts away real quick as they get in close to the enemy. Light infantry can go in very light indeed. You could put a light infantry battalion and their light weapons (assault rifles, machine guns, and mortars) on three or four 747 wide-body jets. These guys would still need food, medical support, and ammunition resupply, but they could, for example, hold the airport they landed at against lightly armed opponents.

Light infantry has its advantages, but it is not the solution for every little war that pops up.

QUICK LOOK: The United Nations and Little Wars

During the cold war, the UN generally kept its head down lest it be torn apart by superpower conflicts. Now that the cold war is over, the UN has rapidly emerged as the principal international peacekeeping organization. This was as it was originally meant to be. The UN had been active in peacekeeping operations ever since its founding in 1945. One of the first peacekeeping actions was in Korea, where the UN presided over a full-scale war. This pleased no one, and didn't really change anything either. Thus the UN's major problem is that it has yet to come up with a method of sorting out those situations that it can handle from those that it cannot.

Further complicating this problem is that the UN has built up a bureaucracy increasingly independent of control by any nation or group of nations. No one, or no nation, can complain too loudly about peacekeeping efforts; thus the UN peacekeeping moves forward, trying to intervene in any little war where UN funds and troops can be scraped together. But therein lies the UN's major problem. The UN has no powers to levy taxes or raise troops. The member nations voluntarily pay their assessments to the UN and, if any nation so desires, make troops available for UN peacekeeping. In the area of world public opinion, no nation can come out against peacekeeping. But when it comes time to send money to the UN, or offer troops, inaction speaks loudly enough. But with 178 member nations, 23,000 employees, and over $4 billion to spend each year, the UN has enough resources to get things started. After that, these peacekeeping initiatives often acquire a life of their own. Consider the list below, showing the

UN peacekeeping operations in effect when the cold war ended, as well as those that were set up in the years after the cold war ended. The UN's main problem is not getting these operations started (who could be against peacemaking), but keeping them going. Optimism springs eternal and past failures are easily forgotten.

The earliest peacekeeping operations were qualified successes. Israel and India/Pakistan were both situations that took place before the cold war got under way in earnest. But then the Korean War came along in 1950 and, after a fashion, made it clear that the decades-long struggle between the capitalist East and Communist West was now under way. Until the late 1980s, the UN could, only with great difficulty, assert itself as a peacemaker. The superpowers had divided the world among themselves and preferred to do their own peacekeeping, or to prevent anyone else from attempting it.

But when the cold war ended abruptly in 1989, the UN found itself in a rather new situation. The superpowers were no longer at each other's throats. In 1991 the Soviet Union disintegrated, thus withdrawing itself from any strong positions, pro or con, on UN intervention anywhere. That left the United States, which also soon lost its taste for peacekeeping.

The list below (of currently active UN peacekeeping operations) shows that the early 1990s will be seen as something of a golden age of peacekeeping, with the UN taking on just about every hot spot in sight. Before 1989, there were several peacekeeping operations that came and, after a fashion, went. The largest one was in Korea, where the United States led a UN-sanctioned army against Communist forces. Technically, that one is still on. There were also some rescue missions in Africa during the 1960s.

Year	Operation
1948	UNMOGIP—United Nations Military Observer Group in India and Pakistan
1948	UNTSO—United Nations Truce Supervision Organization (Palestine)
1964	UNFICYP—United Nations Force in Cyprus

1974	UNDOF—United Nations Disengagement Observer Force (Middle East)
1978	UNIFIL—United Nations Interim Force in Lebanon
1991	MINURSO—United Nations Mission for the Referendum in Western Sahara
1991	ONUSAL—United Nations Observer Mission in El Salvador
1991	UNAVEM—United Nations Angola Verification Mission
1991	UNIKOM—United Nations Iran-Kuwait Observation Mission
1991	UNOSOM—United Nations Operation in Somalia
1992	UNPROFOR—United Nations Protection Force (Yugoslavia)
1992	UNTAC—United Nations Transitional Authority in Cambodia
1993	UNOMIG—United Nations Observer Mission in Georgia
1993	UNOMIL—United Nations Monitoring Group in Liberia
1993	UNOMOZ—United Nations Operation in Mozambique
1993	UNOMUR—United Nations Observer Mission Uganda-Rwanda
1994	UNHIM—United Nations Haiti Inspection Mission

In reality, the UN had then, and has now, serious restrictions on its peacekeeping activity. These handicaps fall into three general areas.

Political. The UN has to get a favorable vote among its members before it can attempt to intervene. Now, you may think, who could vote against peace? Well, no one, but many nations would vote against the UN, or any other nation, intruding on what may be considered the internal affairs of a sovereign nation. This is, has always been, and will continue to be a controversial point. While the UN exists to protect the independence of its member nations, situations that might call for UN intervention are often civil wars or rebellions within nations. The government of the afflicted nation doesn't always invite the UN in, and increasingly, the UN doesn't even ask for an invitation. This makes a lot of countries with current, or potential, internal unrest uncomfortable with giving the UN too much authority to unilaterally enter nations with what the rest of the world considers major problems.

Fiscal. It's expensive to send in the troops. Someone has to pay for it, and many nations, including the United States, are behind in their payments to the UN. The UN cannot borrow much money; it often scrapes along by delaying payment for services rendered. A military intervention usually involves more civilian UN employees than troops. There is also the humanitarian aid (food, medicine, and the like). It's the aid and the civilians that cost the most, as permanent UN employees are paid at U.S. wage levels. Locals are hired more cheaply, and, most important, the troops are paid at about half the going rate for troops from an industrialized nation. Actually, troops from wealthy nations are often not paid for by the UN, but their prepaid services are "donated" by the country they came from. Less industrialized nations only send troops if the soldiers can be paid. The lower rate the UN pays for these third world troops is quite a bit more than the troops are usually paid, and the money goes to the nation the soldiers come from. The troops get the same pay they always get (plus, at times, a small bonus) and the nation supplying the troops makes a nice profit, in hard currency, for the peacekeeping efforts of their lads. But the UN has to scrounge up the money for all of this before or, all too often, after the troops are sent in. A fall-off of contributions usually makes peacekeeping operations chancy propositions as fiscal problems prevent sending in additional troops or even adequately supporting the ones that are already there.

Emotional. Electronic media has made the world an electronic village. Everyone knows, or thinks they know, what everyone else is doing. With more democracies, it is easier for outrages in far-off lands to excite the passions of citizens worldwide and generate calls for "something to be done." The elected officials get the message, the issue is raised in the UN, and before you know it, another peacekeeping mission is under way. Long-range aircraft and fast ships allow troops and their equipment to be quickly dispatched to any part of the globe. But the emotions often cool as quickly as they were enflamed. The troops are out there, doing a difficult task, when they note that the folks back home have changed their minds. The peacekeeping operations are not like wars, where both sides are allowed to battle on until one side or another has prevailed. Peacekeeping involves trying to get two or more groups to stop, at least temporarily, fighting each other. If the locals really don't want to stop, the peacekeepers are unlikely to receive authorization to take on all the locals and impose a peace.

The folks back home are unlikely to allow this either. Most people have an image of peacekeeping as, well, peaceful. A bunch of blue-helmeted good guys standing around with guns and white armored vehicles, who by their very presence create a peaceful atmosphere. The reality is quite different, with locals regarding the UN troops as another bunch of targets. And those white vehicles are so easy to see, and take aim at.

By 1995 even the peace-loving bureaucrats at the UN were beginning to understand that peacekeeping was a chancy proposition. Intervening in civil wars creates some strange situations. All the warring factions see the UN aid and staff as resources to be used to further their cause. Aid is hijacked, or exorbitant "transit fees" (extortion by any other name, a "protection racket") are charged for aid moving through a factious territory. At times even the UN troops, especially the low-paid ones from third world nations, add their own corruption. This is usually in the form of black market activity, or theft and resale of relief supplies.

The weaker side in the local fighting uses the UN soldiers and civilians as a shield and refuge for their civilians and fighters. For this reason, even getting out of a peacekeeping operation can be risky, as the UN staff and troops are liable to find their exit blocked by women and children, or even armed men. All sides in the local fighting will use and exploit the UN any way they can, just as they exploit the international media to position themselves as the victims in need of more protection, more aid, more sympathy, more of anything they can get. Civil wars are desperate affairs and the various factions show little restraint in grabbing any advantage that comes their way. For the UN staff and soldiers, it's a job; for the locals it's a matter of life and death, and whatever passions got them going in the first place.

There is also a perverse effect of UN intervention on the local culture and economy. Typically, the UN brings in food, shelter, medical workers, and other forms of aid. The local economy is never completely destroyed, but it now has a difficult time competing with the free largess offered by the UN. Local farmers have no reason to grow food when it can be gotten for free from the UN. The UN often becomes a major employer of locals. In the poor parts of the world where the UN often operates, the locals soon find that they rather like all the good things the UN has brought in. The local population will thus protest, often violently, when the UN decides to leave.

The UN isn't the only peacemaker in the world; there are many local attempts at stopping, stalling, or otherwise thwarting local conflicts. Nigerian-led African troops in Liberia and NATO forces in the Balkans both prefer to operate under the UN flag. That makes some diplomatic sense, as troops from nations in the region would, for various historical reasons, be looked on with suspicion by one faction or another. The UN is a new entity (1945) and, more than any other in the world, seen as relatively neutral. But as the situation in the Balkans and Liberia has demonstrated, peacekeeping troops under a UN flag are not a magic formula for peace. These two operations also show the shortcomings of peacekeeping. In neither situation are the warring factions eager for peace. The only options the peacekeepers have is to stay put and get shot at, get out, or go to war with everyone and keep fighting until all the locals are disarmed.

The situation in the Balkans is particularly galling because NATO, and its European members, are acutely aware that, peace or no peace, it's going to cost them. The refugees from the fighting run for nearby countries, and it's difficult to turn them away. Taking the refugees is expensive and causes political unrest in the host countries. Trying to keep peace in the war zone is liable to get your own troops killed and that causes political unrest back home. It's a no-win situation.

The list of dead and wounded UN peacekeepers is getting longer, and the peacekeeping efforts are often unavailing. Peacekeeping is not the same as peacemaking. The former assumes that the warring parties have agreed to stop fighting; the latter implies that UN-controlled forces will impose peace. Peacemaking is bloody and likely to escalate. The UN bureaucrats are not military commanders, and don't want to be. But there has been a tendency to send peacekeeping troops into situations that require peacemaking. The Balkans and Somalia are bloody examples. This has provided a reality check for the UN, and the nations that supply the troops. For the rest of the decade, we can expect a more hard-headed, and hard-hearted, attitude toward peacekeeping, from both the UN and the nations that supply the arms and money.

QUICK LOOK: How Money Runs the World

Make no mistake: During the cold war money was *the* principal weapon. Superpower cash, spread into far corners of the planet, both kept the peace and fed the "armed struggle."

Now the cold war money pot is empty. Only the guns are left.

Money, however, as in capital, has become even more important. Most of the world's nagging little wars are a result of there not being enough cash available to buy and build peace.

Yes, people can buy peace. It's been done for thousands of years. Purchased peace is not a perfect peace, but it's preferable to the violent alternative.

The 1996 world economy is a $25- to $26-trillion-dollar-a-year enterprise; it requires trillions of dollars of annual savings and profits a year to keep going. The popular political expression "to create jobs" usually glosses over the fact that it costs a lot of money to "create" a job, and if you don't have competent management in charge of the process, the job won't last long. Creating a job requires anywhere from tens to hundreds of thousands of dollars. If the job is not well managed, if the job is not profitable and does not generate sufficient profit to provide money to replace the workers' tools and keep up with technology, the job, and its investment, largely disappears.

Most of the corporate profits and savings are truly international, because money can move rapidly from danger, and toward opportunity. Capital goes where there appears to be the best opportunity to make the most profit. That is where the jobs show up. Where money lands, it creates jobs. Communist China showed what could happen when a market economy was installed in a formerly Communist state. China stopped squandering its capital and began letting profit-driven entrepreneurs create profitable jobs that created more jobs. China since the late 1970s has had one of the fastest-growing economies on the planet. With nearly a quarter of the planet's population, China's economic awakening is a matter of major import. Yet China is having a rough ride. The Chinese legal system is shaky—even primitive in terms of economic operations—and the social order is unsettled. China's experiment with capitalism could still turn into nothing more than a pile of gilded wreckage.

The change from statist, controlled economies to open, free market economies is a major feature and major hurdle of this post–cold war era. The cold war's ideological struggle was a key component of that conflict. The West backed capitalism and the free market. The East preached socialism and state control of the economy. The Western system was based on thousands of years of experience and development. The capitalist system was not perfect (which is why socialists and Communists tried to develop grand alternatives), but in the long run capitalism works best.

As an economic and political idea, socialism (meaning where all economic assets are owned jointly by everyone and allegedly used for the common good) also goes back thousands of years. Tribal communities are often "socialist" in a broad sense. Communism arose in the nineteenth century as a means of bringing about socialism by means of force and revolution. In theory, the Communist version of socialism was to exist with democracy. Communism preached that a dictatorship would be needed temporarily until universal socialism was achieved. But no Communist state was able to do away with their "temporary" dictators.

All Communists and most socialists, however, make very fundamental errors when it comes to understanding how a successful economy actually operates. Socialism and communism play down the role of individual initiative, individual desires, and even basic greed. "Socialism that works" (i.e., socialism producing much wealth and distributing the wealth equally) requires selfless behavior by a large number of people. As the collapse of communism in the 1980s demonstrated, such continual, large-scale selflessness is not as widespread a trait in the human race as are personal desires "for something better" and greed.

Capitalism and the free market is a rough but workable method of controlling the greed and encouraging the selflessness. It does so by establishing rules for the players and reminding the incipient robber barons that sharing the wealth from time to time is a form of insurance against civil disorder.

Capitalism encourages people to save their money and invest it in profitable enterprise in order to make more money. Some people do get filthy rich. In the eighteenth and nineteenth centuries many capitalists simply built marginal enterprises and required outrageous working hours from their workers in order to keep them afloat economically. Business was king and anything that got in the way of business, like revolution or economic depression, focused attention on a practical way to deal with the problem so that everyone could get on with the business of business. Striking workers and revolution were bad for business. Too many poverty-stricken people was bad for social order, so the conservative aristocrats of mid-nineteenth-century Germany established a workers' pension system. The Great Depression in America led to another array of social programs. Twentieth-century capitalists also took note of the need to have a lot of well-paid consumers so that the free market would have buyers as well as sellers. The paradox of capitalism is that greed and self-interest often produce a more effective form of economic generosity.

The Communists concentrated economic power, control of the money, in a group of people who were not driven by the profit motive. So the wealth of Communist states was squandered in unprofitable, but politically attractive, or simply self-indulgent, schemes. Many of the new, post-1945, nations, fell for the Communist/socialist line. With the United States and the Soviet Union handing out large amounts of cash, free food, and cheap weapons, it was possible for many a national leader to "socialize" his economy and keep the illusion that "socialism works" going for a decade or so. The cheap guns kept the local critics at bay, and the foreign aid went to pay the people holding the guns and such other staff as were required to run the socialist state. This charade eventually led to the collapse of many of these national economies. Zaire, typical of many African "socialist states," saw its per capita income fall by more than half, from independence in the early 1960s to total economic collapse in the 1990s. But even new nations that espoused capitalism, like oil-rich Nigeria, found that the right slogans were not enough. More was needed.

Those nations that went for a free market and capitalism realized that one needs money to make money. The spectacular economic growth of nations like Korea, Taiwan, and Japan was fueled by savings rates of 20–30 percent (i.e., people put into banks 20–30 percent of what they earned). Those savings, and corporate profits, are the only source of capital with which to build new factories and, equally important, maintain the ones that already exist. America has a low savings rate, about half that of most industrial nations. That would be (and eventually will be) a catastrophe if it were not for that other component of capitalism—the capitalist. Kings and dictators have always been at odds over the independent entrepreneurs who turned capital into more capital. Those people control the economy and don't always do what kings and dictators want them to do. Modern democracy represents the victory of capitalists over kings; of taking care of business over taking care of whatever the king or dictator wanted to do (which often made no economic sense). The Communists thought they could beat the capitalists by restricting consumption among their own people and piling up more capital. But without free-wheeling capitalists to make the most of the capital, all that treasure shrinks. That is what happened in the Communist nations. Vast amounts of cash went into things that made no economic sense and, worst of all, created no additional wealth. Even the Communists caught on to this problem by the early 1990s. Which is why many of the "former" Communists in former Communist nations still hold power (they are professional politicians), but also back the market economy and the efforts of their local capitalists to create more wealth.

For the free market to work, you also need rules. Capitalism doesn't work under the law of the jungle. Hong Kong and Taiwan attribute much of their success to the establishment of a legal system that provides a consistent way to settle commercial disputes. Celebrity murder trials may grab the headlines, but courts earn their keep by giving capitalists an alternative to forming their own private armies. Nations blessed with natural resources and a free market economy still stumble when they can't guarantee safe streets and the rule of law. Russia is learning this lesson the hard way, as is mainland China and "capitalist" Nigeria.

Once a Communist economy frees its financial system and allows capital to flow in and out, the money will mostly flow out if the nation does not make it possible for business to do business and make a profit. Thus in the initial stages of establishing a "free economy," cash mainly flowed out of Russia and China, until the government could reassure capitalists that their capital was safe. In new and unsettled capitalist nations the newly made profits are as likely to be shipped abroad as they are to be invested locally.

It isn't just former Communist nations that have to worry about "capital flight." In the 1980s, capital flows were examined in nations receiving large amounts of foreign aid. It showed that in unstable nations, the money went out about as quickly as it came in. Whether the money had been stolen, or doled out to legitimate enterprises, the money fled if conditions in the nation were not conducive to economic growth.

Even seemingly healthy nations can suffer from capital flight. Take the United States, for example. In the 1990s, America was still running a budget deficit, spending more money than it was earning. That was flooding the world with dollars. Meanwhile, Japan, whose people saved twice as much of their income as Americans, and sold more goods than they bought, was being paid a lot of those dollars for Japanese goods. Currency traders, who exchange one currency for another on an international scale, began to find out that there were far more dollars wanting to be turned into yen (the Japanese currency) than the other way around. So it became more expensive to buy yen with dollars. Simple supply and demand. In 1980 a dollar would buy you 250 yen. By 1995, a buck bought less than 100 yen. People were losing confidence in the dollar, because the country that backed it could not balance its own books. Now you know why there is such enthusiasm for balancing the budget. In 1945, Great Britain was in the same position as the United States today, and in the next thirty years Britain saw its standard of living go from one of the highest in the world to one that doesn't even make the top ten anymore.

Money (capital) keeps the whole world moving. Ideology can get in the way and bloody dictators can slow the process, but as long as people want to better their lives, they will need money to build and create. Money has to come from somewhere and if you can't save it or borrow it, in the contemporary world you will not grow. If a nation can't maintain order, or prevent too much of the money from being stolen (i.e., stop or limit corruption, a real problem in Mexico, for example), the money the nation needs to develop and prosper will flee.

This is another tough economic-historical rule of thumb: If an economy fails to grow, it will die. That is precisely what is happening in many nations that never paid attention to the need to nurture, feed, and protect capital.

Part 6
DATABANK ON WARS AND ARMIES, PRESENT AND POTENTIAL

This section is designed to present a brief introduction to current international and internal wars, with notes on each. The next time you hear about some obscure conflict, a quick check with this chapter will bring you up-to-date on the background of the situation.

The chart that begins on page 651 shows key data on most of the world's nations.

One very important thing to keep in mind is that a small number of nations possess the majority of the world's economic power and population. Just eight nations (United States, China, Japan, Germany, France, India, Great Britain, and Russia) possess two thirds of the world's economic activity (GDP), 51 percent of the population, and 31 percent of the real estate. This small group of nations, out of some two hundred on the planet, also have admitted they have nuclear weapons. Very few other nations have armed forces that can do much more than fight internal foes, or neighbors.

HOW TO READ THE CHART

Averages and Totals gives the averages, or totals, for each column, as appropriate.

Summary Data

This section of the chart summarizes and analyzes country data on the basis of geography. Statistics are summarized by continent. For details on the nations in each continent, see the individual nation data below.

COUNTRY PROFILE

Country—Nation for which the information is provided.

Rank—Rank within region by war-making power.

War State—Degree of involvement in war. 1—nothing much going on at all; 5—pretty serious insurgency or disorder or armed tensions with neighbor but not out of control; 9—major war.

Government's Stability (1–9)—An indication of the ability of the government to act without fear of overthrow or disintegration. 1—chaos (as in Somalia); 9—rock solid (as any government can get). Less stable governments often lead to war, either as an attacker or as a victim.

War Power—Relative ability of nation to engage in warfare: a combination of qualitative factors and number of troops under arms. This is largely the nation's ability to defend itself. For a large nation like Russia or China, this combat capability is spread out along the nation's vast borders and, in effect, consists of up to half a dozen separate entities. This must be taken into account when considering the war-making power of a large country with long borders and many enemies. Even a country as relatively small as Iraq must disperse its forces over a wide area to counter a host of potential enemies. Once in the battle area, this value can change considerably depending on how the forces are deployed and used. If one side lacks sufficient supplies of food, fuel, and ammunition in the combat area, their war-making power degrades accordingly. Things are rarely "equal" on the battlefield.

Attack Power—Relative ability to make war beyond one's borders. This covers the resources needed to move combat forces long distances and keep them supplied. Nations with large fleets and air forces can do this. The superpowers, especially the United States, is unique in that it can move enormous amounts of combat power to any part of the globe. That is a unique capability, which no other nation possesses.

Total Quality—Overall qualitative value of nation's military forces. It consists of the following items that were rated (but are not shown on the chart). Leaders—Officer quality and training. Equipment—Quality and quantity of equipment available. Experience—Quality of recent military experience, with an average rating indicating sound experience, but in lengthy peacetime operations only. A politically active military would tend to be rated lower here. An armed force with recent combat experience would be rated higher. Support—Quality of logistical apparatus, maintenance capacity, and general ability to sustain combat operations. Mobilization—Ability to rapidly expand forces beyond current active duty manpower. This depends on the availability of trained manpower, equipment, and the availability of technical and managerial skills in the population pool. Tradition—Quality of psychological factors such as culture, military history, and tradition.

GEOGRAPHIC PROFILE—SUMMARY OF GEOGRAPHIC DATA ABOUT EACH COUNTRY

Area of sq km (in thousands)—Surface area of nation in thousands of square kilometers. Larger nations require larger forces to cover all that territory. But the larger spaces also make it easier to defend, as the invader has to occupy more ground and travel longer distances in hostile territory in order to succeed.

Military Environment Index—Suitability of the country for military operations, on a scale of 0–9. 0 is highly unfavorable conditions; 9, highly favorable. A combination of country size, terrain, climate patterns, border length, and location, plus the vulnerability of vital civil, economic, and military resources to an invading army.

Population (per sq km)—A good indicator of how much civilians can be expected to suffer. The denser the population, the more likely civilians will be caught in the crossfire.

Pop Total (in millions)—Total resident population in millions. Rounded and projected to late 1990s. Note that many, if not most, nations do not run a regular census and have only a rough idea of their populations. These are the best estimates based on several sources.

Percent of Literacy—Percent of the population technically able to read and write (often merely an indication of ability to sign one's name). If a nation is not yet industrialized, this is a good indication of their potential to industrialize.

Life Expectancy—Average life expectancy in years. The female's is usually 10–15 percent longer than the male's, except in the poorest countries, where it is about equal. A prime indicator of what the real quality of life in a nation is. More accurate than GDP.

ECONOMIC PROFILE—INDICATORS OF ECONOMIC STRENGTH

GDP—Gross Domestic Product in billions of dollars for the most recent year available. Total value of goods and services produced for internal consumption. GNP (gross national product, which is often used interchangeably) is a similar number, but includes overseas activities. As with population data, GDP is often difficult to calculate. International trade is easily tracked and valued, but most nations generate the bulk of their wealth internally. Many nations have only crude internal accounting capabilities. As a consequence, GDP data is often an estimate. We have collected such data from several sources (the UN, banks, government documents, etc.) and come up with a reasonable composite.

Per Capita GDP (in thousands of dollars)—Note that nations with per capita GDP of only a few hundred dollars a year understate the actual income of the people. In these very poor nations much of the population is surviving through a noncash economy. It usually involves subsistence farming (growing enough for themselves) as well as "underground economy" activity that often doesn't make it to the official GDP figures. A more recent yardstick, more accurate but not fully accepted, is purchasing power parity (PPP). That yardstick translates GDP into local buying power. It costs a lot less to live in some nations than in others, and this new yardstick calculates that. It gives nations like China and India much higher GDPs, but does not, like traditional GDP, translate local economic activity to a common currency (in this case U.S. dollars).

MILITARY CAPABILITY—A SUMMARY OF THE COUNTRY'S MILITARY CAPACITY

Active Manpower—Number or men and women on active service in the armed forces expressed in thousands.

Military Budget—Annual expenditures on defense in millions of dollars. This is another slippery figure, even more so than GDP. There is no standard way of accounting for military expenditures (although the more industrialized nations have reached some consensus in this area). We make our usual estimates based on all the (often conflicting) information available to us.

Percent of GDP—Defense expenditures as a percent of GDP. Shows emphasis nation places on military power.

Budget per Man—The amount of money spent on each active duty soldier. The more is spent per man, the better equipped the troops are. Training and leadership are another matter, though.

Equivalent Divisions—Number of equivalent divisions available from active and reserve army units, combining smaller units into "equivalent" divisions (eight to twelve infantry and tank battalions, plus some artillery and other units). Basically the number of major combat units a nation can fight a war with.

Armored Fighting Vehicles—Total number of tanks, infantry combat vehicles, scout cars, armored assault guns, and amphibious assault vehicles. A good indicator of how mechanized and mobile a nation's ground forces are.

Combat-Capable Aircraft—Total number of combat-capable airplanes and helicopters. Once the war starts and one side gains control of the air, and keeps it, the other side is at a grave disadvantage.

Navy—Numeric value of the nation's naval forces, on a scale of 0 to 10, with 0 representing none; 1, minimal; 2–3, coastal fleets of increasing strength; 4–6, for fleets of high seas capability; 7–9, the fleets ranking just behind 10. The U.S. Navy possesses more than half the naval combat power in the world.

THE GREAT DISARMAMENT OF THE 1990s

A note on the end of the cold war. With the collapse of Eastern European communism, the virtual disappearance of the Warsaw Pact and a major European arms reduction treaty, nearly all European nations are experiencing major declines in defense spending and force levels. This will continue through the late 1990s, except for those few nations that have already developed serious disputes with their neighbors (Romania, Hungary, Bulgaria, and Turkey, for example). The long-festering economic problems of Russia and Eastern Europe must now be attended to and this will put military affairs into the background for a decade or so.

LITTLE WARS AND TINY CONFLICTS

As the chart demonstrates, some nations have small armed forces and even smaller combat power. Thus a civil war in many African nations amounts to little more than a few thousand lightly armed troops firing a few shots and one faction deciding to flee across the border or into the bush. The winners move into the capital and take over. In many nations, in Africa and elsewhere, an ongoing "rebellion" would, in the days before CNN and satellite news, be considered little more than "a bandit problem." Put an eloquent bandit in front of a camera and you have a revolutionary. Yet if war is a matter of degree, then there are few nations on our planet capable of getting a proper war going. For the remainder, any action is basically large-scale police work.

Small nations not shown on the chart include Bahamas, Bahrain, Belize, Brunei, Cape Verde Islands, Comoro Islands, Cyprus (Greek), Cyprus (Turkish), Djibouti, Equatorial Guinea, Fiji, Gambia, Guyana, Iceland, Luxembourg, Maldives, Malta, Mauritius, Qatar, São Tomé and Principe, Seychelle Islands, Suriname.

Country	Rank	War State	Government's Stability	War Power	Attack Power	Total Quality	Area of sq km (in thousands)	Military Environment Index	Population (per sq km)	Population Total (in millions)	Percent of Literacy	Life Expectancy
Averages & Totals		3	6	65,215	963	9	130,492	5	44	5,789	67	63
Africa		3	4	79	1	4	21,352	5	26	563	37	51
Americas		2	7	1,152	574	9	38,712	5	20	770	81	68
Europe		3	6	1,624	210	17	27,668	5	32	875	94	72
Middle East		3	6	556	11	14	13,503	7	23	313	52	64
South Asia		4	6	492	16	12	5,441	4	235	1,279	37	54
Southeast Asia		2	7	1,317	150	16	23,816	5	84	1,989	80	66
African Nations												
South Africa	1	3	7	27	1	33	1,221	5	34	42.0	55	63
Nigeria	2	4	4	13	0	15	911	3	132	120.0	28	48
Ethiopia	3	4	4	8	0	8	1,127	4	45	51.0	34	51
Angola	4	5	4	8	0	8	1,247	4	9	12.0	20	43
Eritrea	5	2	7	4	0	17	121	5	26	3.2	40	55
Zimbabwe	6	3	4	3	0	7	387	4	29	11.0	47	61
Tanzania	7	2	5	3	0	5	886	3	32	28.0	79	51
Rwanda	8	5	4	2	0	14	26	7	308	8.0	30	51
Somalia	9	7	1	2	0	4	627	5	11	7.0	60	53
Kenya	10	3	5	2	0	7	569	6	51	29.0	47	61
Chad	11	4	3	1	0	4	1,259	6	5	6.6	16	39
Uganda	12	5	5	1	0	3	200	4	95	19.0	52	50
Cameroon	13	3	4	1	0	4	469	3	29	14.0	65	50
Senegal	14	4	5	1	0	6	202	6	45	9.0	11	50
Zaire	15	2	3	0	0	1	2,268	2	19	43.0	42	52

(continued)

		Country Profile					Geographic Profile		Population Profile			
Rank	Country	War State	Government's Stability	War Power	Attack Power	Total Quality	Area of sq km (in thousands)	Military Environment Index	Population (per sq km)	Population Total (in millions)	Percent of Literacy	Life Expectancy
16	Mozambique	3	5	0	0	1	784	3	23	18.0	14	46
17	Gabon	1	6	0	0	6	258	5	5	1.4	65	52
18	Ghana	2	5	0	0	3	230	4	75	17.0	30	59
19	Madagascar	1	5	0	0	1	582	5	23	14.0	52	51
20	Ivory Coast	1	6	0	0	2	318	4	44	14.0	24	53
21	Zambia	2	5	0	0	1	741	5	13	9.6	53	55
22	Niger	2	4	0	0	3	1,267	4	7	9.0	8	49
23	Mauretania	3	5	0	0	1	1,030	5	2	2.3	17	45
24	Guinea-Bisseau	2	5	0	0	2	28	4	43	1.2	15	45
25	Burundi	3	5	0	0	1	25	4	248	6.2	38	51
26	Mali	3	4	0	0	2	1,220	5	8	9.8	10	45
27	Sierra Leone	6	3	0	0	1	72	9	63	4.5	15	44
28	Liberia	6	2	0	0	2	96	5	31	3.0	20	54
29	Congo	3	3	0	0	1	342	4	9	3.0	80	56
30	Botswana	1	6	0	0	1	585	6	3	1.5	33	59
31	Namibia	1	6	0	0	1	805	3	3	2.1	69	50
32	Malawi	2	2	0	0	1	94	5	106	10.0	25	48
33	Guinea	2	5	0	0	1	246	5	31	7.7	48	42
34	Burkina Faso	2	2	0	0	1	274	7	39	10.6	7	47
35	Togo	1	5	0	0	1	54	4	81	4.4	18	55
36	Central Afr. Rep.	2	2	0	0	1	623	6	6	3.5	20	46
37	Benin	1	5	0	0	1	111	6	50	5.6	11	49

Lesotho	38	2	7	0	0	1	30	9	67	2.0	66	60
Swaziland	39	1	6	0	0	1	17	7	59	1.0	69	50
American Nations												
United States	1	2	9	1,000	572	61	9,166	3	29	262.0	99	76
Brazil	2	3	6	51	1	14	8,456	3	19	163.0	76	66
Canada	3	1	8	24	0	32	9,858	5	3	29.0	99	77
Colombia	4	4	6	12	0	8	1,039	3	34	35.0	88	66
Chile	5	2	7	12	0	12	749	7	19	14.0	94	72
Peru	6	3	7	11	0	9	1,280	4	19	24.0	80	63
Argentina	7	2	7	10	0	14	2,736	7	12	34.0	94	70
Cuba	8	3	6	9	0	10	111	7	103	11.0	98	73
Mexico	9	1	8	8	0	4	1,923	5	49	95.0	89	70
Venezuela	10	1	7	4	0	4	882	6	25	22.0	85	70
El Salvador	11	4	5	3	0	8	21	7	276	5.8	65	62
Ecuador	12	2	6	3	0	4	277	3	43	12.0	86	66
Nicaragua	13	3	6	2	0	12	120	4	38	4.5	87	62
Bolivia	14	2	4	1	0	3	1,084	4	7	8.1	62	54
Uruguay	15	1	6	1	0	5	174	7	18	3.2	94	71
Dominican Rep.	16	1	7	0	0	2	48	5	167	8.0	74	62
Paraguay	17	1	5	0	0	3	397	5	13	5.0	81	69
Guatemala	18	3	6	0	0	1	108	4	98	11.0	50	61
Costa Rica	19	1	8	0	0	4	51	3	65	3.3	93	76
Panama	20	1	6	0	0	2	76	7	36	2.7	90	73
Honduras	21	3	6	0	0	1	112	6	53	5.9	56	65
Jamaica	22	2	7	0	0	6	11	8	236	2.6	74	76
Trinidad	23	1	8	0	0	5	5	8	260	1.3	98	70
Haiti	24	3	5	0	0	1	28	5	257	7.2	23	55

(continued)

	Country Profile						Geographic Profile		Population Profile			
Country	War Rank	War State	Government's Stability	War Power	Attack Power	Total Quality	Area of sq km (in thousands)	Military Environment Index	Population (per sq km)	Population Total (in millions)	Percent of Literacy	Life Expectancy
European Nations												
Russia	1	4	6	417	154	24	17,075	4	9	149.0	95	69
France	2	2	9	188	18	46	546	5	106	58.0	99	75
Germany	3	2	9	178	13	46	350	6	234	82.0	99	74
Turkey	4	4	6	168	7	31	771	5	80	62.0	70	64
Britain	5	2	8	130	9	48	242	6	244	59.0	99	75
Ukraine	6	2	6	75	2	15	604	4	86	52.0	98	69
Italy	7	2	6	69	2	20	294	5	201	59.0	93	76
Poland	8	1	6	64	2	23	305	8	128	39.0	98	70
Spain	9	2	7	38	1	17	499	5	80	40.0	97	77
Yugoslavia	10	5	6	35	0	26	102	5	103	11.0	91	73
Bosnia	11	6	5	28	0	26	51	4	84	4.3	99	75
Romania	12	1	6	26	0	11	230	6	102	23.0	98	70
Greece	13	3	6	24	0	14	131	5	84	11.0	95	77
Croatia	14	5	6	21	0	19	57	5	84	4.8	99	73
Czech Republic	15	1	8	13	0	13	71	6	146	10.0	99	71
Netherlands	16	1	8	13	0	18	34	7	465	16.0	99	77
Hungary	17	1	8	13	0	16	92	8	114	11.0	99	69
Sweden	18	1	9	12	0	19	412	5	21	8.8	99	77
Belgium	19	2	7	11	0	17	30	9	333	10.0	99	77
Austria	20	2	8	10	0	18	83	6	96	8.0	98	75
Bulgaria	21	1	7	10	0	9	111	7	77	8.6	94	71

Belarus	22	2	6	9	0	10	207	6	53	11.0	99	70
Finland	23	1	9	8	0	23	305	4	17	5.1	99	75
Azerbaijan	24	6	4	8	0	14	87	5	87	7.6	99	70
Armenia	25	6	6	7	0	20	30	4	113	3.4	99	72
Norway	26	1	9	6	0	18	308	4	14	4.3	99	76
Portugal	27	2	7	6	0	11	92	7	120	11.0	84	74
Denmark	28	1	8	5	0	17	42	8	124	5.2	99	75
Uzbekistan	29	4	5	5	0	10	447	3	51	23.0	95	68
Switzerland	30	1	9	4	0	18	40	4	175	7.0	99	78
Albania	31	2	6	4	0	6	27	5	126	3.4	75	73
Slovakia	32	2	6	3	0	7	49	5	114	5.6	96	72
Turkmenistan	33	3	5	3	0	6	488	5	9	4.2	88	65
Georgia	34	6	4	3	0	16	70	5	81	5.7	98	72
Kazakhstan	35	3	5	3	0	6	2,717	5	7	18.0	90	68
Moldova	36	3	3	2	0	13	34	5	132	4.5	97	68
Slovenia	37	5	3	1	0	13	20	4	99	2.0	95	74
Ireland	38	3	6	1	0	8	69	5	52	3.6	99	76
Macedonia	39	1	8	1	0	9	25	3	92	2.3	90	73
Palestine	40	3	5	1	0	9	6	6	323	2.0	80	68
Lithuania	41	4	5	1	0	9	65	6	60	3.9	98	71
Kyrgyzstan	42	1	6	1	0	6	198	5	25	5.0	90	67
Tajikistan	43	2	5	1	0	13	143	4	43	6.2	90	68
Latvia	44	6	4	1	0	10	64	7	42	2.7	99	69
Estonia	45	1	7	0	0	12	45	7	38	1.7	40	55
Middle East Nations												
Iran	1	5	6	128	2	24	1,636	4	41	67.0	49	57
Egypt	2	3	6	104	2	23	995	7	62	62.0	45	59
Israel	3	3	8	87	5	46	21	9	248	5.2	82	77

(continued)

	Country Profile						Geographic Profile		Population Profile			
Country	Rank	War State	Government's Stability	War Power	Attack Power	Total Quality	Area of sq km (in thousands)	Military Environment Index	Population (per sq km)	Population Total (in millions)	Percent of Literacy	Life Expectancy
Iraq	4	4	5	70	2	16	434	7	46	20.0	56	66
Syria	5	1	7	42	0	10	184	6	78	14.0	47	68
Saudi Arabia	6	2	7	29	0	17	2,150	6	9	18.0	52	66
Morocco	7	3	7	23	0	11	446	6	60	28.0	28	64
Algeria	8	4	6	21	0	18	2,382	6	13	30.0	52	65
Jordan	9	2	7	19	0	18	92	8	45	4.1	71	69
Sudan	10	6	5	7	0	6	2,376	7	12	29.0	30	53
Yemen	11	3	5	6	0	9	528	6	21	11.0	20	50
Lebanon	12	3	5	6	0	12	10	7	370	3.7	74	67
United Arab Emir.	13	1	7	5	0	7	84	9	30	2.5	68	70
Libya	14	3	6	3	0	4	1,760	7	3	5.1	55	66
Kuwait	15	2	6	3	0	15	18	9	94	1.7	72	74
Tunisia	16	1	6	2	0	4	155	7	57	8.9	63	69
Oman	17	2	6	2	0	3	212	8	10	2.2	20	56
South Asian Nations												
India	1	2	7	306	15	23	2,974	3	309	920.0	37	57
Pakistan	2	4	5	121	1	19	779	5	166	129.0	27	54
Burma	3	3	6	27	0	9	658	3	70	46.0	78	55
Sri Lanka	4	6	7	18	0	13	65	4	277	18.0	87	69
Bangladesh	5	3	5	10	0	9	134	7	940	126.0	29	53
Nepal	6	3	6	5	0	12	137	2	161	22.0	20	50
Afghanistan	7	7	2	5	0	7	647	4	25	16.0	12	42
Bhutan	8	1	6	0	0	1	47	4	43	2.0	5	48

East Asian Nations	#											
China	1	3	6	528	123	17	9,596	5	135	1,300.0	75	69
Korea, North	2	2	4	183	9	15	121	3	198	24.0	93	69
Korea, South	3	2	7	155	7	23	98	3	469	46.0	93	69
Taiwan	4	2	7	139	4	32	14	6	1,571	22.0	95	73
Vietnam	5	2	7	96	2	16	330	4	224	74.0	78	64
Japan	6	2	8	72	4	28	378	5	333	126.0	99	79
Indonesia	7	3	7	47	1	16	1,827	4	111	202.0	62	59
Thailand	8	2	8	19	0	7	512	5	117	60.0	82	65
Australia	9	1	9	18	0	28	7,618	4	2	18.0	98	77
Malaysia	10	2	7	18	0	14	329	4	61	20.0	65	67
Philippines	11	3	6	14	0	13	298	3	225	67.0	87	66
Singapore	12	1	9	12	0	21	1	8	3,000	3.0	87	74
Cambodia	13	5	5	10	0	11	177	4	62	11.0	48	48
New Zealand	14	1	9	2	0	17	269	5	13	3.6	99	76
Mongolia	15	1	6	2	0	8	1,565	7	1	2.3	80	65
Laos	16	3	4	2	0	4	231	5	21	4.9	85	49
Papua-New Guinea	17	2	5	0	0	2	452	2	10	4.5	33	54

Economic Profile | Military Capability

Country	Rank	GDP (in billions)	Per Capita GDP (in thousands)	Active Manpower (in thousands)	Military Budget (in millions)	Percent of GDP	Budget per Man (in thousands)	Equivalent Divisions	Armored Fighting Vehicles	Combat-Capable Aircraft	Combat Ships	Navy
Averages & Totals		$25,798	$4.5	22,120	$693,066	2.7	$31	1,163	316,153	43,458	3,278	311
Africa		300	1	930	6,917	2.3	7	42	9,098	858	822	N/A
Americas		8,405	11	2,940	283,235	3.4	96	131	52,705	9,491	1,523	N/A
Europe		10,005	11	6,182	244,106	2.4	39	387	147,140	13,774	1,662	N/A
Middle East		581	77	2,910	38,720	6.7	13	149	53,210	4,123	220	N/A
South Asia		423	0	2,437	13,241	3.1	5	94	11,140	1,631	61	N/A
Southeast Asia		6,084	3	6,721	106,847	1.8	16	360	42,860	9,597	624	N/A
African Nations												
South Africa	1	135	3.2	75	3,000	2.2	40	3	4,000	200	15	5
Nigeria	2	33	0.3	77	210	0.6	3	4	900	110	12	3
Ethiopia	3	4	0.1	100	150	3.8	2	6	400	30	8	0
Angola	4	4	0.3	85	800	20.0	9	2	400	90	2	1
Eritrea	5	1	0.3	20	30	3.0	2	1	40	0	3	1
Zimbabwe	6	6	0.5	44	210	3.5	5	3	220	44	0	0
Tanzania	7	4	0.1	50	90	2.3	2	2	270	21	0	2
Rwanda	8	1	0.1	15	55	5.5	4	0	25	0	0	0
Somalia	9	1	0.1	45	0	0.0	0	0	100	0	2	0
Kenya	10	9	0.3	25	220	2.4	9	1	210	60	5	1
Chad	11	2	0.2	30	75	5.0	3	1	122	4	0	0
Uganda	12	4	0.2	46	100	2.9	2	2	50	0	0	0
Cameroon	13	11	0.8	22	125	1.1	6	1	55	18	2	1
Senegal	14	7	0.8	14	144	2.1	10	1	100	8	0	1
Zaire	15	8	0.2	45	245	3.1	5	4	145	20	0	1

16	Mozambique	2	0.1	30	75	3.8	3	2	300	35	0	1
17	Gabon	7	4.7	5	155	2.3	31	0	100	24	1	1
18	Ghana	8	0.5	7	110	1.4	16	1	55	18	0	1
19	Madagascar	4	0.3	21	40	1.1	2	1	115	12	1	1
20	Ivory Coast	10	0.7	14	144	1.4	10	0	50	5	2	1
21	Gambia	4	0.4	24	65	1.6	3	1	145	55	0	0
22	Niger	3	0.3	5	35	1.2	7	0	155	0	0	0
23	Mauretania	1	0.6	15	36	2.6	2	1	140	6	0	1
24	Guinea-Bisseau	0	0.3	9	9	3.0	1	0	65	3	0	1
25	Burundi	1	0.2	15	30	3.0	2	0	60	5	0	0
26	Mali	4	0.4	7	75	2.1	11	1	110	15	0	1
27	Sierra Leone	0	0.1	7	15	3.8	2	0	20	0	0	0
28	Liberia	1	0.3	5	15	1.5	3	0	0	0	0	1
29	Congo	2	0.7	9	60	3.0	7	0	200	18	0	0
30	Botswana	4	2.7	7	185	4.6	26	0	50	18	0	1
31	Namibia	3	1.4	8	60	2.0	8	1	40	0	1	0
32	Malawi	3	0.3	10	25	1.0	3	0	40	2	0	0
33	Guinea	4	0.5	10	55	1.5	6	1	120	11	1	1
34	Burkina Faso	4	0.3	9	110	3.1	12	0	100	10	0	0
35	Togo	2	0.5	7	55	2.8	8	0	90	16	0	1
36	Central Afr. Rep.	1	0.4	5	35	2.5	7	0	50	0	0	0
37	Benin	2	0.4	5	45	1.9	9	0	40	0	0	0
38	Lesotho	1	0.4	2	25	3.6	13	0	16	0	0	0
39	Swaziland	1	1.0	1	4	0.4	4	0	0	0	0	0
	American Nations											
1	United States	6,500	24.8	1,500	260,000	4.0	173	35	42,000	7,500	429	10
2	Brazil	480	2.9	333	5,000	1.0	15	18	1,800	340	25	7
3	Canada	620	21.4	70	8,000	1.3	114	7	1,600	300	25	3

(continued)

Economic Profile | Military Capability

Country	Rank	GDP (in billions)	Per Capita GDP (in thousands)	Active Manpower (in thousands)	Military Budget (in millions)	Percent of GDP	Budget per Man (in thousands)	Equivalent Divisions	Armored Fighting Vehicles	Combat-Capable Aircraft	Combat Ships	Navy
Colombia	4	$48	$1.4	144	$1,000	2.1	$7	5	290	145	8	3
Chile	5	55	3.9	90	1,200	2.2	13	6	500	125	14	6
Peru	6	55	2.3	120	800	1.5	7	11	600	110	32	4
Argentina	7	120	3.5	65	3,000	2.5	46	6	1,100	285	30	6
Cuba	8	11	1.0	85	155	1.4	2	10	2,800	85	30	3
Mexico	9	350	3.7	175	1,500	0.4	9	10	350	135	21	3
Venezuela	10	65	3.0	77	800	1.2	10	4	500	155	14	4
El Salvador	11	7	1.2	30	110	1.6	4	2	90	45	0	1
Ecuador	12	15	1.3	55	550	3.7	10	3	220	85	16	2
Nicaragua	13	2	0.4	15	70	3.5	5	1	200	2	0	1
Bolivia	14	7	0.9	33	125	1.8	4	3	150	60	0	2
Uruguay	15	12	3.8	22	220	1.8	10	2	220	24	3	1
Dominican Rep.	16	9	1.1	22	120	1.3	5	1	45	10	20	1
Paraguay	17	6	1.2	16	80	1.3	5	1	80	20	0	1
Guatemala	18	12	1.1	42	120	1.0	3	2	60	22	0	1
Costa Rica	19	8	2.4	8	100	1.3	13	1	0	2	0	1
Panama	20	7	2.6	12	90	1.3	8	1	0	0	0	1
Honduras	21	4	0.7	16	50	1.3	3	1	80	36	0	1
Jamaica	22	3	1.3	3	30	0.9	9	0	12	0	0	1
Trinidad	23	6	4.6	3	90	1.5	35	0	0	0	0	1
Haiti	24	3	0.4	5	25	0.8	5	0	8	5	0	1

European Nations													
1	Russia	1,200	8.1	1,600	75,000	6.3	47	85	45,000	3,800	845	9
2	France	1,400	24.1	380	36,000	2.6	95	26	7,400	990	83	7
3	Germany	1,900	23.2	360	25,000	1.3	69	15	9,500	710	81	4
4	Turkey	175	2.8	500	7,200	4.1	14	24	9,000	650	50	6
5	Britain	1,200	20.3	250	32,000	2.7	128	8	5,300	720	99	8
6	Ukraine	56	1.1	450	3,000	5.4	7	18	12,000	1,200	3	3
7	Italy	1,250	21.2	310	15,000	1.2	48	7	4,200	460	41	5
8	Poland	90	2.3	260	2,400	2.7	9	15	4,000	480	18	3
9	Spain	590	14.8	200	6,500	1.1	33	12	3,400	190	42	6
10	Yugoslavia	10	1.0	125	900	9.0	7	9	1,300	360	27	3
11	Bosnia	2	0.5	100	800	40.0	8	5	200	0	3	0
12	Romania	40	1.7	220	1,100	2.8	5	11	4,400	450	3	3
13	Greece	81	7.4	160	3,400	4.2	21	15	4,800	330	47	3
14	Croatia	12	2.5	100	800	6.7	8	4	400	30	3	2
15	Czech Republic	30	2.9	90	780	2.6	9	5	3,100	190	0	0
16	Netherlands	350	22.2	65	7,000	2.0	108	3	1,900	180	27	4
17	Hungary	37	3.5	72	600	1.6	8	6	2,600	200	0	0
18	Sweden	250	28.4	60	4,500	1.8	75	15	1,300	450	50	3
19	Belgium	240	24.0	60	4,000	1.7	67	5	1,800	110	4	2
20	Austria	190	23.8	50	1,500	0.8	30	5	700	50	0	0
21	Bulgaria	20	2.3	100	500	2.5	5	5	3,300	320	12	2
22	Belarus	16	1.5	90	420	2.6	5	5	6,500	330	3	0
23	Finland	107	21.0	31	1,500	1.4	48	21	440	110	12	3
24	Azerbaijan	4	0.6	50	133	3.0	3	4	600	44	3	0
25	Armenia	2	0.6	30	75	3.8	3	2	500	12	3	0
26	Norway	120	27.9	33	3,000	2.5	91	5	550	75	64	3
27	Portugal	88	8.0	50	1,500	1.7	30	4	550	75	20	3

(continued)

Economic Profile | Military Capability

Country	Rank	GDP (in billions)	Per Capita GDP (in thousands)	Active Manpower (in thousands)	Military Budget (in millions)	Percent of GDP	Budget per Man (in thousands)	Equivalent Divisions	Armored Fighting Vehicles	Combat-Capable Aircraft	Combat Ships	Navy
Denmark	28	$150	$28.8	25	$2,800	1.9	$112	3	1,000	80	29	2
Uzbekistan	29	14	0.6	44	365	2.6	8	2	800	188	3	0
Switzerland	30	250	35.7	22	4,000	1.6	182	18	1,900	280	0	0
Albania	31	2	0.6	55	90	4.5	2	3	800	70	3	1
Slovakia	32	12	2.1	45	300	2.5	7	3	2,100	150	3	0
Turkmenistan	33	4	1.0	50	133	3.0	3	4	600	44	3	0
Georgia	34	3	0.4	15	90	3.6	6	1	200	30	3	1
Kazakhstan	35	20	1.1	41	400	2.0	10	4	3,600	210	3	0
Moldova	36	4	0.9	12	50	1.3	4	1	180	22	3	0
Slovenia	37	14	7.0	8	250	1.8	31	1	110	2	3	1
Ireland	38	54	15.0	13	500	0.9	38	1	120	31	5	1
Macedonia	39	2	0.9	10	40	2.0	4	1	90	2	3	0
Palestine	40	4	1.8	10	50	1.4	5	1	50	0	3	0
Lithuania	41	3	0.8	9	100	3.0	11	1	20	3	3	1
Kyrgyzstan	42	3	0.6	12	55	1.8	5	1	600	122	3	0
Tajikistan	43	2	0.4	5	125	5.2	25	1	100	22	3	0
Latvia	44	2	0.7	7	60	3.3	9	1	20	2	3	1
Estonia	45	2	1.1	3	90	5.0	36	1	110	0	3	1
Middle East Nations												
Iran	1	60	0.9	500	2,500	4.2	5	20	2,400	250	16	3
Egypt	2	44	0.7	420	1,800	4.1	4	16	7,500	530	42	3
Israel	3	72	13.8	175	7,000	9.7	40	12	8,500	600	28	3

Iraq	4	18	0.9	400	2,800	15.6	7	35	6,000	310	8	3
Syria	5	27	1.9	410	800	3.0	2	14	9,200	700	20	3
Saudi Arabia	6	130	7.1	160	12,000	9.2	75	5	4,600	320	14	3
Morocco	7	30	1.1	190	1,000	3.3	5	8	1,900	125	5	3
Algeria	8	45	1.5	110	1,400	3.1	13	8	2,400	260	24	3
Jordan	9	6	1.5	95	420	7.0	4	5	2,400	125	0	1
Sudan	10	7	0.2	115	750	10.7	7	5	900	65	0	1
Yemen	11	8	0.7	62	400	5.0	6	4	2,100	150	9	3
Lebanon	12	7	1.9	45	350	5.0	8	2	1,100	22	0	1
United Arab Emir.	13	38	15.2	62	2,000	5.3	32	2	700	130	3	3
Libya	14	32	6.3	70	1,200	3.8	17	6	2,500	350	32	3
Kuwait	15	26	15.3	17	2,000	7.7	118	2	450	100	10	1
Tunisia	16	18	2.0	36	500	2.8	14	3	440	36	4	2
Oman	17	13	5.9	43	1,800	13.8	42	2	120	50	5	1
South Asian Nations												
India	1	310	0.3	1,250	7,500	2.4	6	40	4,400	880	67	7
Pakistan	2	54	0.4	580	3,300	6.1	6	22	3,100	440	22	6
Burma	3	15	0.3	270	1,200	8.0	4	15	240	101	1	3
Sri Lanka	4	11	0.6	122	500	4.5	4	3	220	44	0	2
Bangladesh	5	26	0.2	111	400	1.5	4	5	150	66	2	2
Nepal	6	3	0.1	40	40	1.3	1	3	30	0	0	0
Afghanistan	7	3	0.2	60	300	10.0	5	5	3,000	100	0	0
Bhutan	8	0	0.2	4	1	0.3	0.3	1	0	0	0	0
East Asian Nations												
China	1	600	0.5	2,800	7,000	1.2	3	95	12,000	5,800	335	8
Korea, North	2	20	0.8	1,100	2,200	11.0	2	45	11,200	820	37	6
Korea, South	3	350	7.6	620	16,000	4.6	26	46	4,500	630	31	6
Taiwan	4	240	10.9	400	10,000	4.2	25	30	2,600	520	43	5

(continued)

Economic Profile   Military Capability

Country	Rank	GDP (in billions)	Per Capita GDP (in thousands)	Active Manpower (in thousands)	Military Budget (in millions)	Percent of GDP	Budget per Man (in thousands)	Equivalent Divisions	Armored Fighting Vehicles	Combat Capable Aircraft	Combat Ships	Navy
Vietnam	5	$22	$0.3	550	$500	2.3	$1	68	3,500	220	14	5
Japan	6	4,000	31.7	235	50,000	1.3	213	14	1,800	520	82	8
Indonesia	7	145	0.7	270	2,400	1.7	9	14	500	128	21	6
Thailand	8	130	2.2	255	3,600	2.8	14	16	1,300	220	12	5
Australia	9	330	18.0	60	6,500	2.0	108	4	850	177	18	5
Malaysia	10	70	3.5	115	3,000	4.3	26	6	1,020	105	10	2
Philippines	11	60	0.9	105	1,400	2.3	13	9	480	155	10	4
Singapore	12	60	20.0	55	3,300	5.5	60	6	1,200	180	6	3
Cambodia	13	3	0.3	85	50	1.7	1	3	300	20	?	1
New Zealand	14	46	12.8	10	700	1.5	70	1	100	44	5	3
Mongolia	15	1	0.2	22	22	4.4	1	1	1,400	26	0	0
Laos	16	2	0.3	35	105	7.0	3	2	110	30	?	0
Papua-New Guinea	17	6	1.3	4	70	1.2	18	0	0	2	0	1

Notes on Nations' Military Power and Their
Wars

(for those who are not keen on numerical analysis)

What follows is a brief comment on each nation in alphabetical order.

Afghanistan—Ethnic and religious (degrees of Islamic zealotry) rivalries fuel the fighting. No end in sight, save a truce through exhaustion. The fighting will not go much beyond its own borders because of the civil war left in the wake of the Russian withdrawal in 1987. Even after the civil war is settled, Afghanistan will continue to pose no major threat to its neighbors, except for unpredictable raids by one of the many continually warring factions. Alexander the Great encountered this twenty-five hundred years ago, which goes to show you that there are some things that are consistent in history.

Albania—Too small, too obsessed with internal post-Communist disorder, and surrounded by stronger powers. Its major military threat beyond its borders is official or unofficial support to ethnic Albanian populations in neighboring countries, especially Yugoslavia (Kosovo) and Greece. Clan rivalries increase internal trouble.

Algeria—Civil war is between the wealthy minority of old revolutionaries controlling the government and army, versus Islamic fundamentalists. The Berber minority is caught in the middle. The economy is a mess, military in disarray.

Angola—The long war between the formerly Communist MPLA government and the UNITA (formerly a socialist lot) lurches to a conclusion after both sides are abandoned by their cold war patrons. Peace agreements have been signed, but warring parties have not yet sorted out all the details, nor has everyone disarmed. The United States has quit backing UNITA.

Argentina—Still suffering the aftereffects (low morale and reduced budgets) of their 1982 defeat by Great Britain in the Falklands War. Slowly rebuilding. Argentina and Britain have been arguing over the Falkland/Malvinas islands for more than a century.

Armenia—Nagorno-Karabakh is a province in Azerbaijan populated by Armenians. A war has erupted between Azerbaijan and Armenia over who controls it. So far the Armenians are winning. In the process, Armenia's economy has been wrecked.

Australia—Beset by economic problems, and the lack of any immediate threat, their armed forces slowly fade away. Troops are well equipped and professional.

Austria—Officially neutral since the 1950s, and now without a Warsaw Pact threat. Not likely to increase its forces.

Azerbaijan—Has had a series of internal disputes since gaining its independence from the Soviet Union in 1991. It is also involved in an ongoing war with neighboring Armenia over long-disputed territory.

Bahrain—Threatened by Iraq and Iran; friendly to U.S. forces and likely to increase its own fundamentalist internal disorder.

Bangladesh—Poverty-stricken and without any armed threats except from within.

Belarus—Another new nation formed in the wake of the Soviet Union's demise. Poor economy, poor armed forces, and not much else.

Belgium—Never quite able to meet all of its NATO commitments; now retrenching in the face of the nonexistent Warsaw Pact threat.

Belize—Long-standing tension with Guatemala (which claims Belize as a "lost province") produces avid attention to military matters and ties with Great Britain.

Benin—Poor African nation with no active external enemies.

Bhutan—Poverty-stricken monarchy on India's northern border. Nominal defense forces and no disputes with anyone.

Bolivia—Long-festering dispute with Chile over lost access to ocean. Nation is too poor to create an armed force that can do anything about it. Military activity largely against internal opposition.

Bosnia-Herzegovina—Has been torn by civil war among Serb, Muslim, and Croat factions since splitting away from Yugoslavia in 1992. Muslims held control of the government, and most of the troops. Serbs had nearly as many troops, but the alliance of the local Croats with the Muslims gave the Muslim/Croat combination nearly a two-to-one manpower advantage over the Serbs. NATO created a shaky peace in late 1995.

Botswana—Poor, landlocked African nation with minor border disputes with neighbors. Insignificant armed forces. Simmering border dispute with Namibia, Zambia, and Zimbabwe.

Brazil—The major military power in South America. Minor border disputes with Paraguay and Uruguay.

Brunei—Incredibly rich oil state surrounded by Malaysia. No disputes with larger neighbor, but protected by British Gurkha mercenaries and diplomatic alliances.

Bulgaria—Fear of the Turks, and a weakening of its traditional Russian "protector," are likely to keep the military in a strong bargaining position.

Burkina Faso—Landlocked, poor, internal strife, and not much military power.

Burma—Poor nation ruled by junta and beset by many internal disputes. No disputes with neighbors. Ethnic and political opponents to the government operate in remote border areas.

Burundi—Poor, landlocked, no external disputes. Major conflict between majority Hutu people and militarily stronger minority Tutsi. Tutsis and Hutus continue centuries of ethnic conflict that threatens to turn into a mass slaughter similar to what took place in neighboring Rwanda during 1994.

Cambodia—Fifteen-year-old civil war finally ended and UN-supervised elections were conducted. Khmer Rouge continue to defy newly formed government, although they continue to fight mainly to protect the timber-smuggling racket they have established on the Thai border.

Cameroon—Minor border disputes with neighbors, little internal unrest. Nominal armed forces.

Canada—Maintains nominal armed forces; relies on U.S. Fleet for protection from any potential threats.

Cape Verde Islands—Nominal armed forces, no internal or external disputes or significant external threats.

Central African Republic—Poor, landlocked, no external disputes, some internal. Nominal armed forces.

Chad—Nigeria has tried to bring peace to this longtime ethnic dispute, with some factions backed by Libya. France has also been involved in trying to keep the peace. The ongoing civil war is partially fomented by Libya. Some factions are supported by France. Weak central government.

Chile—Strong economy, democratic government, efficient military tradition but shrinking armed forces because of lack of internal or external threat. The Tacna-Arica region provides a long-standing territorial dispute among Chile, Peru, and Bolivia.

China—Increasing unrest, but 1980s decision to shrink, and modernize, armed forces is still under way. Priority is still economic development. Unrest between the locals in Tibet and China has been ongoing since China took over in the 1950s. There is also a looming civil war in China; also, the longtime enmity between mainland China and Taiwan. Both are still officially at war and both are positioned to restart the fighting. China has insisted that it will invade if Taiwan declares independence. Taiwan, with an increasingly democratic government, has already renounced claims to rule all of China and is moving toward independence. This could get ugly. Disputes between China and Russia are dormant for the moment, but the antagonisms over territory remain. In the South China Sea, oil and claims to several small island groups here have led to a dispute among the Philippines, China, Taiwan, and Vietnam.

Colombia—Armed forces partially corrupted by drug traffickers. Paramilitary forces are steadily increased to fight drug lords. Endemic internal disorder for the last forty years. Population is heavily armed and quick to use their guns.

Comoro Islands—Minor dispute with France, but otherwise a militarily insignificant ministate. France rescued the government from a mercenary takeover in 1995.

Congo—Minor dispute with Zaire over border, minor internal opposition. Nominal armed forces.

Costa Rica—No armed forces, only paramilitary troops. No internal or external disputes.

Croatia—Fought its way free from Yugoslav domination in 1993 and defeated its Serb minority in 1995. Well-organized, -equipped, and -led armed forces, usually allied with the Bosnians.

Cuba—Large armed forces, which are rapidly deteriorating; declining economy, no external threats (except the imagined U.S. one), and growing internal opposition.

Cyprus (Greek)—Heavily armed Greek portion of Cyprus faces Turkish forces in other part of island. The UN keeps the peace between Turkish and Greek locals as well as a Turk army in the northern part of the island.

Cyprus (Turkish)—See above.

Czech Republic—No external threats. Declining armed forces due to demise of Warsaw Pact, but planned rebuilding of armed forces using Western equipment.

Denmark—No external or internal threats. Declining armed forces due to demise of Warsaw Pact.

Dhofar—A long-simmering dispute between Oman and Dhofar insurgents. Not much fireworks of late, but plenty of potential.

Djibouti—Dispute with Somalia over border and Somali nomads. Strong ties with France and basically under French protection. Internally, the Somali-speaking Issa tribe struggles against Afar nomads of the Afar-based Front for the Restoration of Unity and Democracy (FRUD), against the government. The government has fifteen thousand troops. The French seem to have lost the ability to mediate, but they control their base and 60 percent of GDP.

Dominican Republic—No external disputes, low-level internal dissent. Weak armed forces.

Ecuador—Border dispute with Peru (Maranon River area; Peru and Ecuador have long argued over their border in the Amazon area), internal disorder. Lackluster armed forces.

Egypt—Long-standing disputes with Sudan and Libya, minor internal disorder. Military is professional and good at getting the most out of a low budget.

El Salvador—Ongoing civil war has laped to criminal peace.

Equatorial Guinea—Minor dispute with Gabon, weak economy, and low-level internal disputes. Lackluster armed forces.

Eritrea—Well-trained and battle-experienced armed forces, but poorly equipped. Dispute with Sudan and potential internal problems, because population is half Christian and half Muslim.

Estonia—Ethnic, commercial, and diplomatic ties to neighboring Finland provide some additional protection from another Russian takeover. Tiny armed forces organized and led by former American Army colonel of Estonian extraction.

Ethiopia—Even with the Communist government gone, ethnic factions battle on. Somalia and Ethiopia dispute ownership of the Ogaden desert region (controlled by Ethiopia), whose normal population (most are refugees now) are Somalis.

Finland—Neutral and well prepared to defend itself.

France—Well-diversified armed forces, from strategic nuclear missiles to intervention forces.

Gabon—Minor dispute with Equatorial Guinea and some internal disputes.

Georgia—Small, but feisty, minority in the Ossetia region in rebellion. New nation wracked by internal disputes among various factions.

Germany—Newly unified; military will be smaller than during the cold war. Most professional and effective armed forces in Europe.

Ghana—Ongoing internal disputes, above average (for Africa) armed forces.

Great Britain—Domestic economic problems and the disappearance of the Warsaw Pact have created a decline in force levels. The problem in Ulster, the last piece of Ireland controlled by Britain, first came along in the twelfth century. The Protestant Irish want to stay with Britain; the Catholics want to join with the Republic of Ireland. Recent (1994–95) peace talks have quieted things down a bit.

Greece—Major military objective is preparation for a war with Turkey, which Greece has little chance of winning. The Aegean Sea supplies a potential conflict between Turkey and Greece. The dispute goes back nearly a thousand years. No resolution in sight, and occasionally there's some shooting.

Guatemala—Claims Belize, but lacks the military force to take it. Much internal dissent, ongoing war with insurgent groups.

Guinea—Very poor nation with equally poor armed forces.

Guinea-Bissau—Very poor nation with equally poor armed forces.

Guyana—Disputes with Venezuela and Suriname. Nominal armed forces and unstable internal situation.

Haiti—Civil unrest continues, even with a democratically elected government. Very poor nation formerly run by armed forces. Nation no longer has any armed forces.

Honduras—Some disputes with Honduras, quite a bit of internal dissent. Armed forces oriented toward suppressing insurgency.

Hungary—Downsizing and restructuring its armed forces in face of demise of the Warsaw Pact and growing potential for war with Romania over territorial dispute.

Iceland—Nominal armed forces; depends on United States.

India—Regional superpower, with lots of good infantry, some tanks, and a few nukes. The struggle among nationalists, the government, and sundry ethnic and religious groups causes some internal instability. The long-standing (since 1948) antagonism between India and Pakistan continues to make another major war possible. A conflict among India, the Kashmiris, and Pakistan over who should control Kashmir serves as the focus of the India-Pakistan dispute. Several territorial disputes remain between China and India. India has been fighting Nagaland insurgents since the late 1940s.

Indonesia—Sundry minor disputes with numerous island neighbors plus some serious internal unrest. Armed forces largely paramilitary. Irian Barat is an area that Indonesia has been trying to pacify for years. In Timor, the locals have been fighting Indonesia for over ten years. At times, it gets quite bloody.

Iran—Demobilized after disastrous war with Iraq in the 1980s. Rebuilding forces on a more professional model. Still faces substantial internal problems and possible renewal of war with Iraq. Iran has an internal conflict. The insurgents are supported by Iraq, but Iran's theocratic rulers have most to fear from a widespread unhappiness with a sagging economy. Iran and Iraq's conflict has been low level since 1988, but armed clashes still occur. Iran wants revenge for the 1980s war and is rearming. In the Persian Gulf, the situation continues to fester, as Iran occupies islands in the Strait of Hormuz and generally behaves like it owns the Gulf (which is what worries Saudi Arabia, the United States, the UAE, Qatar, and Bahrain).

Iraq—So-so armed forces and lots of internal and external enemies. Kurdistan is still in flames, as a UN-administered "safe haven" in northern Iraq encourages Kurd nationalism. Iran and Iraq wait on the sidelines while Kurds and Turks battle each other in eastern Turkey.

Ireland—Nominal armed forces, no real foreign or internal threats.

Israel—Armed to the teeth and very good at combat. Forces lose their edge after many years of inaction, but not as quickly as hostile neighbors in the same situation. Biggest problem is internal, with Arab population. This internal conflict has changed, as Israel agreed in 1994 to give PLO-controlled Palestinians some autonomy. More radical Palestinian factions still wage a terror campaign.

Italy—Conscript-based forces, with many professional segments. Shrinking in face of end of cold war. Major reorganization under way, with an eye toward having only professionals in the armed forces.

Ivory Coast—No local and few internal disputes. Somewhat above-average armed forces for Africa.

Jamaica—Very small, but professional, armed forces. No external, but a few internal, disputes.

Japan—Well-trained and lavishly equipped forces. Without nuclear weapons, not likely to cause neighboring China or Russia any trouble.

Jordan—Small, but professional, armed forces. Not as good as they used to be, but still a cut above all the neighbors (except Israel).

Kazakhstan—Small, well-equipped (because of Soviet Union weapons in place at independence) army and air force. No external threats, but possibility of internal disorder.

Kenya—Increasing internal disputes put the military's traditional professionalism to the test.

Korea, North—Well-trained and -equipped and likely to follow orders (at least initially). Country in danger of political upheaval, which the military may not be able to handle.

Korea, South—Similar to North Korean forces, with somewhat more modern equipment. More politically reliable, if only because the South is a functioning democracy. The 1950–53 war has paused, via an armistice, not ended. South Korea, North Korea, and the United States are still there.

Kuwait—Forces crushed by Iraq in mid-1990, rebuilt in Saudi Arabia, and slated for expansion in the future. Kuwait and Iraq are still technically at war, as Iraq has refused to fully comply with the UN-brokered armistice. Iraq still claims Kuwait as its nineteenth province.

Kyrgyzstan—Small armed forces; nearly half the population consists of ethnic minorities. Tajikistan and Kyrgyzstan have border and ethnic disputes that could lead to war.

Laos—Landlocked backwater with lackluster armed forces and not much to fight over. Vietnam and Laos have some disagreements over real estate and Vietnam's support of Laotian insurgents.

Latvia—Tiny armed forces, about 40 percent of the population is ethnic (mainly Russian) minorities and ever fearful of the Russians taking over again.

Lebanon—Nominally independent, with large Syrian force still occupying the country. Israel occupies southern areas, and pro-Iranian Muslim fundamentalists control areas in the mountains, under Syrian protection. Civil war is largely over, but the Syrians could still annex the country.

Lesotho—Minimal armed forces; depends on South Africa for defense and its very existence.

Liberia—Endemic civil war. Winding down because of mutual exhaustion among the contending groups.

Libya—Lavishly equipped but ineptly trained and led armed forces. Continually interferes with neighbors. Egypt glares at Libya for the latter's intrigues with Sudan. This is an ancient antagonism (going back thousands of years).

Lithuania—Tiny armed forces; about 17 percent of the population is ethnic (mainly Russian) minorities and ever fearful of the Russians taking over again.

Luxembourg—Minimal armed forces; depends on neighbors.

Madagascar—Island nation that disputes ownership of some nearby islands with France. Minimal armed forces.

Malawi—Landlocked, poor, not much military power.

Malaysia—Islamic fundamentalist insurgents are becoming increasingly violent. Some disputes with neighbors of several island groups.

Maldives—Island microstate without much to worry about. Minor dispute over some nearby islands.

Mali—Landlocked, poverty-stricken, not much for the military to do.

Malta—Small island state. Strategic position, theoretical threat from Libya.

Mauritania—Long-standing hostility with Senegal could get serious, although neither side could really afford it.

Mauritius—Small island state without much need for armed forces.

Mexico—Too small to take on the United States up north and much larger than any neighbors to the south. Nominal armed forces.

Moldova—Moldova, whose population is largely Romanian, last belonged to Russia. It is now split by a civil war among Moldovans wanting to be independent, those who want a merger with Romania, and ethnic Russians who want anything but that. These have split off and formed the Trans-Dniester Republic.

Mongolia—Caught between China and Russia, thus only minimal armed forces. China has voiced a desire to get Mongolia "back."

Morocco—Ongoing conflict with separatists in the Western Sahara. Western Sahara-Morocco and Polisario insurgents on verge of making peace. It was supposed to be over years ago, but it isn't. One of the better armed forces in the area.

Mozambique—Ongoing civil war that has finally died down. The nation, including its armed forces, is in disarray.

Nepal—Ongoing internal unrest. Government reluctant to use too much force.

Netherlands—Small but professional military. Scheduled to become smaller with the end of the Warsaw Pact.

New Zealand—Steadily shrinking armed forces. No one in the area to use them on.

Nicaragua—Even with the settlement of the civil war, military remains relatively large but not terribly efficient. Primary objective is internal politics. Insurgents of various flavors still fight the government.

Niger—Landlocked, poor, border dispute with Libya. Chad and Niger have some border and ethnic disputes of long duration.

Nigeria—Military superpower in the region. Lots of quantity, some quality. Threat of another civil war (last one in the 1960s).

Norway—Small but efficient forces, backed by large body of trained reserves.

Oman—Oman and the United Arab Emirates (UAE) still have a long-festering dispute over undefined borders. Not likely to blow up anytime soon, but you never know. Uses a lot of mercenaries; has the money to pay for it.

Pakistan—Fairly large, fairly professional armed forces are faced with many internal threats and one major external one (India). Pakistan has problems with various ethnic groups, special interest groups, Islamic fundamentalists, and tribes.

Palestine—Bit by bit, achieving sovereignty over more territory formerly ruled by Israel. The Palestine Liberation Organization (PLO) has long had bloody internal disputes between insurgents (of various flavors) and the PLO leadership of Yasir Arafat.

Panama—Civil disorder in wake of U.S. 1989 invasion. Only armed forces are primarily paramilitary.

Papua New Guinea—Much of population Stone Age, nominal military. Bougainville, which controls the big Panguna copper mines, wants to separate from Papua New Guinea (PNG). PNG is also fighting an insurgency in Arawa region on big island. Bougainvilleans want to either be free or join one of the Solomons confederations. Armed forces involved are tiny and not heavily armed. Largely a police action.

Paraguay—Landlocked and caught between much larger nations. Low quantity and quality of forces results.

Peru—Beset by internal problems; armed forces organized to deal with it. The Shining Path movement still has some fight left in it. Border conflict with Ecuador.

Philippines—No external enemies, plenty of internal ones. The armed forces reflect this. Still has problems with the Muslim Moros and a few diehard Marxists. Disputes Chinese claims on Spratly Islands.

Poland—Breakup of Warsaw Pact has led to shrinking of army. Morale was low through the 1980s because of internal political strife. Still afraid of Germans and Russians.

Portugal—Big shrinkage after decolonialization of 1970s. Not much rebuilding since. Economy coming back.

Qatar—Another Persian Gulf ministate that tries to purchase the best defense that money can buy.

Romania—Never very efficient in the best of times, has gotten much worse since fall of Communist government in 1989. Still faces possible conflict with Hungary over Transylvania. Romania and Hungary have long argued, and sometimes fought, over who owns Transylvania (currently in Romania, but populated by a large Hungarian minority).

Russia—Massive arms reductions from 1990 treaties, major morale problems, and declines in defense industry efficiency and military budget. But a shadow of what it was in the 1980s, but still formidable, and large. Ingushtia is another Chechnya; in fact, it's right next door in the Caucasus. As of 1995, Russia had not yet responded to the local declarations of independence.

Rwanda—Similar to Burundi, with constant violence between Hutu and Tutsi, except here the Hutus were in charge until the 1994 civil war. Ethnic rivalry between Hutus and Tutsis led to nearly a million (mostly Tutsi) dead in 1994. Millions of Hutus fled as the Tutsi fought back. Now Hutu guerrillas operate out of Zaire.

São Tomé and Principe. Island ministate, of no military significance.

Saudi Arabia—Ancient warrior tradition, but still trying to master the skills of modern soldiering. Continues to suffer from an unending supply of religious zealots, plus an increasingly restive educated class that is more into democracy and less religious (thus further inflaming the zealots).

Senegal—Mauritania and Senegal have a long-standing border dispute. Senegalese troops had a good reputation in the French service during the colonial period. Armed forces a cut above neighboring forces.

Seychelles Islands—Island ministate not much interested in military affairs.

Sierra Leone—Poor, ongoing civil disorder and rebellion. No military power.

Singapore—Small city-state, disproportionately large and efficient armed forces. Robust economy worth defending.

Slovakia—Inherited numerous arms plants building weapons of Russian design. All for export. Local armed forces in bad shape.

Slovenia—Managed to break away from Yugoslavia with minimal damage and has stood apart from the ensuing fighting. Small, but eager, armed forces.

Somalia—Country has been wracked by clan fighting for most of the 1990s. Traditional warriors, have not yet mastered modern warfare. Disputes with all neighbors as well as internal strife. Never a dull moment.

South Africa—Regional superpower. Modern and efficient army, navy, air force, and paramilitary. Probably has nukes. Much internal strife but no neighbors that are a threat. Radical elements of the Xhosa, Zulu, and Boers ethnic groups threaten armed violence.

Spain—Relatively small but gradually modernizing forces. No external threats, although some internal strife.

Sri Lanka—Ongoing civil war, with India looking on, between Sri Lanka and Tamil minority.

Sudan—Ongoing civil war. The dispute between the Arab influenced peoples of the north and the more African groups in the south has been going on for centuries. Libya has provided support to the southerners. Iran now supports the northerners.

Suriname—A shaky government gives rise to various insurgent groups. Ongoing civil strife.

Sweden—Small country, large economy, powerful reserve-based armed forces. A longtime neutral and successful at it.

Switzerland—Same drill as Sweden.

Syria—Long a police state; has a small number of religious, political, and ethnic insurgents. Not much action of late, but the potential is there. At odds with all its neighbors and full of internal strife. Military of questionable efficiency against competent opponent (such as Israel). Syria is discussing peace, and the United States has managed to broker a peace that Jordan can live with.

Taiwan—Losers in 1940s Chinese civil war. Man for man, one of the best armed forces in the region. Some internal strife; still claims rule of mainland China, but unlikely to go to war over it.

Tajikistan—Small, well-equipped (because of Soviet Union weapons in place at independence) army and air force. Tight ties with Russia, which provides armed forces to fight rebels. Some 30 percent of the population are ethnic minorities. Being adjacent to Afghanistan, is beset by Islamic fundamentalist insurgents, as well as Tajiks unhappy with the local dictator.

Tanzania—Minor border disputes, otherwise undistinguished military power.

Thailand—Ongoing problems with several insurgent groups out in the bush. Serious border problems with Cambodia, some internal strife. Armed forces tend toward corruption and lackadaisical performance.

Togo—No significant internal or external threats. Not much in the way of armed forces either.

Trinidad—Island ministate with nominal armed forces.

Tunisia—No internal or external threats and reasonably efficient, but small, armed forces.

Turkey—Some internal strife and disputes with neighbors, but has sufficiently efficient armed forces to handle most situations. Potentially the strongest Muslim power.

Turkmenistan—Small, well-equipped (because of Soviet Union weapons in place at independence) army and air force. No external threats, but possibility of internal disorder. About 20 percent of the population are ethnic minorities.

Uganda—Ongoing civil strife. Still faces ethnic fighting among various tribes.

Ukraine—Crimea, originally conquered by Russia in the nineteenth century, but given to the Soviet Republic of the Ukraine in the 1950s, is now the center of a dispute between Russia and Ukraine over who should now own it.

United Arab Emirates—A collection of oil-rich ministates in the Persian Gulf.

United States—With the decline of Russia's military effectiveness, now the premier world military power.

Uruguay—Surrounded by larger nations, basically a token armed forces whose main task is keeping the population in line.

Uzbekistan—Small, well-equipped (because of Soviet Union weapons in place at independence) army and air force. No external threats, and small possibility of internal disorder because only 10 percent of population are ethnic minorities.

Venezuela—No serious internal or external threats. Competent armed forces for the region.

Vietnam—There are several minor insurgent groups, but the biggest potential problem comes from the populations, unhappy over a shaky economy. Very poor, internal strife, hostile neighbors (particularly China). Lots of combat experience in ill-equipped (but large) armed forces. No combat since 1979, but the bad blood between China and Vietnam remains.

Yemen—Just finished one civil war, may be headed for another. Hostile to large, but less populous, neighbor Saudi Arabia. Lots of warriors, not a lot of well-trained soldiers. Poor. The two Yemens united, and shortly thereafter produced a civil war. That ended, but the tribally based insurgents are still out there (supported by Saudi Arabia).

Yugoslavia/Serbia—No longer really exists except as a Serb-majority state. Is embroiled in several current and potential conflicts. Large armed forces, good fighters. There is great potential for additional conflicts among Serbs, Albanians, and Macedonians. Kosovo—unrest builds in this province of Serbia that contains an Albanian majority.

Zaire—Country, and government, have disintegrated. Many factions vying for local power. Poor, corrupt, internal and external strife. Armed forces largely for keeping population in line.

Zambia—Poor, not many internal or external enemies. Nominal armed forces.

Zimbabwe—Ethnic disputes continue to simmer. One of the better-run nations in Africa. Small armed forces have no chance against more efficient troops in neighboring South Africa.

TERRORIST ORGANIZATIONS AND LITTLE CONFLICTS THAT COULD GET BIGGER

With the end of the cold war, a lot of leftist and anti-NATO/U.S./ West groups (once funded and supported by the USSR) have disappeared. But there are still a lot of disgruntled people out there with a yen for violence.

Belgium—Walloon nationalist movement.

Bulgaria—Turkish nationalists.

Canada—Quebec separatists.

China—Tibetan separatists.

Egypt—Muslim Brotherhood.

France—Basque ("Iparretarrak" movement), Breton (Breton Revolutionary Army), Corsican (Corsican Revolutionary Brigade, Corsican Renaissance Action), and New Caledonian separatist movements; SOS France, anti-immigrant group; many others.

Germany—Ecological activists; neo-Nazi "German Action Groups"

("DA") and "military sports groups"; Anti-Imperialist Cell, militant feminists.

Great Britain—Animal Liberation Front; Welsh nationalist movement; Scottish National Liberation Army.

Iceland—Sea Shepherd, antiwhaling movement.

India—Gurkha separatists; Kashmiri separatists; Tripuran separatists; Bodo separatists.

Indonesia—Holy War Commandos; South Moluccan separatists.

Italy—Friuli separatist movement; Lotta Continua (Continuous Struggle) revolutionary group; neofascist Armed Revolutionary Nuclei (NAR) and Ordine Nuovo (New Order) extremists; Prima Linea (Front Line) anarchist movement; Red Brigades; Sardinian separatists; Ein Tyrol, Tyrolean separatist movement.

Israel—Terror Against Terror; Sicarites, anti-Arab groups.

Japan—Red Revenge Corps, right-wing activists; Japanese Red Army; Religious terrorists Aum Shin Rikyo (Supreme Truth) and other radical religious groups.

Libya—Anti-Qaddafi Al-Borkan (Volcano) movement.

Malagasy Republic—Kung-fu cultists.

Netherlands—South Moluccans.

Niger—Popular Front for the Liberation of Niger; Tuaregs.

Oman—Dhofari separatists.

Philippines—Marcos sympathizers; rightist army-faction.

Pakistan—Baluchi separatists; Shiite extremists.

South Africa—White liberation movement, Afrikaner liberation movement.

Spain—Antiterrorist Liberation Group (GAL), anti-Basque; Basque separatists ("ETA"); Canary Islands Liberation Front; Lucha por la Libertad de Melilla; Catalan Red Liberation Front, Catalan separatists.

Switzerland—Ecological extremists.

Turkey—Armenian Secret Army, Justice Commandos of Armenian Genocide; rightist Gray Wolves.

United States—Animal rights movement; antiabortion/family planning activists; anti-Arab activists; anti-nuclear-power extremists; antipornography activists; Arizona Patriots movement; Armed Resistance Movement and Revolutionary Fighting Group, leftists; Aryan Nations and related neo-Nazis; Black Liberation Army; Committee of the

States; Croatian nationalists; drug traffickers; Earth First! ecology extremists; Jewish Defense League; KKK; Posse Comitatus, right-wing libertarians; Michigan Militia; sundry other militias; Puerto Rican nationalists (Organization of Volunteers for the Puerto Rican Revolution, Puerto Rican National Liberation Front); Red Guerrilla Resistance; religious cults; White Patriots party; United Freedom Front/Sam Melville-Johnathan Jackson Unit; Islamic fundamentalists; and many other armed NUTS.

DATA AND SOURCES, 1996 EDITION

Analysts have to be better than their data. For example, at one point we found five different GDPs for Zaire. That's all right—Zaire probably doesn't know what its GDP was. We used an averaged figure. Here is another typical story: In December 1983, while beginning research on the first edition of *A Quick and Dirty Guide to War,* we found published aggregate foreign-debt estimates for the Philippines that ranged from $17 billion to over $25 billion. That's a difference of more than 40 percent. Both figures, however, indicated that the Philippines had a severe debt problem. You have to forget the trees and see the forest. Given the chaos numerous countries have been experiencing since 1990, many economic and political statistics used in preparation of this edition were also averages based on various sources.

Many of the numbers have gone through the wash and come out scrubbed. They are not, however, squeaky clean. They are colored by the authors' interpretation. We have no doubt made some mistakes in interpretation (we have learned from earlier editions, both from what we got wrong as well as what we got right); our intent, however, has always been to try to penetrate the statistics and understand the big picture.

Different statistics are understandable. Governments, especially dictatorships, purposely lie to their people and the world. That is part of their survival strategy. Even governments in open societies regularly mislead their people. This is called politics or public relations. Everyone has a slant, so research teaches you to allow for wind drift.

Our sources of information are many. There are the obvious ones: *The Economist, International Defense Review, Aviation Week and Space Technology, International Security, U.S. News and World Report, The New York Times, Miami Herald, Houston Chronicle, Washington Post, Wall Street Journal, Christian Science Monitor, Los Angeles Times, Dallas Morning News, Oil and Gas Journal, Le Monde, Die Zeit, Stern, Time,* and half a dozen others. *The San Antonio Express News* (for whom coauthor Austin Bay writes a regular column covering international affairs) was particularly helpful in providing background for the chapter on Mexico.

Some sources are not so obvious: *Focus, The Jerusalem Post, The Week in Germany,* and many other newsletters or international reports. We did not use a scrap of classified evidence or data, though no doubt censors would scream if they found out what a good library our on-line service can provide. We have also used transcripts from *The MacNeil-Lehrer NewsHour,* sources provided by dissidents, propaganda provided by governments. We made use of the U.S. State Department's *Background Notes* series, the CIA's unclassified *World Factbook 1994* (check it out, it's in the library), *Facts on File,* and *Fiche du Monde Arabe. World Press Review* offers constant "good leads" on who-is-doing-what-and-why. World Watch Institute Reports are chock-full of useful analysis. On-line sources have also proven very helpful, whether they be the Internet, Usenet, or commercial services.

The real sources of this book, however, lie in what we'll call "deep background." Machiavelli's *The Prince,* Sun Tzu's *The Art of War,* and Von Clausewitz's *On War* are vital to any adequate understanding of power politics. These theorists have aged well. Their books are utilized by today's power politicians.

Other useful references include Hyam's *Soil and Civilization,* Tuchman's *A Distant Mirror*, Newbigin's *Geographical Aspects of Balkan Problems* (a work of genius and apparently out of print since 1915), Rebecca West's classic *Black Lamb and Grey Falcon* (hey, the Balkans don't change), Thucydides' *The Peloponnesian War*, Fuller's *The Foundations of the Science of War*, Al and Heidi Toffler's *War and Anti-War*, Lord Kinross's *Ataturk*, and Fall's *Street Without Joy*.

INDEX

685